What is VAK?

YOU CAN APPROACH the topic of learning styles with a simple and powerful system—one that focuses on just three ways of perceiving through your senses:

- Seeing, or *visual learning*
- Hearing, or *auditory learning*
- Movement, or *kinesthetic learning*

To recall this system, remember the letters VAK, which stand for **v**isual, **a**uditory, and **k**inesthetic. The theory is that each of us prefers to learn through one of these sense channels. To reflect on your VAK preferences, answer the following questions. Circle the answer that best describes how you would respond. This is not a formal inventory—just a way to prompt some self-discovery.

When you have problems spelling a word, you prefer to

1. Look it up in the dictionary.
2. Say the word out loud several times before you write it down.
3. Write out the word with several different spellings and then choose one.

You enjoy courses the most when you get to

1. View slides, videos, and readings with plenty of charts, tables, and illustrations.
2. Ask questions, engage in small-group discussions, and listen to guest speakers.
3. Take field trips, participate in lab sessions, or apply the course content while working as a volunteer or intern.

When giving someone directions on how to drive to a destination, you prefer to

1. Pull out a piece of paper and sketch a map.
2. Give verbal instructions.
3. Say, "I'm driving to a place near there, so just follow me."

When planning an extended vacation to a new destination, you prefer to

1. Read colorful, illustrated brochures or articles about that place.
2. Talk directly to someone who's been there.
3. Spend time at that destination on a work-related trip before vacationing there.

You've made a commitment to learn to play the guitar. The first thing you do is

1. Go to a library or music store and find an instruction book with plenty of diagrams and chord charts.
2. Listen closely to some recorded guitar solos and see whether you can sing along with them.
3. Buy a guitar, pluck the strings, and ask someone to show you a few chords.

You've saved up enough money to lease a car. When choosing from among several new models, the most important factor in your decision is

1. The car's appearance.
2. The information you get by talking to people who own the cars you're considering.
3. The overall impression you get by taking each car on a test drive.

You've just bought a new computer system. When setting up the system, the first thing you do is

1. Skim through the printed instructions that come with the equipment.
2. Call up someone with a similar system and ask her for directions.
3. Assemble the components as best as you can, see if everything works, and consult the instructions only as a last resort.

You get a scholarship to study abroad next semester in a Spanish-speaking country. To learn as much Spanish as you can before you depart, you

1. Buy a video-based language course on DVD.
2. Download audio podcasts that guarantee basic fluency in just 30 days.
3. Sign up for a short immersion course in which you speak only Spanish.

Name _____ Date _____

Now take a few minutes to reflect on the meaning of your responses. The number of each answer corresponds to a learning style preference.

1 = visual   **2 = auditory**   **3 = kinesthetic**

	Visual	Auditory	Kinesthetic
My totals			

My dominant Learning Style(s): _____

_____

Do you see a pattern in your own answers? A pattern indicates that you prefer learning through one sense channel over the others. Or you might find that your preferences are fairly balanced.

Whether you have a defined preference or not, you can increase your options for success by learning through *all* your sense channels. For example, you can enhance visual learning by leaving room in your class notes to add your own charts, diagrams, tables, and other visuals later. You can also key your handwritten notes into a computer file and use software that allows you to add colorful fonts and illustrations.

To enhance auditory learning, reinforce your memory of key ideas by talking about them. When studying, stop often to summarize key points and add examples in your own words. After doing this several times, dictate your summaries into a voice recorder and transfer the files to an iPod or similar device. Listen to these files while walking to class or standing in line at the store.

For kinesthetic learning, you've got plenty of options as well. Look for ways to translate course content into three-dimensional models that you can build. While studying grammar, for example, create a model of a sentence using different colors of clay to represent different parts of speech. Whenever possible, supplement lectures with real-world audio and video input and experiences, field trips to Spanish-speaking neighborhoods, and other opportunities for hands-on activity. Also recite key concepts from your courses while you walk or exercise.

These are just a few examples. In your path to mastery of learning styles, you can create many more of your own.

Introducing *Cuadros*, a **new** 4-volume, 4-semester articulated Spanish program

Cuadros offers Introductory and Intermediate Spanish students a seamless, individualized experience within an easy-to-use 4-volume, 4-semester framework. Created by the same author team that produced the popular Spanish textbooks, *Nexos* and *Alianzas*, the *Cuadros* series applies a proven methodology to an entirely new language program.

Cuadros adheres to a realistic pace for a seamless transition from Introductory to Intermediate Spanish. (Volumes 1 & 2 cover Introductory Spanish; Volumes 3 & 4 cover Intermediate Spanish.)

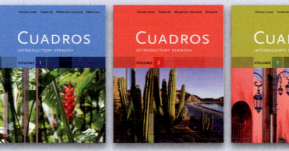

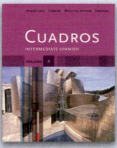

Guided Language Learning

▶ A **VAK** (**V**isual, **A**uditory, and **K**inesthetic) Learning Style Quiz appears at the beginning of each of the 4 volumes to help instructors determine the types of student learners in their class and to accommodate different learning styles. In addition, the VAK offers information to help students understand and make the most of their dominant learning style.

You've just bought a new computer system. When setting up the system, the first thing you do is

1. Skim through the printed instructions that come with the equipment.
2. Call up someone with a similar system and ask her for directions.
3. Assemble the components as best as you can, see if everything works, and consult the instructions only as a last resort.

You get a scholarship to study abroad next semester, which starts in just 3 months. You will travel to a country where Spanish is the most widely spoken language. To learn as much Spanish as you can before you depart, you

1. Buy a video-based language course that's recorded on a DVD.
2. Set up tutoring sessions with a friend who's fluent in Spanish.
3. Sign up for a short immersion course in an environment in which you speak only Spanish, starting with the first class.

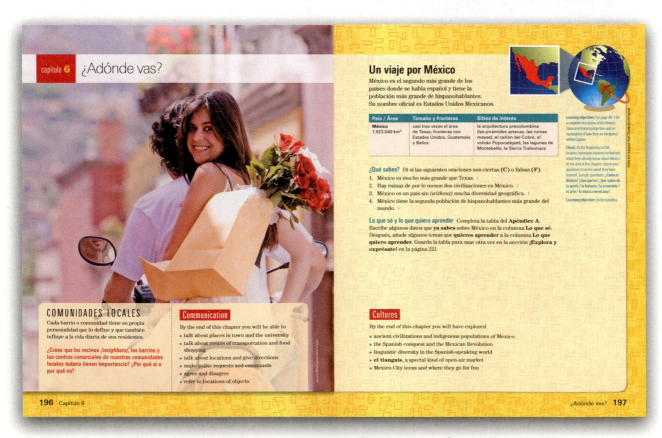

▲ Each *Cuadros* chapter begins with a compelling overview of its communicative and cultural objectives. Chapter themes and regions of focus are introduced to activate background knowledge, which will provide students with a contextualized and personalized learning experience in the chapter sections that follow.

◀ In addition to the five chapters presented in each *Cuadros* volume, Volumes 2, 3, and 4 also include a *Preliminary Chapter*. This chapter allows for a review and recycling of key stuctures and vocabulary, and reinforces skills practiced throughout the previous volume. It also enables instructors to gauge which language topics should be covered or reviewed in class.

Review and recycling is enhanced through the use of the self-test study tool in **iLrn™: Heinle Learning Center**.

▶ A *Repaso y preparación* section at the end of each chapter offers students a guided review of the material they have just completed, as well as a glimpse of what's to come as they prepare for the next chapter.

Contextualized Language

▶ *¡Imagínate!* sections in each chapter introduce active vocabulary through an engaging storyline video. Thematic vocabulary presentations are followed by a wealth of practice opportunities that progress systematically from structured to open-ended.

◀ *¡Prepárate!* sections within each chapter present the use (*Cómo usarlo*) followed by the form (*Cómo formarlo*) of key grammatical structures. Listening and speaking activities incorporate real-world examples to further support students' understanding of each grammar topic.

Authentic Culture for Meaningful Communication

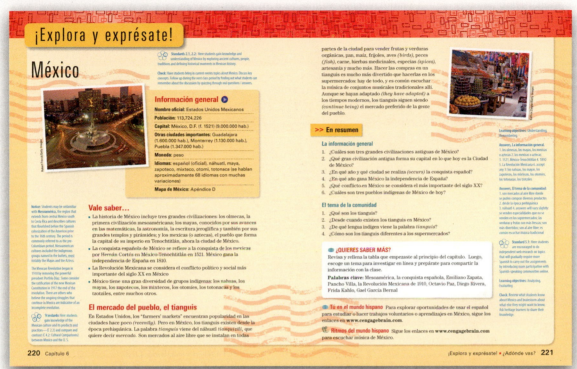

¡Explora y exprésate! sections help students make the connection between real-world topics from a part of the Spanish-speaking world and what they have studied and practiced in the chapter. These connections empower students' further cultural explorations as well as their communication skills.

▶ **Voces de la comunidad** sections direct students to the new **Voces del mundo hispano** video clips, which expose students to authentic language and real-world perspectives. The **Voces de Estados Unidos** box at the bottom of the page highlights successful Spanish speakers in the U.S. today.

Skills Development

▶ **A ver** sections include a video-viewing strategy as well as pre-viewing, viewing, and post-viewing activities.

A ver

Standard 1.2: Through video viewing, students learn interpretive strategies for communication. Activities in this section regularly provide opportunities for students to interpret spoken language.

ESTRATEGIA

Watching facial expressions

As you learned in **Chapter 3**, watching body language aids comprehension. The same is true of watching facial expressions: a smile, a frown, a raised eyebrow, or a laugh. These gestures can give you a better understanding of what the character means.

Antes de ver Estudia las palabras y frases que se usan en el video.

prisa	*hurry*
suerte	*luck*
sueños	*dreams*
Siga derecho...	*Continue straight. . .*
esquina	*corner*
Doble a la derecha...	*Turn to the right. . .*
cuadras	*blocks*

Learning objective: Understanding

▶ **Ver** Mira el video sin sonido *(without sound)* y pon atención en las expresiones faciales.

Después de ver 1 Ahora, mira el video de nuevo con el sonido puesto *(sound on)* y di si las expresiones faciales de estas personas contribuyen al sentido de lo que dicen (**sí o no**).

◀ **A leer** sections offer a variety of reading strategies students can immediately put to use in an authentic reading selection, as well as pre-reading, reading, and post-reading activities.

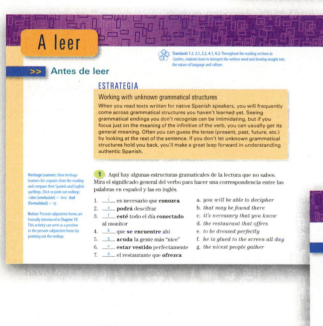

A leer

>> **Antes de leer**

Standards 1.2, 2.1, 2.2, 4.1, 4.2: Throughout the reading sections in Cuadros, students learn to interpret the written word and develop insight into the nature of language and culture.

ESTRATEGIA

Working with unknown grammatical structures

When you read texts written for native Spanish speakers, you will frequently come across grammatical structures you haven't learned yet. Seeing grammatical endings you don't recognize can be intimidating, but if you focus just on the meaning of the infinitive of the verb, you can usually get its general meaning. Often you can guess the tense (present, past, future, etc.) by looking at the rest of the sentence. If you don't let unknown grammatical structures hold you back, you'll make a great leap forward in understanding authentic Spanish.

Heritage Learners: Have heritage learners list cognates from the reading and compare their Spanish and English spellings. Elicit or point out endings: -ción (revolución) → -tion; -dad (formalidad) → -ty

Notice: Present subjunctive forms are formally introduced in Chapter 10. This activity can serve as a preview to the present subjunctive forms by pointing out the endings.

1 Aquí hay algunas estructuras gramaticales de la lectura que no sabes. Mira el significado general del verbo para hacer una correspondencia entre las palabras en español y las en inglés.

1. ___ es necesario que **conozca**
2. ___ **podrá** descifrar
3. ___ **esté** todo el día **conectado** al monitor
4. ___ que **se encuentre** ahí
5. ___ **acuda** la gente más "nice"
6. ___ **estar vestido** perfectamente
7. ___ el restaurante que **ofrezca**

a. *you will be able to decipher*
b. *that may be found there*
c. *it's necessary that you know*
d. *the restaurant that offers*
e. *to be dressed perfectly*
f. *he is glued to the screen all day*
g. *the nicest people gather*

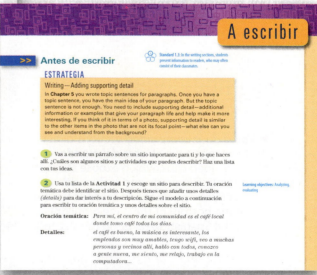

A escribir

>> **Antes de escribir**

Standard 1.3: In the writing sections, students present information to readers, who may often consist of their classmates.

ESTRATEGIA

Writing—Adding supporting detail

In **Chapter 5** you wrote topic sentences for paragraphs. Once you have a topic sentence, you have the main idea of your paragraph. But the topic sentence is not enough. You need to include supporting detail—additional information or examples that give your paragraph life and help make it more interesting. If you think of it in terms of a photo, supporting detail is similar to the other items in the photo that are not its focal point—what else can you see and understand from the background?

1 Vas a escribir un párrafo sobre un sitio importante para ti y lo que haces allí. ¿Cuáles son algunos sitios y actividades que puedes describir? Haz una lista con tus ideas.

2 Usa tu lista de la **Actividad 1** y escoge un sitio para describir. Tu oración temática debe identificar el sitio. Después tienes que añadir unos detalles *(details)* para dar interés a tu descripción. Sigue el modelo a continuación para escribir tu oración temática y unos detalles sobre el sitio.

Learning objectives: Analyzing, evaluating

Oración temática: *Para mí, el centro de mi comunidad es el café local donde tomo café todos los días.*

Detalles: *el café es bueno, la música es interesante, los empleados son muy amables, tengo wifi, veo a muchas personas y vecinos allí, hablo con todos, conozco a gente nueva, me siento, me relajo, trabajo en la computadora...*

▶ **A escribir** sections encourage students' skill development through hands-on strategies and stepped writing practice.

Integrated Video Program

The **Cuadros** video program connects students to the authentic cultures of the Spanish-speaking world while developing listening and viewing skills. There are four distinct types of video:

- **Storyline videos** engage students while reinforcing chapter grammar and vocabulary.

- *Voces del mundo hispano* clips expose students to authentic language and real-world perspectives.

- **Geocultural footage** transports students to the country or region of focus.

- **Grammar tutorials** provide additional support for each structure.

Ana y Manuel

Un cortometraje de Manuel Calvo

Mención especial a la interpretación Femenina (Elena Anaya) y Galán del II Certamen de Cortometrajes Cine en español de la XIV Muestra de Cine Internacional de Palencia y Mención Especial en el VII Premio de Cortometrajes Iberia

DIRECCIÓN: MANUEL CALVO   GUIÓN: MANUEL CALVO BASADO EN UN RELATO DE ISABEL GALÁN   PRODUCCIÓN: ELAMEDIA, ENCANTA FILMS Y KOLDO ZUAZUA PC PRESENTAN   PRODUCCIÓN EJECUTIVA: ROBERTO BUTRAGUEÑO, KOLDO ZUAZUA Y MÓNICA BLAS   DIRECCIÓN DE PRODUCCIÓN: ROBERTO BUTRAGUEÑO Y ALICIA RODRÍGUEZ   FOTOGRAFÍA: DANI SOSA   ARTE: HENAR MONTOYA   SONIDO: SOUNDERS CREACIÓN SONORA   MÚSICA: JOSÉ VILLALOBOS   ACTORES PRINCIPALES: ELENA ANAYA EN EL PAPEL DE ANA Y DIEGO MARTÍN EN EL PAPEL DE MANUEL

Cortometrajes added in Volumes 3 and 4

Volumes 3 and 4 of the **Cuadros** series introduce four contemporary, engaging short films (*cortometrajes*) by Hispanic filmmakers (two films in each Intermediate Spanish text).

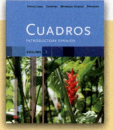
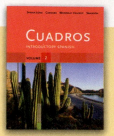

Cuadros
Introductory Spanish

iLrn HEINLE LEARNING CENTER

Heinle's all-in-one online teaching and learning system, now with the media sharing and commenting capability of Share It! Please see the inside front cover for more information.

	Volume 1	Volume 2
	Printed Access Card: 978-1-133-43593-8	Printed Access Card: 978-1-428-27612-3
	Instant Access Code: 978-1-133-43595-2	Instant Access Code: 978-1-428-27611-6

The **Premium Website** offers students complimentary access to the text audio program, Web activities and links, Google Earth™ coordinates, and an iTunes™ playlist. Premium password-protected resources include the SAM audio program, the video program, grammar and pronunciation podcasts, auto-graded quizzes, grammar tutorial videos, and more!

	Volume 1	Volume 2
	Printed Access Card: 978-1-133-50643-0	Printed Access Card: 978-1-428-27610-9
	Instant Access Code: 978-1-133-50700-0	Instant Access Code: 978-1-428-27609-3

The **Student Activities Manual (SAM)** offers students additional reading, writing, viewing, listening, and pronunciation practice opportunities. In addition, the **SAM Audio Program** includes simulated conversations and pronunciation practice.

	Volume 1	Volume 2
	978-1-133-31161-4	978-1-133-31162-1
	978-1-111-35244-8	978-1-111-35244-8

PowerLecture™ The **PowerLecture CD-ROM** houses a robust testing program, complete with four versions of each chapter exam, supplementary activities, PowerPoint decks, and audioscripts/audio files related to the tests' listening comprehension sections.

	Volume 1	Volume 2
	978-1-111-34350-7	978-1-111-34350-7

The **Annotated Instructor's Edition** includes suggestions for activities as well as cultural and linguistic information to support instructors with varying levels of experience. New annotations include *Check* (assessment) annotations and Bloom's taxonomy annotations.

	Volume 1	Volume 2
	978-1-111-34346-0	978-1-111-34346-0

KEY PACKAGES

	Volume 1	Volume 2
Student Edition **+** iLrn Printed Access Card	978-1-133-49799-8	978-1-133-29128-2
Student Edition **+** Student Activities Manual **+** Premium Website PAC	978-1-133-28722-3	978-1-133-29045-2

Program Approach and Philosophy

Cuadros offers Introductory and Intermediate Spanish students an unparalleled individualized experience within an easy-to-use 4-volume, 4-semester framework. Chapters in Volumes 1 and 2 adhere to a steady, realistic pace, supported by a full suite of instructor resources, to enable a seamless transition from Introductory to Intermediate Spanish. Chapters in Volumes 3 and 4 increase in rigor with additional grammar topics and higher-level tasks. Two authentic short films apiece in Volumes 3 and 4, and documentary-style interviews in Volume 4, further engage students at the intermediate level through exposure to real-world Spanish.

In every chapter of Volumes 1 and 2, *Cuadros*

- promotes culture-rich, content-based language learning that incorporates current themes and content with strong student appeal
- profiles successful North American Hispanics in different fields and regions
- reflects a positive, real-world, and diverse view of the Spanish language and its speakers
- contains a complete grammatical infrastructure
- presents contextualized vocabulary through authentic video interviews and video segments about student life
- contains opportunities for language practice and creation in the presentational mode
- encourages communicative oral exchange in class about a wide variety of subjects
- promotes lifelong language learning through humor in each chapter's cartoon
- systematically develops reading strategies and process-based writing through progressive practice
- addresses the intellectual needs of novice language learners by offering analytical activities

In addition, *Cuadros* provides the tools to help students

- discover their dominant learning style (Visual, Auditory, Kinesthetic)
- succeed with grammar-focused support activities designed for their learning style
- identify what they know, what they would like to know, and what they have learned, using KWL charts
- check their mastery of grammar and vocabulary concepts and review for the semester ahead through comprehensive, volume-level diagnostics
- share their knowledge and comment on their peers' informational posts at **ilrn.heinle.com**

Cuadros also provides the tools to help instructors

- identify the learning style preferences of their class
- conduct a thorough review of what students have already learned with teaching tips and lesson plans tailored to the preliminary chapters of Volumes 2 through 4
- highlight common points in need of remediation through language-focused diagnostics
- measure student progress in class with **Check** annotations throughout each chapter

- correlate chapter objectives at the activity level to learning objectives aligned with the Cognitive and Knowledge categories of Bloom's Taxonomy
- expand their classes' visual aids through robust PowerPoint materials that include additional teaching tips and suggestions
- assess student progress through one of four different chapter-level testing styles, with a choice of two versions of each volume's final examination
- gauge students' oral proficiency through volume-level oral assessments complete with volume-specific rubrics

Cuadros and the National Standards

Cuadros is a results-oriented program that draws its contextual and communicative theory and practice from the National Standards for Foreign Language Learning and focuses on implementing and achieving these goals within the Spanish classroom. The program carefully integrates the "5Cs" of Communication, Cultures, Connections, Community, and Comparisons, offering many organized presentational activities and a variety of opportunities to connect, compare, and communicate with local and virtual Spanish-speaking communities.

Integrating the Standards for Foreign Language Learning: Preparing for the 21st Century is at the core of the program's philosophy. The Standards advocate an interconnected approach to language learning through five goal areas (Communication, Cultures, Connections, Comparisons, Communities). The "5Cs" serve as the foundation for the *Cuadros* program, with the aim of producing culturally and linguistically intelligent students of the Spanish language who are able to

- **communicate** in the language
- make **cultural and linguistic comparisons**
- achieve a high level of **cultural appreciation**
- **connect** information in *Cuadros* with disciplines and interests beyond the text
- experience both local and virtual Spanish-speaking **communities**

As language instructors know, the most effective teaching weaves all of the 5Cs into classroom presentations, activities, tasks, and options beyond the classroom. Activities throughout *Cuadros* provide opportunities for interpersonal and presentational communication, and the following sections focus explicitly on specific standards:

- Chapter opener (Cultures, Connections)
- **¡Fíjate!** (Cultures, Comparisons)
- **Voces de la comunidad** (Communities, Cultures)
- **Sonrisas** (Communication, Communities)
- **¡Explora y exprésate!** (Cultures, Communication)
- **¿Quieres saber más?** (Connections, Communities)

Icons and annotations in the AIE margins reference each Standard practiced by name as well as number.

- Communication
- Cultures
- Connections
- Comparisons
- Communities

Cuadros and Backward Design

The incorporation of Backward Design principles throughout *Cuadros* encourages and supports enhanced student engagement with Spanish and Hispanic cultures by personalizing the student experience. In each chapter opener, students first assess cultural information for factual content through discrete-item practice, then establish personalized learning goals at the chapter level by filling in KWL ("what I know," "what I want to know," "what I have learned") charts to record prior knowledge and to detail what they would like to know about the topics and regions presented. Students close the loop at the end of the chapter by documenting what they have learned. A blank KWL chart is provided in the appendix as well as on the **Premium Website** as a downloadable PDF for student use.

For instructors, **Check** annotations accompany chapter openers, **¡Fíjate!** features, chapter-end **¡Explora y exprésate!** and **Repaso y preparación** sections, and other relevant sections. These annotations offer suggestions to assess student's baseline awareness of target cultures and understanding of topics, measure what they have learned, and identify areas that may need further reinforcement.

Cuadros and Bloom's Taxonomy

Learning objectives for selected activities and exercises in each chapter are classified using Bloom's Taxonomy (revised version, 2000). This classification makes learning more accessible through the use of scaffolding via a hierarchy of cognitive skills that range from "knowing," which encompasses the ability to identify, list, and describe, to "understanding," which is demonstrated by the ability to paraphrase, give examples, compare, and identify main ideas, all the way to "synthesizing" or "creating," which entails composing, designing, and producing.

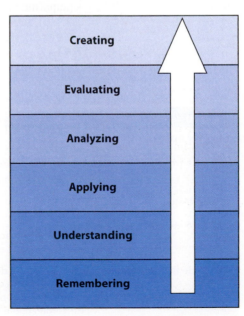

Creating

Evaluating

Analyzing

Applying

Understanding

Remembering

The activities classified using Bloom's Taxonomy provide different entry points for learners at different levels of readiness and with different backgrounds and goals. Learners needing extra support can take advantage of numerous activities that bridge the gap between the lower and higher levels of the hierarchy, while more advanced learners, or learners with specific needs such as heritage speakers, can find engaging work at the higher levels. The classifications also provide a way to vary the pace and demands of class work by alternating between different levels of activities. In addition, they offer a way to review and reinforce material in a challenging manner: the skills acquired through the use of activities at one level can be reviewed and expanded upon using activities at higher levels.

Cuadros and Heritage Learners

Cuadros offers teachers extra help with incorporating heritage learners into the first-year Spanish classroom. Annotations in every chapter provide specific ideas on working with heritage learners, and a set of guidelines addressing the needs of heritage learners is available in the instructor resources section of the *Cuadros* companion site.

Cuadros and Spanish in the United States

The *Cuadros* program is also strongly committed to reminding students and teachers alike that the United States has the third largest Spanish-speaking population in the world. Spanish is truly a second language in the U.S., with extensive commercial, educational, and media applications. With its extensive coverage of global Hispanic communities, implementation of the National Standards, and emphasis on linguistic know-how and technical literacy in Spanish, *Cuadros* prepares students to communicate meaningfully in Spanish and become fully participating members of the global community.

Chapter Organization

Cuadros is organized into easily recognizable sections that present and practice new chapter content.

Section	Description
Chapter opener	Communicative and cultural chapter objectives, cultural information, and comprehension quizzes that activate students' background knowledge. Chapter openers in Volume 4 engage students at a more advanced level, with personalized quizzes and questionnaires.
¡Imagínate!	Contextualized presentation of thematic vocabulary followed by practice that progresses smoothly from structured to open-ended.
A ver	Storyline video segments and viewing strategies accompanied by pre-viewing, viewing, and post-viewing activities.
Voces de la comunidad	Authentic **Voces del mundo hispano** video interviews with native Spanish speakers expose students to Spanish from around the Hispanic world. Profiles of prominent North American Hispanics are accompanied by recorded quotes and thematic opinion questions. Web links contain additional information about the professionals and their fields.

Section	Description
¡Prepárate!	Grammar presentations followed by communicative practice. **Cómo usarlo** focuses on usage explanations while **Cómo formarlo** presents grammatical forms and rules. **Lo básico** boxes explain grammatical terms with examples. Includes two listening-based grammar activities per chapter and video-based tutorials for every grammar topic.
¡Explora y exprésate!	Guides students to apply and expand on knowledge gained from material presented and practiced in the first half of the chapter. This section includes cultural readings, activities, and a video presentation on the featured country or countries.
A leer	Reading strategies and pre-reading, reading, and post-reading practice of authentic (beginning with Ch. 2) texts as well as literary selections.
A escribir	Writing strategies and stepped writing practice in every chapter.
Vocabulario	End-of-chapter active vocabulary summaries with translations.
Repaso y preparación	End-of-chapter review of structures as well as a review of previously learned grammar to help students prepare for what they will learn in the next chapter.
Special Features	
Preliminary chapters	Volumes 2, 3, and 4 of **Cuadros** each include a special preliminary chapter that reviews and recycles key structures and vocabulary while reinforcing skills practiced throughout the previous volume. These chapters also enable instructors to gauge which language topics need to be reviewed in class.
¡Fíjate!	Linguistic notes that focus on cross-cultural comparisons are followed by **Práctica** activities designed to widen students' cultural perspectives.
Sonrisas	Cartoon feature that practices a grammatical or lexical topic in each chapter. **Comprensión** activities for cartoons through Chapter 4 become **Expresión** (extension) activities beginning with Chapter 5.
¿Quieres saber más?	Themes for further exploration of the chapter's country or countries encourage students to complete their KWL charts and refers them to the **Cuadros** premium website to research and prepare presentations to share with classmates through iLrn: Heinle Learning Center.
Tú en el mundo hispano	Points students to a wealth of resources on the **Cuadros** premium website and in iLrn: Heinle Learning Center for study abroad, internship, volunteer opportunities, and student exchanges in the region of focus.
Ritmos del mundo hispano	Descriptions, video links and iTunes playlists for key traditional and contemporary musicians and groups on the **Cuadros** premium website and in iLrn: Heinle Learning Center.
Cortometrajes	Volumes 3 and 4 of the **Cuadros** series introduce four contemporary, engaging short films by Hispanic filmmakers (two films in each Intermediate Spanish text).

Components of *Cuadros*

Cuadros offers a wide array of student and instructor materials to accommodate various learning styles and approaches.

- **Total Adaptability** Offers solutions for traditional face-to-face, hybrid, or online distance learning courses without separate course preparation. **iLrn: Heinle Learning Center** lets instructors manage their courses quickly and efficiently.
- **Program Continuity** Provides a single program solution for departments that offer both face-to-face and online courses, so instructors prepare only once for different course types. The print-page fidelity of the eBook provides students and instructors with a familiar visual presentation for transitioning between traditional learning and online learning.

Instructor Components

Annotated Instructor's Edition

 The **Annotated Instructor's Edition (AIE)** provides marginal annotations with classroom tips, ideas for additional activities, and answers to Student Text activities. It also includes annotations that highlight particular National Standards and goal areas and that provide ideas for working with heritage learners in the classroom. The **Instructor's Guide** material at the beginning of the AIE provides information about the program, ideas for teaching with *Cuadros*, and possible course configurations across varying numbers of semesters or quarters.

PowerLecture Instructor Resource CD-ROM

This CD-ROM contains four separate testing strands to accommodate four types of testing approaches: discrete, discrete and open-ended, open-ended, and holistic. There are two versions of each volume-level final: one discrete and open-ended version and one holistic version. Info-gap activities, grammar and vocabulary activity worksheets, and PowerPoint slides are also provided with the testing strands for each chapter. Volume-level oral assessments provide a study prep for students before their oral assessment, a speaking rubric for students and instructors, and a set of questions targeting the vocabulary and grammar concepts learned in each volume. In addition, teaching suggestions provide sample syllabi and lesson plans for the preliminary chapters in Volumes 2 through 4.

Testing Audio CD

 This CD contains the recorded material corresponding to the listening portions of the Testing Program.

DVD

This multi-tier video program features four types of footage: a storyline video for each lesson in the student text, new **Voces del mundo hispano** authentic interviews with native Spanish speakers, geocultural footage with narrative in Spanish and grammar tutorials for each structure. All clips are also available on the **Premium Website** and via **iLrn: Heinle Learning Center**.

Instructor Site

Resources for this passkey-protected site include

- Instructor's Guide
- Integration Guide
- Transition Guide
- Sample syllabi
- Sample lesson plans
- PowerPoint slides of vocabulary and grammar charts from the text
- Situation cards and guide to situation cards
- Audioscript for the **Text Audio CD**
- Audioscript for the **SAM Audio CD Program**
- SAM Answer Key
- Videoscripts

A list of student components and their descriptions can be found on page iv.

CUADROS STORYLINE VIDEOSCRIPTS

Capítulo 1: ¿Con quién hablo?

(On campus/In Anilú's apartment)

BETO	Perdón.

(Javier's phone rings.)

JAVIER	¡Hola!
ANILÚ	Hola, Beto. ¿Cómo te va?
JAVIER	Bastante bien, pero... ¿Beto? Yo no soy Beto.
ANILÚ	Pues, ¿cómo te llamas?
JAVIER	¿Yo? Soy Javier de la Cruz. Y yo, ¿con quién hablo?
ANILÚ	Me llamo Anilú. Ana Luisa Guzmán. Mucho gusto, Javier de la Cruz.
JAVIER	Encantado, Ana Luisa Guzmán.
ANILÚ	Pero, ¿cuál es tu número de teléfono? Yo marqué el 3-39-71-94.
JAVIER	No, ése no es mi número de teléfono. Mi número es el 371-2812.
ANILÚ	Pues, mira, Javier, voy a marcar el 339-7194 de nuevo.
JAVIER	Muy bien. Ha sido un placer. ¡Adiós!
ANILÚ	Igualmente. ¡Adiós!

(They hang up. Javier's phone rings again.)

JAVIER	¿Aló?
ANILÚ	Buenos días, Javier. ¿Cómo estás?
JAVIER	Pues, terrible, Anilú. Aquí hay un problema.
ANILÚ	Sí, Javier. Tienes el celular de mi amigo Beto.
JAVIER	¡Ay! Y ¿qué hacemos?
ANILÚ	No sé... déjame ver.

(On campus)

BETO	Es tarde.
ANILÚ	Tranquilo, ya debe estar por venir.
BETO	Estoy preocupado.

(Javier arrives.)

ANILÚ	¿Tú eres Javier?
JAVIER	Y tú eres Anilú, ¿no?
ANILÚ	Sí. Beto, quiero presentarte a Javier de la Cruz.
BETO	Mucho gusto, Javier.
JAVIER	Encantado, Beto.
BETO	Aquí está tu celular.
JAVIER	Gracias, Beto. Aquí está tu celular.
BETO	Bueno, ¡tengo que irme! Muchas gracias, Javier. Y gracias a ti también, Anilú.
ANILÚ	Chau.
BETO	Chau.
ANILÚ	Pues, Javier, mucho gusto en conocerte.
JAVIER	El gusto es mío.
ANILÚ	Pues, entonces, ¡nos vemos!
JAVIER	¡Hasta luego! ¡Chau!
ANILÚ	¡Chau!

Capítulo 2: ¡Mentiroso!

(Beto's and Anilú's apartments)

BETO	*(As he types)* ¡Buenas tardes, Autora14!
DULCE	*(As she types)* ¡Buenas tardes, Experto10!
BETO	<u>¿Eres estudiante?</u>
DULCE	<u>Sí, soy estudiante en la Universidad de Costa Rica.</u>
BETO	<u>¡Qué coincidencia! Yo también.</u>
SERGIO	¿Qué haces, Beto? ¿Navegas por Internet?
BETO	Sí. En mensajes instantáneos. <u>Autora14, ¿qué te gusta hacer los domingos?</u>
SERGIO	¿Con quién hablas?
BETO	No sé. Es una estudiante de la Universidad. Su nombre electrónico es Autora14.
SERGIO	Dile que tienes un amigo muy guapo.
DULCE	<u>Los domingos generalmente estudio en la biblioteca.</u>
ANILÚ	¡Qué aburrida!
BETO	<u>¿Estudias?</u>
ANILÚ	Dile que bailas y cantas y... y escuchas música.
BETO	<u>¿No te gusta hacer otras cosas?</u>
DULCE	<u>Pues sí. A veces mis amigos y yo tomamos un refresco en el Jazz Café o alquilamos un video.</u>
ANILÚ	*(Pushing Dulce away)* Con permiso, con permiso. <u>Y tú, Experto10, ¿qué te gusta hacer los domingos?</u>
SERGIO	*(As Beto)* <u>Autora14, soy un hombre activo. Bailo, canto, toco la guitarra, cocino...</u>
BETO	¡Sergio! ¡Mentiroso! ¡No me gusta bailar, no me gusta cantar, no toco la guitarra y no cocino!
SERGIO	¡Qué aburrido eres, hombre!
ANILÚ	<u>¿Cocinas?</u> Un hombre que cocina... y también ¡le gusta bailar y cantar! <u>Experto10, ¿cuál es tu número de teléfono?</u>
DULCE	Anilú, ¿qué haces?
ANILÚ	Ay.
SERGIO	<u>¿Mi número de teléfono?</u> *(Beto turns off computer)* ¡Beto! ¿Qué haces?
BETO	Apago la computadora. Punto. Fin. No más.
SERGIO	Mañana regreso, Autora14. Mañana regreso.

Capítulo 3: Gracias por la entrevista

(On campus)

CHELA	Disculpa. ¿Puedo haceros una entrevista? Disculpa. ¿Puedo haceros...? Disculpa. ¿Puedo haceros una entrevista?
CAMARÓGRAFO	¿Cuántas entrevistas tenemos que hacer?
CHELA	Dos por lo menos.
CAMARÓGRAFO	¿De qué trata el programa?

CHELA	Tú sabes, lo típico, un día en la vida de un universitario, ¿cuántas clases tienes?, ¿cuántas veces por semana?, ¿dónde vives, estudias, comes?, ¿cuánto tiempo pasas navegando por Internet?, etcétera.
CAMARÓGRAFO	Qué aburrido.
CHELA	Con permiso, señorita.
ANILÚ	¿Sí?
CHELA	Quiero hacerle una entrevista para un programa que vamos a transmitir en la página web de la Universidad.
ANILÚ	¿Qué clase de preguntas me vas a hacer?
CHELA	Preguntas sobre la vida universitaria. Para empezar, dime, ¿cuántas clases tienes?
ANILÚ	Ay, ¡qué aburrido!, ¿no crees? Si voy a salir por Internet, quiero hacer más que recitar mis clases: computación, diseño gráfico, psicología, bla, bla, bla, bla, bla.
CHELA	Comprendo que no son las preguntas más interesantes del mundo, pero...
ANILÚ	Prefiero hablar de mi tiempo libre, los sábados, por ejemplo.
CHELA	¿Qué haces los sábados?
ANILÚ	Por la mañana, corro en el parque. A las dos de la tarde, tengo clase de danza afrocaribeña.
CHELA	¿Y por la noche?
ANILÚ	Por la noche escucho música con mis amigos o vamos al cine o a un restaurante.
CAMARÓGRAFO	Uy, ¿qué hora es? ¡Tengo que irme!
CHELA	Pero, ¿adónde vas? ¡Necesito otra entrevista!
CAMARÓGRAFO	¡Tengo clase a las once!
CHELA	Son las once menos cuarto. Espera un minuto, por favor.
CAMARÓGRAFO	Está bien.
CHELA	¿Así que te gustan más los fines de semana que los días de entresemana?
ANILÚ	Pues sí, por supuesto. Los fines de semana son mucho más divertidos. *(Looking at her watch)* Ay, es tarde. Yo también tengo clase a las once.
CHELA	Gracias por la entrevista. Una cosa más, ¿tu nombre, por favor? A la cámara.
ANILÚ	Anilú Guzmán. Oye, ¿cuándo sale la entrevista en la red?
CHELA	Mañana.
ANILÚ	*(Spotting Javier)* ¡Javier!... ¡Adiós! ¡Javi!
CHELA	¡Adiós! ¿Ya? ¿Se grabó?

Capítulo 4: ¿Te gustan los grupos de conversación?

(On campus)

BETO	¡Estoy furioso!
CHELA	Pero, ¿por qué?
BETO	Primero llego tarde a la clase de literatura.
CHELA	Llegar tarde no es una tragedia.

BETO	¡Tenemos examen! Abro mi computadora portátil, pero en la pantalla dice que no tengo suficiente memoria para abrir la aplicación.
CHELA	¿Tienes una computadora portátil de las nuevas? ¿A colores?
BETO	No, es negra, pero si no te molesta, ¡vuelvo a mi historia!
CHELA	Tranquilo, Beto.
BETO	¡Tranquilo! ¿Cómo que tranquilo? ¡Tengo que tomar el examen a mano! ¡Imagínate! ¡Tener que usar un bolígrafo para el examen de literatura!
CHELA	Fíjate que el bolígrafo es un implemento muy útil. Generalmente puedes depender del bolígrafo...
BETO	¡Pero con la computadora puedo escribir más rápido! Con el bolígrafo es un proceso muy lento. Suena el timbre, y ¡no puedo completar el examen!
CHELA	¡Pobre Beto! Siento tu frustración.
BETO	Entonces, empiezo a salir del salón de clases. No sé en dónde, pero entre el salón y la biblioteca, pierdo mi asistente electrónico.
CHELA	Ya me voy. Estoy muy aburrida con tu cuento trágico. Chau.
DULCE	Perdona, pero ¿es éste tu asistente electrónico?
BETO	¡Sí! Muchas gracias. Pero, ¿dónde...?
DULCE	En el escritorio, después del examen. Estoy en tu clase de literatura.
BETO	¡Ah! Muchísimas gracias. ¿Cómo te llamas?
DULCE	Dulce.
BETO	Mucho gusto, Dulce. Y mil gracias por recoger mi asistente electrónico. ¿Quieres tomar un refresco o un café?
DULCE	Sí, ¿por qué no?

(Beto sees that she's carrying a printed email with the name Autora14 on it)

BETO	¿Tú? ¿Tú eres Autora14?
DULCE	Sí, yo soy Autora14. ¿Por qué preguntas?
BETO	No, no, nada. ¿Te gustan los grupos de conversación?
DULCE	No, en realidad, no. Prefiero el correo electrónico.

Capítulo 5: ¡Pelo de bruja!

(Anilú's apartment)

ANILÚ	Mira, ven a ver.
DULCE	¿Qué es?
ANILÚ	Son fotos de mi familia.
DULCE	¿De veras? ¿En la computadora?
ANILÚ	Sí, mi hermanito Roberto tiene una cámara digital. Saca fotos de la familia y me las manda por Internet.
DULCE	¿Quién es este señor?

ANILÚ	Es mi papá. Se enoja cuando Roberto le saca fotos. No le gusta salir en fotos. Dice que se ve muy gordo.
DULCE	¿Qué hace tu papá?
ANILÚ	Es arquitecto. Diseña edificios para negocios.

(The telephone rings.)

ANILÚ	¿Aló?
MAMÁ	¡Hija! ¡Qué gusto oír tu voz! ¡Nunca llamas! Nadie sabe nada de ti. ¿Cómo estás?
ANILÚ	Más o menos bien, mamá. Es que estoy muy ocupada. Tengo mucho trabajo para mis clases y con mi proyecto en la Web, ¡no me queda tiempo para nada ni nadie!
MAMÁ	Bueno, pero siempre hay que hacer tiempo para llamar a tu mamá.
ANILÚ	Sí, mamá, está bien. Perdóname.
MAMÁ	No te preocupes, hija. Algún día vas a tener hijos y entonces vas a saber cómo es...
ANILÚ	Mamá, ¿está Roberto por allí? Necesito hablar con él.
MAMÁ	No puede venir al teléfono. Se está bañando.
ANILÚ	¿Está bañándose? ¿A esta hora?
MAMÁ	Acaba de regresar de su partido de fútbol. ¡Ay! ¡No hay ni toallas ni jabón en el baño! Me tengo que ir. Tengo que llevarle a tu hermano una toalla, el jabón y el champú. Te llamo luego.
ANILÚ	Está bien, mamá. Me saludas a papá, y a Roberto también.
MAMÁ	Sí, hija, cómo no. ¡Hasta lueguito!
ANILÚ	¡Chau, mamá!

(The telephone rings again.)

ANILÚ	¿Aló?
ROBERTO	¡Anilú! Mamá dice que quieres hablar conmigo.
ANILÚ	Sí. Roberto, quiero darte las gracias por las fotos.
ROBERTO	¿Es todo? ¿No quieres decirme algo más?
ANILÚ	No, es todo. ¿Por qué?
ROBERTO	Las fotos. ¿Estás viendo las fotos?
ANILÚ	Sí, ¿por qué?
ROBERTO	¿Ves la foto del cumpleaños del abuelo?
ANILÚ	¡Roberto! ¡Qué foto tan horrible!
ROBERTO	¡Adiós, pelo de bruja!

Capítulo 6: ¿Adónde vas con tanta prisa?

(Javier and Sergio's apartment)

| SERGIO | Oye, ¿adónde vas con tanta prisa? |
| JAVIER | Primero tengo que ir al gimnasio, y después al centro estudiantil. |

SERGIO	Pero, ¿por qué la prisa, hombre?
JAVIER	Después del centro estudiantil, tengo que ir al banco a sacar dinero, y después al "súper" a comprar la comida para la cena.
SERGIO	Dicen que el supermercado es el lugar ideal para conocer a la mujer ideal...
JAVIER	¿Ah, sí?
SERGIO	Sí.
JAVIER	Tal vez hoy es mi día de suerte.
SERGIO	¿Vas en bicicleta?
JAVIER	No, voy a pie. Mi bici se desinfló. Bueno, adiós—¡me tengo que ir!

(Chela and Dulce's apartment)

DULCE	Pero, mujer, ¿adónde vas con tanta prisa?
CHELA	Quiero ir al gimnasio antes de hacer las compras en el supermercado.
DULCE	Pero si no es tarde, son sólo las tres.
CHELA	Ya sé, pero si me da tiempo, quiero ir a la carnicería para comprar unos bistecs.
DULCE	¡A la carnicería! ¿Viene alguna persona especial a cenar?
CHELA	No, desafortunadamente, no.
DULCE	Nunca sabes cuándo vas a conocer a la persona de tus sueños...
CHELA	Es verdad.
DULCE	¡Adiós! ¡Suerte!
CHELA	Gracias. Nos vemos luego.

(Outside the bank)

SEÑORA	Perdone, joven, ¿me puede decir dónde queda el Centro Comercial Paco?
JAVIER	Sí, señora, con mucho gusto. Siga derecho hasta aquella esquina.
SEÑORA	Derecho hasta aquella esquina.
JAVIER	En la esquina, doble a la derecha y camine... dos cuadras.
SEÑORA	Dos cuadras.
JAVIER	En la última cuadra, frente al banco, va a ver el centro comercial.
SEÑORA	Muchas gracias, joven.
JAVIER	De nada.

(Javier and Sergio's apartment)

SERGIO	Ah, por fin regresas. ¿Todavía solo?
JAVIER	Sí, todavía solo.
SERGIO	Algún día, mi amigo, algún día.

(Chela and Dulce's apartment)

DULCE	Veo que tienes las compras, pero no a la persona de tus sueños.
CHELA	Sí, todavía sola.
DULCE	Algún día, mi amiga, algún día.

Capítulo 7: ¡Odio el gimnasio!

(At the fitness center)

SERGIO	¿Viste el partido de fútbol entre Argentina y México ayer?
JAVIER	No, llegué tarde a casa.
SERGIO	Pues, te perdiste un partido buenísimo. Yo lo vi en casa de Arturo.
JAVIER	¿Ah, sí? ¿Y quién ganó?
SERGIO	Argentina, 2 a 1.
JAVIER	Me encanta ver los partidos de fútbol internacional por tele.
SERGIO	Y además del fútbol, ¿qué otros deportes te gustan?
JAVIER	Las competencias de natación, el ciclismo y el boxeo.
SERGIO	¿El boxeo? ¡Guau! Yo prefiero el fútbol nacional, el italiano, el español...
JAVIER	¿Qué piensas de los deportes de invierno?
SERGIO	No sé, hay algunos que me parecen interesantes, como el hockey sobre hielo y el esquí alpino.
JAVIER	Mira, ahí viene Beto. Hola Beto. Qué milagro verte por aquí.
BETO	Ya sé. ¡Odio el gimnasio! No tengo ganas de hacer ejercicio en estas malditas máquinas.
SERGIO	¡Pobre Beto! ¿Qué te pasa? ¿Les tienes miedo a las "maquinitas"?
BETO	No, no seas ridículo. Yo prefiero jugar tenis, pero hoy no puedo porque está lloviendo.
JAVIER	Tienes razón. Y además, hace mucho viento. Ayer salí a correr pero hoy no tuve otra opción que venir aquí.
BETO	Sí. ¡Hace mal tiempo desde el lunes!
SERGIO	¡Pobre Beto! ¿Por qué no levantas pesas un rato? *(Grabbing Beto's arm)* ¡Qué vergüenza! ¡Tienes los músculos de un niño!
JAVIER	Oye, Beto, ¡ten cuidado con esas pesas!
BETO	¡Cállate! ¿No ves que ahí viene Dulce?
DULCE	¡Hola, muchachos! ¿Cómo les va?
SERGIO	Muy bien, Dulce.
BETO	¡Buenas tardes, Dulce!
DULCE	Hola, Beto. ¿Haces ejercicio aquí con frecuencia?
BETO	¡Sí, claro! Todos los días. Vengo a hacer ejercicio y... a levantar pesas.

(Hearing this, Sergio and Javier start to laugh)

DULCE	¡Ah, qué bueno! A mí no me gusta el gimnasio. Prefiero jugar tenis, pero como está lloviendo... *(She sees Sergio and Javier laughing)* ¿Qué pasa? ¿De qué se están riendo?
BETO	No nada, nada.

Capítulo 8: Ya sé exactamente lo que busca

(In a clothing store)

CLERK	¿En qué puedo servirle, señor?
JAVIER	Pues, estoy buscando un regalo para mi mamá pero no sé, no veo nada.
CLERK	Pues, si le gusta la ropa fina, esta blusa de seda es muy bonita y además está rebajada.
JAVIER	No, no le gusta este color.
CLERK	¿Quizás este suéter?
JAVIER	No. Tampoco necesita suéter.
CLERK	Y las joyas, ¿a quién no le gustan las joyas? Venga por aquí, por favor. ¿Quizás estos aretes? Son de oro y le dan ese toque de elegancia a cualquier vestido.
JAVIER	Sí, son muy bonitos. ¿Cuánto cuestan?
CLERK	Usted tiene muy buena suerte, porque hoy estos aretes tienen un 25 por ciento de descuento. Vea...
JAVIER	Muy bien, me parece muy buen precio. Me los llevo.
CLERK	A su madre le van a encantar. ¿Cómo desea pagar, con tarjeta de crédito o en efectivo?
JAVIER	En efectivo. *(He pays the clerk.)*
CLERK	Que le vaya muy bien.
JAVIER	Muchas gracias.

(Javier leaves. Soon after, Chela enters.)

CLERK	Buenas, señorita. ¿En qué puedo servirle?
CHELA	La verdad es que estoy buscando un regalo para el cumpleaños de mi mamá pero no tengo ni la menor idea qué comprarle.
CLERK	Su mamá seguro es una mujer de muy buen gusto. Tal vez esta blusa de seda...
CHELA	Uy, no, ¡a mamá no le gusta ese color!
CLERK	Muy bien. ¿Qué le parece este suéter? Es muy elegante, ¿no?
CHELA	No, no usa ese estilo.
CLERK	¡Ya sé exactamente lo que busca! Venga por aquí, por favor. Estos aretes de oro son preciosos, y están a muy buen precio hoy.
CHELA	¡Qué bonitos! Sí, creo que sí le van a gustar a mi mamá. Voy a llevármelos.
CLERK	Tiene muy buen gusto, señorita. ¿Cómo desea pagar? En efectivo, ¿verdad?
CHELA	Sí, gracias. *(She pays the clerk and leaves.)*
CLERK	¡Parece que una mamá va a recibir regalos idénticos de su hija y de su hijo!

Capítulo 9: Ni por un millón de dólares

(Dulce and Chela's apartment)

DULCE	Anda, dime, me muero de curiosidad, ¿cómo te fue anoche con Sergio?
CHELA	¡Fatal, mujer! ¡Qué hombre más egoísta!
DULCE	*(Facetiously)* ¿Sergio? ¿Egoísta? ¿En serio? No lo sabía.
CHELA	No sé ni por dónde empezar.

DULCE	¡Desde el principio, por supuesto! Quiero todos los detalles.
CHELA	Bueno, desde el principio. A ver. Quedamos en vernos a las ocho en punto en el restaurante. No llegó hasta las ocho y media. Cuando llegó, no ofreció explicaciones y no se disculpó. El camarero nos trajo los menús pero en ese momento sonó el celular de Sergio. Habló por teléfono —no sé con quién— por diez minutos enteros mientras yo esperaba. Por fin colgó y ordenamos. Yo pedí el pollo asado y él pidió el lomo de res. Habló de sí mismo por una eternidad y mientras hablaba no dejaba de arreglarse el pelo. Por fin llegaron los platos. Empezamos a comer. Inmediatamente, Sergio llamó al camarero. ¡Pobre camarero! Sergio fue muy descortés con él. Le dijo que la sopa estaba congelada, que el bróculi no estaba fresco ¡y que la carne estaba cruda! Mandó toda la comida a la cocina. ¡Qué vergüenza! No sabía qué hacer. Mientras esperábamos sus platos, se enfriaron los míos. Por fin llegó el camarero con los platos nuevos. Se los sirvió a Sergio con mucha cortesía. Después de la cena, otro desastre. El camarero nos servía el café cuando sonó el celular de Sergio otra vez. Decidió tomar la llamada en privado. Al levantarse, se pegó en la mesa y tiró el café por todo el mantel.
DULCE	¡Uy, qué horror! ¡Parece de película!
CHELA	Sí, ¡de película de horror! Y ¡no me lo vas a creer!... pero después de todo eso, ¡no le dejó propina al pobre camarero! ¡Yo tuve que regresar a dejársela!
DULCE	No te tengo que preguntar si vuelves a salir con él.
CHELA	¡Ni por un millón de dólares!

Capítulo 10: Soy buen cocinero

(At the park)

DULCE	¡Gracias por la invitación, muy amable! Hace mucho tiempo que no voy de picnic. Y ¡mira! ¿Preparaste tú todo esto?
BETO	Sí, claro. Soy buen cocinero. Cuando era niño, me gustaba preparar la comida para mi familia.
DULCE	¿En serio? Yo creía que a los chicos no les gustaba hacer nada en la casa. Mis hermanos

	siempre decían que el trabajo de la casa era para las mujeres.
BETO	¡Qué anticuado! Yo no pienso así. Me crié en el centro de la ciudad. Y somos muy modernos los hombres de la ciudad.
DULCE	¿De veras? Qué bueno. En mi casa, mis hermanas y yo teníamos que hacer los quehaceres domésticos, mis hermanos sólo hacían lo que tenía que ver con el garaje o el jardín.
BETO	No me parece justo. Yo tendía las camas, pasaba la aspiradora, lavaba los platos igual que mis hermanas.
DULCE	Pues eres único.
BETO	Sí, mi mamá decía que yo era su ayudante preferido. Barría el piso, sacaba la basura, ponía la mesa, limpiaba los baños, planchaba, sacudía las alfombras...
DULCE	Oye, me estás tomando el pelo, ¿verdad? Yo no conozco a ningún niño tan trabajador.
BETO	Pues, exagero un poco, pero sí me gustaban algunos de los quehaceres.
DULCE	¿Como cuáles?
BETO	Pues, a ver, me gustaba limpiar el refrigerador. Y también me gustaba sacar la basura.
DULCE	Pues, qué pena que mis hermanos no fueran así.
BETO	Sí. Cuando yo tenga hijos, quiero que aprendan a ser responsables desde muy pequeños. Quiero que participen en los quehaceres de la casa.
DULCE	*(Pretending to get dreamy-eyed)* ¡Vas a ser un padre excelente!
BETO	*(Trying to change the subject)* Mira, ¿por qué no pruebas los sandwiches de jamón y queso? Están muy sabrosos...
DULCE	Sí, un padre excelente... eres un buen cocinero, te gustan los quehaceres domésticos, quieres que tus hijos sean trabajadores...
BETO	Mira, prueba éstos, los compré en el supermercado.
DULCE	¡En el supermercado! ¿No los preparaste tú?
BETO	No, no los preparé. La verdad es que a mi no me gusta cocinar.
DULCE	*(Laughing)* ¡Yo lo sabía! Tu historia me pareció demasiado fantástica. ¡Planchabas! ¡Limpiabas los baños! ¡Cocinabas! ¡Súper-Chico! ¡El ayudante preferido de su madre! ¡Hombre moderno!

VOCES DEL MUNDO HISPANO VIDEOSCRIPTS

Capítulo 1: ¿Cómo te llamas?

▪ **¿Cómo te llamas y de dónde eres?**

Hola, me llamo Sandra Alvarado… Soy de Puerto Rico.
Yo me llamo Ricardo García Rojas. Yo soy de México.
Me llamo Bruna Moscol. Soy de Perú.
Me llamo Jessica. Yo soy de Cuba.
Me llamo Dayramir González Vicet. Soy de La Habana, Cuba.
Me llamo Claudio Ragazzi. Soy de Buenos Aires, Argentina.

Mi nombre es Javier Melendez y soy de San Juan, Puerto Rico.

Me llamo Ana. Soy de Argentina.

Me llamo Alejandro Zorrilla. Yo soy de Uruguay.

Yo me llamo Marcela Jaramillo. Yo soy de Guayaquil, Ecuador.

Me llamo Ela Quezada. Soy de Puerto Rico.

Yo me llamo David Torres. Soy de Bogotá, Colombia.

Me llamo Patricia de la Rosa Tejera. Yo soy de Barcelona.

Me llamo Aura Suárez. Soy de Honduras.

Me llamo Juan Pedro Paniagua. Yo soy de una ciudad del norte de España. Se llama Bilbao.

Me llamo Constanza Leal. Yo soy de Chile.

Yo soy de la República Dominicana.

Yo soy de Maracaibo, Venezuela.

Yo soy de la Ciudad de México.

Yo soy de La Paz, Bolivia.

Yo soy de Chile.

Soy de la Ciudad de Guatemala.

Soy de Perú.

Soy de Panamá.

Soy de Colombia.

Soy de los Estados Unidos.

- **¿Cuántos años tienes?**

Tengo 24 años.

Tengo 20 años.

Yo tengo 20 años.

Tengo 46 años.

Tengo 40 años.

Yo tengo 39 años.

Yo tengo 24 años.

Tengo 27 años.

Tengo 27 años.

Tengo… déjame ver… ¿hoy? 52 años.

Yo tengo 42 años.

Yo tengo 44 años.

Tengo 26 años.

Tengo 43.

Tengo 19 años.

Tengo 19 años.

Tengo 21 años.

Yo tengo 19 años.

Tengo 24 años.

- **¿Cuál es tu profesión?**

Soy estudiante de sociología.

Yo soy estudiante de sicología.

Soy estudiante.

Yo soy estudiante universitario.

Soy ingeniero civil.

Yo soy asistente ejecutiva.

Soy pianista.

Soy cantante y bailarina profesional.

Yo soy profesora de español.

Soy asistente legal bilingüe.

Yo soy músico, guitarrista, compositor y profesor de música.

Yo soy contadora.

Yo soy administrador de proyectos y yo soy actor.

Soy fotógrafo, fotoperiodista e instructor de yoga.

Soy estudiante de doctorado en biología.

Capítulo 2: ¿Qué te gusta hacer?

- **¿De dónde es tu familia?**

Mi mamá es de Panamá y mi papá es de Guatemala.

Mis padres son de la República Dominicana.

Mi papá es de la República Dominicana y mi mamá es de ascendencia irlandesa.

Mis padres son de Chile.

Mis padres son de Colombia.

- **¿Qué te gusta hacer en tu tiempo libre?**

En mi tiempo libre me gusta acampar, me gusta ir de excursiones, bailar y, bueno, cocinar y compartir con familiares y amistades.

En mi tiempo libre me gusta bailar, me gusta leer y me gusta actuar.

En mi tiempo libre me encanta ir de compras, a comprar ropa y arreglarme las uñas.

En mi tiempo libre me gusta andar en bicicleta.

Me gusta leer libros, me gusta escuchar música, me gusta ver la televisión.

Me gusta leer.

- **En tu opinión, ¿cómo eres?**

En mi opinión soy espontánea, activa y honesta.

Soy carismática, muy generosa, y, bueno, tengo muy buen humor.

Yo soy una persona activa, extrovertida y feliz.

Soy bien apasionada y cariñosa.

Pues, yo soy alegre, soy flexible, soy muy adaptiva a las situaciones, soy muy curiosa.

Soy tímida pero alegre.

- **Según tus amigos y familiares, ¿cómo eres?**

Según mis amigos y familiares, soy activa, responsable e impulsiva.

Soy alegre, leal y divertida.

Soy simpática, bien enfocada y profesional.

Bueno, de acuerdo a mami, soy inteligente, soy su niña chiquita, soy bella. De acuerdo a mis amigos, soy muy trabajadora, soy muy exigente de mí misma, soy buena bailadora.

Reservada. Piensan que soy tímida y un poco callada.

Capítulo 3: ¿Qué clases vas a tomar?

- **¿Qué estudias en la universidad?**

Estudio film.

Estoy estudiando administración de empresas.

Estudio piano y composición en Berklee.

Estudio ingeniería mecánica con sostenibilidad.

- **¿Qué haces entresemana?**

Entresemana yo trabajo en mi casa.

Siempre hago algo con film, o veo películas, o hago películas.

En la semana trabajo jornada parcial y… paso mucho tiempo con mi hija en el tiempo libre.

Entresemana trabajo.

Durante la semana estudio.

Estudio todo el día, y despúes salgo en la noche a bailar salsa con mis amigos.

Entresemana yo ensayo mucho para todos los eventos y espectáculos que yo hago como bailarina y cantante.

Bueno pues, estudio mucho, bailo en prácticas de organizaciones y… voy al cine a veces.

■ **¿Qué haces durante los fines de semana?**

Los fines de semana a veces hago conciertos y a veces salgo con mi familia.

En los fines de semana me relajo. Me gusta ir a bailar o estar con amistades, no hacer cosas de la escuela.

Durante los fines de semana me gusta pasar el tiempo con mi familia, ir al cine, ir al parque, ir a comer… actividades fuera de la casa.

Me gusta mucho bailar, me gusta leer, me gusta actuar y especialmente bailar la salsa en los clubes.

Los fines de semana me gusta ir al cine, me gusta ir al gimnasio, me gusta pasar tiempo con mi familia y mis amistades.

Los fines de semana me gusta salir a bailar a fiestas, me gusta ir al cine y me gusta descansar y relajarme.

En los fines de semana me encanta pasar tiempo con mi familia y ver videos en YouTube.

Capítulo 4: ¿Te interesa la tecnología?

■ **¿Qué aparatos electrónicos tienes?**

Tengo un teléfono celular, tengo una computadora portátil, tengo una televisión y también tengo un reproductor de discos compactos.

Tengo un ordenador portátil, tengo una cámara web, tengo un teléfono celular y tengo una cámara digital.

Tengo mi celular, computadora, mi reproductor MP3.

■ **¿Qué aparato te gusta más y por qué?**

Bueno, el aparato elétronico que me gusta más es el reproductor de discos compactos, porque me gusta como suena y me encanta escuchar la música.

Mi reproductor MP3, que es mi favorito, porque tengo toda mi música.

De mis aparatos eléctronicos me gusta más mi ordenador portátil porque puedo chatear con mi familia y mis amigos en España.

■ **¿Pasas mucho tiempo en Internet? ¿Por qué?**

Normalmente estoy muy ocupada y no tengo tiempo para chatear con mis amigos, pero los fines de semana tengo más tiempo y me conecto frecuentemente.

No, no paso mucho tiempo en el Internet porque es un poco aburrido para mí, y prefiero todavía comunicarme con mis amigos directamente.

Yo intento no pasar mucho tiempo en Internet porque estoy muy ocupado, pero es muy útil para mi para comunicarme con otras personas, también revisar el e-mail, y especialmente utilizo Skype para comunicarme con mi novia que está en España.

Capítulo 5: ¿Qué tal la familia?

■ **¿Qué profesión estudias?**

Estoy estudiando para obtener la certificación de gerente de proyectos.

Yo tengo un asociado en paralegal, y ahora voy a estudiar ciencias políticas.

■ **¿Cuántas personas hay en tu familia y cuáles son sus profesiones?**

En mi familia somos siete. Mis papás están jubilados. Tengo dos hermanos que tienen una fábrica de ventanas. Una de mis hermanas tiene un restaurante y mi hermana menor trabaja en administración de empresas para el gobierno.

En mi familia hay cinco personas. Tengo un hermano que es militar, una hermana que es maestra, otra hermana que es contadora, un sobrino que es ingeniero y una sobrina política que es abogada.

Mi familia en El Salvador son cinco personas: Está mi mamá que hace el trabajo en casa, mi hermano varón, el mayor, que trabaja en San Salvador, en una maquila, y mi hermana, una de mis hermanas que está trabajando en una fábrica en Usulután, y mi hermana menor, que está yendo a la escuela. Y mi hija, que tiene 17 años, que también está yendo a la escuela.

En los Estados Unidos yo tengo cuatro miembros de mi familia. Una es mi esposa y tengo dos hijos: un varón, de diez años, una niña de seis años, y mi hermana que tiene 22 años. Mi esposa trabaja en una lavandería y mis dos hijos están yendo a la escuela. Mi hijo el varón está en el cuarto grado y mi hija la hembra está en kindergarten. En el kínder.

Capítulo 6: ¿Adónde vas?

■ **¿Qué tiendas hay en tu barrio?**

En mi barrio hay papelerías donde venden todas las cosas para la escuela como libretas, lápices… también hay restaurantes y hay tiendas de ropa como boutiques y tiendas donde venden comida, leche, pan… hay muchas panaderías.

En mi barrio hay… a ver… hay un centro comercial que tiene tiendas de ropa, tiendas de zapatos, de deportes, y también hay supermercados.

En mi barrio hay un mercado al aire libre, donde puedes ir a comprar carnes, verduras y frutas.

■ **¿Qué tipos de transporte usas cada día?**

El metro, el bus y el carro.

Bueno, uso auto, pero a veces nos transportamos en combi y en el metro.

Pues yo uso mi patineta, la amo, y pues con eso llego a todas partes, rápido.

■ **¿Adónde vas?**

Bueno, cuando uso el auto, el carro, es a trabajar normalmente, pero cuando uso el transporte público como las combis o el metro es para pasear o para visitar a los amigos.

Yo voy al centro de la Ciudad de México a comer en los restaurantes, a caminar en los parques y a ver el centro histórico.

Cada día uso mi patineta para llegar a todas mis clases.

Capítulo 7: ¿Qué pasatiempos prefieres?

▪ ¿Cuál es tu estación preferida? ¿Por qué?

Mi estación preferida es la primavera, porque todo está verde, luego del invierno, que es todo tan oscuro. Los colores son muy vívidos y la temperatura empieza a subir. La primavera es lo más bonito del año.

Me encanta el otoño. Me encanta el cambio de las hojas…

En Costa Rica hay dos estaciones: la estación seca que va de diciembre a mayo, y la estación lluviosa, que va de mayo a diciembre, y yo prefiero la estación seca.

▪ ¿Cuál te gusta menos? ¿Por qué?

La estación que menos me gusta es el invierno porque es muy frío y muy largo.

La que me gusta menos es la estación lluviosa porque casi todas las tardes llueve y… llueve mucho y es muy difícil hacer actividades afuera.

¡Ach! El invierno. ¡Detesto el invierno! ¡Detesto el frío! ¿Por qué? Porque siempre hay frío, te tienes que poner demasiada ropa, tienes que estar así. No me gusta, no me gusta.

▪ ¿Qué te gusta hacer en tus ratos libres?

En mis ratos libres me gusta hacer artes marciales y me gusta hacer yoga.

En mis ratos libres me gusta salir con amigos a tomar café. Me encanta bailar, me encanta acampar y estar en la naturaleza y compartir con mis amistades.

▪ ¿Qué deportes practicas?

Realmente no practico ningún deporte.

Me encanta el fútbol y me encanta correr y caminar.

Practico artes marciales y el yoga.

Capítulo 8: ¿Cómo defines tu estilo?

▪ ¿Dónde compras tu ropa?

A mí me gusta comprar mi ropa en el centro comercial local, porque tiene varias tiendas y hay mucha variedad.

Compro mi ropa en Sears en Perú, en los Estados Unidos en la tienda Marshalls, y en línea.

Yo compro mi ropa en los almacenes, en las tiendas de ropa o en los boutique.

Yo compro la ropa en mercados artesanales. Hay… en casi todas las ciudades grandes hay un mercado artesanal muy famoso en la ciudad de Otavalo en Imbabura. Pero hay artesanía y ropa artesanal que me gusta mucho en todo el país.

▪ ¿Cuáles son tus prendas favoritas de ropa? ¿Por qué?

Mi prenda favorita de ropa es la mini-falda porque es muy feminina y también es muy cómoda.

Me gustan mucho las camisas porque me hacen sentir cómodo, me gusta como me queda y creo que se me ve bien. Mis prendas favoritas son las faldas porque puedo enseñar mis piernas.

▪ ¿Pones mucha o poca importancia en la moda y la ropa? ¿Por qué?

Yo le pongo mucha importancia a la moda y a la ropa, porque de la manera que tú te vistes, tú le estás dando la cara a la sociedad.

No le pongo mucha importancia a la moda porque soy muy viejo.

Pongo mucha importancia en la moda porque puedo combinar accesorios.

No le doy mucha importancia a la moda, porque no me gusta hacer lo que todo el mundo hace. Si todos van para allá, yo me quiero ir para allá. Quiero ser siempre original. La moda tiende a hacer que la gente toda tenga una misma identidad y yo no, yo no voy por ahí.

Capítulo 9: ¿Qué te apetece?

▪ ¿Cuáles son tus platos y comidas favoritos?

Mi plato favorito es saisi. Es un plato típico, típico boliviano. Tiene carne, tiene vegetables, este, la forma que, la manera en que lo hace mi abuela es riquísimo. Otra comida favorita es la sopa de espinaca que tenemos en Bolivia. Es bien rico, especialmente como lo hace mi abuela.

Mi plato favorito es silpancho. Y… silpancho tiene arroz, y después tiene carne asada, con un huevo, y al final tiene una ensalada de cebollas y tomates.

Bueno, hay muchos platos muy sabrosos. Tenemos la chipa guazú, sopa paraguaya, puchero, so'o , payagua mascada . Hay muchas comidas muy ricas. Mi plato favorito es la sopa paraguaya que es riquísimo. Se prepara con harina de maíz, grasa de chancho, queso Paraguay, leche, huevos y cebolla.

▪ ¿Comes frecuentemente en un restaurante? ¿De qué tipo?

De vez en cuando, como en un restaurante. A mí me gusta cocinar en casa también. Me gusta… restaurantes italianos y también me encanta la comida árabe.

A mí me gusta la comida tailandesa.

Prefiero las churrasquerías que son lugares donde se come mucha carne, carne de diferentes tipos; carne vacuna, de pollo, embutidos y sobre todo hay diferente variedad de pastas.

▪ ¿Prefieres comer en casa o en un restaurante? ¿Por qué?

Prefiero comer en mi casa. No como mucho en restaurantes, porque es más económico comer en casa y más saludable.

Me gustan los dos. Ambos son buenos. Me gusta comer en restaurantes porque alguien te lo está preparando y puedes probar comida típica de otro país, de otra cultura. Pero también me encanta cocinar en casa, porque me gusta cocinar y me gusta estar con mi familia.

Capítulo 10: ¿Dónde vives?

▪ ¿Dónde vives? ¿Cómo es tu apartamento o casa?

Vivo en la Ciudad de Guatemala. Tengo una casa que comparto con mi mamá y mi hermano, y usualmente es bastante fría pero me fascina porque tiene un montón de ventanas y le entra un montón de luz, entonces en general es bastante abierta y amplia.

Yo vivo en Boston. Mi apartamento es un apartamento de dos cuartos. Tiene cocina, tiene refrigeradora, tiene una mesa de cocina… además de eso en la sala tiene un sofá y, además de eso pues tiene el baño.

▪ ¿Cómo es tu habitación? Describe las cosas que están allí.

Honestamente, mi cuarto está bastante desordenado, pero desordenado o no, siempre tiene recortes en las paredes de artistas o cantantes que me gustan.

Mi habitación no es tan grande, ni es tan pequeña. Yo la tengo adornada con cuadros de cultura de Nicaragua. Además de eso, tengo una pequeña mesa donde tengo mi computadora. Y tengo el televisor frente a la cama. Eso significa que cuando estoy trabajando en la noche y quiero ver televisión, simplemente me paso a la cama.

■ **De niño(a), ¿tenías que ayudar con los quehaceres domésticos? ¿Qué hacías?**
Sí, yo tenía que ayudar mucho en lo que eran los quehaceres domésticos de mi familia. Yo era el menor, y a veces me

enojaba mucho porque, este, me hacían hacer todos los mandados de la casa. Entonces mi hermano mayor nunca hacía los mandados. Siempre mis padres, como yo era el menor, me mandaban a hacer todos los mandados y a limpiar la casa.

De niña, mis hermanos y yo nos rotábamos los quehaceres, tales como lavar los platos, sacar la basura y organizar la sala familiar.

GEOCULTURAL VIDEOSCRIPTS

Capítulo 2

San Antonio
La ciudad de San Antonio, en el centro de Texas, se ubica al sudoeste de Houston, a 250 kilómetros de la frontera mexicana.

En San Antonio hay mucha influencia hispana. Los mexicanos han aportado a estas tierras muchas de sus tradiciones.

La ciudad es un destino turístico muy popular, con muchas atracciones y actividades.

"El Mercado" es un mercado mexicano que está en la parte oeste de la ciudad. Es el mercado mexicano más grande de los Estados Unidos.

El Álamo, en el centro de la ciudad, es una misión española parcialmente reconstruida.

Este monumento histórico nacional es un símbolo de la independencia texana.

En San Antonio hay agua en todas partes: en fuentes, cascadas, parques, y por supuesto en el río que cruza la ciudad. El río San Antonio, que pasa por el centro, está bordeado de árboles, flores tropicales, cascadas y caminos.

En el Paseo del Río hay puentes pintorescos y botes turísticos que pasan por las aguas plácidas del río. Allí también hay muchos restaurantes, bares, clubes nocturnos, comercios, hoteles y apartamentos lujosos.

Pero es el sabor que le inyectan los mexicoamericanos lo que hace de San Antonio una ciudad especial.

Miami
Arena blanca, cálidas olas, mar azul. Miami es la puerta de Estados Unidos hacia Latinoamérica y el Caribe.

La ciudad tiene aproximadamente dos millones y medio de habitantes. Los hispanos, que representan más del 65% de la población, son principalmente de origen cubano.

Los cubanos han jugado un papel muy importante en el desarrollo cultural, social y económico de Miami.

Tradiciones, costumbres y aspectos de la cultura cubana en general han sido reconstruidos en el contexto de la ciudad de Miami.

Los hijos y los nietos de los inmigrantes cubanos de mediados del siglo pasado, son cubanoamericanos por denominación étnica.

"La pequeña Habana", una zona que incluye la famosa Calle Ocho, es "hogar" para la comunidad cubana.

Además de los cubanos, en Miami también hay grupos de inmigrantes hispanos de El Salvador, Honduras y Nicaragua.

Miami es una ciudad cosmopolita donde llegan personas de muchos países para trabajar, vivir y pasarlo bien.

En las playas y en los bulevares se vive un ambiente festivo, gracias a su gente; esa gente alegre y amistosa de Miami con ese sabor latino cubanoamericano.

Nueva York
"La Gran Manzana", "La ciudad que nunca duerme", Nueva York.

Es la ciudad más poblada de los Estados Unidos de América, con más de ocho millones de habitantes.

Casi tres millones de puertorriqueños viven en los Estados Unidos. La mayoría vive en las ciudades de Nueva York y Nueva Jersey. Un dato interesante es que en Nueva York viven más puertorriqueños que en San Juan, la capital de Puerto Rico.

Especialmente en las últimas décadas, han llegado de Puerto Rico miles de personas. Para muchos, fue muy difícil adaptarse a la vida de la gran ciudad.

También son importantes en Nueva York otros grupos de inmigrantes hispanos como los dominicanos y los colombianos.

La presencia de medios de comunicación en español, y de comercio estilo latino, refleja la importancia de la población hispana en la ciudad.

¡Un mundo de gente con gente de todo el mundo! Ésa es Nueva York, la gran metrópoli. ¡Cuando la conoces, ya sabes por qué su slogan dice: "Yo amo Nueva York!"
I love New York!

Capítulo 3

Puerto Rico
San Juan, la capital de Puerto Rico, es la ciudad más antigua y mejor conservada de la región del Caribe.

Se conoce como la "Ciudad amurallada" por la impresionante muralla de 60 pies de altura que bordea la ciudad desde 1539.

Éste es el Fuerte de San Felipe del Morro, una edificación militar de seis niveles, estructura clave en el fortalecimiento del Imperio Español en el Nuevo Mundo.

Además de sus edificios históricos y sus calles pintorescas, Puerto Rico es conocido por las artesanías típicas, como las muñecas de trapo, los instrumentos musicales y todo tipo de objetos de madera.

Estas máscaras hechas de papel maché representan la influencia africana en la cultura puertorriqueña.

Al este de San Juan están las playas de Piñones, donde abundan los quioscos con comida típica como los "bacalaítos", una fritura de bacalao.

Hacia el sur, y frente al Mar Caribe, está la segunda ciudad más grande de la isla, Ponce.

En la Plaza los ponceños se refrescan con una piragua mientras disfrutan la tarde junto a la Catedral de la Guadalupe.

El antiguo Parque de Bombas, con sus tradicionales colores rojo y negro, es una de las atracciones de Ponce, al igual que La Guancha, un paseo tablado junto al mar, perfecto para admirar la puesta del sol.

Con costas hacia el Atlántico y el Caribe, Puerto Rico es ideal para las actividades al aire libre, ya sea un picnic, ir de compras o hacer turismo.

Cuba

La República Socialista de Cuba, situada en el Mar Caribe, es la isla más grande de las Antillas Mayores. Su población supera los 11 millones de habitantes, y está conformada por un 51% de mulatos, 37% de descendientes de españoles y cerca de 12% de negros descendientes de africanos.

La Capital de Cuba es La Habana, situada en torno a la Bahía de La Habana, frente al estrecho de La Florida.

La Bahía se comunica con el mar a través de un estrecho canal donde encontramos el Castillo del Morro, con su emblemático faro, la fortificación más antigua construida por los españoles en América.

Desde la entrada de la bahía hasta la desembocadura del río Almendares se extiende El Malecón, la avenida más popular de toda La Habana. El Malecón tiene una extensión de más de 7 kilómetros y a lo largo de su recorrido se pueden ver unas vistas espectaculares, sobre todo a la hora de la puesta del sol.

En la bahía también se encuentra el principal puerto de Cuba y el barrio de La Habana Vieja, el más antiguo de la capital, con edificios antiguos, muchos de ellos construidos en el siglo XVI.

En La Habana Vieja están todos los grandes monumentos antiguos, las fortalezas, los conventos e iglesias, los palacios, las callejuelas, los balcones. La Habana Vieja es el conjunto colonial más rico de Latinoamérica.

En el centro de La Habana llama la atención la cúpula del Capitolio de La Habana, de estilo renacentista, que tiene gran similitud con la Basílica de San Pedro, en Roma.

La Plaza de La Revolución es el símbolo de la revolución cubana.

Parece que el tiempo detuvo su marcha en La Habana de la década de los sesenta: en sus calles transitan autos muy antiguos y gran cantidad de coches halados por caballos.

El punto más alto de la ciudad es el monumento a José Martí, una estatua de mármol de 17 metros con una torre de 142 metros de altura.

Actualmente el turismo es muy importante para la economía del país. Cuba recibe más de 2 millones de turistas internacionales al año.

Los cubanos son gente que se manifiesta con alegría en los bailes populares de las calles y sobre todo en el ámbito artístico de la música y el folclore.

La República Dominicana

Playas, mar verde, artesanías singulares… Santo Domingo, capital de La República Dominicana, es un lugar tropical ideal.

La ciudad de Santo Domingo está situada en la desembocadura del río Ozama, al sur de la isla.

Cristóbal Colón bautizó esta isla "La Española". Aquí en Santo Domingo se encuentra la tumba del descubridor del continente americano. También está el monumento "Faro a Colón", construido en su honor.

Las antiguas construcciones coloniales recuerdan la época de la conquista de América.

En esta isla encontramos las ruinas de la primera Catedral del Nuevo Mundo, Santa María la Menor, fundada en 1530…

la Universidad Santo Tomás de Aquino, fundada en 1538… el Hospital San Nicolás de Bari, fundado en 1503… entre otras edificaciones y fortificaciones que datan del siglo XVI.

El clima agradable de la isla dominicana es ideal para la práctica de actividades al aire libre.

A la mayoría de la gente joven le gusta el béisbol, que es el deporte más popular y más practicado del país.

El clima caribeño de la isla es cálido y hospitalario, como la gente.

Entre la artesanía que es posible comprar por las calles, encontramos múltiples ejemplares de arte popular: collares, platos, vasijas, máscaras, timbales y cuadros como los que se venden en el Mercado Modelo de Artesanía.

La Avenida del Malecón pasa por las hermosas playas de Santo Domingo: Es por las playas de arena blanca, el mar y las palmeras de esta bella tierra… que los habitantes la llaman Quisqueya, "Madre de todas las tierras".

Capítulo 4

Madrid

Madrid, la capital de España, se sitúa en el centro de la península Ibérica.

Su población es de más de tres millones de habitantes.

Es una ciudad dinámica y una de las ciudades con mayor población de la Unión Europea.

También es un centro financiero y cultural importante.

Madrid es una ciudad de muchos atractivos: por sus calles y Plaza Mayor, sus parques, jardines e innumerables museos y restaurantes excelentes.

Una de las avenidas principales es la Gran Vía, situada en la parte antigua de la ciudad.

También en la parte antigua, en la Puerta del Sol, encontramos el Kilómetro Cero, punto de partida de las carreteras radiales de España.

Los Museos del Jamón son tiendas que se especializan en jamones y embutidos de gran tradición española. Son muy visitados por los amantes de este tipo de comida.

En la zona de Atocha están los museos más prestigiosos de Madrid, entre ellos el Centro de Arte Reina Sofía.

Un sitio que recibe muchos visitantes es el Parque del Retiro, reconocido como uno de los parques más bellos del mundo. En sus grandes áreas de recreo la gente va a caminar o simplemente a descansar bajo el sol brillante de Madrid.

Toledo

Toledo, una pequeña ciudad española de grandes tesoros artísticos, está cerca de Madrid en un cerro junto al río Tajo.

Conocida como "La ciudad de las tres culturas", musulmanes, judíos y cristianos convivieron en Toledo durante la Edad Media.

La cultura musulmana se nota en las calles pequeñas y estrechas y en la arquitectura "mudéjar" del siglo XV.

La Sinagoga del Tránsito es testimonio de las contribuciones judías a la ciudad. Allí está hoy el Museo Sefardí.

La presencia cristiana se ve en la catedral, una de las mayores edificaciones de la cristiandad.

Dentro de las murallas de Toledo, encontramos monumentos, iglesias, palacios y museos.

La Casa Museo de El Greco exhibe la obra de este célebre pintor, que vivió en Toledo en el siglo XVI.

En la iglesia de Santo Tomé se encuentra su obra maestra, "El entierro del Conde Orgaz".

Con su aspecto medieval, sus artesanías y obras de arte en metal, y la cerámica que adornan calles y balcones, Toledo es una auténtica joya monumental, nombrada Patrimonio Mundial por la UNESCO.

Capítulo 5

Honduras

Tegucigalpa es la capital y la ciudad más poblada de Honduras. Fundada en el siglo XVI, la ciudad está situada al pie del Cerro El Picacho.

El Parque Nacional del Picacho, o de las Naciones Unidas, es un buen sitio para pasar el tiempo libre. Allí podemos ver una gran estatua de mármol que representa a Cristo resucitado.

Desde el parque del Picacho se pueden ver el estadio de fútbol Francisco Morazán y una extensa vista panorámica del centro de la ciudad.

En Tegucigalpa la arquitectura colonial se conserva en las edificaciones del centro histórico, como la Basílica de Suyapa y la catedral del siglo XVII. La catedral está frente a la Plaza Central, una de las plazas más importantes de la ciudad donde está el monumento a Francisco Morazán, considerado héroe nacional. El Parque Manuel Bonilla, también conocido como el Parque la Leona, es el parque principal de la ciudad. Hay un mirador con vistas espectaculares, caminos y jardines, y una estatua en honor al general Manuel Bonilla, ex presidente hondureño.

La ciudad tiene lugares de interés cultural importantes, como el Teatro Nacional, museos y toda la zona histórica de la ciudad.

Entre los atractivos de Tegucigalpa figura el Mercado la Isla, el más importante del país; bulevares, parques y plazas.

En los puestos de artesanía la gente puede comprar artículos de madera, junco, textiles, barro y otros productos que reflejan la herencia indígena.

La herencia indígena de Honduras tiene su mayor representación en la Escalinata de los Jeroglíficos, en las ruinas mayas de Copán.

Sin ninguna duda, los "catrachos", como se les conoce a los hondureños, tienen muchas razones para sentir orgullo por su país.

El Salvador

El Salvador, el país más pequeño de Centroamérica, tiene una historia larga de erupciones volcánicas y terremotos.

San Salvador, fundada en 1525, es la capital y el centro económico del país. Hoy día es una ciudad moderna y es la segunda más poblada de Centroamérica.

En la Plaza de Las Américas, en San Salvador, está el monumento al Salvador del Mundo.

La Catedral Metropolitana, en el centro de la ciudad, tiene una colorida fachada. Muchas personas visitan la catedral para ver la tumba del arzobispo Óscar Romero, recordado y admirado por su lucha por ayudar a los pobres.

En la Plaza Gerardo Barrios podemos ver el Palacio Nacional, que sufrió daños con los terremotos de 1986 y 2001; es considerado un monumento nacional. También vemos las estatuas de Cristóbal Colón y la Reina Isabel La Católica.

El Teatro Nacional, construido a principios del siglo XX, es monumento nacional y lugar de conciertos, teatro, baile y actos oficiales.

El Mercado de Artesanías está en el edifico del antiguo Monasterio de San Francisco. En este mercado venden artículos del arte y artesanía popular salvadoreña.

El Estadio Cuscatlán, el más grande de Centroamérica, se usa principalmente para partidos de fútbol, pero también para conciertos y eventos culturales y políticos.

Cerca de San Salvador encontramos el pueblo indígena de Panchimalco. Este pueblo pintoresco posee la iglesia colonial más antigua del país.

El Cerro Verde es un volcán extinto que hizo su última erupción hace 2500 años. Durante la erupción, la lava llegó casi hasta el lago Coatepeque.

En la cima de Cerro Verde se encuentra uno de los pocos bosques nebulosos del país, dado su altura de ubicación a 2030 metros sobre el nivel del mar. Desde los miradores ubicados a lo largo de los senderos interpretativos del parque Cerro Verde se pueden apreciar los imponentes volcanes de Santa Ana e Izalco.

Existen muchas actividades que pueden desarrollarse en el parque, una de las favoritas son las caminatas por caminos de exótica flora y fauna, que hacen del Parque nacional Cerro Verde un paraíso natural.

Capítulo 6

México

El Distrito Federal es la capital de México.

Sobre las ruinas de la ciudad azteca de Tenochtitlán los españoles construyeron la Catedral de la Guadalupe y el Palacio del Virrey.

Este es el Zócalo, la cuarta plaza más grande del mundo y centro político y religioso de México.

El Paseo de la Reforma comienza en esta plaza y se extiende por gran parte de la ciudad. En esta gran avenida está el Monumento a la Independencia, conocido también como la Victoria Alada, o el Ángel.

También sobre el Paseo de la Reforma está el Museo de Antropología, un museo importantísimo para conocer la historia de los pueblos antiguos de México.

En este museo hay versiones de la Piedra del Sol, una especie de calendario para medir los ciclos astronómicos. Hay también muchos artefactos precolombinos.

La compleja y diversa historia de México está reflejada en la arquitectura de la ciudad. Edificios, catedrales y templos se entremezclan para contar la historia y un poco de la vida de los mexicanos de hoy.

Capítulo 7

Panamá

La República de Panamá es un país de América Central. Está situada entre Costa Rica y Colombia, el Mar Caribe y el Océano Pacífico.

Su capital es la Ciudad de Panamá. Allí se encuentra el Canal de Panamá; canal interoceánico entre las costas del Océano Atlántico y el Océano Pacífico.

La palabra Panamá es de origen indígena, y significa "Abundancia de Peces".

En general la Ciudad de Panamá tiene un clima tropical, y también su gente es muy calurosa.

Existe una gran diversidad étnica. La mayoría de la población es de origen mestizo, descendientes de indígenas, africanos y españoles.

La Ciudad de Panamá es uno de los centros bancarios más fuertes del mundo y el centro financiero y de seguros más poderoso de toda Latinoamérica.

Es una de las ciudades más avanzadas y cosmopolitas del continente americano, con numerosas atracciones turísticas. El Puente de las Américas, sobre el Canal de Panamá, une el istmo. Fue inaugurado el 12 de octubre de 1962.

El Casco antiguo de Panamá es el barrio histórico de la ciudad. Se le llama Panamá Viejo. En él encontramos estrechos callejones y gran cantidad de casas de vieja tradición adornadas con balcones estilo colonial y otras edificaciones antiguas, como la Catedral, frente a la Plaza de la Independencia, la Iglesia de Nuestra Señora de la Asunción y antiguos edificios de gobierno.

Con su crisol de tradiciones y culturas, rincones históricos y modernos rascacielos, Panamá es, como lo dice su slogan turístico: "La Ruta por descubrir".

Costa Rica

La República de Costa Rica es un país pequeño, que aunque sólo cubre un 0.01% de la masa del planeta Tierra, contiene aproximadamente un 5% de su biodiversidad.

Rodeada de valles y montañas y con costas en el Océano Pacífico y el Mar Caribe, Costa Rica es una república democrática, con una población de 4 millones de habitantes que gozan de la paz y la belleza natural de su país.

San José es la capital de Costa Rica. Algunos lugares interesantes de la ciudad de San José son:

El Teatro Nacional, que está en el corazón de la capital. Fue construido en 1890, con un estilo clásico renacentista. Es una copia pequeña de la famosa Ópera de París.

El Museo Nacional está localizado en un antiguo fuerte. Allí se puede apreciar arte precolombino y de la época colonial de Costa Rica.

Otros sitios de interés histórico y arquitectónico son: la Catedral Metropolitana, que está frente al Parque Central, el Teatro Melico Salazar, el Parque Morazán, y el Parque Nacional, donde está El Monumento Nacional, que representa la victoria de los costarricenses ante los filibusteros en la batalla de 1856.

El Parque Metropolitano La Sabana es donde cientos de "ticos" —como se les conoce a los costarricenses— llegan cada día para hacer deporte o para descansar. La Sabana es considerado un "pulmón" en la ciudad.

Los ticos son gente de naturaleza amable y tranquila, que viven y disfrutan la paz de un país privilegiado. Como dice el himno nacional: "bajo el límpido azul de tu cielo, vivan siempre el trabajo y la paz".

Capítulo 8

Perú

Lima es la capital de Perú y la ciudad más grande del país. Fue fundada por el conquistador español Francisco Pizarro en 1535.

Miraflores es el distrito más cosmopolita de la ciudad. En los restaurantes de la Calle de las Pizzas, turistas y visitantes limeños disfrutan de la comida peruana.

El Parque Kennedy, también en el distrito de Miraflores, tiene múltiples atracciones: la vieja iglesia Virgen Milagrosa, plazas de juegos infantiles, y el Parque del Amor, que tiene una famosa escultura de una pareja dándose un beso.

Otros parques son el Olivar y el Parque de la Muralla, que conserva parte de la muralla que antiguamente protegía la ciudad de los piratas.

Edificios como el Palacio de Justicia y el Teatro Colón son característicos de la ciudad limeña.

La Catedral de Lima y la iglesia de San Francisco son ejemplos del estilo colonial español.

Cerca de la Plaza Mayor hay varios monumentos y edificios gubernamentales, como el Correo Central y el Palacio Municipal.

La Plaza San Martín es una de las plazas principales de la ciudad.

Allí está el monumento en homenaje a José de San Martín, héroe de la independencia peruana.

Otras atracciones de Lima son: el mercado de artesanías, las plazas e iglesias, las playas, el barrio chino, y el maravilloso "circuito mágico del agua", un conjunto de fuentes de agua animadas con luz y sonido.

Ecuador

Rodeada por volcanes, como el Cotopaxi, por la Cordillera Central de los Andes, y situada a 2.850 metros sobre el nivel del mar, Quito, la capital de Ecuador, goza de un clima primaveral todo el año.

Hace 1.500 años los incas construyeron caminos desde el centro de lo que hoy es Quito hacia los cerros de adoración al dios del sol y de la luna.

Los españoles cristianizaron estas rutas religiosas, comerciales y militares, construyendo la Catedral de la Virgen de Quito en 1534.

Poblada por casi un millón y medio de habitantes, la ciudad de Quito es hoy Patrimonio de la Humanidad y el segundo centro histórico más grande de América, después de La Habana, Cuba.

Para conocer el Quito Antiguo hay que visitar la Plaza Grande, rodeada de edificios coloniales como la Catedral Metropolitana, el Palacio Arzobispal y los distintos monasterios e iglesias que pueblan la zona.

Pero Quito es también moderno. Al norte de la ciudad colonial se encuentra la parte moderna de la capital de Ecuador, reflejo de la acelerada vida de los quiteños hoy. Pronto los ecuatorianos celebrarán 200 años de independencia del dominio español, y las raíces indígenas nunca dejaron de ser evidentes.

Un paseo dominical por los pasillos del Mercado Mariscal o por el parque El Ejido ofrece una abundancia de artesanía indígena…y de comidas ecuatorianas.

El Ecuador moderno ofrece historia y cultura indígena y colonial. Y la diversidad de su topografía —costa, montañas y selva amazónica— es excelente para el turismo ecológico.

Capítulo 9

Bolivia

Bolivia es un país con mucha riqueza cultural y arqueológica.

La capital gubernamental es La Paz, que está situada en los Andes a 3.650 metros de altura.

La mayoría de los bolivianos son indígenas aymaras y quechuas. Los mestizos y personas de origen europeo forman una parte menor de la población.

En La Paz se ven grandes contrastes sociales: al oeste y al norte hay barrios pobres y al sur hay barrios ricos.

La ciudad conserva un aspecto de la época colonial en su arquitectura, con su Catedral construida entre los siglos XVI y XVII, el Palacio de Gobierno y el Congreso Nacional. Tiene muchas iglesias, como la iglesia de San Francisco. Cerca está el célebre Museo del Oro.

El centro de la ciudad es de una actividad intensa, con mucho tráfico y gran cantidad de peatones.

El Paseo del Prado, una avenida principal, pasa por la zona comercial y financiera de La Paz.

Los mercados de frutas y los puestos de comida en las calles son muy populares.

En los mercados indígenas de artesanía se pueden comprar artículos muy originales, especialmente tejidos hechos a mano.

En la Plaza Humboldt es posible obtener pinturas de temas andinos y ver a los artistas pintar.

Por su situación geográfica, la zona de La Paz tiene ecosistemas del altiplano y trópico.

La zona andina está a una hora por carretera de la ciudad. Allí encontramos el espectacular lago Titicaca, a 3.900 metros sobre el nivel del mar.

Otros lugares hermosos de Bolivia son: las ruinas precolombinas de Tiahuanaco y Oruro, con sus carnavales y música tradicional indígena.

Paraguay

Paraguay, Tierra del Arpa del Nuevo Mundo.

Asunción, la capital del país, situada en la bahía del Río Paraguay, conserva ruinas y construcciones coloniales. También es una ciudad moderna y cosmopolita.

El área metropolitana tiene una población de aproximadamente 1.400.000 habitantes.

En la zona histórica, el Palacio de Gobierno llama la atención por su bello estilo colonial.

Cerca de esta zona también encontramos el tradicional mercado principal.

La vida artística de Paraguay está relacionada con el arpa paraguaya.

El arpa paraguaya se originó cuando un tañedor de arpas llegó a Paraguay con los conquistadores españoles en 1526. Este instrumento fue adoptado por los habitantes de la época.

Ellos lo perfeccionaron utilizando madera americana.

Así crearon un nuevo tipo de arpa y también un repertorio de música especialmente para ella.

El arpa paraguaya, que tiene 32 o 36 cuerdas, es un instrumento muy liviano, sin partes metálicas.

Paraguay es un país bilingüe. Sus idiomas oficiales son el español y el guaraní.

Esta es la lengua nativa de los guaraníes, un pueblo antiguo de la zona.

Hoy en día se enseñan los dos idiomas en las escuelas del país.

Y los niños aprenden que "Paraguay" es una palabra guaraní, que significa "aguas adornadas".

Capítulo 10

Guatemala

Tierra legendaria de hombres de maíz. Tierra de los mayas. En esta ciudad, las calles de piedra, las casas y las iglesias son muy antiguas.

Los mercados, de gran colorido, tienen mucha vida.

Antigua, fundada a mediados del siglo XVI, parece una escena de otros tiempos.

Esta ciudad es uno de los destinos turísticos más importantes de toda Guatemala.

Las costumbres religiosas de sus habitantes, que son descendientes mayas, son una mezcla de ritos mayas y cristianos.

Chichicastenango es una ciudad muy visitada por peregrinos indígenas.

Ellos se reúnen en la iglesia de Santo Tomás para celebrar antiguos ritos mayas.

Los mercados de artesanía tienen verdaderas obras de arte.

Los huipiles son blusas tradicionales indígenas tejidas según el estilo de cada pueblo o región.

Entre los textiles y otras artesanías encontramos también calendarios mayas.

En Solola, el Lago Atitlán, a 1.500 metros de altura sobre el nivel del mar, es uno de los lagos más bellos del mundo. Desde el lago, se ven los volcanes Atitlán, Tolimán y San Pedro.

Estos volcanes, como los mayas y sus descendientes, forman una parte inseparable de la larga historia de Guatemala.

Nicaragua

Nicaragua, que en la lengua indígena náhuatl significa "junto al agua", es la tierra de los lagos y de los volcanes. Nicaragua es el país más grande de Centroamérica. Managua es la capital y el centro económico de la nación. Está situada en la costa sur del Lago de Managua.

En Nicaragua hay muchos lagos, lagunas y volcanes: El Lago de Nicaragua, que es el lago más grande del país, el Volcán Mombacho, que está inactivo, volcanes activos como el Volcán Masaya, el gran Volcán Momotombo; y la Laguna de Tiscapa, una reserva natural.

En Managua está la famosa silueta de Sandino, que es el monumento al líder de la revolución y héroe nacional Augusto César Sandino.

La ciudad fue reconstruida después del terremoto de 1974, y hoy vemos ejemplos de su desarrollo urbano, con construcciones como rotondas y pasos a nivel, y edificaciones de interés cultural y arquitectónico como la Catedral Nueva y la Concha Acústica.

Otros lugares de interés cultural son el Palacio Nacional de la Cultura, la antigua catedral, y el Teatro Rubén Darío, que lleva el nombre del poeta inmortal del modernismo.

El ambiente en Managua es alegre, como se ve en el parque de Tiscapa, en el malecón y en las plazas importantes de la ciudad.

Granada es la ciudad histórica de Nicaragua. Es una de las ciudades coloniales más bellas de América Central.

La Iglesia y Convento de San Francisco, del siglo XVI, es una de las edificaciones coloniales más antiguas del continente americano.

En el centro de la ciudad está el Parque Central.

Y muy cerca del Parque se encuentran las iglesias principales de Granada y la Casa de los Tres Mundos, que es una institución que promueve proyectos culturales en Nicaragua y América Central.

La ciudad de Masaya es reconocida por su bella artesanía. En sus mercados vemos hamacas, máscaras, textiles y pinturas primitivistas, en un ambiente popular y festivo.

¡Lagos, volcanes, islas, arquitectura colonial, artesanía, eso es Nicaragua!

VOLUME 1

CUADROS

INTRODUCTORY SPANISH

Sheri Spaine Long
University of Alabama at Birmingham

María Carreira
California State University at Long Beach

Sylvia Madrigal Velasco

Kristin Swanson

HEINLE
CENGAGE Learning™

Australia • Brazil • Japan • Korea • Mexico • Singapore • Spain • United Kingdom • United States

HEINLE
CENGAGE Learning™

Cuadros
**Sheri Spaine Long, María Carreira,
Sylvia Madrigal Velasco, &
Kristin Swanson**

Vice President, Editorial Director:
  PJ Boardman

Publisher: Beth Kramer

Senior Acquisitions Editor: Heather
  Bradley Cole

Senior Development Editor: Kim Beuttler

Assistant Editor: Sara Dyer

Editorial Assistant: Claire Kaplan

Senior Media Editor: Morgen Murphy

Senior Marketing Manager: Ben Rivera

Marketing Coordinator: Claire Fleming

Marketing Communications Manager:
  Glenn McGibbon

Senior Content Project Manager: Aileen
  Mason

Senior Art Director: Linda Jurras

Senior Manufacturing Planner: Betsy
  Donaghey

Rights Acquisition Specialist: Mandy
  Grozsko

Production Service: PreMediaGlobal

Text Designers: Carol Maglitta, Susan Gilday

Cover Designer: Harold Burch

Cover Image: ©Marc Le Fèvre/Photolibrary

Compositor: PreMediaGlobal

For product information and technology assistance, contact us at
Cengage Learning Customer & Sales Support, 1-800-354-9706
For permission to use material from this text or product,
submit all requests online at **www.cengage.com/permissions**
Further permissions questions can be emailed to
permissionrequest@cengage.com

Library of Congress Control Number: 2011937474

Student Edition:

ISBN-13: 978-1-111-34114-5

ISBN-10: 1-111-34114-1

Annotated Instructor's Edition:

ISBN-13: 978-1-111-34346-0

ISBN-10: 1-111-34346-2

Heinle
20 Channel Center Street
Boston, MA 02210
USA

Cengage Learning is a leading provider of customized learning solutions with office locations around the globe, including Singapore, the United Kingdom, Australia, Mexico, Brazil and Japan. Locate your local office at **international.cengage.com/region**

Cengage Learning products are represented in Canada by Nelson Education, Ltd.

For your course and learning solutions, visit **www.cengage.com**

Purchase any of our products at your local college store or at our preferred online store **www.cengagebrain.com**

Instructors: Please visit **login.cengage.com** and log in to access instructor-specific resources.

Printed in Canada
1 2 3 4 5 6 7 15 14 13 12 11

To the Student

¡Bienvenidos! Welcome to the *Cuadros* introductory Spanish program. Spanish is one of the most useful languages you can learn; it is spoken by nearly 500 million people across the globe, including over 50 million Hispanics in the United States alone—one out of every six Americans. It is the most spoken language in the world after Mandarin Chinese and English. As you undertake your study of the Spanish language with *Cuadros*, keep in mind the following:

- We strive to present the Spanish-speaking world in all its diversity, with particular attention to indigenous and African-Hispanic populations, as well as European and Latin American immigrant populations.

- We guide you to make cross-cultural comparisons between the cultures you learn about and your own. Too often, the emphasis has been on the differences among cultures, when what may be surprising is the number of things we have in common with Spanish speakers around the world.

- We encourage you to look at your own community and to meet and interact with the Spanish speakers you encounter in both local and global communities. Spanish is all around you—just keep your eyes and ears open for it!

- *Cuadros* is designed to enrich your language-learning experience—while you are learning another language, you are also gathering information *about* the people who speak it and the countries where it is spoken. At first, you may think that you are unable to read or understand much Spanish, but in *Cuadros*, the focus is on getting the main ideas, and the tasks expected of you are limited to what you have already learned or what you can safely deduce from context. You will be surprised to see that you can comprehend more than you think you can!

- *Cuadros* features a variety of resources to help you achieve your language-learning goals more easily. Media icons at relevant points throughout the print book tell you exactly which component to use for additional practice or support. Or, work right from the eBook for direct access to all of the program's resources, including audio recordings of key vocabulary and grammar terms, instant activity feedback, and online chat and commenting functionality.

- Learning a language is easier if you relax and have fun. Keeping this in mind, we've included humorous and contemporary content with the goal of making language learning enjoyable and interesting.

We hope you enjoy your introduction to the Spanish language and its many peoples and cultures. Learning a language sets you on a course of life-long learning. It is one of the most valuable and exciting things you can do to prepare yourself to be a global citizen of the twenty-first century.

—The Authors

Student Components

Student Text

Your **Student Text** contains all the information and activities you need for in-class use. Volumes 1 and 2 each contain a preliminary chapter followed by five regular chapters that contain vocabulary presentations and activities, grammar presentations and activities, video-related practice, cultural information, reading selections, and writing practice. There are also valuable reference sections at the back of each book, including Spanish-English and English-Spanish glossaries and verb charts. In addition, Volume 2 contains an appendix that reviews all of the grammar presented in Volume 1.

Student Activities Manual (SAM): Workbook / Lab Manual / Video Manual

The **Student Activities Manual (SAM)** includes out-of-class practice of the material presented in the Student Text. Volumes 1 and 2 of the SAM are each divided into a Workbook (**Cuaderno de práctica**), which focuses on written vocabulary and grammar practice, reading, and writing; a Lab Manual (**Manual de laboratorio**), which focuses on pronunciation and listening comprehension; and a Video Manual (**Manual de video**), which offers extra practice of the storyline and **Voces del mundo hispano** segments.

iLrn™ Heinle Learning Center

An all-in-one online learning environment, including an audio- and video-enhanced interactive eBook, assignable textbook activities, companion videos, assignable voice-recorded activities, an online workbook and lab manual with audio, interactive enrichment activities, a chapter- and volume-level diagnostic study tool for better exam preparation, and now, media sharing and commenting capability through Share It! The iLrn: Heinle Learning Center is offered separately for Volumes 1 and 2.

Premium Website

You will find a wealth of resources and practice on the *Cuadros* **Premium Website**, accessible for Volumes 1 and 2 at **www.cengagebrain.com.** The **Premium Website** assets should be used as you work through each chapter and as you review for quizzes and exams.

To get access, visit CengageBrain.com

- It provides access to the text audio program, Web activities and links, Google Earth™ coordinates, and an iTunes™ playlist.
- The premium password-protected resources include the SAM audio program, the video program, grammar and pronunciation podcasts, grammar tutorial videos, auto-graded quizzes, and more!
- The web quizzes focus on vocabulary and grammar and provide automatic feedback, which helps you understand errors and pinpoints areas for review.
- The web activities offer the opportunity to explore authentic Spanish-language websites. Cultural web links relate to the **Voces de la comunidad, ¡Fíjate!,** and **¿Quieres saber más?** activities as well as **Tú en el mundo hispano**, which covers volunteer, study abroad, and internship opportunities throughout the Hispanic world and **Ritmos del mundo hispano**, a section that explores traditional and contemporary Hispanic music through music and video links.

Acknowledgments

Reviewers and Contributors

We would like to acknowledge the helpful suggestions and useful ideas of our reviewers, whose commentary was invaluable to us in shaping *Cuadros*.

Many thanks go to the following professors, each of whom offered valuable suggestions through their participation in live and virtual focus groups:

ACTFL: Introductory Spanish Focus Group
Aleta Anderson, *Grand Rapids Community College*
Yolanda González, *Valencia Community College*
Monica Montalvo, *University of Central Florida*
Renee Wooten, *Vernon College*

Pasadena Focus Group
Esther Castro, *San Diego State University*
Mercedes Limón, *Chaffey College*
Ofelia McQueen, *Los Angeles City College*
Markus Muller, *California State University, Long Beach*
Rosalinda Nericcio, *San Diego State University*
Yelgy Parada, *Los Angeles City College*
Victoria Tirado, *Chaffey College*

Philadelphia Focus Group
Norma Corrales-Martin, *Temple University*
Judith R. Downing, *Rutgers University – Camden*
April Jacobs, *Temple University*
Maríadelaluz Matus-Mendoza, *Drexel University*
Patricia Moore-Martinez, *Temple University*
Eva Recio-Gonzalez, *University of Pennsylvania*
Kimberly Ann Vega, *Temple University*

Development Reviews
Karen Berg, *College of Charleston*
Genevieve Breedon, *Darton College*
Matt Carpenter, *Yuba College, Clear Lake Campus*
John Catlett, *Cabrini College*
Daria Cohen, *Rider University*
Carmen García, *Valencia Community College*
Martha García, *University of Central Florida*
Diego Emilio Gómez
Yolanda González, *Valencia Community College*
Laurie Huffman, *Los Medanos College / Florida State College*
Isabel Killough, *Norfolk State University*
Lori Lammert, *Chattanooga State Community College*

Jill Loney, *Urbana University*
Richard McCallister, *Delaware State University*
Meghan Mehlos, *University of Wisconsin – Eau Claire*
Deanna Mihaly, *Eastern Michigan University*
Dianne Moneypenny
Lisa Nalbone, *University of Central Florida*
Janet Norden, *Baylor University*
Catherine Ortíz, *University of Texas at Arlington*
Sieglinde Poelzler-Kamatali, *Ohio Northern University*
Rosalea Postma-Carttar, *University of Kansas*
Laura Ruiz-Scott, *Scottsdale Community College*
Lester Edgardo Sandres Rapalo, *Valencia Community College*
Erika Sutherland, *Muhlenberg College*
David Tate, *Brevard Community College*
Wendy Westmoreland, *Cleveland Community College*
Sandra Wise, *University of Texas at Arlington*

Testing Program Consultants
Bárbara Ávila-Shah, *University at Buffalo, The State University of New York*
Patrick Brady, *Tidewater Community College*
Marta Nunn, *Virginia Commonwealth University*
Helga Winkler, *Ventura County Community College District – Moorpark College*

We would like to extend our gratitude to the Graduate Teaching Assistant and Adjunct Faculty Focus Group, which discussed the tools needed to ensure a successful transition to a new edition and successful use over the course of the semester.

Graduate Teaching Assistant / Adjunct Faculty Focus Group
Alison Atkins, *Boston University*
Alison Carberry, *Boston University*
Alejandra Cornejo, *Boston University*
Daniela Dorfman, *Boston University*
Megan Gibbons, *Boston University*
Rebeca Hey-Colón, *Harvard University*
Magdalena Malinowska, *Boston University*
Glenda Quiñónez, *Harvard University*

Finally, special thanks go to the following professors and writers, who have written the outstanding supplements to accompany this program:

Meghan Allen, *Babson College – Volume-level diagnostics and Web assets*

Flavia Belpoliti, *University of Houston – Bridge chapter teaching suggestions*

María Colina – *Lesson plans*

Juan De Urda, *SUNY Fredonia – Web quizzes*

Karen Haller Beer – *Testing program*

Maribel Lárraga, *Our Lady of the Lake University – Testing program and audio script*

Sarah Link – *PowerPoint presentations*

Jeff Longwell, *New Mexico State University – Volume-level oral assessments*

Nina Patrizio-Quiñones, *Our Lady of the Lake University – Testing program and audioscript*

Joshua Pope, *University of Wisconsin – Madison – Information gap activities*

Nidia Schuhmacher, *Brown University – Web searches*

Sierra Turner, *University of Alabama – Activity worksheets*

A hearty thanks to our fine VAK system, Learning Style worksheet writers: **Carlos Abaunza, Rebeca Hey-Colón** from **Harvard University** and **Magdalena Malinowska** from **Boston University**. Through creativity, hard work, and proactive communication, these writers took full ownership of the project from its incipient stages to create a comprehensive set of intuitive and valuable tools for visual, auditory, and kinesthetic learners.

We would also like to thank the World Languages Group at Heinle Cengage Learning for their ongoing support of this project and for guiding us along the long and sometimes difficult path to its completion! Many thanks especially to Beth Kramer and Heather Bradley for their professional guidance and outstanding support. We would also like to thank Kim Beuttler, our development editor, for her enthusiastic support and dedication to the project, her unflagging energy and enthusiasm, and her unerring eye for detail, Sara Dyer for her creative and focused work on the supplements that support *Cuadros*, and Morgen Murphy for her dedication to the quality of the media package. Thanks also to Aileen Mason, our production editor, for her meticulous care, and for her cheerful and good-humored tenacity in keeping the production side of things moving efficiently, and to Katy Gabel for her excellent project management work. We would like to extend our appreciation to Lindsey Richardson, Marketing Director, and Ben Rivera, Senior Marketing Manager, for their outstanding creative vision and hard work on campus, and to Glenn McGibbon, Senior Marketing Communications Manager, for his phenomenal work on marketing and promotional materials. We would like to acknowledge our copyeditor Janet Gokay, our proofreaders Pilar Acevedo and Jonathan Jucker, our art director, Linda Jurras, for her inspired design work, our illustrators JHS Illustration Studio and Fian Arroyo, Hilary Hudgens for his creative design contributions, and the many other design, art, and production staff and freelancers who contributed to the creation of this program.

¡Mil gracias a todos!

To my inspirational students, who helped shape *Cuadros*, and to *mi querida familia*, John, Morgan, and John, who have accompanied me on my life's magical journey as a Hispanist. *Gracias por el apoyo infinito.*
—S. S. L.

I am particularly appreciative of the help and encouragement of my husband, Bartlett Mel, my father, Domingo Carreira, and my colleagues Ana Roca, Najib Redouane, and Irene Marchegiani Jones.
—M. C.

I would like to thank my parents, Dulce and Óscar Madrigal, for bequeathing to me their language, their culture, their heritage, their passion for life, and their *orgullo* in *México, lindo y querido.*
—S. M. V.

A special thanks to Mac Prichard and to Shirley and Bill Swanson for their constant support and encouragement, both personal and professional.
—K. S.

	TEMAS	COMUNICACIÓN	VOCABULARIO ÚTIL
capítulo 9 **¿Qué te apetece?** 306	Sabores Bolivia y Paraguay	• talk about food and cooking • shop for food • order in a restaurant • talk about what you used to eat and cook • say what you do for others	1. Restaurants and menus **308–309** 2. Recipes and food preparation **312** 3. Setting the table **314**
capítulo 10 **¿Dónde vives?** 346	Los sitios Guatemala y Nicaragua	• talk about your childhood • describe homes and their furnishings • talk about household tasks • indicate numerical order • express possession • talk about the duration of past and present events • say what people want others to do	1. Parts of the city, the house, ordinal numbers **348** 2. Household tasks, furniture, and decorations **350–352** 3. Household appliances **354**

Reference Materials

¡Bienvenidos a la clase de español!

The Spanish alphabet has 29 characters—the same as the English alphabet, plus the extra letters **ch, ll,** and **ñ**. When using a Spanish dictionary to look up words that begin with **ch** and **ll**, note that they do not have a separate listing, but are instead listed alphabetically under the letters **c** and **l**.

In 2010, the **Real Academia de la Lengua Española** updated the Spanish names of some letters. **Ve** and **doble ve** are now **uve** and **doble uve**, and **i griega** has been shortened to **ye**, but the adoption of these names is not universal among Spanish speakers. In addition, **ch** and **ll** have not been considered independent letters since 1994.

Go to the **Pronunciación** section of the preliminary chapter in the *Student Activities Manual* or *eSAM* and practice the sounds of the alphabet.

The purpose of these pages is to introduce you to some of the "nuts and bolts" of Spanish you'll need right away. Familiarize yourself with these words and expressions and do the activities described. Don't worry about memorizing it all—you'll have many more opportunities to work with these words as you progress through *Cuadros*.

Check: Ask students to spell their names in pairs. Listen in to assess their progress. Provide other relevant words such as your state, name of president or college / university, etc.

El alfabeto

a	*a*	**A**rgentina	n	*ene*	**N**icaragua
b	*be*	**B**olivia	ñ	*eñe*	Espa**ñ**a
c	*ce*	**C**osta Rica	o	*o*	**O**taval**o**
ch	*che*	**Ch**ichén Itzá	p	*pe*	**P**araguay
d	*de*	**D**inamarca	q	*cu*	**Q**uito
e	*e*	**E**cuador	r	*erre*	Pe**r**ú
f	*efe*	**F**ilipinas	s	*ese*	**S**antiago
g	*ge*	**G**uatemala	t	*te*	**T**oledo
h	*hache*	**H**onduras	u	*u*	C**u**ba
i	*i*	**I**nglaterra	v	*uve*	**V**enezuela
j	*jota*	**J**alisco	w	*doble uve*	Bots**w**ana
k	*ka*	**K**enya	x	*equis*	Mé**x**ico
l	*ele*	**L**os Ángeles	y	*ye*	**Y**ucatán
ll	*elle*	Va**ll**adolid	z	*zeta*	**Z**acatecas
m	*eme*	**M**arruecos			

Standards: Throughout *Cuadros,* there are many activities based on the *Standards for Foreign Language Learning.* The *Instructor's Guide* contains helpful information about the standards and describes how they are implemented in *Cuadros.* In addition, icons and annotations are used to point out the standard or standards addressed in the various chapter sections and activities. Please go to **actfl.org** for a downloadable Executive Summary of the *Standards for Foreign Language learning.*

Heritage Learners: The letters **b, v, c, ll,** and **w** go by different names in different Spanish-speaking countries. If you have Heritage Learners in your class, ask them how they refer to these letters: **be de burro o be larga, ve de vaca / ve corta / ve chica, che o ce-hache, elle o doble ele, doble u o doble uve,** etc.

Suggestion: Tell students that the names of letters vary across the Spanish-speaking world and that there are many regional variations. Let them know that they will be assessed on the alphabet, but that variants not listed are not incorrect.

Optional: Play Hangman or Scrabble to provide spelling practice.
Suggestion: Model the pronunciation of vowels (**a, e, i, o, u**). Demonstrate the **g**, the silent **h**, **ñ** like *ny* (*canyon* from English), the trilled **rr**, and **v**. Point out that **p, t,** and **c** (with the "k"sound) are aspirated or pronounced with a puff of air in English, unlike Spanish. Demonstrate this with **pan, tan, con. Optional:** In Castilian Spanish the **z (z, ci, ce)** is pronounced like the *th* in English.

Suggestion: For alphabet practice, model the question and act out the answer by writing letters on the board: **¿Cómo se deletrea su / tu / mi nombre?** For example: **Mi nombre es J, u, a, n, G, a, r, c, í, a.**

Check: Ask students to count the number of **personas** in the room. Preview simple words such as **libro, profesor(a), computadora, chico(a)** to be able to count these as well.

Los números 1–100

0	*cero*	20	*veinte*	40	*cuarenta*
1	*uno*	21	*veintiuno*	41	*cuarenta y uno*
2	*dos*	22	*veintidós*	42	*cuarenta y dos*
3	*tres*	23	*veintitrés*	43	*cuarenta y tres*
4	*cuatro*	24	*veinticuatro*	44	*cuarenta y cuatro*
5	*cinco*	25	*veinticinco*	45	*cuarenta y cinco*
6	*seis*	26	*veintiséis*	46	*cuarenta y seis*
7	*siete*	27	*veintisiete*	47	*cuarenta y siete*
8	*ocho*	28	*veintiocho*	48	*cuarenta y ocho*
9	*nueve*	29	*veintinueve*	49	*cuarenta y nueve*
10	*diez*	30	*treinta*	50	*cincuenta*
11	*once*	31	*treinta y uno*	51	*cincuenta y uno*
12	*doce*	32	*treinta y dos*	52	*cincuenta y dos*
13	*trece*	33	*treinta y tres*	53	*cincuenta y tres*
14	*catorce*	34	*treinta y cuatro*	54	*cincuenta y cuatro*
15	*quince*	35	*treinta y cinco*	55	*cincuenta y cinco*
16	*dieciséis*	36	*treinta y seis*	56	*cincuenta y seis*
17	*diecisiete*	37	*treinta y siete*	57	*cincuenta y siete*
18	*dieciocho*	38	*treinta y ocho*	58	*cincuenta y ocho*
19	*diecinueve*	39	*treinta y nueve*	59	*cincuenta y nueve*

60	*sesenta*
70	*setenta*
80	*ochenta*
90	*noventa*
100	*cien*

Suggestion: Practice numbers with math problems. Teach these conventions: + **más,** − **menos,** × **por,** ÷ **dividido por,** = **es igual a.**

Standard 1.2 / Optional: Have students create their own Bingo cards with paper. Playing Bingo practices listening comprehension in the interpretive mode of both letters and numbers. Solving Sudoku puzzles as a group also practices Spanish, quantitative literacy, and listening comprehension.

Heritage Learners: Call attention to the fact that **z** changes to **c** when followed by **i** in words like **dieciocho, dieciséis.** Point out that a similar rule applies when **z** is followed by **e.** Write the following words on the board and ask students to form the plural: **pez (peces), luz (luces), paz (paces).**

Memorize the numbers 1–15.

Notice the pattern for the numbers from 16 to 29: **diez** + **seis** = **dieciséis; veinte** + **uno** = **veintiuno.** Notice that 11–15 do not follow that pattern.

Notice the pattern for the numbers over 30: **treinta** + **uno** = **treinta y uno; cuarenta** + **dos** = **cuarenta y dos; cincuenta** + **tres** = **cincuenta y tres;** etc.

Do not confuse sixty and seventy. Notice that **sesenta** is formed from **seiS,** with an **s,** and **setenta** is formed from **sieTe,** with a **t.**

With a partner, practice counting in Spanish by taking turns (Student 1: **uno;** Student 2: **dos,** etc.). Or, practice a sequence; for example, multiples of three (Student 1: **tres, seis, nueve;** Student 2: **doce, quince, dieciocho,** etc.).

Las personas

With a partner, name ten people you know. Take turns identifying them first by age and gender and then by their relationship to you: **Marcos Martínez—20 años, hombre, amigo.**

Suggestion: Give classroom commands and have students act them out.

| el hombre | la mujer | el muchacho / el chico | la muchacha / la chica | el niño | la niña |

© Cengage Learning 2013

| el estudiante | el profesor | la instructora | el instructor |

la estudiante

la profesora

© Cengage Learning 2013

el amigo

la amiga

la compañera de cuarto

el compañero de cuarto

© Cengage Learning 2013

En el salón de clase

>> **En el libro de texto**

la actividad *activity*
el capítulo *chapter*
el dibujo *drawing*
la foto *photo*
la lección *lesson*
la página *page*

>> **La pregunta** *The question*

¿Cómo se dice… ?
   How do you say . . . ?
¿Qué significa… ?
   What does . . . mean?

>> **La respuesta** *The answer*

Se dice… *It's said . . .*
Significa… *It means . . .*

Review: Numbers, words, and classroom objects are all around us. Have students count classroom objects and spell their names.

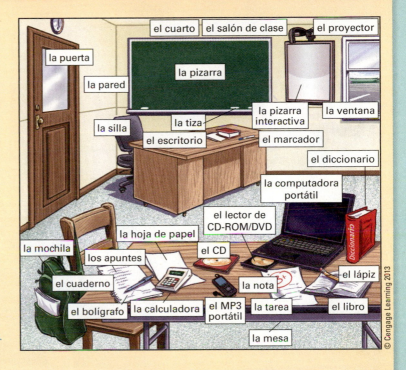

el cuarto · el salón de clase · el proyector · la puerta · la pared · la pizarra · la pizarra interactiva · la ventana · la silla · la tiza · el escritorio · el marcador · el diccionario · la computadora portátil · el lector de CD-ROM/DVD · la hoja de papel · la mochila · los apuntes · el CD · el lápiz · el cuaderno · la nota · el bolígrafo · la calculadora · el MP3 portátil · la tarea · el libro · la mesa

© Cengage Learning 2013

>> **Mandatos comunes** *Classroom commands*

Abran los libros / libros electrónicos. *Open your books / e-books.*
Adivina. / Adivinen. *Guess.*
Cierren los libros / libros electrónicos. *Close your books / e-books.*
Contesta. / Contesten. *Answer.*
Entreguen la tarea. *Turn in your homework.*
Mándenme la tarea por e-mail. *E-mail me your homework.*
Escriban en sus cuadernos / sus computadoras. *Write in your notebooks / computers.*
Escuchen el audio. *Listen to the audio.*
Estudien las páginas… a… *Study pages . . . to . . .*
Hagan la tarea para mañana. *Do the homework for tomorrow.*
Lean el Capítulo 1. *Read Chapter 1.*
Repitan. *Repeat.*

Suggestion: Emphasize the false cognate **nota** by writing A, A−, B, C+, C, etc., on the board. Also, you may want to give contrastive cultural information about grading systems in different Spanish-speaking countries: **sobresaliente, notable, suficiente, aprobado / no aprobado.**

With a partner, take turns pointing out objects shown in the illustration that you can see in your classroom.

Your instructor will practice the most common classroom commands with the entire class and before you know it, you will know them by heart! Do not worry about memorizing them.

Suggestion: Point out as many classroom words as possible to introduce words in context. Bring supplies to show students the visual image of the written word. Classroom vocabulary: (1) Students can physically label items in the classroom. (2) Teach **¿Dónde está…?** by acting it out and writing it on the board. Ask questions and have students point at the item or object: **¿Dónde está la ventana?, ¿Dónde está el libro de Luis?,** etc. Then have them quiz a partner.

¿Cómo te llamas?

LA IDENTIDAD PERSONAL

As individuals we value our uniqueness while drawing strength from the similarities and experiences we share with others.

How do you define yourself, both as an individual and as a member of different groups?

Communication

By the end of this chapter you will be able to

- exchange addresses, phone numbers, and e-mail addresses
- introduce yourself and others, greet, and say goodbye
- make a phone call
- tell your and others' ages
- address friends informally and acquaintances politely
- write a personal letter

Jeremy Woodhouse/Getty Images

Learning objectives: See pages AIE-3—AIE-4 for a complete description of the Bloom's Taxonomy learning objectives and an explanation of how they are integrated within *Cuadros*.

Un viaje por el mundo hispanohablante

1.

Gen Productions/Shutterstock

2.

Jozef Sedmak/Shutterstock

3.

Dmitry Rukhlenko/Shutterstock

Check: At the beginning of this chapter, interview students to find out what they already know about the world's Spanish-speaking populations. At the end of the chapter, repeat your questions to assess what they have learned.

¿Qué sabes? *(What do you know?)*

1. Match the names of these famous locations in the Spanish-speaking world with their photos.
   a. la Pirámide del Sol, Teotihuacán, México
   b. las Cataratas de Iguazú, Puerto Iguazú, Argentina
   c. la Catedral de la Sagrada Familia, Barcelona, España

2. There are 21 official Spanish-speaking countries in the world, not including the United States. Can you place them in the correct areas of the world? Use the information below to make a list of the six areas. Then list the countries that you think belong in each one. Save your work to check in the **¡Explora y exprésate!** section on page 33.

Áreas: África, El Caribe, Centroamérica, Europa, Norteamérica, Sudamérica

Países: Argentina, Bolivia, Chile, Colombia, Costa Rica, Cuba, Ecuador, El Salvador, España, Guatemala, Guinea Ecuatorial, Honduras, México, Nicaragua, Panamá, Paraguay, Perú, Puerto Rico, República Dominicana, Uruguay, Venezuela

Lo que sé y lo que quiero aprender Complete the chart in **Appendix A**. Write some facts you *already know* about the Spanish-speaking world in the **Lo que sé** column. Then add some things you *want to learn* about in the **Lo que quiero aprender** column. Save the chart to use again in the **¡Explora y exprésate!** section on page 33.

Learning objectives: Understanding

Culture: Find out what students already know and then use Google Earth to show these sites, while providing some general information.
La Sagrada Familia: large landmark Roman Catholic cathedral in Barcelona, Spain, designed by architect Antoní Gaudí. Construction began in 1882 and is scheduled for completion in 2026.
Iguazú Falls: mammoth waterfalls on the border of Brazil and Argentina. Considered a natural wonder of the world. **Panama Canal:** ship canal in Panama joining the Atlantic and Pacific oceans. Built between 1904 and 1914.
Pyramid of the Sun (Teotihuacán): one of the largest Pre-Columbian pyramids in Mesoamerica, and world's third largest. Begun by the ancient **teotihuacanos** around 100 A.D.; the Aztecs later continued construction. Located near modern-day Mexico City; designated a UNESCO World Heritage Site in 1987.

Check: In *Cuadros*, the **Lo que sé y lo que quiero aprender** activities allow students to build on cultural knowledge. Also included are suggested "checks" in the margin to assess student progress. Use the chart to recheck students' knowledge of basic facts later in the chapter.

Cultures

By the end of this chapter you will have explored

- Spanish around the world
- a brief history of the Spanish language
- some statistics about Spanish speakers
- a few comparisons between Spanish and English
- Spanish in the professional world
- Spanish-language telephone conventions

¡Imagínate!

▶ >> ## Vocabulario útil 1

Standards 5.1, 5.2: Examples of some standards that will be met in Ch. 1 are: Communities—contact Spanish-speaking communities online; and Communities—interpret irony in cartoon strip based on experiential enrichment.

© Cengage Learning 2013

JAVIER:	**¡Hola!**
ANILÚ:	Hola, Beto. **¿Cómo te va?**
JAVIER:	**Bastante bien,** pero… ¿Beto? Yo no soy Beto.

Spanish has formal and informal means of address: singular formal *(s. form.)*, singular familiar *(s. fam.)*, and plural *(pl.)* for more than one person, formal or informal. You will learn more about how to address people on pages 23–24.

Notice: These conversational scenes from the *Cuadros* video present the vocabulary in context. Video viewing activities appear later in the chapter.

Suggestion: One way to present this vocabulary is to model a two-way conversation. Greet a student, ask how he/she is, and sign off. If the student is not able to respond, ask the rest of the class for **ayuda** or **socorro.** Teach these words to your class. You will use them over and over again! Greet other students and carry on mini-conversations until they all catch on. Practice both informal and formal greetings. Finally, have students conduct mini-conversations with their neighbors.

>> ### Para saludar *How to greet*

Hola. *Hello.*
¿Qué tal? *How are things going?*
¿Cómo estás (tú)? *How are you? (s. fam.)*
¿Cómo está (usted)? *How are you? (s. form.)*
¿Cómo están (ustedes)? *How are you? (pl.)*
¿Cómo te va? *How's it going with you? (s. fam.)*
¿Cómo le va? *How's it going with you? (s. form.)*
¿Cómo les va? *How's it going with you? (pl.)*
¿Qué hay de nuevo? *What's new?*
Buenos días. *Good morning.*
Buenas tardes. *Good afternoon.*
Buenas noches. *Good night. Good evening.*

>> ### Para responder *How to respond*

Bien, gracias. *Fine, thank you.*
Bastante bien. *Quite well.*
(No) Muy bien. *(Not) Very well.*
Regular. *So-so.*
¡Terrible! / ¡Fatal! *Terrible! / Awful!*
No mucho. *Not much.*
Nada. *Nothing.*
¿Y tú? *And you? (s. fam.)*
¿Y usted? *And you? (s. form.)*

ACTIVIDADES

1 **Conversaciones** With a classmate, take turns greeting each other and responding. Choose an appropriate response from those provided.

I

1. Hola, ¿qué tal?
   a. Buenos días.
   (b.) Muy bien, gracias.
   c. ¿Y tú?

2. Buenas tardes. ¿Qué hay de nuevo?
   (a.) No mucho.
   b. Bastante bien.
   c. Terrible.

3. Buenas noches. ¿Cómo le va?
   a. Nada.
   b. ¿Y usted?
   (c.) Fatal.

4. Buenos días. ¿Cómo están?
   (a.) Regular.
   b. Buenas noches.
   c. No mucho.

5. Hola, ¿cómo está?
   a. ¿Cómo te va?
   (b.) Bien, gracias, ¿y usted?
   c. Nada.

6. Buenas tardes.
   a. Terrible.
   (b.) Buenas tardes. ¿Qué hay de nuevo?
   c. No muy bien. ¿Y tú?

¿Qué tal?

¡Fatal! ¿Y tú?

© Cengage Learning 2013

2 **Saludos** Exchange greetings with a classmate. Follow the cues.

M

1. **Greeting:** It is morning, and you want to know how your classmate is doing. *(sample answers):* Buenos días. ¿Cómo te va?

   Response: You had a terrible night and don't feel well. ¡Fatal!

2. **Greeting:** It is evening, and you run into two classmates; you want to know if anything new has come up. Buenas noches. ¿Qué hay de nuevo?

   Response: Not much has happened since you last saw your friend. No mucho.

3. **Greeting:** You run into a professor in the afternoon; you want to know how things are going. Buenas tardes. ¿Cómo está usted?

   Response: You're doing quite well and want to know how your student is doing. Bastante bien, gracias. ¿Cómo estás tú?

3 **¿Qué tal?** Have a conversation with one of your friends when you first see him or her that day.

C

MODELO   Tú: *¡Hola, Adriana! ¿Cómo te va?*
          Compañero(a): *Bien, gracias, Rosa. Y tú, ¿cómo estás?*
          Tú: *Regular.*

Optional: If students want to know how to say "text messaging" or "instant messaging," you can give them the expressions **enviar un mensaje de texto** and **enviar un mensaje instantáneo.** They will learn this as active vocabulary in **Chapter 4.**

© Cengage Learning 2013

ANILÚ: Pues, ¿cómo te llamas?

JAVIER: ¿Yo? **Soy** Javier de la Cruz. Y yo, ¿con quién hablo?

ANILÚ: **Me llamo** Anilú. Ana Luisa Guzmán. … Pero, **¿cuál es tu número de teléfono?** Yo marqué el 3-39-71-94.

JAVIER: No, ése no es mi número de teléfono. **Mi número es el 3-71-28-12.**

Spanish speakers often ask **¿Cuál es tu / su e-mail?**, using the English term rather than **dirección electrónica.**

In an e-mail address in Spanish, @ is pronounced **arroba** and **.com** is pronounced **punto com.**

>> **Para pedir y dar información personal**
Exchanging personal information

¿Cómo te llamas? *What's your name? (s. fam.)*
¿Cómo se llama? *What's your name? (s. form.)*

Me llamo... *My name is. . .*
(Yo) soy... *I am. . .*

¿Cuál es tu número de teléfono? *What's your phone number? (s. fam.)*
¿Cuál es su número de teléfono? *What's your phone number? (s. form.)*

Mi número de teléfono es el 3-71-28-12. *My phone number is 371-2812.*
Es el 3-71-28-12. *It's 371-2812.*

¿Dónde vives? *Where do you live? (s. fam.)*
¿Dónde vive? *Where do you live? (s. form.)*

Vivo en... *I live in / at / on. . .*
  la avenida... *avenue*
  la calle... *street*
  el barrio... / la colonia... *neighborhood*

¿Cuál es tu dirección? *What's your address? (s. fam.)*
¿Cuál es su dirección? *What's your address? (s. form.)*
Mi dirección es... *My address is. . .*

¿Cuál es tu dirección electrónica? *What's your e-mail address? (s. fam.)*
¿Cuál es su dirección electrónica? *What's your e-mail address? (s. form.)*
Aquí tienes mi dirección electrónica. *Here's my e-mail address. (s. fam.)*
Aquí tiene mi dirección electrónica. *Here's my e-mail address. (s. form.)*

Optional: Some students may respond **Mi nombre es...** Be prepared to show this alternative to **Me llamo...**

Optional: You may want to point out that abbreviations for **calle** and **avenida** are commonly seen in addresses: **C/Otero; Avda. Reina Mercedes.**

Optional: Students who live in dorms often give the name of a dorm instead of a street name. Be prepared to add: **Vivo en la residencia estudiantil...**

Optional: You may want to teach students **¿Cuál es tu celular?** or **Dame el número de tu celular.**

ACTIVIDADES

I **4** **Respuestas** Pick from the second column the correct response to the questions in the first column.

1. ¿Dónde vives? d
2. ¿Cuál es su dirección electrónica? c
3. ¿Cómo se llama? a
4. ¿Cuál es tu número de teléfono? b

a. Yo soy Rita Rivera.
b. Es el 4-87-26-91.
c. Es Irene29@yahoo.com.mx.
d. En la colonia Villanueva.

Learning objective: Remembering

Suggestion: Remind students to give their phone numbers by using pairs after the first digit: **Mi número es el ocho, veintidós, cuarenta y siete, treinta y cinco.**

Check: To assess progress, have random students recite their phone numbers to the whole class.

Optional: Have students circulate and ask as many classmates as possible for their personal information. If they want, they can ask for e-mail or Twitter addresses as well.

M/C **5** **En la reunión** You are at the first meeting of the International Hispanic Student Association at your college. You have been elected secretary and must record in Spanish the name, address, and phone number of every member. With a male and female classmate playing the parts of the members, ask for the information you need. Without looking at the book, listen to their responses and type or write out their personal information. Then ask your partners for their real personal information and record that. *All items follow the pattern of the model.*

MODELO Jorge Salinas, avenida B 23, 2-91-66-45
　　　　　Tú: *¿Cómo te llamas?*
　　　　　Compañero(a): *Me llamo Jorge Salinas.*
　　　　　Tú: *¿Dónde vives?*
　　　　　Compañero(a): *Vivo en la avenida B, veintitrés.*
　　　　　Tú: *¿Cuál es tu número de teléfono?*
　　　　　Compañero(a): *Es el dos, noventa y uno, sesenta y seis, cuarenta y cinco.*

1. Amanda Villarreal, calle Montemayor 10, 8-13-02-55
2. Diego Ruiz, Colonia del Valle, calle Iturbide 89, 7-94-71-30
3. Irma Santiago, avenida Flores Verdes 12, 9-52-35-27
4. Baldemar Huerta, calle Otero 39, 7-62-81-03
5. Ingrid Lehmann, avenida Aguas Blancas 62, 4-56-72-93
6. ¿… ?
7. ¿… ?

> Notice in the **MODELO** how, except for the first example, all digits of a telephone number in Spanish are given in pairs. Spanish speakers in the United States might not use this convention.

> Notice that unlike in English, the street name precedes the number in addresses in Spanish: **Calle Iturbide 12** vs. *12 Iturbide Street.*

C **6** **¡Mucho gusto!** With a classmate, role-play a cell phone conversation in which one of you has reached the wrong number. You are curious about the person you have accidentally reached. Try to get as much information from each other as possible.

MODELO —Hola. ¿Marcos?
　　　　　—No, yo no soy Marcos.
　　　　　—Bueno, ¿cómo se llama usted?
　　　　　—…

¿Dónde vives?
¿ …?

© Cengage Learning 2013

Check: Create a fictitious name, phone number, and e-mail address. Check student listening skills by reading aloud. Students write what they hear. Review correct answers to see how much they capture.

Heritage Learners: Here heritage learners and high beginners may want to review additional phone expressions: **¿Diga?, ¿Dígame?, ¿Mande?, ¿Sí?, ¿Quién es?, Buenos días,** etc.

Check: To help establish an interactive classroom, ask volunteers to role-play a cell phone conversation in front of the whole class. This activity will alert students to the fact that they will be asked to present for the class what they practice in small groups.

¡Fíjate! Los celulares

Cellular phone technology has revolutionized telecommunications throughout the entire world. Cell phones are as popular in Latin America and Spain as they are in the United States. With the advent of the smartphone, cell phones are now routinely used for e-mail, photos, video, text messaging, games, applications, face-to-face phone conversations, GPS directions, and almost anything else you can do online.

Unas chicas usan su celular para hablar con un amigo.

Although customs for speaking on the phone vary from one Spanish-speaking country to another, here are some useful phrases to get you started.

Familiar Conversation

—¡Hola!	*Hello?*
—Hola. ¿Qué estás haciendo?	*Hi. What are you doing?*
—Nada, ¿y tú?	*Nothing, and you?*
—¿Quieres hacer algo?	*Do you want to do something?*
—Claro. ¿Nos vemos donde siempre?	*Sure. See you at the usual place?*
—Está bien. Hasta luego.	*OK. See you later.*
—Chau.	*Bye.*

Formal Conversation

—¡Hola! / ¿Aló?	*Hello?*
—Hola. ¿Puedo hablar con… ?	*Hi, may I speak with . . . ?*
—Sí. Aquí está.	*Yes. Here he/she is.*
—Lo siento. No está.	*Sorry. He's/she's not here.*
—Por favor, dígale que llamó (nombre). Mi número es el…	*Please tell him/her that (name) called. My number is . . .*
—Muy bien.	*OK.*
—Muchas gracias.	*Thank you very much.*
—De nada. Adiós.	*You're welcome. Goodbye.*
—Adiós.	*Goodbye.*

Práctica With a partner, role-play two different phone calls, using the expressions provided. In the first call, you dial a friend's cell phone and speak to him or her. In the second call, you dial a friend's home number and speak to his grandmother. In the second case, the person you are trying to reach is not in and you need to leave a message. Don't forget to use the correct level of address (familiar or formal).

Vocabulario útil 3

© Cengage Learning 2013

ANILÚ:	Beto, **quiero presentarte a** Javier de la Cruz.
BETO:	**Mucho gusto**, Javier.
JAVIER:	**Encantado**, Beto.
BETO:	Aquí está tu celular.
JAVIER:	Gracias, Beto. Y aquí está tu celular.
BETO:	**Bueno, ¡tengo que irme! Muchas gracias**, Javier. Y gracias a ti también, Anilú.
ANILÚ:	Pues, Javier, **mucho gusto en conocerte**.
JAVIER:	**El gusto es mío.**
ANILÚ:	Pues, entonces, **¡nos vemos!**
JAVIER:	¡Hasta luego! Chau.

>> **Para presentar a alguien**   *Introducing someone*

Soy... *I am . . .*
Me llamo... / Mi nombre es...
   My name is . . .
Quiero presentarte a... *I'd like to introduce you (s. fam.) to . . .*

Quiero presentarle a... *I'd like to introduce you (s. form.) to . . .*
Quiero presentarles a... *I'd like to introduce you (pl.) to . . .*

>> **Para responder**   *How to respond*

Mucho gusto. *My pleasure.*
Mucho gusto en conocerte. *A pleasure to meet you (s. fam.).*
Encantado(a). *Delighted to meet you.*

Igualmente. *Likewise.*
El gusto es mío. *The pleasure is mine.*
Un placer. *My pleasure.*

>> **Para despedirse**   *Saying goodbye*

Adiós. *Goodbye.*
Hasta luego. *See you later.*
Hasta mañana. *See you tomorrow.*
Hasta pronto. *See you soon.*

Nos vemos. *See you later.*
Chau. *Bye.*
Bueno, tengo que irme. *Well / OK, I have to go.*

Suggestion: Dramatize the scene with handshaking, kisses, and hugs. These sociolinguistic norms vary from country to country in the Spanish-speaking world. Give an example of differences in physical contact and spatial closeness compared with typical customs in the U.S.

The word **chau** comes from the Italian word *ciao,* which means both *hello* and *goodbye.* In Spanish, it is only used to say *goodbye.* The spelling has been changed to reflect Spanish pronunciation.

Suggestion: Other common ways to end conversations are **Hasta la vista** and **Hasta la próxima.**

ACTIVIDADES

I **7** **¿Cómo respondes?** Choose the best response to each statement.

1. Me llamo Rubén.
   a. Adiós.   **b.** Un placer.   c. Hasta mañana.

2. Quiero presentarte a Cristina.
   a. Igualmente.   b. Bueno, tengo que irme.   **c.** Mucho gusto.

3. Mucho gusto en conocerte.
   a. Chau.   **b.** Igualmente.   c. Mi nombre es Santiago.

4. Bueno, tengo que irme.
   a. Hasta luego.   b. Encantado(a).   c. El gusto es mío.

Suggestion: After doing **Activity 8** in groups or pairs, have several sets of students act out these dialogs in front of the class.

Check: For a formal assessment of **Activity 8,** you may want to rate student or group performance with a score of 1 to 5 for pronunciation, accurate communication, completeness, and creativity.

8 **Quiero presentarte a…** Introductions are a normal part of everyday life.
M Study the drawing and, with a partner, create four short conversations in which one person introduces another person to a third party. In each conversation, pick one of the characters in the group and play that role. The labels show the four groups.

Grupo 1

Grupo 2

Grupo 3

Grupo 4

© Cengage Learning 2013

M **9** **Fiesta** You're at a party and you meet someone you really like who speaks only Spanish. Write out the conversation you might have with that person. Include the following:

Learning objective: Understanding

> greeting
> response
> introduction
> exchange of phone numbers and e-mail addresses
> exchange of addresses
> goodbyes

C **10** **Un e-mail** Write an e-mail to your Spanish instructor introducing yourself. In it, give your name, address, e-mail address, phone number, and any other information you think your Spanish instructor should know about you. Send it!

Learning objective: Applying

Standard 1.3: This e-mail activity allows students to meet the presentational standard by identifying the audience to which the student will present specific information.

Optional: You may want to encourage students to create fictional names, phone numbers, and e-mail addresses to avoid having them reveal too much personal information online.

Suggestion: Give several examples of e-mail messages that emphasize the difference in register and tone that one uses addressing an instructor versus a close friend.

Heritage Learners: Have students say whether the following e-mail greetings and closings are appropriate for their instructor, a classmate, a close friend, or a parent: **Estimado(a), Queridísimo(a), Besos y abrazos, Saludos, Con afecto, Atentamente.**

¡Hola, profesora!

Me llamo Gretchen Murray. Soy estudiante en su clase de español. Mi dirección electrónica es gmurray@xyzmail.com. Vivo en el campus. Mi número de teléfono es el 5-12-49-47. ¡Nos vemos pronto!

Saludos,
Gretchen

© Cengage Learning 2013

11 **¡Mucho gusto en conocerte!**

C You are at a party with a group of four or five classmates. Greet each other, introduce yourselves, present at least one other member of the group to the others, and then carry on as lively a conversation as you can, exchanging as much personal information as you normally would. Find a natural way to end the conversation and then say goodbye to each other.

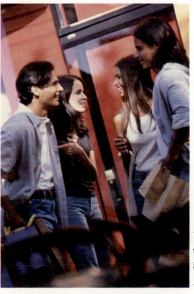

Juan Silva/Getty Images

A ver

Standard 1.2: Through video viewing students learn interpretive strategies for communication. Activities in this section regularly provide opportunities for students to interpret spoken language.

ESTRATEGIA

Viewing a segment several times

When you first hear authentic Spanish, it may sound very fast. Stay calm! Remember that you don't have to understand everything and that, with video, you have the opportunity to replay. The first time you view the segment, listen for the general idea. The second time, listen for details.

Antes de ver 1 How many of the characters in this video segment do you already know? Go back to pages 8, 10, and 13 and identify the people you see in the photos there. *Anilú, Javier, Beto*

Antes de ver 2 Review some of the key words and phrases used in the video.

Ha sido un placer.	*It's been a pleasure.*
Marqué…	*I dialed . . .*
¡Tengo prisa!	*I'm in a hurry!*
Voy a marcar…	*I'm going to dial . . .*

Antes de ver 3 Before you watch the video, read items 1–3. Then, as you watch, listen for this information.

1. Las personas que hablan por celular: ¿Cómo se llaman? *Javier, Anilú*
2. Las personas al final: ¿Cómo se llaman? *Javier, Anilú, Beto*
3. _____Javier_____ tiene *(has)* el celular de _____Beto_____.

© Cengage Learning 2013

▶ **Ver** Now watch the video segment as many times as necessary to answer the questions in **Antes de ver 3**.

Después de ver Are the following statements about the video segment true **(cierto)** or false **(falso)**? Correct the false statements.

1. Javier tiene el celular de Anilú. *falso; Javier tiene el celular de Beto.*
2. Anilú es una amiga de Javier. *falso; Anilú es una amiga de Beto.*
3. Beto es un amigo de Anilú. *cierto*
4. El número del teléfono celular que tiene Javier es el 3-39-71-94. *cierto*
5. El número de teléfono de Beto es el 3-39-71-94. *cierto*
6. Anilú le presenta Javier a Beto. *cierto*

>> Voces del mundo hispano

© Cengage Learning 2013

In this video segment, people from around the Spanish-speaking world introduce themselves. First read the statements below. Then watch the video as many times as needed to say whether the statements are true **(cierto)** or false **(falso)**.

1. Ela y Sandra son de Puerto Rico. C
2. Aura y Dayramir son de Honduras. F
3. Claudio tiene 42 años *(is 42 years old).* F
4. David tiene 19 años. C

5. Ricardo es estudiante universitario. C
6. Patricia y Constanza son profesoras de español. F

Standards, 2.1, 2.2, 3.2: Students read about successful Spanish speakers in the U.S. and acquire cultural information that features distinctive viewpoints of Spanish-speaking people.

📢 >> Voces de Estados Unidos

Track 2

Spanish speakers in North America

Comstock Images/Thinkstock

In 1787, Thomas Jefferson had this advice for his nephew, Peter Carr: ❝Apply yourself to the study of the Spanish language with all of the assiduity you can. It and the English covering nearly the whole of America, they should be well known to every inhabitant who means to look beyond the limits of his farm.❞

Today, the U.S. is the fourth-largest Spanish-speaking country in the world. The 44 million Hispanics (or Latinos) who make their home in this country represent the fastest-growing segment of the U.S. population, comprising nearly 16.66% of the total population. For its part, Canada is also home to a thriving community of over 300,000 Hispanics.

U.S. Hispanics are enjoying a period of unprecedented prosperity. Their estimated buying power of $800 billion a year more than doubles the combined buying power of all other Spanish-speaking countries in the world. Through Spanish-language websites, publications, and advertising aimed at the lucrative Hispanic market, U.S. companies are continually striving to better understand, entice, and serve Latino consumers.

The **Voces de la comunidad** section of Chapters 2–20 of *Cuadros* features an outstanding North American Hispanic from these and other areas, people whose contributions have direct relevance to the theme of the chapter.

¿Y tú? What are your reasons for studying Spanish? Do you want to use it for personal or professional reasons?

Optional: According the U.S. Census Bureau, *Hispanics* or *Latinos* are those people who *classified themselves* in one of the specific categories listed on the Census questionnaire— "Mexican, Mexican Am., Chicano," "Puerto Rican," or "Cuban"—as well as those who indicate that they are "other Spanish / Hispanic / Latino." Origin can be viewed as the heritage, nationality group, lineage, or country of birth of the person or the person's parents or ancestors before their arrival in the United States. People who identify their origin as Spanish, Hispanic, or Latino can be of any race.

¡Prepárate!

>> ## Gramática útil 1

 Standard 4.1: Grammar explanations frequently compare similarities and differences between English and Spanish usage such as gender.

Identifying people and objects: Nouns and articles

Cómo usarlo

Nouns identify people, places, and things: **señora Velasco, calle,** and **teléfono** are all nouns. *Articles* supply additional information about the noun.

1. *Definite* articles refer to a specific person, place, or thing.

> **La** Avenida Central es **la** calle más importante de **la** universidad.
> *(You already know which avenue and university you are talking about.)*

> *Central Avenue is **the** most important street in **the** university.*

2. *Indefinite* articles refer to a noun without identifying a specific person, place, or thing.

> **Un** amigo es **una** persona que te gusta.
> *(You are making a generalization, true of any friend.)*

> *A friend is **a** person you like.*

Suggestion: Dramatize this concept in the classroom. Hold up *Cuadros* and say **Es el libro de español.** Then pick up any other book without identifying it and say **Es un libro.**

Cómo formarlo

The idea of gender for non-person nouns and for articles does not exist in English, although it is a feature of Spanish and other languages. When learning new Spanish words, memorize the article with the noun to help remember gender.

LO BÁSICO

- *Number* indicates whether a word is singular or plural: **la calle** *(sing.),* **las calles** *(pl.),* **un escritorio** *(sing.),* **unos escritorios** *(pl.)*
- *Gender* indicates whether a word is masculine or feminine: **una avenida** *(fem.),* **el teléfono** *(masc.)*

3. Noun gender and number

- **Gender:** Often you can tell the gender of a Spanish noun by looking at its ending. Here are some general guidelines.

Optional: You may want to show students other cognates that end in **-ción** and are feminine: **acción, ficción, información, interacción, investigación, pronunciación,** etc.

When nouns ending in **-ión** become plural, they lose the accent on the **o: la corporación,** but **las corporaciones.**

Masculine	Feminine
1. Nouns ending in **-o: el amigo, el muchacho**	Exception to rule #1: **la mano** *(hand)*
Exceptions to rule #2: words ending in **-ma: el sistema, el problema, el tema, el programa;** also **el día, el mapa**	2. Nouns ending in **-a: la compañera de cuarto, una chica**
Exceptions to rule #3: **el avión, el camión**	3. Nouns ending in **-ión, -dad, -tad,** and **-umbre** are usually feminine: **la información, una universidad, una costumbre** *(custom)*

Nouns referring to people often reflect gender by changing a final **o** to an **a** (**chico / chica, amigo / amiga**) or adding an **a** to a final consonant (**profesor / profesora**). For nouns ending in -**e**, -**ista**, or -**a** that refer to people, the article or context indicates gender (**el estudiante / la estudiante, el guitarrista / la guitarrista, Juan / Juanita es atleta**).

■ **Number:** Spanish nouns form their plurals in several ways.

Singular	Plural
Ends in vowel: **calle**	Add **s: calles**
Ends in consonant: **universidad**	Add **es: universidades**
Ends in -**z: lápiz**	Change **z** to **c** and add **es: lápices**

Décima Feria de las Mascotas

sábado, 11 de mayo, 10:00 a 14:00, Plaza Central

¡Ven a ver y a llevarte algunos de los perros, gatos, pájaros, lagartos y serpientes más raros del mundo!

Photos: Ameng Wu/iStockphoto.com (Boa); Eric Isselee/iStockphoto.com (Dog and Cat); Ameng Wu/iStockphoto.com (Chameleon); Content: © Cengage Learning 2013

How many plural nouns can you identify in this poster for a pet fair? Can you find the two definite articles?

Answers: Mascotas, perros, gatos, pájaros, lagartos, serpientes; las, los

4. Definite and indefinite articles

■ Here are the Spanish definite articles, which correspond to the English article *the*.

	Singular	Plural
Masculine	**el amigo** *the friend (male)*	**los amigos** *the friends (male or mixed group)*
Feminine	**la amiga** *the friend (female)*	**las amigas** *the friends (female)*

In the past, **los** and **unos**, rather than **las** and **unas**, were used to refer to groups containing one or more males. The **Real Academia de la Lengua Española** recently ruled that the feminine forms should be used for groups with more females than males, but usage is changing slowly.

- Here are the Spanish indefinite articles, which correspond to the English articles *a*, *an*, and *some*.

	Singular	Plural
Masculine	**un amigo** a friend *(male)*	**unos amigos** some friends *(male or mixed group)*
Feminine	**una amiga** a friend *(female)*	**unas amigas** some friends *(female)*

Notice: The absence of the indefinite article before one's profession will need to be reinforced repeatedly. Model and practice: **Soy profesor(a). Soy estudiante. …es presidente,** etc.

When the noun is modified, the article is used: **Liana es una profesora excelente.**

- Remember that you use masculine articles with masculine nouns and feminine articles with feminine nouns. When a noun is in the plural, the corresponding plural article (masculine or feminine) is used: **el hombre, los hombres.**
- When referring to a person's *profession*, the article is omitted: **Liana es profesora y Ricardo es dentista.**
- However, when you use a *title* to refer to someone, the article is used: **Es el profesor Gómez.** When you address that person directly, using their title, the article is not used: **Buenos días, profesor Gómez.**

The following titles are typically used with the article when referring to a person, and without the article when addressing that person directly.

señor (Sr.)	*Mr.*	**señorita (Srta.)**	*Miss / Ms.*
señora (Sra.)	*Mrs. / Ms.*	**profesor / profesora**	*professor*

ACTIVIDADES

 Standard 1.2: In this activity students must understand spoken language.

1 **¿Femenino o masculino?** Listen to the speaker name a series of items and people. First, write whether the noun mentioned is masculine **(M)** or feminine **(F)**, or both **(M/F)**. Next, write the singular form of the noun with its correct definite article. Lastly, write the plural noun with its correct definite article.

Track 3
I

Audioscript, Act. 1, ¿Femenino o masculino?: *Modelo: libro* 1. *bolígrafo* 2. *pizarra* 3. *mesa* 4. *escritorio* 5. *amigo* 6. *estudiante* 7. *artista* 8. *ventana*

MODELO *M*
el libro
los libros

Answers, Act. 1: 1. M, el bolígrafo, los bolígrafos 2. F, la pizarra, las pizarras 3. F, la mesa, las mesas 4. M, el escritorio, los escritorios 5. M, el amigo, los amigos 6. M/F, el / la estudiante, los / las estudiantes 7. M/F, el / la artista, los / las artistas 8. F, la ventana, las ventanas

Learning objective: Applying

2 **¿Definido o indefinido?** Work with a partner. Try to guess from the context whether it makes more sense to use the definite article, the indefinite article, or no article in each of the following pairs of sentences. Then say which article to use if one is required. If no article is required, mark X.
M

1. Es ___una___ calle en mi colonia.
   Es ___la___ calle central de mi colonia.

2. Es ___X___ profesor en mi universidad.
   Es ___el___ profesor de español.

3. Es ___la___ estudiante (*fem.*) más (*most*) inteligente de mi clase.
   Es ___X___ estudiante.

4. Es _____la_____ avenida más importante de mi colonia.

   Es _____una_____ avenida en mi colonia.

5. Es _____una_____ universidad en mi estado *(state)*.

   Es _____la_____ universidad más importante de mi estado.

3 **Presentaciones** With a partner, complete the following introductions
M with the correct definite or indefinite articles where needed. If no article is
needed, mark with an X.

Learning objectives: Understanding,
Applying

1. —Sra. Oliveros, quiero presentarle a _____la_____ Srta. Martínez.

   —Un placer. ¿Dónde vive usted?

   —Vivo en _____la_____ calle Colón, en _____la_____ colonia Robles.

2. —Oye, Ricardo, quiero presentarte a mi amiga Rebeca. Ella es _____X_____
   dentista.

   —¡Mucho gusto, Rebeca! Yo soy _____X_____ profesor de matemáticas.

   —¿De veras? Yo tengo *(I have)* _____un_____ amigo que es profesor también.

3. —Buenas tardes. Yo soy _____el_____ Sr. Bustelo.

   —Sr. Bustelo, ¿cuál es su número de teléfono?

   —Es _____el_____ 8-21-98-32.

4. —¡Hola!

   —Buenos días. ¿Puedo hablar con _____el_____ Sr. Lezama?

   —Lo siento. No está.

   —Por favor, dígale que llamó _____la_____ Sra. Barlovento. Tenemos *(We have)*
   clase de administración mañana y necesito darle *(I need to give him)*
   _____los_____ apuntes.

4 **Más presentaciones** Introduce yourself to another classmate. Exchange
C information about where you live, phone numbers, and e-mail addresses. Then
prepare to introduce your classmate to the entire class.

Standard 1.1: Students
practice interpersonal
communication by making
introductions and exchanging
information.

© Cengage Learning 2013

>> Gramática útil 2

Identifying and describing: Subject pronouns and the present indicative of the verb **ser**

Estar, which you have already used in the expression **¿Cómo estás?**, also means *to be*. You will learn other ways to use **estar** in **Chapter 4**.

Standard 4.1: In comparing the English *to be* with the two verbs in Spanish, you may want to conjugate *to be*: *I am, you are, he/she is, . . .*

Cómo usarlo

The Spanish verb **ser** can be used to identify people and objects, to describe them, to make introductions, and to say when something will take place. It is one of two Spanish verbs that are the equivalents of the English verb *to be*.

Mi teléfono **es** el 2-39-71-49.

Yo **soy** Mariela y ella **es** Elena.

La fiesta **es** el miércoles.

*My telephone number **is** 2-39-71-49.*

*I **am** Mariela and this **is** Elena.*

*The party **is** on Wednesday.*

Cómo formarlo

LO BÁSICO

- *Pronouns* are words used to replace nouns. (Some English pronouns are *it, she, you, him*, etc.)
- Verbs change form to reflect *number* and *person*. *Number* refers to singular versus plural. *Person* refers to different subjects.
- A verb's *tense* indicates the time frame in which an event takes place (for example, *talk, talked, will talk*). The *present indicative tense* refers to present-time events or conditions (*I talk, I am talking*).

1. Subject pronouns

- Subject pronouns are pronouns that are used as the subject of a sentence. Here are the subject pronouns in Spanish.

¿**Tú** eres Javier?

Singular		Plural	
yo	*I*	**nosotros / nosotras**	*we*
tú	*you (fam.)*	**vosotros / vosotras**	*you (fam.)*
usted (Ud.)	*you (form.)*	**ustedes (Uds.)**	*you (fam., form.)*
él, ella	*he, she*	**ellos, ellas**	*they*

© Cengage Learning 2013

- The **vosotros / vosotras** forms are primarily used in Spain. They allow speakers to address more than one person informally. In most other places, Spanish speakers use **ustedes** to address several people, regardless of the formality of the relationship. The **vosotros** forms of verbs are provided in *Cuadros* so that you can recognize them, but they are not included for practice in activities.

2. Formal vs. familiar

English has a single word—*you*—to address people directly, regardless of how well you know them. As you have already seen, Spanish has two basic forms of address: the **tú** form and the **usted** form.

- **Tú** is used to address a family member, a close friend, a child, or a pet.
- **Usted** (often abbreviated **Ud.**) is a more formal means of address used with older people, strangers, acquaintances, and sometimes with colleagues.
- Remember that the **ustedes** form is normally used to address more than one person in both *informal* and *formal* contexts (except in Spain, where **vosotros**(as) is used in informal contexts).

Levels of formality vary throughout the Spanish-speaking world, so it's important when traveling to listen to how **tú** and **usted** are used and to follow the local practice.

In some countries, you will hear **vos** forms (Argentina and parts of Uruguay, Chile, and Central America). This is a variation of **tú** that is used only in these regions.

To show respect, you sometimes hear the titles **don** and **doña** used with people you address as **usted**. **Don** and **doña** are used with the person's first name: **don Roberto, doña Carmen**.

3. The present tense of the verb **ser**

The present indicative forms of the verb **ser** are as follows. Note the subject pronouns associated with each form.

ser *(to be)*	
Singular	
yo soy	*I am*
tú eres	*you (s. fam.) are*
usted es	*you (s. form.) are*
él es	*he is*
ella es	*she is*
Plural	
nosotros / nosotras somos	*we are*
vosotros / vosotras sois	*you (pl. fam.) are*
ustedes son	*you (pl. form. or pl. fam.) are*
ellos son	*they (masc. or mixed) are*
ellas son	*they (fem.) are*

In Spanish, it is not always necessary to use the subject pronoun with the verb, as long as the subject is understood. For example, it's less common to say **Yo soy Rafael**, because **Soy Rafael** is clear enough on its own.

Suggestion: Act out several conversations with **un(a) amigo(a)** and another with **el presidente**, emphasizing the difference in register and pronoun.

Standard 4.1: Have students think about how they talk to various people to express formality and respect. Do they vary the language used when talking to friends, family, a supervisor, an instructor, a clerk in a store, or a stranger on the street? Ask them to give some examples of different ways to phrase the same piece of information for each audience. For example, if they needed to ask a favor of a friend, a family member, a supervisor, an instructor, or a complete stranger, how would they modify the request?

Learning objective: Understanding

5 **Descripciones** With a partner, match each of the following descriptions with the correct group of individuals.

I

__d__	1. two teens		a.	Son compañeras de cuarto.
__b__	2. one professor		b.	Es profesor de periodismo (*journalism*).
__a__	3. two roommates		c.	Somos profesores en la universidad.
__c__	4. two professors		d.	Son estudiantes.

M **6** **Manuel** Manuel writes an e-mail to a new Facebook friend describing himself and his two best friends. Complete his e-mail with the correct forms of **ser**.

¡Hola! Yo (1) __soy__ Manuel Ybarra. (2) __Soy__ estudiante en la Universidad Nacional Autónoma de México, que (3) __es__ una de las universidades más importantes de las Américas. ¡La población estudiantil (4) __es__ de más de 270.000 estudiantes!

Tengo dos amigos íntimos. Mi amiga Susana (5) __es__ una persona muy sincera. Ella y yo (6) __somos__ inseparables. Mi amigo Hernán (7) __es__ muy cómico. Hernán y yo (8) __somos__ compañeros de cuarto. Susana y Hernán (9) __son__ buenos amigos también. Y tú, ¿cómo (10) __eres__?

M/C **7** **¿Quiénes son?** Use **ser** to say who the following people are.

1. [Nombre] __es__ mi compañero(a) de clase.
2. [Nombre] __es__ el profesor (la profesora) de español.
3. [Nombre] __es__ el instructor (la instructora) en la clase de español.
4. Nosotros __somos__ estudiantes de español.
5. Tú… eres
6. Usted… es
7. Ustedes… son
8. Ellos… son

8 **Le presento a…** In groups of three or four, act out an introduction in front of the class. Decide beforehand the ages and the social standing of the people you are role-playing, as well as how informal or formal the situation is. The class must guess whether the introduction is formal or informal. Follow the model.

C

MODELO (formal)
—*Buenos días, profesora García.*
—*Buenos días, Susana.*
—*Profesora García, le presento a mi amigo Paul.*
—*Encantada, Paul.*

Gramática útil 3

Expressing quantity: **Hay** + nouns

Cómo usarlo

1. **Hay** is the Spanish equivalent of *there is* or *there are* in English.

Hay una reunión en la cafetería.	*There is a meeting in the cafeteria.*
Hay tres estudiantes en la clase.	*There are three students in the class.*
Hay unos libros en la mesa.	*There are some books on the table.*
Hay una fiesta el viernes.	*There is a party on Friday.*

2. **Hay** is used with both singular and plural nouns, and in both affirmative and negative contexts.

   Hay un bolígrafo, pero no **hay** lápices en la mesa.

3. **Hay** can be used with numbers or with indefinite articles (**un, una, unos, unas**), but it is never used with definite articles (**el, la, los, las**).

¡**Hay** tres profesores en la clase, pero sólo **hay** una estudiante!	*There are three professors in the class, but there is only one student!*

4. With a plural noun or negative, typically no article is used with **hay** unless you are providing extra information.

Hay papeles en la mesa.	*There are papers on the table.*
No hay libros en el escritorio.	*There aren't (any) books on the desk.*
Hay quince personas en la clase.	*There are fifteen people in the class.*

   BUT:

Hay unas personas interesantes en la clase.	*There are some interesting people in the class.*

Aquí **hay** un problema.

Suggestion: Reinforce examples by stating *Hay* **es una forma invariable.** Write the word **invariable** on the board. Then write **Hay un libro. Hay unos libros.** Model the question **¿Qué hay en el salón de clase?** Have students generate answers with **hay** + classroom vocabulary. Don't forget to write **hay** on the board and then cross out the **h**, saying **No se pronuncia la hache.**

Cómo formarlo

Hay is an *invariable verb form* because it never changes to reflect number or person. That is why **hay** can be used with both singular and plural nouns.

ACTIVIDADES

Learning objective: Understanding

Standards 1.1, 1.2: Students have numerous opportunities to communicate in Spanish in guided and open activities within grammar sections.

I **9** **¿Sí o no?** Look at the form and then answer the questions using **hay** or **no hay.** Follow the model.

> **Nombre:** Alicia Monteverde Salinas
> **Dirección:** 1742 NE Cleary Street, Portland, OR 97208
> **Número de teléfono:**
>   **casa:** _____   **celular:** 971-555-2951   **oficina:** 503-555-8820
> **Contacto personal:** _____
> **Dirección electrónica:** Alims@netista.org
> **Referencia:** _____

© Cengage Learning 2013

MODELOS ¿Hay... *un nombre?*
              Sí, hay.
              ¿Hay... *un número de teléfono de la casa?*
              No, no hay.

¿Hay...

1. ...una dirección? Sí, hay.
2. ...un número de teléfono de la oficina? Sí, hay.
3. ...un número del celular? Sí, hay.
4. ...un contacto personal? No, no hay.
5. ...una dirección electrónica? Sí, hay.
6. ...una referencia? No, no hay.

Answers, Act. 10: 1. Hay quince computadoras en el laboratorio. 2. Hay dos policías en la calle. 3. Hay cinco libros en el escritorio. 4. Hay tres profesores en la reunión. 5. Hay cuarenta estudiantes en la cafetería. 6. Hay veinte personas en la fiesta. 7. Hay treinta y cinco verbos en la pizarra. 8. Hay un celular en la mochila.

M **10** **Hay...** Say how many of the following things are in the places mentioned.

MODELO ventana (5): salón de clase
            Hay cinco ventanas en el salón de clase.

1. computadora (15): laboratorio
2. policía (2): calle
3. libro (5): escritorio
4. profesor (3): reunión
5. estudiante (40): cafetería
6. persona (20): fiesta
7. verbo (35): pizarra
8. celular (1): mochila

Learning objective: Applying

C **11** **¿Cuántos (How many) hay?** In groups of four or five, find out how many of the following objects there are in your group.

MODELO *Hay tres teléfonos celulares en el grupo.*

1. teléfonos celulares
2. cuadernos
3. diccionarios
4. computadoras portátiles
5. MP3 portátiles
6. ¿... ?

C **12** **¿Hay o no hay...?** With a classmate, take turns asking and answering whether the items indicated are in the classroom.

Objetos posibles: una computadora, un escritorio, un libro, un mapa, una mesa, una mochila, una pizarra digital interactivo, una ventana, ¿... ?

Sonrisas

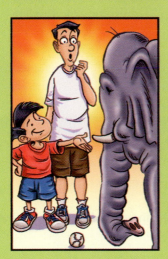

Comprensión Answer the following questions about the cartoon.

1. Según (*According to*) Dieguito, ¿qué hay en su cuarto? un elefante
2. En realidad, ¿qué hay en el cuarto de Dieguito? un elefante
3. Según el papá de Dieguito, ¿qué hay en el jardín (*garden*)? un elefante
4. En realidad, ¿hay un elefante en el jardín? no

Standards 1.2, 5.2: In Sonrisas cartoons, students interpret written language and examine language through humor, irony, and common sense. This technique guides students toward personal enjoyment and life-long uses of the language.

>> Gramática útil 4

Suggestion: Give the lesson on **tener** a personal dimension. Prepare a short list of things that you own, or bring a bag of objects to class. Recycle vocabulary already presented or use cognates. Next, engage students in a group conversation about their possessions: **¿Qué tienes en la mochila? ¿Qué tienes en casa? ¿Qué tiene tu compañero en casa?**, etc.

Expressing possession, obligation, and age: **Tener, tener que, tener + años**

Tienes el cellular de mi amigo Beto.

Optional: You may want to expand with examples showing omission of the article: **¿Tienes computadora mochila / amigos hispanos / amigos internacionales? Tengo (No tengo) calculadora / compañero de cuarto / fotos de la familia.**

Cómo usarlo

1. The verb **tener** means *to have*. It is used in Spanish to express possession and to give someone's age. You can also use it with **que** and another verb to say what you have to do: **Tengo que irme.** *(I have to go.)*

Tengo dos teléfonos en casa.	*I **have** two telephones in my house.*
Elena **tiene** veinte años. ¿Cuántos años **tienen** Sergio y Dulce?	*Elena **is** twenty years old. How old **are** Sergio and Dulce?*
Tengo que irme porque **tengo** clase.	*I **have to** go because I **have** class.*

2. When **tener** is used to express possession, the article is usually omitted, unless number is emphasized or you are referring to a specific object.

3. Note that where Spanish uses **tener… años** to express age, the English equivalent is *to be . . . years old.*

Remember, it's better to use the verb without a subject pronoun unless the subject is unclear or you want to emphasize it.

Suggestion: Expand further by adding numbers before nouns.

In Spanish the word for birthday is **cumpleaños**, which literally means "completes **(cumple)** years **(años)**." Many Spanish speakers celebrate their saint's day **(el día de su santo)**, which is the birthday of the saint whose name is the same as or similar to their own. For example: **El 19 de marzo es el día de San José.**

Notice: Reinforce that the names of the months are generally not capitalized in Spanish.

Cómo formarlo

1. Here are the forms of the verb **tener** in the present indicative tense.

tener *(to have)*			
yo	**tengo**	nosotros / nosotras	**tenemos**
tú	**tienes**	vosotros / vosotras	**tenéis**
Ud., él, ella	**tiene**	Uds., ellos, ellas	**tienen**

2. When talking about age, it's helpful to know the months of the year so that you can say when people's birthdays are celebrated.

¿Cuándo es tu cumpleaños? *When is your birthday?*

enero	julio
febrero	agosto
marzo	septiembre
abril	octubre
mayo	noviembre
junio	diciembre

Suggestion: Have students sort themselves by birth month into different sectors of the room. After they return to their seats, see who can remember the most classmates' birth months.

Optional: If time permits, preview the seasons. Say: **Los meses de la primavera son marzo, abril y mayo. Los meses del verano son junio, julio y agosto. Los meses del otoño son… . Los meses del invierno son… .**

3. When giving dates in Spanish, the day of the month comes first: **el quince de abril** = *April 15th.* When writing the date with numbers, the day always comes before the month: 15/4/10 = **el quince de abril de 2010**.

Suggestion: For additional practice, write dates on the board (2/12, 5/6, etc.) and have students read them. Be sure they remember that the day precedes the month in Spanish. Preview larger numbers **(mil = 1000)** by teaching the current year. For example: **2012 = dos mil doce.** The formal presentation of larger numbers is in Chapter 8.

ACTIVIDADES

M **13** **¿Qué tienen?** Say what each person has or has to do.

MODELO Yo *tengo* un cuaderno en el escritorio.

1. Yo ___tengo___ un celular en la mochila.
2. Nosotros ___tenemos___ que leer el libro.
3. Ellos ___tienen___ unos apuntes en el cuaderno.
4. Tú ___tienes___ dos libros en la mochila.
5. El profesor ___tiene___ cinco lápices en el escritorio.
6. Ustedes ___tienen___ que escuchar el audio.

14 **¿Cuántos años tienen?** Tell a friend the birthdays and ages of the
M following people.

MODELO Arturo (28/3; 25 años)
El cumpleaños de Arturo es el veintiocho de marzo.
Tiene veinticinco años. El cumpleaños de…

1. Martín (12/4; 21 años) …Martín es el doce de abril. Tiene veintiún años.
2. Sandra y Susana (14/7; 24 años) …Sandra y Susana es el catorce de julio. Tienen veinticuatro años.
3. mamá (16/6; 45 años) …mamá es el dieciséis de junio. Tiene cuarenta y cinco años.
4. papá (22/2; 47 años) …papá es el veintidós de febrero. Tiene cuarenta y siete años.
5. Gustavo (7/9; 17 años) …Gustavo es el siete de septiembre. Tiene diecisiete años.
6. Irma y Daniel (19/1; 19 años) …Irma y Daniel es el diecinueve de enero. Tienen diecinueve años.

15 **La fiesta** Listen to the conversation between Marta and Juan. They are
Track 4 talking about the birthdays and ages of various friends. Write down the age and
M the birthday of each person.

	Edad	Cumpleaños
1. Miguel	22 años	30 de julio
2. Arturo	25 años	27 de julio
3. Enrique	24 años	1 de agosto
4. Isabel	26 años	5 de agosto

16 **Yo tengo…** With a classmate, take turns asking and telling which of the
C following objects you have and don't have with you today. Follow the model.

MODELO Tú: *¿Tienes un libro?*
Compañero(a): *Sí. Tengo tres libros.*

Objetos posibles: bolígrafo, celular, computadora portátil, cuaderno, diccionario, lápiz, marcador, mochila, ¿…?

The number **veintiuno** shortens to **veintiún** when it's used with a noun: **veintiún años**.

Learning objective: Understanding

Audioscript, Act. 15, La fiesta:

[Marta]: Es una gran fiesta. Celebramos el cumpleaños de varias personas.

[Juan]: ¿Ah, sí? ¿De quién?

[Marta]: Pues, Miguel tiene veintidós años.

[Juan]: ¿Cuándo es su cumpleaños?

[Marta]: El 30 de julio.

[Juan]: Y ¿cuándo es el cumpleaños de Arturo?

[Marta]: El cumpleaños de Arturo es el 27 de julio.

[Juan]: ¿Ah, sí? Y ¿cuántos años tiene? ___

[Marta]: ¡Uy! Arturo es viejo. Tiene veinticinco años.

[Juan]: ¿Celebran otros cumpleaños?

[Marta]: Sí, el cumpleaños de Enrique es el primero de agosto. Cumple veinticuatro años. Y el cumpleaños de Isabel es el cinco de agosto y ella cumple veintiséis años.

[Juan]: ¡Qué maravilla! Nos vamos a divertir.

¡Explora y exprésate!

El español: ¡una lengua global!

Standards 2.1, 2.2, 3.1: Throughout *Cuadros*, the **Explora y exprésate** sections explore Spanish-speaking cultures and reinforce and further knowledge of other disciplines—in this case geography, history, and statistics.

Check: Assess what students have learned about the world's Spanish-speaking populations by repeating your questions from student interviews at the beginning of the chapter. For a quick additional check, have students close their books and see how many Spanish-speaking countries they can name, by continent.

Información general ▶

- Spanish is the official language of 21 countries.
- With almost 500 million native and second-language speakers internationally, Spanish is one of the most widely spoken languages in the world.
- Spanish ranks second worldwide for number of native speakers, with 329 million. (Chinese is first, with 1.2 billion native speakers, and English is a close third, with 328 million speakers.)
- Spanish is spoken by 34.5 million people in the United States and by approximately 480,000 people in Canada. It is one of the most widely studied and fastest-growing languages in both countries.

Top 5 languages on the Internet	Internet users by language	Internet users as percentage of total
English	536,564,837	27.3%
Chinese	444,948,013	22.6%
Spanish	153,308,074	7.8%
Japanese	99,143,700	5.0%
Portuguese	82,548,200	4.2%

Adapted from Top Ten Languages Used in the Web chart at http://www.internetworldstats.com/stats7.htm, Copyright © 2010, Miniwatts Marketing Group. All rights reserved worldwide.

Ryan McVay/Getty Images

Vale saber…

- Spanish originated on the Iberian Peninsula as a descendant of Latin.
- King Alfonso X tried to standardize the language for official use in the 13th century in the Castile region of Spain.
- By 1492, when Christopher Columbus headed for the Western Hemisphere, Spanish had already become the spoken and written language that we would recognize today.
- Spanish was brought to the New World by explorers who colonized the new territories under the Spanish flag for the Spanish Empire. At its peak, *el Imperio español* was one of the largest empires in world history.
- Today, there are far more Spanish speakers in Latin America than there are in Spain.

Prisma Archivo/Alamy

Note: Throughout *Cuadros*, the **Vale saber…** sections highlight a selection of key facts and events. In this chapter it is not intended to present a comprehensive historical analysis of the Spanish language.

■ El Imperio español

© Cengage Learning 2013

Idioma

- Spanish is referred to as either **español** or **castellano**.
- Like all languages, Spanish exhibits some regional variations, limited mainly to vocabulary and pronunciation. In spite of these variations, Spanish speakers from all over the world communicate without difficulty.
- Spanish and English share many cognates, due to the fact that many of their words have the same linguistic roots in Latin and Arabic.

| family | *familia* | computer | *computadora* |

Profesiones

- Here are just a few of the professions where Spanish is in high demand in the United States:

law	investment banking
medicine	sales and marketing
tourism	government
social sciences	human resources
education	interactive media

Marty Lederhandler/AP Images

Learning objectives:
Understanding, Remembering

>> En resumen

La información general

1. In how many countries is Spanish the official language? 21
2. In what place does Spanish rank in terms of numbers of native speakers? Second
3. Where did Spanish originate? Iberian Peninsula
4. Who tried to standardize Spanish in the 13th century? King Alfonxo X
5. What do English and Spanish have in common? cognates; Latin and Arabic linguistic roots

Los países de habla hispana

Los países de habla hispana Did you place the countries in the correct areas? With a partner, check your list from **¿Qué sabes?** on page 7 against the list below to see how many you got right.

África	Guinea Ecuatorial
El Caribe	Cuba, Puerto Rico*, República Dominicana
Centroamérica	Costa Rica, El Salvador, Guatemala, Honduras, Nicaragua, Panamá
Europa	España
Norteamérica	Canadá, Estados Unidos**, México
Sudamérica	Argentina, Bolivia, Chile, Colombia, Ecuador, Paraguay, Perú, Uruguay, Venezuela

*Es un Estado Libre Asociado (Commonwealth), no un país independiente.
**Se habla español, pero el español no es la lengua oficial.

Los beneficios de hablar el español With a partner, discuss your reasons for studying Spanish. What professional or personal benefits do you expect to get out of your study of this language? Do a search for key words such as "medical careers in Spanish" to find out why knowing Spanish will be useful to you in your career.

🌐 ¿QUIERES SABER MÁS?

Return to the chart that you started at the beginning of the chapter. Add all the information that you already know in the column **Lo que aprendí**. Then look at the column labeled **Lo que quiero aprender**. Are there some things that you still don't know? Pick one or two of these, or choose from the topics listed below, to investigate further online. You can also find more key words for different topics at **www.cengagebrain.com**. Be prepared to share this information with the class.

Palabras clave: (Historia) la Península Ibérica, la influencia árabe, el Nuevo Mundo, Cristóbal Colón **(Profesiones)** derecho, medicina, finanzas, tecnología, turismo, traducción **(Hispanos históricos célebres)** Alfonso X de Castilla y León, los Reyes Católicos.

🌐 **Tú en el mundo hispano** To explore opportunities to use your Spanish to study, volunteer, or hold internships in any part of the Spanish-speaking world, follow the links at **www.cengagebrain.com**.

🎵 **Ritmos del mundo hispano** Follow the links at **www.cengagebrain.com** to hear music from across the Spanish-speaking world.

Suggestion: Explain that **habla hispana** = donde se habla español; **hispanohablante** = una persona que habla español.

Suggestion: Before beginning, model pronunciation of country names for repetition.

Suggestion: Send the more ambitious learners on an Internet search to find out which places listed in the chart have a co-official language with Spanish: Equatorial Guinea (French); Puerto Rico (English); Peru (Quechua); Paraguay (Guaraní); Bolivia (Quechua, Aymara).

Optional: Have students study country capitals and then quiz each other: **¿Cuál es la capital de Chile?**

Learning objectives: Analyzing, Evaluating

Standard 5.1: In the **¿Quieres saber más?** sections, students are encouraged to do independent web research on topics that will gradually require more Spanish to carry out the assignments by introducing more participation with Spanish-speaking communities on the Web.

A leer

 Standards 1.2, 2.1, 2.2, 4.1, 4.2: Throughout the reading sections in *Cuadros*, students learn to interpret the written word and develop insight into the nature of language and culture.

ESTRATEGIA

Identifying cognates to aid comprehension

You have already learned a number of *cognates*—words that look similar in both Spanish and English but are pronounced differently. Some cognates you have already learned are **regular, terrible,** and **teléfono**. Cognates help you get a general idea of content, even if you don't know a lot of words and grammar.

¡**OJO!** *False cognates* are words that look similar in English and Spanish but mean different things. For example, **dirección** usually means *address*, not *direction*, in English. If a word that looks like a cognate doesn't make sense, you may need to look it up in a dictionary to discover its true meaning.

Suggestion: Show students the gesture for ¡OJO!

¡**OJO!** (literally, "Eye!") is used in Spanish to direct a person's attention to something. It is similar to saying "Watch out!" or "Be careful!" in English.

Learning objective: Analyzing

1 Look at the headline and the four sections of the following article. See if you can get the main idea of the article by relying on cognates and words you already know.

1. Put a check mark by the words that you already know in the title and the four bulleted sections.
2. Underline the cognates that appear in these sections. Can you guess their general meaning, based on context and where they appear in the sentence?

2 Now read the article, concentrating on the cognates and words you already know. Then answer the following questions, based on what you have read.

1. Según *(According to)* el artículo, las personas que tienen una dirección electrónica con su nombre son…
   a. misteriosas   c. emocionales
   ⓑ honestas   d. introvertidas

2. Las personas que son lógicas y poco emocionales tienen una dirección electrónica…
   ⓐ con números   c. de fantasía
   b. con su nombre   d. descriptiva

3. Las personas que se describen *(describe themselves)* con su dirección electrónica son…
   ⓐ un poco inocentes   c. agresivas
   b. aventureras   d. introvertidas

4. ¿Cuál es el nombre de fantasía que usan en el artículo? frodo4ever@ciberifico.net

5. En tu opinión, ¿es correcta o falsa la información sobre tu personalidad?

Answers will vary.

LECTURA

¡Tu dirección electrónica revela tu personalidad!

¿Es simbólica la dirección electrónica que usas? Muchas personas creen[1] que no, pero en realidad, los "nombres de computadora" que usamos revelan información importante sobre nuestras características más secretas. ¿Revela todo[2] tu dirección electrónica? ¡Vamos a ver!

Escoge[3] el tipo de dirección electrónica más similar a la tuya[4]…

Nombre

ejemplo: lucidíaz@woohoo.net

En este caso, la dirección electrónica puede[5] representar a una persona directa y honesta. Prefiere la realidad y es práctica y realista. No le interesa el misterio o la fantasía. Estas personas son muy aptas para los negocios[6] a causa de su estilo directo.

Números

ejemplo: 1078892@compluservicio.com

Las personas con los números en las direcciones electrónicas no tienen mucho interés en las cortesías diarias o las interacciones sociales. ¡Prefieren el mundo[7] súper racional de los números y las matemáticas puras! Otra explicación es que prefieren ser anónimos —quieren[8] mantener su misterio con un nombre que revela muy poco[9]!

Autodescripción

ejemplo: románticoloco29@universidad.edu

Las personas que se describen con la dirección electrónica necesitan comprensión y cariño[10]. Pueden ser amables, afectuosas y un poco ingenuas o inocentes. Pero, ¡cuidado[11]! ¡Estos nombres pueden ser totalmente falsos! Los nombres que indican que una persona es honesta o responsable pueden distorsionar la realidad completamente…

Fantasía

ejemplo: frodo4ever@ciberífico.net

Por lo general, estas personas consideran el ciberespacio como una oportunidad para la reinvención personal. Prefieren identificarse como un personaje imaginario para participar en lo que es, para ellos, ¡un drama cibernético! Pueden ser aventureras, emocionales y extrovertidas. Estos nombres también pueden atraer a las personas introvertidas que tienen la fantasía de presentarse completamente diferente de su realidad diaria.

[1]think [2]everything [3]Choose [4]yours [5]can [6]business [7]world [8]they want to [9]very little [10]affection [11]careful

---

>>

Después de leer Learning objectives: Remembering, Understanding

3 With a partner, try to invent as many names in each of the last two categories (**autodescripción** and **fantasía**) as you can. Use cognates from the reading when possible and be as creative as you can!

Optional: After students do **Activity 3**, have them share their favorite creation with the class.

4 Now take the list of e-mail names you created in **Activity 3** and add your own e-mail name to the list. (Or, if your e-mail name is simply your name or number, create a name that you would like to use.) Then, with your partner from **Activity 3**, form a group with two other pairs. Share your lists and see if you can guess each other's e-mail addresses.

All of the reading passages in *Cuadros* include translations of key (but not all) unknown words. Try to get the gist of the passage before you look for the definitions. Saving them as a last resort allows you to read the passage more quickly and to concentrate on getting the main idea.

A escribir

 Standard 1.3: In the writing sections, students present information to readers, who may often consist of their classmates.

As you use *Cuadros,* you will learn to write by using a *process* that moves from prewriting (identifying ideas and organizing them) through writing (creating a rough draft) and ends with revising (editing and commenting on writing). In each **A escribir** section, you will learn strategies that help you improve your techniques in each of the three phases of the writing process.

ESTRATEGIA

Prewriting—Identifying your target audience

Before you write, consider who will read your work. Your intended reader's identity is the crucial element that helps you establish the format, tone, and content of your written piece. Imagine you are writing two descriptions of the same event. How would your description vary if you were writing it for a close friend or for someone you have never met? Remembering your audience is the first step toward creating an effective written piece.

1 You are going to write an e-mail to your new Spanish-speaking roommate whom you have not yet met. With a partner, create a list of the information you should include in your message and identify its tone.

2 Taking your list of information from **Activity 1**, study the following partial model and see if you have included everything you need.

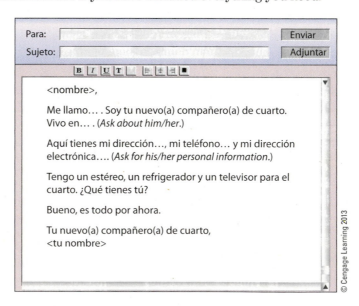

<nombre>,

Me llamo…. Soy tu nuevo(a) compañero(a) de cuarto. Vivo en…. (*Ask about him/her.*)

Aquí tienes mi dirección…, mi teléfono… y mi dirección electrónica…. (*Ask for his/her personal information.*)

Tengo un estéreo, un refrigerador y un televisor para el cuarto. ¿Qué tienes tú?

Bueno, es todo por ahora.

Tu nuevo(a) compañero(a) de cuarto,
<tu nombre>

Para: Enviar
Sujeto: Adjuntar

© Cengage Learning 2013

>> Composición

3 Using the previous model, write a rough draft of your e-mail. Try to write freely without worrying too much about mistakes or misspellings. You will have an opportunity to revise your work later. Here are some additional words and phrases.

una cafetera	*coffee maker*
Es todo por ahora.	*That's all for now.*
un estéreo	*stereo*
una impresora	*printer*
una lámpara	*lamp*
un microondas	*microwave oven*
para el cuarto	*for the room*
un refrigerador	*refrigerator*
un televisor	*television set*

Yellow Dog Productions/Getty Images

>> Después de escribir

4 Exchange your rough draft with a partner. Read each other's work and comment on its content and structure. For example, put a check mark next to places where you would like more information. Put a star by the sentence you like best. Put a question mark where the meaning is not clear. Underline any places where you are not certain the spelling and grammar are correct.

5 Now go back over your letter and revise it. Incorporate your partner's comments. Use the following checklist to check your final copy. Did you . . .

- make sure you included all the necessary information?
- match the tone of your writing to your audience?
- follow the model provided in **Activity 2**?
- check to make sure you used the correct forms of **ser** and **tener**?
- watch to make sure articles and nouns agree?
- look for misspellings?

Suggestion: For additional practice, have pairs revise one of their e-mails to make it more formal. Have them imagine it is addressed to the head of the residence hall instead of to their future roommate. Ask: *How would you modify the language in the existing letter to make it more courteous and formal?*

Vocabulario

Para saludar   *How to greet*

Hola. *Hello.*

¿Qué tal? *How are things going?*

¿Cómo estás (tú)? *How are you? (s. fam.)*

¿Cómo está (usted)? *How are you? (s. form.)*

¿Cómo están (ustedes)? *How are you? (pl.)*

¿Cómo te va? *How's it going with you? (s. fam.)*

¿Cómo le va? *How's it going with you? (s. form.)*

¿Cómo les va? *How's it going with you? (pl.)*

¿Qué hay de nuevo? *What's new?*

Buenos días. *Good morning.*

Buenas tardes. *Good afternoon.*

Buenas noches. *Good night. Good evening.*

Para responder   *How to respond*

Bien, gracias. *Fine, thank you.*

Bastante bien. *Quite well.*

(No) Muy bien. *(Not) Very well.*

Regular. *So-so.*

¡Terrible! / ¡Fatal! *Terrible! / Awful!*

No mucho. *Not much.*

Nada. *Nothing.*

¿Y tú? *And you? (s. fam.)*

¿Y usted? *And you? (s. form.)*

Para pedir y dar información personal   *Exchanging personal information*

¿Cómo te llamas? *What's your name? (s. fam.)*

¿Cómo se llama? *What's your name? (s. form.)*

Me llamo… *My name is . . .*

(Yo) soy… *I am . . .*

¿Cuál es tu número de teléfono? *What's your phone number? (s. fam.)*

¿Cuál es su número de teléfono? *What's your phone number? (s. form.)*

Mi número de teléfono es es el 3-71-28-12. *My phone number is 371-2812.*

Es el 3-71-28-12. *It's 371-2812.*

¿Dónde vives? *Where do you live? (s. fam.)*

¿Dónde vive? *Where do you live? (s. form.)*

Vivo en… *I live at . . .*

    la avenida… *avenue . . .*

    la calle… *street . . .*

    el barrio… / la colonia… *neighborhood . . .*

¿Cuál es tu dirección? *What's your address? (s. fam.)*

¿Cuál es su dirección? *What's your address? (s. form.)*

Mi dirección es… *My address is . . .*

¿Cuál es tu dirección electrónica? *What's your e-mail address? (s. fam.)*

¿Cuál es su dirección electrónica? *What's your e-mail address? (s. form.)*

Aquí tienes mi dirección electrónica. *Here's my e-mail address. (s. form.)*

Aquí tiene mi dirección electrónica. *Here's my e-mail address. (pl.) (s. form.)*

arroba @

punto com *.com*

Para presentar a alguien   *Introducing someone*

Soy… *I am . . .*

Me llamo… / Mi nombre es… *My name is . . .*

Quiero presentarte a… *I'd like to introduce you (s. fam.) to . . .*

Quiero presentarle a… *I'd like to introduce you (s. form.) to . . .*

Quiero presentarles a… *I'd like to introduce you (pl.) to . . .*

Para responder   *How to respond*

Mucho gusto. *My pleasure.*

Mucho gusto en conocerte. *A pleasure to meet you.*

Encantado(a). *Delighted to meet you.*

Igualmente. *Likewise.*

El gusto es mío. *The pleasure is mine.*

Un placer. *My pleasure.*

Para despedirse *Saying goodbye*

Adiós. *Goodbye.*
Hasta luego. *See you later.*
Hasta mañana. *See you tomorrow.*
Hasta pronto. *See you soon.*

Nos vemos. *See you later.*
Chau. *Bye.*
Bueno, tengo que irme. *Well / OK, I have to go.*

Para hablar por teléfono *Talking on the telephone*

Familiar

—**¡Hola!** *Hello?*
—**Hola. ¿Qué estás haciendo?** *Hi. What are you doing?*
—**Nada, ¿y tú?** *Nothing, and you?*
—**¿Quieres hacer algo?** *Do you want to do something?*
—**Claro. ¿Nos vemos donde siempre?** *Sure. See you at the usual place?*
—**Está bien. Hasta luego.** *OK. See you later.*
—**Chau.** *Bye.*

Formal

—**¡Hola! / ¿Aló?** *Hello?*
—**Hola. ¿Puedo hablar con…?** *Hi, may I speak with . . . ?*
—**Sí. Aquí está.** *Yes. Here he/she is..*
—**Lo siento. No está.** *Sorry. He's/she's not here.*
—**Por favor, dígale que llamó (nombre).** *Please tell him/her that (name) called.*
  Mi número es el… *My number is . . .*
—**Muy bien.** *OK.*
—**Muchas gracias.** *Thank you very much.*
—**De nada. Adiós.** *You're welcome. Goodbye.*
—**Adiós.** *Goodbye.*

¿Cuándo es tu cumpleaños? *When is your birthday?*

enero *January*
febrero *February*
marzo *March*
abril *April*
mayo *May*
junio *June*

julio *July*
agosto *August*
septiembre *September*
octubre *October*
noviembre *November*
diciembre *December*

Palabras útiles *Useful words*

Títulos

don *title of respect used with male first name*
doña *title of respect used with female first name*
señor / Sr. *Mr.*
señora / Sra. *Mrs., Ms.*
señorita / Srta. *Miss, Ms.*

Los artículos definidos
el, la, los, las *the*

Los artículos indefinidos
un, una *a*
unos, unas *some*

Los pronombres personales
yo *I*
tú *you (fam.)*
usted (Ud.) *you (form.)*

él *he*
ella *she*
nosotros / nosotras *we*
vosotros / vosotras *you (fam. pl.)*
ustedes (Uds.) *you (fam. or form. pl.)*
ellos / ellas *they*

Los verbos
estar *to be*
hay *there is, there are*
ser *to be*
tener *to have*
tener… años *to be . . . years old*
tener que *to have to (+ verb)*

Expresiones
Tengo prisa. *I'm in a hurry.*

Repaso y preparación

Preparation: Have students review this material and complete the activities here, in the SAM, and online before they begin **Chapter 2**.

Complete these activities to check your understanding of the new grammar points in **Chapter 1** before you move on to **Chapter 2**.

The answers to the activities in this section can be found in **Appendix B**.

Check: The **Repaso** section not only reviews grammar and vocabulary for the student but it offers a built-in performance assessment. By doing review activities with students, you can assess concepts that you may need to continue to reinforce in future classes.

Nouns and articles (p. 18)

1 For each blank, decide whether an article is needed. If it is, write the correct definite or indefinite article. If no article is needed, write X.

Rudyanto Wijaya/iStockphoto

1. ¡Bienvenida a ___la___ Doctora Silvina Madrones! Ella es
2. ___X___ profesora de estadísticas y tiene su doctorado de
3. ___la___ Universidad Autónoma de México. Además (*Besides*) de ser
4. ___X___ profesora, es 5. ___X___ escritora y 6. ___X___ autora de
7. ___unos___ libros de texto muy populares. Ella es 8. ___una___ adición agradable a 9. ___los___ Departamentos de Matemáticas y Ciencias Sociales.

Subject pronouns and the present indicative of the verb **ser** (p. 22)

2 For sentences 1–3, write in the missing subject pronouns. For sentences 4–6, write in the missing forms of the verb **ser** in the present indicative.

1. ___Tú___ eres dentista.
2. ___Nosotros___ somos profesores.
3. ___Yo___ soy veterinario.

4. Ella ___es___ taxista.
5. Uds. ___son___ arquitectos.
6. Nosotras ___somos___ actrices.

Hay + nouns (p. 25)

Remember to leave out the indefinite article with **no hay: Hay una silla, pero no hay escritorio.**

3 Say whether the drawing shows the following items. If you see more than one of an item, say how many there are.

© Cengage Learning 2013

1. ¿una chica? Hay dos chicas.
2. ¿un hombre? Hay un hombre.
3. ¿una mujer? Hay una mujer.
4. ¿un niño? No hay niño.

5. ¿una computadora? No hay computadora.
6. ¿una mochila? No hay mochila.
7. ¿una serpiente? Hay una serpiente.
8. ¿un elefante? No hay elefante.

Tener, tener que, tener + años (p. 28)

4   Complete each sentence with the correct present indicative form of **tener**.

1. Marcos, ¿___tienes___ un bolígrafo?
2. Profesor Martín, ¿___tiene___ la tarea?
3. Yo ___tengo___ tu dirección.
4. Nosotras ___tenemos___ muchos amigos.
5. Ellos no ___tienen___ el libro.
6. Tú ___tienes___ las fotos.

5   Write forms of **tener que** to tell what the following people have to do.

1. Yo ___tengo que___ presentarte a mis amigos.
2. ¡Ellos ___tienen que___ conocerte!
3. Nosotros ___tenemos que___ entregar la tarea.
4. Él ___tiene que___ contestar la pregunta.
5. Tú ___tienes que___ escuchar el audio.
6. Ustedes ___tienen que___ leer el capítulo.

6   Say how old each person is, based on the year he or she was born. *Answers will vary depending on current year.*

1. tú (1957)   Tú tienes... años.
2. ellos (2005)   Ellos tienen... años.
3. usted (1962)   Usted tiene... años.
4. ella (1975)   Ella tiene... años.
5. yo (1992)   Yo tengo... años.
6. nosotros (1990)   Nosotros tenemos... años.
7. ustedes (1983)   Ustedes tienen... años.
8. tú y yo (1995)   Tú y yo tenemos... años.

LWA/Dann Tardif/Getty Images

¿Cuántos años tiene?

>> Preparación para el Capítulo 2   **Learning objective:** Evaluating

Starting in **Chapter 2,** the **Preparación** section provides review and practice of grammar topics presented in *previous* chapters. The objective of this section is to help you remember previously learned structures that will be useful when you learn new grammar topics in the next chapter. Because this is the first chapter, however, there is no previous grammar to review.

To prepare for **Chapter 2,** reread **Chapter 1: Gramática útil 1.**

¿Qué te gusta hacer?

GUSTOS Y PREFERENCIAS

We express aspects of our personalities through our likes and dislikes. In this chapter, we explore the relationship between personalities and preferences.

How do you think that the activities you like and dislike define who you are?

Communication

By the end of this chapter you will be able to

- express likes and dislikes
- compare yourself to other people and describe personality traits
- ask and answer questions
- talk about leisure-time activities
- indicate nationality

Felix Sánchez/Getty Images

Un viaje por las áreas hispanohablantes de Estados Unidos

Estos diez estados *(states)* tienen las poblaciones más grandes *(biggest)* de hispanohablantes de Estados Unidos. ¿Puedes *(Can you)* identificar los cinco estados con las poblaciones más grandes?

Orden	Estado
California	Arizona
Texas	California
Florida	Colorado
Nueva York	Florida
Illinois	Georgia
	Illinois
	Nueva Jersey
	Nuevo México
	Nueva York
	Texas

Check: At the beginning of this chapter, interview students to find out how much they already know about U.S. Hispanics, including information on heritage and demographics across the country. At the end of the chapter, repeat your questions to assess what they have learned.

Some U.S. states have Spanish equivalents that are fairly common in speech, while others do not. *Cuadros* provides the Spanish state name only if it is frequently used by native speakers, e.g., Nueva York, Nuevo México. Otherwise, the English name is provided, e.g., Rhode Island, Massachusetts.

¿Qué sabes? Di si las siguientes oraciones son **C (ciertas)** o **F (falsas)**.

1. No hay ningún *(none)* estado del Medio Oeste *(Midwest)* en la tabla. F
2. La mayoría *(Most)* de los estados con muchos hispanohablantes están en el Sur *(South)*, el Suroeste *(Southwest)* o el Oeste. C
3. Los nombres de algunos *(some)* de los estados son de origen español. C

Lo que sé y lo que quiero aprender Completa la tabla del **Apéndice A**. Escribe algunos datos que **ya sabes** sobre los hispanohablantes de Estados Unidos en la columna **Lo que sé** *(What I already know)*. Después, añade *(add)* algunos temas que **quieres aprender** a la columna **Lo que quiero aprender** *(What I want to learn)*. Guarda *(Save)* la tabla para usarla otra vez en la sección **¡Explora y exprésate!** en la página 71.

Cultures

By the end of this chapter you will have explored

- world nationalities
- bilingual culture in the U.S. and Canada
- some statistics about Hispanics in the U.S.
- Hispanic groups in the U.S.: brief overview of their history and culture
- some famous U.S. Hispanics talking about themselves and their heritage

¡Imagínate!

>> ## Vocabulario útil 1

Standards 3.1, 4.2, 5.1: Examples of the other standards that will be met in **Chapter 2** are Connections—geography through nationalities; Comparisons—inviting in English- and Spanish-speaking cultures; Communities—Spanish-language media in the U. S.

© Cengage Learning 2013

BETO: Autora14, ¿**qué te gusta hacer** los domingos?

DULCE: Los domingos generalmente **estudio** en la biblioteca.

ANILÚ: ¡Qué aburrida!

BETO: ¡**Estudias!**

ANILÚ: Dile que **bailas** y **cantas** y **escuchas** música.

BETO: ¿No te gusta hacer otras cosas?

DULCE: Pues sí. A veces mis amigos y yo **tomamos un refresco** en el Jazz Café o **alquilamos un video**.

Notice: In this section, **me gusta, te gusta, le gusta,** and **les gusta** are presented lexically, followed by an infinitive. Students will learn this structure formally in the second grammar presentation of the chapter.

Suggestion: Point out that the days of the week are not capitalized in Spanish.

Suggestion: You may want to write the three cues for these scenes on the board as headings: **A mí me gusta…, A mi amiga le gusta…, A mis amigos les gusta…** Have students study the drawings with labeled vocabulary and generate both orally and in writing things that the characters in the drawings like to do. Write the activities on the board under the headings. This will serve as an introduction to the vocabulary in the chapter. Then personalize the activity by asking students what they like to do based on this vocabulary: **¿A ti te gusta…?**

Suggestion: Since so many students rent their movies by downloading them, you may want to teach **bajar / descargar un video / una película.** Students may also watch movies online, which is also called **streaming** in Spanish.

>> ### Las actividades *Activities*

A ti, ¿qué te gusta hacer los fines de semana (los viernes, los sábados y los domingos)?

What do you like to do on the weekends (Fridays, Saturdays, and Sundays)?

© Cengage Learning 2013

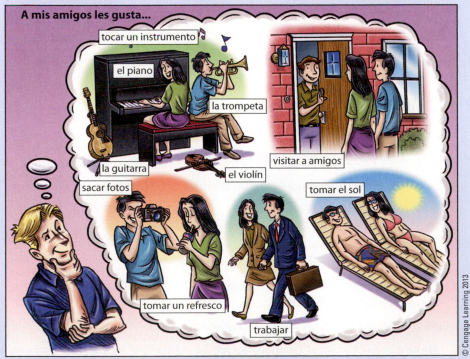

ACTIVIDADES

Optional: Have students mime or act out the activities and the class can identify them in Spanish.

I **1** **Los verbos** What Spanish verbs do you associate with the following? Choose from the list. (Some items can have more than one answer.)

1. ___b, h, i___ los murales
2. ___c, e___ la música
3. ___f, i___ los deportes
4. ___a, e, h___ una presentación oral
5. ___c, e, f___ un instrumento musical
6. ___d, e, g___ la familia

   a. preparar
   b. pintar
   c. tocar
   d. visitar
   e. escuchar
   f. practicar
   g. conversar
   h. estudiar
   i. mirar

Learning objectives: Understanding, Applying

Preparation: Encourage students to follow the models in the activities where **gustar** is used.

M **2** **Le gusta…** Your friends like to participate in certain activities. Say what they like to do, based on the information provided.

MODELOS Ernestina: murales
     Le gusta pintar.
     Leo: orquesta de música clásica
     Le gusta tocar un instrumento musical.

Answers, Act. 2: 1. Le gusta bailar. 2. Le gusta cantar. 3. Le gusta cocinar. 4. Le gusta sacar fotos. 5. Le gusta escuchar música. 6. Le gusta mirar televisión. 7. Le gusta hablar por teléfono. 8. Le gusta navegar por Internet.

1. Neti: ballet
2. Antonio: himnos y ópera
3. Javier: paella y enchiladas
4. Clara: cámara
5. Ernesto: estéreo
6. Beti: programas de comedia, noticias
7. Susana: celular
8. Luis: páginas web

C **3** **Mis actividades favoritas**

Standard 1.1: Preparation: Stress that students must generate activities (infinitive verb forms), not things. With true beginners, you may need to cue students with question on board and review silent **h**: **¿Qué te gusta hacer?**

Check: Assess whether students differentiate between **gusta/gustan** when listening. Have them write what they hear, repeating each sentence twice: 1. Me gusta caminar. 2. Te gustan los libros electrónicos. 3. Nos gusta leer y escribir. 4. A él le gusta la clase. 5. ¿Les gusta la actividad?

1. Make a list of five activities you like to do.

MODELO *Me gusta patinar en el parque.*

2. Now ask three other students what their favorite activities are and record their responses.

MODELO —*¿Qué te gusta hacer?*
     —*Me gusta caminar.*
     You write: *A Heather le gusta caminar.*

3. Compare responses to see who, if anyone, has similar favorite activities, and share this list with the class.

MODELO *A Marta y a Juan les gusta sacar fotos.*

4. Make a list of the most frequent activities mentioned by your classmates. Write a short paragraph about what students like to do and what activities they don't like to do.

¡Fíjate! "Spanglish": la mezcla de dos idiomas

When two cultures are in close proximity, eventually their languages will influence each other. Because native speakers of Spanish and native speakers of English have lived side by side for hundreds of years in the United States, a new hybrid form of the two languages has begun to spring up in conversation on the street, in poetry and fiction, and even in the articles of academic linguistic journals.

Strict language purists, including parents who want their children to be fluent and literate in both languages, and intellectuals who view the mixing of languages as a degradation of the original languages, do not approve of the casual use of Spanglish among the newer generations of Latino Americans. Ilan Stavans, a Mexican native, award-winning essayist, and the Lewis-Sebring professor in Latin American and Latino Culture at Amherst College, illustrates this point in his book *Spanglish: The Making of a New American Language*:

> Asked by a reporter in 1985 for his opinion on el espanglés, . . . Octavio Paz, the Mexican author of *The Labyrinth of Solitude* (1950) and a recipient of the Nobel Prize for Literature, is said to have responded with a paradox: "ni es bueno ni es malo, sino abominable"—it is neither good nor bad but abominable. This wasn't an exceptional view: Paz was one of scores of intellectuals with a distaste for the bastard jargon, which, in his eyes, didn't have gravitas.

Spanglish is not easy to master. It takes a profound understanding of the nuances of both English and Spanish in order to syncopate the linguistic components of each and produce a comprehensible and communicative statement. Bilingual puns, bilingual wordplay, and bilingual sentence fusion can be found in the works of many Latino American writers such as Francisco Alarcón, Julia Álvarez, Sandra Cisneros, Cristina García, Tato Laviera, and Junot Díaz.

Even Stavans admits, "Over the years my admiration for Spanglish has grown exponentially. . . ," and he continues:

> And, atención, Spanglish isn't only a phenomenon that takes place en los Unaited Esteits: in some shape or form, with English as a merciless global force, it is spoken—and broken: no es solamente hablado sino quebrado—all across the Hispanic world, from Buenos Aires to Bogotá, from Barcelona to Santo Domingo.
> Beware: Se habla el espanglés everywhere these days!

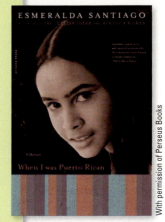

With permission of Perseus Books

"Cover of Ballantine edition", copyright © 1993 by Ballantine, from DREAM IN CUBAN by Cristina Garcia. Used by permission of Ballantine, a division of Random House, Inc.

Práctica

1. How do you feel about the mixing of two languages? Can you find any other instances in the history of the world where this has occurred?
2. Do you know any bilingual speakers? Do you know of any books that use the fusion of Spanish and English in some form? Do some research in your community or on the web and try to find two or three examples of a bilingual statement that amuses you.

Optional: Students may notice that García and Díaz are typically written with an accent in Spanish. Frequently last names are anglicized in the U.S., and they are no longer written with the accent over the **i**.

Optional: Brainstorm with students about their experiences with examples of Spanglish.

▶ >> Vocabulario útil 2

SERGIO: ¿Con quién hablas?

BETO: No sé. Es una estudiante de la Universidad. Su nombre electrónico es Autora14.

SERGIO: Dile que tienes un amigo muy **guapo.**

Suggestion: Ask a variety of questions based on the art to recycle concepts of age, how many dogs, what elements in the drawing students can identify, etc. **¿Cuántos años tiene ella/él? ¿Qué hay en el dibujo? ¿Te gusta el perro?**

>> **Características físicas** *Physical traits*

Notice that you say **Tiene el pelo negro / rubio / castaño**, etc., but when someone is a redhead, you say **Es pelirrojo(a)**. You can also say **Es rubio(a)** to indicate that someone is a blond. **Es moreno(a)** may indicate that someone is either a brunette or has dark skin.

Optional: If needed, teach **Tiene el pelo blanco** or **Tiene muchas canas**.

Heritage Learners: Some of the vocabulary words in this chapter have variants that may be more commonly used by heritage learners. Give or solicit examples: **rubio = güero; castaño = color café / oscuro; guapo = buen mozo / atractivo; perezoso = flojo, vago.**

ACTIVIDADES

I **4** **Sergio, Beto, Anilú y Dulce** Complete the following descriptions of the video characters.

1. Sergio…
   a. es rubio. b. es muy, muy pequeño. c. es guapo.

2. Anilú…
   a. es pelirroja. b. tiene el pelo castaño. c. es gorda.

3. Beto…
   a. es viejo. b. es gordo. c. es delgado.

4. Dulce…
   a. tiene el pelo negro. b. tiene el pelo rubio. c. es baja.

M **5** **Descripciones** Describe the people in the illustrations below. Use as many physical descriptions as you can.

1. **Eduardo**

   Eduardo es alto y delgado. Es joven. Es pelirrojo.

2. **el señor Bernal**

   El señor Bernal es bajo. Es viejo. Tiene el pelo castaño.

3. **Sofía**

   Sofía es pequeña. Tiene el pelo negro. Es joven.

4. **Roque**

   Roque es feo y gordo.

© Cengage Learning 2013

Heritage Learners: Point out that **pelirrojo** has two **r's**, but **rojo** has only one. Other words that follow this pattern are **puertorriqueño / Puerto Rico; pararrayos, rayos.**

C **6** **¿Cómo soy yo?** Describe yourself in a paragraph for your Internet blog. You can also include activities that you like to do. Read your description to your partner. Then have him or her read their description to you.

Learning objectives: Creating, Understanding

MODELO *Soy alta y tengo el pelo negro. Me gusta tomar el sol y escuchar música.*

▶ >> Vocabulario útil 3

ANILÚ: Y tú, Experto10, ¿qué te gusta hacer los domingos?

SERGIO: Autora14, soy un hombre **activo.** Bailo, canto, toco la guitarra, cocino…

BETO: ¡Sergio! **¡Mentiroso!** ¡No me gusta bailar, no me gusta cantar, no toco la guitarra y no cocino!

SERGIO: ¡Qué **aburrido** eres, hombre!

>> **Características de la personalidad** *Personality traits*

aburrido(a)	divertido(a); interesante	*boring / fun; interesting*
activo(a)	perezoso(a)	*active / lazy*
antipático(a)	simpático(a)	*unpleasant / pleasant*
extrovertido(a)	introvertido(a); tímido(a)	*extroverted / introverted; timid, shy*
generoso(a)	egoísta	*generous / selfish, egotistic*
impaciente	paciente	*impatient / patient*
impulsivo(a)	cuidadoso(a)	*impulsive / cautious*
inteligente	tonto(a)	*intelligent / silly, stupid*
mentiroso(a)	sincero(a)	*liar / sincere*
responsable	irresponsable	*responsible / irresponsible*
serio(a)	cómico(a)	*serious / funny*
trabajador(a)	perezoso(a)	*hard-working / lazy*

▌ ACTIVIDADES ▐

7 **Diferentes** You and a partner have differing opinions of the same person. Your partner will say that this imaginary person is a certain way, and you will counter by saying they are just the opposite. Take turns describing several imaginary people this way. Follow the model.

MODELO Tú: *Arturo es activo.*
Compañero(a): *¡No! Arturo es perezoso.*

Compañero(a): *Carmela es impulsiva.*
Tú: *¡No! Carmela es cuidadosa.*

I **8** **¿Cómo son?** Benjamín describes himself and several of his friends and relatives. Which adjective best describes each person?

Learning objective: Understanding

Optional: Follow up by dropping names of individuals known to your students such as President Obama, Lady Gaga, Daniel Radcliffe, etc., and have them do descriptions.

1. No me gusta mirar televisión. Prefiero practicar deportes o levantar pesas.
   a. serio   b. activo   c. impulsivo

2. A mi amiga Marta le gusta ayudar *(to help)* a sus amigos.
   a. antipática   b. mentirosa   c. generosa

3. Mi profesora es una maestra muy buena. Explica la lección y repite todas las instrucciones.
   a. paciente   b. impaciente   c. interesante

4. Mi amigo Joaquín tiene una imaginación muy buena. Le gusta inventar historias falsas.
   a. tímido   b. tonto   c. mentiroso

5. Mi amigo Alberto habla y habla y habla… ¡pero no es muy interesante!
   a. aburrido   b. serio   c. divertido

6. Mi amiga Linda tiene muchas ideas buenas sobre qué hacer los fines de semana. Además es una persona muy cómica.
   a. inteligente   b. tonta   c. divertida

M **9** **La clase de psicología** What personality traits does it take to succeed in various professions? Choose characteristics on the right that you think best fit the professions on the left. Follow the model.

Learning objective: Applying

Standard 1.1: In **Activities 9** and **10,** students provide information and express opinions.

MODELO *Los políticos tienen que ser honestos,…*

Profesiones	Características	
los políticos	sistemáticos	serios
los artistas	deshonestos	estudiosos
los criminales	honestos	sinceros
los actores	inteligentes	pacientes
los científicos	creativos	talentosos
los doctores	simpáticos	impulsivos
los policías	extrovertidos	egoístas
los estudiantes	trabajadores	mentirosos
	curiosos	cuidadosos
	temperamentales	¿…?
	responsables	

C **10** **Mis amigos** Describe two people from your family to your partner. Provide both physical and personality traits in your descriptions. Then have your partner describe two people from his or her family.

MODELO —*Es una persona alta y delgada. Tiene el pelo castaño. También (Also) es una persona cómica y divertida…*

Notice that you use the **-a** form of all the adjectives in this activity because the adjectives modify the feminine noun **persona**. You will learn more about adjective endings later in this chapter.

Antes de ver Review these key words and phrases used in the video.

apagar   *to turn off*
Dile que...   *Tell him/her that . . .*
No sé.   *I don't know.*

ESTRATEGIA

Using questions as an advance organizer

One way to prepare yourself to watch a video segment is to familiarize yourself with the questions you will answer after viewing. Look at the questions in **Después de ver 1**. Before you watch the video, use these questions to create a short list of the information you need to find. Example: **la dirección electrónica de Beto, la dirección electrónica de Dulce, el nombre del amigo de Beto**, etc.

© Cengage Learning 2013

▶ **Ver** Now watch the video segment as many times as needed to find the information in your list.

Después de ver 1 Answer (in Spanish) the following questions about the video.

1. ¿Cuál es la dirección electrónica de Beto? ¿Y la de Dulce? Experto10, Autora14
2. ¿Cómo se llama el amigo de Beto? ¿Y la amiga de Dulce? Sergio, Anilú
3. ¿Cuáles son las actividades preferidas de Dulce? estudiar, tomar un refresco o alquilar un video con amigos
4. Según *(According to)* Sergio, ¿cuáles son las actividades preferidas de Experto10? bailar, cantar, tocar la guitarra, cocinar

Después de ver 2 Now say whether the following statements about the video segment are true (**cierto**) or false (**falso**).

1. Según Anilú, Dulce es una persona muy aburrida. cierto
2. Sergio es una persona muy sincero. falso
3. Dulce generalmente estudia en casa los domingos. falso
4. A Beto le gusta bailar, cantar y tocar la guitarra. falso
5. Según Anilú, un hombre que cocina y canta y baila es el hombre ideal. cierto
6. Sergio apaga la computadora porque Anilú quiere *(wants)* su número de teléfono. falso

Preparation: Show the video segment once, having students pick out cognates to help them relax and listen for similarities between Spanish and English. Let students call out the cognates in Spanish or English after the first showing. Then direct students to **Después de ver 1** and have them focus on the information they need to look for in the second viewing. Follow up with a third showing of the segment, so that students can confirm their answers.

Learning objective: Remembering

▶ >> Voces del mundo hispano

© Cengage Learning 2013

In this video segment, the speakers say where their families are from and talk about their personalities and pastimes. First read the statements below. Then watch the video as many times as needed to say whether the statements are true **(cierto)** or false **(falso)**.

1. La mamá de Nicole es de Guatemala. F
2. El papá de Liana es de la República Dominicana. C
3. Según Inés, ella es activa, extrovertida y feliz *(happy)*. C
4. Según los amigos y familiares de Inés, ella es alegre, cuidadosa y tímida. F
5. A Constanza le gusta caminar. F
6. A Jessica y Ana María les gusta leer. C

🔊 >> Voces de Estados Unidos

Track 5

Isabel Valdés, ejecutiva y autora

Courtesy of Isabel Valdéz

❝Hispanics are becoming more and more entrenched in American society. Their participation is reflected in the growing number of Hispanic associations, libraries, research centers, and businesses throughout the United States. Furthermore, Hispanics are increasingly active in government at the federal, state, county, and city levels. They have also made significant contributions to American art, theater, literature, film, music, and sports.❞

Isabel Valdés es responsable de muchas campañas publicitarias en español en Estados Unidos y Latinoamérica. Sus clientes incluyen firmas tales como PepsiCO y Frito-Lay. Esta chilena-estadounidense es autora de cuatro libros sobre el mercado *(market)* hispano en Estados Unidos. Es además la directora de IVC, una empresa *(business)* consultora que ofrece servicios estratégicos a compañías para alcanzar *(to reach)* a consumidores multiculturales en EEUU y los mercados globales. Valdés dedica mucho tiempo al trabajo voluntario para ayudar a *(help)* varias organizaciones, entre ellas *The Nacional Council of La Raza* y *The Latino Community Foundation.*

¿Y tú? What are your interests? Do you identify yourself as part of a market segment? If so, which one(s)?

¡Prepárate!

>> ## Gramática útil 1

Describing what you do or are doing:
The present indicative of regular -ar verbs

Bailo, canto, toco la guitarra, **cocino**...

Cómo usarlo

Suggestion: Reinforce the translations of the present tense on the board, underlining options: **(Yo) estudio.** I study. I _do_ study. I _am_ studying. I _am going to_ study. Students will learn other ways to talk about the future in **Chapters 3** and **13.**

In English we use a variety of structures to express different present-tense concepts. In Spanish many of these are communicated with the same grammatical form. The present indicative tense in Spanish can be used. . .

- to describe routine actions:

  ¡Estudias mucho!   *You study a lot!*

- to say what you are doing now:

  Estudias matemáticas hoy.   *You are studying*
                                                mathematics today.

- to ask questions about present events:

  ¿**Estudias** con Enrique todas   *Do you study with Enrique*
    las semanas?   *every week?*

- to indicate plans in the immediate future:

  Estudias con Enrique el viernes, ¿no?   *You're going to study with*
                                                Enrique on Friday, right?

The use of the present tense to talk about future plans is used more in some regions of the Spanish-speaking world than others.

Notice: Students will learn **-er/-ir** conjugations in **Chapter 3.**

Notice how the same form in Spanish, **estudias**, can be translated four different ways in English.

Cómo formarlo

LO BÁSICO

- An *infinitive* is a verb before it has been conjugated to reflect person and tense. **Bailar** *(To dance)* is an infinitive.
- A *verb stem* is what is left after you remove the **-ar, -er,** or **-ir** ending from the infinitive. **Bail-** is the verb stem of **bailar.**
- A conjugated verb is a verb whose endings reflect person *(I, you, he/she, we, you, they)* and tense *(present, past, future, etc.).* **Bailas** *(You dance)* is a conjugated verb (person: *you familiar singular;* tense: *present*).

Suggestion: For students with limited English grammar experience, model the conjugation of a few verbs in English to enhance their linguistic awareness.

1. Spanish infinitives end in **-ar**, **-er**, or **-ir**. For now, you will learn to form the present indicative tense of verbs ending in **-ar**. To form the present indicative tense of a regular **-ar** verb, simply remove the **-ar** and add the following endings.

bailar *(to dance)*			
yo	bail**o**	nosotros / nosotras	bail**amos**
tú	bail**as**	vosotros / vosotras	bail**áis**
Ud., él, ella	bail**a**	Uds., ellos, ellas	bail**an**

2. Remember, as you learned in **Chapter 1**, you do not need to use the subject pronouns (**yo, tú, él, ella**, etc.) unless the meaning is not clear from the context of the sentence, or you wish to clarify, add emphasis, or make a contrast.

   Camino en el parque todos los días.　　*I walk in the park every day.*
   But:
   Yo camino en el parque, pero Lidia　　*I walk in the park, but Lidia*
   　　camina en el gimnasio.　　　　　　　*walks in the gymnasium.*

3. You may use certain conjugated present-tense verbs with infinitives. However, do not use two conjugated verbs together unless they are separated by a comma or the words **y** *(and)*, **pero** *(but)*, or **o** *(or)*.

   Necesitamos trabajar el viernes.　　*We have to work on Friday.*
   Los sábados, **trabajo, practico**　　*On Saturdays I work, play*
   　　deportes y **visito** a amigos.　　*sports, and visit friends.*
   Los domingos, **dejo de trabajar**.　　*On Sundays I stop working.*
   　　¡**Bailo, canto** o **escucho** música!　　*I dance, sing, or listen to music!*

4. To say what you don't do or aren't planning to do, use **no** before the conjugated verb.

   ¡**No estudio** los fines de semana!　　*I don't study on the weekends!*

5. Add question marks to turn a present-tense sentence into a *yes/no* question.

   ¿**No estudias** los fines de semana?　　*Don't you study on the weekends?*
   ¿**Tienes que estudiar** este fin　　*Do you have to study this*
   　　de semana?　　　　　　　　　　*weekend?*

6. Other regular **-ar** verbs:

apagar	*to turn off*	**llegar**	*to arrive*
acabar de (+ infinitive)	*to have just done something*	**necesitar** (+ infinitive)	*to need (to do something)*
buscar	*to look for*	**pasar**	*to pass (by); to happen*
cenar	*to eat dinner*	**preparar**	*to prepare*
comprar	*to buy*	**regresar**	*to return*
dejar de (+ infinitive)	*to leave; to stop (doing something)*	**usar**	*to use*
descansar	*to rest*	**viajar**	*to travel*
llamar	*to call*		

Notice that in this usage, Spanish infinitives are often translated into English as *-ing* forms: *I stop working.*

The expression **acabar de** can be used with any infinitive to say what activity you and others have just completed: **Acabo de llegar.** *(I just arrived.)* **Acabamos de cenar.** *(We just ate dinner.)*

M **1** **Beto** Beto describes his day in an e-mail to a friend. Complete his description with the correct form of the verb in parentheses.

A las siete de la mañana, (1. caminar) a la universidad. (2. Llegar) a las siete y media. Si tengo tiempo, (3. estudiar) un poco antes de las clases.

A veces (4. necesitar) comprar unos libros. (5. Comprar) los libros en la librería. Generalmente (6. cenar) en la cafetería. Después (7. pasar) por un café y (8. tomar) un café o un té. (9. Regresar) al dormitorio a las siete de la noche. (10. Hablar) con mis amigos por teléfono o (11. navegar) por Internet.

M **2** **Anilú y Sergio** Anilú and Sergio do different things. Say what each of them does. Use **pero** *(but)* to contrast what they do. Follow the model.

MODELO Anilú: cenar en un restaurante; Sergio: cocinar en casa
Anilú cena en un restaurante, pero Sergio cocina en casa.

1. Anilú: bailar; Sergio: levantar pesas   Anilú baila, pero Sergio levanta pesas.
2. Anilú: trabajar; Sergio: descansar   Anilú trabaja, pero Sergio descansa.
3. Anilú: tomar un refresco; Sergio: tomar café   Anilú toma un refresco, pero Sergio toma café.
4. Anilú: estudiar; Sergio: navegar por Internet   Anilú estudia, pero Sergio navega por Internet.
5. Anilú: alquilar un video; Sergio: mirar televisión   Anilú alquila un video, pero Sergio mira televisión.
6. Anilú: escuchar música rap; Sergio: tocar la guitarra   Anilú escucha música rap, pero Sergio toca la guitarra.

 3 **Tú** Interview a partner about his or her activities.
C

MODELO estudiar en la biblioteca
Tú: *¿Estudias en la biblioteca?*
Compañero(a): *Estudio en la biblioteca.*

1. caminar a la universidad   (No) Camino…
2. tocar la guitarra   (No) Toco…
3. visitar mucho a la familia   (No) Visito…
4. trabajar los fines de semana   (No) Trabajo…
5. cenar en la cafetería   (No) Ceno…
6. necesitar una computadora   (No) Necesito…

4 **Ellos y nosotros** Work in pairs to compare the activities of you and your
C friends (**nosotros**) and someone else's friends (**ellos**).

MODELO estudiar
Nosotros estudiamos en la biblioteca. Ellos estudian en casa.

1. estudiar   Verb forms: estudiamos, estudian
2. cenar   cenamos, cenan
3. trabajar   trabajamos, trabajan
4. visitar a la familia   visitamos, visitan
5. necesitar   necesitamos, necesitan
6. llegar a la universidad   llegamos, llegan
7. navegar por Internet   navegamos, navegan
8. ¿…?   Answers will vary.

5 **Los fines de semana** What do you generally do on the weekends? First, make a chart like the one below and fill in the **Yo** column. Compare your list with those of two classmates. Then write a paragraph comparing your typical weekend to theirs. (**¡OJO!: por la mañana / tarde / noche** = *in the morning / afternoon / night*)

C

Learning objectives: Creating, Analyzing

Standard 1.1/Suggestion, Act. 5: Start this activity by modeling a few things that you do during the weekends. **Durante los fines de semana, trabajo en casa, ceno con mi familia, compro comida en mi supermercado favorito**, etc. Then have students fill out the chart. As an alternative to the written paragraph, have students report orally to the whole class or in groups. This activity encourages students to communicate in Spanish (C 1.1: Interpersonal Communication).

¿Cuándo?	Yo	Amigo(a) #1	Amigo(a) #2
viernes por la noche:	*Descanso en casa.*		
sábado por la mañana:			
sábado por la tarde:			
sábado por la noche:			
domingo por la mañana:			
domingo por la tarde:			
domingo por la noche:			

MODELO *Los viernes por la noche generalmente descanso en casa.*
Mi amigo Eduardo generalmente…

6 **¿Quién?** You work at a dating service and you have to decide who to introduce to whom. You have some descriptions in writing and some on audio. First read the following profiles. Then listen to the audio descriptions. For each description you hear, write the person's name next to the profile below that is most compatible with that person.

Track 6

Standard 1.2/Suggestion: Students should listen to the audio two or three times to facilitate interpretive listening.

Audioscript, Act. 6, ¿Quién?: *1. Me llamo Andrés. Me gusta mirar televisión. No soy muy activo. 2. Me llamo Marta. Soy muy trabajadora. Estudio todos los días. 3. Yo soy Jorge. Me gusta bailar y cantar. Soy extrovertido. 4. Yo soy Ángela. Visito a mis amigos por las tardes. Me gusta tomar refrescos con ellos y conversar. 5. Me llamo Rudy. Me gusta navegar por Internet. Soy un poco tímido. 6. Me llamo Sara. Me gusta practicar deportes. Soy muy activa.*

Perfiles: Andrés, Marta, Jorge, Ángela, Rudy, Sara

Rosa: Me gusta escuchar música de todo tipo. ¡Soy muy divertida!
Sugerencia para Rosa: ___Jorge___

Isidro: Levanto pesas tres veces por semana. Soy muy atlético.
Sugerencia para Isidro: ___Sara___

Roberta: Me gusta mirar películas. No practico deportes.
Sugerencia para Roberta: ___Andrés___

Carmen: Uso Internet mucho en mis estudios. Soy introvertida.
Sugerencia para Carmen: ___Rudy___

José Luis: Estudio mucho. Soy un poco serio.
Sugerencia para José Luis: ___Marta___

Antonio: Todos los días hablo por teléfono con mis amigos. Mis amigos son muy divertidos.
Sugerencia para Antonio: ___Ángela___

Now use the information above to find the best match for you and your classmates, based on the information you provided in **Activity 5.**

MODELO *Antonio es la persona más compatible con* (with) *Katie.*

>> Gramática útil 2

Saying what you and others like to do: Gustar + infinitive

Un hombre que cocina...
y también **¡le gusta bailar
y cantar!**

© Cengage Learning 2013

Standard 4.1/Suggestion:
Here *to like* in English is compared to **gustar** in Spanish. Capitalize on the English word *gusto* (He lives his life with gusto) to connect these concepts.

Cómo usarlo

The Spanish verb **gustar** can be used with an infinitive to say what you and your friends like to do. Note that **gustar**, although often translated as *to like*, is really more similar to the English *to please*. **Gustar** is always used with pronouns that indicate *who is pleased* by the activity mentioned.

—**Me gusta bailar** salsa.

I like to dance salsa.
(Dancing salsa pleases me.)

—¿**Te gusta bailar** también?

Do you like to dance, too?
(Does dancing please you, too?)

—No, pero a **Luis le gusta** mucho.

No, but Luis likes it a lot. (No, but it pleases Luis a lot.)

Cómo formarlo

LO BÁSICO

The pronouns used with **gustar** are indirect object pronouns. They show the person who is being pleased or who likes something. You will learn more about them in **Chapter 8**.

1. When **gustar** is used with one or more infinitives, it is always used in its third-person singular form **gusta**. Sentences with **gusta** + *infinitive* can take the form of statements or questions without a change in word order.

—**Nos gusta cocinar** y **cenar** en restaurantes.

We like to cook and to eat dinner in restaurants.

—¿**Te gusta cocinar** también?

Do you like to cook also?

¡OJO! Do not confuse
me, te, le, nos, os, and
les with the subject
pronouns **yo, tú, él, ella,
Ud., nosotros, vosotros,
ellos, ellas,** and **Uds.**
that you have already
learned.

2. **Gusta** + *infinitive* is used with the following pronouns.

gusta + *infinitive*	
Me gusta cantar. *I like to sing.*	**Nos** gusta cantar. *We like to sing.*
Te gusta cantar. *You like to sing.*	**Os** gusta cantar. *You (fam. pl.) like to sing.*
Le gusta cantar. *You (form.) / He / She like (s) to sing.*	**Les** gusta cantar. *You (pl.) / They like to sing.*

3. When you use **gusta**, you can also use **a** + *person* to emphasize or clarify *who* it is who likes the activity mentioned. Clarification is particularly important with **le** and **les,** because they can refer to several people.

Le gusta navegar por Internet.	*He/She likes to browse the Internet. (Who does?)*
A Beto / A él le gusta navegar por Internet.	*Beto / He likes to browse the Internet.*
A ellos les gusta cantar.	*They like to sing.*
A nosotros nos gusta conversar.	*We like to talk.*
A Sergio y a Anilú les gusta bailar.	*Sergio and Anilú like to dance.*

4. If you want to emphasize or clarify what you or a close friend like, use **a mí** (with **me gusta**) and **a ti** (with **te gusta**).

A mí me gusta alquilar películas, pero **a ti te gusta** mirar televisión.	*I like to rent movies, but you like to watch television.*

Notice that **mí** has an accent, but **ti** does not.

Suggestion: A graphic representation of **gustar** + *inf.* on the board may be helpful for students who prefer formulas. Arrange the following in 5 columns:

Col. 1	Col. 2	Col. 3
A	mí	me
	ti	te
	Ud.	le
	él	nos
	ella	os
	nosotros	les
	vosotros	
	ellos	
	ellas	
	Uds.	

Col. 4	Col. 5
gusta	bailar
	estudiar
	conversar
	etc.

5. To create negative sentences with **gusta** + *infinitive*, place **no** before the *pronoun* + **gusta**.

No nos gusta trabajar.	*We don't like to work.*
A Roberto **no le gusta cocinar**.	*Roberto doesn't like to cook*.

6. To express agreement with someone's opinion, use **también**. If you want to disagree, use **no** or **tampoco**. If you want to ask a friend if they like an activity you've already mentioned, ask **¿Y a ti?**

—¿Te gusta cocinar?	*Do you like to cook?*
—**A mí, no.** No me gusta. Me gusta comer en restaurantes. **¿Y a ti?**	*No, not me. I don't like it. I like to eat in restaurants. And you?*
—**A mí también.** Pero no me gusta comer en restaurantes elegantes.	*Me too. But I don't like to eat in fancy restaurants.*
—**¡A mí tampoco!**	*Me neither!*

Suggestion: Practice **A mí también** and **A mí tampoco** by expressing likes and by saying to students: **A mí me gusta mucho cocinar. ¿Y a ti? No me gusta estudiar. ¿Y a ti?**

A mí me gusta sacar fotos.

Konstantin Sutyagin/Shutterstock

M **7** **Atleta 23** Can you tell what the following people like to do, based on their online names? Pick their preferred activities from the column to the right.

MODELO   Cantante29
   A Cantante29 le gusta cantar.

1. Pianista18
2. Atleta23
3. Artista12
4. Estudiante31
5. Fotógrafo11
6. Cocinero13
7. Bailarina39

estudiar
cocinar
cantar
tocar el piano
sacar fotos
bailar
practicar deportes
pintar

8 **En el parque** With a partner, describe what everyone in the illustration
M likes to do.

© Cengage Learning 2013

Melinda y Celia

Miguel y Natalia

David

Héctor

Ana

Elena y Francisco

Carlos

Answers, Act. 8: A Melinda y a Celia les gusta patinar. A Elena y a Francisco les gusta bailar. A Miguel y a Natalia les gusta practicar deportes. A Ana le gusta hablar por teléfono. A Héctor le gusta escuchar música. A David le gusta sacar fotos. A Carlos le gusta tocar la guitarra.

Check: Propose that students write a brief description of a classmate including a physical description and his/her likes/dislikes. Have students read their descriptions to classmates without revealing identities. While the class guesses who is being described, assess progress in listening for accuracy and ability to communicate information based on concepts introduced previously.

9 🔊 **Les gusta** Susana and Alberto like to participate in certain activities together, but prefer to do other things alone. First listen to what they say and decide who likes to do the activity mentioned. After you listen, use the verbs indicated to create a sentence saying who likes to do what. Follow the models.

Track 7

Learning objectives: Understanding, Applying

Standard 1.2: This activity provides practice in interpretive communication.

MODELOS *(A Susana y a Alberto) Les gusta bailar.*

	Susana	Alberto	Susana y Alberto
bailar			x

(A Susana) Le gusta caminar en el parque.

	Susana	Alberto	Susana y Alberto
caminar en el parque	x		

	Susana	Alberto	Susana y Alberto
1. hablar por teléfono	Le gusta hablar por teléfono.		
2. cocinar comida mexicana			Les gusta cocinar comida mexicana.
3. sacar fotos	Le gusta sacar fotos.		
4. navegar por Internet			Les gusta navegar por Internet.
5. tocar la guitarra		Le gusta tocar la guitarra.	

Audioscript, Act. 9, Les gusta:

Modelos:

Los fines de semana, nos gusta ir a una discoteca a bailar. También bailamos en casa.

Camino en el parque los domingos. Me gusta mucho.

1. ¡Susana habla por teléfono todos los días! Habla con los amigos y con la familia. 2. Nos gusta mucho la comida mexicana. Los fines de semana cocinamos comida mexicana en mi casa. 3. ¡Susana saca muchas fotos! Saca fotos muy buenas. 4. A nosotros nos gusta navegar por Internet. ¡Es muy divertido! 5. Alberto toca la guitarra en un café todos los fines de semana. Toca muy bien.

C **10** **El estudiante hispanohablante** A new Spanish-speaking student is arriving at your dorm today. You want to let him know what activities you and your friends like to do so he can think about which activities he'd like to do with you. Write a note to post on your door that tells him what you and your friends typically like to do and where, so that when he arrives, he can decide what he wants to do with you.

Learning objective: Applying

1. First fill out the following chart to help you organize the information. Here are some possible locations: **el parque, el gimnasio, el restaurante, la cafetería, la residencia estudiantil, la biblioteca, la discoteca, el café, la oficina**.

Me gusta…	Nos gusta…	¿Dónde?

2. Once you complete the chart, use the information to write a note to welcome the new student, telling what you and your friends like to do and where, so that he can make plans to join you or not.

>> Gramática útil 3

Describing yourself and others: Adjective agreement

Cómo usarlo

Creative Study Gat®, "Se busca" advertisement for www.bitsandcream.com. Used with permission from Gat Publicidad.

Find at least three adjectives in this advertisement from a Spanish magazine. What nouns do they modify?

Answers: The adjectives are **divertidas, extrovertidas, dinámicas** and **positiva.** All modify **personas,** except **positiva,** which modifies **actitud.** If students ask, **artistas** is a noun; the adjective is **artísticos.**

As you learned in **Chapter 1,** Spanish nouns must agree with definite and indefinite articles in both gender and number. This agreement is also necessary when using Spanish adjectives. Their endings change to reflect the number and gender of the nouns they modify.

Anilú es **delgada**.	*Anilú is **thin**.*
Sergio y Beto son **inteligentes**.	*Sergio and Beto are **intelligent**.*
Sergio es un hombre **alto**.	*Sergio is a **tall** man.*
Dulce y Anilú son mujeres **jóvenes**.	*Dulce and Anilú are **young** women.*

Notice that in these cases the adjectives go *after* the noun, rather than before, as in English.

Cómo formarlo

LO BÁSICO

A *descriptive adjective* is a word that describes a noun. It answers the question *What is . . . like?*

To modify is to limit or qualify the meaning of another word. A descriptive adjective *modifies* a noun by specifying characteristics that apply to that noun: **un estudiante** vs. **un estudiante inteligente**.

1. **Gender**: If an adjective is used to modify a masculine noun, the adjective must have a masculine ending. If it is used to modify a feminine noun, it must have a feminine ending.

- The masculine ending for adjectives ending in **-o** is the **o** form.
- The feminine ending for adjectives ending in **-o** is the **a** form.
- Adjectives ending in **-e** or most consonants don't change to reflect gender.
- Adjectives ending in **-or** add **a** to the ending for the feminine form.

Un professor	Una profesora
simpátic**o**	simpátic**a**
interesant**e**	interesant**e**
trabajad**or**	trabajad**ora**

2. **Number**: If an adjective is used to modify a plural noun or more than one noun, it must be used in its plural form.

- To create the plural of an adjective ending in a vowel, add **s**.
- To create the plural of an adjective ending in a consonant, add **es**.
- To create the plural of an adjective ending in **-or**, add **es** to the masculine form and **as** to the feminine form.
- To create the plural of an adjective ending in **-z**, change the **z** to **c** and add **es**.

El profesor	Los profesores	Las profesoras
simpátic**o**	simpátic**os**	simpátic**as**
interesant**e**	interesant**es**	interesant**es**
trabajad**or**	trabajad**ores**	trabajad**oras**
feli**z**	feli**ces**	feli**ces**

3. As with articles and subject pronouns, adjectives that apply to mixed groups of males and females typically use the masculine form.

4. Most descriptive adjectives are used *after* the noun, rather than before.

5. If you want to use more than one adjective, you can use **y** *(and)* or **o** *(or)*.

El estudiante es simpático **y** trabajador.
¿Es el profesor alto **o** bajo?
Mis amigos son activos, generosos **y** cómicos.
¿Son ellas extrovertidas **o** introvertidas?

- If **y** appears before a word that begins with an **i**, it changes to **e**.
  La instructora es divertida **e** interesante.

- If **o** appears before a word that begins with an **o**, it changes to **u**.
  Hay siete **u** ocho estudiantes buenos en la clase.

Numbers do not change to match the number or gender of the nouns they describe. They go *before* the noun, rather than after.

Note that Spanish does not use a serial comma, as English does optionally. In the following English sentence, the comma after *generous* can be kept or omitted: *My friends are active, generous, and funny.* In Spanish, you do not use a comma after **generosos**: **Mis amigos son activos, generosos y cómicos.**

Suggestion for p. 64: Give some examples of nationalities in a context: **Soy norteamericana. Mi madre es alemana. Mi padre es norteamericano. Mis amigos son chilenos, norteamericanos y cubanos.** This will reinforce not only agreement in number and gender, but also demonstrate that no article is necessary between the verb and the nationality, as in some cases in English.

Suggestion for p. 64: Point out that nationalities and languages are not capitalized in Spanish. Names of countries are always capitalized.

> Remember that Puerto Ricans are U.S. citizens.

6. Adjectives of nationality follow slightly different rules. These adjectives add **a / as** feminine endings for nationalities whose names end in **-l, -s,** and **-n.** See the nationalities in the following group for examples. Adjectives of nationality are always used after the noun.

Nacionalidades		
África		
ecuatoguineano(a) Guinea Ecuatorial		
Asia		
chino(a) China	**indio(a)** India	
coreano(a) Corea	**japonés, japonesa** Japón	
Australia		
australiano(a) Australia		
Centroamérica y el Caribe		
costarricense Costa Rica	**guatemalteco(a)** Guatemala	**panameño(a)** Panamá
cubano(a) Cuba	**hondureño(a)** Honduras	**puertorriqueño(a)** Puerto Rico
dominicano(a) República Dominicana	**nicaragüense** Nicaragua	**salvadoreño(a)** El Salvador
Europa		
alemán, alemana Alemania	**francés, francesa** Francia	**italiano(a)** Italia
español, española España	**inglés, inglesa** Inglaterra	**portugués, portuguesa** Portugal
Norteamérica		
canadiense Canadá	**estadounidense** Estados Unidos	**mexicano(a)** México
Sudamérica		
argentino(a) Argentina	**colombiano(a)** Colombia	**peruano(a)** Perú
boliviano(a) Bolivia	**ecuatoriano(a)** Ecuador	**uruguayo(a)** Uruguay
chileno(a) Chile	**paraguayo(a)** Paraguay	**venezolano(a)** Venezuela

> **Estados Unidos** is often abbreviated as **EEUU** or **EE.UU.** in Spanish. Some native speakers do not use the article **los** with **EEUU: en Estados Unidos** or **en EEUU.**

7. Several adjectives in Spanish may be used *before* or *after* the noun they modify. Three common adjectives of this type are **bueno** *(good),* **malo** *(bad),* and **grande** *(big, large).* When **bueno** and **malo** are used before a singular masculine noun, they have a special shortened form. Whenever **grande** is used before any singular masculine or feminine noun, its shortened form **gran** is used. Note that **grande** has different meanings when used *before* the noun *(great, famous)* and *after* the noun *(big, large).*

> Notice the umlaut on the **ü** in **nicaragüense.** It is called a **diéresis** in Spanish. The **diéresis** is placed on the **u** in the syllables **gue** and **gui** to indicate that the **u** needs to be pronounced. Compare: **bilingüe, pingüino** and **guerra, Guillermo.**

un estudiante bueno	BUT:	un **buen** estudiante
una estudiante buena		una buena estudiante
un día malo	BUT:	un **mal** día
una semana mala		una mala semana
un hotel grande	BUT:	un **gran** hotel
una universidad grande	BUT:	una **gran** universidad

Optional: Point out that some Spanish speakers use USA instead of EEUU.

Notice: Nationalities should be used to allow students to choose the ones most applicable to their heritage when talking about origin. Add relevant nationalities as necessary, for example: **nigeriano, filipino, sueco,** etc. Point out how to pluralize as necessary. You may want to designate which nationalities students are to learn for active use and which are for recognition only.

I **11 El profesor y la profesora** Say whether the description refers to **la profesora, el profesor**, or if it could refer to both of them.

MODELO Es trabajadora.
la profesora

1. Es serio. el profesor
2. Es activo. el profesor
3. Es extrovertida. la profesora
4. Es responsable. el profesor o la profesora
5. Es inteligente. el profesor o la profesora
6. Es cuidadosa. la profesora
7. Es paciente. el profesor o la profesora
8. Es interesante. el profesor o la profesora
9. Es sincera. la profesora
10. Es generoso. el profesor

M **12 Marcos y María** Marcos and María are two of your best friends. They are not at all similar. Describe what they are like. Follow the model.

MODELO Marcos es divertido.
María no es divertida. Es aburrida.

1. Marcos es paciente.
2. María es responsable.
3. Marcos es extrovertido.
4. María es perezosa.
5. Marcos es sincero.
6. María es antipática.
7. Marcos es rubio.
8. María es delgada.

Answers, Act. 12: 1. María no es paciente. Es impaciente. 2. Marcos no es responsable. Es irresponsable. 3. María no es extrovertida. Es introvertida. 4. Marcos no es perezoso. Es trabajador. 5. María no es sincera. Es mentirosa. 6. Marcos no es antipático. Es simpático. 7. María no es rubia. Es morena / pelirroja. 8. Marcos no es delgado. Es gordo.

Suggestion: Expand **Activity 12** by having students describe their own friends; for example: **Mi amigo John es divertido, pero no es trabajador.**

Rocío

13 También Your partner tells you that a person you both know has a certain personality or physical trait. Say that two of your friends are just like that person.

M

Answers will vary for second sentence.

MODELO Compañero(a): *Rocío es alta.*
Tú: *Tomás y Marcelo también son altos.*

1. Gerardo

Gerardo es atlético.

2. Ángela
Ángela es pelirroja.

3. Miguel
Miguel es cómico.

4. Carmela
Carmela es perezosa.

5. Pablo
Pablo es trabajador.

6. Jimena
Jimena es impaciente.

© Cengage Learning 2013

14 Las nacionalidades With your partner, take turns asking the nationalities
C   of the following people. Then mention another person of the same nationality.

> **MODELO** Orlando Bloom (Inglaterra)
>   Tú: *¿De qué nacionalidad es Orlando Bloom?*
>   Compañero(a): *Es inglés.*
>   Tú: *¿De veras? Robert Pattinson es inglés también.*
>   *Answers will vary for second sentence of each reply.*

1. Penélope Cruz y Rafael Nadal (España) Son españoles.
2. Manny Ramírez (República Dominicana) Es dominicano.
3. Sonia Sotomayor (Puerto Rico) Es puertorriqueña.
4. Audrey Tautou (Francia) Es francesa.
5. Diego Luna y Gael García Bernal (México) Son mexicanos.
6. Gabriel García Márquez (Colombia) Es colombiano.
7. Rigoberta Menchú (Guatemala) Es guatemalteca.
8. Venus y Serena Williams (Estados Unidos) Son estadounidenses.
9. Celia Cruz y Fidel Castro (Cuba) Son cubanos.

15 Personas famosas In groups of four or five, each person takes a turn
C   describing a famous person. The rest of the group tries to guess who is being
described.

Palabras útiles: actor (actriz), atleta, cantante, músico(a), político(a)

> **MODELO** Tú: *Es actriz. Es estadounidense. Es alta, delgada y rubia. Es muy
>   inteligente y simpática. Habla inglés, francés y español. ¿Quién es?*
>   Grupo: *Es Gwyneth Paltrow.*

Learning objectives: Creating,
Applying

16 Tus cualidades You are appearing in a play and the director wants you to
C   write a short bio for the theatre program. First, make a list of the personal and
physical qualities you want to include. Then make a list of all of your favorite
and least favorite activities. (If you want to use adjectives and activities you
haven't learned yet, look for them in a Spanish-English dictionary.) Exchange
your lists with a classmate and suggest changes you think would be helpful.

Learning objectives:
Understanding, Analyzing

17 Tu descripción Now, using the information you listed in **Activity 16,**
C   write your description. Make sure you write at least five complete sentences,
using the third person, since that is how these descriptions normally appear in
theatre programs. Then, in groups of three or four, exchange your descriptions
and see if you can guess whose ad is whose. If possible, as a follow-up, post
your description on the class website under a false name and see if others can
guess who it is.

> **MODELOS** *Shannon Silvestre es una actriz buena... También es... Le gusta...*
>   *Shaun Perales es un actor cómico... No le gusta..., pero sí le gusta...*

Sonrisas

Comprensión Answer the following questions about the cartoon.

1. Según el gato (cat), ¿cómo es? *Es activo.*
2. Según el perro, ¿cómo es? *También es activo.*
3. En realidad, ¿cómo es el gato? ¿Y el perro? *En realidad, el gato es perezoso y mentiroso. El perro es activo.*
4. ¿Tienen consecuencias serias las mentiras del gato? En tu opinión, ¿son sinceras o mentirosas las personas cuando se comunican por Internet? *Answers will vary.*

 Standard 5.2: Here students interpret the language and situation for enrichment and consider ethical behavior as a life-long issue.

¡Explora y exprésate!

Standards 2.1, 2.2: Here students gain knowledge and understanding of Hispanic American culture, with a focus on identities and demographics, and explore cultural products in art, music, and literature.

Doble identidad: Los latinos en EEUU y Canadá

Andresr/Shutterstock

Los cinco grupos de latinos de mayor número en Estados Unidos son los méxicoamericanos (o los chicanos), los puertorriqueños, los cubanoamericanos, los dominicanos y los salvadoreños. Cada grupo tiene una historia larga y distinta. Sin embargo, tienen en común la doble identidad del bilingüe. El censo de 2010 indica que hay más de 50 millones de latinos en Estados Unidos.

En Canadá, viven 480.000 hispanos de varios países. La población va creciendo *(is increasing)*, aumentando un 6% cada año.

When expressing numbers with numerals, Spanish uses a period where English uses a comma (480.000 rather than 480,000). It also uses a comma instead of a period to express decimals (6,5 rather than 6.5).

The addition of **americanos** to each cultural group varies in usage. **Méxicoamericanos** and **cubanoamericanos** are commonly heard to distinguish Americans of Mexican and Cuban descent from Mexican and Cuban natives. **Puertorriqueños** do not add the term **americanos** because they are American citizens whether they live in Puerto Rico or in the U.S. **Dominicanos** and **salvadoreños** have not yet begun adding the term **americanos** to their group name, although this may change for future generations.

Latinos en Estados Unidos*	
mexicanos	31.673.700
puertorriqueños	4.411.604
salvadoreños	1.736.221
cubanos	1.677.158
dominicanos	1.360.476
guatemaltecos	1.077.412
colombianos	916.616
hondureños	624.533
españoles	613.585
ecuatorianos	611.457
peruanos	557.107

*Pewhispanic.org, 2009

Los cinco estados con las poblaciones hispanas más concentradas*	
California	14.014.000
Texas	9.461.000
Florida	4.224.000
Nueva York	3.417.000
Illinois	2.028.000

*http://pewhispanic.org/files/reports/140.pdf

Notice: Population figures are never static. It can be difficult to obtain statistics that compare the same groupings at the same time period. This list of Hispanics by nationality dates back to 2009, while state populations and other demographic data are drawn from 2010 U.S. census figures.

Optional: Remind students that the Latino population has grown and continues to grow, so the fact there is a great deal of interest in the Latino market does not come as a surprise. Ask students: Are there Spanish ads or classified ads in your local newspapers? Do you get a Spanish-language television station in your home? Encourage students to obtain ads and view Spanish programs and compare them to English-language ads and TV programs.

Check: Interview students again, using the same questions from the beginning of the chapter, to assess what they now know and would still like to know about U.S. Hispanics. Have students examine the population data and ask if they are aware that Hispanics now represent the largest minority population in the U.S.

Los méxicoamericanos o chicanos

Vale saber...

Throughout *Cuadros*, the **Vale saber...** section will highlight important historical events. In this chapter, it is not intended to be a comprehensive historical analysis of each group.

- After the Mexican-American War in 1848, Mexico ceded California, Texas, and parts of New Mexico, Arizona, Utah, Nevada, Colorado, Kansas, and Wyoming to the U.S. The majority of Mexicans in these areas elected to stay and were granted citizenship.
- The Chicano movement was born in the 1960s as Mexican-Americans attempted to regain a sense of pride in their Mexican heritage and culture.
- The integration of Mexican culture can be seen in vibrant areas such as the Riverwalk in San Antonio, Texas, the Pilsen and La Villita communities in Chicago, and the Mission District in San Francisco.

The term "Chicano" was adopted by Americans of Mexican descent during the American civil rights movement to distinguish themselves from Mexicans native to Mexico. There are many theories about its origin, none of which can be proven. The term was used by Mexican American activists who wanted to claim a unique ethnic and political identity.

Los grandes muralistas chicanos

Diego Rivera, José Orozco y David Siquieros eran *(were)* grandes muralistas mexicanos que usaban sus murales para expresar su visión política y reclamar sus orígenes indígenas. El arte del mural como expresión cultural ha sido adoptado *(has been adopted)* por los chicanos en EEUU.

Justin Sullivan/AP Images

Los puertorriqueños

Vale saber...

- In 1898, after the Spanish American War, Spain ceded Puerto Rico to the U.S. Nine years later, President Woodrow Wilson signed the Jones Act, which granted American citizenship to all Puerto Ricans.
- Many Puerto Ricans settled in New York City or in other parts of New York State, but younger Puerto Ricans have moved to Texas, Florida, Pennsylvania, New Jersey, Massachusetts and other states.
- El Museo del Barrio, La Marqueta, and el Desfile Puertorriqueño de Nueva York are all testimony to the bicultural life of the "Nuyoricans", also known as "nuyorquinos" or "nuevarriqueños."

Los poetry slams

Miguel Algarín, profesor de Rutgers, empezó *(began)* The Nuyorican Poets Café en su apartamento del East Village en 1973. Hoy día el Café es una organización sin fines de lucro *(non-profit agency)* que se ha transformado en un foro para poesía, música, hip hop, video, artes visuales, comedia y teatro. Los Poetry Slams son eventos muy populares en el Café.

Philip Scalia/Alamy

Culture: Point out that Cubans have come as refugees to the U.S. since 1959 for political reasons. Nearly one million Cubans now reside in the U.S.

Los cubanoamericanos

Vale saber…

- All of Florida and Louisiana were provinces of Cuba prior to the Louisiana Purchase and the Adams-Onís Treaty of 1819.
- The largest community of Cuban Americans in the United States is in Miami-Dade County in Florida.
- La Pequeña Habana in Miami is the cultural center of Cuban American life.

Jeff Greenberg/PhotoEdit

La música

El Buena Vista Social Club era un club en La Habana donde se juntaban los músicos en los años 40. La ilustre historia musical de Cuba sigue en los Estados Unidos con los cantantes Jon Secada, Albita, Celia Cruz, Gloria Estefan y el saxofonista Paquito D'Rivera—todos ganadores del premio Grammy.

Los dominicanos y los centroamericanos

Vale saber…

- New York City has had a Dominican population since the 1930s. They largely settled in Quisqueya Heights, an area of Washington Heights in Manhattan. Nowadays, Dominicans also reside in New Jersey, Massachusetts, and Miami.
- In the 1980s and 90s, Dominican immigration to the United States was at its height.
- In the 1980s, political conflicts in Guatemala, El Salvador, and Nicaragua led to a big wave of immigration to the U.S. Many Central Americans made their homes in cities like Los Angeles, Houston, Washington, D.C., New York, and Miami.

LatinContent/Getty Images

La literatura revolucionaria

El conflicto produce la literatura. La tarea del escritor es captar la verdad *(truth)* de la vida diaria. En países que pasan por una revolución, es urgente describir las condiciones del ser humano por escrito *(in writing)*. Testimonio de la necesidad de escribir en tiempos de conflicto es la importante literatura centroamericana de escritores como Gioconda Belli, Rigoberta Menchú Tum, Claribel Alegría, Ernesto Cardenal y Roque Dalton.

>> En resumen

La información general Say which Hispanic group each statement describes.

Learning objectives: Understanding, Remembering

1. Los **nuyoricans** son personas de este grupo que viven *(live)* en Nueva York. puertorriqueños
2. Este grupo en Estados Unidos adopta esta forma de arte como expresión cultural. méxicoamericanos / chicanos
3. Los conflictos en los países de origen de este grupo produce una literatura revolucionaria. centroamericanos
4. **Chicano** es otro nombre para una persona de este grupo. méxicoamericanos
5. Esta sección de Miami es el centro cultural de este grupo. cubanoamericanos
6. La inmigración de este grupo a Estados Unidos ocurre principalmente en las décadas de los 80 y los 90. dominicanos

🌐 ¿QUIERES SABER MÁS?

Return to the chart that you started at the beginning of the chapter. Add all the information that you already know in the column **Lo que aprendí.** Then, look at the column labeled **Lo que quiero aprender.** Are there some things that you still don't know? Pick one or two of these, or from the topics listed below, to further investigate online. You can also find more key words on different topics at **www.cengagebrain.com.** Be prepared to share this information with the class.

Palabras clave: (méxicoamericanos): the Mexican-American War, Treaty of Guadalupe Hidalgo, 5 de mayo**; (puertorriqueños):** Treaty of Paris, Jones Act, Luis Muñoz Rivera; **(cubanoamericanos):** calle Ocho, Ybor City, Louisiana Purchase, Adams-Onís Treaty; **(dominicanos y centroamericanos):** *El Norte*, Rafael Trujillo, Anastasio Somoza, Sandinistas, Civil War in El Salvador

Learning objectives: Analyzing, Evaluating

Check: Reviewing the table of information from earlier in the chapter provides a ready list of student-generated items to research.

🌐 **Tú en el mundo hispano** To explore opportunities to use your Spanish to study, volunteer, or do internships in the U. S. and Canada, follow the links at **www.cengagebrain.com**.

🎧 **Ritmos del mundo hispano** Follow the links at **www.cengagebrain.com** to hear music in Spanish from the U.S. and Canada.

A leer

>> **Antes de leer**

ESTRATEGIA

Looking up Spanish words in a bilingual dictionary

When reading in Spanish, try to understand the general meaning of what you read and don't spend time looking up every unknown word. But if there are key words you can't understand, using a dictionary can save you time.

Try to look up only one or two words from each page of text. Focus on words that you cannot guess from context and that you must understand to get the reading's general meaning. When you do look up the word, don't settle on the first definition! Look at the different English translations provided. Which one seems to best fit with the overall content of the reading?

When looking up verbs, remember that you must look up the infinitive form (**-ar**, **-er**, or **-ir**) and not the conjugated form. (**Ser** instead of **soy**, **hablar** instead of **hablas**, etc.) When you look up adjectives, look up the masculine form (**bueno** instead of **buena**, etc.).

For more on using a bilingual dictionary, see the **A escribir** section on page 76.

Answers, Act. 1, number 1: Possible words include: **orgullosos/ orgullosa/orgullo, nuestra, rechazar, pelotero, sino, trata de, ropa, enamorada, moda, entrenador, Encantador, perros, agradecido**

Suggestion: It may be helpful to bring several bilingual dictionaries to class (or show some online) so that students can see some titles, prices, or sites. There are many dictionaries on the market and on the Internet, and it can be overwhelming. Also, don't forget to take this opportunity to familiarize students with the bilingual glossary at the back of *Cuadros*.

Optional: Take the opportunity to warn students about the limitations of online translation sites.

1 When celebrities are interviewed, they often describe themselves and talk about their backgrounds. The point of the interview is to share personal information with the viewer and reader.

1. Look at the quotes of the seven U.S. Hispanics featured on pages 73–74. Read the translated words at the bottom of each page, then skim the quotes themselves. What words don't you know that you might need in order to get the main idea? Make a list of 5 to 10 words.

2. Can you guess from context any of the words you identified? For example, Albert Pujols is listed as a **pelotero** and in his photo he is wearing a uniform. Based on that information, can you guess what a **pelotero** is?

3. Of the remaining words, how many do you really need to know in order to understand the basic idea of what the person is saying? With a partner, create a list that contains only the words you think are necessary to get the main idea.

2 Now that you have narrowed down your list of unknown but key words, work with a partner to look them up in the dictionary. Be sure to read all the English definitions. Which one(s) fit(s) best in the context of the article?

LECTURA

¿Cómo soy yo?

Charles Sykes/AP Images

Carlos Santana
músico de ascendencia mexicana

"Soy un músico serio, como Paco de Lucía. Serio, pero divertido. Nunca invertí[1] energía en ser rico o famoso".

Culture: Paco de Lucía is a Spanish guitarist who plays primarily flamenco music. He was one of the creators of the New Flamenco style during the 1960s and 70s.

Roberto Pfeil/dapd/AP Images

Zoe Saldana
actriz de ascendencia puertorriqueña y dominicana

"Como latina, pienso que[2] tenemos que sentirnos[3] muy orgullosos de nuestra herencia. Tendemos[4] a buscar raíces[5] europeas y a rechazar las indígenas y las africanas, y eso es un asco, una vergüenza[6]. El latino es una composición de todos".

Isabel Toledo
diseñadora de ropa de ascendencia cubana

"Ser latina es ser quien soy, no cómo me defino... Es una cultura enamorada de la moda".

Kathy Willens/AP Images

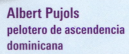

Albert Pujols
pelotero de ascendencia dominicana

"Yo quiero que la gente me recuerde[7], no sólo como Albert Pujols el buen pelotero, sino por la persona que yo soy, bien humilde[8] y que trata de ayudar[9] a los que lo necesitan".

MLB Photos via Getty Images

[1]*I never invested* [2]*I think that* [3]*to feel* [4]*We tend to* [5]*roots* [6]**un...**: *it's disgusting and a shame* [7]**Yo...:** *I want people to remember me* [8]*humble* [9]**trata...:** *that tries to help*

Eva Longoria
actriz de ascendencia mexicana

"Somos mexicanos de quinta[10] generación en Texas y estoy[11] orgullosa de ser latina y de representar a los latinos en todas partes... Ser mexicana es muy importante en quién soy yo".

Helga Esteb/Shutterstock

Henny Garfunkel/Retna Ltd./Corbis

Wilmer Valderrama
actor de ascendencia venezolana

"Yo soy muy agradecido por mis raíces latinas... A mí me da mucha dicha[12] y un orgullo muy grande cuando la gente latina admira cualquier[13] trabajo que he hecho[14]".

César Millán
entrenador de perros ("El Encantador de Perros"), de ascendencia mexicana

"Sólo soy un tipo instintivo que vive en el momento".

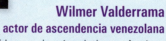

Douglas Kirkland/Corbis

[10]*fifth* [11]**I am** [12]**me...:** *it gives me a lot of happiness* [13]*whatever* [14]**he...:** *I have done*

>> Después de leer

 3 Now work with a partner to match the descriptions on the right with each person on the left.

_f_ 1. Carlos Santana	a. Es muy agradecido por su herencia latina.
_d_ 2. Zoe Saldana	b. Vive en el presente, no en el futuro.
_e_ 3. Albert Pujols	c. Es mexicana y muy orgullosa de su herencia.
_g_ 4. Isabel Toledo	d. Habla de ser una composición de culturas.
_b_ 5. César Millán	e. Es una persona muy humilde.
_c_ 6. Eva Longoria	f. Es serio, pero divertido.
_a_ 7. Wilmer Valderrama	g. Es de una cultura enamorada de la moda.

4 With a classmate, take turns interviewing each other and writing down your responses. Answer the following questions based on your own personality or that of a famous celebrity.

Learning objective: Applying

1. ¿Cuál es tu herencia? (Soy de ascendencia...)
2. ¿Cómo eres? (Soy...)
3. ¿Qué te gusta hacer? (Me gusta...)

5 Now, choose a famous Spanish speaker and do a search for him or her online. Find enough information to answer the three questions in **Actividad 4** about that person—**¡en español, por favor!** Be prepared to share your information with the class.

Rafael Nadal, España

Paulina Rubio, México

A escribir

ESTRATEGIA

Prewriting—Looking up English words in a bilingual dictionary

Since no textbook can provide you with all the words you may want to use when you write, you will want to use a bilingual dictionary to supplement the words you already know. Here's how to use the dictionary most effectively.

1. Decide on the English word you want to translate: for example, *lively.*

2. Think of several English synonyms for that word: *vivacious, energetic.*

3. Look up the original English word in the English-Spanish part of the dictionary and write down all the Spanish equivalents given. Note that semicolons are used to separate groups of words that are similar in meaning. Example: *lively:* **vivo, vivaz, vivaracho; rápido, apresurado; gallardo, galán, airoso; vigoroso, brioso, enérgico; animado, bullicioso; eficaz, intensivo.**

4. Take a Spanish equivalent from each group and look it up in the Spanish part of the dictionary. What is given as its English equivalent? As you look up each word, you'll see that often the different Spanish words express very different ideas in English.

   Example: **Rápido** and **apresurado** are words that apply more to actions, since they are translated as *rapid, quick, swift* and *brief, hasty.*

5. Now look up the English synonyms you listed in step #2 and see what Spanish equivalents are given. Are any of them the same as those that turned up for the first word? Example: *vivacious:* **vivaz, animado, vivaracho;** *energetic:* **enérgico, activo, vigoroso.**

6. Focus on the words that came up more than once: **vivaz, vivaracho, animado, enérgico.** If you need to, look these words up a final time. Which best expresses the shade of meaning you want to use?

1 You are going to write a short description of a sculpture by Fernando Botero, the well-known Colombian painter and sculptor.

Look at the photo of the sculpture on page 77. What words might you need to describe it? Here are some to get you started, but look up any new words you might require in a bilingual dictionary. **¡OJO!** Remember to cross-check the words you choose in order to get the one that best fits what you are trying to say.

Palabras útiles: escultura *(sculpture)*, **estatua** *(statue)*, **montado a caballo** *(on horseback)*, **sombrero** *(hat).*

La escultura *Hombre montado a caballo* de Fernando Botero

>> Composición

Learning objective: Creating

2 Write three to five sentences that describe the sculpture, using the list of words you generated in **Actividad 1.** Try to write freely without worrying too much about mistakes and misspellings.

>> Después de escribir

3 Now go back over your review and revise it. Use the following checklist to guide you. Did you . . .

- include all the necessary information?
- check to make sure that the adjectives and nouns agree in gender and number?
- make sure that the verbs agree with their subjects?
- look for misspellings?

Vocabulario

Para expresar preferencias *Expressing preferences*

¿Qué te gusta hacer? *What do you like to do?*
A mí me gusta... *I like . . .*
A ti te gusta... *You like . . .*
A... le gusta... *You/He/She like(s) . . .*
A... les gusta... *You (pl.)/They like . . .*
¿Y a ti? *And you?*

alquilar videos / películas *to rent videos/movies*
bailar *to dance*
caminar *to walk*
cantar *to sing*
cocinar *to cook*
escuchar música *to listen to music*
estudiar en la biblioteca / en casa *to study at the library/at home*
hablar por teléfono *to talk on the phone*
levantar pesas *to lift weights*

mirar televisión *to watch television*
navegar por Internet *to browse the Internet*
patinar *to skate*
pintar *to paint*
practicar deportes *to play sports*
sacar fotos *to take photos*
tocar un instrumento musical *to play a musical instrument*
   la guitarra *the guitar*
   el piano *the piano*
   la trompeta *the trumpet*
   el violín *the violin*
tomar un refresco *to have a soft drink*
tomar el sol *to sunbathe*
trabajar *to work*
visitar a amigos *to visit friends*

Para describir *Describing*

¿Cómo es? *What is he/she/it like?*

muy *very*

Características de la personalidad *Personality traits*

aburrido(a) *boring*
activo(a) *active*
antipático(a) *unpleasant*
bueno(a) *good*
cómico(a) *funny*
cuidadoso(a) *cautious*
divertido(a) *fun, entertaining*
egoísta *selfish, egotistic*
extrovertido(a) *extroverted*
generoso(a) *generous*
impaciente *impatient*
impulsivo(a) *impulsive*
inteligente *intelligent*
interesante *interesting*

introvertido(a) *introverted*
irresponsable *irresponsible*
malo(a) *bad*
mentiroso(a) *dishonest, lying*
paciente *patient*
perezoso(a) *lazy*
responsable *responsible*
serio(a) *serious*
simpático(a) *nice*
sincero(a) *sincere*
tímido(a) *shy*
tonto(a) *silly, stupid*
trabajador(a) *hard-working*

Características físicas *Physical traits*

alto(a) *tall*
bajo(a) *short*
delgado(a) *thin*
feo(a) *ugly*
gordo(a) *fat*
grande *big, great*
guapo(a) *handsome, attractive*
joven *young*

lindo(a) *pretty*
pequeño(a) *small*
viejo(a) *old*

Es pelirrojo(a) / rubio(a). *He/She is redheaded/ blond(e).*
Tiene el pelo negro / castaño / rubio. *He/She has black/brown/blond hair.*

Nacionalidades *Nationalities*

alemán (alemana) *German*
argentino(a) *Argentinian*
australiano(a) *Australian*
boliviano(a) *Bolivian*
canadiense *Canadian*
chileno(a) *Chilean*
chino(a) *Chinese*
colombiano(a) *Colombian*
coreano(a) *Korean*
costarricense *Costa Rican*
cubano(a) *Cuban*
dominicano(a) *Dominican*
ecuatoguineano(a) *Equatorial Guinean*
ecuatoriano(a) *Ecuadoran*
español(a) *Spanish*
estadounidense *U. S. citizen*
francés (francesa) *French*

guatemalteco(a) *Guatemalan*
hondureño(a) *Honduran*
indio(a) *Indian*
inglés (inglesa) *English*
italiano(a) *Italian*
japonés (japonesa) *Japanese*
mexicano(a) *Mexican*
nicaragüense *Nicaraguan*
panameño(a) *Panamanian*
paraguayo(a) *Paraguayan*
peruano(a) *Peruvian*
portugués (portuguesa) *Portuguese*
puertorriqueño(a) *Puerto Rican*
salvadoreño(a) *Salvadoran*
uruguayo(a) *Uruguayan*
venezolano(a) *Venezuelan*

Los verbos

acabar de *(+ inf.)* *to have just done something*
apagar *to turn off*
buscar *to look for*
cenar *to eat dinner*
comprar *to buy*
dejar *to leave*
dejar de *(+ inf.)* *to stop (doing something)*
descansar *to rest*

llamar *to call*
llegar *to arrive*
necesitar *to need*
pasar *to pass (by)*
preparar *to prepare*
regresar *to return*
usar *to use*

Otras palabras

los fines de semana *weekends*
los viernes *Fridays*
los sábados *Saturdays*
los domingos *Sundays*
el gato *cat*

el perro *dog*
pero *but*
también *also*
tampoco *neither*

Repaso y preparación

Repaso del Capítulo 2

Check: The **Repaso** section not only reviews grammar and vocabulary for the student but also offers a built-in performance assessment. By doing review activities with students, you can assess concepts that you may need to continue to reinforce in future classes.

Complete these activities to check your understanding of the new grammar points in **Chapter 2** before you move on to **Chapter 3**.

The answers to the activities in this section can be found in **Appendix B**.

Preparation: Have students review this material and complete the activities here, in the SAM, and online before they begin **Chapter 3**.

Answers, Act. 1: 1. Esteban y Carolina caminan. 2. Usted pinta. 3. Loreta levanta pesas. 4. Yo saco fotos. 5. Nosotros tomamos el sol. 6. Tú cocinas. 7. Ustedes hablan por teléfono. 8. Tú y yo patinamos.

The present indicative of regular -ar verbs (p. 54)

1 Look at the illustrations and say what the people indicated are doing.

1.
Esteban y Carolina

2.
usted

3.
Loreta

4.
yo

© Cengage Learning 2013

5.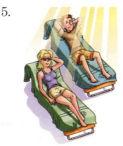
nosotros

6.
tú

7.
ustedes

8.
tú y yo

Gustar + infinitive (p. 58)

Answers, Act. 2: 1. A mí me gusta estudiar. 2. A ti te gusta mirar televisión. 3. A usted le gusta visitar a amigos. 4. A nosotras nos gusta pintar. 5. A ustedes les gusta practicar deportes.

2 Read the description of each person. Then say what activity he or she likes to do, choosing from the list. Follow the model.

Actividades: estudiar, mirar televisión, pintar, practicar deportes, visitar a amigos, trabajar.

MODELO Ellos son muy trabajadores.
A ellos les gusta trabajar.

1. Yo soy muy serio.
2. Tú eres muy perezosa.
3. Usted es muy extrovertido.
4. Nosotras somos muy artísticas.
5. Ustedes son muy activos.

Adjective agreement (p. 62)

Answers, Act. 3: 1. Gretchen y Rolf son alemanes. Son muy sinceros. 2. Brigitte es francesa. Es muy divertida. 3. Nosotras somos españolas. Somos simpáticas. 4. Yo soy estadounidense. Soy muy generosa. 5. Usted es japonesa. Es muy interesante. 6. Tú eres italiano. Eres muy activo.

3 Use forms of **ser** to describe each person using the cues provided.

1. Gretchen y Rolf / Alemania / sincero
2. Brigitte / Francia / divertido
3. nosotras / España / simpático
4. yo (feminino) / Estados Unidos / generoso
5. usted (feminino) / Japón / interesante
6. tú (masculino) / Italia / activo

>> Preparación para el Capítulo 3

Nouns and articles (Chapter 1)

4 Complete the description with the definite and indefinite articles that are missing. Make sure the articles agree with the nouns they modify.

A mí me gustan 1. __las__ clases que tengo hoy. 2. __El__ profesor de historia es muy inteligente y 3. __la__ profesora de español es muy interesante. Tengo 4. __unos__ amigos en 5. __la__ clase de ingeniería y por eso es muy divertida. Solamente tengo 6. __una__ clase por la tarde. Pero no es 7. __un__ día normal. Normalmente tengo clases por 8. __la__ mañana y también por 9. __la__ tarde. ¡Pero por lo menos, no tengo clases por 10. __las__ noches!

> Complete these activities to review some previously learned grammatical structures that will be helpful when you learn the new grammar in **Chapter 3**.
>
> Be sure to reread **Chapter 2: Gramática útil 1** and **2** before moving on to the **Chapter 3** grammar sections.

Subject pronouns and the present indicative of the verb **ser** (Chapter 1)

5 Match the illustrations on the left with the sentences on the right. Then write in the missing forms of the verb **ser**.

1. __f__

2. __d__

3. __a__

4. __g__

5. __b__

6. __e__

7. __c__

a. Ella __es__ muy tímida.

b. Nosotros __somos__ muy perezosos.

c. Yo __soy__ muy extrovertida.

d. Usted __es__ muy impaciente.

e. Tú __eres__ generoso.

f. Él __es__ activo.

g. Ustedes __son__ inteligentes.

© Cengage Learning 2013

capítulo 3 ¿Qué clases vas a tomar?

¡VIVIR ES APRENDER!

Los estudiantes asisten a clases formales y estudian muchas materias. Pero en un sentido *(sense)* menos formal, todos somos estudiantes. Aprendemos algo nuevo todos los días—de nuestros *(our)* amigos, familiares y experiencias.

Para ti, ¿cuál es la mejor manera *(the best way)* de aprender?

Communication

By the end of this chapter you will be able to

- talk about courses and schedules and tell time
- talk about present activities and future plans
- talk about possessions
- ask and answer questions

Glowimages RF

Un viaje por Cuba, Puerto Rico y la República Dominicana

Estos tres países están situados en el mar Caribe y tienen un clima tropical. Todos también tienen montañas. La República Dominicana comparte *(shares)* una isla con Haití.

País / Área	Tamaño y fronteras *(Size and Borders)*	Sitios *(Places)* de interés
Cuba 110.860 km²	un poco más pequeño que Pensilvania	las cavernas de Bellamar, la Vieja Habana, la península de Guanahacabibes
Puerto Rico 8.950 km²	casi tres veces *(almost three times)* el área de Rhode Island	Vieques, El Morro, Viejo San Juan
República Dominicana 48.380 km²	más de dos veces el área de Nuevo Hampshire; frontera con Haití	Pico Duarte, la sierra *(mountains)* de Samaná, La Universidad Autónoma de Santo Domingo

¿Qué sabes? Di si las siguientes oraciones son ciertas (**C**) o falsas (**F**).

1. Estos tres países están en el mar Caribe. C
2. La República Dominicana es casi dos veces el tamaño de Puerto Rico. F
3. No hay una zona vieja en Cuba. F

Lo que sé y lo que quiero aprender Completa la tabla del **Apéndice A**. Escribe algunos datos que **ya sabes** sobre estos países caribeños en la columna **Lo que sé**. Después, añade algunos temas que **quieres aprender** a la columna **Lo que quiero aprender**. Guarda la tabla para usarla otra vez en la sección **¡Explora y exprésate!** en la página 111.

Cultures

By the end of this chapter you will have explored

- facts about Puerto Rico, Cuba, and the Dominican Republic
- Cuba: the campaign for literacy
- Puerto Rico: the bilingual education of the **boricuas**
- República Dominicana: the oldest university in the New World
- the 24-hour clock
- three unusual schools in the Caribbean

¡Imagínate!

Standard 5.2: The spirit of this chapter lays the groundwork for lifelong language learning by providing the tools so that students can begin to use Spanish for their personal enjoyment and enrichment.

© Cengage Learning 2013

CHELA: Para empezar, dime, ¿cuántas clases tienes?

ANILÚ: Ay, ¡qué aburrido!, ¿no crees? Si voy a salir por Internet, quiero hacer más que recitar mis clases: **computación, diseño gráfico, psicología**, bla, bla, bla…

CHELA: Comprendo que no son las preguntas más interesantes del mundo, pero…

ANILÚ: Prefiero hablar de mi tiempo libre, los **sábados**, por ejemplo.

Suggestion: Point out to students Anilú's classes and ask: **¿Estudias computación, diseño gráfico o psicología?** Reinforce pronunciation as needed.

Notice that many of the courses of study are cognates of their English equivalents. Be sure to notice the difference in spelling, accentuation, and pronunciation, for example: **geografía**: geography.

Suggestion: To prepare students to recite their classes, preview that **y → e** before words beginning with **i** and **hi: Tengo clase de arquitectura e ingeniería. Estudio geografía e historia.**

Check: Have students spell out loud at least two of their classes and then pronounce the names. This helps assess progress with the subject words as well as the alphabet.

Optional: With the growing popularity of double majors, you may elect to ask who has a **doble especialidad**.

Heritage Learners: Use this vocabulary to review some basic rules of orthography and accentuation in Spanish. Point out to students that words that end in **-cion** or **-sion** always take an accent, as do names of languages or nationalities that end in **-es** (**inglés, japonés, francés**). Many names of disciplines that end in **-ía** require an accent, but not all. Contrast the sound of the last syllable in **Asia** and **hacía**, pointing out that the latter requires an accent.

>> **Campos de estudio**

Los cursos básicos
la arquitectura
las ciencias políticas
la economía
la educación
la geografía
la historia
la ingeniería
la psicología

Las humanidades
la filosofía
las lenguas / los idiomas
la literatura

Heritage Learners: In Spanish, two spellings are accepted: **psicología** and **sicología**. Similarly, **psiquiatra** and **siquiatra**.

Las lenguas / Los idiomas
el alemán
el chino
el español
el francés
el inglés
el japonés

Las matemáticas
el cálculo
la computación / la informática
la estadística

Las ciencias
la biología
la física
la medicina
la química (chemistry)
la salud (health)

Los negocios
la administración de empresas
la contabilidad (accounting)
el mercadeo (marketing)

La comunicación pública
el periodismo (journalism)
la publicidad

Las artes
el arte
el baile
el diseño gráfico
la música
la pintura

Suggestion: When presenting the vocabulary, ask students about their classes, majors, and minors to familiarize and create a personalized context for these words. Ask questions: **En nuestra universidad, ¿es más popular la ingeniería o la psicología? ¿Te gusta más la historia o la biología? ¿Qué estudias? ¿Cuál es tu especialidad? ¿Tienes otra concentración de estudios?** You may also want to ask about subjects they like to study using **gustar estudiar: ¿Te gusta estudiar ciencias políticas?** Also survey students on **¿Cuál es tu clase favorita?**

Check: To practice accentuation, ask students to raise their hand if the word requires an accent: **geología, ecología, dislexia, primaria, historia, carpintería, secundaria, antropología, fotografía, astronomía, bacteria, librería, astrología, magia, enciclopedia, biología, hotelería, farmacia, secretaria, comedia.** Elicit spelling correspondences between English and Spanish: **farmacia**, pharmacy (**f** v. **ph**); **antropología**, anthropology (**t** v. **th**); **ciencias**, sciences (**c** v. **sc**); **comercio**, commerce (**m** v. **mm**); **administración**, administration (**ción** v. **tion**); **química**, chemistry (**qu** v. **ch**).

>> Lugares en la universidad

¿**Dónde tienes la clase de...?**	*Where does your . . . class meet?*
En el centro de computación.	*In the computer center.*
...el centro de comunicaciones.	*. . . the media center.*
...el gimnasio.	*. . . the gymnasium.*
la cafetería	*the cafeteria*
la librería	*the bookstore*
la residencia estudiantil	*the dorm*

Notice that the week begins on Monday in most Spanish-speaking countries. Also notice that the days of the week are not capitalized in Spanish as they are in English.

>> Los días de la semana

lunes	martes	miércoles	jueves	viernes	sábado	domingo
8	9	10	11	12	13	14

To say that something happens *on* a certain day, use the singular article with the day of the week: **La fiesta va a ser *el* sábado.**

To say that something happens on the same day every week, use the plural article with the day of the week: ***Los* sábados visito a mi madre.** Notice that there is no preposition **en** *(on)* in these cases.

ACTIVIDADES

I 1 Las carreras Say what course you would take if you were interested in a certain career.

MODELO journalist
            el periodismo

1. psychologist la psicología
2. accountant la contabilidad
3. software programmer la computación / la informática
4. architect la arquitectura
5. graphic designer el diseño gráfico
6. teacher la educación

2 Las clases de Mariana With a partner, say on which days Mariana has each of her classes, based on her class schedule.

MODELO economía
            Mariana tiene economía los lunes, los miércoles y los viernes.

1. psicología
2. literatura
3. francés
4. contabilidad
5. pintura
6. música

	lunes	martes	miércoles	jueves	viernes
8:00	economía		economía		economía
10:00	psicología	literatura	psicología	literatura	
11:30	francés	francés	francés	francés	francés
3:00		contabilidad		contabilidad	
4:00	pintura		música	pintura	música

Learning objective: Understanding

Answers, Act. 2: 1. Mariana tiene psicología los lunes y los miércoles. 2. Mariana tiene literatura los martes y los jueves. 3. Mariana tiene francés los lunes, los martes, los miércoles, los jueves y los viernes. 4. Mariana tiene contabilidad los martes y los jueves. 5. Mariana tiene pintura los lunes y los jueves. 6. Mariana tiene música los miércoles y los viernes.

Notice: On many Spanish calendars, the days of the week are abbreviated: **L M M J V S D** or **Lu, Ma, Mi, Ju, Vi, Sa, Do.** In Spain it is more common to use **L M X J V S D.**

Optional: Name other careers to prompt additional associations:
pharmacist → **la química**
trainer → **la salud**
public relations executive → **el mercadeo**
writer → **la literatura**
zoologist → **la biología**, etc.

3 Mis clases Create a chart with your class schedule. Include days, times, and locations. Then, with a partner, ask each other questions about each day of the week. Be sure to save your schedule for later activities.

MODELO Tú: *¿Qué clases tienes los lunes?*
Compañero(a): *Los lunes tengo psicología, arte y computación.*

4 ¿Dónde? Ask your partner where he/she does certain activities.

MODELO levantar pesas
Tú: *¿Dónde levantas pesas?*
Compañero(a): *En el gimnasio.*

1. visitar a tus amigos
2. navegar por Internet
3. escuchar los CDs de la clase de español
4. practicar deportes
5. comprar libros
6. vivir
7. tener clase de baile
8. estudiar

5 Entrevista Imagine that you are like Chela in the video and you must approach someone in your class for an interview about their daily schedule. Use as much language as you can from previous chapters. Make a list of questions beforehand. Then record the interview and upload for the class to view or summarize the interview in class. You can use the following questions or make up your own.

Preguntas:
Buenos días, ¿qué tal?
¿Cómo te llamas?
¿De dónde eres?
¿Cuántos años tienes?
¿Qué te gusta hacer los domingos?
¿Qué estudias?
¿Cuántas clases tienes?
¿Dónde tienes la clase de…?
¿Cuál es tu clase preferida?
¿Qué día de la semana te gusta más?

6 Mi blog Write a blog post about the interview you did in Activity 5. What were some of the interesting things you learned about your partner?

MODELO *Mi compañero estudia psicología, pero su clase preferida es la clase de baile.*

¡Fíjate! El reloj de veinticuatro horas

The 24-hour clock is used globally, and in all Spanish-speaking countries, for schedules and official times. The system is based on counting the hours of the day from zero through twenty-four. The first twelve hours of the day (from midnight until noon) are represented by the numbers 0–12. Any time after noon is represented by that time +12. The **h** after the time stands for **horas**.

Robert Fried/Alamy

For example:
1:00 P.M. = 1:00 + 12 = 13:00h
2:30 P.M. = 2:30 + 12 = 14:30h
5:45 P.M. = 5:45 + 12 = 17:45h

To go from a 24-hour clock time to a 12-hour clock time, you must subtract 12 hours from the 24-hour clock time.

For example:
13:00h – 12 = 1:00 P.M.
14:30h – 12 = 2:30 P.M.
17:45h – 12 = 5:45 P.M.

The 24-hour clock is almost always used in written form. In conversation, Spanish speakers use the 12-hour format, adding **de la mañana** (morning, A.M.), **de la tarde** (afternoon, P.M.), and **de la noche** (evening, P.M.) for clarification.

Práctica 1 With a partner, look at the schedules below. Convert the times on the 24-hour clock to the 12-hour clock. Follow the model.

MODELO 21:20h = *9:20 P.M.*
1. 23:20h = 11:20 P.M.
2. 14:45h = 2:45 P.M.
3. 18:30h = 6:30 P.M.
4. 16:25h = 4:25 P.M.
5. 15:10h = 3:10 P.M.
6. 19:15h = 7:15 P.M.

Práctica 2 With a partner, look at the schedules that you used in **Activity 3**. Convert the times on your schedules to hours on the 24-hour clock. Follow the model.

MODELO Tú: *Mi (My) clase de matemáticas es a las 3:00 de la tarde.*
Compañero(a): *Tu (Your) clase de matemáticas es a las 15:00 horas.*

Optional: Ask students to review schedules in **Activity 3** to add the day of the week as well as the class name and hour as a follow-up.

Optional: Point out that one advantage of the 24-hour clock is that you don't have to add A.M. or P.M. after the time. In the U. S., the 24-hour clock is rarely used, except by the military and some government offices. Ask students: **Why do you think that might be? Do you like the idea of using a 24-hour clock? Why or why not?**

Suggestion: Have your class identify whether these times should be followed by **de la mañana, de la tarde,** or **de la noche**: 9:50h, 14:10h, 23:30h, 1:25h, 20:05h, 16:55h

Check: For a simple assessment, divide your class into teams and show clock faces or write time on the board. Have teams compete to see who can tell the correct 24-hour time the most quickly.

Check: Have students reshuffle in pairs to review personal schedules. They can recite their classes, class times, and days of the week. Select two students to present their schedules to the whole class.

Optional: Read the following sentences. Ask students to raise their right hand if the time mentioned is A.M., and raise their left hand if it's P.M. **Siempre desayuno a las ocho. Son las diez y tengo clase de psicología. Vamos a la cafetería a las cinco y media. Vamos al cine a las siete y veinte.**

>> Vocabulario útil 2

CHELA: ¿Qué haces los sábados?

ANILÚ: **Por la mañana**, corro por el parque. **A las dos de la tarde**, tengo clase de danza afrocaribeña.

CHELA: ¿Y **por la noche**?

ANILÚ: Por la noche escucho música con mis amigos o vamos al cine o a un restaurante.

CAMARÓGRAFO: Uy, **¿qué hora es?** ¡Tengo que irme!

CHELA: Pero, ¿adónde vas? ¡Necesito otra entrevista!

CAMARÓGRAFO: ¡Tengo clase **a las once**!

CHELA: **Son las once menos cuarto.** Espera un minuto, por favor.

Point out: When you ask the time, use **¿qué?** and when asking what time something takes place, use **¿a qué?**

Compare the following two questions and responses.

¿Qué hora es? *(What time is it?)*

Es la una. *(It's one o'clock.)*

¿A qué hora es la clase de español? *([At] What time is Spanish class?)*

Es a la una. *(It's at one o'clock.)*

Preparation: Some students will prefer practicing with an old-fashioned clock face. Draw a large circle on the board, add numbers to the clock and clock hands; you can quickly erase to change the time. To the right side of the clock write **y** (+) and to the left write **menos** (–). Outside the clock face, label **cuarto** and **media** and draw a sun on the upper right and a moon to the upper left.

Notice: It takes a lot of practice for true beginners to be able to tell time efficiently. Practice random hours. Use a clock prop with movable arms or list times on a board and practice: 5:35, 2:15, 1:12, 10:45, 6:17, 7:07, 8:56, 3:32, 4:47, 9:25, 11:20, 12:05, 7:48, 10:10, 1:16, etc. Take advantage of all digital clocks on computers, organizers, and phones.

>> Para pedir y dar la hora *Asking for and giving the time*

¿Qué hora es? *What time is it?*

Es la una.

Son las dos.

Son las cinco y cuarto.
Son las cinco y quince.

Son las cinco y media.

Son las cinco y diez.

Son las cinco menos cuarto.
Faltan quince par las cinco.

—¿**Tienes tiempo** para tomar un café?

—**Sí, es temprano.** / —¡Ay, no, **ya es muy tarde**!

Mañana, tarde o noche
Mira **el reloj** para **decir la hora.**

Morning, afternoon, or night
Look at the clock to tell the time.

Son las ocho de la mañana.

Son las tres de la tarde.

Son las nueve de la noche.

© Cengage Learning 2013

Es mediodía.
Es medianoche.
Es tarde.
Es temprano.

It's noon.
It's midnight.
It's late.
It's early.

Suggestion: Point out to students that when these expressions are preceded by **a—al mediodía / a la medianoche**— they mean *at noon* and *at midnight.*

Optional: To recycle these concepts, ask the day, date, and time at some point during every class meeting.

ACTIVIDADES

7 **¿Qué hora es?** Ask your partner what time it is. He/She will tell you
M what time it is. Take turns asking the time.

MODELO 1:00 P.M.
Tú: *¿Qué hora es?*
Compañero(a): *Es la una de la tarde.*

1. 3:15 P.M.
2. 2:45 P.M.
3. 10:30 A.M.
4. 12:00 noon
5. 6:55 A.M.
6. 9:25 P.M.

8 **Mi horario** Get out the agenda page that you completed for **Activity 3.**
C Ask your partner about his/her class schedule. You name a day and a time,
and your partner tells you what class he/she has at that time. Talk about all five
days of the week.

Learning objectives: Understanding, Applying

MODELO Tú: *Es lunes y son las diez de la mañana.*
Compañero(a): *Tengo clase de cálculo.*

9 **Tu horario** Exchange your agenda page with your partner. Your partner
C names a day and a time, and you tell him/her where he/she is at that time. Take
turns with each other's schedules.

Learning objective: Understanding

MODELO Compañero(a): *Es viernes y son las dos de la tarde. ¿Dónde estoy?*
Tú: *Estás en la clase de danza afrocaribeña.*

De la mañana is used for the morning hours between midnight and noon. **De la tarde** is used for daylight hours after noon. **De la noche** is used only for nighttime hours. These hours vary from country to country, given that in some countries it gets dark earlier or stays light later.

Compare the use of **de** and **por** in the following sentences.

La clase es a las diez **de la mañana**.

En general estudio **por la mañana**.

Note that you use **de la mañana / tarde / noche** to give a specific time of day. You use **por la mañana / tarde / noche** to give a more general time frame.

Optional: If many students in a class will likely study abroad, add that airline officials typically announce the **hora local** upon landing in a Spanish-speaking country.

Answers, Act. 7: 1. Son las tres y cuarto de la tarde. / Son las tres y quince de la tarde. 2. Son las tres menos cuarto de la tarde. / Son las dos y cuarenta y cinco de la tarde. / Faltan quince para las tres de la tarde. 3. Son las diez y media de la mañana. 4. Es mediodía. / Son las doce de la tarde. 5. Son las seis y cincuenta cinco de la mañana. / Faltan cinco para las siete de la mañana. / Son las siete menos cinco de la mañana. 6. Son las nueve y veinticinco de la noche.

Suggestion: Reinforce the words **laboratorio** and **práctica** *(internship)* here: **Los viernes tengo laboratorio de química y la clase de inglés. Por la tarde a las cuatro, voy a mi práctica en el museo de ciencias naturales.**

Vocabulario útil 3

© Cengage Learning 2013

CHELA: ¿Así que te gustan más los fines de semana que los días de **entresemana**?

ANILÚ: Pues sí, por supuesto. Los fines de semana son mucho más divertidos. Ay, **es tarde**. Yo también tengo clase a las once.

CHELA: Gracias por la entrevista. …

ANILÚ: Oye, ¿cuándo sale la entrevista en la red?

CHELA: **Mañana.**

Suggestion: For oral practice, have mini-conversations like: ¿A qué fecha estamos?, ¿Cuál es la fecha de tu cumpleaños?, ¿Te gusta más tu cumpleaños durante el fin de semana o entresemana?, ¿Cuál es la fecha del cumpleaños de tu mamá? Also ask students about their work or study habits. ¿Cuándo trabajas / estudias?, ¿Con quién(es)?, ¿Dónde?, ¿Qué días?, ¿A qué hora?

Optional: Expansion Activity. **La fiesta.** Charge your Spanish class with finding a common meeting time and date for a class party. Name a time and a day, and students will have to say whether they can come. The student with a conflict must suggest another time. The entire class must find a common meeting time, even if it means the party will be on Sunday at 3 A.M.!

Optional: Another way to find a common meeting time is through Doodle.com. In Doodle, change the settings to Spanish. Demonstrate the free tool to the students. Assign several students another engagement for which the class members need to find a common time. The Doodle poll can be used for oral practice by having one or two students explain the poll's results to the whole class.

>> **Para hablar de la fecha** *Talking about the date*

¿Qué día es hoy? *What day is today?*
Hoy es martes treinta. *Today is Tuesday the 30th.*

¿A qué fecha estamos? *What is today's date?*
Es el treinta de octubre. *It's the 30th of October.*
Es el primero de noviembre. *It's the first of November.*

¿Cuándo es el Día de las Madres? *When is Mother's Day?*
Es el doce de mayo. *It's May 12th.*

el día *day*
la semana *week*
el fin de semana *weekend*
el mes *month*
el año *year*
todos los días *every day*
entresemana *during the week/on weekdays*

ayer *yesterday*
hoy *today*
mañana *tomorrow*

M **10** **¿Qué es?** Say what each of the following time periods are.

MODELO febrero
       el mes

1. enero el mes
2. sábado y domingo el fin de semana
3. 2012 el año
4. el 7 de septiembre el día / la fecha
5. 7 de noviembre a 14 de noviembre la semana
6. hoy el día

11 **Las fechas** Form pairs and look at a current yearly calendar. Your
C professor will give each team five minutes to answer the following questions.
Write out your answers in Spanish. There are some words that you might not
know. Try to guess at their meaning, but don't let it hold you up!

Preparation: Bring calendars to class to use as a visual aid. Also have students bring or open their planners or e-calendars to be able to record important dates in Spanish.

1. ¿Qué día de la semana es Navidad (25 de diciembre) este año?
2. ¿Qué día de la semana es el Día de la Independencia (4 de julio) este año?
3. ¿Qué día de la semana es el Día de los Enamorados (14 de febrero) este año?
4. ¿A qué fecha estamos? ¿Cuándo es el próximo *(next)* examen de español?
5. ¿Cuándo son las próximas vacaciones? ¿Qué día regresan los estudiantes
    de las próximas vacaciones?

C **12** **Fechas importantes** Write out in Spanish ten to fifteen dates that are
important for you. Then copy them into your calendar. The following are some
examples of the dates you might include.

los cumpleaños de los miembros de mi familia
los cumpleaños de mis amigos
el Día de las Madres
el Día del Padre
las fechas de las vacaciones
el aniversario de…
las fechas de mis exámenes finales

© Cengage Learning 2013

A ver

ESTRATEGIA

Using body language to aid in comprehension

When you observe the body language of the person speaking, you can get clues to a person's meaning by watching facial expressions, gestures, hand movements, and so on. For example, if you ask someone a question and the person shrugs and walks away, the meaning is clear, even if no words were uttered!

> As a previewing strategy to help guide your comprehension of the video segment, read the items in **Después de ver 1** *before* you view the video.

© Cengage Learning 2013

Suggestion: While watching the video without sound, have students jot down words to describe types of body language that they may observe. Words like **animado, indiferente, activo,** or other descriptive words can be written on the board and students can choose from the list.

Learning objective: Remembering

Antes de ver Review these key words used in the video.

la entrevista	*the interview*
transmitir	*to transmit*
la red	*the Internet*

▶ **Ver** Now watch the video segment for **Chapter 3** without sound. Pay special attention to the characters' body language.

Después de ver 1 Say whether statements 1-4 are true (**cierto**) or false (**falso**), based on your observation of the characters' body language. Then watch again with sound and complete statements 5–9.

1. Muchos estudiantes prefieren no participar en la entrevista con Chela. cierto
2. Chela indica algo *(something)* al estudiante con la cámara. cierto
3. El estudiante con la cámara no tiene prisa *(is not in a hurry)*. falso
4. Anilú observa a Javier (el estudiante que aparece al final del segmento) con mucho interés. cierto
5. En la opinión del estudiante con la cámara y de Anilú, el tema del programa de Chela es __aburrido__.
6. Anilú tiene clases de computación, diseño gráfico y __psicología__.
7. Los __sábados__, Anilú corre en el parque.
8. Los sábados por la noche, Anilú escucha música con amigos o va al __cine__ o a un restaurante.
9. El estudiante con la cámara tiene clase a las __once__.

Después de ver 2 With a partner, dramatize one of the following situations.

- You are the reporter and you are attracted to the interviewee. Try to get the interviewee's phone number.
- You are the interviewee and you are attracted to the cameraman. Try to get the cameraman's phone number.
- You are the interviewee and you don't like the reporter's attitude. Try to evade the reporter's questions.

▶ >> Voces del mundo hispano

In this video segment, the speakers talk about their studies and pastimes. First read the statements below. Then watch the video as many times as needed to say whether the statements are true (**cierto**) or false (**falso**).

1. Sandra estudia administración de empresas. C
2. Jessica estudia química. F
3. A Javier le gusta ver *(to see)* películas. C
4. A Dayramir le gusta bailar salsa con sus amigos. C
5. Durante los fines de semana, Ela va *(goes)* al parque. C
6. Durante los fines de semana, Inés visita a su familia. F

© Cengage Learning 2013

Note: Organizations such as the Hispanic Association of Colleges and Universities (HACU) champion the cause of Hispanics in higher education and offer resources (scholarships, internships, and more) to support students of Hispanic heritage.

🔊 >> Voces de Estados Unidos

Track 8

Sonia Sotomayor, jueza, Corte Suprema de Estados Unidos

Pablo Martínez Monsiváis/AP Images

❝Creo que si las caras de los jueces *(judges' faces)* no reflejan la población a la que sirven, la gente va a tener menos confianza en el sistema de justicia. Es importante que todos los grupos de Estados Unidos estén representados en la función más importante de la sociedad.❞

Sonia Sotomayor, la primera persona de ascendencia hispana en la Corte Suprema de los Estados Unidos, es la personificación del sueño *(dream)* americano. Nacida *(Born)* en un proyecto público en El Bronx a padres puertorriqueños, la jueza es conocida por su inteligencia, capacidad de trabajo y respeto por sus raíces. Dos tragedias en su niñez forman su carácter: la muerte *(death)* de su padre a los nueve años y la diabetes juvenil. Con la ayuda *(help)* de su madre, Sotomayor triunfa sobre estas adversidades. Asiste a Princeton, y después a la escuela de derecho de Yale. Sin embargo, la jueza nunca olvida sus raíces *(never forgets her roots)*. Sus experiencias como empleada en una dulcería *(candy store)* y una tienda de ropa *(clothing store)* y como camarera *(waitress)* le dan una especial sensibilidad hacia las necesidades de las personas comunes.

¿Y tú? ¿ Are you interested in working in the public sector? Why or why not?

Optional: To expand on ¿Y tú?, put some infinitives on the board to stimulate the discussion: **investigar, crear, inventar, construir, organizar, formular, servir**, etc. These words and subject words allow students to hint at a career path.

Standards 2.1, 2.2, 3.2, 5.1: Students read about successful Spanish speakers in the U.S. and acquire cultural information that features distinctive viewpoints of Spanish-speaking people. Encourage them to research other U.S. Hispanics with careers in government, public service, or not-for-profits that serve the Hispanic population. Ask students to research volunteer activities locally to plant the seed of practicing Spanish beyond the classroom.

¡Prepárate!

Gramática útil 1

Asking questions: Interrogative words

¿Cuántas entrevistas tenemos que hacer?

Suggestion: Clarify that interrogative words are question words, then ask, **¿Qué tienen todos los interrogativos?** (¡Acentos!) You may want to mention examples such as **que** *(that)* and **como** *(like)*, whose meanings change entirely when they are written with accents. Preview **por qué** and **porque**.

Heritage Learners: Interrogatives always require an accent, but it is not always obvious to heritage learners where the accent is placed. For those students who have difficulty hearing the location of the written accent, have them practice saying interrogative words out loud in an exaggerated manner. This should make it easier to locate the stressed syllable.

You may want to point out that **cuál** + noun is also used, depending on the region.

Cómo usarlo

You have already seen, learned, and used a number of interrogative words to ask questions. **¿Cómo te llamas?, ¿Cuál es tu dirección electrónica?, ¿Dónde vives?**, and **¿Qué tal?** are all questions that begin with interrogatives: **cómo, cuál, dónde, qué.**

As in English, we use interrogatives in Spanish to ask for specific information. Here are the Spanish interrogatives.

¿Cuál(es)?	*What? Which one(s)?*	**¿Dónde?**	*Where?*
¿Qué?	*What? Which?*	**¿Adónde?**	*To where?*
¿A qué hora?	*(At) What time?*	**¿De dónde?**	*From where?*
¿De qué?	*About what? Of what?*	**¿Quién(es)?**	*Who?*
¿Cuándo?	*When?*	**¿De quién(es)?**	*Whose?*
¿Cuánto(a)?	*How much?*	**¿Cómo?**	*How?*
¿Cuántos(as)?	*How many?*	**¿Por qué?**	*Why?*

1. **¿Qué?** and **¿cuál?** may appear interchangeable at first sight, but they are used in very specific ways.

   ¿Qué? is . . .
   - used to ask for a definition: **¿Qué es el reloj de veinticuatro horas?**
   - used to ask for an explanation or further information: **¿Qué vas a estudiar este semestre?**
   - generally used when the next word is a noun: **¿Qué libros te gustan más? ¿Qué clase tienes a las ocho?**

   ¿Cuál? is . . .
   - used to express a choice between specified items: **¿Cuál de los libros prefieres?**
   - used when the next word is a form of **ser** but the question is *not* asking for a definition: **¿Cuál es tu número de teléfono? ¿Cuáles son tus clases favoritas?**

2. **¿Dónde?** is used to ask where something is.

   ¿Dónde está la biblioteca?   ***Where** is the library?*

3. **¿Adónde?** is used to ask where someone is going.

    ¿Adónde vas ahora?   *Where are you going now?*

4. **¿De quién es?** and **¿De quiénes son?** are used to ask about possession. You answer using **de**.

    —¿**De quién** es la computadora?   ***Whose*** *computer is this?*
    —**Es de** Miguel.   ***It's*** *Miguel's.*

    —¿**De quiénes** son los libros?   ***Whose*** *books are these?*
    —**Son de** Anita y Manuel.   ***They're*** *Anita's and Manuel's.*

5. Questions using **¿por qué?** can be answered using **porque** *(because)*.

    —¿**Por qué** tienes que trabajar?   ***Why*** *do you have to work?*
    —¡**Porque** necesito el dinero!   ***Because*** *I need the money!*

Cómo formarlo

1. Interrogatives are always preceded by an inverted question mark (**¿**). The question requires a regular question mark (**?**) at the end.

2. Notice that in a typical question the subject *follows* the verb.

    ¿Dónde **estudia Marcos**?   *Where does **Marcos study**?*
    ¿Qué instrumento **tocan** ustedes?   *What instrument do **you play**?*

3. **¿Quién?** and **¿cuál?** change to reflect number.

    ¿**Quién** es el hombre alto? / ¿**Quiénes** son los hombres altos?
    ¿**Cuál** de los libros tienes? / ¿**Cuáles** son tus idiomas favoritos?

4. **¿Cuánto?** changes to reflect both number and gender.

    ¿**Cuánto** dinero tienes?   ***How much*** *money do you have?*
    ¿**Cuánta** comida compramos?   ***How much*** *food should we buy?*
    ¿**Cuántos** años tienes?   ***How many*** *years old are you? /*
                                  How old *are you?*

    ¿**Cuántas** personas hay?   ***How many*** *people are there?*

5. When you want to ask *how much* in a general way, use **¿cuánto?**

    ¿Cuánto es?   **¿Cuánto necesitamos?**

6. Note that interrogatives always require an accent.

7. You have already learned how to form simple *yes/no* questions by adding **no** to a sentence.

    ¿**No escribes** e-mails   ***Aren't you writing*** *any*
       hoy?   *e-mails today?*

8. You can also form simple *yes/no* questions by adding a tag question, such as **¿verdad?** *(Isn't that right?)* and **¿no?** to the end of a statement.

    Cantas en el coro con   *You sing in the chorus with*
       Ana, **¿no?**   *Ana, **right?***
    Enrique baila salsa muy   *Enrique dances salsa very*
       bien, **¿verdad?**   *well, **right?***

1 Las preguntas What question would you have to ask to produce the response shown? You will hear three questions. Choose the correct one.

__b__	1.	La clase de informática es a las once de la mañana.
__c__	2.	Tengo que ir al centro de computación para la clase de informática.
__a__	3.	La computadora portátil es de mi compañero de cuarto.
__b__	4.	Hay que comprar tres libros para la clase de informática.
__a__	5.	Porque me gustan mucho las computadoras y quiero aprender a programarlas.
__c__	6.	La señora Delgado es la profesora de informática.

2 En la cafetería You overhear a conversation between two students in the cafeteria. Fill in the correct form of the question words to complete their conversation.

—¿(1) __Qué__ clases tienes este semestre?
—Tengo arte, literatura, cálculo, química y economía.

—¿(2) __Cuáles__ son tus clases favoritas?
—El arte y la literatura.

—¿(3) __Quiénes__ son tus autores favoritos?
—Gabriel García Márquez, Mario Vargas Llosa, Julia Álvarez e Isabel Allende.

—¿(4) __Quién__ es tu profesor de literatura?
—El señor Banderas.

—¿(5) __Cuántos__ libros necesitas para la clase de literatura?
—Diez, más o menos, pero son libros que puedo sacar de la biblioteca.

—¿A (6) __qué__ hora tienes la clase de literatura?
—A las diez de la mañana.

—¿(7) __Adónde__ vas ahora?
—Al centro de computación.

—¿(8) __Por qué__ vas allí?
—Porque necesito usar las computadoras para hacer mi tarea.

—Pero tienes computadora portátil. ¿(9) __De quién__ es la computadora portátil?
—Es de mi compañero de cuarto. ¡Haces demasiadas *(You ask too many)* preguntas!

†† 3 Más preguntas For each activity indicated, take turns asking and
M/C answering questions with a partner.

> **MODELO** bailar (cuándo)
> Estudiante #1: *¿Cuándo bailas?*
> Estudiante #2: *Bailo los viernes.*

1. estudiar (qué)
2. visitar a amigos (cuándo)
3. hablar con la profesora (por qué)
4. caminar (adónde)
5. tener años (cuánto)
6. imprimir los informes (dónde)

††† 4 ¡Qué curiosidad! In groups of three or four, take turns coming up with
C as many questions as you can for each activity listed. (Take turns writing down
the questions or keep your own list.) Then compare your group's questions with
another group to see who has the most questions for each activity.

1. correr
2. comer
3. tener muchos amigos
4. escuchar música
5. comprar muchos libros
6. tomar clases

††† 5 Encuesta #1 In the chapter activities labeled **"Encuesta"** you will
C gather information from your fellow students in order to write a description
of life at your college or university in the **A escribir** section at the end of the
chapter.

Learning objective: Applying

Suggestion, Act. 5: To help students
get started formulating questions,
have them look back at the questions
in **Activity 2.**

1. First prepare a questionnaire by creating two questions for each category,
   using the cues provided or coming up with your own.

   El horario: clases por día / semana, lugar preferido para estudiar

   El trabajo: lugar de trabajo, horas de trabajo

   La computadora: tiempo que pasas en la computadora, sitios interesantes
   en Internet

   La universidad: clases difíciles y fáciles, las horas por semana que
   estudias, profesores buenos y malos

2. Now work with another group and ask the members to answer your
   questionnaire. Be sure to answer their questions as well. Keep track of
   your results. You will need them later in the chapter.

Gramática útil 2

Talking about daily activities: The present indicative of regular -er and -ir verbs

Cómo usarlo

Por la mañana, **corro** en el parque.

In **Chapter 2,** you learned how to use the present indicative of regular **-ar** verbs to talk about daily activities. The present indicative of **-er** and **-ir** verbs are used in the same contexts.

Remember:

1. The present indicative, depending on how it is used, can correspond to the following English usages: *I read* (in general), *I am reading, I am going to read, I do read*, and, if used as a question, *Do you read?*

2. You can often omit the subject pronoun when the subject is clear from the verb ending used or from the context of the sentence.

   Leo en la biblioteca todos los días.   *I read in the library every day.*
   Lees en la residencia estudiantil, ¿no? *You read in the dorm, right?*

3. You may use an infinitive after certain conjugated verbs.

   ¿Tienes que imprimir esto?   *Do you have to print this?*
   ¿Necesitas leer este libro?   *Do you need to read this book?*
   ¡Dejo de leer después de medianoche!   *I stop reading after midnight!*

4. However, do not use two verbs conjugated in the present tense together unless they are separated by a comma or the words **y** *(and)* or **o** *(or).*

   Leo, estudio y **escribo**   *I read, study, and write*
   composiciones en la biblioteca.   *compositions in the library.*

5. Remember that you can negate sentences in the present indicative tense to say what you don't do or aren't planning to do.

   No comemos en la   *We're not eating in the*
   cafetería hoy.   *cafeteria today.*
   No leo todos los días.   *I don't read every day.*

Cómo formarlo

To form the present indicative tense of **-er** and **-ir** verbs, simply remove the **-er** or **-ir** and add the following endings.

comer *(to eat)*			
yo	**como**	nosotros / nosotras	**comemos**
tú	**comes**	vosotros / vosotras	**coméis**
Ud. / él / ella	**come**	Uds. / ellos / ellas	**comen**

© Cengage Learning 2013

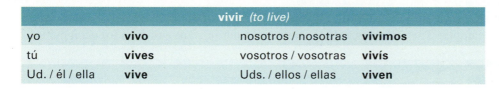

vivir *(to live)*			
yo	**vivo**	nosotros / nosotras	**vivimos**
tú	**vives**	vosotros / vosotras	**vivís**
Ud. / él / ella	**vive**	Uds. / ellos / ellas	**viven**

Here are some commonly used **-er** and **-ir** verbs.

-er verbs			
aprender a (+ infinitive)	*to learn to (do something)*	**creer (en)**	*to believe (in)*
beber	*to drink*	**deber** (+ infinitive)	*should, ought (to do something)*
comer	*to eat*	**leer**	*to read*
comprender	*to understand*	**vender**	*to sell*
correr	*to run*		

-ir verbs			
abrir	*to open*	**escribir**	*to write*
asistir a	*to attend*	**imprimir**	*to print*
compartir	*to share*	**recibir**	*to receive*
describir	*to describe*	**transmitir**	*to broadcast*
descubrir	*to discover*	**vivir**	*to live*

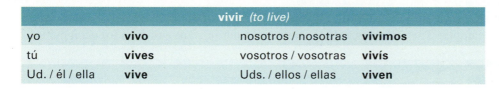

Notice that the present indicative endings for **-er** and **-ir** verbs are identical except for the **nosotros** and **vosotros** forms.

Heritage Learners: To make proper use of the dictionary, it is important for heritage language speakers to be able to produce the infinitive form of a verb. Elicit infinitives for: **entiendo, escuchan, empieza, traen, bebiendo, estoy, voy, pidiendo, producen, sabiendo, llueve, volvemos, bailamos, quieren.**

Suggestion: To present these verbs, prepare a brief autobiography as a model. Don't forget to pantomime verbs as you model: (**Yo**) **vivo en**... **Como mucho en casa con mi familia. En mi tiempo libre, corro todos los días. Para mi trabajo, leo y escribo. ¿Qué haces tú?** Then ask questions like these using the **-er** and **-ir** verbs and recycling interrogative words: **¿Dónde vives? ¿Con quién vives? ¿Comes en casa o en la cafetería universitaria? ¿Asistes a clases todos los días? ¿Escribes mucho para tus clases? En tu tiempo libre, ¿corres? ¿Recibes muchos mensajes de texto?** etc.

ACTIVIDADES

I **6 ¿Qué hacen?** Based on the information provided, what do the people indicated do? Choose verbs from the list. Follow the model.

MODELOS Carlos ya no necesita esa cámara digital.
Vende la cámara.

Tú y yo necesitamos hacer ejercicio.
Corremos en el parque.

Verbos posibles: aprender / asistir / comer / compartir / correr / vender

1. ¡Olivia tiene la clase de biología a las tres y ya son las tres y cinco! <u>Corre</u> a la universidad.
2. A Susana no le gusta esa bicicleta. <u>Vende</u> la bicicleta.
3. Raúl y Enrique tienen que viajar a Puerto Rico en dos meses. <u>Aprenden</u> español.
4. Elena y yo no comprendemos las lecturas del libro. <u>Asistimos</u> a una clase de estudio.
5. No me gustan los restaurantes aquí. <u>Como</u> en la cafetería todos los días.
6. Susana vive con una compañera de cuarto. <u>Comparte</u> el apartamento con ella.

M **7** **La vida estudiantil** Say what the people indicated are doing today on campus. The numbers indicate how many actions are going on for each person.

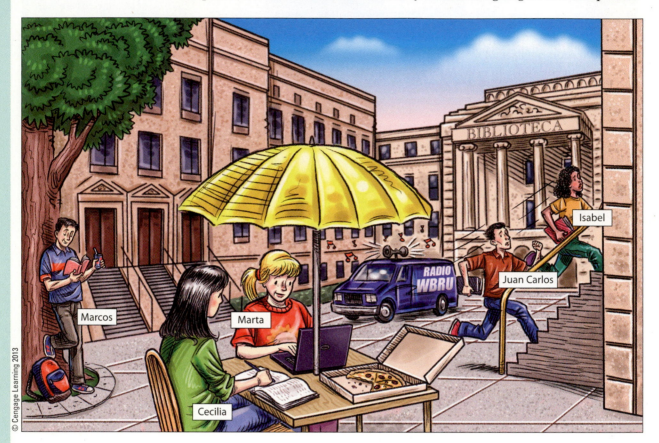

1. Juan Carlos e Isabel (1)   Juan Carlos e Isabel corren.
2. Marcos (2)   Marcos lee. Marcos bebe (un refresco). / Marcos lee y bebe un refresco.
3. Cecilia y Marta (2)   Cecilia y Marta comen (pizza). Cecilia y Marta escriben. / Cecilia y Marta escriben y comen (pizza).
4. Radio WBRU (1)   Radio WBRU transmite.
5. Y tú, ¿qué haces (*what are you doing*)?   Answers will vary.

M/C **8** **¿Y tú?** With a partner, take turns asking and answering the following questions.

1. ¿Cuándo asistes a tu primera clase del día?
2. ¿Vives en un apartamento o en una residencia?
3. ¿A qué hora comes la cena (*dinner*)?
4. ¿Recibes muchos e-mails de tu familia?
5. ¿Escribes muchos informes?
6. ¿Dónde lees los libros para tus clases?

C **9** **¿Qué hacemos?** Using an element from each of the three columns, create eight sentences describing what you and people you know do in and around campus.

MODELO *Yo asisto a clases los lunes, los miércoles y los jueves.*

A	**B**	**C**
yo	aprender a hablar	café por la mañana
tú	español	en el centro de comunicaciones
compañero(s)	asistir a	clases *(número)* días de la semana
de cuarto	beber	correspondencia electrónica todos los
profesor(es)	comprender	días
estudiante(s)	correr	en el estadio
amigo(s)	creer (en)	la importancia de Internet
	escribir	clases los *(día de la semana)*
	leer	novelas latinoamericanas en el parque
	recibir	poemas para la clase de literatura
		las lecturas del libro
		mensajes de texto *(text messages)*
		¿...?

👤👤👤 **10** **Encuesta #2** Use the cues provided to create a questionnaire. Use the
C interrogatives you learned earlier in the chapter along with the cues provided. Once your group has completed the questionnaire, ask the questions to members of another group. Remember to save your responses for use later in the chapter.

1. leer libros / por semana
2. compartir cuarto / con compañero(a) de cuarto
3. asistir a clase / todos los días / todas las semanas
4. comer en la cafetería / por semana
5. vender / libros de texto

C **11** **La vida universitaria** Write a message to a friend describing your university life. Mention the following things or anything else you might want to talk about. Save your work for use later in the chapter.

- cuántas clases tienes y los días que asistes a clase
- dónde y cuándo comes
- dónde vives
- qué libros lees
- qué actividades te gustan (correr, levantar pesas, mirar televisión, navegar por Internet, leer, escribir, etc.)

Gramática útil 3

Talking about possessions: Simple possessive adjectives

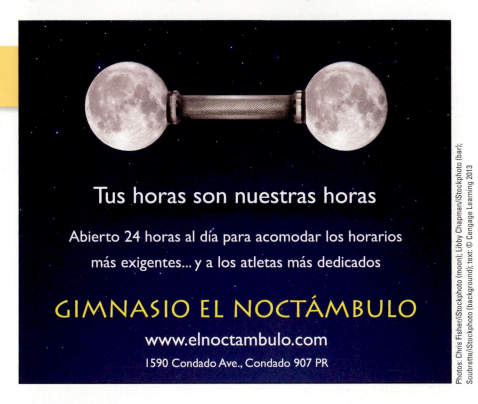

Tus horas son nuestras horas

Abierto 24 horas al día para acomodar los horarios
más exigentes... y a los atletas más dedicados

GIMNASIO EL NOCTÁMBULO

www.elnoctambulo.com

1590 Condado Ave., Condado 907 PR

Photos: Chris Fisher/iStockphoto (moon); Libby Chapman/iStockphoto (bar); Soubrette/iStockphoto (background); text: © Cengage Learning 2013

Cómo usarlo

1. You already have learned to express possession using **de** + a noun or name.

Es la computadora portátil **de la profesora**.	It's **the professor's** laptop computer.

2. You can also use possessive adjectives to describe your possessions, other people's possessions, or items that are associated with you. You are already familiar with some possessive adjectives from the phrases **¿Cuál es <u>tu</u> dirección?** and **Aquí tienes <u>mi</u> número de teléfono**.

—¿Cuándo es **tu** clase de historia?	*When is **your** history class?*
—A las dos. Y **mi** clase de español es a las tres.	*At two. And **my** Spanish class is at three.*

3. When you use **su** (which can mean *your, his, her, its,* or *theirs*), the context will usually clarify who is meant. If not, you can follow up with **de** + name.

Es **su** libro. Es **de la profesora**.	*It's **her** book. It's **the professor's**.*

LO BÁSICO

Possessive adjectives modify nouns in order to express possession. In other words, they tell who owns the item.

1. Here are the simple possessive adjectives in Spanish.

mi **mis**	*my*	**nuestro / nuestra** **nuestros / nuestras**	*our*
tu **tus**	*your (fam.)*	**vuestro / vuestra** **vuestros / vuestras**	*your (fam. pl.)*
su **sus**	*your (form.), his, her, its*	**su** **sus**	*your (pl.), their*

The subject pronoun **tú** *(you)* has an accent on it to differentiate it from the possessive adjective **tu** *(your)*.

> **Tú** trabajas los lunes, ¿verdad?
>
> **Tu** libro está en mi casa.

2. Notice that . . .

- all possessive adjectives change to reflect number: **mi clase, mis clases; nuestro compañero de cuarto, nuestros compañeros de cuarto.**
- **mi, tu**, and **su** do not change to reflect gender, but **nuestro** and **vuestro** do: **nuestro libro, nuestros amigos, vuestras clases,** but **mi libro, mi clase.**
- unlike other adjectives, which often go after the noun they modify, simple possessive adjectives always go before the noun: **su profesora, nuestras amigas.**

ACTIVIDADES

I **12** **¿De quién es?** Say to whom the following things belong.

MODELO computadora portátil (yo)
Es mi computadora portátil.

1. apuntes, tarea, CDs, silla (yo) mis, mi, mis, mi
2. bolígrafos, lápiz, celular, examen (María) sus, su, su, su
3. calculadoras, cuadernos, dibujo, mochilas (nosotros) nuestras, nuestros, nuestro, nuestras
4. diccionario, notas, escritorio, DVDs (tú) tu, tus, tu, tus
5. libros, tiza, cuarto, papeles (la profesora Roldán) sus, su, su, sus
6. computadora, fotos, salón de clase, apuntes (ustedes) su, sus, su, sus

Optional: Circulate around the classroom and look for items like the ones in **Activity 12**. Pick up items and ask **¿De quién es?** Get students to answer **Es de...; es su libro**. You can line these items up in front of the class, and see who can remember all of the owners.

M **13** **¿Es de quién?** Look at the pictures and state what each person has.

Marta

MODELO *Marta tiene su guitarra.*

1.

Martín

2.

Felipe y Eusebio

3.

Sarita y Estela

4.

tú y yo

5.

tú

6.

ustedes

© Cengage Learning 2013

C **14** **Conversaciones** You just met someone from Cuba. Write a message to him or her asking for more information. Use the following ideas for your message or make up your own questions.

- dirección
- número de teléfono
- cumpleaños
- clases

- amigos / compañeros de cuarto
- actividades favoritas
- ¿...?

C **15** **Nuestros amigos** Make two semantic maps like the one below—one each for two of your friends. Put your name at the bottom of each map. In groups of four, give one map to each person. The person whose map it is has to start the conversation. Then, each of the others must say something about the friend using a possessive adjective. Notice whom you're addressing!

Mi amigo(a) se llama _____. ¿Cómo es?

¿nacionalidad?	¿características físicas?	¿características de personalidad?	¿nacionalidad de sus papás?
_____	_____	_____	_____

MODELO

Estudiante #1: *Mi amigo es puertorriqueño.*

Estudiante #2: *Tu amigo puertorriqueño es alto.* (talking to Estudiante #1)

Estudiante #3: *Su amigo puertorriqueño es responsable.* (talking to others)

Estudiante #4: *Su amigo se llama Carlos y sus padres son puertorriqueños también.* (talking to others)

Sonrisas

© Cengage Learning 2013

Comprensión In your opinion, how would you describe the characters in the cartoon?

1. En tu opinión, ¿es generoso y romántico o manipulador el hombre? ¿Por qué? *manipulador*
2. En tu opinión, ¿es inocente y romántica o manipuladora la mujer? ¿Por qué? *inocente y romántica*
3. ¿Crees que los contratos prenupciales son una buena idea o una mala idea? *Answers will vary.*

Optional: In groups, compile lists that reflect the items that most people are willing to share and those that they are least willing to share. Have students compare lists with the rest of the class. **¿Cuáles son las cosas más típicas / no típicas? ¿Quiénes son las personas más generosas de la clase?**

Gramática útil 4

Indicating destination and future plans: The verb **ir**

Quiero hacerle una entrevista para un programa que **vamos a transmitir** en la página web de la Universidad.

You have already used similar expressions: **necesitar** + infinitive *(to need to do something)*, **tener que** + infinitive *(to have to do something)*, and **dejar de** + infinitive *(to stop doing something)*.

Check: During class, have students conjugate **ir** from memory and generate corresponding subject pronouns on paper. This quick check helps instructors and students see how much they can produce.

Heritage Learners: Point out that the **a** is not always audible, for example, in cases such as **voy a hablar** and **voy a abrir**. When writing, this **a** must always be included.

Suggestion: Emphasize that **él** *(he /him)* does not contract. Point out that contraction takes place only with the article **el** *(the)*.

Suggestion: In pairs, have students interview each other to get as much information about a classmate's after-class plans as possible. First, model interview questions with a student: **Después de la clase de español, ¿adónde vas? ¿Con quién vas? ¿Quién es? ¿Por qué vas? ¿A qué hora vas?**

Cómo usarlo

You can use the Spanish verb **ir** to say where you and others are going. You can also use it to say what you and others are going to do in the near future.

Vamos a la biblioteca mañana.	***We're going** to the library tomorrow.*
Vamos a estudiar.	***We're going to study.***

Cómo formarlo

LO BÁSICO

An *irregular verb* is one that does not follow the normal rules, such as **tener**, which you learned in **Chapter 1**.

A *preposition* links nouns, pronouns, or noun phrases to the rest of the sentence. Prepositions can express location, time sequence, purpose, or direction. *In, to, after, under,* and *for* are all English prepositions.

1. Here is the verb **ir** in the present indicative tense. **Ir**, like the verbs **ser** and **tener** that you have already learned, is an irregular verb.

ir *(to go)*			
yo	**voy**	nosotros / nosotras	**vamos**
tú	**vas**	vosotros / vosotras	**vais**
Ud. / él / ella	**va**	Uds. / ellos / ellas	**van**

2. Use the preposition **a** with the verb **ir** to say where you are going.

Voy a la cafetería.	***I'm going to** the cafeteria.*

3. When you want to use the verb **ir** to say what you are going to do, use this formula: **ir** + **a** + *infinitive*.

Vamos a comer a las cinco hoy. Después, **vamos a ir** al concierto.	***We're going to eat** at 5:00 today. Afterward, **we're going to go** to the concert.*

4. When you use **a** together with **el**, it contracts to **al**. The same holds true for **de** + **el**: **del**.

> a + el = **al**   de + el = **del**

Voy **a la** biblioteca y luego **al** gimnasio. Después, **al** mediodía, voy a estudiar en la biblioteca **del** centro de comunicaciones.

© Cengage Learning 2013

ACTIVIDADES

I **16** **Vamos a...** Say what the people indicated plan to do and where they are going to do it.

MODELO yo (estudiar: biblioteca)
Voy a estudiar. Voy a la biblioteca.

1. Pedro y Rafael (levantar pesas: gimnasio)
2. mi compañero de cuarto y yo (correr: parque)
3. Fabiola (escuchar los CDs de español: centro de comunicaciones)
4. Tomás, Andrea y yo (tomar un refresco: cafetería)
5. tú (comprar libros: librería)
6. Lourdes (descansar: residencia estudiantil)
7. tú (leer libros: biblioteca)
8. David y Patricia (comer: restaurante caribeño)

🔊 **17** **¡Pobre Miguel!** Listen as Miguel describes his schedule to his best friend
Track 10 Cristina. As you listen, write down where he goes on each day of the week.
M Then use **ir** + **a** to create seven complete sentences that describe his schedule.

1. los lunes: Los lunes va a la(s) clase(s) de español, (de) biología y (de) química.
2. los martes: Los martes va a la clase de música por la mañana y a la clase de psicología por la tarde.
3. los miércoles: Los miércoles va a la(s) clase(s) de español, (de) biología y (de) química.
4. los jueves: Los jueves va a la clase de música por la mañana, a la clase de psicología por la tarde y al laboratorio de lenguas por la noche.
5. los viernes: Los viernes va a la biblioteca a trabajar por la tarde.
6. los sábados: Los sábados va a la biblioteca a trabajar por la tarde.
7. los domingos: Los domingos va al parque a leer el periódico y a tomar un refresco.

👥 **18** **Encuesta #3** You need to get more information about student life for the
C description you will be writing later in this chapter. Find out as much as you
can about your partner's leisure activities. Ask questions such as the following
and take notes. Then, as a class, tally the information you collected.

El tiempo libre

1. ¿Adónde vas los viernes y los sábados por la noche? ¿Con quién vas?
2. ¿Adónde vas entresemana cuando no estudias? ¿Con quién vas?
3. ¿...?

Vocabulario útil: un club, una discoteca, el cine *(movie theater)*, un
restaurante, un centro comercial *(mall)*, un partido *(game)* de fútbol
americano / de básquetbol, pasar tiempo en línea, ir a una fiesta, etc.

¡Explora y exprésate!

Standards 2.1, 2.2: Here students gain knowledge and understanding of Caribbean culture and explore cultural products such as educational institutions.

Check: Many students confuse the Caribbean islands. Project a blank map of the islands and have students fill in the names to assess their geographical knowledge. Look over this section and jot down 3-4 items related to Caribbean culture that you want students to know. Then decide what you will emphasize in the ¡Explora y exprésate! section to help students retain this information.

Cuba

Christian Kober/Getty Images

Información general

Nombre oficial: República de Cuba

Población: 11.477.459

Capital: La Habana (f. 1515) (2.200.000 hab.)

Otras ciudades importantes: Santiago (450.000 hab.), Camagüey (300.000 hab.)

Moneda: peso cubano

Idiomas: español (oficial)

Mapa de Cuba: Apéndice D

Notice that **f.** is the abbreviation for **fundado(a)**, which means *founded.* La Habana, the capital city of Cuba, was founded in 1515.

Notice that **hab.** is the abbreviation for **habitantes**, which means *inhabitants.* This is how population statistics are written in Spanish.

Vale saber…

- La población de la isla es una mezcla *(mixture)* de los nativos originales (taínos), descendientes de esclavos africanos y europeos, mezcla que produce una cultura única. También hay una población china significante, resultado de la inmigración china a Norteamérica y al Caribe durante los años 1800.
- Raúl Castro (hermano de Fidel) es el actual presidente de Cuba.

La educación para todos

Cuba se distingue por tener uno de los mejores sistemas de educación del mundo. Desde la revolución cubana en 1959, el sistema de educación ha sido

Chine Nouvelle/SIPA/Newscom

(has been) prioridad del gobierno cubano, empezando con la Campaña Nacional de Alfabetización en Cuba en 1960. El objetivo de la campaña fue *(was)* eliminar el anafalbetismo y llevar maestros *(to bring teachers)* y escuelas *(schools)* a todas las áreas del país. La educación, ¡para todos!

Puerto Rico

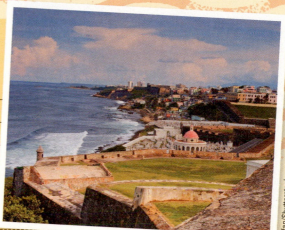

Información general ▶

Nombre oficial: Estado Libre Asociado de Puerto Rico (Commonwealth of Puerto Rico)

Población: 3.997.663

Capital: San Juan (f. 1521) (450.000 hab.)

Otras ciudades importantes: Ponce (200.000 hab.), Caguas (150.000 hab.)

Moneda: dólar estadounidense

Idiomas: español, inglés (oficiales)

Mapa de Puerto Rico: Apéndice D

Vale saber…

- A los puertorriqueños también se les conoce como *(are also known as)* "boricuas", ya que antes de la llegada de los europeos en 1493 la isla se llamaba *(was called)* Borinquen.

- Los puertorriqueños son ciudadanos *(citizens)* estadounidenses, pero no votan en elecciones de Estados Unidos.

La educación bilingüe

La educación en Puerto Rico está garantizada constitucionalmente y es gratuita hasta el nivel secundario *(secondary level)*. El español es el idioma de instrucción, pero los estudiantes toman clases de inglés en todos los grados. Los estudios universitarios son iguales al sistema estadounidense: el bachillerato *(bachelor's degree)*, la maestría *(master's degree)* y finalmente el doctorado *(Ph.D)*. Ser boricua es ser bilingüe.

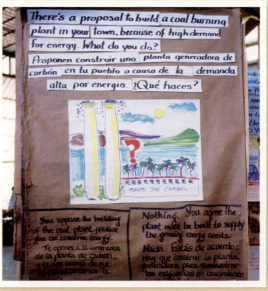

República Dominicana

Información general ▶

Nombre oficial: República Dominicana

Población: 9.794.487

Capital: Santo Domingo (f. 1492) (2.500.000 hab.)

Otras ciudades importantes: Santiago de los Caballeros (2.000.000 hab.), La Romana (300.000 hab.)

Moneda: peso dominicano

Idiomas: español

Mapa de República Dominicana: Apéndice D

Vale saber…

Optional: To emphasize that that the Dominican Republic shares the island of Hispaniola with Haiti, show an image of the two sovereign nations.

- La isla que comparten la República Dominicana y Haití se llama La Hispaniola. Estuvo bajo *(It was under)* control español hasta 1697, cuando la parte oeste *(western)* pasó a ser territorio francés.

- Santo Domingo es la primera ciudad del Nuevo Mundo *(New World)*. En esta ciudad capital, se construyeron *(were built)* la primera catedral, el primer hospital y la primera universidad del Nuevo Mundo.

La universidad más antigua del Nuevo Mundo

La Universidad Santo Tomás de Aquino, ahora conocida como la Universidad Autónoma de Santo Domingo, se puede considerar *(can be considered)* la universidad más antigua del Nuevo Mundo. Fundada en 1538—unos cien años antes que Harvard en 1636 y Yale en 1701—empezó *(it began)* con cuatro facultades: medicina, derecho *(law)*, teología y artes. ¡Cómo han cambiado los tiempos! *(How times have changed!)* Hoy día la Universidad ofrece muchos más cursos, entre ellos: ingeniería, arquitectura, economía e informática, por supuesto.

Suggestion: Challenge students to answer 1-6 in Spanish (or at least bilingually)!

La información general Answer these questions in English.

1. Look at the maps on page 83. What is the Spanish name of the area in which these three countries are located? El Caribe
2. Which of the three countries is closest to the United States? Cuba
3. Which two countries are islands and which one shares an island with another country? Cuba and Puerto Rico; Dominican Republic
4. Why are Puerto Ricans called **boricuas**? Because the island used to be known as Borinquen
5. Which island citizens are also American citizens? Puerto Ricans
6. Which country boasts the first city in the New World? Dominican Republic

El tema de la educación

1. What was the objective of Cuba's "Campaña Nacional de Alfabetización"?
2. Why are "boricuas" bilingual?
3. What were the first four academic departments established in the oldest university of the New World?

Answers, El tema de la educación:
1. eliminate illiteracy; get teachers and schools in all areas of the country 2. because they are required to take English in every grade 3. medicine, law, theology, arts

🌐 ¿QUIERES SABER MÁS?

On the chart that you started at the beginning of the chapter, add what you already know under **Lo que aprendí.** For the **Lo que quiero aprender** column, pick one or two of the things you would still like to learn, or one or two of the key words below to investigate online. Be prepared to share this information with the class.

Palabras clave: (Cuba) la revolución cubana, José Martí, Celia Cruz; **(Puerto Rico)** Estado Libre Asociado de Puerto Rico, Rosario Ferré, Tito Puente; **(República Dominicana)** Juan Pablo Duarte, las hermanas Mirabal, Sammy Sosa

Culture/Check: Culture is everchanging. Have students investigate additional interests of their own choosing about the cultures of the Caribbean. To do a check of this information, have students report it back to the class in a brief presentation. Use broad categories to rate student mini-presentations. For example: (1) level of interest of the topic to the class, (2) amount of information, (3) clarity of communication. Use a rating of 1-5 for each category.

🌐 **Tú en el mundo hispano** To explore opportunities to use your Spanish to study, volunteer, or do internships in Cuba, Puerto Rico, and the Dominican Republic, follow the links on **www.cengagebrain.com**.

🎬 **Ritmos del mundo hispano** Follow the links at **www.cengagebrain.com** to hear music from Cuba, Puerto Rico, and the Dominican Republic.

A leer

>> Antes de leer

ESTRATEGIA

Using visuals to aid in comprehension

When visuals accompany a text, looking at them first can help you determine the subject. When you approach a reading, look first at the visuals and any captions that accompany them to see if they help you understand the content.

Heritage Learners: Encourage heritage learners to share with the class samples of music, art, and films from their country of origin or from the countries in this chapter.

1 Look at the following article about three different schools (**escuelas**) in the Caribbean. Focus on the photos, captions, and headlines, then match the general information on the right with the photos on the left.

1. __b__ Foto A
2. __c__ Foto B
3. __a__ Foto C

a. Aquí los estudiantes estudian técnicas para filmar programas de televisión y cine.
b. Los estudiantes de esta escuela toman clases de música.
c. Esta escuela ofrece cursos de bellas artes, ilustración, diseño gráfico y diseño digital.

Learning objective: Analyzing

2 The following are some unknown words and phrases you will encounter in the reading passages. Although not all the words are cognates, they are somewhat similar to their English counterparts. See if you can match them up.

1. __c__ sin pagar nada
2. __i__ se han graduado
3. __h__ está afiliada con
4. __e__ se admiten
5. __f__ construyó
6. __b__ villa
7. __a__ fue inaugurado
8. __j__ se ofrecen
9. __d__ edición
10. __g__ han recibido

a. *was inaugurated*
b. *village*
c. *without paying anything*
d. *editing*
e. *are admitted*
f. *constructed*
g. *have received*
h. *is affiliated with*
i. *have graduated*
j. *are offered*

3 Now, using the information you gained from looking at the visuals, read the article, and focus on getting the main idea. Don't forget to use cognates and active vocabulary to help you understand the content. Try not to worry about unknown words and just focus on getting the main information.

LECTURA

Tres escuelas interesantes del Caribe

A. El saxofonista puertorriqueño David Sánchez, uno de los graduados famosos de "La Libre"

Redferns/Getty Images

La Escuela Libre[1] de Música Ernesto Ramos Antonini

En Puerto Rico muchos estudiantes de música toman cursos sin pagar nada, gracias a cinco escuelas públicas de educación musical. Establecidas a finales de los años 40 por un político local, estas escuelas han graduado a miles[2] de estudiantes. Entre los graduados famosos están el saxofonista de jazz David Sánchez y el cantante salsero Gilberto Santa Rosa.

La escuela más grande es la de San Juan, que está afiliada con el prestigioso Berklee College of Music en Boston. Los cursos de estudio incluyen la música clásica, rock, jazz, contemporánea y tradicional, y el currículum prepara a los estudiantes para estudiar cursos más avanzados en el Conservatorio de Música de Puerto Rico. En San Juan sólo se admiten 100 estudiantes al año, aunque se reciben solicitudes[3] de más de 600 personas, así que los estudiantes de la escuela son unos de los más talentosos de la isla.

La Escuela de Diseño Altos de Chavón

Esta escuela data de los años 70 cuando la República Dominicana construyó un centro cultural en la pequeña villa de Altos de Chavón. La Escuela de Diseño, que forma parte del centro, fue inaugurado por Frank Sinatra en 1982 y está afiliada con el famoso Parsons The New School for Design en la ciudad[4] de Nueva York.

Los 110 estudiantes de La Escuela de Diseño se especializan en campos de estudio como bellas artes e ilustración, diseño gráfico, diseño de modas[5], diseño digital y diseño de interiores.

Más de 1.000 estudiantes dominicanos e internacionales se han graduado de la escuela. Los graduados de la escuela son elegibles para transferirse directamente a Parsons en Nueva York o París.

B. Unos estudiantes de arte de La Escuela de Diseño

Courtesy of Altos de Chavon/Alex Otero

La Escuela Internacional de Cine y Televisión

En la Escuela Internacional de Cine y Televisión (EICTV) de San Antonio de los Baños, Cuba, se ofrecen cursos de formación audiovisual para estudiantes cubanos e internacionales. La EICTV fue inaugurada en 1986 y es presidida por el famoso escritor colombiano Gabriel García Márquez. Los profesores, además de ser instructores, son cineastas profesionales que dirigen[6] películas y documentales a nivel mundial[7].

C. Un estudiante de la Escuela Internacional de Cine y Televisión

Paul Bennett/Corbis

Los estudiantes de la EICTV estudian siete especialidades en el curso regular: guión[8], producción, dirección, fotografía, sonido[9], edición y documentales. También se presentan unos veinte talleres[10] especializados cada año. Más de 1.500 estudiantes de unos treinta países se han graduado de la EICTV desde su incepción y los graduados de la escuela han recibido más de 100 premios[11] en varios festivales nacionales e internacionales

[1]*Free* [2]*thousands* [3]**aunque**…: *although they receive applications* [4]*city* [5]*fashion* [6]*they direct* [7]**a**…: *worldwide* [8]*script* [9]*sound* [10]*workshops* [11]*prizes*

4 Answer the following questions about the readings to see how well you understood them.

1. ¿Quiénes son dos graduados famosos de la Escuela Libre de la Música?
2. ¿Con qué institución estadounidense está afiliada la Escuela Libre de la Música?
3. ¿Cuáles son tres tipos de música que los estudiantes estudian en la Escuela Libre?
4. ¿Con qué institución estadounidense está afiliada la Escuela de Diseño Altos de Chavón?
5. ¿Cuáles son cuatro campos de estudio que se ofrecen en la Escuela de Diseño?
6. ¿Cuántos graduados de la Escuela de Diseño hay?
7. ¿Qué autor está afiliado con la EICTV?
8. ¿Cuáles son cuatro campos de estudio que se ofrecen en la EICTV?

 5 With a partner, answer the following questions about the reading and about your own interests.

1. ¿Cuál de las tres escuelas les interesa *(interests you)* más?
2. ¿Cuál de los campos de estudio de esa escuela les interesa más?
3. ¿Conocen *(Are you familiar with)* unas escuelas similares en Estados Unidos? ¿Cómo se llaman?

Esta escuela está en Providence, Rhode Island. ¿Sabes *(Do you know)* cómo se llama y cuál es su especialización?

Andre Jenny / Alamy

Antes de escribir

ESTRATEGIA

Prewriting—Brainstorming ideas

When you are planning to write and need ideas, try brainstorming. You can do this verbally with a partner, writing down your ideas, or on your own, writing freely and without restriction. The key thing is to write ideas as they occur, without evaluating them. Then take the list of ideas and decide which work best.

> It is important to try to brainstorm in Spanish. This will get you to start "thinking" in Spanish, which in turn will lead to increased comfort and ease with the language.

1 Retrieve the information from the three **Encuesta** activities (**Activity 5** on p. 97, **Activity 10** on p. 101, and **Activity 18** on p. 107). With a partner, study the results and brainstorm ideas to describe the life of a typical student at your university.

2 Look at the following partial diary entry, and organize your information into a similar format. Try to use only words you've already learned.

> viernes, 10 de octubre
>
> ¡Tengo muchas actividades hoy! A las ocho, tengo clase de química. Luego, voy a ir al café para estudiar para el examen de historia a las diez...
> Por la tarde, tengo que... Por la noche, voy a...

© Cengage Learning 2013

> **Suggestion:** If class time will not permit this series of activities, it may be modified and assigned to teams to do outside of class as a group project. Have students report on results of surveys in class.

Composición

3 Using the previous model, work with your partner on a rough draft of your diary entry. For now, just write freely without worrying about mistakes. Here are some additional words and phrases that may be useful as you write.

primero	*first*	**finalmente**	*finally*
luego	*later*	**mucho que hacer**	*a lot to do*
entonces	*then*	**un día (muy) ocupado**	*a (very) busy day*
después	*after that*	**con**	*with*

Después de escribir

4 Now, with your partner, go back over your diary entry and revise it.

Did you . . .

- make sure you included all the necessary information?
- check to make sure the verbs are conjugated correctly?
- make sure articles, nouns, and adjectives agree?
- use possessive adjectives correctly?
- look for misspellings?

> **Notice:** Sharing writing in class is an important part of the process approach to writing that helps build class community and editing skills, while providing an audience for student writing.

Vocabulario

Campos de estudio *Fields of study*

Los cursos básicos *Basic courses*
la arquitectura *architecture*
las ciencias políticas *political science*
la economía *economics*
la educación *education*
la geografía *geography*
la historia *history*
la ingeniería *engineering*
la psicología *psychology*

Las humanidades *Humanities*
la filosofía *philosophy*
las lenguas / los idiomas *languages*
la literatura *literature*

Las lenguas / Los idiomas *Languages*
el alemán *German*
el chino *Chinese*
el español *Spanish*
el francés *French*
el inglés *English*
el japonés *Japanese*

Las matemáticas *Mathematics*
el cálculo *calculus*
la computación *computer science*

la estadística *statistics*
la informática *computer science*

Las ciencias *Sciences*
la biología *biology*
la física *physics*
la medicina *medicine*
la química *chemistry*
la salud *health*

Los negocios *Business*
la administración de empresas *business administration*
la contabilidad *accounting*
el mercadeo *marketing*

La comunicación pública *Public communications*
el periodismo *journalism*
la publicidad *public relations*

Las artes *The arts*
el arte *art*
el baile *dance*
el diseño gráfico *graphic design*
la música *music*
la pintura *painting*

Lugares en la universidad *Places in the university*

¿Dónde tienes la clase de...?
Where does your . . . class meet?
En el centro de computación.
In the computer center.
...el centro de comunicaciones.
. . . the media center.
...el gimnasio. *. . . the gymnasium.*

la cafetería *the cafeteria*
la librería *the bookstore*
la residencia estudiantil *the dorm*

Los días de la semana *The days of the week*

lunes *Monday*	**miércoles** *Wednesday*	**viernes** *Friday*	**domingo** *Sunday*
martes *Tuesday*	**jueves** *Thursday*	**sábado** *Saturday*	

Para pedir y dar la hora *Asking for and giving the time*

Mira el reloj para decir la hora... *Look at the clock to tell the time . . .*
¿Qué hora es? *What time is it?*
Es la una. *It's one o'clock.*
Son las dos. *It's two o'clock.*
Son las... y cuarto. *It's . . . fifteen.*
Son las... y media. *It's . . . thirty.*

Son las... menos cuarto. *It's a quarter to . . .*
Faltan quince para las... *It's a quarter to . . .*

tarde *late*
temprano *early*
¿A qué hora es la clase de español? *(At) What time is Spanish class?*
Es a la / a las... *It's at . . .*

Mañana, tarde o noche *Morning, afternoon, or night*

de la mañana *in the morning* (with precise time)
de la tarde *in the afternoon* (with precise time)
de la noche *in the evening* (with precise time)

Es mediodía. *It's noon.*
Es medianoche. *It's midnight.*

por la mañana *during the morning*
por la tarde *during the afternoon*
por la noche *during the evening*

Para hablar de la fecha *Talking about the date*

¿Qué día es hoy? *What day is today?*
Hoy es martes treinta. *Today is Tuesday the 30th.*

¿A qué fecha estamos? *What is today's date?*
Es el treinta de octubre. *It's the 30th of October.*
Es el primero de noviembre. *It's the first of November.*

¿Cuándo es el Día de las Madres? *When is Mother's Day?*
Es el doce de mayo. *It's May 12th.*

el día *day*
la semana *week*
el fin de semana *weekend*
el mes *month*
el año *year*
todos los días *every day*
entresemana *during the week/on weekdays*

ayer *yesterday*
hoy *today*
mañana *tomorrow*

Para hacer preguntas *Asking questions*

¿Cómo? *How?*
¿Cuál(es)? *What? Which one(s)?*
¿Cuándo? *When?*
¿Cuánto(a)? *How much?*
¿Cuántos(as)? *How many?*
¿De quién es? *Whose is this?*

¿De quiénes son? *Whose are these?*
¿Dónde? *Where?*
¿Por qué? *Why?*
¿Qué? *What? Which?*
¿Quién(es)? *Who?*

Verbos

abrir *to open*
aprender *to learn*
asistir a *to attend*
beber *to drink*
comer *to eat*
compartir *to share*
comprender *to understand*
correr *to run*
creer (en) *to believe (in)*
deber *should, ought*
dejar de *to stop (doing something)*

describir *to describe*
descubrir *to discover*
escribir *to write*
imprimir *to print*
ir *to go*
ir a *to be going to (do something)*
leer *to read*
recibir *to receive*
transmitir *to broadcast*
vender *to sell*
vivir *to live*

Adjetivos posesivos

mi(s) *my*
tu(s) *your (fam.)*
su(s) *your (sing. form., pl.) his, her, their*

nuestro(a) / nuestros(as) *our*
vuestro(a) / vuestros(as) *your (pl. fam.)*

Contracciones

al (a + el) *to the*
del (de + el) *from the, of the*

Otras palabras

porque *because*
escuela *school*

Repaso y preparación

>> ## Repaso del Capítulo 3

Preparation: Have students review this material and complete the activities here, in the SAM, and online before they begin **Chapter 4**.

Complete these activities to check your understanding of the new grammar points in **Chapter 3** before you move on to **Chapter 4**.

The answers to the activities in this section can be found in **Appendix B**.

Check: The **Repaso** section not only reviews grammar and vocabulary for the student but also offers a built-in performance assessment. By doing review activities with students, you can assess concepts that you may need to continue to reinforce in future classes.

Interrogative words (p. 94)

1 Complete each sentence in the chat with an interrogative word (**cuál, cuándo, cuántas, por qué, qué, quien**), capitalizing as needed.

> **Finita7:** Marcos, ¿_____qué_____ estudias?
>
> **Marcosis:** Historia. ¿_____Por qué_____?
>
> **Finita7:** ¡Necesito tu ayuda! ¡Por favor!
>
> **Marcosis:** ¿_____Cuál_____ es tu problema?
>
> **Finita7:** ¡Tengo que escribir un informe!
>
> **Marcosis:** ¿Para _____cuándo_____ tienes que entregar la tarea?
>
> **Finita7:** ¡Mañana!
>
> **Marcosis:** ¿_____Cuántas_____ páginas?
>
> **Finita7:** ¡Cinco!
>
> **Marcosis:** ¿_____Quién_____ es el profesor?
>
> **Finita7:** ¡Martínez!
>
> **Marcosis** ¡Noooooooooo! Este problema no tiene solución...
>
> **Finita7:** :-O

The present indicative of regular -er and -ir verbs (p. 98)

2 Complete each sentence with the present-tense form of the verb indicated.

1. Marta ___escribe___ (escribir) la tarea para la clase de ciencias políticas.
2. Tú y yo ___debemos___ (deber) ir a la biblioteca.
3. Yo ___como___ (comer) pizza mientras estudio.
4. Uds. ___viven___ (vivir) en la Residencia Central, ¿verdad?
5. La profesora de literatura ___lee___ (leer) muchas novelas.

Simple possessive adjectives (p. 102)

3 Complete each sentence with a possessive adjective.

1. No comprendo a ___mis___ padres.
2. ¿Tienes ___tus___ notas?
3. Escribimos ___nuestra___ tarea.
4. Ella lee ___sus___ papeles.
5. Ellos abren ___sus___ libros.
6. Aquí tienes ___mi___ número.

The verb ir (p. 106)

4 Complete the sentences with the present-indicative forms of **ir**.

1. Si yo ___voy___ a la biblioteca, ¿qué ___van___ a hacer ustedes?
2. Mi amiga ___va___ a correr, pero nosotros ___vamos___ al gimnasio.
3. Tú ___vas___ a la librería, ¿verdad?

118 Capítulo 3

Gustar + infinitive (Chapter 2)

5 Use the cues to create complete sentences. Follow the model.

MODELO (a Marta) / gustar correr
A Marta le gusta correr.

1. (a mí) / gustar leer
2. (a nosotros) / gustar comer
3. (a ustedes) / gustar bailar
4. (a ti) / gustar cocinar
5. (a él) / gustar patinar
6. (a mí) / gustar cantar

The present indicative of regular -ar verbs (Chapter 2)

6 Complete the description with present indicative forms.

Tengo dos compañeros de cuarto. Roque es muy serio y 1. __estudia__ (estudiar) mucho. También 2. __cocina__ (cocinar) la cena. ¡Es un chef fantástico! El otro, Raul, 3. __toca__ (tocar) la guitarra y 4. __canta__ (cantar). A veces, él y Roque 5. __levantan__ (levantar) pesas y 6. __practican__ (practicar) deportes, como el tenis y el fútbol. Nosotros 7. __miramos__ (mirar) televisión y 8. __alquilamos__ (alquilar) videos por las noches. ¿Y yo? Pues, yo 9. __trabajo__ (trabajar) mucho y a veces 10. __visito__ (visitar) a amigos. ¡Yo no 11. __paso__ (pasar) mucho tiempo allí!

Present indicative of ser (Chapter 1), Adjective agreement (Chapter 2)

7 Use an adjective from the list to write a sentence with **ser** about each person.

MODELO *Neli es muy trabajadora.*

Adjetivos: activo(a), divertido(a), egoísta, generoso(a), impaciente, perezoso(a), tímido(a) trabajador(a)

Neli

1.

Rogelio y Mauricio

2.

tú

3.

nosotros

4.

yo

5.

Sandra

6.

Néstor y Nicolás

Answers, Act. 5: 1. A mí me gusta leer. 2. A nosotros nos gusta comer. 3. A ustedes les gusta bailar. 4. A ti te gusta cocinar. 5. A él le gusta patinar. 6. A mí me gusta cantar.

Answers, Act. 7: 1. Rogelio y Mauricio son muy egoístas. 2. Tú eres muy impaciente. 3. Nosotros somos muy perezosos. 4. Yo soy muy activo(a). 5. Sandra es muy generosa. 6. Néstor y Nicolás son muy tímidos.

¿Te interesa la tecnología?

CONEXIONES VIRTUALES Y PERSONALES

Las nuevas tecnologías tienen un impacto tremendo en las áreas de las comunicaciones, los negocios y las relaciones personales, entre otras. ¡Nuestro mundo está cambiando *(is changing)* todos los días!

¿Cuáles son tus aparatos electrónicos favoritos y para qué los usas?

Communication

By the end of this chapter you will be able to

- talk about computers and technology
- identify colors
- talk about likes and dislikes
- describe people, emotions, and conditions
- talk about current activities
- say how something is done

British Retail Photography/Alamy

Un viaje por España

España es el único país europeo donde el español es la lengua oficial. España forma la Península Ibérica con Portugal, y por eso tiene costas en el Atlántico, el mar Mediterráneo y el mar Cantábrico. También tiene varias sierras, entre ellas la sierra de Guadarrama en la parte central del país y la sierra Nevada en el sur.

Check: At the beginning of this chapter, interview students to find out what they already know about Spain. At the end of the chapter, repeat your questions to assess what they have learned.

Globe Art: Adapted from Shutterstock/rtguest

País / Área	Tamaño y fronteras	Sitios de interés
España 499.542 km²	un poco más de dos veces el área de Oregón; fronteras con Portugal, Francia y Andorra y con Marruecos (Ceuta y Melilla)	la Alhambra, el Museo del Prado, el Museo Guggenheim, las Islas Canarias, las Islas Baleares

¿Qué sabes? Di si las siguientes oraciones son ciertas (**C**) o falsas (**F**).

1. España está situada completamente en Europa. F
2. Varios grupos de islas también forman parte de España. C
3. Hay unos museos importantes en España. C
4. España es más pequeña que Oregón. F

Lo que sé y lo que quiero aprender Completa la tabla del **Apéndice A.** Escribe algunos datos que **ya sabes** sobre España en la columna **Lo que sé**. Después, añade algunos temas que **quieres aprender** a la columna **Lo que quiero aprender**. Guarda la tabla para usarla otra vez en la sección **¡Explora y exprésate!** en la página 151.

Cultures

By the end of this chapter you will have explored

- the Spanish empire
- the great artists and writers of Spain
- the Arabic influence on Spanish architecture
- Buika, a Spanish singer who blends many musical styles
- a popular Spanish social networking site
- borrowed words on the Internet

¡Imagínate!

Standards 3.1, 3.2: Throughout this chapter, you will see examples (general chapter theme, technological vocabulary, social network reading, Internet use surveys, etc.) of making connections with technology in Spanish.

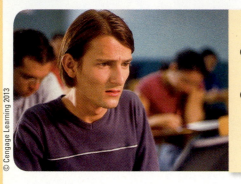

BETO:	¡Estoy furioso!
CHELA:	Pero, ¿por qué?
BETO:	Primero llego tarde a la clase de literatura.
CHELA:	Llegar tarde no es una tragedia.
BETO:	¡Tenemos examen! Abro mi **computadora portátil**, pero en la **pantalla** dice que no tengo suficiente **memoria** para abrir la **aplicación**.

>> La tecnología
El hardware

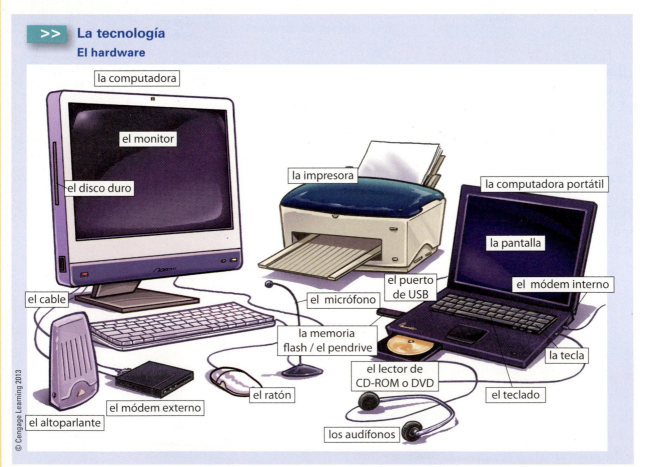

- la computadora
- el monitor
- el disco duro
- el cable
- el altoparlante
- el módem externo
- el ratón
- el micrófono
- la memoria flash / el pendrive
- la impresora
- el puerto de USB
- el lector de CD-ROM o DVD
- los audífonos
- la computadora portátil
- la pantalla
- el módem interno
- la tecla
- el teclado

Notice: In Spain, **la computadora** is called **el ordenador**. **El computador** is also used, mostly in Latin America. Another term for **hacer clic** is **pulsar**.

>> La tecnología

El software
la aplicación *application*
los archivos *files*
  el archivo PDF *PDF attachment*
el ícono del programa
  program icon
el juego interactivo
  interactive game
el programa antivirus *antivirus program*
el programa de procesamiento de textos *word processing program*

Funciones de la computadora
archivar *to file*
bajar / descargar *to download*
conectar *to connect*
enviar *to send*
funcionar *to function*
grabar *to record*
guardar *to save*
hacer clic / doble clic *to click / double-click*
instalar *to install*
subir / cargar *to upload*

> **PDF** stands for **el formato de documento portátil** and is pronounced **pe-de-efe**.

> To describe the hard drive of your computer or its processor, use:
> - **un disco duro con capacidad de 500 GB (gigabytes)**
> - **un procesador a 2.4 o 2.53 GHz (gigahercio)**

Suggestion: Begin a conversation with: **Mi impresora tiene cuatro colores: rojo, azul, amarillo, etc. Los otros colores son…** Always introduce colors with objects (**Mi libro es rojo**). Continue with simple, personalized questions: **¿De qué color es tu libro / tu bolígrafo / tu lápiz etc.? ¿Cuál es tu color preferido?**

>> Los colores

azul   amarillo   anaranjado   blanco   café, marrón   gris

morado   negro   rojo   rosa, rosado   verde

© Cengage Learning 2013

> When a color is used as an adjective, it comes after the noun it modifies.
> - If it ends in **-o**, it changes to match the gender and number of that noun: **la silla negra**, **los cuadernos rojos**.
> - If the color ends in **-e**, add an **s** to the plural: **las pizarras verdes**.
> - If the color ends in a consonant, add **es** to the plural: **los libros azules**.
> - **Marrón** in the plural changes to **marrones**, with no accent. Can you figure out why, for pronunciation reasons, it loses the accent?
> - Note that **rosa** and **café** change to reflect number, but not gender.
> - If you want to say that a color is dark, use **fuerte** or **oscuro**. For example, **amarillo fuerte** or **amarillo oscuro**. If you want to say that a color is light, use **claro**. For example, **azul claro**.

── ACTIVIDADES ──

I **1** **La computadora** Un amigo necesita hacer *(needs to do)* ciertas cosas en la computadora. ¿Qué parte de la computadora va a necesitar para hacer lo que quiere? Escoge de la segunda columna.

Learning objective: Understanding

1. __e__ Necesito imprimir el correo electrónico.
2. __b__ Necesito ver un video de YouTube.
3. __f__ Necesito conectar el teclado al monitor.
4. __a__ Necesito escuchar música mientras trabajo.
5. __c__ Necesito escribir un documento.
6. __d__ Necesito archivar un documento.
7. __g__ Necesito grabar un mensaje para enviar a mis amigos.
8. __h__ Necesito instalar el programa de procesamiento de textos.

a. los audífonos
b. la pantalla
c. el teclado
d. la memoria flash
e. la impresora
f. el cable
g. el micrófono
h. el lector de DVD-ROM

> Starting in this chapter, many of the activity direction lines will be presented in Spanish. Here are a few words that will help you understand Spanish direction lines: **di** *(say)*, **haz** *(do)*, **escoge** *(choose)*, **luego** *(then, later)*, **siguiente** *(following)*, **oración** *(sentence)*, **párrafo** *(paragraph)*.

2 **El sitio web** Tu compañero(a) quiere buscar información sobre ciertos temas en el servicio ¡VIVA! Latino. Tú le dices *(You tell him/her)* en qué ícono debe hacer doble clic. Luego, él o ella te dirige a los íconos que corresponden a tus intereses.

In some countries, the Internet is referred to as **la Internet**, in others as **el Internet**, and in others still, it is referred to simply as **Internet**, with no article to indicate gender.

¡VIVA! Latino

Directorio de sitios web

Arte y cultura
Literatura, Teatro, Museos, Guías

Internet y computadoras
WWW, Aplicaciones, Chat, Redes

Educación
Primaria, Secundaria, Universidades

Medios de comunicación
Radio, TV, Revistas, Periódicos

Deportes y ocio
Deportes, Fútbol, Juegos, Turismo

Salud
Medicina, Enfermedades, Ejercicio, Dietas

Espectáculos y diversión
Cine, Actores, Música, Humor

Materias de consulta
Bibliotecas, Diccionarios

Culture: **El Museo del Prado** is one of the most visited art museums in the world. Located in Madrid, Spain, **el Prado** principally houses paintings and sculpture from the twelfth to the nineteenth centuries and is considered to be one of the finest collections of European art.

MODELO el Museo del Prado en Madrid
Tú: *Necesito más información sobre el Museo del Prado en Madrid.*
Compañero(a): *Haz doble clic en el ícono rojo.*

1. una dieta vegetariana   el ícono gris
2. mi actor (actriz) favorito(a)   el ícono morado
3. un diccionario español / inglés   el ícono blanco
4. la Copa Mundial de Fútbol   el ícono anaranjado
5. un programa de procesamiento de textos   el ícono azul
6. la Universidad Complutense de Madrid   el ícono amarillo
7. el periódico *El País* de Madrid   el ícono verde
8. ¿…?   Answers will vary.

Culture: **La Universidad Complutense de Madrid** is one of the oldest, largest, and top-ranked public universities in Spain. The campus is located in an area in Madrid called **la Ciudad Universitaria.**

Culture: **La Copa Mundial de Fútbol** or the Soccer World Cup (FIFA World Cup) organizes the world championships for soccer every four years. Spain won the World Cup in 2010. Other Spanish-speaking countries that have won the World Cup include Argentina and Uruguay.

3 **Mi computadora** ¿Puedes describir tu computadora? Incluye en tu descripción todos los componentes de tu computadora y menciona el color de cada uno si es apropiado.

If you want to describe the colors of your mousepad, you can say **almohadilla de ratón**, or simply **mousepad**.

MODELO *El monitor de mi computadora es azul y blanco. Los cables son grises. El ratón es blanco. Los altoparlantes son negros. Las teclas en el teclado son blancas…*

¡Fíjate! El lenguaje de Internet

The Internet is a source of entirely new words in English, a development that has created language issues for translators and Internet users alike. Online word forums in which people from different countries discuss how to translate Internet terms into their own languages are useful in dealing with these issues. In many cases, the universal Internet terms have simply stayed in English. Here are some examples of words that have commonly (or infrequently) used Spanish translations, and others that do not yet (and may never!) have translations.

Pedro Armestre/AFP/Getty Images/Newscom

Blog: This is an abbreviated form of Web-log, and is usually referred to simply as *blog*, losing the *We* of Web. In Spanish, it is common to simply say **blog**, but it can also be defined as: **un diario personal en un sitio web que contiene reflexiones, comentarios, fotos, video o enlaces**.

Forum: Foro is the common Spanish translation. If you are referring to an announcement board, you would say **un tablón de anuncios**. A message board is **un tablón de mensajes**.

Podcast: Un podcast is a radio broadcast that is Portable On Demand. If you want to use only Spanish words, you could say **una emisora radial en Internet**. **Los podcasts** are downloaded to **un teléfono inteligente** or **un smartphone**, where the user can listen to them at leisure.

Video conferencing: Chat with your friends via Internet using **un sistema de video conferencia**.

Wifi: Most Spanish speakers simply say **wifi**, with a wide variation in pronunciation from country to country. To be technically correct, you could refer to it as **la red inalámbrica**. (**Alambre** means *wire,* which is why **inalámbrica** means *wireless.)* Although you would be understood with this mouthful of a phrase, you would probably be considered rather geeky. Stick with **wifi** for now.

Text messaging: Everyone texts these days. In Spanish this would be **enviar un mensaje de texto**.

Instant messaging: If you instant message someone, this is referred to as **enviar un mensaje instantáneo**.

Sound files: Music downloads are **archivos de sonido** or **MP3s** that can be transferred directly to **MP3 portátiles** or **los smartphones**.

Las redes sociales: Social networking sites like Facebook and Twitter have become the preferred mode of communication for many people throughout the world.

Without a doubt, the Internet will continue to create new functions and new words as its uses multiply. Don't panic! You can find a site online that will help you find just the Spanish expression you are looking for!

Práctica Escribe una lista de términos de Internet en inglés que no sabes decir en español. Con un(a) compañero(a), busca en Internet un sitio con las traducciones y las pronunciaciones, o simplemente verifica que lo más común es usar el término en inglés.

Notice: Point out that the capitalization of **Wifi** or **wifi** varies and has not been standardized in the Spanish language.

Optional: Consider introducing *correo basura (spam)* and recycle words from earlier chapters with questions like: **¿Recibes mucho correo basura? ¿Cuántos correos basura recibes al día? ¿Recibes más correo basura por la noche o por la mañana? ¿Qué tipo de correo basura recibes? ¿Lees el correo basura? ¿Abres el correo basura?**

Check: To measure progress with new vocabulary, if you are teaching in a technology-rich classroom, go to places like your e-mail, junk mail, keyboard, and informally quiz the class with **¿Cómo se llama _____?** Using the same technique, demonstrate *to download, to record, to upload, to send,* etc.

Heritage Learners: Ask heritage learners if they have Spanish-language sites that they like to visit or can recommend to the class.

>> Vocabulario útil 2

BETO: Empiezo a salir del salón de clases. No sé en dónde, pero entre el salón y la biblioteca, pierdo mi **asistente electrónico**.

CHELA: Ya me voy. Estoy muy **aburrida** con tu cuento trágico.

Suggestion: Go around the class and whisper in students' ears some of the emotion words (in random order). Then have students act out their assigned emotion in front of the class or in smaller groups. The rest of the class guesses the emotion. Be sure to emphasize gender with this activity [i. e., **estás furioso(a)**].

>> Las emociones

aburrido(a) *bored*
cansado(a) *tired*
contento(a) *happy*
enfermo(a) *sick*
enojado(a) *angry*
furioso(a) *furious*
nervioso(a) *nervous*
ocupado(a) *busy*
preocupado(a) *worried*
seguro(a) *sure*
triste *sad*

Suggestion: Have a discussion with students about their computers and other electronic items. ¿Tienes una computadora portátil / cámara digital / videocámara, etc.? ¿Para qué se usa? ¿Para escribir? ¿Para escuchar música? **¿Para sacar fotos?** To practice colors, introduce the word **funda** *(case)* and ask about the color of their phone or laptop cases.

Products like the iPod®, the iPhone®, Android™, the Blackberry®, Bluetooth®, etc., can all be referred to in English when speaking in Spanish. For example, **¿Tienes un iPhone? ¿De qué color es tu iPod?**

>> Aparatos electrónicos

el asistente electrónico *electronic notebook*
la cámara digital *digital camera*
la cámara web *webcam*
el MP3 portátil *portable MP3 player*
el reproductor / grabador de discos compactos *CD player / burner*
el reproductor / grabador de DVD *DVD player / burner*
la tableta *tablet computer*
el teléfono inteligente / smartphone *smartphone*
la videocámara *videocamera*

© Cengage Learning 2013

ACTIVIDADES

M **4 Las emociones** Las siguientes personas están en ciertas situaciones. ¿Cómo crees que están? *Answers may vary.*

1. A Raúl le gusta navegar por Internet y jugar videojuegos. Hay una tormenta *(thunderstorm)* y por eso no hay electricidad en su casa. No tiene nada *(nothing)* que hacer. Está aburrido.

2. Blanca acaba de comprar una computadora portátil pero cuando llega a casa, no funciona. Está furiosa / enojada.

3. Julio tiene que escribir una composición de diez páginas para su clase de historia mañana y todavía no ha empezado *(hasn't begun)*. Está nervioso.

4. Mañana Luis tiene que ir al trabajo por tres horas, estudiar para un examen y hacer una investigación en Internet para la clase de filosofía. Está ocupado.

5. Sabrina trabaja diez horas en la biblioteca, va a su clase de aeróbicos y camina a casa del gimnasio. Está cansada.

6. Marcos y Marina toman un refresco, escuchan música y conversan en un café en la Plaza Mayor. Están contentos.

👥 **5 ¿Eres un(a) tecnogeek o un(a) tecnófobo(a)?** With a partner, come up
C with a list of items related to technology. Use a point system of 1–5 to rate how tech-savvy someone is (1 = the least advanced and 5 = the most advanced). Then, in groups of four or five, ask each person in the group about each item. Based on your findings, decide who is the most technologically advanced and who is the most technologically inexperienced in the group. Report your findings to the class.

Sample items

teléfono inteligente

computadora portátil

tableta

perfil *(profile)* en Facebook

más de una dirección de e-mail

revista *(magazine)* de tecnología

tomar clases virtuales en línea *(take classes online)*

bajar videos de YouTube

👥 **6 El Corte Inglés** El Corte Inglés es el almacén *(department store)* más
C grande en España. Con un(a) compañero(a), busca el sitio web del Corte Inglés. Entren en el Departamento de Electrónica y contesten las siguientes preguntas.

1. ¿Cuáles son las subcategorías en el Departamento de Electrónica?

2. Entren en la subcategoría DVD & Blu Ray. Nombren tres productos que hay allí y sus precios en euros (€).

3. Quieren comprarle un regalo *(gift)* a un amigo a quien le gusta la música. Busquen un regalo apropiado. ¿Qué es? ¿Cuánto cuesta?

4. Quieren comprarle un regalo a una amiga a quien le gusta grabar videos, pero no tienen mucho dinero *(money)*. Busquen la videocámara con el precio más bajo *(lowest price)*.

5. ¿Qué producto electrónico quieres comprar? ¿Cuánto cuesta?

Learning objective: Analyzing

Culture: The concept of the **plaza mayor** or the main square is historically an urban-organizing feature in many European cities that dates back to Roman times. The main square hosted markets, and was also used for bullfights. Many cities and towns in Spain and Latin America today have main squares that are used for public gatherings such as concerts, or house cafés, restaurants, and shops.

Optional: Write the following question: **Antes de clase, ¿qué acabas de hacer?** Then pinpoint an actual time that occurred before your class, for example, **a las doce y cuarto, antes de clase...** Act out examples using activities from your pre-class routine, such as **Acabo de mandar un correo electrónico a mis estudiantes. Acabo de trabajar con unos estudiantes en mi oficina.** Then refer back to the question and have students fill in the blank with things that they have just recently done: **Acabo de _____.** Stress the use of the infinitive.

Optional: Encourage students who use social neworks such as Facebook and Twitter to switch their language settings to Spanish, and to "like" pages in Spanish. Also, you may want to model with students how to "hispanicize" the pronunciation of words like Facebook and Twitter, so that they understand that although these words look like English words, they will not necessarily sound like English in a Spanish conversation.

Learning objectives: Understanding, Applying

Answers, Act. 6: 1. Televisión, DVD & Blu Ray, Home Cinema, Sonido Hifi, Sonido Portátil, Videocámaras, Fotografía, Servicio de revelado digital, Telescopios, Instrumentos musicales, Electrónica Automóvil, Telefonía, Recargas telefónicas, Accesorios Electrónica 2.–5. *Answers will vary.*

▶ >> Vocabulario útil 3

BETO: ¿Tú? ¿Tú eres Autora14?

DULCE: Sí, yo soy Autora14. ¿Por qué preguntas?

BETO: No, no, nada. ¿Te gustan los **grupos de conversación**?

DULCE: No, en realidad, no. Prefiero el **correo electrónico**.

You are learning two words for e-mail: **correo electrónico** and **e-mail**. **Correo electrónico** refers more to the whole system of e-mail or a group of e-mails, while **el e-mail** refers to a specific e-mail message.

To say you are going to post something on your Facebook page, you can say:

Voy a publicar un post en mi página de Facebook.

Voy a publicar mi estado *(status).*

Voy a publicar mis noticias *(news).*

Voy a publicar algo en el muro *(wall)* **de mi amigo Javier.**

Voy a subir / bajar fotos / videos a mi página de Facebook.

Optional: This vocabulary can be expanded with more specific questions about students' online habits and sites. For example: **¿Visitas las librerías electrónicas? ¿Cuáles? ¿Cómo se llaman? ¿Qué compras allí? (¿Libros? ¿MP3s? ¿Películas?) ¿Tienes un sitio web favorito o personal?**

>> Funciones de Internet

acceder *to access*
el blog *blog*
el buscador *search engine*
el buzón electrónico *electronic mailbox*
chatear *to chat online*
el ciberespacio *cyberspace*
la conexión *connection*
hacer una conexión *to get online*
cortar la conexión *to get offline, disconnect*
la contraseña *password*
el correo electrónico / el e-mail *e-mail*
en línea *online*
el enlace *link*
el foro *forum*
el grupo de conversación *chat room*
el grupo de noticias *news group*
la página web *web page*
el proveedor de acceso *Internet provider*
la red mundial *World Wide Web*
la red social *social networking site*
el sitio web *website*
el usuario *user*
el wifi *wifi, wireless connection*

© Cengage Learning 2013

Standards: While working through the survey, students will interpret written language (C 1.2: Interpretive Communication) and express opinions (C 1.1: Interpersonal Communication).

7 **¡Gran sorteo!** Completa el cuestionario para el concurso *(contest)* de
I la revista *DIGITAL en Español*. Compara tus respuestas con las respuestas de diez compañeros de clase. Haz una gráfica como la de la página 130 que muestre *(shows)* los resultados de tu cuestionario. Llena los espacios en blanco *(Fill in the blanks)* con el número de estudiantes que marcaron *(marked)* esa respuesta.

Digital en Español

¡GRAN SORTEO!

Participe en el sorteo de *Digital en Español* y gánate una impresora multifunción que puede colocarse perfectamente sobre cualquier escritorio. Además, resulta fácil de usar y funciona como impresora, escáner, copiadora y fax. Este modelo puede ser conectado fácilmente a tu computadora con conexiones inalámbricas Bluetooth 2.0 o Wi-Fi.

1. ¿Usas computadora portátil o una de escritorio?
_____ portátil
_____ de escritorio
_____ ninguna de las dos

2. ¿Tienes teléfono inteligente o celular sin capacidades de computadora?
_____ inteligente
_____ celular

3. ¿Tienes tableta?
_____ sí
_____ no

4. ¿Cuál de tus aparatos electrónicos usas con más frecuencia?
_____ teléfono inteligente
_____ teléfono celular
_____ tableta
_____ computadora portátil
_____ otro aparato

5. ¿Cómo usas tu teléfono con más frecuencia?
_____ para hablar por teléfono
_____ para enviar mensajes de texto
_____ para navegar Internet
_____ para publicar en las redes sociales como Facebook y Twitter
_____ otro

6. ¿Para qué usas Internet principalmente? Indica sólo tres usos.
_____ compras
_____ servicios de banco
_____ investigaciones
_____ correo electrónico
_____ redes sociales
_____ para mantener mi sitio web
_____ para publicar un blog
_____ ver videos en YouTube
_____ otro

7. ¿Cuántas veces por día publicas algo en Facebook?
_____ 0
_____ 1-3
_____ 4-6
_____ más de 7

8. ¿Cuál es tu modo preferido de comunicación con tus amigos?
_____ hablar por teléfono
_____ enviar mensajes de texto
_____ enviar e-mails
_____ publicar en Facebook
_____ tuitear
_____ persona a persona
_____ otro

1. _____ portátil		5.	_____ para hablar por teléfono	
_____ de escritorio			_____ para enviar mensajes de texto	
_____ ninguna de las dos			_____ para navegar Internet	
			_____ para publicar en las redes sociales como Facebook y Twitter	
			_____ otro	
2. _____ inteligente		6.	_____ compras	
_____ celular			_____ servicios de banco	
			_____ investigaciones	
			_____ correo electrónico	
			_____ social media	
			_____ para mantener mi sitio web	
			_____ para publicar un blog	
			_____ ver videos en YouTube	
			_____ otro	
3. _____ sí		7.	_____ 0	
_____ no			_____ 1–3	
			_____ 4–6	
			_____ más de 7	
4. _____ teléfono inteligente		8.	_____ hablar por teléfono	
_____ teléfono celular			_____ enviar mensajes de texto	
_____ tableta			_____ enviar e-mails	
_____ computadora portátil			_____ publicar en Facebook	
_____ otro aparato			_____ tuitear	
			_____ persona a persona	
			_____ otro	

8 **¿Cómo usas Internet?** ¿Qué más quieres saber sobre *(do you want to know about)* los hábitos de tus compañeros acerca de Internet? Escribe cinco preguntas más como las del cuestionario en la **Actividad 7**. Luego, hazle las preguntas a tu compañero(a) de clase y que él o ella te haga *(have him or her ask you)* sus preguntas.

C

MODELO *¿Te gustan las redes sociales? ¿Cuántas horas al día pasas en las redes sociales?*
¿Tienes un blog? ¿Cuántas veces por semana escribes en tu blog?

Learning objective: Creating

C **9** **Mi blog** Escribe un blog para describir como usas Internet. Ponle todos los detalles que puedas *(that you can)*. Usa las ideas de la **Actividad 8**, de la lista o inventa otras.

Opciones:

- ¿qué te gusta hacer en Internet?
- ¿usas el teléfono inteligente para acceder a Internet?
- ¿cuáles son tus aparatos electrónicos preferidos?
- ¿qué clase de videos te gusta bajar o subir?
- ¿usas la computadora para ver programas de la televisión?
- ¿cuál es tu modo de comunicación preferido?
- ¿…?

C **10** **La red social** Escribe tu perfil en español para tu página en la red social. Además de la información básica, escribe un párrafo sobre tu personalidad. Explica un poco sobre tu relación con la tecnología. ¿Eres tecnofóbico o tecnomaestro?

Learning objectives: Applying, Analyzing

11 **¿Qué estás pensando?** Ten una conversación con un(a) compañero(a)
C sobre un post que piensas publicar en la página de tu red social. El post describe cómo vas a usar la tecnología hoy.

MODELO Tú: *Voy a compartir unas fotos en mi red social.*
Compañero(a): *¡Qué divertido! ¿Estás tú en las fotos?*

12 **Los cursos virtuales** Hoy en día es posible tomar cursos virtuales por
C Internet. Hay muchas universidades de habla española que ofrecen una gran variedad de cursos a distancia.

En grupos de cuatro, escojan *(choose)* un país de la lista de abajo. Visiten los sitios web que corresponden a ese país, usando la lista de enlaces que está en **www.cengagebrain.com**.

Países: España, México, Argentina

1. ¿Qué cursos virtuales ofrece la universidad o escuela?
2. ¿En el sitio web es posible hacer una visita virtual? ¿Hay información sobre los profesores de los cursos? ¿Sobre los otros estudiantes?
3. Después de obtener toda la información sobre este sitio web, compárenla con la información de los otros grupos.

Culture: Spain has been at the forefront of web-based, distance learning with a large public university called **la Universidad Nacional de la Educación a Distancia (UNED)**.

Optional: Have a discussion about online courses: **¿Hay ventajas en tomar un curso virtual en español? ¿Cuáles son? ¿Cuáles son las desventajas? ¿Te gusta más la idea de matricularte en un curso virtual de una universidad de habla española o la de visitar el país para tomar el curso en persona? ¿Por qué?**

Standard 5.1: Students use Spanish through virtual educational communities beyond the school setting.

© Shutterstock/enigmatico

ESTRATEGIA

Watching without sound

Sometimes it helps to watch a segment first without the sound, especially when it contains a lot of action. As you watch, focus on the characters' actions and interactions. What do you think is happening? Once you have gotten some ideas, watch the segment a second time with the sound turned on.

Antes de ver Lee la lista de eventos que ocurren en este episodio.

_____ Beto descubre que su computadora no tiene suficiente memoria.

_____ Dulce tiene el asistente electrónico de Beto.

_____ Beto está furioso porque tiene que escribir el examen con bolígrafo y papel.

_____ Beto llega tarde a clase.

_____ Beto ve una hoja de papel con el e-mail de Autora14.

_____ Beto deja su asistente electrónico en el salón de clase.

▶ **Ver** Mira el episodio para el **Capítulo 4** sin sonido *(sound)*.

Después de ver 1 Ahora vuelve a *(go back to)* **Antes de ver** y usa números para poner *(to put)* la lista en el órden correcto. 2, 5, 3, 1, 6, 4

Después de ver 2 Mira el episodio otra vez—ahora con sonido—y completa las oraciones siguientes.

1. Beto llega tarde a la clase de _____literatura_____.
2. Según Chela, ella está muy _____aburrida_____ con la historia trágica de Beto.
3. La dirección electrónica de _____Dulce_____ es Autora14.
4. Dulce prefiere el correo electrónico a _____los grupos de conversación_____.

Después de ver 3 En tu opinión, ¿de qué hablan Dulce y Beto mientras salen juntos al final del episodio? Basándote en lo que ya sabes de sus personalidades, escribe una conversación breve entre ellos mientras se conocen *(they get to know each other)* un poco mejor.

© Cengage Learning 2013

Learning objective: Remembering

Standard 3.1: Students use Spanish while they make connections with other disciplines (e. g., sociology, business).

>> Voces del mundo hispano

© Cengage Learning 2013

En el video para este capítulo Juan Pedro, Patricia y Sergio hablan de los aparatos tecnológicos y sus hábitos con relación a Internet. Lee las siguientes oraciones. Después mira el video una o más veces para decir si las oraciones son ciertas (**C**) o falsas (**F**).

1. Juan Pedro y Patricia tienen una cámara digital. **F**
2. Sergio tiene un reproductor de MP3. **C**
3. A Juan Pedro le gusta mucho su reproductor de discos compactos. **C**
4. A Patricia le gusta usar su ordenador (computadora) para chatear. **C**
5. Patricia sólo usa Internet durante los días de entresemana. **F**
6. A Sergio no le gusta usar e-mail ni *(nor)* Skype. **F**

🔊 >> Voces de Estados Unidos

Track 11

Thaddeus Arroyo, director ejecutivo de información

PRN Images

En la escuela, las matemáticas y la lógica siempre fueron las materias preferidas de Thaddeus Arroyo. Hoy en día, Arroyo, que es Director Ejecutivo de Información *(Chief Information Officer)* en AT&T, es uno de los líderes del campo de la informática y uno de los ejecutivos más importantes del país. Arroyo es conocido mundialmente *(worldwide)* por hacer posible la fusión *(merger)* de Cingular Wireless y AT&T Wireless, creando así la mayor red del país, con unos 60 millones de usuarios. De padre español y madre mexicana, Arroyo explica su éxito *(success)* profesional de esta manera:

❝**Mi mamá y mi papá, los dos, fueron inmigrantes y se concentraron en la educación. Ellos no me permitieron creer que existían barreras insuperables. Creo que más que otra cosa es la fe en el arte de la posibilidad.**❞ *("Both my parents were immigrants and focused on education. They would never let me believe there was any barrier I couldn't overcome. I think more than anything else it was believing in the art of the possibility.")*

¿Y tú? En tu opinión, ¿qué tipo de preparación escolar y características personales son necesarias para ser un líder en el campo de la tecnología?

¡Prepárate!

Expressing likes and dislikes: **Gustar** with nouns and other verbs like **gustar**

© Cengage Learning 2013

¿**Te gustan** los grupos de conversación?

> Remember that when you use **gustar** + infinitive you only use **gusta: Les gusta comer en la cafetería.**

Standard 4.1: Emphasize that the person doing the liking is expressed by the indirect object in Spanish. Compare **me gusta** with the English construction *it is pleasing to me.*

Optional: Explain examples with the translation *to be pleasing* (i.e., it is pleasing to me, they are pleasing to me) emphasizing that the person (**me, te, le,** etc.) is receiving the action.

Notice: For true beginners, point out the **formas singulares** and **formas plurales** of **gustar** and pronouns for awareness and reinforcement.

> You will learn more about Spanish indirect object pronouns in **Chapter 8.**

Heritage Learners: Give a dictation with a series of statements with **gustar** to train heritage learners to notice pronouns, verb endings, and grammatical nuance.

Cómo usarlo

As you learned in **Chapter 2,** you can use **gustar** with an infinitive to say what activities you and other people like to do.

Me gusta estudiar en la biblioteca, pero **a Vicente le gusta estudiar** en la cafetería.	*I like to study in the library, but Vicente likes to study in the cafeteria.*

You can also use **gustar** with nouns, to say what thing or things you (and others) like or dislike. In this case, you use **gusta** with a single noun and **gustan** with plural nouns or a series of nouns.

—¿**Te gusta** esta **computadora?**	*Do you like this computer?*
—Sí, ¡pero **me gustan** más estas **portátiles**!	*Yes, but I like these laptops more!*

When you make negative sentences with **gusta** and **gustan,** you use **no** before the pronoun + **gusta / gustan.**

Nos gustan los programas de diseño gráfico, pero **no nos gustan** los programas de arte.	*We like the graphic design programs, but we don't like the art programs.*

Cómo formarlo

LO BÁSICO

- In Spanish, an *indirect object pronoun* is used with **gustar** to say who likes something. Because **gustar** literally means to *please,* the indirect object answers the question: *Pleases whom?*
- A *prepositional pronoun* is a pronoun that is used after a preposition, such as **a** or **de.**

1. As you have already learned, you must use forms of **gustar** with the correct indirect object pronoun.

Me gusta	el foro.	**Nos gusta**	el foro.
Me gustan	los foros.	**Nos gustan**	los foros.
Te gusta	el foro.	**Os gusta**	el foro.
Te gustan	los foros.	**Os gustan**	los foros.
Le gusta	el foro.	**Les gusta**	el foro.
Le gustan	los foros.	**Les gustan**	los foros.

2. As you have learned, if you want to *emphasize* or *clarify* who likes what, you can use **a** + name or noun, or **a** + prepositional pronoun. Note that when **a** + prepositional pronoun is used, there is often no direct translation in English. Notice that except for **mí** and **ti**, the prepositional pronouns are the same as the subject pronouns you already know.

Prepositional pronoun	Indirect object pronoun	Form of **gustar** + noun
A mí	**me**	gustan los videojuegos.
A ti	**te**	gustan los videojuegos.
A Ud. / a él / a ella	**le**	gustan los videojuegos.
A nosotros / a nosotras	**nos**	gustan los videojuegos.
A vosotros / a vosotras	**os**	gustan los videojuegos.
A Uds. / a ellos / a ellas	**les**	gustan los videojuegos.

Notice that while **mí** takes an accent, **ti** does not.

A mí me gustan los MP3 portátiles pero **a Elena** no le gustan.
A ella le gustan los teléfonos inteligentes que también tocan MP3s.

*I like MP3 players, but **Elena** doesn't like them.*
***She** likes smartphones that also play MP3s.*

Suggestion: With heritage learners and high beginners, point out additional verbs like **gustar: doler** *(to hurt, pain, ache)*, **faltar** *(to be missing, lack)*, **hacer falta** *(to need)*, **parecer** *(to seem, appear)*, **quedar** *(to have left, remain)*, **sorprender** *(to be surprising)*.

3. A number of other Spanish verbs are used like **gustar.** These verbs are usually just used in two forms, as is **gustar.**

—**Me interesan** mucho estos celulares.
—¿No **te molesta** la recepción mala aquí?

I'm interested in these cell phones.
Doesn't the bad reception here bother you?

Other verbs like **gustar**	
encantar *to like a lot*	**¡Me encanta** la tecnología!
fascinar *to fascinate*	A Ana **le fascinan** esos sitios web.
importar *to be important to someone; to mind*	**Nos importa** tener acceso a Internet. ¿**Te importa** si usamos la computadora?
interesar *to interest, to be interesting*	A ellos **les interesan** las redes sociales.
molestar *to bother*	**Nos molestan** las computadoras viejas.

Optional: To practice these courtesy expressions, have students get up out of their seats, pretend to bump into each other, and come up with an appropriate exchange. Model one exchange with a student before beginning the activity.

In Spanish-speaking cultures, courtesy is of utmost importance. It is very common to use phrases like **¿Le importa?** or **¿Le molesta?** to ask someone a question. **¿Le importa si uso la computadora?** would be more likely heard than **Voy a usar la computadora** or **¿Puedo usar la computadora?** It's also common to use **por favor** when asking a question and **gracias** upon receiving the answer. Other common expressions of courtesy are:

¡Perdón! / ¡Disculpe! / ¡Lo siento! *Pardon me! / Excuse me! / I'm sorry!*

No hay de qué. / No se preocupe.

No problem. / Not to worry.

Con permiso. *Excuse me. . . / With your permission. . .*

Cómo no. *Of course. / Certainly.*

ACTIVIDADES

I **1** **¿Te gusta?** Di si te gustan o no las siguientes cosas.

MODELO (Me gustan / No me gustan) las computadoras portátiles.
Me gustan las computadoras portátiles.

1. (Me gustan / No me gustan) los juegos interactivos de tenis.
2. (Me gusta / no me gusta) el sitio web de YouTube.
3. (Me gustan / No me gustan) las clases virtuales.
4. (Me gustan / No me gustan) los aparatos electrónicos.
5. (Me gusta / No me gusta) el nuevo CD de Paulina Rubio.
6. (Me gustan / No me gustan) los sitios web y foros sobre España.

M **2** **Los gustos** Para cada persona, di si le gustan o no las cosas indicadas.

MODELO los teléfonos inteligentes / Marío (no)
A Mario no le gustan los teléfonos inteligentes.

1. las computadoras portátiles / tú (sí)
2. las cámaras digitales / Sara y Laura (sí)
3. los juegos interactivos / usted (no)
4. las redes sociales / nosotros (sí)
5. los foros sobre los autos / ustedes (no)
6. los podcasts / tú (no)
7. los grupos de noticias / yo (¿…?)
8. las tabletas / yo (¿…?)

M **3** **¿Qué les gusta o gustan?** Mira los dibujos y di qué les gusta (o gustan) a las personas indicadas. Sigue el modelo y usa **gusta** o **gustan** según la(s) cosa(s) o la actividad indicadas.

MODELOS Martina / navegar en Internet
A Martina le gusta navegar en Internet.

1.

Roque / las computadores portátiles

2.

ustedes / jugar juegos interactivos

3.

nosotros / las tabletas

4.

tú / tu videocámara

5.

yo / mi teléfono inteligente

6.

los niños / ver los videos en la computadora

4 **¿Y ustedes?** Pregúntales a varios compañeros de clase sobre sus gustos.

M/C

MODELO Facebook (Twitter, Yelp, Foursquare, ¿…?)
   Tú: *¿Les gusta Facebook?*
   Compañero(a): *Sí, me gusta Facebook, pero no me gusta Twitter.*

1. el grupo de noticias de profesores de español (de artistas chilenos, de actores de teatro, ¿…?)
2. la página web de Yahoo! en español (de *People en español*, de *Newsweek* o *CNN en español*, ¿…?)
3. el foro de estudiantes de español (de profesores de español, de estudiantes de francés, ¿…?)
4. los juegos interactivos (de mesa, de niños, ¿…?)
5. las computadoras portátiles (PC, Mac, ¿…?)
6. el programa de arte (de diseño gráfico, de contabilidad, ¿…?)

5 **¿Te interesa?** Pregúntale a un(a) compañero(a) qué opina *(feels)* sobre varios aspectos de la tecnología.

C

MODELO interesar: los blogs de personas desconocidas *(strangers)*
   Tú: *¿Te interesan los blogs de personas desconocidas?*
   Compañero(a): *No, no me interesan los blogs de personas desconocidas.*

1. molestar: recibir mucha correspondencia electrónica
2. interesar: grupos de noticias
3. gustar: enviar mensajes de texto
4. molestar: buscadores muy lentos *(slow)*
5. interesar: sitios web comerciales
6. gustar: chatear con personas en otros países
7. importar: recibir e-mails de personas desconocidas

Suggestion: Warm up or follow up Activity 5 with additional questions: ¿Te gusta recibir correo electrónico? ¿De quién? ¿Te interesan los cursos virtuales? ¿Te gustan los teléfonos celulares? ¿Te molesta el uso de los teléfonos celulares en los coches? ¿En clase? ¿En restaurantes?, etc.

Answers, Act. 5: 1. ¿Te molesta recibir mucha correspondencia electrónica? 2. ¿Te interesan los grupos de noticias? 3. ¿Te gusta enviar mensajes de texto? 4. ¿Te molestan los buscadores muy lentos? 5. ¿Te interesan los sitios web comerciales? 6. ¿Te gusta chatear con personas en otros países? 7. ¿Te importa recibir e-mails de personas desconocidas?

Learning objectives: Applying, Analyzing

6 **Encuesta** Haz una encuesta con tus compañeros de clase. Pregúntales si les gustan las cosas y actividades indicadas. Después, con la clase entera, comparen los resultados para ver cuáles son los gustos y preferencias de todos los estudiantes.

C

_____ ¿los juegos interactivos o los juegos tradicionales?
_____ ¿los textos digitales o los libros?
_____ ¿las clases en la universidad o las clases virtuales?
_____ ¿estudiar en la biblioteca o estudiar en un café?
_____ ¿escuchar música cuando estudias o estudiar sin música?
_____ ¿ver películas en la computadora o ver películas en el televisor?

7 **La tecnología** Pregúntales a seis compañeros qué les gusta de la tecnología y qué les molesta. Escribe un resumen sobre los resultados.

C

MODELO *¿Cuáles son tres cosas que te gustan de la tecnología?*
   ¿Cuáles son tres cosas que te molestan?

Learning objectives: Applying, Analyzing

Gramática útil 2

Describing yourself and others and expressing conditions and locations: The verb **estar** and the uses of **ser** and **estar**

Estoy muy **aburrida** con tu cuento trágico.

Suggestion: Reinforce this grammar topic with the statement: <u>Estar se usa para describir el estado y para decir dónde.</u> Write these terms on the board, and ask students to come up with 5–7 examples of each: **Estado = Estoy nerviosa. Dónde = Estoy en clase.**

Heritage Learners: The rules that govern the use of **ser** and **estar** in U.S. Spanish are not always the same as those of standard Spanish. In particular, the verb **estar** is sometimes used in cases where standard Spanish uses **ser.** For this reason, it is important go over the uses of **ser** and **estar** carefully with native speakers. U.S. Spanish: **El apartamento está pequeño.** Standard Spanish: **El apartamento es pequeño.**

Preparation: Bring a ball or other object(s) that can be tossed, moved, or passed around the classroom. Locate the object(s) with **¿Dónde está / están?**

Cómo usarlo

You already know that the verb **ser** is translated as *to be* in English. You have already used the verb **estar**, which is also translated as *to be*, in expressions such as **¿Cómo estás?** While both these Spanish verbs mean *to be*, they are used in different ways.

1. Use **estar . . .**
   - to express location of people, places, or objects.

     La profesora Suárez **está** en la biblioteca. | *Professor Suárez **is** in the library.*
     Los libros **están** en la mesa. | *The books **are** on the table.*

   - to talk about a physical condition.

     —¿Cómo **está** usted? | *How **are** you?*
     —**Estoy** muy bien, gracias. | *I'm well, thank you.*
     —Yo **estoy** un poco cansada. | *I'm a little tired.*

   - to talk about emotional conditions.

     El señor Albrega **está** un poco nervioso hoy. | *Mr. Albrega **is** a little nervous today.*
     Estoy muy ocupada esta semana. | *I'm very busy this week.*

2. Use **ser . . .**
   - to identify yourself and others.

     Soy Ana y ésta **es** mi hermana Luisa. | *I'm Ana and this **is** my sister Luisa.*

   - to indicate profession.

     Pablo Picasso **es** un artista famoso. | *Pablo Picasso **is** a famous artist.*

   - to describe personality traits and physical features.

     Somos altos y delgados. | *We **are** tall and thin.*
     Somos estudiantes buenos. | *We **are** good students.*

   - to give time and date.

     Es la una. Hoy **es** miércoles. | *It **is** one o'clock. Today **is** Wednesday.*

   - to indicate nationality and origin.

     —**Eres** española, ¿no? | *You **are** Spanish, right?*
     —Sí, **soy** de España. | *Yes, I **am** from Spain.*

   - to express possession with **de.**

     Este celular **es de Anita.** | *This **is Anita's** cell phone.*

   - to give the location of an event.

     La fiesta **es** en la residencia estudiantil. | *The party **is** in the dorm.*

Notice that expressing the location of people, places, and things (other than events) requires the use of **estar. Ser** is used only to indicate *where an event will take place*.

Cómo formarlo

1. Here are the forms of the verb **estar** in the present indicative tense.

estar *(to be)*			
yo	**estoy**	nosotros / nosotras	**estamos**
tú	**estás**	vosotros / vosotras	**estáis**
Ud. / él / ella	**está**	Uds. / ellos / ellas	**están**

2. In the **¡Imagínate!** section you learned some adjectives that are commonly used with **estar** to describe physical and emotional conditions.

aburrido(a)   nervioso(a)
cansado(a)   ocupado(a)
contento(a)   preocupado(a)
enfermo(a)   seguro(a)
enojado(a)   triste
furioso(a)

Don't forget that when you use adjectives with **estar,** as with any other verb, they need to agree with the person or thing they are describing in both gender and number.

Los estudiantes están
  preocupados por Miguel.
Elena está nerviosa a causa
  del examen.

The students are worried
  about Miguel.
Elena is nervous because of
  the exam.

ACTIVIDADES

I **8** **¿Dónde están?** Todos participan en diferentes actividades en diferentes lugares de la universidad. ¿Dónde están?

MODELO   Ricardo y Juana estudian. (Está / <u>Están</u>) en la biblioteca.

1. Javier toma un refresco. (Está / Estás) en la cafetería. Está
2. Mi compañero(a) de cuarto y yo descansamos. (Estoy / Estamos) en la residencia estudiantil. Estamos
3. Paula y Pedro navegan por Internet. (Estamos / Están) en el centro de computación. Están
4. La profesora Martínez lee una novela. (Estás / Está) en el parque. Está
5. Usted escribe en la pizarra. (Está / Están) en el salón de clase. Está
6. Nosotros escuchamos el audio de la clase de español. (Estoy / Estamos) en el centro de comunicaciones. Estamos
7. Teresa levanta pesas. (Está / Están) en el gimnasio. Está
8. Tú compras un libro para la clase de filosofía. (Estás / Está) en la librería. Estás

M **9** **¿Cómo están?** Tú y varias personas están en las siguientes situaciones. Usa **estar** + adjetivo para describir cómo están. Usa adjetivos de la lista.

Adjetivos: aburrido(a), cansado(a), contento(a), enfermo(a), enojado(a), nervioso(a), ocupado(a), preocupado(a), triste

MODELO Sales bien en el examen de francés, tomas el sol por la tarde, cenas con tu mejor amigo(a) y alquilas un video que te gusta mucho.
Estoy contento(a).

1. Tienes una entrevista con el director de la universidad para un trabajo que necesitas. Estoy nervioso(a).

2. Carlos tiene una infección y tiene que ir al hospital. Está enfermo.

3. Marta y Mario no tienen nada *(nothing)* que hacer *(to do)* —no hay nada interesante en la tele y su computadora no funciona. Están aburridos.

4. Compras una nueva computadora. Llegas a casa y cuando tratas de usarla, no funciona. La tienda de computadoras no abre hasta el lunes. Estoy enojado(a).

5. Tú y tu familia tienen mucho que hacer. Entre los estudios, el trabajo, los deportes, la familia y los amigos, no hay suficiente tiempo en el día para hacerlo todo. Estamos ocupados.

6. Elena practica deportes por la mañana, trabaja en la biblioteca por la tarde y estudia por la noche. Cuando llega a casa, descansa. Está cansada.

7. La tarea de matemáticas es muy difícil —Martín no comprende las instrucciones. Es muy tarde para llamar a un amigo. Tiene que entregar la tarea muy temprano por la mañana. Está preocupado.

8. El abuelo *(grandfather)* de Pedro y Delia está muy enfermo. Pedro y Delia lo visitan en el hospital. Están tristes / preocupados.

Learning objective: Understanding M **10** **Yo soy…** Completa las oraciones con la forma correcta de **ser** o **estar**.

MODELO Yo _____ estudiante. _____ en clase.
Yo soy estudiante. Estoy en clase.

1. El señor Ortega ___está___ muy ocupado.
___Está___ en la oficina.

2. Nosotros ___somos___ divertidos.
___Estamos___ contentos ahora.

3. Rogelio ___es___ profesor.
___Es___ alto y delgado.

4. Alejandro y yo ___somos___ de Barcelona.
___Estamos___ aquí en Estados Unidos por un año.

5. Pedro y Arturo ___están___ enfermos.
___Están___ en el hospital.

6. Esta computadora ___es___ de Lucía.
Lucía ___es___ una estudiante muy trabajadora.

11 ***¿Ser o estar?*** Trabaja con un(a) compañero(a) de clase para completar
C las oraciones. Lean las oraciones y juntos decidan si se debe usar **ser** o **estar**.
Escriban la forma correcta del verbo. Luego, escriban por qué se usa **ser** o **estar**.

MODELO *Soy* María Hernández Catina.
   razón *(reason): identidad*

Razones: característica física, característica de personalidad, estado físico,
estado temporáneo, fecha, hora, identidad, lugar de un evento, nacionalidad,
posesión, posición *(location)*, profesión

1. ¿Cómo ____está____ usted, profesor Taboada? razón: estado físico
2. Yo ____estoy____ un poco cansado hoy. razón: estado físico
3. Isabel ____es____ de España. razón: nacionalidad
4. ¿Dónde ____está____ la biblioteca? razón: posición
5. Mi padre ____es____ profesor de lenguas. razón: profesión
6. Hoy ____es____ miércoles, el 22 de octubre. razón: fecha
7. Nati ____es____ alta, delgada y tiene el pelo castaño. razón: característica física
8. Esta semana Leonardo ____está____ muy ocupado. razón: estado temporáneo
9. Este libro, ¿ ____es____ de la profesora? razón: posesión
10. ¿Dónde ____es____ la clase de filosofía? razón: lugar de un evento

12 ***¡Pobre Mónica!*** Trabaja con un(a) compañero(a) de clase. Miren
C el dibujo y juntos escriban una descripción de Mónica y de la situación en
general. Traten de usar **ser** o **estar** en cada oración y de escribir por lo menos
cinco oraciones.

Suggestion, Act. 11: Model
contrasting statements to warm up
for **Activity 11:** Hernando es alto y
muy delgado. Es estudiante. Está
ocupado. Está preocupado. Then
select a class member and ask the
class to describe him/her: **¿Cómo
es** *(name)?* ¿Cómo está en este
momento?

Answers, Act. 12: *Possible answers:*
Mónica es alta y muy delgada.
Es estudiante. Está ocupada. Está
preocupada. Hoy es martes. La fiesta
es hoy en casa de Mónica.

In Spanish-speaking
countries, **martes 13,** or
Tuesday the 13th, rather
than Friday the 13th,
is considered an
unlucky day.

Sonrisas

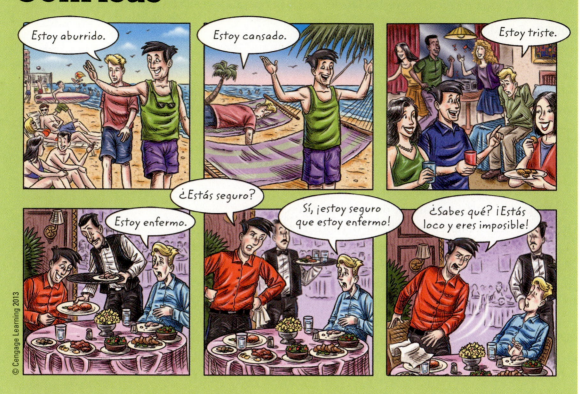

Comprensión En tu opinión, ¿cuáles de los siguientes adjetivos describen al hombre rubio? Y al hombre moreno?

- ¿Quién está…?

  aburrido / cansado / contento / enfermo / furioso / nervioso / ocupado / preocupado / seguro / triste

- ¿Quién es…?

  activo / antipático / cómico / cuidadoso / divertido / egoísta / extrovertido / impaciente / introvertido / perezoso / serio / simpático / tonto

Answers, Comprensión: El hombre rubio está aburrido, cansado, enfermo, nervioso, preocupado, seguro y triste. El hombre moreno está contento y furioso. El hombre rubio es antipático, egoísta, serio y tonto. El hombre moreno es activo, divertido, extrovertido y simpático.

Gramática útil 3

Talking about everyday events: Stem-changing verbs in the present indicative

Cómo usarlo

In **Chapters 1** and **2** you learned the present indicative forms of regular **-ar, -er,** and **-ir** verbs in Spanish. There are other Spanish verbs that use the same endings as regular **-ar, -er,** and **-ir** verbs in this tense, but they also have a small change in their stem. (Remember that the stem is the part of the infinitive that is left after you remove the **-ar / -er / -ir** ending.)

¡Pobre Beto! **Siento** tu frustración.

© Cengage Learning 2013

—¿Qué **piensas** de este MP3 portátil?

—Me gusta, pero **prefiero** éste.

—¿Verdad? Bueno, ¿por qué no le **pides** el precio al dependiente?

*What **do you think** of this MP3 player?*

*I like it, but I **prefer** this one.*

*Really? Well, why don't **you ask** the sales clerk the price?*

Cómo formarlo

1. There are three categories of stem-changing verbs in the present indicative.

	o → ue: encontrar (to find)	e → ie: preferir (to prefer)	e → i: pedir (to ask for)
yo	encuentro	prefiero	pido
tú	encuentras	prefieres	pides
Ud. / él / ella	encuentra	prefiere	pide
nosotros / nosotras	encontramos	preferimos	pedimos
vosotros / vosotras	encontráis	preferís	pedís
Uds. / ellos / ellas	encuentran	prefieren	piden

Suggestion: Show students that these are "boot" verbs to help them remember which forms have the stem change. Write out the conjugation of a stem-changing verb (**un verbo que tiene un cambio en el radical o la raíz**) in two columns (singular and plural). Then draw a line only around the forms that have a stem change. You should be left with a line drawing of a boot.

2. Note that the stem changes in all forms except the **nosotros / nosotras** and **vosotros / vosotras** forms.

3. Remember, all the endings for the present indicative are the same for these verbs as for the other regular verbs you've learned: **-o, -as, -a, -amos, -áis, -an** for **-ar** verbs; **-o, -es, -e, -emos / -imos, -éis / -ís, -en** for **-er** and **-ir** verbs. The only thing that is different here is the change in the stem.

Heritage Learners: Some heritage speakers may use stem changes in the **nosotros** forms of these verbs as well as in the infinitive form (i.e., **piensar, encuentrar,** etc.) Point out that in standard Spanish these forms are not stem-changing.

4. Here are some commonly used Spanish verbs that experience a stem change in the present indicative tense.

Suggestion: Clarify and contrast **pensar de** and **pensar en**: ¿Qué piensas del presidente? vs. ¿Piensas mucho en el futuro?

e → ie

cerrar	*to close*
comenzar (a)	*to begin (to)*
empezar (a)	*to begin (to)*
entender	*to understand*
pensar de	*to think (of), have an opinion about*
pensar en	*to think about, to consider*
perder	*to lose*
preferir	*to prefer*
querer	*to want, to love*
sentir	*to feel*

Suggestion: To present the verbs in context, model a brief narration using as many of these verbs as possible. As you say each, write it on the board and underline the stem change to draw students' attention to the change. For example, **Quiero comprar una computadora nueva. Prefiero comprar una Macintosh. Sueño con una computadora portátil. Probablemente pido la nueva computadora para mi cumpleaños.**

o → ue

contar	*to tell, to relate; to count*
dormir	*to sleep*
encontrar	*to find*
jugar*	*to play*
poder	*to be able to*
sonar	*to ring, to go off (phone, alarm clock, etc.)*
soñar (con)	*to dream (about)*
volver	*to return*

e → i

pedir	*to ask for something*
repetir	*to repeat*
servir	*to serve*

*__Jugar__ is the only **u → ue** stem-changing verb in Spanish. It's grouped with the **o → ue** verbs, because its change is most similar to those.

ACTIVIDADES

I **13** **En la clase de computación** Estás en la clase de computación. Escoge la forma correcta del verbo entre paréntesis para describir lo que hacen todos.

1. Yo (pido / pide) el número de teléfono del nuevo estudiante. pido
2. La profesora (repite / repiten) las instrucciones de la actividad. repite
3. Nosotros (sirvo / servimos) refrescos después de la clase. servimos
4. Él (prefiere / prefieren) usar los mensajes de texto para comunicarse con su familia. prefiere
5. Tú (encontramos / encuentras) la clase muy difícil. encuentras
6. Ellos (piden / pedimos) la dirección electrónica de la universidad. piden
7. Nosotras (preferimos / prefieren) ir a un café con wifi después de clase. preferimos
8. Yo (encuentras / encuentro) la clase muy divertida. encuentro

👥 **14 ¿Entiendes?** Tú tienes que presentar el nuevo sistema de software a un
M grupo diverso de asistentes administrativos. Les preguntas si entienden cómo
hacer ciertas cosas con los nuevos programas. Tu compañero(a) te contesta.

MODELO ¿_____ (ustedes) cómo instalar el programa antivirus? (sí)
Tú: ¿*Entienden cómo instalar el programa antivirus?*
Compañero(a): *Sí, entendemos cómo instalar el programa antivirus.*

1. ¿ _____ (ustedes) cómo abrir la aplicación? (no)
2. ¿ _____ (usted) cómo archivar los documentos al disco duro? (sí)
3. ¿ _____ (tú) cómo funciona el buscador? (no)
4. ¿ _____ (ellos) cómo cortar la conexión a Internet? (sí)
5. ¿ _____ (ustedes) cómo entrar en los foros? (no)
6. ¿ _____ (tú) cómo pedir apoyo técnico (*tech support*)? (sí)

Answers, Act. 14: 1. —¿Entienden cómo abrir la aplicación? —No, no entendemos… 2. —¿Entiende usted cómo archivar los documentos al disco duro? —Sí, entiendo… 3. —¿Entiendes cómo funciona el buscador? —No, no entiendo… 4. —¿Entienden cómo cortar la conexión a Internet? —Sí, entienden… 5. —¿Entienden cómo entrar en los foros? —No, no entendemos… 6. —¿Entiendes cómo pedir apoyo técnico? —Sí, entiendo…

🔊 **15 ¿A qué hora vuelves?** Un amigo te pregunta cuándo vuelven a casa tú,
Track 12 tus amigos y varios miembros de tu familia. Escucha la pregunta y escribe la
M respuesta correcta en una oración completa. Estudia el modelo.

MODELO Ves: 10:30 A.M.
Escuchas: ¿*A qué hora vuelves de la clase de computación?*
Escribes: *Vuelvo de la clase de computación a las diez y media de
la mañana.*

1. 4:00 P.M.
2. 1:00 A.M.
3. 3:15 P.M.
4. 8:00 P.M.
5. 7:00 P.M.
6. 11:30 A.M.

Answers, Act. 15: 1. Vuelven del colegio a las cuatro de la tarde. 2. Volvemos de la fiesta a la una de la mañana. 3. Vuelve del trabajo a las tres y cuarto (quince) de la tarde. 4. Volvemos de la universidad a las ocho de la noche. 5. Vuelve de la oficina a las siete de la tarde (noche). 6. Vuelvo del gimnasio a las once y media de la mañana.

Audioscript, Act. 15, ¿A qué hora vuelves?: *Modelo: ¿A qué hora vuelves de la clase de computación? 1. ¿A qué hora vuelven tus amigos Mario y Marcos del colegio? 2. ¿A qué hora vuelven ustedes de la fiesta? 3. ¿A qué hora vuelve tu mamá del trabajo? 4. ¿A qué hora vuelven tú y tus compañeros de la universidad? 5. ¿A qué hora vuelve tu papá de la oficina? 6. ¿A qué hora vuelves del gimnasio los sábados?*

M **16 En la clase de español** Todos los estudiantes en la clase de español
están en medio de alguna actividad. Di lo que hace cada persona.

MODELO Olga (no entender las instrucciones)
Olga no entiende las instrucciones.

1. Joaquín (cerrar el texto digital) Joaquín cierra el texto digital.
2. Iris (perder su lugar en el capítulo) Iris pierde su lugar en el capítulo.
3. Paulo (dormir en su escritorio) Paulo duerme en su escritorio.
4. Lisa (empezar a hacer la tarea) Lisa empieza a hacer la tarea.
5. Arturo (pensar en las vacaciones) Arturo piensa en las vacaciones.
6. Andrés y Marta (jugar en la computadora) Andrés y Marta juegan en la computadora.
7. Roberto y Humberto (querer ir al gimnasio) Roberto y Humberto quieren ir al gimnasio.
8. Ingrid (preferir hacer la tarea en la computadora) Ingrid prefiere hacer la tarea en la computadora.
9. Francisco (no poder abrir la aplicación) Francisco no puede abrir la aplicación.
10. la profesora (volver a repetir la tarea) La profesora vuelve a repetir la tarea.
11. yo (pedir el número de la página de la lectura) Yo pido el número de la página de la lectura.
12. yo (repetir la pregunta) Yo repito la pregunta.

Volver a + *infinitive*
means to go back and do
something, or to do it
over.

17 **Trucos para tecnófobos** Con un(a) compañero(a) miren el anuncio de un programa de televisión sobre trucos para las personas que no saben mucho de tecnología. Después, contesten las preguntas a continuación.

M/C

¿Eres tecnófobo?

¡En este show puedes aprender 50 cosas fáciles para ayudarte con todos tus aparatos! ¿Quieres saber más? Pues, ¡a ver! Canal 22, 19:30

© Cengage Learning 2013

cosas: *things*

1. ¿Cuántas cosas fáciles pueden hacer con estos trucos *(tricks)*? cincuenta
2. ¿Prefieren aprender a usar los trucos o piensan que son una pérdida *(waste)* de tiempo?
3. ¿Pueden usar sus celulares para hacer otras funciones? ¿Cuáles?
4. ¿Tienen todos estos aparatos? ¿Quieren comprar otros aparatos electrónicos? ¿Por qué sí o no?

18 **¿Quieres ir?** Pregúntale a tu compañero(a) si quiere hacer una actividad contigo. Él o ella te dice que prefiere hacer otra cosa.

C

Actividades: ir a tomar un refresco, ver un video, estudiar en la biblioteca, mirar television, navegar por Internet, tomar el sol, visitar a amigos, bailar, ¿…?

MODELO Tú: *¿Quieres ver un video?*
    Compañero(a): *No, prefiero jugar un juego interactivo.*

19 **La vida universitaria** ¿Es la vida del estudiante muy difícil hoy en día? Con tres compañeros de clase, contesten las siguientes preguntas sinceramente. Basándose en las respuestas de sus compañeros, decidan juntos si la vida universitaria produce mucho estrés para el estudiante. Presenten su conclusión a la clase.

C

1. ¿Sientes mucho estrés? ¿Por qué?
2. ¿A qué hora vuelves a la residencia estudiantil de la universidad?
3. ¿A qué hora duermes? ¿Dónde duermes? ¿Cuántas horas duermes por noche? ¿Duermes lo suficiente?
4. ¿Juegas videojuegos? ¿Juegos interactivos? ¿Juegos en la red? ¿Cuánto tiempo pasas a diario jugando estos juegos?
5. ¿Pierdes tus llaves *(keys)* con frecuencia? ¿Tus gafas *(glasses)*? ¿Tu dinero *(money)*? ¿Tu tarea? ¿Tus libros? ¿Tus cuadernos? ¿Tu mochila?
6. ¿Piensas mucho en el futuro? ¿Puedes imaginar tu futuro?

20 Los hábitos del universitario Haz una gráfica como la de abajo. Usa las frases indicadas para crear preguntas. (Si quieres, puedes escribir tus propias preguntas.) Luego, hazles las preguntas a diez compañeros de clase. Según sus respuestas, apunta el número de estudiantes en la columna apropiada. Luego, escribe una descripción de tus resultados.

Learning objective: Analyzing

Frases para las preguntas	Número de estudiantes
dormir más de seis horas por noche:	6
no dormir más de seis horas por noche:	4
preferir hablar por teléfono para comunicarse:	
preferir escribir e-mail para comunicarse:	
preferir enviar un mensaje de texto para comunicarse:	
jugar un deporte:	
jugar videojuegos:	
sentir mucho estrés:	
no sentir mucho estrés:	
pensar en su futuro todos los días:	
no pensar en su futuro todos los días:	
encontrar la vida universitaria difícil:	
encontrar la vida universitaria fácil:	
¿…?	

MODELO *Seis estudiantes duermen más de seis horas por noche.*
Cuatro estudiantes no duermen más de seis horas por noche.

21 Mi blog Escribe un perfil personal para tu blog en Internet. Describe tus características físicas, tu personalidad, tus clases preferidas, tus hábitos en la universidad, tus emociones y lo que te gusta, molesta o interesa, etc. Ponle a tu descripción todo el detalle que puedas.

Suggestion, Act. 21: Review physical characteristics (**delgado, viejo, joven, pelirrojo, moreno,** etc.) and personality traits (**activo, generoso, serio, perezoso,** etc.) from **Chapter 2** by making up examples to start **Mi blog:** *En mi blog me gusta escribir de mi mejor amigo. Es alto, joven y tiene el pelo castaño. No es impulsivo. Trabaja en una firma publicitaria. Para su trabajo tiene que ser creativo y responsable. Es serio y sincero…*

>> Gramática útil 4

Describing how something is done: Adverbs

Personalidades famosas

Carla Royo-Villanova

Fundadora de Carla Bulgaria Roses Beauty

"Para mi innovar es una filosofia de vida. Procuro innovar en cada momento profesional y personal y asi no caer nunca en la rutina. Que cada dia sea diferente. La idea original de mi empresa fue precisamente gracias a ese espiritu innovador que me caracteriza".

« Anterior   Siguiente »

Slide of Carla Royo Villanova from *Muy Interestante*, http://premioinnova.muyinteresante.es/index.php. Used with permission from Gruner y Jahr and Carla Royo Villanova.

Cómo usarlo

When you want to say how an activity is carried out (slowly, thoroughly, generally, etc.), you use an adverb.

Generalmente, prefiero usar una contraseña secreta.

Escribo más **rápido / rápidamente** en computadora que con bolígrafo.

Este programa es **muy** lento.

Generally, *I prefer to use a secret password.*

I write more ***rapidly*** *on the computer than I do with a pen.*

This program is ***very*** *slow.*

Standard 4.1: Here students benefit from comparing Spanish **-mente** to English *-ly*.

Cómo formarlo

LO BÁSICO

An adverb is a word that modifies a verb, an adjective, or another adverb. (Sometimes adjectives can also be used as adverbs—for example, *fast*). *Generally, rapidly,* and *very* are all adverbs. You can identify an adverb by asking the question, *"How?"*

1. To form an adverb from a Spanish adjective, it is often possible to add the ending **-mente** to the adjective: **fácil → fácilmente**. If the adjective ends in an **-o**, change it to **-a** before adding **-mente: rápido → rápidamente**.

2. Here are some frequently used Spanish adjectives that can be turned into **-mente** adverbs.

fácil *(easy)*	→	**fácilmente**
difícil *(difficult)*	→	**difícilmente**
lento *(slow)*	→	**lentamente**
rápido *(fast)*	→	**rápidamente**

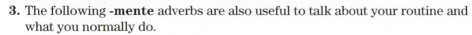

3. The following **-mente** adverbs are also useful to talk about your routine and what you normally do.

frecuentemente	*frequently*	**normalmente**	*normally*
generalmente	*generally*		

4. Here are some other common Spanish adverbs.

bastante	*somewhat, rather*	Este sistema es **bastante** lento.
bien	*well*	Tu computadora funciona **bien**.
demasiado	*too much*	Navego **demasiado** por Internet.
mal	*badly*	¡Mi cámara web funciona muy **mal**!
mucho	*a lot*	Me gustan **mucho** los juegos interactivos.
muy	*very*	Guardo archivos **muy** frecuentemente.
poco	*little*	Chateo **poco** por Internet.

> Remember, adverbs can be used to modify other adverbs, so it's perfectly acceptable to use **muy** with **frecuentemente** or **mal**, for example!

ACTIVIDADES

🔊 Track 13 M **22** **¿Cómo?** Escucha a Miriam mientras describe su vida a una amiga. Completa sus oraciones. Escoge el adjetivo más lógico del grupo y conviértelo en un adverbio añadiendo el sufijo **-mente**.

Adjetivos: constante, cuidadoso, directo, fácil, frecuente, general, inmediato, lento, normal, paciente, rápido, tranquilo.

1. Puedes instalar el programa antivirus ___fácilmente___.
2. Yo chateo por Internet ___frecuentemente___.
3. Hay algunos sitios web que funcionan ___lentamente___.
4. ___Normalmente___, navego por Internet dos o tres horas por día.
5. Con este módem interno, puedo hacer una conexión ___rápidamente___.
6. Instalo los programas de software en mi computadora ___cuidadosamente___.
7. Tengo tarea ___constantemente___.
8. Los domingos prefiero pasar el día ___tranquilamente___.

Audioscript, Act. 22, ¿Cómo?:
1. Es fácil instalar el programa antivirus. 2. Me gusta chatear por Internet con frecuencia. 3. Ese sitio web es muy lento. 4. Para mí es normal navegar por Internet dos o tres horas por día. 5. Con este módem interno, es rápido hacer una conexión a Internet. 6. Soy muy cuidadosa cuando instalo los programas de software en mi computadora. 7. Tengo tarea todos los días. Es constante. 8. Los domingos descanso, bebo un cafecito, escucho música… todo muy tranquilo.

👤👤👤 C **23** **¿Cómo te sientes?** Averigua *(Find out)* cómo se sienten tus compañeros de clase en ciertas situaciones. Hazles las siguientes preguntas a varios compañeros y apunta sus respuestas. Luego, dale los resultados de tu encuesta a la clase.

Learning objectives: Applying, Creating

¿Cómo te sientes cuando…
1. vas a tener un examen?
2. tu computadora no funciona bien?
3. recibes la cuenta *(bill)* de tu teléfono celular?
4. la batería de tu teléfono no funciona?
5. pierdes los archivos de tu tarea?
6. ¿…?

Posibles respuestas

bien	bastante nervioso (triste, preocupado, etc.)
mal	demasiado nervioso (cansado, furioso, etc.)
muy bien	no me afecta
muy mal	¿…?

¡Explora y exprésate!

España

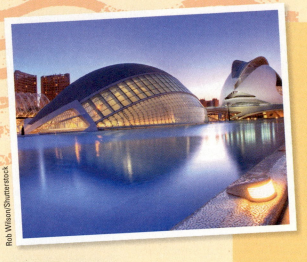

Rob Wilson/Shutterstock

Información general

Nombre oficial: Reino de España

Población: 40.548.753

Capital: Madrid (f. siglo X) (3.300.000 hab.)

Otras ciudades importantes: Barcelona (1.600.000 hab.), Valencia (840.000 hab.), Sevilla (710.000 hab.), Toledo (85.000 hab.)

Moneda: euro

Idiomas: castellano (oficial), catalán, vasco, gallego

Mapa de España: Apéndice D

Spain is often seen as one big culture when, in fact, it is the amalgamation of former kingdoms and separate regions. Many of these are autonomous states and have separate languages and/or dialects, and distinct cultural customs. Spanish is referred to as "castellano" in areas where there is an additional native language. Typically these are bilingual zones.

Vale saber…

- El Imperio español fue *(was)* el primer imperio global y uno de los más grandes en toda la historia mundial. En su apogeo *(peak)*, España tenía territorios en todos los continentes menos Antártida.

- España ha producido muchos artistas ilustres. En la literatura, se distingue Miguel de Cervantes, escritor de *El ingenioso hidalgo Don Quijote de la Mancha*, que se considera la primera novela moderna. En las artes, los grandes maestros de la pintura española incluyen a El Greco, Diego de Velázquez y Francisco de Goya. En el siglo *(century)* XX, Pablo Picasso, Joan Miró y Salvador Dalí son los innovadores más importantes del arte moderno.

- La influencia árabe en la arquitectura del siglo VIII, construida por los colonizadores musulmanes comúnmente llamados "los moros", es evidente por todo el sur de España, en particular en Granada, Córdoba y Sevilla.

Buika, artista universal

Paul White/AP Images

Concha Buika, conocida profesionalmente como Buika, es cantante española, hija de ecuatoguineanos y una maravillosa estudiante de todos los estilos musicales del mundo. Boleros, flamenco, jazz, funk, soul y el ritmo africano todos forman parte de su obra musical. Además, le fascinan los ritmos electrónicos y dice que para ella sus 'joyas' *(jewels)* son los aparatos electrónicos que utiliza para hacer música. Con sus ritmos globales y su uso de la tecnología, Buika es una artista universal que rompe *(breaks)* todas las barreras.

>> En resumen

La información general

Learning objectives: Understanding, Remembering

1. ¿Qué país fue *(was)* el primer imperio global? España
2. ¿En qué continentes tenía *(had)* España territorios? En todos los continentes menos Antártida
3. ¿Quién es el autor de la primera novela moderna? Miguel de Cervantes
4. ¿Quiénes son los grandes maestros de la pintura española? El Greco, Diego de Velázquez, Francisco de Goya
5. ¿Quiénes son los artistas españoles que se consideran innovadores del arte moderno? Pablo Picasso, Joan Miró, Salvador Dalí
6. ¿Qué tres ciudades españolas tienen una influencia árabe en su arquitectura? Granada, Córdoba, Sevilla

El tema de la música electrónica

1. ¿De dónde son los padres de Buika? Guinea Ecuatorial
2. ¿Qué estilos musicales incorpora Buika en su obra musical? boleros, flamenco, jazz, funk, soul, ritmo africano
3. ¿Qué considera Buika sus 'joyas'? los aparatos electrónicos que usa para hacer música
4. ¿Qué hace de Buika una artista universal? sus ritmos globales y su uso de la tecnología

🌐 ¿QUIERES SABER MÁS?

En la tabla que empezaste al principio del capítulo, añade toda la información que ya sabes en la columna **Lo que aprendí.** Escoge uno o dos de los temas que escribiste en la columna **Lo que quiero aprender,** o uno o dos de los temas a continuación para investigar en línea. Prepárate para compartir la información con la clase.

Palabras clave: el Imperio español; la Guerra Civil español; la influencia musulmana; Pedro Almodóvar; Penélope Cruz; Rafael Nadal

🌐 **Tú en el mundo hispano** Para explorar oportunidades de usar el español para estudiar o hacer trabajos voluntarios o aprendizajes en España, sigue los enlaces en el sitio web de **www.cengagebrain.com.**

🎬 **Ritmos del mundo hispano** Sigue los enlaces en **www.cengagebrain.com** para escuchar música de España.

A leer

>> Antes de leer

ESTRATEGIA

Using format clues to aid comprehension

In **Chapter 3,** you looked at the visuals that accompanied an article to get an idea of its content. It is also very helpful to look at an article's format. The headline, a section title, and any kind of highlighted or boxed text (often called sidebars) can give you a general idea of the article's content.

1 Mira el artículo en la página 153. ¿Cuántas de las siguientes claves *(clues)* de formato puedes identificar en el artículo? Basándote en esas claves, ¿de qué trata el artículo?

- título de sección
- texto del lado *(sidebar)*
- fotos
- título de artículo
- citas *(quotations)*
- ilustraciones o gráficos

2 Ahora lee el artículo en la página 153 y busca las ideas principales.

>> Después de leer

3 Di si las siguientes oraciones son **ciertas (C)** o **falsas (F)**.

1. ___F___ Este artículo habla de una plataforma tecnológica de hardware.
2. ___C___ Tuenti es un sitio exclusivo.
3. ___C___ Muchas de las personas que trabajan para Tuenti son jóvenes.
4. ___F___ Para Tuenti, la privacidad no es muy importante.
5. ___F___ Todas las personas que trabajan para Tuenti son españoles.

4 Contesta las preguntas con un(a) compañero(a).

1. ¿Puedes usar Tuenti con tu celular? sí
2. Según Tuenti, ¿cuántas personas usan el sitio web cada día? millones de personas
3. ¿Cuáles son las nacionalidades de los cofundadores? Dos son españoles y dos son norteamericanos.
4. ¿Cuántas invitaciones recibe cada nuevo usuario? tres
5. ¿Dónde está la oficina de Tuenti? en Madrid
6. ¿Qué significa Tuenti? tu entidad
7. En tu opinión, ¿puede tener éxito *(be successful)* un sitio como Tuenti en Estados Unidos?

LECTURA

Sólo con invitación

Algunos trabajadores de Tuenti (¡y otro inanimado!).

El País Photos/Newscom

¿Qué es Tuenti?

Tuenti es una red social española que es uno de los sitios web más populares del país. Es la creación de dos españoles, Felix Ruiz y Joaquín Ayuso, y dos norteamericanos, Zaryn Dentzel y Kenny Bentley. Y, a diferencia de otras redes sociales como Facebook, es necesario recibir una invitación personal antes de poder juntarse[1] a esta comunidad virtual.

> **"Si no eres tú mismo, no eres nadie[2] en Tuenti"**
> —**Zaryn Dentzel, uno de los cofundadores de Tuenti**

¿Por qué requiere Tuenti una invitación?

Según Dentzel, "Anteponemos[3] la privacidad de nuestro público al crecimiento sin control[4]. De ese modo cuando entras en la red ya tienes, al menos, un amigo".

Esta decisión resulta en una exclusividad bastante inflexible. Cada nuevo usuario recibe sólo tres invitaciones — ¡así que tiene que pensarlo bien antes de usarlas!

Unos datos sobre Tuenti

- El nombre es una abreviatura de "tu entidad".
- Está basado en Madrid.
- La edad media de las personas que trabajan para Tuenti es de 24 años. Ellos son de más de quince países diferentes.

☺) tuenti

¿Qué es Tuenti?

Tuenti es una plataforma social privada, a la que se accede únicamente por invitación. Cada día la usan millones de personas para comunicarse entre ellas y compartir información.

 Social
Conéctate, comparte y comunícate con tus amigos, compañeros de trabajo y familia.

 Local
Descubre servicios locales y participa con las marcas que realmente te importan.

 Móvil
Accede a Tuenti desde tu móvil en tiempo real estés donde estés.

Courtesy of © tuenti 2011

únicamente: *only* **marcas:** *brands*

[1] *to join* [2] *no one* [3] *We give preference to* [4] **al…:** *over uncontrolled growth*

A escribir

ESTRATEGIA

Prewriting—Narrowing your topic

After you choose a topic for a piece of writing, but before you begin the writing process, you need to narrow your topic to fit the scope of your written piece. For example, in this section, you will write a note to a friend who is interested in technology. Since most notes are short, you don't want to choose a huge topic to cover.

One way to narrow a topic is to take it and ask yourself questions about it. For example, if your general topic is "computers," ask, "What kind of computer?" You might answer, "A laptop." The next question might be, "Why do you want a laptop?" The answer might be, "Because I like to be able to take it with me." You could then ask, "Where do you want to use your laptop?" with the answer, "At the coffee shop down the corner with free wifi." Once you have progressed through a series of narrowing questions like this, you have narrowed your topic from "computers" to "ways having a laptop can help you save money."

Learning objectives: Applying, Analyzing, Creating

1 Piensa en dos o tres temas generales que puedes usar para escribir a un(a) amigo(a) que es muy aficionado(a) *(a big fan)* a la tecnología. Un ejemplo de un tema general puede ser **las computadoras**, **el Internet**, etc.

2 Go back to the list of topics you created in **Actividad 1**. Ahora, elige *(choose)* uno de los temas y practica la técnica de la **Estrategia** para hacer el tema más específico.

3 Ahora, lee el mensaje modelo a continuación donde Magali habla de sus clases y tarea relacionadas con la tecnología y también de sus planes para el fin de semana. ¿Contiene su mensaje palabras o frases que puedes usar en tu composición? Si hay, apúntalas. Si necesitas otras palabras que no sabes *(you don't know)*, búscalas en un diccionario bilingüe antes de escribir.

Hola, ¿cómo estás?

Buscar mensaje 🔍   **+ Nuevo mensaje**

◀ Volver a Mensajes | Marcar como no leído | Denunciar correo no deseado | Eliminar | ▲ | ▼

Entre Tú y Magali Fulanita

Magali Fulanita 19 de enero, 18:00

Hola, ¿Cómo estás? Todo va bien aquí. 😊 Tengo muchos planes para el fin de semana. Primero, voy a trabajar un poco en la computadora.
Tengo que crear la plantilla *(template)* de un sitio web para mi clase de diseño gráfico. ¡Sólo podemos usar los tres colores principales! Muy fácil, ¿verdad? 😊 Bueno, a mí me gustan mucho los colores vivos – el rojo, el amarillo… Entonces, ¡va a ser un programa brillante! Después de trabajar en la computadora, voy a salir el sábado con Laila y Marta. (¿Por qué no vienes?) Y el domingo tengo tarea para la clase de programación.
Así que voy a estar muy ocupada… y un poco cansada! 😟
Bueno, ¡escríbeme pronto para decirme tus noticias!

Un abrazo, Magali

Respuesta

Responder

>> ## Composición

4 Ahora, escribe un borrador *(rough draft)* de tu mensaje. Incluye información sobre el tema que desarrollaste *(that you developed)* en las **Actividades 1** y **2**. También debes incluir un poco de información personal para tu amigo(a), como en el mensaje modelo. Trata de escribir rápidamente, sin preocuparte *(without worrying)* demasiado por los errores.

>> ## Después de escribir

5 Mira tu borrador otra vez. Usa la siguiente lista para revisarlo *(to revise it)*.

- ¿Tiene tu mensaje toda la información necesaria? ¿Está bien organizado?
- ¿Corresponden los sujetos de las oraciones a los verbos?
- ¿Corresponden las formas de los artículos, los sustantivos y los adjetivos?
- ¿Usas correctamente **ser** y **estar**, los verbos con cambio en la raíz *(stem)* y los verbos como **gustar**?
- ¿Hay errores de puntuación o de ortografía *(spelling)*?

Vocabulario

La tecnología   *Technology*

El hardware   *hardware*

La computadora   *computer*
el altoparlante   *speaker*
el cable   *cable*
el disco duro   *hard drive*
la memoria flash / el pendrive   *flash drive*
el módem externo   *external modem*
el micrófono   *microphone*
el monitor   *monitor*
el puerto de USB   *USB port*
el ratón   *mouse*

La computadora portátil   *Laptop computer*
los audífonos   *earphones*
el módem interno   *internal modem*
la impresora   *printer*
el lector de CD-ROM o DVD   *CD-ROM / DVD drive*
la pantalla   *screen*
la tecla   *key*
el teclado   *keyboard*

El software   *Software*

la aplicación   *application*
los archivos   *files*
el archivo PDF   *PDF attachment*
el ícono del programa   *program icon*
el juego interactivo   *interactive game*
el programa antivirus   *antivirus program*
el programa de procesamiento de textos   *word processing program*

Funciones de la computadora   *Computer functions*

archivar   *to file*
bajar / descargar   *to download*
conectar   *to connect*
enviar   *to send*
funcionar   *to function*
grabar   *to record*
guardar   *to save*
hacer clic / doble clic   *to click / double-click*
instalar   *to install*
subir / cargar   *to upload*

Los colores   *Colors*

amarillo(a)   *yellow*
anaranjado(a)   *orange*
azul   *blue*
blanco(a)   *white*
café / marrón   *brown*
gris   *gray*

morado(a)   *purple*
negro(a)   *black*
rojo(a)   *red*
rosa / rosado(a)   *pink*
verde   *green*

Las emociones   *Emotions*

aburrido(a)   *bored*
cansado(a)   *tired*
contento(a)   *happy*
enfermo(a)   *sick*
enojado(a)   *angry*
furioso(a)   *furious*

nervioso(a)   *nervous*
ocupado(a)   *busy*
preocupado(a)   *worried*
seguro(a)   *sure*
triste   *sad*

Aparatos electrónicos   *Electronic devices*

el asistente electrónico   *electronic notebook*
la cámara digital   *digital camera*
la cámara web   *webcam*
el MP3 portátil   *portable MP3 player*
el reproductor / grabador de discos compactos   *CD player / burner*

el reproductor / grabador de DVD   *DVD player / burner*
la tableta   *tablet computer*
el teléfono inteligente / smartphone   *smartphone*
la videocámara   *videocamera*

Funciones de Internet *Internet functions*

acceder *to access*	**el enlace** *link*
el blog *blog*	**el foro** *forum*
el buzón electrónico *electronic mailbox*	**el grupo de conversación** *chat room*
el buscador *search engine*	**el grupo de noticias** *newsgroup*
chatear *to chat online*	**la página web** *web page*
el ciberespacio *cyberspace*	**el proveedor de acceso** *Internet provider*
la conexión *the connection*	**la red mundial** *World Wide Web*
hacer una conexión *to get online*	**la red social** *social networking site*
cortar la conexión *to get offline, disconnect*	**el sitio web** *website*
la contraseña *password*	**el (la) usuario(a)** *user*
el correo electrónico / e-mail *e-mail*	**el wifi** *wifi, wireless connection*
en línea *online*	

Verbos como *gustar*

encantar *to like a lot*	**interesar** *to interest, to be interesting*
fascinar *to fascinate*	**molestar** *to bother*
importar *to be important to someone; to mind*	

Otros verbos*

cerrar (ie) *to close*	**perder (ie)** *to lose*
comenzar (ie) *to begin*	**poder (ue)** *to be able to*
contar (ue) *to tell, to relate; to count*	**preferir (ie)** *to prefer*
dormir (ue) *to sleep*	**querer (ie)** *to want; to love*
empezar (ie) *to begin*	**repetir (i)** *to repeat*
encontrar (ue) *to find*	**sentir (ie)** *to feel*
entender (ie) *to understand*	**servir (i)** *to serve*
jugar (ue) *to play*	**sonar (ue)** *to ring, to go off (phone, alarm clock, etc.)*
pedir (i) *to ask for something*	**soñar (ue) con** *to dream (about)*
pensar (ie) de *to think, have an opinion about*	**volver (ue)** *to return*
pensar (ie) en *to think about, to consider*	

Adjetivos

difícil *difficult*	**lento** *slow*
fácil *easy*	**rápido** *fast*

Adverbios

difícilmente *with difficulty*	**bastante** *somewhat, rather*
fácilmente *easily*	**bien** *well*
frecuentemente *frequently*	**demasiado** *too much*
generalmente *generally*	**mal** *badly*
lentamente *slowly*	**mucho** *a lot*
normalmente *normally*	**muy** *very*
rápidamente *rapidly*	**poco** *little*

*Starting here, stem-changing verbs will be indicated in vocabulary lists with the stem change in parentheses.

Repaso y preparación

 Repaso del Capítulo 4

Preparation: Have students review this material and complete the activities here, in the SAM, and online before they begin **Chapter 5**.

Complete these activities to check your understanding of the new grammar points in **Chapter 4** before you move on to **Chapter 5**.

The answers to the activities in this section can be found in **Appendix B**.

Check: The **Repaso** section not only reviews grammar and vocabulary for the student but it offers a built-in performance assessment. By doing review activities with students, you can assess concepts that you may need to continue to reinforce in future classes.

Gustar with nouns and other verbs like gustar (p. 134)

1 Completa las oraciones con un pronombre de objeto indirecto y escoge la forma correcta del verbo indicado.

1. A ellos ___les gustan___ (gusta / gustan) los blogs.
2. A mí ___me encanta___ (encanta / encantan) mi teléfono inteligente.
3. A él ___le molesta___ (molesta / molestan) perder acceso a Internet.
4. A nosotros ___nos interesan___ (interesa / interesan) los foros sobre la tecnología.
5. A ti no ___te importa___ (importa / importan) cambiar tu contraseña frecuentemente.
6. A usted ___le gusta___ (gusta / gustan) el nuevo programa antivirus.

The verb estar and the uses of ser and estar (p. 138)

2 Completa las oraciones con una forma de **ser** o **estar**.

1. Oye, Marcos ¿ ___estás___ enojado?
2. Nosotros ___estamos___ en la biblioteca.
3. Yo ___soy___ estudiante.
4. Ellos ___son___ altos y rubios.
5. ¡Tengo examen! ___Estoy___ muy nervioso.
6. Ella no puede dormir. ___Está___ cansada.
7. Hoy ___es___ miércoles.
8. El celular ___es___ de Marisa.
9. Mi computadora ___está___ en mi mochila.
10. Mis amigos ___son___ españoles.
11. La fiesta ___es___ en el café.
12. Los altoparlantes ___están___ en la mesa.

Stem-changing verbs in the present indicative (p. 143)

Answers, Act. 3: 1. Tú duermes mucho. 2. Yo cierro la computadora portátil. 3. Ella entiende las instrucciones. 4. Nosotras jugamos el juego interactivo. 5. Usted repite la contraseña. 6. Ellos quieren un MP3 portátil. 7. Yo puedo instalar el programa. 8. Nosotros preferimos ir a un café con wifi.

3 Haz oraciones completas con los sujetos y verbos indicados.

1. tú / dormir mucho
2. yo / cerrar la computadora portátil
3. ella / entender las instrucciones
4. nosotras / jugar el juego interactivo
5. usted / repetir la contraseña
6. ellos / querer un MP3 portátil
7. yo / poder instalar el programa
8. nosotros / preferir ir a un café con wifi

Adverbs (p. 148)

4 Escoge un adjetivo de la lista, cámbialo a un adverbio con **-mente** y úsalo para completar una de las siguientes oraciones.

Adjetivos: fácil, general, lento, rápido

1. No me gusta escribir. Escribo muy ___lentamente___.
2. ¡Está computadora es fantástica! Funciona muy ___rápidamente___.
3. ___Generalmente___ me gusta navegar en Internet, pero no me gusta este sitio web.
4. Ella aprende nuevos programas muy ___fácilmente___. No son difíciles para ella.

The present indicative of regular -ar, -er, and -ir verbs (Chapters 2 and 3)

5 Completa las oraciones del anuncio *(advertisement)* con la forma correcta del verbo indicado.

Complete these activities to review some previously learned grammatical structures that will be helpful when you learn the new grammar in **Chapter 5**.

Be sure to reread **Chapter 4: Gramática útil 2** and **3** before moving on to the new **Chapter 5** grammar sections.

¡Súper rápido, súper ligero!
Y esta semana, ¡una súper oferta!

El Incre-Libre 2020
____debe____ **(deber) ser tu nueva computadora si tú...**

- ___envías___ **(enviar) o___recibes___ (recibir) archivos grandes por e-mail,**
- ___grabas___ **(grabar) muchos videos o___instalas___(instalar) programas de software que requieren mucha memoria,**
- ___llevas___ **(llevar) tu portátil siempre contigo y___trabajas___(trabajar) con ella en muchos sitios, ...ésta es la computadora para ti.**

Nuestros clientes ___hablan___ (hablar) de su satisfacción con el Incre-Libre:

"¡Esta computadora___funciona___(funcionar) muy rápidamente! Yo___bajo___(bajar) y___subo___ (subir) archivos a mi sitio web todos los días sin problema."

–Pilar Torres García, diseñadora de sitios web

"¡El Incre-Libre no ___pesa___(pesar—*to weigh*) nada! Voy a un café, ___saco___ (sacar) la computadora de mi mochila,___accedo___(acceder) a Internet y___leo___(leer) las noticias del mundo. No importa dónde estoy."

–Javier Salazar Rojas, profesor

"Los altoparlantes son increíbles. Cuando mi hermanos y yo___usamos___(usar) la computadora para mirar videos, ellos siempre___comentan___(comentar) la calidad del audio."

–Marcos Villarreal Barrios, estudiante

¡Esta semana, nosotros___ofrecemos___(ofrecer) el Incre-Libre por sólo 1.200 euros!

Es nuestra portátil más popular –___vendemos___(vender) casi 100 de ellas cada semana.

¡Si quieres una,___debes___(deber) actuar AHORA! Nuestros expertos en la computación personal están listos para atenderles.

¿Qué tal la familia?

Stephen Simpson/Getty Images

RELACIONES FAMILIARES

En el mundo hispanohablante, las relaciones familiares son un aspecto muy importante de la identidad personal.

¿Es tu familia una parte importante de tu vida diaria? ¿Cuánto tiempo pasas con miembros de tu familia en una semana? ¿En un mes?

Communication

By the end of this chapter you will be able to

- talk about and describe your family
- talk about professions
- describe daily routines
- indicate ongoing actions

Un viaje por El Salvador y Honduras

Learning objectives: See pages AIE-3–AIE-4 for a complete description of the Bloom's Taxonomy learning objectives and an explanation of how they are integrated within *Cuadros*.

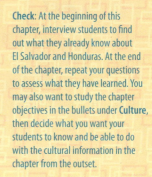

Estos países centroamericanos comparten una frontera y una costa pacífica. Honduras también tiene una costa atlántica. Los dos tienen un clima tropical.

País / Área	Tamaño y fronteras	Sitios de interés
El Salvador 20.720 km²	un poco más pequeño que Massachusetts; fronteras con Guatemala y Honduras	el bosque lluvioso (*rain forest*) del Parque Nacional Montecristo; los volcanes de Izalco, Santa Ana y San Vicente; las ruinas mayas de Joya de Cerén; las playas (*beaches*) del Pacífico
Honduras 111.890 km²	un poco más grande que Tennessee; fronteras con El Salvador, Guatemala y Nicaragua	las ruinas mayas de Copán, las islas de la Bahía, la arquitectura colonial de Tegucigalpa y San Pedro Sula, el bosque tropical de la región de la Mosquitia

Check: At the beginning of this chapter, interview students to find out what they already know about El Salvador and Honduras. At the end of the chapter, repeat your questions to assess what they have learned. You may also want to study the chapter objectives in the bullets under **Culture**, then decide what you want your students to know and be able to do with the cultural information in the chapter from the outset.

¿Qué sabes? Di si las siguientes oraciones son ciertas **(C)** o falsas **(F)**.

Learning objective: Understanding

1. Estos dos países tienen más o menos el mismo (*same*) tamaño. F
2. Hay ruinas mayas en Honduras, pero no en El Salvador. F
3. El Salvador tiene muchos volcanes. C
4. Hay ejemplos de arquitectura colonial en Honduras. C

Lo que sé y lo que quiero aprender Completa la tabla del **Apéndice A**. Escribe algunos datos que **ya sabes** sobre estos países en la columna **Lo que sé**. Después, añade algunos temas que **quieres aprender** a la columna **Lo que quiero aprender**. Guarda la tabla para usarla otra vez en la sección **¡Explora y exprésate!** en la página 187.

Cultures

By the end of this chapter you will have explored

- facts about Honduras and El Salvador
- a unique course of study in Honduras
- a financial cooperative in El Salvador
- careers where knowledge of Spanish is helpful
- the Afro-Hispanic **garífuna** culture of Honduras

¡Imagínate!

Standard 2.1: The **Garífuna** culture reflects Afro-Caribbean and Central American roots. The practices and the perspectives of the **Garífuna** culture are explored in this chapter.

>> Vocabulario útil 1

Learning objectives: Applying, Analyzing

Preparation: Present family terms in the context of an appropriate real-world family: yours, the current U.S. president's, a well-known pop culture family, a Central American family, a royal family, etc. Write a simple, brief paragraph and read it as a model in class.

© Cengage Learning 2013

ANILÚ: Son fotos de mi **familia**.

DULCE: ¿De veras? ¿En la computadora?

ANILÚ: Sí, mi **hermanito** Roberto tiene una cámara digital. Saca fotos de la familia y me las manda por Internet.

Preparation: You may have students who are sensitive about talking about their families. Always give students the option of talking about a family other than their own. Be prepared to field questions on lexical items such as **está muerto(a), está divorciado(a)**, if asked.

In Spanish, the masculine plural **hermanos** can mean both *brothers* (all males) and *brothers and sisters / siblings* (both males and females).

To refer to a couple, use **la pareja**. For example: **Es una pareja muy elegante.** Also, to ask about someone's partner, you can say: **¿Quién es la pareja de Juan?** Or: **Su pareja es doctor.**

Notice that **parientes** is a false cognate: it does *not* mean *parents*; it means *family members*. **Los padres** is the correct term for *parents*.

In some countries, the **-astro(a)** ending might be viewed as pejorative, and speakers might refer to **la esposa de mi padre** instead of **mi madrastra**. Be conscious of these nuances.

>> La familia nuclear

la madre (mamá) *mother*	**la tía** *aunt*
el padre (papá) *father*	**el tío** *uncle*
los padres *parents*	**la prima** *female cousin*
la esposa *wife*	**el primo** *male cousin*
el esposo *husband*	**la sobrina** *niece*
la hija *daughter*	**el sobrino** *nephew*
el hijo *son*	**la abuela** *grandmother*
la hermana (mayor) *(older) sister*	**el abuelo** *grandfather*
el hermano (menor) *(younger) brother*	**la nieta** *granddaughter*
	el nieto *grandson*

>> La familia política

la suegra *mother-in-law*	
el suegro *father-in-law*	
la nuera *daughter-in-law*	
el yerno *son-in-law*	
la cuñada *sister-in-law*	
el cuñado *brother-in-law*	

>> Otros parientes

la madrastra *stepmother*	
el padrastro *stepfather*	
la hermanastra *stepsister*	
el hermanastro *stepbrother*	
la media hermana *half-sister*	
el medio hermano *half-brother*	

In Spanish, diminutives are common. You form the diminutive by adding **-ito** or **-ita** to a noun: **hermano → hermanito**. (Other diminutives are formed by adding **-cito / -cita: coche → cochecito**.)

A diminutive is used: 1) to indicate that something or someone is small, or younger. **Una casita** is a small house; **una hermanita** is a younger sister. 2) to express love or fondness. For example, Anilú probably refers to her grandmother as **abuelita** to indicate that she loves her dearly.

To express affection, Spanish speakers also use nicknames. In the video, **Anilú** is a nickname for Ana Luisa, **Beto** for Roberto, and **Chela** for Graciela.

Heritage Learners: Caribbean or Costa Rican students may use the suffix **-ico(a)** to form the diminutive of vowel-final words with a t in their final syllable: **rata → ratica, tomate → tomatico**. This is not a stigmatized linguistic trait but merely a dialectal variant; it should not be corrected or criticized.

Heritage Learners: Ask heritage learners to describe the role of the **madrina** and **padrino** in Hispanic families.

Suggestion: Ask students to comment on this popular Spanish saying: **La familia es el corazón y el espíritu de la cultura latina.**

ACTIVIDADES

Learning objective: Understanding

I **1** **Los parientes** Completa las oraciones con la respuesta correcta para describir las relaciones entre los parientes de Anilú. Usa el árbol genealógico *(family tree)* de Anilú para identificar las relaciones.

Arturo Villa González y Beatriz Vega Chapa de Villa Rodrigo Guzmán Corona y Adela Flores Romero de Guzmán

Carlos Irene Amelia Pedro Hernán Rosa

Tomás Rafael Gloria Anilú Roberto Alberto Sonia

1. Rodrigo es ____a____ de Adela.
   a. el esposo b. el suegro c. el tío
2. Tomás y Rafael son ____c____.
   a. hermanas b. primos c. hermanos
3. Sonia es ____b____ de Anilú.
   a. la tía b. la prima c. la hermanastra
4. Roberto es ____a____ de Rosa.
   a. el sobrino b. el nieto c. el yerno
5. Gloria es ____c____ de Rodrigo y Adela.
   a. la suegra b. la hija c. la nieta
6. Adela es ____c____ de Amelia.
   a. la madrastra b. la cuñada c. la suegra

Check: Have students fill out a blank family tree to see what they remember and how well they spell. Collect papers to see where gaps in learning persist.

👥 **2** **La familia de Anilú** Con un(a) compañero(a) de clase, háganse
M preguntas sobre el árbol genealógico *(family tree)* de Anilú de la **Actividad 1.** Túrnense nombrando la persona y diciendo cuál es su relación con Anilú.

MODELO Compañero(a): *¿Quién es Beatriz Vega Chapa?*
Tú: *Es la abuela de Anilú.*

👥 **3** **El árbol genealógico** Dibuja el árbol genealógico de tu familia. Empieza
C con tus abuelos y sigue con el resto de tu familia. Luego, en grupos de tres, intercambien sus árboles y háganse preguntas sobre sus familias.

Learning objective: Applying

MODELO Tú: *¿Tom es tu hermano?*
Compañero(a): *Sí, es mi hermano menor. Tiene quince años y es muy divertido.*
Tú: *¿Quién es Elisa?*
Compañero(a): *Es mi sobrina. Es la hija de mi hermana mayor.*

👥 **4** **Mi familia** Escribe un párrafo corto sobre cada miembro de tu familia
C nuclear. Para cada individuo, di quién es, cómo se llama y cuántos años tiene. Incluye algunas características físicas y también unas de personalidad. Luego, en grupos de tres, lean sus descripciones al grupo. El grupo te hace preguntas sobre cada miembro de tu familia y tú contestas. **Learning objective:** Creating

Suggestion: Locate a graphic organizer for a family tree on the Internet or draw your own. Use it to present vocabulary words in the context of an authentic family, mentioning names and where people live. Point out relationships between relatives and emphasize gender. Take the opportunity to recycle interrogative words with questions like **¿Cómo se llama mi / tu / su madre / padre / etc. ? ¿Cuántos tíos tengo? ¿Dónde vive mi prima?**

> Notice that two surnames are given for Anilú's grandparents. In some Spanish-speaking countries, the first surname is the father's, and the second one is the mother's. Anilú's full name is Anilú Guzmán Villa. If she marries someone whose first surname is Rodríguez, Anilú may add it to become Anilú Guzmán Villa de Rodríguez, or Sra. Rodríguez. This tradition is changing, however, and in many Spanish-speaking countries women do not change their names.

Suggestion/Preparation: Jot down the diminutive nicknames in one column and proper names in another. See if students can match them.
1. Maripili   a. Mercedes
2. Chavela   b. María Pilar
3. Meche   c. Guadalupe
4. Memo   d. José
5. Paco   e. Isabel
6. Pepe   f. Guillermo
7. Lupe   g. Francisco
Answers: 1. b 2. e 3. a 4. f 5. g 6. d 7. c

© Cengage Learning 2013

▶ >> Vocabulario útil 2

DULCE: ¿Quién es este señor?

ANILÚ: Es mi papá. Se enoja cuando Roberto le saca fotos. No le gusta salir en fotos. Dice que se ve muy gordo.

DULCE: ¿Qué hace tu papá?

ANILÚ: Es **arquitecto**. Diseña edificios para negocios.

Notice: Students never know enough vocabulary to cover all of the possibilities. Teach them the phrase "X **trabaja en…**" to give more options while talking about what their relatives and friends do. Help students with new terms and list them on the board.

Suggestion: Practice family terms and professions at the same time with questions like **¿En qué trabaja tu padre / tu madre / tu tío, etc.?**

When describing someone's profession, don't use an article as we would in English: **Es abogada** translates as *She is a lawyer*.

El policía means a single policeman. **La policía** can mean a single policewoman or the entire police force. You have to extract the correct meaning from context. Other professions whose meaning depends on the context and the article are: **el químico / la química, el físico / la física, el músico / la música, el matemático / la matemática, el guardia / la guardia**.

La mujer policía is also used for a single policewoman.

>> Las profesiones y las carreras

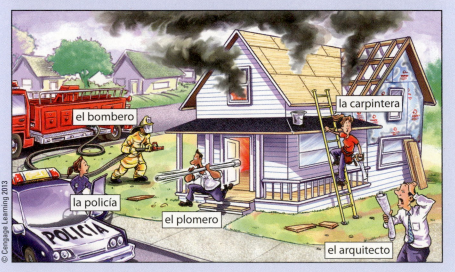

>> Más profesiones

el actor / la actriz *actor / actress*	**el (la) gerente de…** *manager of. . .*
el (la) asistente *assistant*	**el hombre / la mujer de**
el (la) camarero(a) *waiter / waitress*	**negocios** *businessman /*
el (la) cocinero(a) *cook, chef*	*businesswoman*
el (la) contador(a) *accountant*	**el (la) ingeniero(a)** *engineer*
el (la) dentista *dentist*	**el (la) maestro(a)** *teacher*
el (la) dependiente *salesclerk*	**el (la) mecánico(a)** *mechanic*
el (la) director(a) de social	**el (la) peluquero(a)** *barber /*
media *director of social media*	*hairdresser*
el (la) diseñador(a) gráfico(a)	**el (la) programador(a)** *programmer*
graphic designer	**el (la) secretario(a)** *secretary*
el (la) dueño(a) de… *owner of. . .*	**el (la) trabajador(a)** *worker*
el (la) enfermero(a) *nurse*	**el (la) veterinario(a)** *veterinarian*

Suggestion: Give compound examples of work titles so that students can be more descriptive about prospective careers or positions held by people that they know: **Directora de Operaciones Internacionales, Gerente Regional, Director Ejecutivo, Abogado Internacional, Coordinador de Diseño, Diseñador Multimedia…**

As of this printing, no established translation for social media has been agreed upon by Spanish speakers. Most simply use the English "social media."

ACTIVIDADES

Optional: Also get students thinking about work preferences: **¿Te interesa el teletrabajo? ¿…trabajar en una oficina, en una escuela, en una clínica, en una compañía multinacional, al aire libre…? ¿…viajar para tu trabajo? ¿…trabajo tecnológico?**

I **5** **¿Qué hace?** Escoge la profesión más lógica para cada persona.

1. Alejandro trabaja en un hospital. Es… c
2. Catalina trabaja en el teatro. Es… d
3. Pedro trabaja en un restaurante. Es… a
4. El señor Cortez trabaja en una escuela secundaria *(high school)*. Es… e
5. Amelia trabaja en el centro de computación. Es… f
6. Irene trabaja en un hospital para animales. Es… b

a. cocinero(a)
b. veterinario(a)
c. enfermero(a)
d. actor / actriz
e. maestro(a)
f. programador(a)

👥 **6** **Quiere ser…** Tú y tu compañero(a) hablan de varios amigos. Tú le dices
M a tu compañero(a) qué es lo que estudia esa persona y tu compañero(a) te dice qué quiere ser esa persona.

MODELO medicina
Tú: *Marcos estudia medicina.*
Compañero(a): *Quiere ser médico.*

1. contabilidad
2. administración de empresas
3. ingeniería
4. informática
5. diseño gráfico
6. arte
7. pedagogía
8. periodismo

Answers, Act. 6: All begin with **Quiere ser…** 1. contador(a) 2. hombre / mujer de negocios 3. ingeniero(a) 4. programador(a) 5. diseñador(a) gráfico(a) 6. artista 7. maestro(a) / profesor(a) 8. periodista

Suggestion: Expand with statements like: 1. **Estudia medicina pero quiere trabajar con animales.** 2. **Le gusta servir. Trabaja en un restaurante.** 3. **Es creativo. Trabaja mucho con la computadora.**

M **7** **Presentaciones** Estás en la fiesta de un amigo. Él te presenta a varios miembros de su familia. Lee sus presentaciones. Luego, para cada persona, indica cuál es su relación con el narrador y su profesión.

1. Quiero presentarte a Antonio. Él es el hijo de mi tía Rosa. Antonio trabaja en el Hospital Garibaldi. Ayuda a las personas enfermas.
   Nombre: Antonio   *Relación:* ___primo___   *Profesión:* ___enfermero / médico___

2. Te presento a Miranda. Miranda es la hija de mi tío Ricardo. Miranda enseña francés en el Colegio Del Valle.
   Nombre: Miranda   *Relación:* ___prima___   *Profesión:* ___maestra___

3. Mira, te presento a Olga. Olga trabaja para el periódico *El Universal*. Olga es la esposa de mi hermano.
   Nombre: Olga   *Relación:* ___cuñada___   *Profesión:* ___periodista___

4. Quiero presentarte a César. César es el hijo de mi hermano. César trabaja en una pizzería después del colegio.
   Nombre: César   *Relación:* ___sobrino___   *Profesión:* ___camarero, cocinero___

5. Éste es Raúl. Raúl es el hermano de mi padre. Él diseña casas y edificios.
   Nombre: Raúl   *Relación:* ___tío___   *Profesión:* ___arquitecto___

6. Te presento al señor Domínguez, el padre de mi esposa. Él escribe software para una compañía multinacional.
   Nombre: señor Domínguez   *Relación:* ___suegro___   *Profesión:* ___programador___

C **8** **¿Qué quieres ser?** En grupos de tres, hablen sobre sus planes para el futuro.

MODELO   Tú: *¿Qué profesión te interesa?*
Compañero(a): *¿A mí? Yo quiero ser director de social media.*
Tú: *¿Dónde quieres trabajar?*
Compañero(a): *Quiero trabajar aquí, en Los Ángeles.*

C **9** **El español y las profesiones** En Estados Unidos, hay muchas oportunidades profesionales para personas que hablan español. Aquí hay algunas carreras que utilizan el español.

- abogado(a)
- académico(a)
- enfermero(a)
- intérprete
- médico(a)
- periodista
- policía
- profesor(a) o maestro(a) de español
- secretario(a) bilingüe
- trabajador(a) social

Con un(a) compañero(a) de clase, contesten las siguientes preguntas.

1. ¿Te interesa alguna de estas carreras? ¿Por qué? ¿Crees que poder hablar español es importante para tu futuro?

2. En Europa, los estudiantes de colegio aprenden inglés y muchas veces otro idioma además de su lengua nativa. ¿Crees que es buena idea? ¿Por qué? ¿Crees que los estadounidenses deben aprender otro idioma además del inglés? ¿Por qué?

¡Fíjate! Las profesiones y el mundo

Gracias a la tecnología, el mundo va cambiando *(is changing)* muy rápido. Algunas profesiones que no existían ayer, existen hoy. Antes, más profesiones eran locales, es decir, consistían en lo que se podía hacer dentro de *(consisted of what could be done within)* la comunidad: policía, bombero, dentista, doctor, profesor. Ahora es posible elegir una profesión que puede tener un impacto global. ¿En qué campos existen profesiones internacionales?

Marvin Newman/Photolibrary

Science Faction / SuperStock

Asistencia sanitaria internacional	*International health care*
Banca internacional	*International banking*
Consultoría de negocios	*Consulting*
Derecho internacional	*International law*
Ingeniería multinacional	*International engineering*
Mercadotecnia internacional	*International marketing*
Política exterior	*Foreign policy*
Programas de conservación ambiental	*Environmental programs*
Servicios financieros	*Financial services*
Tecnología ambiental	*"Green" technology*
Telecomunicaciones	*Telecommunications*

Práctica Ve a Internet y busca tres profesiones internacionales que te interesan. ¿En qué campo están? ¿Qué puedes hacer en tus estudios para empezar a prepararte para cada profesión?

With some professions, there is a lot of confusion about how to specify gender, especially for traditionally male professions like **piloto, bombero, ingeniero, general, mecánico, plomero**. The ambiguity is also due to the number of options for specifying gender. Some professions change the ending, like **el actor** and **la actriz; el maestro** and **la maestra; el alcalde** *(mayor)* and **la alcaldesa**. Other professions simply change the article, with no change to the noun, like **el gerente** and **la gerente, el dentista** and **la dentista**. Sometimes, the word **mujer** or **señora** is used to specify the gender: **la señora juez** *(judge)*, **la mujer policía**.

Suggestion: Ask students to jot down on a piece of paper some examples of gender expressions in English that they hear in spoken language to make it easier to compare with Spanish examples in the text (e.g., *the lady fireman*).

Standards 4.1, 4.2: The **¡Fíjate!** cultural and linguistic notes throughout *Cuadros* encourage students to connect and compare information about cultures, cultural practices, languages, and linguistic history. Topics usually relate to the chapter theme and vocabulary, and help students understand the nature of cultural practices and language usage.

Check: For a quick comprehension and spelling check of the professions listed in **¡Fíjate!**, ask students to sort and group them under the following labels: **Salud, Negocios, Medioambiente, Otro**. Some will fit into several categories. Students can compare groupings and check spelling during the class check.

⊙ >> Vocabulario útil 3

ANILÚ: Mamá, ¿está Roberto por allí? Necesito hablar con él.

MAMÁ: No puede venir al teléfono. Se está bañando.

ANILÚ: ¿Está bañándose? ¿A esta hora?

MAMÁ: Acaba de regresar de su partido de fútbol. ¡Ay! ¡No hay ni **toallas** ni **jabón** en el baño! Me tengo que ir. Tengo que llevarle a tu hermano una toalla, el jabón y el **champú**…

>> **En el baño** *In the bathroom*

ACTIVIDADES

M **10** **¿Qué necesitan comprar?** Según la situación, ¿qué necesita comprar cada persona?

MODELO *Él necesita comprar champú.*

1.

2.

3.

4.

5.

6.

11 **El HiperMercado** Tú y tu hermano(a) C ven un anuncio para el HiperMercado en el periódico. Tú le dices qué quieres comprar y él o ella te dice cuánto dinero necesitas para comprar ese artículo.

(**¡OJO!** *Dollars* = **dólares** y *cents* = **centavos**.)

MODELO Tú: *¿Quiero comprar un cepillo y un peine.*
Hermano(a): *Necesitas tres dólares y setenta y nueve centavos para comprar el cepillo y el peine.*

> Unlike grocery stores, which focus mostly on food items, **hipermercados** in Spanish-speaking countries are similar to supermarkets, but tend to sell an even wider range of household products.

HiperMercado
¡Todo para la familia!
¡Los mejores precios de la ciudad!

Cepillo y peine "La Bella":
 $4,39 **$3,79**

Champú "Largo y limpio":
$3,39 **$2,79**

Cepillo de dientes y pasta de dientes "Brillante":
$4,75 **$3,75**

Desodorante "Frescura":
$2,69 **$1,99**

Jabón antibacterial "Sanitario":
$1,49 **$1,19**

Máquina de afeitar "El Varonil":
$24,99 **$19,99**

Paquete de seis rasuradoras "Para ella":
$3,97 **$3,47**

Paquete de dos toallas de mano "Elegantes":
$4,99 **$3,99**

A ver

Standard 1.2: Through video viewing, students learn interpretive strategies for communication. Activities in this section regularly provide opportunities for students to interpret spoken language.

ESTRATEGIA

Listening for the main idea

A good way to organize your viewing of authentic video is to focus on getting the main idea of the segment (or of each of its parts). Don't try to understand every word; just try to get the gist of each scene. Later, with the help of the textbook activities, some of the other details of the segment will emerge.

Antes de ver Mira las fotos a la izquierda *(on the left)*. Haz correspondencia entre *(Match)* las fotos y los diálogos.

ⓐ

ⓑ

ⓒ

© Cengage Learning 2013

_____c_____ 1. Dulce: ¿Qué hace tu papá?

Anilú: Es arquitecto. Diseña edificios para negocios.

_____b_____ 2. Mamá: Bueno, pero siempre hay que hacer tiempo para llamar a tu mamá.

Anilú: Sí, mamá, está bien. Perdóname.

_____a_____ 3. Anilú: Mira, ven a ver.

Dulce: ¿Qué es?

© Cengage Learning 2013

Learning objective: Analyzing

▶ **Ver** Ahora mira el video para el **Capítulo 5.** Trata de entender la idea principal de cada escena.

Después de ver Haz correspondencia entre las escenas y las ideas principales.

1. _____d_____ **Escena 1:** Anilú está mirando *(is looking at)* la computadora.

2. _____a_____ **Escena 2:** Anilú habla con su mama.

3. _____e_____ **Escena 3:** Anilú y Dulce miran una foto en la impresora.

4. _____c_____ **Escena 4:** Roberto llama a Anilú.

5. _____b_____ **Escena 5:** Anilú mira la foto de la fiesta de cumpleaños del abuelo.

a. La mamá de Anilú dice que ella nunca la llama.

b. A Anilú no le gusta la foto pero Roberto cree que es muy cómica.

c. Roberto quiere saber *(to know)* si a Anilú le gustan las fotos.

d. Anilú dice *(says)* que tiene unas fotos digitales.

e. Ven una foto del papá de Anilú.

>> Voces del mundo hispano

En el video para este capítulo Mirna, José y Aura hablan de las profesiones y de sus familias. Lee las siguientes oraciones. Después mira el video una o más veces para decir si las oraciones son ciertas (**C**) o falsas (**F**).

1. Mirna estudia para ser diseñadora gráfica. F
2. José ya es paralegal y estudia para ser abogado. F
3. Una de las hermanas de Mirna trabaja en administración de empresas. C
4. Aura tiene un hermano y dos hermanas. C
5. Una hermana de Aura es contadora. C
6. José tiene seis miembros de su familia en Estados Unidos. F

>> Voces de Estados Unidos

Track 14

Gloria G. Rodríguez, fundadora de Avance

Gloria Rodriguez

❝Essentially, to be Hispanic is to value children . . . Rarely are children as welcomed and visible with adults as in the Latino culture. Indeed, los hijos son la riqueza de los padres, son nuestro gran tesoro.❞

La doctora Gloria G. Rodríguez es fundadora de Avance, una organización nacional que ayuda a familias latinas pobres con niños pequeños. En su libro, *Raising Nuestros Niños: Bringing Up Latino Children in a Bicultural World*, Rodríguez explica la filosofía de Avance así:

> Los padres tienen la esperanza y el deseo, hope and desire, that their children succeed, and that they feel un gran orgullo, a great sense of pride, when they do. Esta esperanza y orgullo de los padres, this hope and pride, become tremendous driving forces for Latino parents (p. 3).

Esta méxicoamericana de orígenes muy pobres es ganadora de muchos premios y reconocimientos por su labor con familias hispanas.

¿Y tú? ¿Es importante tu familia en tu vida estudiantil? ¿Qué papel juega la familia en la educación de los niños?

Standards 2.1, 2.2, 3.2: Students read about successful Spanish speakers in the U.S. and acquire cultural information that features distinctive viewpoints of Spanish-speaking people.

¡Prepárate!

Gramática útil 1

Describing daily activities: Irregular-**yo** verbs in the present indicative, **saber** vs. **conocer**, and the personal **a**

Cómo usarlo

1. You have already learned the present indicative tense of many verbs. These include regular **-ar**, **-er**, and **-ir** verbs (**hablar, comer, vivir**, etc.), some irregular verbs (**ser, tener, ir**), and some stem-changing verbs (**pensar, poder, dormir**, etc.).

Suggestion: You may want to do some old-fashioned drilling to see that students can produce irregular forms. Call out a random subject (**yo, tú, él, ella, ustedes**…) and infinitives from this section. Have students conjugate orally in chorus.

2. Now you will learn some verbs that are regular in all forms of the present indicative except the **yo** form. Like other verbs in the present indicative tense, these verbs can be used to say what you routinely do, what you are doing at the moment, or what you plan to do in the future.

Todos los días **salgo** para la universidad a las ocho.	*Every day **I leave** for the university at 8:00.*
Ahora mismo, **pongo** mis libros en la mochila y **digo** "hasta luego" a mi compañera de cuarto.	*Right now, **I put / I'm putting** my books in my backpack and **I say / I'm saying**, "See you later" to my roommate.*
Esta noche, **traigo** mis libros a casa otra vez y **hago** la tarea.	*Tonight, **I bring / I'll bring** my books home again and **I do / I'll do** my homework.*

Cómo formarlo

Irregular-yo verbs

Many irregular-**yo** verbs in the present indicative fall into several recognizable categories. Others have to be learned individually.

Suggestion: After checking forms, try more meaningful practice. Have a conversation about students' life at the university: **¿A qué hora sales de tu casa para la universidad? ¿Qué traes a la universidad? ¿Conduces a la universidad? ¿Conoces a mucha gente en la universidad? ¿A quién(es)?**, etc.

1. -go endings:

hacer	*to make; to do*	**hago**, haces, hace, hacemos, hacéis, hacen
poner	*to put*	**pongo**, pones, pone, ponemos, ponéis, ponen
salir	*to leave, to go out (with)*	**salgo**, sales, sale, salimos, salís, salen
traer	*to bring*	**traigo**, traes, trae, traemos, traéis, traen

Conducir is used more frequently in Spain to talk about driving. In most of Latin America, the verbs **manejar** and **guiar** (both regular **-ar** verbs) are used. (**Guiar** uses an accent on the **i** in these forms: **guío, guías, guía, guían.**)

2. -zco endings:

conducir	*to drive; to conduct*	**conduzco**, conduces, conduce, conducimos, conducís, conducen
conocer	*to know a person; to be familiar with*	**conozco**, conoces, conoce, conocemos, conocéis, conocen
traducir	*to translate*	**traduzco**, traduces, traduce, traducimos, traducís, traducen

3. Other irregular-**yo** verbs:

dar	*to give*	**doy**, das, da, damos, dais, dan
oír	*to hear*	**oigo**, oyes, oye, oímos, oís, oyen
saber	*to know a fact;* *to know how to*	**sé**, sabes, sabe, sabemos, sabéis, saben
ver	*to see*	**veo**, ves, ve, vemos, veis, ven

Note that **oír** requires a **y** in the **tú, él / ella / Ud.,** and **ellos / ellas / Uds.** forms.

4. Two irregular-**yo** verbs (**-go** verbs) with a stem change:

decir	*to say, to tell*	**digo**, dices, dice, decimos, decís, dicen
venir	*to come, to attend*	**vengo**, vienes, viene, venimos, venís, vienen

5. Remember that most of these verbs are irregular only in the **yo** form. Otherwise, they follow the rules for regular **-ar, -er**, and **-ir** verbs that you have already learned. **Oír** uses the regular endings but includes a spelling change: the addition of **y** to all forms except the **yo** form. **Decir** and **venir** also have a stem change in addition to the irregular-**yo** form, but they still use **-ir** present-tense endings.

Suggestion: To clarify the **saber / conocer** contrast, ask students questions about their classmates: **¿Conoces a Jim de nuestra clase? ¿Qué sabes de él?** (su especialidad, su dirección electrónica, etc.)

Saber vs. conocer

Saber and **conocer** both mean *to know*. It's important to know when to use each one.

- Use **saber** to say that you know a fact or information, or that you know how to do something.

Algún día vas a tener hijos y entonces vas a **saber** cómo es.

Eduardo **sabe** hablar alemán, jugar tenis y bailar flamenco. Además **sabe** dónde están todos los restaurantes buenos de la ciudad.	*Eduardo **knows how** to speak German, play tennis, and dance flamenco. He also **knows** where all the good restaurants in the city are.*

- Use **conocer** to say that you know a person or are familiar with a thing.

—¿**Conocen** a Sandra?	*Do you **know** Sandra?*
—No, pero **conocemos** a su hermana.	*No, but we **know** her sister.*
—¿**Conoces** bien Tegucigalpa?	*Do you **know** Tegucigalpa well?*
—Sí, pero no **conozco** las otras ciudades de Honduras.	*Yes, but I don't **know** the other cities in Honduras.*

One way to remember the difference between **saber** and **conocer** is that **saber** is usually followed by either a verb or a phrase, while **conocer** is often followed by a noun and is never followed by an infinitive.

The personal **a** can also be used with pets: **Adoro a mi perro.**

The personal a

When you use **conocer** to say that you know a person, notice that you use the preposition **a** before the noun referring to the person. This preposition is known as the personal **a** in Spanish and it must be used whenever a person receives the action of any verb (not just **conocer**). It has no equivalent in English.

In **Chapter 3** you learned that **a** + **el** = **al**. The personal **a** is no exception: **Veo al profesor.**

Conocemos **a** Nina y **a** Roberto.	*We know Nina and Roberto.*
¿Ves **a** tus amigos frecuentemente?	*Do you see your friends frequently?*

I **1** **¿Sí o no?** Lee las oraciones y decide si requieren la **a** personal o no. Añade la **a** personal si es necesaria o marca con una **X** si no es necesaria.

1. Veo _____a_____ mis hermanos todos los días.
2. Hago mi tarea con _____X_____ ellos.
3. Les digo las noticias de casa _____a_____ ellos también.
4. Oigo _____X_____ sus comentarios sobre la universidad.
5. Conozco _____a_____ muchos de sus amigos.
6. Conduzco el auto cuando visito _____a_____ mi familia.

Answers, Act. 2: 1. Salgo del trabajo a las cinco. 2. Generalmente, traigo trabajo a casa. 3. Cuando llego a casa, vengo muy cansada. 4. Hago la cena a las siete. 5. Pongo la mesa antes de hacer la cena. 6. Cuando la cena está preparada, digo "todo está listo". 7. Conozco a mis hijos muy bien. 8. Sé que tengo que llamarlos varias veces. 9. Por fin, oigo a los niños apagar la tele. 10. Doy las gracias por otro día más o menos normal.

Expansion, Act. 2: To practice third-person singular forms, have students go back through **Activity 2** and begin each sentence with **La mamá de Anilú.**

M **2** **La mamá de Anilú** La mamá de Anilú le describe un día normal a una amiga. Da su descripción desde su punto de vista *(viewpoint)*.

1. salir del trabajo a las cinco
2. generalmente, traer trabajo a casa
3. cuando llego a casa, venir muy cansada
4. hacer la cena *(dinner)* a las siete
5. poner la mesa *(set the table)* antes de hacer la cena
6. cuando la cena está preparada, decir "todo está listo"
7. conocer a mis hijos muy bien
8. saber que tengo que llamarlos varias veces
9. por fin, oír a los niños apagar la tele
10. dar las gracias por otro día más o menos normal

M/C **3** **¿Sabes…?** Con un(a) compañero(a), formen preguntas con las siguientes frases. Túrnense para hacerse las preguntas. Luego, inventen nuevas preguntas usando el verbo en cada frase y háganse esas preguntas.

MODELO conducir para llegar a la universidad
Tú: *¿Conduces para llegar a la universidad?*
Compañero(a): *No, no conduzco para llegar a la universidad.*
Tú: *¿Conduces todos los días?*
Compañero(a): *No, conduzco tres días por semana.*

1. conocer al (a la) presidente de la universidad
2. dar tu contraseña a tus amigos
3. decir siempre la verdad
4. hacer la tarea puntualmente
5. saber escribir programas para los teléfonos inteligentes
6. salir frecuentemente con amigos
7. traducir poemas del inglés al español
8. traer la computadora portátil a la clase
9. venir cansado(a) o aburrido(a) de las clases
10. ver televisión por la mañana, la tarde or la noche

4 **¿Saber o conocer?** Con un(a) compañero(a), túrnense para hacer las
M/C siguientes preguntas. La persona que hace las preguntas tiene que decidir entre
los verbos **saber** o **conocer**.

> **MODELO** ¿(Saber / Conocer / Conocer a) hablar español?
> Tú: *¿Sabes hablar español?*
> Compañero(a): *Sí, sé hablar español.*

1. ¿(Saber / Conocer / Conocer a) el (la) compañero(a) de cuarto de…?
2. ¿(Saber / Conocer / Conocer a) Nueva York, París o Londres?
3. ¿(Saber / Conocer / Conocer a) tocar el violín?
4. ¿(Saber / Conocer / Conocer a) Honduras?
5. ¿(Saber / Conocer / Conocer a) preparar comida hondureña o salvadoreña?

Preparation: Remind students that
the **a personal no se traduce al
inglés.** Examples: **Conozco a su papá.
¿A quién buscas?**

Answers, Act. 4: 1. ¿Conoces al (a la)
compañero(a) de cuarto de…?
2. ¿Conoces Nueva York, París o
Londres? 3. ¿Sabes tocar el violín?
4. ¿Conoces Honduras? 5. ¿Sabes
preparar comida hondureña o
salvadoreña?

Learning objective: Understanding

 5 **Sé y conozco** Escribe cinco cosas que **sabes** hacer. Luego escribe
C el nombre de cinco personas o lugares que **conoces**. Intercambia tu lista
con un(a) compañero(a). Tu compañero(a) tiene que informarle a la clase
lo que tú **sabes** y **conoces** y tú tienes que hacer lo mismo con la lista de tu
compañero(a).

> **MODELO** Tu lista: *Sé jugar tenis.*
> *Conozco a muchas personas que juegan tenis.*
> Tu compañero(a): *Javier sabe jugar tenis.*
> *Conoce a muchas personas que juegan tenis.*

6 **Cuestionario** Primero, escribe tus respuestas a las preguntas. Luego, en
C grupos de tres, háganse las preguntas del siguiente cuestionario. Si quieren,
pueden añadir algunas preguntas al cuestionario. Cada uno en el grupo debe
contestar cada pregunta.

Learning objective: Applying

1. **Tu horario**
   ¿Cuándo haces ejercicio?
   ¿Cuándo haces la tarea?
2. **Tu vida social**
   ¿Sales por la noche? ¿Adónde vas?
   ¿Con quién sales los fines de semana?
3. **Tu medio de transporte preferido**
   ¿Tienes coche? ¿Conduces a la universidad?
   ¿Conduces todos los días o usas otro medio de transporte?
4. **Tu tiempo libre**
   ¿Sabes jugar algún deporte?
   ¿Sabes tocar un instrumento? ¿Cuál?
5. **¿Conoces el mundo?**
   ¿Conoces los países de Latinoamérica? ¿Cuáles?
   ¿Conoces África o Asia?

>> Gramática útil 2

Describing daily activities: Reflexive verbs

Ya es hora de despertarse a una nueva clase de hotel de negocios.

Hotel Calidad Ejecutiva
www.calidadejecutiva.com 1-800-444-4444
7800 Avenida Norte, San Salvador 2901-8720

This ad for a business hotel in El Salvador uses a reflexive verb. What is it and what does it mean?

Answers: despertarse, to wake up

The reflexive pronoun and verb must always match the subject of the sentence: **Nosotros nos bañamos, Ellos se afeitan, Mateo se lava**, etc.

Heritage Learners: Heritage language speakers may need help with the orthographic conventions that apply to these and other pronouns in Spanish. Point out that pronouns following gerunds or infinitives are attached to the verb but that those preceding the verb are written as a separate word. Use the following dictation to practice this rule: **1. Los médicos que no se lavan las manos cuidadosamente después de cada consulta pueden enfermarse. 2. Usualmente, Juan se despierta a las 7:00 para llegar a tiempo a su clase a las 8: 00. Hoy va a despertarse más tarde porque no hay clase. 3. Nos conocimos hace un año, pero no comenzamos a vernos hasta el mes pasado.**

Cómo usarlo

1. So far, you have learned to use Spanish verbs to say what actions people are doing or to describe people and things.

Elena **habla** por teléfono.	*Elena **talks** on the phone.*
Tu hermano **está** cansado.	*Your brother **is** tired.*

2. Spanish has another category of verbs, called *reflexive* verbs, where the action of the verb *reflects back* on the person who is doing the action. When you use reflexive verbs in Spanish, they are often translated in English as *with* or *to myself, yourself, himself, herself, ourselves, yourselves, themselves.*

Lidia **se maquilla**.	*Lidia **puts makeup on (herself)**.*
Antes de ir a clase, yo **me ducho**, **me visto** y **me peino**.	*Before going to class, **I shower**, **get dressed**, and **comb my hair**.*

3. Notice how a reflexive verb is always used with a reflexive pronoun. These pronouns always match the subject of the sentence. The action of the verb *reflects back* on the person when the pronoun is used.

Yo me acuesto a las once.	***I go to bed (put myself to bed) at eleven.***
Tú te despiertas a las diez los fines de semana.	***You get up (wake yourself up) at ten on the weekends.***
Nosotros nos bañamos antes de salir de casa.	***We bathe (ourselves) before** we leave the house.*
Ellos se afeitan todos los días.	***They shave (themselves)** every day.*

4. Most reflexive verbs can also be used without the reflexive pronoun to express non-reflexive actions, that is, actions that are performed on someone other than oneself.

Mateo **se baña** todos los días.	*Mateo **bathes** every day.*
Mateo **baña** a su perro.	*Mateo **bathes (washes)** his dog.*

5. Reflexive pronouns can also be used to indicate *reciprocal actions.*

Leo y Ali **se cortan** el pelo.	*Leo and Ali **cut each other's** hair.*

Cómo formarlo

LO BÁSICO

- A *reflexive verb* is one in which the action described reflects back on the subject.
- A *reflexive pronoun* is a pronoun that refers back to the subject of the sentence. English reflexive pronouns are *myself, herself, ourselves,* etc.

1. You conjugate reflexive verbs the same way you would any other verb. The only difference is that you must always include the reflexive pronoun.

2. Here is the reflexive verb **lavarse** conjugated in the present indicative tense.

lavarse *(to wash oneself)*	
yo	**me lav<u>o</u>**
tú	**te lav<u>as</u>**
Ud. / él / ella	**<u>se</u> lav<u>a</u>**
nosotros(as)	**<u>nos</u> lav<u>amos</u>**
vosotros(as)	**<u>os</u> lav<u>áis</u>**
Uds. / ellos / ellas	**<u>se</u> lav<u>an</u>**

3. The only difference in the way that reflexive and non-reflexive verbs are conjugated is the addition of the reflexive pronoun to the verb form. Verbs that are irregular or stem-changing when used non-reflexively have the same irregularities or stem changes when used with a reflexive pronoun.

| **Me despierto** a las seis y media. | *I wake (myself) up at 6: 30.* |
| **Despierto a mi esposo** a las siete. | *I wake my husband up at 7: 00.* |

4. When you use a reflexive verb in its infinitive form, the reflexive pronoun may attach at the end of the infinitive (most commonly) or go at the beginning of the entire verb phrase.

Voy a acostarme a las once.	OR: **Me voy a acostar** a las once.
Necesito acostarme a las once.	**Me necesito acostar** a las once.
Tengo que acostarme a las once.	**Me tengo que acostar** a las once.

Notice that with **gustar** (and similar verbs), the reflexive pronoun *must* be attached at the end of the infinitive.

Me gusta acostar<u>me</u> a las once.

5. Here are some common reflexive verbs, many of which refer to daily routine. Many reflexive verbs have a stem change, which is indicated in parenthesis.

acostarse (ue) *to go to bed*	**levantarse** *to get up*
afeitarse *to shave oneself*	**maquillarse** *to put on makeup*
bañarse *to take a bath*	**peinarse** *to brush / comb one's hair*
cepillarse el pelo *to brush one's hair*	**ponerse (la ropa)** *to put on (clothing)*
cepillarse los dientes *to brush one's teeth*	**prepararse** *to get ready*
despertarse (ie) *to wake up*	**quitarse (la ropa)** *to take off (clothing)*
ducharse *to take a shower*	**secarse el pelo** *to dry one's hair*
lavarse *to wash oneself*	**sentarse (ie)** *to sit down*
lavarse el pelo *to wash one's hair*	**vestirse (i)** *to get dressed*
lavarse los dientes *to brush one's teeth*	

Standard 4.1: Take this opportunity to contrast more examples of reflexive verbs in Spanish, with equivalents in English in written form, to demonstrate that the reflexive pronouns do not necessarily translate tangibly to English:

me lavo	*I wash (myself)*
te cepillas	*you brush (your teeth)*
nos vestimos	*we dress / we get dressed*
se duchan	*they shower*

Remember that when you use a reflexive verb as an infinitive, you still need to change the pronoun to match the subject of the sentence: **Voy a acostarme a las once, pero tú vas a acostar<u>te</u> a medianoche**.

Suggestion: To present these verbs, act out and "ham up" your daily routine using these verbs. A few props like a brush, comb, razor, or makeup will make the presentation memorable and create a context for learning the verbs. Then mime different verbs and have students tell what you're doing; for example, **te acuestas, te afeitas**. Have students mime actions for classmates to identify. Organize TPR-type activities to associate movements with actions.

6. Some Spanish verbs are used with reflexive pronouns to emphasize a change in state or emotion. Spanish has many more verbs that are used this way than English does. Note that some of these verbs (**casarse, comprometerse,** etc.) are usually used to express reciprocal actions, due to the nature of their meaning.

casarse *to get married*	**irse** *to leave, to go away*
comprometerse *to get engaged*	**pelearse** *to have a fight*
despedirse (i) *to say goodbye*	**preocuparse** *to worry*
divertirse (ie) *to have fun*	**quejarse** *to complain*
divorciarse *to get divorced*	**reírse (i)** *to laugh*
dormirse (ue) *to fall asleep*	**relajarse** *to relax*
enamorarse *to fall in love*	**reunirse** *to meet, to get together*
enfermarse *to get sick*	**separarse** *to separate*

7. Here are some common words and phrases to use with these verbs.

a veces *sometimes*	**siempre** *always*
antes *before*	**todas las semanas** *every week*
después *after*	**todos los días** *every day*
luego *later*	**...veces al día /** *. . . times a day /*
nunca *never*	**por semana** *per week*

ACTIVIDADES

MODELO

7 **Necesito...** Para vernos y sentirnos bien, Track 15 todos tenemos que hacer ciertas cosas antes o después de participar en ciertas actividades. Escucha las descripciones y escoge el dibujo que le corresponde a cada descripción.

1. c
2. e
3. f

4. d
5. b
6. a

8 De visita

M Estás de visita en la casa de tu compañero(a) y quieres saber más de la rutina diaria de él o ella y de su familia. Hazle las preguntas de la lista y si quieres, también inventa otras.

MODELO Tú: *¿A qué hora (acostarse) tus padres?*
Tú: *¿A qué hora se acuestan tus padres?*
Compañero(a): *Mis padres se acuestan a las diez o las once de la noche.*

1. ¿Tú (lavarse) el pelo todos los días?
2. ¿Cuántas veces por semana (afeitarse) tu abuelo?
3. ¿(Despertarse) tarde o temprano tu madre?
4. ¿(Ducharse) por la mañana o por la noche tu hermano?
5. ¿(Maquillarse) tu hermana antes de salir para la universidad?
6. ¿A qué hora (acostar) tu compañero(a) de cuarto?
7. ¿A qué hora (levantarse) tu padre?
8. ¿(Peinarse) antes de salir para el colegio tu primo?
9. ¿Cuántas veces por día (lavarse) los dientes tú y tus hermanos?

9 La telenovela

M Miguel y Marta son los protagonistas de una telenovela famosa. Tú eres el (la) guionista *(script writer)* y tienes que escribir una descripción del desarrollo de su relación. Sigue el modelo.

MODELO divertirse en la fiesta de unos amigos
Miguel y Marta se divierten en la fiesta de unos amigos.

1. enamorarse después de un mes
2. comprometerse después de un año
3. casarse en la casa de los padres de Marta
4. pelearse frecuentemente
5. quejarse mucho a sus amigos
6. separarse por seis meses
7. divorciarse después de dos años de matrimonio
8. despedirse en el aeropuerto
9. irse a diferentes regiones del país
10. por fin reunirse

10 Preguntas personales

C Tú y tu compañero(a) quieren saber más sobre sus vidas. Háganse las siguientes preguntas. Luego, inventen cinco preguntas más que usen los verbos de la rutina diaria o los otros verbos reflexivos en las páginas 177–178.

1. ¿A qué hora te acuestas durante la semana? ¿Los fines de semana?
2. ¿A qué hora te levantas durante la semana? ¿Los fines de semana?
3. ¿Te preocupas mucho por tus estudios?
4. ¿Cuántas veces por semana te reúnes con tus amigos?
5.–9. ¿…?

Answers, Act. 8: 1. ¿Te lavas el pelo todos los días? 2. ¿Cuántas veces por semana se afeita tu abuelo? 3. ¿Se despierta tarde o temprano tu madre? 4. ¿Se ducha por la mañana o por la noche tu hermano? 5. ¿Se maquilla tu hermana antes de salir para la universidad? 6. ¿A qué hora se acuesta tu compañero(a) de cuarto? 7. ¿A qué hora se levanta tu padre? 8. ¿Se peina antes de salir para el colegio tu primo? 9. ¿Cuántas veces por día se lavan los dientes tú y tus hermanos?

Check: Be sure to follow up group work regularly (as in **Activity 8**) with spot checks that are both oral and written. By doing so, students will be aware that they are responsible for producing during group time, and instructors can assess performance levels for progress.

Answers, Act. 9: 1. Miguel y Marta se enamoran después de un mes. 2. Miguel y Marta se comprometen después de un año. 3. Miguel y Marta se casan en la casa de los padres de Marta. 4. Miguel y Marta se pelean frecuentemente. 5. Miguel y Marta se quejan mucho a sus amigos. 6. Miguel y Marta se separan por seis meses. 7. Miguel y Marta se divorcian después de dos años de matrimonio. 8. Miguel y Marta se despiden en el aeropuerto. 9. Miguel y Marta se van a diferentes regiones del país. 10. Miguel y Marta por fin se reúnen.

Learning objective: Understanding

Learning objective: Applying

Gramática útil 3

Describing actions in progress: The present progressive tense

Cómo usarlo

Las fotos. **¿Estás viendo** las fotos?

Heritage Learners: Keep in mind that heritage language students may use the gerund in ways that are consistent with English rather than Spanish grammar. Be particularly attentive to incorrect usage* of the gerund in three cases:

a. In subject position: *Nadando (nadar) es un buen ejercicio.

b. After a preposition: Lo pusieron en cárcel por *robando (robar) un carro.

c. In reference to future action: *Estamos teniendo (vamos a tener) una fiesta la semana que viene.

© Cengage Learning 2013

1. The present progressive tense is used in Spanish to describe actions that are in progress at the moment of speaking. It is equivalent to the *is / are + -ing* structure in English.

En este momento **estamos llamando** a los abuelos.
*Right now, **we are calling** the (our) grandparents.*

Están comiendo ahora.
***They are eating** right now.*

2. Note that the present progressive tense is used *much* more frequently in English than it is in Spanish. Whereas in English it is used to describe future plans, in Spanish the present indicative or the **ir** + **a** + infinitive structure is used instead.

Salimos con la familia este viernes.
***We are going out** with the family this Friday.*

Vamos a salir con la familia este viernes.
***We are going to go out** with the family this Friday.*

3. Use the present progressive in Spanish only to describe actions in which people are engaged at the moment. Do not use it to describe routine ongoing activities (use the present indicative), to describe generalized action (use the infinitive), or to describe future actions.

Right now:	No puedo hablar. **Estamos estudiando.**	*I can't talk. **We're studying** (right now).*
BUT:		
Routine:	**Estudio** español, biología, historia e informática.	*I am studying / I study Spanish, biology, history, and computer science.*
Generalized action:	**Estudiar** es importante.	*Studying is important.*
Future:	**Estudio** con Mario el lunes.	*I will study with Mario on Monday.*

Cómo formarlo

LO BÁSICO

A *present participle* is the verb form that expresses a continuing or ongoing action. In English, present participles end in *-ing*: *laughing, reading.*

1. Form the present progressive tense by using the present indicative forms of the verb **estar** (which you learned in **Chapter 4**) and the present participle.

> **estoy / estás / está / estamos / estáis / están** + present participle

2. Here's how to form the present participle of regular **-ar**, **-er**, and **-ir** verbs.

-ar verbs	-er / -ir verbs
Remove the **-ar** from the infinitive and add **-ando**.	Remove the **-er** / **-ir** from the infinitive and add **-iendo**.
caminar → **caminando**	ver → **viendo**
	escribir → **escribiendo**

Estamos caminando al centro.   *We're walking* downtown.
Estoy viendo la televisión.   *I'm watching* television.
Chali **está escribiendo** su trabajo.   *Chali is writing* her paper.

3. A few present participles are irregular.

leer: **leyendo**   oír: **oyendo**

4. All **-ir** stem-changing verbs show a stem change in their present participle as well.

e → i			
despedirse	**despidiéndose**	reírse	**riéndose**
divertirse	**divirtiéndose**	repetir	**repitiendo**
pedir	**pidiendo**	servir	**sirviendo**
o → u			
dormir	**durmiendo**	morir	**muriendo**

5. As you may have noticed in the list above, to form the present participle of reflexive verbs, you may attach the reflexive pronoun to the end of the present participle, or place it before the entire verb phrase, the same as when you use reflexive verbs in the infinitive. Note that when the pronoun is attached, the new present participle form requires an accent to maintain the correct pronunciation.

Lina está levantándose ahora mismo. /   *Lina is getting up* right now.
Lina se está levantando ahora mismo.

Estoy divirtiéndome mucho. /   *I'm having* a lot of *fun*.
Me estoy divirtiendo mucho.

ACTIVIDADES

11 **Preparaciones** La familia González va a una boda *(wedding)* y todos están preparándose. Escucha la conversación telefónica de un miembro de la familia y escoge la oración que dice qué está haciendo cada persona mencionada.

Track 16

I

MODELO __X__ La prima está peinándose. / _____ La prima está riéndose.

1. _____ El padre está vistiéndose. / __X__ El padre está afeitándose.

2. _____ La madre está duchándose. / __X__ La madre está bañándose.

3. __X__ El hermano está lavándose los dientes. / _____ El hermano está lavándose las manos.

4. __X__ La hermana está secándose el pelo. / _____ La hermana está sentándose.

5. __X__ Los abuelos están vistiéndose. / _____ Los abuelos están bañándose.

6. _____ Las tías están cepillándose el pelo. / __X__ Las tías están maquillándose.

12 **¿Qué están haciendo?** Básandote en los dibujos, pregúntale a un(a) compañero(a) qué está haciendo la persona del dibujo. Menciona la profesión de la persona también.

M

MODELO camarero (servir la comida)
Tú: *¿Qué está haciendo el camarero?*
Compañero(a): *Está sirviendo la comida.*

© Cengage Learning 2013

1. la profesora 2. la médica 3. la directora de social media 4. el cocinero 5. la asistente 6. la actriz

13 **¡Imagínense!** Trabaja con un(a) compañero(a) de clase. Juntos hagan una lista de diez personas famosas. Luego, digan qué (en su opinión) están haciendo en este momento. Escriban por lo menos dos frases para cada persona. ¡Sean creativos!

C

14 **¡Chismosos!** Ahora, intercambien sus frases de la **Actividad 13** con las de otra pareja. Juntos escriban una columna de chismes *(gossip)* para una revista semanal. Traten de escribir de una manera interesante y descriptiva. Pueden incluir dibujos de las personas, si quieren. Learning objective: Creating

C

Sonrisas

© Cengage Learning 2013

Expresión Trabaja con un(a) compañero(a) de clase para imaginar cómo es el día de un(a) presidente de una compañía internacional (o de otra profesión). ¿Cuál es su rutina diaria? Hagan un horario de un día típico.

MODELO *Son las ocho de la mañana. Está preparándose para una reunión.*

Honduras

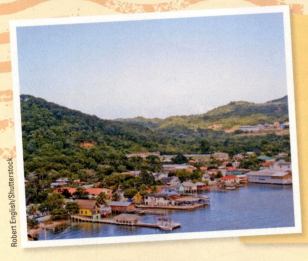

Robert English/Shutterstock

Información general

Nombre oficial: República de Honduras

Población: 7.989.415

Capital: Tegucigalpa (f. 1762) (1.200.000 hab.)

Otras ciudades importantes: San Pedro Sula (640.000 hab.), El Progreso (90.000 hab.)

Moneda: lempira

Idiomas: español (oficial), idiomas amerindios

Mapa de Honduras: Apéndice D

Christian Wilkinson/Shutterstock

Vale saber…

- Honduras tiene una gran historia de pueblos indígenas, entre ellos los lencas, los garífunas, los miskitos, los chortis, los pech, los tolupanes, los tawahkas y los mayas.

- En su cuarto y último viaje al Nuevo Mundo, Cristóbal Colón llega a las costas de Honduras en 1502. La conquista española de Honduras empieza dos décadas después, bajo órdenes de Hernán Cortés, y termina en 1537, con la muerte *(death)* de Lempira, guerrero héroe de orígenes maya-lenca.

- Copán, un centro gubernamental y ceremonial de la antigua civilización maya, se encuentra a orillas *(is located on the shores)* del río Copán, cerca de la frontera con Guatemala. Se considera uno de los sitios arqueológicos más importantes del Período Clásico.

- Honduras basa su economía en la agricultura, especialmente en las plantaciones de banana, cuya comercialización empezó *(began)* en 1889 con la fundación de Standard Fruit Company.

El Salvador

Información general ▶

Nombre oficial: República de El Salvador

Población: 6.052.064

Capital: San Salvador (f. 1524) (400.000 hab.)

Otras ciudades importantes: San Miguel (250.000 hab.), Santa Ana (250.000 hab.)

Moneda: dólar estadounidense

Idiomas: español (oficial), náhuatl, otras lenguas amerindias

Mapa de El Salvador: Apéndice D

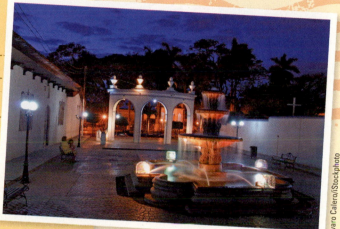

Vale saber...

- El Salvador es el país más pequeño de Centroamérica pero el más denso en población.

- Durante la época precolombina, El Salvador fue habitado por los pipiles y los lencas.

- Joya de Cerén, un Monumento de la Humanidad de la UNESCO en El Salvador, es un descubrimiento de gran importancia. Es un pueblo *(town)* entero sepultado en el siglo VII por una erupción volcánica. Como una Pompeya americana, Joya de Cerén es de inestimable valor arqueológico e histórico.

- Entre 1980 y 1990, El Salvador vivió en guerra civil. Durante esos años, muchos salvadoreños emigraron a Estados Unidos.

La mecatrónica

Courtesy of Unitec

En la Universidad Tecnológica Centroamericana (Unitec) de Honduras, puedes hacer la licenciatura en Mecatrónica, un curso de estudio que combina la mecánica, la electrónica y la informática. ¿Qué aprendes si estudias mecatrónica? Cómo diseñar y construir productos mecatrónicos, como los instrumentos médicos, las cámaras fotográficas, los 'chips' que automatizan a las máquinas, aparatos biomédicos y productos innovadores en varios campos como la bioingeniería. ¿Tienes aptitud para la mecatrónica?

COMEDICA, una cooperativa médica

Hace cuatro décadas *(four decades ago)*, once médicos salvadoreños deciden hacer algo revolucionario para pagar sus costos educativos. Con 100 colones de cada uno, abren una cooperativa para obtener crédito y ahorrar *(save)*. Hoy día, COMEDICA cuenta con $27.12 millones. Entre sus clientes hay médicos, odontólogos, psicólogos, químicos, farmacéuticos y enfermeros. Muchos médicos han adquirido *(have gotten)* sus casas, sus vehículos, equipo para sus clínicas y también sus estudios posgrados con la ayuda de COMEDICA. Los once médicos ilustran el dicho "¡Sí se puede!"

Photo Courtesy of COMEDICA

>> En resumen

Learning objectives: Understanding, Remembering

La información general

Di a qué país o países se refiere cada oración.

1. Un sitio arqueológico muy importante se encuentra en este país.
2. Las plantaciones de banana son una parte importante de la economía de este país.
3. Es el país más pequeño de Centroamérica.
4. Lempira es un gran héroe de este país.
5. El pueblo indígena de los lencas habita este país.
6. Este país pasó por *(underwent)* una guerra civil que duró *(lasted)* diez años.

El tema de las profesiones

1. ¿Qué áreas de estudio combina la mecatrónica?
2. ¿Qué productos aprendes a diseñar y construir en la mecatrónica?
3. ¿Quién empezó *(started)* la cooperativa COMEDICA?
4. ¿Qué dicho ilustra las acciones de los once médicos salvadoreños?

> ### ⊕ ¿QUIERES SABER MÁS?
> Revisa y rellena la tabla que empezaste al principio del capítulo. Luego, escoge un tema para investigar en línea y prepárate para compartir la información con la clase. También puedes escoger de las palabras clave a continuación o en **www.cengagebrain.com**.
>
> **Palabras clave: (Honduras)** los mayas, Lempira, los garífunas, los Miskito, José Antonio Velásques**; (El Salvador)** Tazumal, Acuerdos de Paz de Chapultepec, Óscar Arnulfo Romero, Claribel Alegría

Standard 5.1: Here students are encouraged to do independent web research on topics that will gradually require more Spanish to carry out the assignments by introducing more participation with Spanish-speaking communities online.

Learning objectives: Analyzing, Evaluating

⊕ **Tú en el mundo hispano** Para explorar oportunidades de usar el español para estudiar o hacer trabajos voluntarios o aprendizajes en Honduras y El Salvador, sigue los enlaces en **www.cengagebrain.com**.

⊕ **Ritmos del mundo hispano** Sigue los enlaces en **www.cengagebrain.com** para escuchar música de Honduras y El Salvador.

A leer

>> Antes de leer

ESTRATEGIA

Skimming for the main idea

When reading authentic materials, it's more important to focus on getting the main idea than to understand every word. Skimming is a reading strategy that helps you get the main idea of each paragraph. When you skim, you read quickly, looking for key words and phrases. Together, these techniques give you the main idea of each paragraph.

1 Mira la información sobre la cultura garífuna y completa las oraciones a continuación.

Jim Whitmers

Los garífunas son de ascendencia africana, arauaca e indio-caribe. Sus antepasados, exiliados de la isla de San Vicente en 1797, viajaron *(they traveled)* a la costa Atlántica de Belice y Honduras y a las islas de Barlovento de Nicaragua. Viven allí y en otras regiones cercanas *(close)* con la mayor parte de su cultura intacta, incluso su música y arte tradicionales.

1. La cultura garífuna tiene aproximadamente (150 / 220 / 250) años. 220
2. Los garífunas son de origen (africano / español / inglés). africano
3. Los garífunas todavía tienen su propia (país / cultura / presidente). cultura

Notice: L1 reading research shows that good readers know when they understand what they read and when they do not. They also have strategies for figuring out the material that they do not understand. These strategies include: using contextual clues such as looking ahead or back in the reading, using background information on the topic, paraphrasing a difficult sentence, seeking help, and making correct use of the dictionary. Use the readings in this chapter to give students practice with these skills. First, ask them to identify where in the reading the difficulty occurs. Next, ask them to state precisely what they do not understand. Lastly, model for students the use of deciphering strategies.

2 Trabaja con un(a) compañero(a) para hacer correspondencia entre las frases de la lectura a la izquierda y sus equivalentes en inglés a la derecha. Usen los cognados en negrilla *(boldface)* como guía.

1. __e__ a las **culturas** que los rodeaban
2. __f__ querían que los dejaran en **paz**
3. __c__ están **separados** por fronteras **nacionales**
4. __b__ se mantienen… **unidos**
5. __a__ los **antecesores** han legado
6. __d__ han permanecido fieles a su **pasado**

a. the **ancestors** have left to them
b. they maintain themselves **united**
c. they are **separated** by **national borders**
d. have remained faithful to their **past**
e. to the **cultures** that surround them
f. they wanted to be left in **peace**

3 Ahora lee rápidamente el siguiente artículo sobre la cultura garífuna de Centroamérica. Presta atención en particular a las frases en negrilla. Éstas son importantes para entender la sección. Después de cada sección, vas a tener la oportunidad de ver si entiendes bien las ideas principales.

LECTURA

La cultura garífuna

Durante siglos[1] los garífunas, que constituyen un **grupo étnico disperso a lo largo de las costas de cinco países, se han mantenido apartados**[2] de los demás pueblos[3]. Desde el principio, sus antepasados **no buscaron**[4] **conquistar ni asimilarse a las culturas** que los rodeaban. Sólo querían que los dejaran en paz.

Aunque están separados por fronteras nacionales, los garífunas se mantienen no obstante unidos en su determinación por preservar su cultura, rica en influencias africanas y americanas.

Esteban Felix/AP Images

¿Cierto o falso?   Learning objective (all ¿**Cierto o falso?** activities): Remembering

1. Los garífunas querían *(wanted to)* asimilarse a otras culturas.

2. La cultura garífuna es rica en influencias europeas.

Las comunidades garífunas **conservan celosamente**[5] **su arte, su música, sus artesanías y sus creencias religiosas**, que en conjunto[6] constituyen una forma de vida muy particular. Los antecesores han legado a los garífunas su **música característica, que incorpora canciones y ritmos africanos y americanos**, y un **expresivo lenguaje** que contiene elementos arauacos y caribes—los idiomas originales de los indios caribes—y yoruba, una lengua proveniente de África Occidental. Los garífunas **han permanecido fieles a su pasado**.

¿Cierto o falso?

3. Mantener las tradiciones del arte, de la música y de las creencias religiosas es muy importante para los garífunas.

4. La música garífuna tiene elementos africanos y europeos.

5. La lengua garífuna tiene elementos de lenguas caribes y de una lengua africana.

A través de[7] los siglos, los garífunas sin duda han mantenido el fuego[8] de su vida cultural. En la actualidad, **la libre práctica de sus antiguas tradiciones asegura el conocimiento de su singular historia** y contribuye a acrecentar[9] la riqueza cultural de los países que los albergan[10], compartiendo las sagradas creencias y las ricas expresiones artísticas de sus orgullosos[11] antepasados.

¿Cierto o falso?

6. En realidad, los garífunas no pueden conservar sus tradiciones antiguas.

7. Los garífunas hacen contribuciones culturales a los países donde viven.

Check yourself: 1. F 2. F 3. C 4. F 5. C 6. F 7. C

[1]*centuries* [2]**se…:** *they kept themselves separate* [3]*grupos étnicos* [4]**no…:** *did not seek to* [5]*jealously* [6]**en…:** *como un grupo* [7]**A…:** *Across, Throughout* [8]*fire* [9]*to strengthen, increase* [10]**los…:** *shelter them* [11]*proud*

Excerpt from "Los fuertes lazos ancestrales," from *Américas* magazine, the official publication of the Organization of American States (OAS), published bimonthly in identical English and Spanish editions. Used with permission.

4 Ahora que entiendes las ideas principales de las secciones del artículo, trabaja con un(a) compañero(a) de clase. Lean los párrafos otra vez y luego contesten las siguientes preguntas.

1. ¿Dónde viven los garífunas? en las costas de cinco países, entre ellos Honduras, Nicaragua y Belice

2. ¿Cómo es la lengua garífuna? Tiene elementos de lenguas caribeñas y de yoruba.

3. ¿Cómo es la música garífuna? Incorpora ritmos africanos y americanos.

Learning objectives: Remembering, Understanding

 5 Lee rápidamente la siguiente información sobre los garífunas en Estados Unidos y con un(a) compañero(a), contesten las preguntas a continuación.

Text: © Cengage Learning 2013
Poster: Ivan Moreira

Hay comunidades de garífunas en Estados Unidos también. Una de las más grandes y activas está en y cerca de *(near)* la Ciudad de Nueva York—es la población más grande de garífunas fuera de Centroamérica. La organización Garifuna Coalition USA, Inc. promueve la cultura garífuna de Nueva York y sirve como centro de información sobre sus eventos, noticias y celebraciones.

Todos los años la Coalición organiza el Mes de la Herencia Garífuna y presenta premios *(awards)* a las personas que han promovido *(have promoted)* la cultura garífuna y sus intereses en Estados Unidos. Recientemente organizó una campaña para educar a los garífunas de su comunidad sobre la importancia de identificarse como garífuna en los formularios del Censo 2010.

Answers, Act. 5: 1. en y cerca de Nueva York. 2. Promueve la cultura garífuna de Nueva York. 3. la importancia de identificarse como garífuna en los formularios del Censo 2010.

1. ¿Dónde hay una población grande de garífunas en Estados Unidos?

2. ¿Qué hace la Coalición?

3. ¿De qué trata *(What is it about)* una campaña reciente de la Coalición?

Learning objective: Evaluating

Preparation: Note that the reading does not offer explicit answers for **Activity 6**. Brainstorming a few advantages and disadvantages as a class will help groups get into the activity.

6 En grupos de tres o cuatro estudiantes, identifiquen uno o dos grupos culturales de Estados Unidos o de otros países que mantienen sus tradiciones y costumbres diferentes de las de sus países de residencia. En su opinión, ¿es la preservación de tradiciones y costumbres una consecuencia del aislamiento? ¿Hay beneficios de mantenerse aislados? ¿Hay desventajas *(disadvantages)*?

Antes de escribir

Standard 1.3: In the writing sections, students present information to readers, who may often consist of their classmates.

ESTRATEGIA

Writing—Creating a topic sentence

On page 189, you looked for the main idea, which is usually expressed by the topic sentence. A good paragraph contains a topic sentence and supporting details. When you write, focus on the information you want to convey and write a topic sentence for each paragraph that summarizes its key idea.

 1 Con un(a) compañero(a) de clase, miren el artículo en la página 189. Analicen cada párrafo para identificar la oración que mejor presente la idea principal del párrafo. Ésta es la **oración temática** *(topic sentence)*.

MODELO **Párrafo 1:** *Durante siglos los garífunas, que constituyen un grupo étnico disperso a lo largo de las costas de cinco países, se han mantenido apartados de los demás pueblos.*

2 Vas a escribir unas oraciones temáticas para una composición de tres párrafos sobre tu profesión futura. Piensa en los tres párrafos que vas a usar y escribe una oración temática para cada uno.

MODELO **Tema:** *Las profesiones*
Aspecto específico del tema: *Mi profesión del futuro*
Párrafo 1: (Description of the profession)
Oración temática: *Me interesa el diseño gráfico.*
Párrafo 2: (Reason you want to have this profession)
Oración temática: *Me gusta dibujar y trabajar en la computadora.*
Párrafo 3: (What you need to do to prepare yourself for this profession)
Oración temática: *Para prepararme, necesito tomar una combinación de cursos de diseño gráfico, de arte y de computación.*

Answers, Act. 1: *(Only the first few words in each sentence are provided.)* **Párrafo 2:** Aunque están separados**... Párrafo 3:** Las comunidades garífunas conservan**... Párrafo 4:** En la actualidad**...**

For extra help narrowing your topic, refer to the **A escribir** section in **Chapter 4**.

Learning objective: Creating

Composición

Learning objective: Creating

3 Ahora, usa las tres oraciones temáticas que escribiste para la **Actividad 2** y escribe una composición de tres párrafos sobre tu profesión futura.

Después de escribir

4 Mira tu borrador otra vez. Usa la siguiente lista para revisarlo.

- ¿Tienen tus oraciones temáticas toda la información necesaria?
- ¿Corresponden los sujetos de las oraciones a los verbos correctos?
- ¿Corresponden las formas de los artículos, los sustantivos y los adjetivos?
- ¿Usas correctamente los verbos reflexivos y los verbos irregulares?
- ¿Hay errores de puntuación o de ortografía?

Vocabulario

Suggestion: To review vocabulary, as a synthesis activity have students review their family trees orally and identify their family members and each one's profession.

La familia   *The family*

La familia nuclear   *The nuclear family*

la madre (mamá) *mother*
el padre (papá) *father*
los padres *parents*
la esposa *wife*
el esposo *husband*
la hija *daughter*
el hijo *son*
la hermana (mayor) *(older) sister*
el hermano (menor) *(younger) brother*
la tía *aunt*
el tío *uncle*
la prima *female cousin*
el primo *male cousin*
la sobrina *niece*
el sobrino *nephew*
la abuela *grandmother*
el abuelo *grandfather*
la nieta *granddaughter*
el nieto *grandson*

La familia política   *In-laws*

la suegra *mother-in-law*
el suegro *father-in-law*
la nuera *daughter-in-law*
el yerno *son-in-law*
la cuñada *sister-in-law*
el cuñado *brother-in-law*

Otros parientes   *Other relatives*

la madrastra *stepmother*
el padrastro *stepfather*
la hermanastra *stepsister*
el hermanastro *stepbrother*
la media hermana *half-sister*
el medio hermano *half-brother*

Las profesiones y carreras   *Professions and careers*

el (la) abogado(a) *lawyer*
el (la) asistente *assistant*
el actor / la actriz *actor / actress*
el (la) arquitecto(a) *architect*
el (la) artista *artist*
el (la) bombero(a) *firefighter*
el (la) camarero(a) *waiter / waitress*
el (la) carpintero(a) *carpenter*
el (la) cocinero(a) *cook, chef*
el (la) contador(a) *accountant*
el (la) dentista *dentist*
el (la) dependiente *salesclerk*
el (la) director(a) de social media *director of social media*
el (la) diseñador(a) gráfico(a) *graphic designer*
el (la) dueño(a) de... *owner of . . .*

el (la) enfermero(a) *nurse*
el (la) gerente de... *manager of . . .*
el hombre / la mujer de negocios *businessman / businesswoman*
el (la) ingeniero(a) *engineer*
el (la) maestro(a) *teacher*
el (la) mecánico(a) *mechanic*
el (la) médico(a) *doctor*
el (la) peluquero(a) *barber / hairdresser*
el (la) periodista *journalist*
el (la) plomero(a) *plumber*
el (la) policía *policeman / policewoman*
el (la) programador(a) *programmer*
el (la) secretario(a) *secretary*
el (la) trabajador(a) *worker*
el (la) veterinario(a) *veterinarian*

En el baño   *In the bathroom*

el cepillo *hairbrush*
el cepillo de dientes *toothbrush*
el champú *shampoo*
el desodorante *deodorant*
el jabón *soap*
el maquillaje *makeup, cosmetics*

la máquina de afeitar *electric razor*
la pasta de dientes *toothpaste*
el peine *comb*
la rasuradora *razor*
la toalla *towel*
la toalla de mano *hand towel*

Verbos con la forma **yo** irregular

conducir (-zc) *to drive; to conduct*
conocer (-zc) *to know a person; to be familiar with*
dar (doy) *to give*
decir (-g) (i) *to say, to tell*
hacer (-g) *to make; to do*
oír (oigo) *to hear*

poner (-g) *to put*
saber (sé) *to know a fact; to know how to*
salir (-g) *to leave; to go out (with)*
traducir (-zc) *to translate*
traer (-go) *to bring*
venir (-g) (ie) *to come*
ver (veo) *to see*

Verbos reflexivos

Acciones físicas   *Physical actions*
acostarse (ue) *to go to bed*
afeitarse *to shave oneself*
bañarse *to take a bath*
cepillarse el pelo *to brush one's hair*
cepillarse los dientes *to brush one's teeth*
despertarse (ie) *to wake up*
dormirse (ue) *to fall asleep*
ducharse *to take a shower*
lavarse *to wash oneself*
lavarse el pelo *to wash one's hair*
lavarse los dientes *to brush one's teeth*
levantarse *to get up*
maquillarse *to put on makeup*
peinarse *to brush / comb one's hair*
ponerse (la ropa) *to put on (clothing)*
prepararse *to get ready*
quitarse (la ropa) *to take off (clothing)*
secarse el pelo *to dry one's hair*
sentarse (ie) *to sit down*
vestirse (i) *to get dressed*

Estados / emociones   *States / emotions*
casarse *to get married*
comprometerse *to get engaged*
despedirse (i) *to say goodbye*
divertirse (ie) *to have fun*
divorciarse *to get divorced*
enamorarse *to fall in love*
enfermarse *to get sick*
irse *to leave, to go away*
pelearse *to have a fight*
preocuparse *to worry*
quejarse *to complain*
reírse (i) *to laugh*
relajarse *to relax*
reunirse *to meet, to get together*
separarse *to get separated*

Otros verbos

bañar *to swim; to give someone a bath*
despertar (ie) *to wake someone up*
lavar *to wash*
levantar *to raise, to lift*

manejar *to drive*
quitar *to take off*
secar *to dry something*
vestir (i) *to dress someone*

Otras palabras y expresiones

a veces *sometimes*
antes *before*
después *after*
luego *later*
nunca *never*

siempre *always*
todas las semanas *every week*
...veces al día / por semana
  . . . times a day / per week

Repaso y preparación

>> **Repaso del Capítulo 5**

Preparation: Have students review this material and complete the activities here, in the SAM, and online before they begin **Chapter 6**.

Complete these activities to check your understanding of the new grammar points in **Chapter 5** before you move on to **Chapter 6**.

The answers to the activities in this section can be found in **Appendix B**.

Check: The **Repaso** section not only reviews grammar and vocabulary for the student but it offers a built-in performance assessment. By doing review activities with students, you can assess concepts that you may need to continue to reinforce in future classes.

Answers, Act. 2: 1. Tú conoces Buenos Aires. 2. Ellos saben jugar golf. 3. Yo sé todas las respuestas. 4. Usted conoce a mis primos. 5. Nosotras conocemos al chef. 6. Ella sabe cocinar bien.

Answers, Act. 4: 1. Ella está hablando con un paciente. 2. Yo estoy escribiendo un artículo. 3. Ellos están preparando la comida. 4. Nosotros estamos pintando. 5. Usted está sirviendo la comida. 6. Él está trabajando en la computadora.

Irregular-yo verbs (p. 172) *Answers will vary for Sí/No column.*

1 Completa la encuesta con las formas correctas de los verbos indicados. Después indica si las oraciones son ciertas (**Sí**) o falsas (**No**) para ti.

Yo...		Sí	No	Yo...		Sí	No
1. ...(saber) hablar francés.	Sé			4. ...(hacer) mi tarea todos los días.	Hago		
2. ...(conocer) a una persona famosa.	Conozco			5. ...(salir) todas las noches.	Salgo		
3. ...(conducir) todos los días.	Conduzco			6. ...(ver) a familia todas las semanas.	Veo		

Saber vs. conocer (p. 173)

2 Mira cada cosa o actividad y di si la persona indicada **sabe** o **conoce** cada una. Escribe oraciones completas y no olvides usar la **a** personal cuando sea necesario.

1. tú / Buenos Aires
2. ellos / jugar golf
3. yo / todas las respuestas
4. usted / mis primos
5. nosotras / el chef
6. ella / cocinar bien

Reflexive verbs (p. 176)

3 Completa las oraciones con las formas correctas de los verbos indicados.

1. Martina __se maquilla__ (maquillarse) todos los días.
2. Frecuentemente yo __me acuesto__ (acostarse) muy tarde.
3. Ustedes __se reunen__ (reunirse) todos los miércoles.
4. ¿Tú __te levantas__ (levantarse) temprano o tarde?
5. Nosotros nunca __nos enfermamos__ (enfermarse).
6. Ellos __se pelean__ (pelearse) casi todos los días.

The present progressive tense (p. 180)

4 Haz una oración para decir qué está haciendo cada persona en este momento. Usa las actividades de la lista y sigue el modelo.

MODELO   Tú eres actriz.
Estás maquillándote.

Actividades: escribir un artículo, hablar con un paciente, maquillarse, pintar, preparar la comida, servir la comida, trabajar en la computadora

1. Ella es médica.
2. Yo soy periodista.
3. Ellos son cocineros.
4. Nosotros somos artistas.
5. Usted es camarera.
6. Él es secretario.

194 Capítulo 5

Preparación para el Capítulo 6

Learning objective: Evaluating

Adjective agreement (Chapter 2)

5 Tu amigo habla de su familia. Completa sus comentarios con las formas correctas de los adjetivos indicados.

Tengo una familia 1. ___grande___ (grande). Pero todas las personas son muy 2. ___extrovertidas___ (extrovertido). Mis hermanas son bastante 3. ___simpáticas___ (simpático) pero mi hermanito es un poco 4. ___tonto___ (tonto). Mis primos normalmente están 5. ___contentos___ (contento) pero hoy están muy 6. ___nerviosos___ (nervioso). Mis abuelos son 7. ___viejos___ (viejo) y muy 8. ___divertidos___ (divertido). Me gustan mucho mis familiares y estoy 9. ___triste___ (triste) que no puedo ver a mi familia más frecuentemente.

> Complete these activities to review some previously learned grammatical structures that will be helpful when you learn the new grammar in **Chapter 6.**
>
> Be sure to reread **Chapter 5: Gramática útil 1** before moving on to the new **Chapter 6** grammar sections.

The present indicative of regular -ar verbs (Chapter 2), regular -er and -ir verbs (Chapter 3), and stem-changing verbs (Chapter 4)

6 Escribe oraciones completas con las formas correctas de los verbos indicados.

1. mi tío / lavar su auto todas las semanas
2. mis abuelos / no dormir mucho
3. mis primas / preferir estudiar en la residencia estudiantil
4. mi hermano y yo / correr en el parque los sábados
5. tú / manejar todos los días
6. mi madre / vestir a mi hermanita por las mañanas
7. yo / mirar una película
8. mi madre y yo / vivir en un apartamento grande

Answers, Act. 6: 1. Mi tío lava su auto todas las semanas. 2. Mis abuelos no duermen mucho. 3. Mis primas prefieren estudiar en la residencia estudiantil. 4. Mi hermano y yo corremos en el parque los sábados. 5. Tú manejas todos los días. 6. Mi madre viste a mi hermanita por las mañanas. 7. Yo miro una película. 8. Mi madre y yo vivimos en un apartamento grande.

The verb estar (Chapter 4)

7 Di dónde están las personas indicadas.

MODELO *yo / café*
Yo estoy en el café.

1. la mujer de negocios / oficina
2. tú y yo / salón de clase
3. el Doctor Méndez / hospital
4. los programadores / centro de computación
5. la policía / parque
6. yo / biblioteca
7. los cocineros / restaurante
8. tú / gimnasio

Answers, Act. 7: 1. La mujer de negocios está en la oficina. 2. Tú y yo estamos en el salón de clase. 3. El Doctor Méndez está en el hospital. 4. Los programadores están en el centro de computación. 5. La policía está en el parque. 6. Yo estoy en la biblioteca. 7. Los cocineros están en el restaurante. 8. Tú estás en el gimnasio.

VOLUME 2

CUADROS

INTRODUCTORY SPANISH

Sheri Spaine Long
University of Alabama at Birmingham

María Carreira
California State University at Long Beach

Sylvia Madrigal Velasco

Kristin Swanson

HEINLE
CENGAGE Learning™

Australia • Brazil • Canada • Mexico • Singapore • Spain • United Kingdom • United States

VOLUME 2

CUADROS

INTRODUCTORY SPANISH

Sheri Spaine Long
University of Alabama at Birmingham

María Carreira
California State University at Long Beach

Sylvia Madrigal Velasco

Kristin Swanson

HEINLE
CENGAGE Learning™

Australia • Brazil • Japan • Korea • Mexico • Singapore • Spain • United Kingdom • United States

Mi identidad

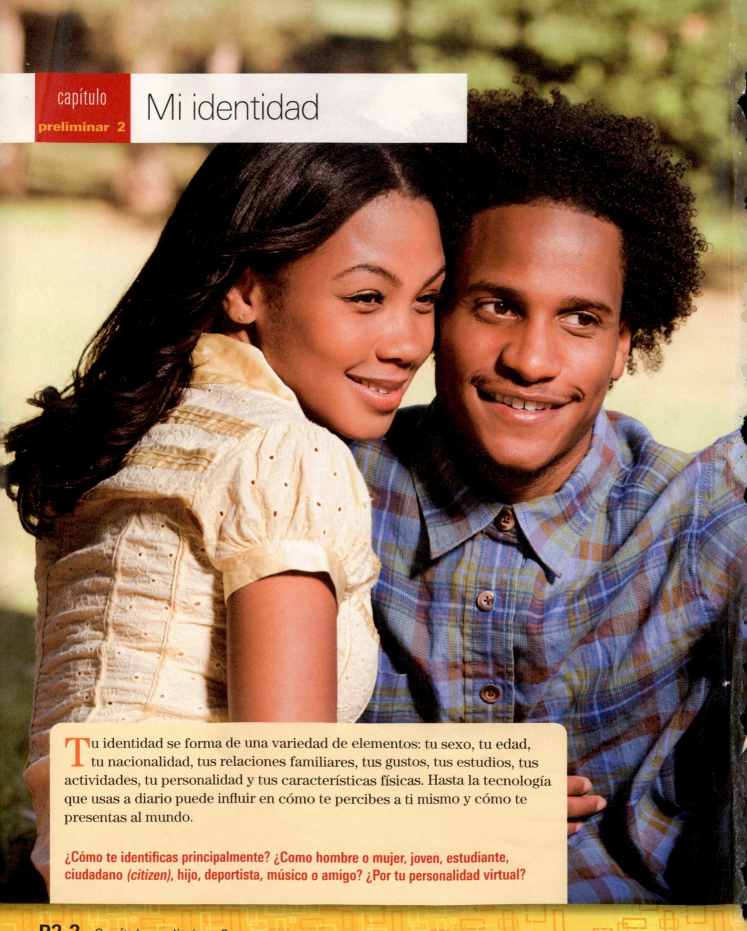

Tu identidad se forma de una variedad de elementos: tu sexo, tu edad, tu nacionalidad, tus relaciones familiares, tus gustos, tus estudios, tus actividades, tu personalidad y tus características físicas. Hasta la tecnología que usas a diario puede influir en cómo te percibes a ti mismo y cómo te presentas al mundo.

¿Cómo te identificas principalmente? ¿Como hombre o mujer, joven, estudiante, ciudadano *(citizen)*, hijo, deportista, músico o amigo? ¿Por tu personalidad virtual?

In this chapter, you will review

Communication

- **identity:** personal information, greetings, introductions, phone calls
- **likes and dislikes:** interests, activities, personal and physical descriptions
- **studies:** classes, schedules, time and dates
- **technology:** hardware, software, Internet, electronics, emotions
- **family:** family members, professions, daily routines, personal care items

Grammar

- **hay** with nouns
- nouns, articles, and adjectives
- the present indicative tense of regular, irregular, stem-changing and irregular-**yo** verbs
- **gustar** and verbs like **gustar**
- interrogative words
- simple possessive adjectives
- **ser** vs. **estar**
- adverbs
- reflexive verbs
- the present progressive

Culture

- un podcast de una estudiante méxicoamericana

iofoto.com/Big

A repasar

Activity 1 practices **hay** with nouns, using **Volume 1 Preliminary Chapter** vocabulary.

1 ¿Qué hay? Con un(a) compañero(a), túrnense para decir si las siguientes cosas están en el salón de clase. **¡OJO!** No deben usar el artículo con los sustantivos plurales, ni tampoco en las oraciones negativas con **hay**.

MODELO   Tú: *Hay un diccionario en el salón de clase.*
             Compañero(a): *No hay notas en el salón de clase.*

Cosas: una calculadora, una computadora, un diccionario, un escritorio, un lápiz, unos libros, una mesa, unas mochilas, unas notas, una pizarra, unas sillas, unas ventanas

Activity 2 practices nouns, articles, and adjectives with the verb **ser**, using vocabulary from **Volume 1, Chapters 1, 2,** and **3**.

2 ¿Cómo son? Con un(a) compañero(a), túrnense para describir las siguientes cosas y personas, usando adjetivos de la lista.

MODELO   *Los libros de la serie* The Hunger Games *son interesantes.*

Cosas: la canción (título), la clase de..., el libro (título), la película (título), el programa de televisión (título), ¿...?
Personas: el actor (nombre), la actriz (nombre), tu mejor amigo(a), el presidente de Estados Unidos, el profesor de..., la profesora de..., ¿...?
Adjetivos: aburrido, antipático, cómico, divertido, estúpido, extrovertido, fantástico, inteligente, introvertido, mentiroso, simpático, serio, tonto, ¿...?

Activity 3 practices the present indicative of regular **-ar, -er, -ir** verbs and the verb **ir,** using vocabulary from **Volume 1, Chapters 2** and **3**.

3 ¿Qué hace? Trabajen en grupos de tres o cuatro personas para crear una historia larga usando verbos de la lista u otros verbos. La primera persona empieza con una oración corta. Después, la segunda persona repite la oración original y añade otra parte, usando un verbo nuevo. Sigan así hasta que la historia llegue a ser *(becomes)* tan larga que nadie pueda recordarla. Después empiecen otra historia con un sujeto nuevo.

MODELO   Tú: *El estudiante perezoso va a la biblioteca.*
             Compañero(a) 1: *El estudiante perezoso va a la biblioteca, pero no estudia.*
             Compañero(a) 2: *El estudiante perezoso va a la biblioteca, pero no estudia. En vez de eso (Instead), habla con sus amigos...*

Verbos: abrir, asistir a, bailar, caminar, cantar, cocinar, comer, compartir, conversar, correr, escribir, estudiar, hablar, ir, leer, mirar, patinar, trabajar, vivir, ¿...?

Designpics/Glow Images

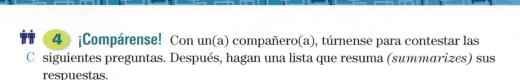

👥 **4** **¡Compárense!** Con un(a) compañero(a), túrnense para contestar las
C siguientes preguntas. Después, hagan una lista que resuma *(summarizes)* sus
respuestas.

Activity 4 practices **tener,
tener que,** and **tener años,**
using vocabulary from
Volume 1, Chapters 1 and **3.**

MODELO   Tú: *Tengo dos libros en la mochila y también tengo...*
Heather: *Tengo tres libros en la mochila y también tengo...*
(Resumen): *En las mochilas tenemos libros y también tenemos...*

1. ¿Cuáles son dos cosas que tienes en la mochila o en la bolsa *(purse)*?
2. ¿Qué clases tienes este semestre o trimestre? ¿Qué clases tienes hoy?
3. ¿Cuántos años tienes? ¿Cuántos años tiene tu madre o tu padre?
4. ¿Qué tienes que hacer hoy? ¿Qué tienes que hacer esta semana? ¿Y este
   fin de semana?

👥 **5** **Preferencias** Con un(a) compañero(a), túrnense para decir si le gustan o
C no las cosas y actividades indicadas. Después, escribe un resumen de lo que les
gustan y lo que no les gustan.

Activity 5 practices
gustar and verbs like
gustar, using vocabulary
from **Volume 1,
Chapters 2, 3,** and **4.**

MODELO   (Resumen): *A mí me gustan... pero a Abe no le gustan...*
A nosotros nos gusta...

1.   2.   3.

4.   5.   6.

7.   8.   9. ¿...?

👥👥 **6** **Preguntas, preguntas** Trabajen en grupos de cuatro. Cada persona
C debe escribir los nombres de tres clases que tiene este semestre o trimestre.
Las otras personas del grupo tratan de adivinar cuáles son las clases, usando
palabras interrogativas para hacer preguntas. Después, túrnense para adivinar
las clases de las otras personas.

Activity 6 practices
interrogative words,
using **Volume 1
Preliminary Chapter** and
Chapter 3 vocabulary.

MODELO   Compañero(a) 1: *¿Quién es el profesor?*
Compañero(a) 2: *¿A qué hora está?*
Compañero(a) 3: *¿Qué día de la semana tienes esta clase?*

Palabras interrogativas: ¿a qué hora?, ¿cómo?, ¿cuándo?, ¿cuál?,
¿cuántos(as)?, ¿dónde?, ¿por qué?, ¿qué?, ¿quién?

7 **Presentaciones** Trabajen en grupos de cuatro personas, dividiéndose en dos parejas. Cada pareja debe turnarse para hacerle las siguientes preguntas a su compañero(a) y anotar las respuestas. (Pueden contestarlas según sus datos personales o inventar otros.) Después, en su grupo original de cuatro, túrnense para presentar a la persona que entrevistaron al grupo completo. Sigan el modelo.

Activity 7 practices the simple possessive adjectives, using vocabulary from **Volume 1, Chapters 2** and **3**.

MODELO Entrevista: —*¿De dónde es tu familia?*
—*Mi familia es de...*
Presentación: *Quiero presentarles a Cassidy Caitlin O'Brien.*
Su familia es de...

1. ¿Cuál es tu nombre completo?
2. ¿De dónde es tu familia?
3. ¿Cuántos años tienes?
4. ¿Cuál es tu clase favorita?
5. ¿Cuál es tu clase menos favorita?
6. ¿Cuáles son tus libros favoritos?
7. ¿Cuáles son tus películas favoritas?
8. ¿Cuáles son tus canciones *(songs)* favoritas?

8 **¿Ser o estar?** Con un(a) compañero(a), túrnense para escribir ocho oraciones completas, usando palabras de las tres columnas. Cuando sea posible, añadan detalles a sus oraciones para hacerlas más interesantes. Sigan el modelo.

Activity 8 practices the verbs **ser** and **estar**, using vocabulary from **Volume 1, Chapter 4**.

MODELO *Yo estoy cansada después de mi clase de computación porque es muy difícil.*

A	B	C
yo	estar	cansado(a)
tú	ser	de...
él		en el centro de computación
ella		mi profesor(a) de...
nosotros		nervioso(a)
ellos		un(a) estudiante...
¿...?		¿...?

9 **Generalmente...** Con un(a) compañero(a), usen los siguientes adjetivos para crear adverbios. Luego, túrnense para usar los adverbios para decir cómo hacen las actividades indicadas.

Activity 9 practices adverbs, using vocabulary from **Volume 1, Chapter 4**.

Adjetivos: correcto, difícil, eficiente, fácil, (no) frecuente, lento, rápido, seguro

Actividades: cambiar tu contraseña, correr, escribir mensajes de texto, hablar, jugar videojuegos, instalar nuevas aplicaciones, sacar fotos, ¿...?

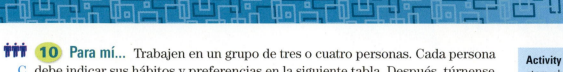

10 **Para mí...** Trabajen en un grupo de tres o cuatro personas. Cada persona
C debe indicar sus hábitos y preferencias en la siguiente tabla. Después, túrnense
para resumir los resultados, según el modelo.

Activity 10 practices
stem-changing verbs in
the present indicative,
using vocabulary from
Volume 1, Chapter 4.

MODELO   *Yo prefiero dormir ocho horas por noche, pero Emma y Keegan
prefieren dormir seis horas. Todos nosotros comenzamos a
estudiar a las...*

1. ¿Cuántas horas prefieres dormir por noche?	4. ¿Quieres comprar una nueva computadora o tableta este año?
2. ¿A qué hora comienzas a estudiar?	5. ¿Puedes programar una computadora?
3. ¿Cuántas horas juegas videojuegos al día?	6. ¿Pierdes tus cosas frecuentemente?

11 **Preguntas personales** Con un(a) compañero(a), túrnense para contestar
C las siguientes preguntas.

Activity 11 practices
irregular-**yo** verbs in the
present indicative, using
vocabulary from
Volume 1, Chapter 5.

1. ¿Conoces a una persona famosa?
2. ¿Sabes hablar francés?
3. ¿Sales todas las noches de la semana?
4. ¿Dices mentiras *(lies)* de vez en cuando?
5. ¿Haces la tarea todos los días?
6. ¿Cuántas horas de televisión ves al día?

12 **Mi rutina** Con un(a) compañero(a), túrnense para decir cuándo haces
cada una de las actividades indicadas. Después, escriban un resumen que
compare sus hábitos.

Activity 12 practices
reflexive verbs, using
vocabulary from
Volume 1, Chapter 5.

MODELO   Tú: *Mi hermana y yo nos peleamos cuando tenemos que compartir
la computadora.*
   (Resumen): *Nate y su hermana se pelean cuando... Sophie y su
madre se pelean cuando...*

Actividades: acostarse, divertirse, enfermarse, levantarse, pelearse,
preocuparse, quejarse, reírse

13 **¿Qué están haciendo?** Haz una lista de cinco familiares que conoces
bien. Después, trabaja con un(a) compañero(a) y túrnense para comentar lo
que crees que cada uno(a) está haciendo en este momento.

Activity 13 practices
the present progressive
tense, using vocabulary
from **Volume 1,
Chapter 5**.

MODELO   *Mi primo Ian está trabajando en la computadora.*

A escuchar

ESTRATEGIA

Listening for the main idea

When you are listening to Spanish, it can sometimes be hard to know what to focus on. There are often words you don't understand. Also, the difference between seeing words on the printed page and hearing them spoken can be huge. A good way to organize your listening task is to focus on getting the main idea of the segment. Don't try to understand every single word, but instead try to get the overall meaning, tone, and feeling of the speaker. Later, with the help of textbook activities and as many listenings as you need, some of the other details will emerge.

1 Trabaja con un(a) compañero(a) para contestar las siguientes preguntas.

1. ¿Qué es un podcast? ¿Qué clase de persona graba y publica podcasts? ¿Para quién son los podcasts? ¿Cuál es el motivo para publicar un podcast?
2. Piensen en los temas de las actividades en la sección **A repasar.** ¿Cuáles de esos temas les parecen *(seem)* ideales para grabar en un podcast?
3. El nombre del podcast es "El día a día de una estudiante cansada". ¿De qué creen que se va a tratar *(is going to be about)*?
4. Lean la información biográfica de la autora del podcast.

Jenkedco/Shutterstock

Nombre: Olivia Reyes
Edad: veinte años
Nacionalidad: méxicoamericana
Profesión: estudiante en University of Texas at Austin
Familia: los padres (Óscar y Yolanda), dos hermanos (Gabriel y Agustín), una hermana (Teresa)
Pasatiempos: tocar la guitarra, mirar televisión y películas por *streaming*, salir con amigos, jugar juegos interactivos

2 Para prepararte a escuchar el podcast de Olivia, haz una correspondencia entre las frases a la izquierda y sus equivalentes en inglés a la derecha.

1. me identifico c	a. *I remember*
2. no me malinterpreten f	b. *again*
3. la mayoría h	c. *I identify myself*
4. me acuerdo a	d. *I fall asleep*
5. qué sé yo i	e. *someone tell me*
6. me quedo dormida d	f. *don't misinterpret me*
7. adivinar j	g. *facets*
8. de nuevo b	h. *the majority*
9. facetas g	i. *what do I know*
10. alguien dígame e	j. *to guess*

>> Escuchar

🔊
Track 17

3 Ahora escucha el podcast "El día a día de una estudiante cansada" en la que Olivia describe un día en su vida universitaria.

>> Después de escuchar

4 Contesta las siguientes preguntas sobre el podcast de Olivia para identificar la idea principal y comentar algunos de los detalles. Escucha el podcast otra vez si necesitas buscar algunas de las respuestas.

1. ¿Cuál es la idea principal del podcast?
   a. Es importante tener muchos pasatiempos.
   b. La vida de estudiante es difícil.
   c. A Olivia no le gustan los estudios.
2. ¿Dónde vive Olivia?
3. ¿Cuál es la identidad que ocupa la mayoría de las veinticuatro horas de su día?
4. ¿Cuándo son sus únicos momentos de libertad *(freedom)*?
5. ¿Qué hace después de su última clase?
6. ¿Qué hace ella con sus padres y hermanos durante los fines de semana?
7. ¿Cuáles son tres cosas que ella hace con sus amigos durante los fines de semana?
8. ¿Cuándo recuerda Olivia que ella es mucho más que una estudiante?

👥 **5** Con un(a) compañero(a) de clase, comparen sus rutinas semanales con las de Olivia. Contesten las siguientes preguntas y después hagan un resumen de sus respuestas. Al final, júntense con otra pareja para compartir y comparar sus resúmenes.

1. ¿Cuáles son las diferentes partes que forman su identidad personal en su totalidad?
2. ¿Cómo son sus rutinas de lunes a viernes?
3. ¿Cómo son sus rutinas los fines de semana?
4. En general, ¿cómo son sus vidas? ¿ocupadas? ¿fáciles? ¿difíciles? ¿aburridas? ¿divertidas? ¿...?
5. Completen las siguientes oraciones:
   ■ En mi opinión, lo bueno de ser estudiante es...
   ■ En mi opinión, lo malo de ser estudiante es...

Answers, Act. 4: *Wording of answers to 4-8 may vary slightly.* 1. b 2. Austin, Texas 3. estudiante 4. cuando va a la cafetería en bicicleta 5. va a la biblioteca para estudiar 6. habla con ellos por teléfono 7. *three of the following*: salir, tomar un refresco, jugar un juego interactivo, escuchar música, ver algo en la tele (por *streaming*) 8. los fines de semana

A escribir

Antes de escribir

ESTRATEGIA

Using a bilingual dictionary

You've already learned a variety of writing strategies in your introductory study of Spanish. As you write, always focus on a mix of strategies to help you approach a specific task. Given the nature of this task, this is one strategy that will help you prepare your information before you write.

Since no textbook can provide all the words you need when you write, you will want to use bilingual dictionaries and online sources to supplement the words you already know. Follow these steps to get the best Spanish equivalent for the word you need.

- Look up the word you want to translate, along with several other words that are close to it. (For example, *weird, odd, strange*.) Compare to see which Spanish words come up as the best translation for each. If the same Spanish word comes up several times, it is likely a good translation.

- Choose one of the Spanish equivalents that came up more than once and look it up to see what its English translation is. Is it your original word or one of its synonyms? If so, it is probably the word you want. If not, focus on another option until you find one that matches.

1 Mira la información biográfica de Olivia en la página P2-8. Después, crea una tarjeta como la de abajo que incluya tus datos personales.

| Nombre: |
| Edad: |
| Nacionalidad: |
| Profesión: |
| Familia: |
| Pasatiempos: |

2 Vas a escribir un guión *(script)* para un podcast. Como ya sabes, los podcasts tienen un enfoque específico y comparten algunas de las opiniones o ideas del (de la) autor(a). Por ejemplo, el podcast de Olivia se enfoca en "El día a día de una estudiante cansada". Con un(a) compañero(a), hagan una lista de por lo menos cinco ideas para un podcast. Pueden tratar los temas de las actividades en la sección **A repasar**, la **Actividad 5** de la sección **A escuchar** u otros, según sus preferencias.

3 Ahora, selecciona una de tus ideas para elaborar en tu podcast. Antes de escribir, crea una lista de palabras relacionadas al tema. Usa un diccionario bilingüe para buscar palabras desconocidas *(unknown)*. Después, piensa en algunos detalles *(details)* relacionados al tema que quieres incluir en tu podcast.

4 Escucha otra vez el podcast de Olivia. ¿Cómo está organizado? ¿Cuál es su tono? Puedes usar su podcast como modelo. También repasa la siguiente lista de sugerencias para los podcasts antes de escribir.

- ¿Quién y cómo eres? Debes presentarte al principio del podcast, igual como lo hace Olivia. Usa los datos de la **Actividad 1** (y, si quieres, otra información pertinente).
- Debes incluir ideas y opiniones interesantes y tratar de presentarlas de una manera divertida.
- Usa un estilo informal y familiar y recuerda que las oraciones cortas *(short)* son más fáciles de entender que las oraciones más largas.
- No presentes demasiada información – escoge un tema muy específico y limita el número de detalles que incluyes.

>> Composición

5 Ahora, escribe el borrador de tu podcast. Incluye la información de las **Actividades 1** y **3** y usa el podcast de Olivia como un modelo. Trata de escribir un podcast interesante y personal que va a divertir a tu audiencia.

mascough/iStockphoto

>> Después de escribir

6 Mira tu borrador otra vez. Usa la siguiente lista para revisarlo.

- ¿Tiene tu podcast un enfoque específico y detalles interesantes?
- ¿Hay concordancia *(agreement)* entre los artículos, sustantivos y adjetivos?
- ¿Usas las formas correctas de todos los verbos?
- ¿Usas bien los adverbios y los verbos como **gustar**?
- ¿Hay errores de puntuación o de ortografía?

¿Adónde vas?

COMUNIDADES LOCALES

Cada barrio o comunidad tiene su propia personalidad que lo define y que también influye a la vida diaria de sus residentes.

¿Crees que los vecinos *(neighbors)*, los barrios y los centros comerciales de nuestras comunidades locales todavía tienen importancia? ¿Por qué sí o por qué no?

Communication

By the end of this chapter you will be able to

- talk about places in town and the university
- talk about means of transportation and food shopping
- talk about locations and give directions
- make polite requests and commands
- agree and disagree
- refer to locations of objects

Un viaje por México

México es el segundo más grande de los países donde se habla español y tiene la población más grande de hispanohablantes. Su nombre oficial es Estados Unidos Mexicanos.

Globe Art: Adapted from Shutterstock/rtguest

País / Área	Tamaño y fronteras	Sitios de interés
México 1.923.040 km²	casi tres veces el área de Texas; fronteras con Estados Unidos, Guatemala y Belice	la arquitectura precolombina (las pirámides aztecas, las ruinas mayas), el cañón del Cobre, el volcán Popocatépetl, las lagunas de Montebello, la Sierra Trahumara

¿Qué sabes? Di si las siguientes oraciones son ciertas (**C**) o falsas (**F**).

1. México es mucho más grande que Texas. C
2. Hay ruinas de por lo menos dos civilizaciones en México. C
3. México es un país sin *(without)* mucha diversidad geográfica. F
4. México tiene la segunda población de hispanohablantes más grande del mundo. F

Lo que sé y lo que quiero aprender Completa la tabla del **Apéndice A**. Escribe algunos datos que **ya sabes** sobre México en la columna **Lo que sé**. Después, añade algunos temas que **quieres aprender** a la columna **Lo que quiero aprender**. Guarda la tabla para usar otra vez en la sección **¡Explora y exprésate!** en la página 221.

Learning objectives: See pages AIE-3—AIE-4 for a complete description of the Bloom's Taxonomy learning objectives and an explanation of how they are integrated within *Cuadros*.

Check: At the beginning of this chapter, interview students to find out what they already know about Mexico. At the end of the chapter, repeat your questions to assess what they have learned. Sample questions: **¿Conoces México? ¿Qué partes? ¿Qué sabes de la gente / la historia / la economía / el arte / la música mexicana?**

Learning objective: Understanding

Cultures

By the end of this chapter you will have explored

- ancient civilizations and indigenous populations of Mexico
- the Spanish conquest and the Mexican Revolution
- linguistic diversity in the Spanish-speaking world
- **el tianguis**, a special kind of open-air market
- Mexico City teens and where they go for fun

¡Imagínate!

>> Vocabulario útil 1

Standards 1.1, 2.1: At the beginning of this chapter, interview (C 1.1) your class to find out what students know about Mexico (C 2.1). At the end of the chapter, repeat the same questions and compare. Sample questions: **¿Conoces México? ¿Qué partes? ¿Qué sabes de la gente / la historia / la economía / el arte / la música mexicana?**

SERGIO: Oye, ¿adónde vas con tanta prisa?

JAVIER: Primero tengo que ir al gimnasio, y después al **centro estudiantil**.

SERGIO: Pero, ¿por qué la prisa, hombre?

JAVIER: Después del centro estudiantil, tengo que ir al **banco** a sacar dinero y después al **súper** para comprar la comida para la cena.

Preparation: Distribute copies or project an image of your campus map. Have students label the places on the map in Spanish and/or move a stick figure or pointer around on the map and ask: **¿Dónde está Pedro? ¿Adónde va?**

>> En la universidad

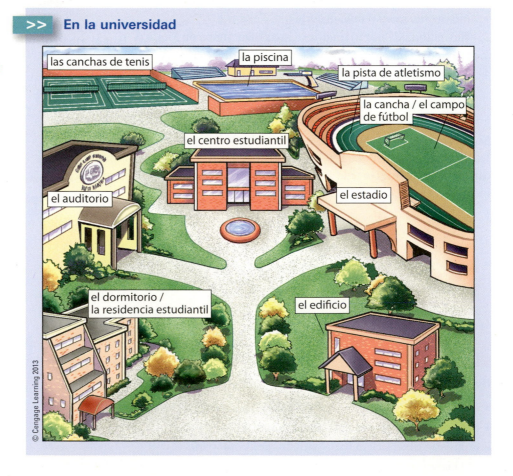

- las canchas de tenis
- la piscina
- la pista de atletismo
- la cancha / el campo de fútbol
- el centro estudiantil
- el estadio
- el auditorio
- el dormitorio / la residencia estudiantil
- el edificio

En la ciudad o en el pueblo

el aeropuerto *airport*	**el museo** *museum*
el almacén *department store*	**la oficina** *office*
el apartamento *apartment*	**la oficina de correos** *post office*
el banco *bank*	**la papelería** *stationery store*
el barrio *neighborhood*	**el parque** *park*
el cajero automático *automated*	**la pizzería** *pizzeria*
teller machine (ATM)	**la plaza** *plaza*
la casa *house*	**el restaurante** *restaurant*
el centro comercial *mall*	**el supermercado** *supermarket*
el cine *cinema*	**el teatro** *theater*
el cuarto *the room*	**la tienda...** *store*
la estación de trenes / autobuses	**...de equipo deportivo**
train/bus station	*sporting goods store*
el estacionamiento *parking lot*	**...de juegos electrónicos**
la farmacia *pharmacy*	*electronic games store*
el hospital *hospital*	**...de ropa** *clothing store*
la iglesia *church*	**el (la) vecino(a)** *neighbor*
la joyería *jewelry store*	
el mercado... *market*	
...al aire libre *open air-market;*	
farmer's market	

ACTIVIDADES

I **1** **¿Dónde está Javier?** Javier necesita varias cosas. ¿Dónde está él? Escoge de los lugares en la tercera columna.

1.  b

2.  d

    a. la joyería

    b. el cajero automático

    c. el supermercado

3.  a

4. f

    d. la farmacia

    e. la oficina de correos

5.  e

6.  c

    f. la tienda de ropa

The names of many places in the city are cognates. With a partner, take turns reading each other as many of the cognates as you can while the other guesses the English translation.

Other places of worship besides **la iglesia** are: **la mezquita** *(mosque),* **la sinagoga, el templo**.

In some varieties of Spanish, to indicate playing a sport, **jugar** is used with the preposition **a: jugar al tenis, jugar al fútbol**. Usage of **a** with **jugar** varies from region to region.

M

2 En la ciudad Indica adónde debe ir cada persona, según lo que quiere hacer o comprar. ¡No te preocupes si no entiendes todas las palabras!

1. —Es hora de comer. Tengo muchas ganas de comerme una pizza enorme.
2. —Tengo que estudiar las pinturas de Picasso para mi clase de arte.
3. —No puedo hacer las compras todavía. Primero necesito ir a sacar dinero.
4. —El doctor dice que necesito esta medicina para controlar mi alergia.
5. —No quiero cocinar en casa. Quiero salir a comer.
6. —Necesito comprar muchas cosas y después de las compras, podemos ir al cine.
7. —Voy a visitar a Mariana y para llegar a su casa, tengo que tomar el autobús.

C

3 ¿Adónde van? Habla con varios compañeros. ¿Adónde van después de clase? ¿Qué van a hacer en ese sitio? También diles adónde vas tú y por qué vas allí.

MODELO Tú: *¿Adónde vas después de clase?*
Compañero(a): *Voy al dormitorio.*
Tú: *¿Qué vas a hacer allí?*
Compañero(a): *Estoy cansado(a). Voy a descansar.*

Opciones: cenar, cocinar, correr, dormir, estudiar, hacer la tarea, jugar (al) tenis / fútbol, levantar pesas, mirar televisión, nadar, trabajar

¡Fíjate! La diversidad lingüística en el mundo de habla hispana

Todas las lenguas exhiben variaciones geográficas. El español de México no es exactamente igual al español de Puerto Rico ni al español de España. Estas variantes regionales de una lengua se llaman *dialectos*.

En general, el léxico o vocabulario es lo que más varía de una zona dialectal a otra en el mundo hispano. Por ejemplo, algunas de las palabras referentes a los medios de transporte exhiben variación dialectal: **carro, máquina, auto, automóvil** y **coche** se usan en diferentes zonas del mundo hispano. De la misma manera, **autobús, bus, guagua, colectivo, camión, ómnibus** y **micro** son diferentes maneras de referirse a *bus*.

La fonología o pronunciación del español también varía de una zona dialectal a otra. Por ejemplo, en algunos lugares del mundo hispano, la letra **s** se puede pronunciar con aspiración, como el sonido inicial de la palabra *hand*. En los dialectos que aspiran, la palabra **español** se pronuncia frecuentemente como [ehpañol].

Es importante recordar que las diferencias entre los dialectos del español son relativamente pocas. Por esta razón, dos hablantes del español de zonas dialectales muy distantes generalmente pueden comunicarse con facilidad.

Práctica ¿Puedes dar unos ejemplos de variación léxica dentro de EEUU o entre los países de habla inglesa del mundo?

>> Vocabulario útil 2

© Cengage Learning 2013

Optional: Point out **subterráneo** as a variant of **metro** in Argentina.

SERGIO: ¿Vas **en bicicleta**?

JAVIER: No, voy **a pie**. Mi bici se desinfló. Bueno, adiós —¡me tengo que ir!

>> Medios de transporte

a pie *on foot, walking*	**en metro** *on the subway*
en autobús *by bus*	**en tren** *by train*
en bicicleta *on bicycle*	**en / por avión** *by plane*
en carro / coche / automóvil *by car*	

ACTIVIDADES

I 4 Para llegar… Quieres llegar de un sitio a otro. ¿Cuál es la forma más lógica para llegar?

Learning objective: Understanding

1. ¿Estoy en el dormitorio y quiero ir a la biblioteca. Voy…
   a. en avión.   (b.) a pie.   c. en tren.

2. Estoy en Los Ángeles y quiero ir a Nueva York. Voy…
   a. en bicicleta.   b. a pie.   (c.) en avión.

> In Mexico, **carro** is more commonly used than **coche**, and **camión** is more common for *bus* than **autobús**.

3. Estoy en casa y quiero ir al parque qué está a dos millas de mi casa. Quiero hacer ejercicio. Voy…
   (a.) en bicicleta.   b. en tren.   c. en autobús.

4. Estoy en la Calle 16 y quiero llegar a la Calle 112. Voy…
   (a.) en metro.   b. en avión.   c. a pie.

5. Estoy en la universidad y quiero visitar a mis padres. Tengo muchas cosas que llevar y quiero hacer muchas paradas *(make many stops)*. Voy…
   a. en bicicleta.   b. a pie.   (c.) en carro.

Optional: Review reflexive verbs after **Actividad 5** by using the prompt: **¿Cómo te preparas para la fiesta? Me ducho, me visto, me voy…** Have students ask each other the question and then expand it to what they do after the party; see reflexive verbs in Chapter 5, p.177: **Me quito la ropa, me lavo los dientes, me acuesto,** etc.

5 ¿Vas a pie? Tu compañero(a) tiene que ir a varios sitios.
C Pregúntale cómo piensa llegar a esos sitios. Inventa destinos lógicos para cada forma de transporte.

Answers, Act. 5: *Questions will vary. Answers:* 1. Voy a ir en tren. 2. Voy a ir en bicicleta. 3. Voy a ir en / por avión. 4. Voy a ir a pie. 5. Voy a ir en coche / carro / automóvil. 6. Voy a ir en metro.

MODELO Tú: *¿Cómo piensas ir a la fiesta de Carmen?*
Compañero(a): *Voy a ir en autobús.*

1.   2.   3.   4.   5.   6.

© Cengage Learning 2013

Vocabulario útil 3

DULCE: Pero, mujer, ¿adónde vas con tanta prisa?

CHELA: Quiero ir al gimnasio antes de **hacer las compras** en el supermercado.

DULCE: Pero si no es tarde, son sólo las tres.

CHELA: Ya sé, pero si me da tiempo, quiero ir a la **carnicería** para comprar unos **bistecs.**

In Spanish-speaking countries, the ending -**ía** indicates a store that specializes in a certain product. It is clear what the store specializes in because the name of the store contains the product. Notice the names of stores that end in -**ía** in **Vocabulario útil 1**. Notice that the **í** always carries an accent. Can you name any other specialty stores that end this way?

>> **Hacer las compras…**

En la carnicería

CARNICERÍA

la salchicha

el jamón

el pavo | el bistec | la chuleta de puerco | el pollo

Suggestion: Converse with students about what they buy where and what products they prefer. Sample questions: **¿Qué compras en la carnicería? ¿Te gusta el bistec / el jamón / el pollo? ¿Comes carne? ¿Qué compras en el supermercado? ¿Prefieres los refrescos o la leche? ¿Cómo vas al supermercado? ¿Qué supermercado prefieres?**

Notice: Carnicería and carnecería are linguistic variants.

>> **En el supermercado**

La comida

el queso

el pan

la leche

los huevos

los vegetales

las papitas fritas

los refrescos

las frutas

el yogur

6 En el barrio Hoy en día, las tiendas especializadas como la carnicería y
la panadería no son tan comunes como en el pasado. En las ciudades grandes
es más típico ir a un supermercado grande para comprar todos los comestibles
en un solo sitio. El movimiento "verde", bajo el lema "Piensa globalmente,
actúa localmente" ha producido mercados al aire libre donde uno puede
comprar productos locales y orgánicos. Los mercados al aire libre y las tiendas
especializadas no pueden competir con los precios de los supermercados
más grandes, pero sí ofrecen la oportunidad de hablar con los vecinos y los
vendedores en un ambiente agradable e íntimo. Formen grupos de cuatro.
Contesten las siguientes preguntas y presenten sus respuestas a la clase.

1. ¿Dónde prefieres hacer las compras, en un supermercado, en pequeñas
   tiendas especializadas o en mercados al aire libre? ¿Por qué?
2. ¿Cuál es el mejor lugar cerca de la universidad para comprar pan? ¿carne?
   ¿fruta? ¿vegetales?
3. ¿Comes carne? ¿Cuántas veces a la semana comes carne? ¿Dónde?
4. ¿Comes mucha fruta y vegetales? ¿Dónde compras la fruta y los vegetales?
5. ¿Qué te importa más cuando haces las compras, el precio de los productos,
   su calidad (quality), si son orgánicos o productos locales, la comodidad
   de comprar todo en un mismo lugar o la amabilidad (friendliness) de las
   personas que trabajan en la tienda?
6. ¿Crees que la idea de ir de compras a varias tiendas especializadas es más
   común en Estados Unidos o en Europa y otros países? ¿Y la idea de los
   mercados al aire libre? ¿de productos locales y órganicos?

7 Las compras Formen grupos de cuatro. Cada persona en el grupo
debe preparar una lista de las compras que tiene que hacer. Intercambien
(Exchange) las listas entre el grupo. Túrnense para describir lo que cada
persona quiere comprar. Después preparen recomendaciones para cada
persona sobre dónde ir de compras.

MODELO *Mark necesita comprar unas salchichas y unos vegetales. Mark debe
ir a la carnicería para las salchichas y al mercado al aire libre
para los vegetales.*

8 El día de hoy Formen grupos de tres. Cada persona debe preparar una
descripción de sus hábitos de consumidor. Intercambien las descripciones y
túrnense para leerlas en voz alta. El grupo tiene que adivinar a quién describe
cada descripción.

MODELO *Descripción: Nunca voy al supermercado porque prefiero comer en
restaurantes de comida rápida (fast food). Cuando invito a
amigos a comer en casa, voy a una pizzería y compro todo lo que
necesito.*
Grupo: ¡Es Julio!

Suggestion: While discussing farmers'
markets (**mercados al aire libre**),
there are concepts that are more
specific to U.S. culture that may be
useful such as **orgánico** *(organic)*,
productos locales *(locally grown)*,
consumo local *(locally bought)*.

Optional: Expand these activities
with a class chat about transportation.
Sample questions: **¿Vas de compras
a pie, en coche, en metro? ¿Cuáles
son unas ciudades norteamericanas
con metro? ¿Conoces unas ciudades
en Europa o en otros lugares con
metro? ¿Cuánto cuesta ir en metro
en...? En nuestro(a) pueblo /
ciudad / campus universitario,
¿cuál es un sitio agradable para ir
en bicicleta? ¿Hay autobuses en
nuestro(a) pueblo / ciudad / campus
universitario? ¿Dónde te gusta ir a
pie? ¿Te gusta viajar en avión?**

Standard 1.2: Through video viewing, students learn interpretive strategies for communication. Activities in this section regularly provide opportunities for students to interpret spoken language.

ESTRATEGIA

Watching facial expressions

As you learned in **Chapter 3**, watching body language aids comprehension. The same is true of watching facial expressions: a smile, a frown, a raised eyebrow, or a laugh. These gestures can give you a better understanding of what the character means.

Antes de ver Estudia las palabras y frases que se usan en el video.

prisa	*hurry*
suerte	*luck*
sueños	*dreams*
Siga derecho...	*Continue straight. . .*
esquina	*corner*
Doble a la derecha...	*Turn to the right. . .*
cuadras	*blocks*

Learning objective: Understanding

© Cengage Learning 2013

▶ **Ver** Mira el video sin sonido *(without sound)* y pon atencíon en las expresiones faciales.

Después de ver 1 Ahora, mira el video de nuevo con el sonido puesto *(sound on)* y di si las expresiones faciales de estas personas contribuyen al sentido de lo que dicen **(sí o no)**.

1. **Javier:** Primero tengo que ir al gimnasio y después al centro estudiantil. no
2. **Sergio:** Dicen que el supermercado es el lugar ideal para conocer a la mujer ideal. sí
3. **Dulce:** ¿A la carnicería? ¿Viene alguna persona especial a cenar? sí
4. **Chela:** Gracias. Nos vemos luego. no
5. **Javier:** Siga derecho hasta aquella esquina. no
6. **Sergio:** Algún día, mi amigo, algún día. sí

Después de ver 2 Mira el video una vez más y pon las actividades de Javier y Chela en el orden correcto.

Javier: ___3___ ir al banco, ___1___ ir al gimnasio, ___2___ ir al centro estudiantil, ___4___ ir al supermercado

Chela: ___1___ ir al gimnasio, ___3___ ir a la carnicería, ___2___ ir al supermercado

Voces de la comunidad

>> Voces del mundo hispano

En el video para este capítulo Verónica, Ricardo y Paola hablan de sus barrios, los medios de transporte y los lugares adónde van frecuentemente. Lee las siguientes oraciones. Después mira el video una o más veces para decir si las oraciones son ciertas (C) o falsas (F).

1. Hay muchos restaurantes y supermercados en el barrio de Ricardo. F

2. Hay un mercado al aire libre en el barrio de Paola. C

3. Verónica frecuentemente usa auto y tren para transportarse. F

4. A Ricardo le gusta usar su patineta *(skateboard)* para ir a todas partes. C

5. Cuando Verónica usa transporte público es para ir al trabajo. F

6. Paola va al centro de la Ciudad de México para comer, caminar y ver películas. F

>> Voces de Estados Unidos

Track 18

Joe Reyna, fundador y director ejecutivo

❝Todos los empresarios somos soñadores *(dreamers)*. Tomamos riesgos *(risks)* y esperamos que den fruto y hacemos todo lo posible por hacerlos funcionar.❞

Courtesy of Viva Markets.

Joe Reyna es el fundador y director ejecutivo de Viva! Markets, una nueva cadena de mercados latinos en el noroeste de Estados Unidos. Criado en Estados Unidos y México y con extensa experiencia en el mundo de los negocios, el joven texano posee las habilidades culturales y profesionales justas para triunfar en este ambicioso emprendimiento *(undertaking)*. Reyna equipa cada uno de sus mercados con una panadería, carnicería, restaurante, cremería, pastelería, tortillería, pescadería y hasta un bazar con otros vendedores. Además, los mercados ofrecen productos asiáticos y polinesios a modo de *(as a way to)* atraer a otros consumidores de la zona.

Reyna ha recibido numerosos reconocimientos por sus logros *(achievements)* en el mundo de los negocios y contribuciones filantrópicas. Entre ellos, fue reconocido por *Utah Business Magazine* como una de las 100 personas más influyentes del estado.

¿Y tú? ¿Qué opinas de los mercados de Reynas? ¿Te interesa visitar uno? ¿Por qué sí o no?

Standards 2.1, 2.2, 3.2, 5.1: Students read about successful Spanish speakers in the U.S. and acquire cultural information that features distinctive viewpoints of Spanish-speaking people. Encourage them to research other U. S. Hispanics with careers in government, public service, or not-for-profits that serve the Hispanic population. Ask students to research volunteer activities locally to plant the seed of practicing Spanish beyond the classroom.

¡Prepárate!

>> ## Gramática útil 1

Indicating location: Prepositions of location

© Cengage Learning 2013

En la última cuadra, **frente al** banco, va a ver el centro comercial.

Cómo usarlo

Use prepositions of location to say where something is positioned in relation to other objects, or where it is located in general.

El restaurante está **frente a** la iglesia.

*The restaurant is **facing** the church.*

El café está **dentro del** almacén.

*The café is **inside** the department store.*

Cómo formarlo

1. Commonly used prepositions of location include the following.

Suggestion: Write **de** + **el** = **del**; **a** + **el** = **al** on the board for emphasis.

Usage of **enfrente de, delante de,** and **frente a** varies from country to country. However, they are more or less equivalent to each other.

Some of these prepositions can be used without the **de** as adverbs. For example, **El museo está cerca.**

Remember that when **de** or **a** follows a preposition of location, they combine with **el** to form **del** and **al**: **frente al hotel, dentro del refrigerador.**

Optional: Return to the concept of the campus map and describe spatial relationships between buildings such as **frente a, lejos de, cerca de,** etc.

al lado de	*next to, on the side of*	La farmacia está **al lado del** hospital.
entre	*between*	La farmacia está **entre el** hospital y la oficina de correos.
delante de	*in front of*	La joyería está **delante del** hotel.
enfrente de	*in front of, opposite*	La joyería está **enfrente del** hotel.
frente a	*in front of, facing, opposite*	La joyería está **frente al** hotel.
detrás de	*behind*	El hotel está **detrás de** la joyería.
debajo de	*below, underneath*	Los libros están **debajo de** la mesa.
encima de	*on top of, on*	El cuaderno está **encima de** los libros.
sobre	*on, above*	La comida está **sobre** la mesa.
dentro de	*inside of*	El libro está **dentro de** la mochila.
fuera de	*outside of*	El pan está **fuera del** refrigerador.
lejos de	*far from*	El súper está **lejos de** la universidad.
cerca de	*close to*	La panadería está **cerca del** hotel.

2. Since these prepositions provide information about *location*, they are frequently used with the verb **estar**, which, as you learned in **Chapter 4**, is used to say where something is located.

Suggestion: Use yourself, objects, and students to illustrate the prepositions of location. For example, have two or three students stand in front of the class, place yourself between them to illustrate: **Estoy entre A y B.** Walk to the classroom door and show yourself inside and outside of the classroom. Place an object on top of and another object below your desk. Hint: Students will always remember **debajo de** if you can crawl under your desk! Move from presentation to practice. Gradually elicit prepositions of location from students by placing a pen, book, or student in different locations or using a simple board drawing.

ACTIVIDADES

1 **¿Dónde está…?** Di dónde están las siguientes cosas. Usa estas
M preposiciones: **al lado de, debajo de, enfrente de, encima de.** También
debes escribir el artículo definido de la segunda cosa, según el modelo.

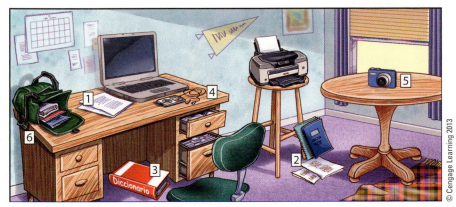

© Cengage Learning 2013

MODELO   La impresora está _al lado del_ escritorio.

1.   Los apuntes están ___al lado de la___ computadora portátil.
2.   Los cuadernos están ___debajo de la___ impresora.
3.   El diccionario de español está ___debajo del___ escritorio.
4.   El MP3 portátil está ___enfrente del___ computadora portátil.
5.   La cámera digital está ___encima de la___ mesa.
6.   La mochila está ___encima del___ escritorio.

2 **Treviño**   En grupos de tres, estudien
C el mapa de Treviño. Luego, túrnense
para describir dónde están situados por
lo menos diez edificios o sitios. Usen las
preposiciones en la página 206.

3 **Nuestro salón de clase**   En grupos
C de tres, describan dónde están varios
objetos en su salón de clase. Usen las
preposiciones en la página 206.

4 **Nuestra universidad**   Ahora,
C trabajen en grupos de tres a cinco para
dibujar un mapa de su universidad.
Incluyan por lo menos seis edificios
principales. Luego, túrnense para
describir la posición de uno de los
edificios. El grupo tiene que adivinar
qué edificio se describe.

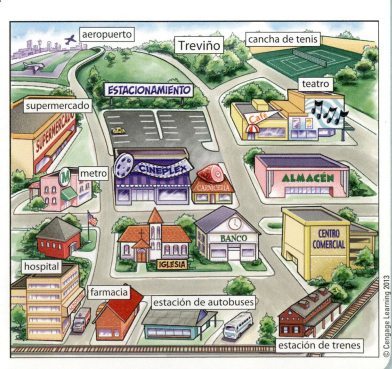

© Cengage Learning 2013

Gramática útil 2

Telling others what to do: Commands with **usted** and **ustedes**

Cómo usarlo

1. You have already been seeing command forms in direction lines. In Spanish, there are two sets of singular command forms, since there are two ways to address people directly (**tú** and **usted**). The informal commands, which you will learn in **Chapter 7**, are used with people you would address as tú. In this chapter you will learn formal commands, as well as plural commands with **ustedes**.

2. Command forms are not used as frequently in Spanish as they are in English. For example, in **Chapter 4** you learned that courteous, softening expressions are often used instead of commands: **¿Le importa si uso la computadora?** instead of **Déjeme** (*Let me*) **usar la computadora.**

3. However, one situation in which command forms are almost always used is in giving instructions to someone, such as directions to a specific location.

Siga derecho hasta la esquina. Allí **doble** a la izquierda.

Continue straight ahead until the corner. Turn left there.

Camine tres cuadras hasta llegar a la farmacia. Allí **doble** a la derecha y **cruce** la calle. La carnicería está al lado del banco.

Walk three blocks until you arrive at the pharmacy. There, turn right and cross the street. The butcher shop is next to the bank.

There are three **usted** command forms in this postcard advertising a tour of historic Mexican theaters. What are they?

Answers: Póngase, Participe, Presente

¡Póngase en escena!

Participe en nuestro tour de los teatros históricos de México, donde las estrellas verdaderas tienen más de 100 años.

Palacio de Bellas Artes, México D.F.   Teatro Calderón, Zacatecas   Teatro Juárez, Guanajuato   Teatro Degollado, Guadalajara

¡Presente esta postal para recibir un descuento de 20%!

EL CONSEJO PARA LA PRESERVACIÓN DE LOS MONUMENTOS NACIONALES

Photos (left to right): Jeri71/Dreamstime; Rfoxphoto/Dreamstime; Afagundes/ Dreamstime; Rfoxphoto/Dreamstime; text: © Cengage Learning 2013

Cómo formarlo

LO BÁSICO

A *command* form, also known as an *imperative* form, is used to issue a direct order to someone you are addressing: **Vaya a la esquina y doble a la derecha.** (**Go** to the corner and **turn** right.)

1. The chart below shows the singular formal (**usted**) and plural (**ustedes**) command forms of the verb **seguir** (*to go*, *to follow*).

	Singular	Plural
affirmative	siga	sigan
negative	no siga	no sigan

2. Here are the rules for forming the usted and ustedes command forms of most verbs. These are true for the affirmative and negative commands.

   - Take the **yo** form of the verb in the present indicative. Remove the **o** and add **e** for **-ar** verbs or **a** for **-er / -ir** verbs, to create the **usted** command.

     poner: → pongo → pong- + a → **ponga**

   - Add an **n** to the **usted** command form to create the **ustedes** command.

     ponga → **pongan**

> By using the **yo** form of the present indicative, you have already incorporated any irregularities in the verb. Now they automatically carry over into the command form.

infinitive	yo form minus the -o ending	plus e / en for -ar verbs OR a / an for -er / -ir verbs	usted / ustedes command forms
hablar	habl-	+ e / en	**hable / hablen**
pensar	piens-	+ e / en	**piense / piensen**
tener	teng-	+ a / an	**tenga / tengan**
decir	dig-	+ a / an	**diga / digan**
escribir	escrib-	+ a / an	**escriba / escriban**
servir	sirv-	+ a / an	**sirva / sirvan**

> **Heritage Learners:** Some U.S. Spanish speakers may tend to use the diphthongs **ie** and **ue** in infinitives such as **pensar, tener, sentir,** and **empezar.** Emphasize the standard infinitive forms of stem-changing verbs.

3. A few command forms require spelling changes to maintain the original pronunciation of the verb.

   - verbs ending in **-car:** change the **c → qu:**

     buscar: → busco → **busque / busquen**

   - verbs ending in **-zar:** change the **z → c:**

     empezar: → empiezo → **empiece / empiecen**

   - verbs ending in **-gar:** change the **g → gu:**

     pagar: → pago → **pague / paguen**

> **Heritage learners:** The syllabary used to teach Spanish-speaking children to read and write offers a good way to practice the spelling changes in **-gar, -car** and **-zar** verbs. Dictate the following sequences: **Ca, que, qui, co, cu; Ga, gue, gui, go gu,** and **za, ce, ci, zo, zu.**

4. A few verbs have irregular **usted** and **ustedes** command forms: **dar (dé / den), estar (esté / estén), ir (vaya / vayan), saber (sepa / sepan),** and **ser (sea / sean).**

Note that you add a written accent to the stressed syllable of the affirmative command form to retain the original pronunciation.

5. For the command forms of reflexive verbs, attach the reflexive pronoun to the *end* of *affirmative* **usted** / **ustedes** commands and place it *before negative* **usted** / **ustedes** commands.

Prepárese para una sorpresa.	*Prepare yourself for a surprise.*
No se ponga nervioso.	*Don't get nervous.*

6. Here are words and phrases for giving directions.

¿Me puede decir cómo llegar a...?	*Can you tell me how to get to . . .?*
¿Me puede decir dónde queda...?	*Can you tell me where . . . is located?*
Cómo no. Vaya...	*Of course. Go . . .*
... a la avenida... / la calle...	. . . to the avenue . . . / street . . .
... a la derecha / izquierda / la esquina.	. . . to the right / the left / the corner.
... (dos) cuadras.	. . . (two) blocks.
... (todo) derecho.	. . . (straight) ahead.

bajar (baje)	*to get down from, to get off of (a bus, etc.)*
caminar (camine)	*to walk*
cruzar (cruce)	*to cross*
doblar (doble)	*to turn*
seguir (i) (siga)	*to continue*
subir (suba)	*to go up, to get on*

One commonly used command in Spanish is **¡Vamos!** *(Let's go!),* which the speaker uses to refer to several people, including himself or herself. Because it includes the speaker in the action, it is used instead of an **ustedes** command form.

Suggestion: Play "Simon Says" (**Simón dice**). Sample prompts: **Digan "adiós", Toquen la mochila / mesa, Toquen su libro de español, Escriban su nombre en el aire, Den su libro a un compañero, Saquen sus apuntes, Abran el libro, etc. Simón dice** serves as a simple comprehension check of formal commands.

7. You may soften commands by adding **por favor** or by using these phrases.

Me gustaría / Quisiera (+ infinitive)...	*I'd like (+ infinitive) . . .*
Por favor, ¿(me) puede (+ infinitive)**?**	*Please, can you (+ infinitive) (me)?*
¿Pudiera / Podría usted (+ infinitive)**?**	*Could you (+ infinitive)?*

—**Me gustaría** comer. **¿Pudiera** recomendarme un restaurante?

—Cómo no. El Farol del Mar es buenísimo.

—¿**Me puede** decir si está lejos?

—Está muy cerca. ¿**Quisiera** saber cómo llegar?

—Sí. ¡Muchas gracias! Y también **me gustaría** tener la dirección.

M **5** **¿Cómo llego...?** Indica el mandato correcto para completar cada oración. **Learning objective:** Understanding

1. (seguir) usted todo derecho hasta la plaza con la iglesia. *Sigue*
2. (doblar) ustedes aquí en la Calle Federal. *Doblen*
3. (subir) ustedes esta calle todo derecho hasta la esquina con Quinteros. *Suban*
4. (cruzar) usted aquí y (caminar) dos cuadras. *Cruce , camine*
5. No (ir) ustedes hasta el parque. *vayan*
6. No (preocuparse) si no llegan inmediatamente. Está un poco lejos. *se preocupen*

M **6** **Los anuncios** El campo de la publicidad hace uso frecuente de los mandatos formales para tratar de convencer al público que compre o use su producto. Completa los anuncios con mandatos, usando la forma de **usted** de los verbos entre paréntesis.

Answers, Act. 6: 1. Abra, Ponga, Tenga 2. Venga, Cocine, Compre 3. espere, Llame, Sirva 4. trabaje, Venga, Descubra 5. Levante, Haga, Reciba 6. Use, Navegue, Visite, Tome

1. (abrir, poner, tener)

> **BANCO MUNDIAL** $
>
> ___ una cuenta en Banco Mundial.
> ___ su dinero en nuestras manos.
> ___ confianza en nuestros profesionales.

2. (venir, cocinar, comprar)

> **SUPERMERCADO CENTRAL**
>
> ___ al Supermercado Central para hacer las compras.
> ___ con la comida más fresca y más natural de la ciudad.
> ___ las comidas favoritas de sus hijos.

3. (esperar, llamar, servir)

> **PIZZERÍA ITALIA**
>
> No ___ .
> ___ al 555-6677 para ordenar su pizza.
> ___ la pizza más fresca y deliciosa en su propia casa en menos de treinta minutos.

4. (trabajar, venir, descubrir)

> *Restaurante París*
>
> *Esta noche, no ___ en la cocina.*
> *___ al Restaurante París para disfrutar de nuestro ambiente relajante y nuestro excelente servicio.*
> *___ nuestra riquísima cocina francesa.*

5. (levantar, hacer, recibir)

> GIMNASIO LA SALUD
>
> ___ pesas en un ambiente agradable.
> ___ ejercicio todos los días para mantenerse en forma.
> ___ un relajante masaje después de su sesión de ejercicios.

6. (usar, navegar, visitar, tomar)

> **CAFÉ CAFÉ**
>
> ¡___nuestro wifi gratis!
> ___ por Internet.
> ___ con amigos.
> ___ un café.

© Cengage Learning 2013

M 7 **¡Niños!** Los padres también usan los mandatos con frecuencia al hablar con sus hijos. La señora Díaz tiene que salir esta noche. ¿Qué les dice a sus hijos? Indica sus mandatos con la forma de **ustedes**.

1. empezar la tarea al llegar a casa Empiecen la tarea al llegar a casa.
2. apagar la computadora después de terminar la tarea Apaguen la computadora después de terminar la tarea.
3. ser pacientes con la niñera *(babysitter)* Sean pacientes con la niñera.
4. no abrir la puerta No abran la puerta.
5. no jugar fútbol dentro de la casa No jueguen fútbol dentro de la casa.
6. no salir de la casa No salgan de la casa.
7. no ir a visitar a sus amigos No vayan a visitar a sus amigos.
8. no comer papitas fritas antes de cenar No coman papitas fritas antes de cenar.
9. acostarse a las diez Acuéstense a las diez.
10. cepillarse los dientes antes de acostarse Cepíllense los dientes antes de acostarse.
11. dormir bien Duerman bien.
12. estar tranquilos Estén tranquilos.

Standard 1.3: Activity 8 practices presentational communication.

Check: Activity 8 also offers an opportunity for assessment. Rank student performances 1-5, with 5 being the best, in one or two of the following categories: communications, accuracy, creativity, pronunciation, and completeness.

Learning objective, Act. 8: Applying

8 **¡Compre, compre, compre!** Ahora, con un(a) compañero(a), escriban un
C anuncio comercial para la televisión. Usen el mandato formal con **usted** para convencer a su público. Presenten el anuncio a la clase.

Optional, Act. 9: To expand on directions, tell students to form groups of three and to pretend that they are throwing a dinner party with three courses for the entire Spanish class. Each course will be at a different residence. Each student gives directions to his/her home.

Optional, Act. 9: Have students use MapQuest® or another map program online and change settings to Spanish language. Search a route and students can see directions and commands in a familiar context. You may want to have students try some searches to well-known places near your campus. Students can read the directions to their classmates. Have students try to guess the hypothetical destinations correctly before they are revealed.

Learning objectives, Act. 10: Understanding, Analyzing

9 **¿Cómo llego?** Tu compañero(a) es turista y te pregunta cómo llegar
C a varios sitios. Dile cómo llegar y dile qué medio de transporte debe usar. Luego, haz tú el papel *(role)* del (de la) turista; tu compañero(a) te va a dar instrucciones. Pueden usar el mapa de la página 207 y añadir los sitios que no están, o pueden decirse cómo llegar a sitios en su comunidad.

1. el supermercado
2. el centro comercial
3. el metro
4. la estación de trenes
5. la estación de autobuses
6. la cancha de tenis
7. la oficina de correos
8. el banco

🔊 10 **La oficina de correos** Escucha la conversación entre un señor y una
Track 19 señorita. La primera vez que escuches la conversación, apunta la información
C que vas a necesitar. Luego, escribe las instrucciones que le da la señorita al señor para llegar a la oficina de correos. Usa los siguientes verbos en tus oraciones.

1. caminar Camine dos cuadras.
2. doblar Doble a la derecha.
3. seguir Siga derecho por una cuadra.
4. cruzar Cruce la calle Central.
5. doblar Doble a la izquierda.
6. caminar Camine otra cuadra.

Sonrisas

Expresión En grupos de tres o cuatro personas, piensen en las órdenes que les gustaría dar a los profesores de la universidad. Luego, escriban una lista de sus ideas.

MODELO *No den tarea para los fines de semana.*

Audioscript: Act. 10, La oficina de correos:
[Señor]:   Perdone, ¿me puede decir cómo llegar a la oficina de correos?
[Señorita]:   Sí, por supuesto. Mire, primero camine dos cuadras. Luego doble a la derecha.
[Señor]:   Dos cuadras y doblo a la derecha.
[Señorita]:   Sí, precisamente. Luego, siga derecho por una cuadra.
[Señor]:   Derecho por una cuadra.
[Señorita]:   Así es. Después de una cuadra, va a llegar a la calle Central. Entonces, cruce la calle Central.
[Señor]:   Cruzo la calle Central.
[Señorita]:   Sí. Doble a la izquierda, camine otra cuadra y allí va a ver la oficina de correos. Es un edificio pequeño. Está entre una
                       farmacia y una tienda de videos.
[Señor]:   Muchas gracias, señorita.
[Señorita]:   De nada.

Optional: For expansion, have students generate a detailed list of typical classroom commands and another list of commands used with family members at home. Compare lists.

Optional: Expand this activity to have students write at least five commands for their classmates that require moving around or doing something in the classroom. Have some students "command" the class while the class acts these out.

Standards 1.2, 5.2: In **Sonrisas** cartoons, students interpret written language and examine language through humor, irony, and common sense. This technique guides students toward personal enjoyment and life-long uses of the language.

Gramática útil 3

Affirming and negating: Affirmative and negative expressions

Cómo usarlo

¿Viene **alguna** persona especial a cenar?

Standard 4.1: Emphasize the comparison of the languages by stressing use or giving more examples of double negatives in Spanish and pointing out that double negatives in English are considered incorrect (except *neither / nor*) and are only present in colloquial speech.

Heritage learners: Point out that **nadien** corresponds to **nadie** in the standard language.

1. There are a number of words and expressions that are used to express affirmatives and negatives in Spanish. Notice that a double negative form is often used in Spanish, where as it is hardly ever used in English.

No conozco a **nadie** aquí.	*I don't know anyone here.*
¿Conoces **a alguien** aquí?	*Do you know anyone here?*
No quiero ni este libro **ni** ése.	*I don't want this book or that one.*

2. Remember to use the personal **a** that you learned in **Chapter 5** when you refer to people: **No conozco <u>a</u> nadie aquí.**

Cómo formarlo

1. Here are some frequently used affirmative and negative words in Spanish. You have already learned some of these, such as **también, siempre**, and **nunca**.

alguien	*someone*	**nadie**	*no one, nobody*
algo	*something*	**nada**	*nothing*
algún / alguno (a, os, as)	*some, any*	**ningún / ninguno(a)**	*none, no, not any*
siempre	*always*	**nunca / jamás**	*never*
también	*also*	**tampoco**	*neither, not either*
o... o...	*either / or*	**ni... ni...**	*neither / nor*

2. Most of these words do not change, regardless of the number or gender of the words they modify. However, the words **alguno** and **ninguno** can also be used as *adjectives*. In this case, they must change to agree with the nouns they modify. Additionally, when they are used before a masculine noun they shorten to **algún** and **ningún**.

—¿Tienes **algún** libro sobre la informática?	*Do you have **a (any)** book about computer science?*
—No, no tengo **ningún** libro sobre ese tema. Pero tenemos **algunos** libros muy interesantes sobre las redes sociales.	*No, I don't have **a (any)** book on that subject. But we do have **some** very interesting books about social networks.*
—No, gracias, ya tengo **algunas** revistas. ¿No tienes **ninguna** sugerencia sobre otros libros?	*No, thanks, I already have **some** magazines. You don't have **any** suggestions for other books?*

3. Alguno and **ninguno** can also be used as *pronouns* to replace a noun already referred to. In this case, they match the number and gender of that noun.

—¿Quieres estos **libros?**   *Do you want these **books**?*

—No, gracias, ya tengo **algunos.**   *No, thanks, I already have **some.***

—¿No quieres una **revista?**   *Don't you want a **magazine**?*

—No, no necesito **ninguna**.   *No, I don't need **any (one)**.*

4. Notice how in Spanish, unlike English, even when more than one negative expression is used in a sentence, the meaning remains negative.

Nunca hay **nadie** aquí.   *There's **never anyone** here.*

No está **ni** Leo **ni** Ana **tampoco**.   *__Neither__ Leo **nor** Ana is here **either**.*

The plural forms of **ninguno** and **ninguna**— **ningunos** and **ningunas**—are not frequently used.

Notice that when a negative word precedes the verb, the word **no** is not used: **Nadie viene.** When the negative word comes after the verb, however, you must use **no** directly before the verb: **No viene nadie.**

ACTIVIDADES

I **11** **¿Qué pasa?** Escoge la palabra o palabras correctas para completar cada oración.

1. ¡Me encanta el café! (Nunca / Siempre) tomo una taza *(cup)* por la mañana. Siempre
2. No tengo (algo / nada) para comer. Voy a ir a mi restaurante favorito. nada
3. A mis amigos les gusta ese almacén y a mí (también / tampoco). también
4. (Alguien / Nadie) hace las compras en ese mercado. Los precios son muy altos. Nadie
5. Yo no como carne y mis amigos (también / tampoco) la comen. tampoco
6. Necesito unos vegetales. ¿Tienes (algunos / ningunos)? algunos

12 **¡Yo también!** Un(a) amigo(a) está en tu casa y tú le explicas algunas cosas sobre los hábitos de tu familia. Él (Ella) dice que su familia es igual. Con un(a) compañero(a), improvisen esta situación. El (La) amigo(a) siempre usa **también** o **tampoco** en su respuesta.

Learning objective: Understanding

MODELO Tú: *Mis tíos nunca cenan antes de las ocho de la noche.*
    Amigo(a): *Mis tíos tampoco.*

1. Mis primos siempre se levantan temprano. Mis primos también.
2. Mi abuelo nunca se viste informalmente. Mi abuelo tampoco.
3. Mi abuela siempre se viste elegantemente. Mi abuela también.
4. A mis padres les encanta salir a comer. A mis padres también.
5. Mi hermana es fanática de la música rap. Mi hermana también.
6. A mis hermanos no les gusta levantarse temprano. A mis hermanos tampoco.
7. Yo siempre me baño y me visto elegantemente si voy a una fiesta. Yo también.

Ahora describe los hábitos verdaderos de tu familia. Tu compañero(a) te dice si su familia es igual o no.

Audioscript, Act.13, El visitante:

Modelo: ¿Hay alguna estación de trenes en el barrio?

1. *¿Hay algún supermercado en el barrio?*
2. *¿Alguien puede decirme cómo llegar al centro comercial?*
3. *¿Siempre compras la carne en la Carnicería La Villita?*
4. *¿Tienes alguna tienda de ropa preferida?*
5. *¿Hay alguna cancha de tenis en el barrio?*
6. *¿Hay algo bueno en el cine?*

Answers, Act. 13: 1. No, no hay ningún supermercado en el barrio. 2. No, nadie puede decirte cómo llegar al centro comercial. 3. No, nunca compro la carne en la Carnicería La Villita. 4. No, no tengo ninguna tienda de ropa preferida. 5. No, no hay ninguna cancha de tenis en el barrio. 6. No, no hay nada bueno en el cine.

Answers, Act. 14: 1. Sí, algunos de los estudiantes van a la biblioteca después de clases./ No, nadie va a la biblioteca después de clases. 2. Sí, me gusta comer algo antes de clases./ No, no me gusta comer nada antes de clases. 3. Sí, hay algunos cajeros automáticos en la universidad./ No, no hay ningún cajero automático en la universidad. 4. Sí, siempre voy en metro a la universidad./ No, nunca voy en metro a la universidad. 5. Sí, hay algunas tiendas de video cerca de la universidad./ No, no hay ninguna tienda de video cerca de la universidad. 6. O estudio antes de clases o estudio después de clases./ No estudio ni antes de clases ni después de clases.

Learning objective: Applying

13 **El visitante** Un visitante pasa el fin de semana en tu casa. Te hace preguntas sobre tu barrio. Contesta sus preguntas en el negativo.

MODELO Escuchas: ¿Hay alguna estación de trenes en el barrio?
Escribes: *No, no hay ninguna estación de trenes en el barrio.*

14 **Encuesta** En parejas, túrnense para hacer y contestar las siguientes preguntas. Contesten primero en afirmativo y luego en negativo. Usen las palabras entre paréntesis en sus respuestas.

MODELO ¿Comes en la cafetería de la universidad? (siempre / nunca)
Sí, siempre como en la cafetería de la universidad.
No, nunca como en la cafetería de la universidad.

1. ¿Algunos de los estudiantes van a la biblioteca (algunos / nadie)
2. ¿Te gusta comer algo antes de clase? (algo / nada)
3. ¿Hay algún cajero automático en la universidad? (algunos / ningún)
4. ¿Vas en metro a la universidad? (siempre / nunca)
5. ¿Hay alguna tienda de video cerca de la universidad? (algunas / ninguna)
6. ¿Estudias antes de clase o después de clase? (o… o… / ni… ni…)

15 **El fin de semana** Vas a pasar el fin de semana en casa de tu compañero(a). Le haces varias preguntas para determinar cómo vas a pasar el fin de semana. Escoge *(Choose)* ideas de la lista o inventa otras. Luego, cambia de papel *(role)* con tu compañero(a). Usa las palabras afirmativas y negativas que acabas de aprender en tus preguntas y tus respuestas.

Ideas posibles: divertido en la tele, comer en el refrigerador, libro de cocina mexicana, escritora mexicana preferida, revista de música popular, juego interactivo, disco compacto de Paulina Rubio, ¿…?

MODELO Tú: *¿Hay algo divertido en la tele?*
Compañero(a): *No, no hay nada divertido en la tele.*

16 **Aquí…** En grupos de tres o cuatro escriban una lista de las preferencias de los estudiantes de su universidad. Usen palabras y expresiones de las tres columnas. Luego, trabajen juntos para escribir un resumen de sus opiniones.

A	B	C
todo el mundo	nunca	comer en…
algunas personas	siempre	comprar algo / nada en…
nadie	jamás	ir a…
		¿…?

Gramática útil 4

Indicating relative position of objects: Demonstrative adjectives and pronouns

Derecho hasta **aquella** esquina...

Cómo usarlo

Demonstrative adjectives and pronouns indicate *relative distance* from the speaker. **Este** is something very close to the speaker, **ese** is something a little farther away, and **aquel** is something at a distance (*over there*).

1. Demonstrative adjectives:

   Esta casa es bonita. También me gusta **esa** casa, pero **aquella** casa es fea.

   This house is pretty. I also like *that* house but *that* house (*over there*) is ugly.

2. Demonstrative pronouns:

   De los autos me gusta **éste**, pero **ése** también es bueno. **Aquél** no me gusta.

   *Of the cars I like **this one**, but **that one** is also good. I don't like **that one** (over there).*

> In everyday speech **ese** and **aquel** are often used interchangeably.

> **Preparation:** Bring three objects to class. Place one close to you, another at medium distance from you, and the third far away from you. Dramatize demonstratives, using Spanish only. Choose objects that will illustrate gender differences.

Cómo formarlo

LO BÁSICO

> A demonstrative adjective modifies a noun. A demonstrative pronoun is used instead of a noun.

1. Demonstrative adjectives and pronouns change to reflect gender and number. Demonstrative *adjectives* reflect the gender and number of the nouns they *modify*. Demonstrative *pronouns* reflect the gender and number of the nouns they *replace*.

	Demonstrative adjectives	Demonstrative pronouns
this; these *(close)*	este, esta; estos, estas	éste, ésta; éstos, éstas
that; those *(farther)*	ese, esa; esos, esas	ése, ésa; ésos, ésas
that; those *(at a distance)*	aquel, aquella; aquellos, aquellas	aquél, aquélla; aquéllos, aquéllas

2. Use these words with demonstrative adjectives and pronouns: **aquí** (*here*, often used with **este**), **allí** (*there*, often used with **ese**), and **allá** (*over there*, often used with **aquel**).

3. **Esto** and **eso** are neutral pronouns that refer to a concept or something that has already been said: <u>Eso es lo que dijo la profesora. Todo esto es muy interesante.</u>

> The only spelling difference between demonstrative adjectives and pronouns is that the pronouns are usually written with an accent. Although accents on demonstrative pronouns were required in the past, the **Real Academia de la Lengua Española** has ruled that they are not necessary. However, most Spanish speakers continue to use these accents. This textbook uses them for the purpose of clarity.

> **Heritage Learners:** Tell students that **allí** and **ahí** are synonymous. Remind them that **ahí** is always written with **h**.

> **Heritage Learners:** You may want to point out that **esto** and **eso** are never written with an accent.

> **Esto** and **eso** do not change their forms; they are invariable forms.

I **17** **¡Ayuda, por favor!** Completa las siguientes conversaciones con el pronombre o adjetivo demostrativo apropiado entre paréntesis.

1. TÚ: Hola, ¿pudiera usted decirme cómo llegar a las canchas de tenis?

   HOMBRE: Cómo no. Siga usted (esta / aquella) calle aquí hasta (esta / esa) esquina allí, la esquina con la avenida Quintana. Luego vaya todo derecho hasta llegar a un parque muy grande. Las canchas de tenis están en (aquel / este) parque. esta, esa, aquel

2. TÚ: Buenos días. Por favor, ¿pudiera usted decirme cómo ir al aeropuerto?

   MUJER: Claro. Usted debe tomar (ese / aquel) autobús allí en la calle Francisco. A ver, tengo la ruta aquí en (aquella / esta) guía.

   TÚ: Muy bien. Entonces, ¿(ese / este) autobús es el que necesito tomar?

   MUJER: Sí. (Este / Ese) autobús lo lleva directamente al aeropuerto. ese, esta, ese, Ese

3. TÚ: Perdón. ¿Puede usted recomendar un restaurante bueno?

   HOMBRE: Seguro. (Éste / Aquél) que está aquí cerca es bastante bueno. Pero hay otro allí, mire, al otro lado de la calle, La Criolla. (Ése / Éste) sirve comida muy rica. Creo que (ése, aquél), La Criolla, es mi favorito. Éste, Ése, ése

4. TÚ: Hola, busco la sección de literatura latina.

   MUJER: Muy bien. (Esos / Estos) libros aquí son de autores cubanos. Allí, en la próxima sección, (esos / estos) libros son de autores mexicanos. Y allá, (estos / aquellos) libros son de otros autores latinamericanos.

   TÚ: ¿Y (esos / estos) libros aquí en la mesa?

   MUJER: ¿(Éstos / Aquéllos) aquí? (Estos / Esos) libros son de autores españoles. Estos, esos, aquellos, estos, Éstos, Estos

M **18** **¿Qué pasa aquí?** Completa las oraciones con el adjetivo o pronombre demostrativo correcto.

1. En el cine: Podría ver ____ese____ horario de películas allí?
2. En el dormitorio: ¿Me puedes pasar ____aquel____ libro allá?
3. En el mercado: No me gustan esos bistecs. Prefiero ____éstos____ aquí.
4. En la pizzería: No quiero una pizza con salchicha. Me gusta más ____ésa____ allí con los vegetales.
5. En la papelería: Necesito un cuaderno grande. Ese cuaderno es bueno pero ____aquél____ allá es aún mejor.
6. En casa: ¿Dónde pongo ____esta____ silla que tengo aquí — al lado del sofá o al lado de la mesa?
7. En la estación de trenes: ¡ ____Esto / Eso____ es terrible! ¡Nuestro tren llega muy tarde!

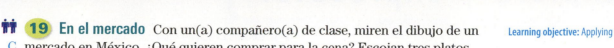

19 En el mercado Con un(a) compañero(a) de clase, miren el dibujo de un
C mercado en México. ¿Qué quieren comprar para la cena? Escojan tres platos
para preparar y hablen de las cosas que necesitan, usando los adjetivos y
pronombres demostrativos correctos.

Learning objective: Applying

MODELO Tú: *¿Qué quieres comprar? ¿Compramos ese queso?*
　　　　　Amigo(a): *Sí, y también estas salchichas. ¿Qué más?*
　　　　　Tú: *Aquellos huevos, ¿no crees?*

20 Adónde vamos? Con un(a) compañero(a) de clase, hagan una lista de
C cinco de los siguientes lugares en tu comunidad u otros que prefieren. Incluyan
sitios que están muy cerca de la universidad, un poco lejos y muy lejos.

restaurantes　　　　museos　　　　　　tiendas de música
cafés　　　　　　　tiendas de ropa　　　pizzerías

Ahora, hablen de los varios sitios de su lista, usando adjetivos y pronombres
demostrativos.

MODELO Tú: *¿Quieres ir al restaurante Chimichangas? Sirven comida*
　　　　　　mexicana.
　　　　　Amigo(a): *No, no me gusta ese restaurante. ¿Por qué no vamos a*
　　　　　　éste, McMurray's? Sirven comida estadounidense.

México

Robert Frerck/Getty Images

Información general

Nombre oficial: Estados Unidos Mexicanos

Población: 113,724,226

Capital: México, D.F. (f. 1521) (9.000.000 hab.)

Otras ciudades importantes: Guadalajara (1.600.000 hab.), Monterrey (1.130.000 hab.), Puebla (1.347.000 hab.)

Moneda: peso

Idiomas: español (oficial), náhuatl, maya, zapoteco, mixteco, otomi, totonaca (se hablan aproximadamente 68 idiomas con muchas variaciones)

Mapa de México: Apéndice D

Vale saber…

- La historia de México incluye tres grandes civilizaciones: los olmecas, la primera civilización mesoaméricana; los mayas, conocidos por sus avances en las matemáticas, la astronomía, la escritura jeroglífica y también por sus grandes templos y pirámides; y los mexicas (o aztecas), el pueblo que forma la capital de su imperio en Tenochtitlán, ahora la ciudad de México.

- La conquista española de México se refiere a la conquista de los mexicas por Hernán Cortés en México-Tenochtitlán en 1521. México gana la independencia de España en 1810.

- La Revolución Mexicana se considera el conflicto político y social más importante del siglo XX en México

- México tiene una gran diversidad de grupos indígenas: los nahuas, los mayas, los zapotecos, los mixtecos, los otomíes, los totonacas y los tzotziles, entre muchos otros.

El mercado del pueblo, el tianguis

En Estados Unidos, los "farmers' markets" encuentran popularidad en las ciudades hace poco *(recently)*. Pero en México, los tianguis existen desde la época prehispánica. La palabra *tianguis* viene del náhuatl *tianquiztli*, que quiere decir *mercado*. Son mercados al aire libre que se instalan en todas partes de la ciudad para vender frutas y verduras orgánicas, pan, maíz, frijoles, aves (*birds*), peces (*fish*), carne, hierbas medicinales, especias (*spices*), artesanía y mucho más. Hacer las compras en un tianguis es mucho más divertido que hacerlas en los supermercados: hay de todo, y es común escuchar la música de conjuntos musicales tradicionales allí. Aunque se hayan adaptado (*they have adapted*) a los tiempos modernos, los tianguis siguen siendo (*continue being*) el mercado preferido de la gente del pueblo.

Kathrin Ziegler/Getty Images

>> En resumen

Learning objectives: Understanding, Remembering

La información general

1. ¿Cuáles son tres grandes civilizaciones antiguas de México?
2. ¿Qué gran civilización antigua forma su capital en lo que hoy es la Ciudad de México?
3. ¿En qué año y qué ciudad se realiza (*occurs*) la conquista español?
4. ¿En qué año gana México la independencia de España?
5. ¿Qué conflicto en México se considera el más importante del siglo XX?
6. ¿Cuáles son tres pueblos indígenas de México de hoy?

Answers, La información general.
1. los olmecas, los mayas, los mexicas o aztecas 2. los mexicas o aztecas 3. 1521, México-Tenochtitlán 4. 1810 5. La Revolución Mexicana 6. accept any 3: los nahuas, los mayas, los zapotecos, los mixtecos, los otomíes, los totonacas, los tzotziles

El tema de la comunidad

1. ¿Qué son los tianguis?
2. ¿Desde cuando existen los tianguis en México?
3. ¿De qué lengua indígen viene la palabra *tianguis*?
4. ¿Cómo son los tianguis diferentes a los supermercados?

Answers, El tema de la comunidad: 1. son mercados al aire libre donde se puden comprar diversos productos 2. desde la época prehispánica 3. náhuatl 4. answers will vary slightly: se venden especialidades que no se venden en los supermercados; las verduras y frutas son más frescas; son más divertidos; son al aire libre; es común escuchar música tradicional

Standard 5.1: Here students are encouraged to do independent web research on topics that will gradually require more Spanish to carry out the assignments by introducing more participation with Spanish-speaking communities online.

Learning objectives: Analyzing, Evaluating

Check: Review what students know about Mexico and brainstorm about what else they might want to know. Ask heritage learners to share their knowledge.

🌐 ¿QUIERES SABER MÁS?

Revisa y rellena la tabla que empezaste al principio del capítulo. Luego, escoge un tema para investigar en línea y prepárate para compartir la información con la clase.

Palabras clave: Mesoamérica, la conquista española, Emiliano Zapata, Pancho Villa, la Revolución Mexicana de 1910, Octavio Paz, Diego Rivera, Frida Kahlo, Gael García Bernal

🌐 **Tú en el mundo hispano** Para explorar oportunidades de usar el español para estudiar o hacer trabajos voluntarios o aprendizajes en México, sigue los enlaces en **www.cengagebrain.com**.

🎞 **Ritmos del mundo hispano** Sigue los enlaces en **www.cengagebrain.com** para escuchar música de México.

A leer

>> **Antes de leer**

ESTRATEGIA

Working with unknown grammatical structures

When you read texts written for native Spanish speakers, you will frequently come across grammatical structures you haven't learned yet. Seeing grammatical endings you don't recognize can be intimidating, but if you focus just on the meaning of the infinitive of the verb, you can usually get its general meaning. Often you can guess the tense (present, past, future, etc.) by looking at the rest of the sentence. If you don't let unknown grammatical structures hold you back, you'll make a great leap forward in understanding authentic Spanish.

Heritage Learners: Have heritage learners list cognates from the reading and compare their Spanish and English spellings. Elicit or point out endings: **-ción (revolución)** = *-tion;* **-dad (formalidad)** = *-ty*.

Notice: Present subjunctive forms are formally introduced in **Chapter 11.** This activity can serve as a preview to the present subjunctive forms by pointing out the endings.

1 Aquí hay algunas estructuras gramaticales de la lectura que no sabes. Mira el significado general del verbo para hacer una correspondencia entre las palabras en español y las en inglés.

1. __c__ es necesario que **conozca**
2. __a__ **podrá** descifrar
3. __f__ **esté** todo el día **conectado** al monitor
4. __b__ que **se encuentre** ahí
5. __g__ **acuda** la gente más "nice"
6. __e__ **estar vestido** perfectamente
7. __d__ el restaurante que **ofrezca**

a. *you will be able to decipher*
b. *that may be found there*
c. *it's necessary that you know*
d. *the restaurant that offers*
e. *to be dressed perfectly*
f. *he is glued to the screen all day*
g. *the nicest people gather*

Answers, Act. 2: 1. conozca, presente; 2. podrá, futuro; 3. esté, presente / conectado, presente; 4. se encuentre, presente; 5. acuda, presente; 6. estar vestido, presente; 7. ofrezca, presente

> It's not necessary to understand all the unknown words in the article to do the activities on page 224.

2 Ahora, mira las frases de la **Actividad 1.** ¿Cuáles son las formas gramaticales que no sabes? Con un(a) compañero(a), hagan una lista de las siete formas gramaticales. ¿Son del tiempo presente o futuro? Hagan una lista de las formas y sus tiempos.

3 Vas a leer un artículo sobre los jóvenes de la Ciudad de México y adónde van para divertirse. Mientras lees, trata de entender los verbos sin pensar demasiado en las estructuras gramaticales que no sabes. Enfoca en las ideas principales del artículo.

LECTURA

Los jóvenes mexicanos se divierten

Alejandro Esquivel

¿Eres telemaníaco(a)...

¿Usted sabe cómo se divierten los "teens"? Las maneras de entretenerse en estos tiempos de revolución electrónica, videojuegos, DVDs, equipos MP3 y antros son tan heterogéneas como la población que ocupa[1] solamente el Distrito Federal… Es necesario que conozca ciertos perfiles de los jóvenes contemporáneos para entender más su manera de ir por la vida. Es así como podrá descifrar algunos de los códigos[2] de la juventud para saber adónde van y qué hacen…

El telemaníaco

Una de las formas de entretenimiento más "ancestrales" es el observar televisión por más de cuatro horas seguidas[3]. A esta joven especie[4] no le interesa ni en lo más mínimo la vida social, pues prefiere observar un maratón entero de Los Simpson a tomar un buen café con sus cuates[5]… Algunos padres prefieren que su "hijito" esté todo el día conectado al monitor, argumentando que es preferible que se encuentre ahí a estar vagabundeando en las calles.

El peace & love

En cuanto a este tipo de jóvenes, les preocupa más lo natural, el amor y la fraternidad entre razas. A diferencia del telemaníaco, éste trata de[6] pasar el menor tiempo posible frente a un televisor. Dentro de sus principales maneras de divertirse está el acudir[7] todos los domingos a la Plaza de Coyoacán, para buscar algún libro y observar los espectáculos culturales que semana a semana ahí se presentan.

El fresa[8]

Este "teen modelo" gusta de asistir a lugares a los cuales acuda la gente más "nice" de la ciudad. Otra forma de diversión son las cenas y los cafés que regularmente se realizan[9] en restaurantes y cafeterías ubicadas[10] en la zona de Bosques de las Lomas y Santa Fe. Al fresa le late[11] bastante asistir a "antros[12]" donde la música comercial sea el hit.

El raver

Los ravers son los encargados de llenar[13] los festivales de música electrónica o raves, ya que éstos sólo son posibles gracias a la asistencia de más de 3 mil personas… La música que se toca es la electrónica y durante los raves se baila sin parar[14] por más de nueve horas continuas y sólo bebiendo agua embotellada. El raver también acude a antros donde solamente se toque electrónica.

El fashion

Otro espécimen fácil de identificar, ya que su preocupación más grande es estar vestido perfectamente. Entre sus grandes pasatiempos está leer revistas de moda[15], pero a la hora de salir trata siempre de asistir al lugar que acaban de inaugurar o al lugar más fashion. También prefiere las cenas en compañía de sus amigos en el restaurante que ofrezca lo último[16] en cocina.

...fresa...u otro tipo?

[1]*vive en* [2]*codes* [3]*continuas* [4]*species* [5]*amigos* [6]**trata...:** *tries to* [7]*ir* [8]*affluent youth* [9]**se...:** *take place* [10]*located* [11]**le...:** *le gusta* [12]*bars or clubs, the "in" places* [13]**encargados...:** *in charge of filling* [14]**sin...:** *without stopping* [15]**revistas…** *fashion magazines* [16]**lo...:** *the latest*

Después de leer

 4 Con un(a) compañero(a), escriban el nombre del grupo de jóvenes que va a cada lugar indicado. En algunos casos, más de un grupo va a ese lugar.

Lugar	Grupo
1. antros	fresas, ravers
2. raves	ravers
3. la Plaza de Coyoacán	peace & love
4. festivales de música electrónica	ravers
5. la zona de Bosques de las Lomas	fresas
6. casa	telemaníacos
7. los lugares más "fashion"	fashion
8. restaurantes	fresas, fashion
9. cafés	fresas

Answers Act. 5: *Any 6 of the following:* teens, DVDs, MP3, monitor, peace & love, teen, nice, hit, raver, rave, fashion

Expansion: Ask students why they think English loanwords are so common in Spanish and other languages. Allow them to respond in English if necessary.

 5 En el **Capítulo 4** hay una nota sobre los préstamos del inglés al español. Este artículo tiene muchos ejemplos de este tipo de palabra. Trabaja con un(a) compañero(a) de clase. ¿Pueden encontrar seis préstamos del inglés al español?

6 Trabaja en un grupo de tres o cuatro estudiantes. ¿Pueden identificar cinco grupos de "tipos" entre los jóvenes estadounidenses? Escriban una lista de los grupos, unas de sus características y adónde van para divertirse. Luego, compartan su lista con la clase entera.

Diane Diederich/iStockphoto

>> Antes de escribir

Standard 1.3: In the writing sections, students present information to readers, who may often consist of their classmates.

ESTRATEGIA

Writing—Adding supporting detail

In **Chapter 5** you wrote topic sentences for paragraphs. Once you have a topic sentence, you have the main idea of your paragraph. But the topic sentence is not enough. You need to include supporting detail—additional information or examples that give your paragraph life and help make it more interesting. If you think of it in terms of a photo, supporting detail is similar to the other items in the photo that are not its focal point—what else can you see and understand from the background?

1 Vas a escribir un párrafo sobre un sitio importante para ti y lo que haces allí. ¿Cuáles son algunos sitios y actividades que puedes describir? Haz una lista con tus ideas.

2 Usa tu lista de la **Actividad 1** y escoge un sitio para describir. Tu oración temática debe identificar el sitio. Después tienes que añadir unos detalles *(details)* para dar interés a tu descripicón. Sigue el modelo a continuación para escribir tu oración temática y unos detalles sobre el sitio.

Learning objectives: Analyzing, evaluating

Oración temática: *Para mí, el centro de mi comunidad es el café local donde tomo café todos los días.*

Detalles: *el café es bueno, la música es interesante, los empleados son muy amables, tengo wifi, veo a muchas personas y vecinos allí, hablo con todos, conozco a gente nueva, me siento, me relajo, trabajo en la computadora...*

>> Composición

Learning objective: Creating

3 Usa la oración temática y los detalles de la **Actividad 2** para escribir un párrafo breve en el que describes el sitio, cómo es y qué haces allí.

>> Después de escribir

4 Mira tu borrador otra vez. Usa la siguiente lista para revisarlo.

- ¿Tiene toda la información necesaria?
- ¿Los detalles relacionan bien con la oración temática?
- ¿Corresponden los sustantivos y adjetivos?
- ¿Corresponden las formas de los verbos y los sustantivos?
- ¿Hay errores de puntuación o de ortografía?

Vocabulario

En la universidad *At the university*

el apartamento *apartment*	**el dormitorio / la residencia estudiantil** *dormitory*
el auditorio *auditorium*	**el edificio** *building*
la cancha / el campo de fútbol *soccer field*	**el estadio** *stadium*
la cancha de tenis *tennis court*	**la oficina** *office*
el centro estudiantil *student center*	**la piscina** *swimming pool*
el cuarto *room*	**la pista de atletismo** *athletics track*

En la ciudad o en el pueblo *In the city or in the town*

el aeropuerto *airport*	**el museo** *museum*
el almacén *store*	**la oficina de correos** *post office*
el banco *bank*	**la papelería** *stationery store*
el barrio *neighborhood*	**el parque** *park*
el cajero automático *automated teller machine (ATM)*	**la pizzería** *pizzeria*
la casa *house*	**la plaza** *plaza*
el centro comercial *mall*	**el restaurante** *restaurant*
el cine *cinema*	**el supermercado** *supermarket*
la estación de trenes / autobuses *train / bus station*	**el teatro** *theater*
el estacionamiento *parking lot*	**la tienda...** *store*
la farmacia *pharmacy*	**...de equipo deportivo** . . . *sporting goods store*
el hospital *hospital*	**...de juegos electrónicos** . . . *electronic games store*
la iglesia *church*	**...de ropa** . . . *clothing store*
la joyería *jewelry store*	**el (la) vecino(a)** *neighbor*
el mercado... *market*	
...al aire libre *open-air market; farmer's market*	

Hacer las compras... *Shopping . . .*

En la carnicería *At the butcher shop*

el bistec *steak*
la chuleta de puerco *pork chop*
el jamón *ham*
el pavo *turkey*
el pollo *chicken*
la salchicha *sausage*

En el supermercado *At the supermarket*

la comida *food*
las frutas *fruits*
los huevos *eggs*
la leche *milk*
el pan *bread*
las papitas fritas *potato chips*
el queso *cheese*
los refrescos *soft drinks*
los vegetales *vegetables*
el yogur *yogurt*

Medios de transporte *Means of transportation*

a pie *on foot, walking*	**en metro** *on the subway*
en autobús *by bus*	**en tren** *by train*
en bicicleta *on bicycle*	**en / por avión** *by plane*
en carro / coche / automóvil *by car*	

Para decir cómo llegar   *Giving directions*

¿Me puede decir cómo llegar a…?
  Can you tell me how to get to . . . ?
¿Me puede decir dónde queda…?
  Can you tell me where . . . is located?
Cómo no. Vaya… *Of course. Go . . .*
  …a la avenida… *. . . to the avenue . . .*
  …a la calle… *. . . to the street . . .*
  …a la derecha *. . . to the right*
  …a la esquina *. . . to the corner*

  …a la izquierda *. . . to the left*
  …(dos) cuadras *. . . (two) blocks*
  …(todo) derecho *. . . (straight) ahead*
bajar *to get down from, to get off of (a bus, etc.)*
cruzar *to cross*
doblar *to turn*
seguir (i) *to continue*
subir *to go up, to get on*

Expresiones de cortesía

Me gustaría (+ infinitive)**…**
  I'd like (+ infinitive) . . .
¿Por favor, me puede decir?
  Please, can you tell me . . . ?

¿Pudiera / Podría Ud. (+ infinitive)**…?**
  Could you (+ infinitive) . . . ?
Quisiera (+ infinitive)**…** *I'd like (+ infinitive) . . .*

Expresiones afirmativas y negativas

algo *something*
alguien *someone*
algún, alguno(a, os, as) *some, any*
jamás *never*
nada *nothing*
nadie *no one, nobody*
ni… ni… *neither / nor*

ningún, ninguno(a) *none, no, not any*
nunca *never*
o… o… *either / or*
siempre *always*
también *also*
tampoco *neither, not either*

Preposiciones

al lado de *next to, on the side of*
cerca de *close to*
debajo de *below, underneath*
delante de *in front of*
dentro de *inside of*
detrás de *behind*
encima de *on top of, on*

enfrente de *in front of, opposite*
entre *between*
frente a *in front of, facing, opposite*
fuera de *outside of*
lejos de *far from*
sobre *on, above*

Adjetivos demostrativos

aquel, aquella; aquellos, aquellas *that; those*
  (over there)
ese, esa; esos, esas *that; those*

este, esta; estos, estas *this; these*

Pronombres demostrativos

aquél, aquélla; aquéllos, aquéllas *that one; those*
  (over there)
ése, ésa; ésos, ésas *that one; those*
eso *that*

éste, ésta; éstos, éstas *this one; these*
esto *this*

Otras palabras y expresiones

allá *over there*
allí *there*
aquí *here*

Repaso y preparación

>> ## Repaso del Capítulo 6

Preparation: Have students review this material and complete the activities here, in the SAM and online before they begin **Chapter 7**.

Complete these activities to check your understanding of the new grammar points in **Chapter 6** before you move on to **Chapter 7**.

The answers to the activities in this section can be found in **Appendix B**.

Check: The **Repaso** section not only reviews grammar and vocabulary for the student but it offers a built-in performance assessment. By doing review activities with students, you can assess concepts that you may need to continue to reinforce in future classes.

Answers, Act. 1: El perro está lejos del auto. 2. El perro está delante del auto. 3. El perro está detrás del auto. 4. El perro está debajo del auto. 5. El perro está dentro del auto. 6. El perro está entre los autos.

Prepositions of location (p. 206)

1 Di dónde está el perro, según las ilustraciones.

Preposiciones: debajo de, delante de, dentro de, detrás de, entre, lejos de, sobre

MODELO *El perro está sobre el auto.*

1.
2.
3.

4.
5.
6.

Commands with **usted** and **ustedes** (p. 208)

2 Completa los anuncios (*ads*) con mandatos con **usted** y **ustedes**.

1. ____Vengan____ (venir) ustedes al Almacén Novomoda. ¡No ____pierdan____ (perder) nuestras ofertas!
2. ____Ponga____ (poner) usted su confianza en la Farmacia Benéfica. ____Hable____ (hablar) con nuestros farmacéuticos para recibir una consultación de salud gratis.
3. ____Haga____ (hacer) su reservación con el Restaurante MundiCultura. ____Llame____ (llamar) ahora para recibir un aperitivo complementario.

Affirmative and negative expressions (p. 214)

3 Completa la narración con palabras afirmativas y negativas de la lista.

Palabras afirmativas y negativas: algo, alguien, alguno(a, os, as), nada, nadie, ningún, nunca, siempre, también, tampoco

1. ____Siempre____ voy al Café Milano para tomar un café con leche. 2. ____También____ como un pastel y hablo con 3. ____algunos____ de los clientes. Después, si no tengo 4. ____nada____ urgente, voy al mercado porque normalmente hay 5. ____algo____ que necesito comprar. Si no veo a 6. ____nadie____ que conozco, hago las compras y salgo rápidamente para el parque.

All art: © Cengage Learning 2013

Demonstrative adjectives and pronouns (p. 217)

4 Usa adjetivos y pronombres demostrativos para completar las oraciones.

1. No quiero _____estos_____ huevos aquí. Prefiero _____ésos_____ allí.
2. No quiero _____aquella_____ leche allá. Prefiero _____ésta_____ aquí.
3. No quiero _____esos_____ vegetales allí. Prefiero _____aquéllos_____ allá.
4. No quiero _____esta_____ pizza aquí. Prefiero _____ésa_____ allí.
5. No quiero _____aquellas_____ frutas allá. Prefiero _____éstas_____ aquí.
6. No quiero _____este_____ yogur aquí. Prefiero _____ése_____ allá.

>> Preparación para el Capítulo 7

Irregular-**yo** verbs in the present indicative (Chapter 5)   Learning objective: Evaluating

5 Tu amiga habla de su rutina diaria. Completa sus comentarios con las formas de yo correctas de los verbos indicados.

Siempre 1. _____salgo_____ (salir) temprano de casa y 2. _____traigo_____ (traer) el almuerzo *(lunch)* conmigo. 3. _____Pongo_____ (poner) todo en mi mochila y 4. _____conduzco_____ (conducir) hasta la universidad. Allí 5. _____veo_____ (ver) a algunos de mis amigos y hablamos un rato. 6. Como _____conozco_____ (conocer) a mucha gente, a veces paso media hora hablando. 7. _____Oigo_____ (oír) sus noticias y también 8. _____hago_____ (hacer) planes con algunos de ellos para reunirnos después de las clases. Después, ¡a trabajar! Si 9. _____digo_____ (decir) la verdad, 10. ¡_____sé_____ (saber) que debo estudiar más y hablar menos!

Complete these activities to review some previously learned grammatical structures that will be helpful when you learn the new grammar in **Chapter 7**.

Be sure to reread **Chapter 6: Gramática útil 2** before moving on to the new **Chapter 7** grammar sections.

Reflexive verbs (Chapter 5)

6 Completa las oraciones con las formas correctas de los verbos reflexivos. Presta atención a la forma verbal que requiere cada una.

1. Tú _____te preparas_____ (prepararse: *present indicative*) para ir al cine.
2. Yo _____me acuesto_____ (acostarse: *present indicative*) tarde después de ir al teatro.
3. Nosotros _____nos preocupamos_____ (preocuparse: *present indicative*) porque el tren llega tarde.
4. Mis amigos _____se están divirtiendo / están divirtiéndose_____ (divertirse: *present progressive*) en el parque.
5. Sé que a ustedes no les gusta ir al museo, ¡pero no _____se quejen_____ (quejarse: *command*) tanto, por favor!
6. _____Siéntese_____ (sentarse: *command*) usted aquí y _____relájese_____ (relajarse: *command*) un poco.

¿Qué pasatiempos prefieres?

TIEMPO PERSONAL

A muchas personas les gusta estar siempre ocupadas y trabajando. Para otras personas los ratos libres (*free time*) son muy importantes.

¿Trabajas para vivir o vives para trabajar? ¿Cuáles son más importantes para ti—los ratos libres o los objetivos profesionales?

Communication

By the end of this chapter you will be able to

- talk about sports and leisure activities
- talk about seasons and the weather
- say how you feel using **tener** expressions
- describe your recent leisure activities
- suggest activities and plans to friends

Gaston Piccinetti/age fotostock

Un viaje por Costa Rica y Panamá

Costa Rica y Panamá comparten una frontera y tienen costas en el mar Caribe y en el océano Pacífico. Costa Rica tiene una geografía más variada que Panamá.

Learning objectives: See pages AIE-3–AIE-4 for a complete description of Bloom's Taxonomy learning objectives and an explanation of how they are integrated within the chapter.

Check: At the beginning of this chapter, interview students to find out what they know about Costa Rica and Panama. At the end of the chapter, repeat the questions to assess what they have learned.

País / Área	Tamaño y fronteras	Sitios de interés
Costa Rica 50.660 km^2	un poco más pequeño que Virginia Occidental; fronteras con Nicaragua y Panamá	sistema grande de parques nacionales, el Teatro Nacional en San José, las plantaciones de café, algunos de los mejores sitios del mundo para navegar en rápidos
Panamá 75.990 km^2	un poco más pequeño que Carolina del Sur; fronteras con Costa Rica y Colombia	el canal de Panamá; las islas de Kuna Yala (antes San Blas) con los kuna, una población indígena; el Parque Nacional de Darién; algunas de las mejores playas centroamericanas para el surfing

¿Qué sabes? Di si las siguientes oraciones son ciertas (**C**) o falsas (**F**).

Learning objective: Understanding

1. Costa Rica es un país más pequeño que Virginia Occidental y Carolina del Sur. C
2. Panamá es ideal para navegar en rápidos y hacer surfing. F
3. Costa Rica y Panamá son países vecinos porque comparten una frontera. C
4. El café es un producto importante para Costa Rica. C

Lo que sé y lo que quiero aprender Completa la tabla del **Apéndice A**. Escribe algunos datos que **ya sabes** sobre estos países en la columna **Lo que sé**. Después, añade algunos temas que **quieres aprender** a la columna **Lo que quiero aprender**. Guarda la tabla para usarla otra vez en la sección **¡Explora y exprésate!** en la página 259.

Cultures

By the end of this chapter you will have explored

- facts about Costa Rica and Panama
- a special boat race from the Atlantic to the Pacific
- why Costa Rica is a paradise for ecotourism
- whitewater rafting in Costa Rica
- Fahrenheit and Celsius temperatures; seasons and the equator

¡Imagínate!

Standard 3.1: Throughout the chapter, refer students to the map of Central America in **Appendix D**. A standards-based approach emphasizes *content* and *context*, which links Central America with sports, climate, history, and natural resources.

>> ## Vocabulario útil 1
Learning objectives: Applying, Analyzing

© Cengage Learning 2013

Remind: Students already know **correr, caminar,** and **levantar pesas.** Review with them: ¿Corres maratones?, ¿Cuál es un sitio popular para correr? Es buena idea caminar rápidamente veinte minutos al día, ¿cierto o falso?, ¿Dónde levantas pesas en tu universidad?, etc.

Optional: Additional sports that may be useful for class discussion: **el patinaje artístico, el patinaje de velocidad, los saltos de esquí, los saltos de trampolín,** etc.

Suggestion: Ask ¿Qué deportes son interesantes / aburridos? ¿Por qué? ¿Te gusta observar o participar en...?

Optional: If students ask, *extreme sports* can be called **deportes extremos** or **deportes de alto riesgo.**

SERGIO:	¿Viste el **partido de fútbol** entre Argentina y México ayer?
JAVIER:	No, llegué tarde a casa.
SERGIO:	Pues, te perdiste un partido buenísimo. Yo lo vi en casa de Arturo.
JAVIER:	¿Ah, sí? ¿Quién ganó?
SERGIO:	Argentina, 2 a 1.
JAVIER:	Me encanta ver los partidos de fútbol internacional por tele.
SERGIO:	Y además del fútbol, ¿qué otros deportes te gustan?
JAVIER:	Las **competencias de natación**, el **ciclismo** y el **boxeo**.
SERGIO:	¿El boxeo? ¡Guau! Yo prefiero el fútbol nacional, el italiano, el español…
JAVIER:	¿Qué piensas de los deportes de **invierno**?
SERGIO:	No sé, hay algunos que me parecen interesantes, como el **hockey sobre hielo** y el **esquí alpino**.

In South America, **correr olas**, literally, "to run waves," is used for surfing.

Remember, as you learned in **Chapter 6, jugar** is used with the preposition **a** in a number of Spanish-speaking countries: **jugar al tenis, jugar al fútbol.** Usage of **a** varies from region to region.

>> ### Los deportes

el boxeo *boxing*
el esquí acuático *water skiing*
el esquí alpino *downhill skiing*
el golf *golf*
el hockey sobre hielo *ice hockey*
la natación *swimming*
el snowboarding *snowboarding*

>> ### Actividades deportivas

entrenarse *to train*
esquiar *to ski*
jugar (al) tenis / (al) béisbol / etc. *to play tennis / baseball / etc.*
levantar pesas *to lift weights*
nadar *to swim*
navegar en rápidos *to go whitewater rafting*
patinar sobre hielo *to ice skate*
practicar / hacer alpinismo *to (mountain) climb, hike*
practicar / hacer surfing *to surf*

>> ### Más palabras sobre los deportes

la competencia *competition*
el equipo *team*
ganar *to win*
el lago *lake*
el partido *game, match*
el peligro *danger*
peligroso(a) *dangerous*
la pelota *ball*
la piscina *pool*
el río *river*
seguro(a) *safe*
la tabla de snowboard *snowboard*

>> Otros deportes

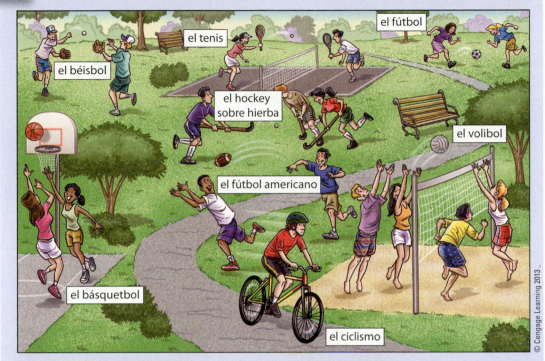

el fútbol

el tenis

el béisbol

el hockey sobre hierba

el volibol

el fútbol americano

el básquetbol

el ciclismo

© Cengage Learning 2013

remar

pescar

montar a caballo

montar en bicicleta

hacer ejercicio

patinar en línea

© Cengage Learning 2013

Sports vocabulary in Spanish contains a lot of words that come from English, for example, **jonrón, gol, béisbol, bate, derbi**, and **fútbol.** It is important to remember that the spelling, pronunciation, and grammatical use of these borrowed words follow the rules of Spanish. All the vowels and consonants of *homerun* are adapted to create **jonrón**; it is pronounced with the rolling **r (la erre)**, and its plural is **jonrones.**

There are pastimes other than sports that you might be interested in: **el póker en línea** *(online poker)*, **jugar a las cartas** *(to play cards)*, **los juegos de mesa** *(board games)*, **el bridge** *(bridge)*, **el ajedrez** *(chess)*, **las damas** *(checkers)*, **el billar americano** *(pool)*, **el billar inglés** *(snooker)*, **el solitario** *(solitaire)*, **el dominó** *(dominoes)*, and **los juegos interactivos** *(interactive games)*. If there are other games that you would like to know how to say in Spanish, go to an online word reference forum or a dictionary app and find out their Spanish equivalent.

>> **Las estaciones**

el verano

julio

el invierno

la primavera

abril

el otoño

© Cengage Learning 2013

ACTIVIDADES

Learning objective: Understanding

Preparation: Point out to students that the names of the months, seasons, and days of the week are not capitalized in Spanish.

Check: Review months of the year so that you can incorporate them into activities to learn the seasons. Have students write them out from memory, and do a quick in-class check on spelling and review pronunciation.

Sample Answers, Act. 1: el parque: levantar pesas, entrenarse, jugar béisbol / básquetbol / fútbol...; **el océano:** hacer surfing, nadar, remar, pescar, hacer esquí acuático; **el lago:** remar, pescar, nadar, hacer esquí acuático; **la cancha:** jugar tenis / básquetbol / volibol / béisbol; **las montañas:** esquiar, hacer esquí alpino, hacer alpinismo; **el gimnasio:** entrenarse, jugar básquetbol / volibol, levantar pesas, el boxeo; **la piscina:** nadar, jugar volibol, entrenarse; **el río:** navegar en rápidos, remar, pescar, hacer esquí acuático

M **1** **En las montañas** Mira la siguiente tabla. Luego, indica qué deportes se pueden practicar en cada lugar. En algunos casos, puede haber varias posibilidades. Limita tus respuestas a un máximo de tres actividades o deportes por cada lugar.

el parque	el océano	el lago	la cancha
las montañas	el gimnasio	la piscina	el río

C **2** **Atletas famosos** Con un(a) compañero(a) de clase, hagan una lista de atletas y otros jugadores famosos. Luego, digan con qué deporte o juego se asocia cada persona.

MODELOS   *Misty May-Treanor*
Misty May-Treanor juega volibol.
Michael Phelps
Michael Phelps practica la natación.

3 ¡Peligro! Con un(a) compañero(a) de clase, digan qué deportes creen

C que son peligrosos y cuáles no lo son. Hagan una lista. Luego, intercambien su lista con la de otra pareja. ¿Tienen las mismas opiniones?

Suggestion: Expand comparing sports by asking: ¿Cuáles son los deportes fáciles? ¿y los difíciles? ¿Cuáles son deportes caros? ¿y económicos? Defiende tu opinión.

4 **El deporte o juego preferido** En grupos de tres o cuatro estudiantes,

C hagan una lista de sus tres actividades o deportes preferidos. Luego hagan una lista de los tres deportes o actividades que no les gustan mucho. Cada grupo tiene que darle sus resultados a la clase.

Optional: After groups determine the most popular sports from their lists, survey the class as a whole to see which activities are the most popular.

MODELO *En nuestro grupo el fútbol, el snowboarding y el surfing son los deportes preferidos.*

En nuestro grupo el golf, la natación y el béisbol son los deportes que menos nos gustan.

5 **Las estaciones** ¿Sabes que los hemisferios norte y sur están en

M/C estaciones opuestas durante todo el año? Durante el verano en el hemisferio norte, es invierno en el hemisferio sur. Con un(a) compañero(a) de clase, mira la tabla e indica la estación que corresponde con cada país y mes.

Learning objective: Understanding

Optional: ¿Qué país sudamericano de habla española está en los hemisferios norte y sur a la vez? (Respuesta: **Ecuador**)

País / mes	Estación
1. Argentina, julio	invierno
2. España, febrero	invierno
3. México, octubre	otoño
4. Uruguay, septiembre	primavera
5. Paraguay, diciembre	verano
6. Cuba, octubre	otoño
7. Panamá, agosto	verano
8. Bolivia, octubre	primavera

6 **En el otoño…** Trabaja con un(a) compañero(a) de clase. Digan qué

C deportes y actividades les gusta hacer en cada estación.

Preparation for Act. 6: If your students need extra help / practice with **gustar,** model several examples using your own sports preferences and emphasizing **gusta** + singular, **gustan** + plural, **gusta** + infinitive.

1. en la primavera
2. en el verano
3. en el otoño
4. en el invierno

JAVIER: Hola, Beto. Qué milagro verte por aquí.

BETO: Ya sé. ¡Odio el gimnasio! No **tengo ganas** de hacer ejercicio en estas malditas máquinas.

SERGIO: ¡Pobre Beto!... ¿Les **tienes miedo** a las "maquinitas"?

BETO: No, ¡no seas ridículo!

Optional: Dramatize the **tener** expressions by having students act them out for their group or for the whole class to guess.

Heritage Learners: Native speakers need explicit instructions on the use of the **diéresis.** Point out that without the use of the **diéresis, tener vergüenza** would be pronounced with the same sound that appears in **guerra.** Similarly, without the **diéresis, pingüino** would be pronounced with the same sound as that which appears in **guitarra.** Give a dictation of the following to reinforce these concepts: 1. **lingüística** 2. **cigüeña** 3. **manguera** 4. **Guillermo** 5. **guante** 6. **averigüe** 7. **guerrilla** 8. **vergüenza** 9. **nicaragüense**

>> **Expresiones con *tener***

tener cuidado *to be careful*
tener ganas de *to feel like (doing)*
tener miedo (de, a) *to be afraid (of)*
tener razón *to be right, correct*
tener vergüenza *to be embarrassed*

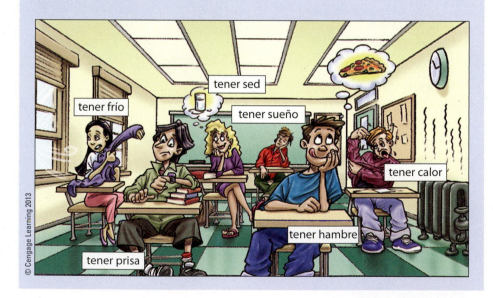

M **7** **¡Tengo sueño!** Indica cómo te sientes en las siguientes situaciones. En algunos casos hay más de una respuesta posible.

1. Tienes un examen muy difícil. Tengo miedo.
2. Es el verano y no tienes aire acondicionado. Tengo calor.
3. Tienes una nueva raqueta de tenis. Tengo ganas de jugar tenis.
4. Ya son las ocho de la noche y todavía no has cenado (*haven't eaten dinner*). Tengo hambre.
5. Acabas de jugar básquetbol por tres horas. Tengo sed. / Tengo calor. / Tengo sueño.
6. Ves una película de terror. Tengo miedo.
7. Son las tres de la mañana y acabas de estudiar. Tengo sueño.
8. Es el invierno y no llevas chaqueta. Tengo frío.
9. Ya son las diez y tu clase de cálculo empieza a las 9:40. Tengo prisa.
10. Sabes las respuestas correctas a todas las preguntas. Tengo razón.

8 **¿Qué tienes?** Usa la siguiente lista. Pasea por la clase y busca una
C persona que tenga una de las emociones que se describen en la lista. Escribe los nombres al lado de las emociones. Luego escribe un resumen de tu encuesta. (¡Es posible que no encuentres nombres para todas las categorías!)

Esta persona...	Nombre
siempre tiene calor:	
tiene miedo de las serpientes:	
tiene ganas de viajar a Nepal:	
tiene vergüenza cuando tiene que hablar enfrente de mucha gente:	
nunca tiene sueño:	
siempre tiene razón:	
nunca tiene prisa:	
tiene ganas de hacer surfing:	

MODELO *Kelly y Sandra siempre tienen calor. Y Jessie…*

Optional: To expand on **Activity 8**, make sure students understand that they must ask and answer questions in Spanish. Model as needed. Pointing at the book and signing without a conversational exchange is not acceptable. If you have time, students can compete for as many signatures by each item as they can find in the class during a set amount of time.

Vocabulario útil 3

BETO: Yo prefiero jugar tenis, pero hoy no puedo porque **está lloviendo**.

JAVIER: Tienes razón. Y además, **hace mucho viento**. Ayer salí a correr pero hoy no tuve otra opción que venir aquí.

BETO: Sí. ¡**Hace mal tiempo** desde el lunes!

Hace frío.

Hace calor.

Hace viento.

Está nevando. Nieva.

Está nublado.

Está lloviendo. Llueve.

© Cengage Learning 2013

>> El tiempo

¿Qué tiempo hace? *What's the weather like?*
Hace buen tiempo. *It's nice weather.*
Hace mal tiempo. *It's bad weather.*
Hace fresco. *It's cool.*
Hace sol. *It's sunny.*

>> La temperatura

grados Celsio(s) / centígrados *degrees Celsius*
grados Fahrenheit *degrees Fahrenheit*
La temperatura está a 20 grados Celsio(s) / centígrados. *It's 20 degrees Celsius.*
La temperatura está a 70 grados Fahrenheit. *It's 70 degrees Fahrenheit.*

Standards: C 3.1 (Making Connections) is met in **Chapter 7** through mathematics with conversions between Celsius and Fahrenheit. Warm up with a few **cierto / falso** items about Celsius and Fahrenheit and get a sense of general knowledge level: **1. Cuando la temperatura está a 30° Celsio(s), hace mucho frío. (F) 2. Cuando la temperatura está a 10° Celsio(s), hace mucho frío. (F)**, etc.

If students want to know how to say *climate change* in Spanish, tell them it's **el cambio climático**.

Note that **grados Celsio(s)** and **centígrados** both refer to measurements on the Celsius scale. **Centígrados** is an older term that has been replaced by **Celsio(s)**. Also notice that whether the plural form of **Celsio** is used varies from country to country.

To convert between Fahrenheit and Celsius:

Grados C → Grados F: (C° × 1,8) + 32 = F°
Ejemplo: (30°C × 1,8) + 32 = 86°F

Grados F → Grados C: (F° − 32) ÷ 1,8 = C°
Ejemplo: (86° F − 32) ÷ 1,8 = 30°C

Suggestion: Review the inversion of the comma (,) and period (.). To review this concept, ask students to rewrite the following numbers as they would appear in the Spanish-speaking world: 1, 234.5 / .075 / 1,786,905 / 1.33

Learning objective: Understanding

ACTIVIDADES

M **9** **El tiempo** Di qué tiempo hace por lo general durante las estaciones o meses indicados.

1. el mes de marzo en tu ciudad
2. el mes de agosto en tu ciudad
3. el mes de enero en tu ciudad
4. el mes de octubre en tu ciudad

5. en invierno en Buenos Aires
6. en invierno en Seattle
7. en verano en Miami
8. en invierno en Chicago

10 **Prefiero…** Trabaja con un(a) compañero(a) de clase. Identifiquen por lo
C   menos dos actividades que les gusta hacer y dos que no les gusta hacer cuando
hace el tiempo indicado. Luego, escriban oraciones completas para hacer un
resumen de sus preferencias.

1. cuando hace calor
2. cuando hace frío
3. cuando hace mucho viento
4. cuando nieva
5. cuando llueve

¡Fíjate!   ¿Qué tiempo hace?

Cuando hablas del tiempo y de la temperatura en español, hay
varias cosas importantes que debes saber. Primero, como viste en la
Actividad 5, los países al norte y al sur del ecuador están en estaciones
opuestas. Es decir, cuando en el norte estamos en invierno, los países
al sur están en verano. Cuando es otoño en EEUU, allá es primavera.

Segundo, EEUU y los países de habla española usan dos sistemas
diferentes para medir *(to measure)* la temperatura. Aquí usamos el sistema
Fahrenheit, mientras que en Latinoamérica y España usan el sistema Celsio.

Finalmente, México, los países del Caribe y varios países de
Centroamérica y Sudamérica tienen temporadas de lluvias y temporadas
secas *(dry)*. Aunque esto es más común en los países más cerca del
ecuador, también puede ocurrir cuando corrientes del océano crean
condiciones especiales, como en el noroeste Pacífico de EEUU y en Perú.

Práctica Miren las siguientes tablas y contesten las preguntas sobre
el tiempo en las dos ciudades. (**tormenta** = *thunderstorm*, **chaparrón** =
cloudburst, downpour)

1. ¿Cuál es la temperatura máxima en San José? ¿Y la temperatura mínima?
2. ¿Crees que se dan estas temperaturas en grados Celsio o Fahrenheit?
3. ¿Qué tiempo hace en San José el martes 28 de agosto? ¿Qué tiempo va a hacer el miércoles? ¿Y el sábado?
4. ¿Cuál es la temperatura máxima en la Ciudad de Panamá? ¿Y la temperatura mínima?
5. ¿Hace más calor en la Ciudad de Panamá o en San José?
6. ¿Cuál es el pronóstico para los días entre el jueves y el sábado en la Ciudad de Panamá?
7. ¿Cuándo es la temporada de lluvias en cada país?

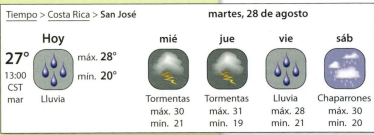

Tiempo > Costa Rica > **San José**   **martes, 28 de agosto**

	Hoy	mié	jue	vie	sáb
27° 13:00 CST mar	máx. **28°** mín. **20°** Lluvia	Tormentas máx. 30 min. 21	Tormentas máx. 31 min. 19	Lluvia máx. 28 min. 21	Chaparrones máx. 30 min. 20

Tiempo > Panamá > **Ciudad de Panamá**   **martes, 28 de agosto**

	Hoy	mié	jue	vie	sáb
Chaparrones	máx. **33°** mín. **26°**	Tormentas máx. 32 min. 25	Chaparrones máx. 34 min. 23	Chaparrones máx. 33 min. 26	Chaparrones máx. 34 min. 25

© Cengage Learning 2013

Standards 4.1, 4.2:
The **¡Fíjate!** cultural and
linguistic notes throughout *Cuadros*
encourage students to connect and
compare information about cultures,
cultural practices, languages, and
linguistic history. Topics usually relate
to the chapter theme and vocabulary,
and help students understand the
nature of cultural practices and
language usage.

Preparation/Optional: For the
presentation of **¿Qué tiempo hace?,**
bring in a large colorful weather page
from a newspaper or use the Internet.
Review colors, and ask where the
weather is nice, hot, cool, etc.

Check: Project the Weather Channel
in Spanish (español.weather.com)
and go to **El tiempo de hoy** and play.
Before you replay, ask students to
identify at least 1–2 places to report
the temperature and the weather to
the class. This activity checks both
interpretation and production.

Answers, Práctica: 1. 28°, 20° 2. Celsio
3. Llueve. Van a tener tormentas el
miércoles y chaparrones el sábado.
4. 33°, 26° 5. Hace más calor en la
Ciudad de Panamá. 6. Van a tener
chaparrones. 7. El verano es la
temporada de lluvias.

A ver

 Standard 1.2: Through video viewing, students learn interpretive strategies for communication. Activities in this section regularly provide opportunities for students to interpret spoken language.

ESTRATEGIA

Listening for details

You have learned to listen for the main idea of a video segment. Knowing in advance what to listen for will help you find key information. **Antes de ver 2** will help you focus on this specific information.

Preparation: Start students thinking about what they will see in the video by chatting about working out: ¿Haces ejercicio? ¿Dónde? ¿Con quién(es)? ¿Vas al gimnasio frecuentemente o con poca frecuencia? ¿Cuándo haces ejercicio (por la mañana, por la tarde, por la noche)? ¿Te gusta usar las máquinas? ¿Levantas pesas? ¿Corres?

Answers, Antes de ver 1: 1. los deportes 2. el fútbol nacional 3. miedo 4. ganas 5. lloviendo 6. viento

Answers, Antes de ver 2: A Javier: le gusta el fútbol / la natación / el ciclismo / el boxeo; no le gusta X (no se indica); **A Sergio:** le gusta el fútbol / el hockey sobre hielo / el esquí alpino; no le gusta X (no se indica); **A Beto:** le gusta el tenis; no le gusta hacer ejercicio en las máquinas (en el gimnasio); **A Dulce:** le gusta jugar tenis; no le gusta el gimnasio

Antes de ver 1 Mira las fotos y el texto en las páginas 232, 236 y 238 del **Vocabulario útil**. Luego, completa las siguientes oraciones sobre las personas de las fotos.

1. Javier y Sergio hablan de (los cursos / los deportes).
2. Sergio prefiere (el fútbol nacional / el hockey sobre hielo) sobre el boxeo.
3. Según Beto, él no les tiene (sueño / miedo) a las máquinas del gimnasio.
4. Además, Beto no tiene (ganas / vergüenza) de hacer ejercicio en el gimnasio.
5. Beto no puede jugar tenis porque está (lloviendo / nevando).
6. Hoy también hace mucho (frío / viento).

Antes de ver 2 Ahora mira la siguiente tabla y fíjate en la información que necesites del video para completarla.

	A Javier	A Sergio	A Beto	A Dulce
le gusta...				
no le gusta...				

▶ **Ver** Mira el video para el Capítulo **7** y completa la tabla en **Antes de ver 2**. Si el video no tiene la información necesaria, pon una X.

Después de ver 1 Escribe frases completas para indicar qué le gusta hacer a cada persona que se menciona en **Antes de ver 2**.

MODELO *A Dulce le gusta jugar tenis, pero no le gusta...*

Learning objectives: Remembering

Answers, Después de ver 2: 1. Hablan del partido de fútbol entre Argentina y México. 2. No 3. Dice que Beto tiene los músculos de un niño. 4. Porque ve que Dulce está en el gimnasio. 5. Le dice que va al gimnasio todos los días para levantar pesas. Es falso. 6. Dulce juega tenis.

Después de ver 2 Con un(a) compañero(a) de clase, contesta las siguientes preguntas sobre el video.

1. ¿De qué hablan Javier y Sergio al principio de la escena?
2. ¿Va Beto al gimnasio con frecuencia?
3. ¿Qué dice Sergio sobre la condición física de Beto?
4. ¿Por qué empieza Beto a hacer ejercicio con mucho entusiasmo?
5. ¿Qué le dice Beto a Dulce sobre su rutina diaria? ¿Es cierto o falso?
6. ¿Qué hace Dulce cuando hace ejercicio?

© Cengage Learning 2013

Voces de la comunidad

▶ >> Voces del mundo hispano

En el video para este capítulo Essdras, Nicole y Andrés
hablan de sus pasatiempos y las estaciones del año. Lee las
siguientes oraciones. Después mira el video una o más veces
para decir si las oraciones son ciertas (C) o falsas (F).

© Cengage Learning 2013

1. A Essdras le gusta el invierno porque todo es muy
   oscuro. F

2. Nicole prefiere el otoño porque le gusta el cambio de
   las hojas *(leaves)*. C

3. A Andrés no le gusta la estación lluviosa porque es difícil salir afuera. C

4. A Essdras le gusta hacer yoga y levantar pesas. F

5. Nicole prefiere bailar y acampar. C

6. Andrés no practica ningún deporte. C

◀))) >> Voces de Estados Unidos

Track 21

Brenda Villa, waterpolista

Cameron Spencer/Getty Images

❝Los medios de comunicación hispanos deben poner de su
parte *(do their part)* para dar publicidad a los atletas
hispanos en deportes no-tradicionales. Así los padres
pueden conocer todas las opciones que hay para sus hijos❞.

Brenda Villa es la mejor waterpolista femenina de la década
2000–2009, según la Federación Internacional de Natación.
Nacida *(Born)* en East L.A. de padres mexicanos, Villa aprendió a
jugar polo a los seis años con sus dos hermanos. Después, en Bell Gardens
High School, jugó para el equipo masculino porque la escuela no tenía
equipo femenino. Villa es graduada de Stanford, donde se especializó
en ciencias políticas. Actualmente es entrenadora de polo en Cerritos
College en California y también juega para el equipo italiano Orizzonte.
Esta súper atleta tiene la distinción de ser la primera latina en el equipo de
waterpolo de los EEUU. Sus honores incluyen varias medallas Olímpicas
y de campeonatos mundiales y también el **Trofeo Peter J. Cutino** del
National Collegiate Athletic Association (NCAA), el más prestigioso honor
a nivel *(level)* individual en el waterpolo universitario norteamericano.

¿Y tú? En tu opinión, ¿cuáles son algunos deportes que no reciben la
atención o el interés público que merecen *(they deserve)*? ¿Crees que los
medios de comunicación deben hacer un esfuerzo para promocionarlos?

Standards 2.1, 2.2, 3.2:
Students read about
successful Spanish speakers in the U.S.
and acquire cultural information that
features distinctive viewpoints of
Spanish-speaking people.

The forms **jugó, aprendió**
and **se especializó** are
all past-tense forms.
You'll learn more about
them on page 242.

¡Prepárate!

>> Gramática útil 1

Talking about what you did: The preterite tense of regular verbs

¿Quién **ganó**?

Spanish uses another past tense called the *imperfect* to talk about past actions that were routine or ongoing. You will learn more about this tense in **Chapter 9.**

Heritage Learners: Research indicates that heritage learners have a better command of the preterite than the imperfect. Verbs referring to state of mind—for example, **ser, sentir, saber**—are an exception to this rule. They are acquired in the imperfect before the preterite because they refer to actions without a clear beginning or end and that go on for a period of time.

Cómo usarlo

LO BÁSICO

A *verb tense* is a form of a verb that indicates the time of an action: the past, present, or future. You have already been using the present indicative **(Estudio en la biblioteca)** and the present progressive **(Estoy hablando por teléfono)** tenses.

When you want to talk in Spanish about actions that occurred and were completed in the past, you use the *preterite tense*. The preterite is used to describe

- actions that began and ended in the past;
- conditions or states that existed completely within the past.

Me desperté, leí el periódico y **salí** para el gimnasio.
Fui secretario bilingüe por dos años.
Estuve muy cansada ayer.

I woke up, I read the newspaper, and I left for the gym.
I was a bilingual secretary for two years.
I was very tired yesterday.

Cómo formarlo

1. To form the preterite tense of regular **-ar**, **-er**, and **-ir** verbs, you remove that ending from the infinitive and add the following endings to the verb stem.

Note that reflexive verbs use the same endings. **Lavarse: me lavé, te lavaste, se lavó, nos lavamos, se lavaron. Reunirse: me reuní, te reuniste, se reunió, nos reunimos, se reunieron.**

	-ar verb: **bailar**		**-er** and **-ir** verbs: **comer / escribir**		
yo	**-é**	bail**é**	**-í**	com**í**	escrib**í**
tú	**-aste**	bail**aste**	**-iste**	com**iste**	escrib**iste**
Ud. / él / ella	**-ó**	bail**ó**	**-ió**	com**ió**	escrib**ió**
nosotros / nosotras	**-amos**	bail**amos**	**-imos**	com**imos**	escrib**imos**
vosotros / vosotras	**-asteis**	bail**asteis**	**-isteis**	com**isteis**	escrib**isteis**
Uds. / ellos / ellas	**-aron**	bail**aron**	**-ieron**	com**ieron**	escrib**ieron**

2. Notice that the preterite forms of **-er** and **-ir** verbs are the same.

Heritage Learners: Many heritage language speakers add an **s** to the preterite form of the second-person singular: *comistes, *hablastes, *vivistes. When correcting this, point out that many people throughout the Spanish-speaking world also exhibit this tendency. The reason this practice is so widespread is because every other instance of a second-person singular conjugation in Spanish carries an **s.** Emphasize that the practice does not correspond to the rules of standard Spanish and should be avoided.

3. Notice that only the **yo** and **Ud. / él / ella** forms are accented.

4. The **nosotros** forms of the preterite and the present indicative of **-ar** and **-ir** verbs are the same. You can tell which is being used by context.

    Bailamos todos los fines de semana.   (present)
    Bailamos salsa con Mario ayer.   (past)

5. All stem-changing verbs that end in **-ar** or **-er** are regular in the preterite.

    Me desperté a las ocho cuando   *I woke up at 8:00 when the*
        sonó el teléfono.   *telephone **rang**.*
    Volví temprano de mis vacaciones   *I returned early from my vacation*
        porque **perdí** mi pasaporte.   *because **I lost** my passport.*

6. Many of the verbs you have already learned are regular in the preterite tense. A few have some minor changes.

    - Verbs that end in **-car, -gar**, and **-zar** have a spelling change in the **yo** form to maintain the correct pronunciation.

        -car: c → qu   sacar: **saqué**, sacaste, sacó, sacamos, sacasteis, sacaron
        -gar: g → gu   llegar: **llegué**, llegaste, llegó, llegamos, llegasteis, llegaron
        -zar: z → c   cruzar: **crucé**, cruzaste, cruzó, cruzamos, cruzasteis, cruzaron

    - Verbs that end in **-eer**, as well as the verb **oír**, change **i** to **y** in the two third-person forms. Note the accent on the **-íste, -ímos**, and **-ísteis** endings.

        leer: leí, leíste, leyó, leímos, leísteis, leyeron
        creer: creí, creíste, creyó, creímos, creísteis, creyeron
        oír: oí, oíste, oyó, oímos, oísteis, oyeron

7. You have already learned the word **ayer.** Here are some other useful time expressions to use with the preterite tense: **anoche** *(last night)*, **anteayer** *(the day before yesterday)*, **la semana pasada** *(last week)*, **el mes pasado** *(last month)*, **el año pasado** *(last year)*.

> Stem-changing verbs that end in **-ir** also have stem changes in the preterite. You will learn these forms in **Chapter 8.**

Optional: For a simple game that will practice the production of preterite verb endings, divide the class into 2–3 groups. Put students in 2–3 lines ready to approach the blackboard. Call out a subject (**tú, mi padre y yo**, etc.) and an infinitive (**bailar, comer, cruzar**, etc.). Remember to avoid stem-changing **-ir** verbs at this point. The first students in each line approach the board and write the correct conjugation. Rotate students and track points.

Optional: Try a dictation with respect to the use of [c] and [g] in the verbal paradigm, as well as the presence or absence of the accent: **1. navegar / navegué / navegue 2. indicar / indiqué / indique 3. brincar / brinqué / brinque 4. rezar / recé / rece 5. abrazar / abracé / abrace**

Notice: Emphasize practice with **jugar (g → gu)** which will be used throughout the chapter. Stress the **yo** form by asking questions like ¿**Jugaste algún deporte ayer / la semana pasada?**

ACTIVIDADES

🔊 **1 ¿Presente o pasado?** Escucha las oraciones e indica si las actividades
Track 22 que se describen ocurren en el presente o el pasado.
I

		Presente	Pasado
1.	Javier y Lidia / esquiar	X	
2.	Susana / entrenarse	X	
3.	yo / navegar en rápidos		X
4.	mi padre / pescar		X
5.	tú / remar	X	
6.	tú / jugar golf		X
7.	yo / patinar sobre hielo	X	
8.	yo / nadir		X

Audioscript, Act. 1, ¿Presente o pasado?:

1. *Javier y Lidia esquían frecuentemente.*
2. *Susana se entrena todos los días.*
3. *Yo navegué en rápidos durante las vacaciones.*
4. *Mi padre pescó casi todos los días el verano pasado.*
5. *Tú remas muy bien.*
6. *¿Jugaste golf esta mañana?*
7. *Patino sobre hielo en el lago en el invierno.*
8. *Nadé en el océano el verano pasado.*

M **2** **El calendario de Rosario** Usa el siguiente calendario para decir qué hizo *(did)* Rosario la semana pasada.

lunes 17	martes 18	miércoles 19	jueves 20	viernes 21	sábado 22	domingo 23
A.M.: estudiar con Lalo	**A.M.:** trabajar en la biblioteca	**A.M.:** almorzar con Neti	**A.M.:** leer en la biblioteca	**A.M.:** correr dos millas	**A.M.:** desayunar con Sergio	**A.M.:** ¡descansar!
P.M.: jugar tenis con Fernando	**P.M.:** salir con Lalo	**P.M.:** sacar la basura	**P.M.:** escribir el ensayo para la clase de literatura	**P.M.:** ¡bailar en la discoteca!	**P.M.:** entrenarse en el gimnasio	**P.M.:** comer con Lalo

© Cengage Learning 2013

MODELOS *El lunes por la mañana Rosario estudió con Lalo.*
O: *El lunes por la mañana Rosario y Lalo estudiaron.*

M **3** **Ayer** Di qué hicieron *(did)* las siguientes personas ayer.

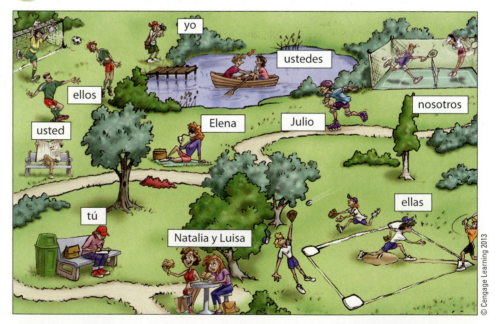

© Cengage Learning 2013

👥 **4** **La semana pasada** Ahora, usa el horario de la **Actividad 2** como
C modelo y complétalo con tu propia información sobre la semana pasada. Luego, trabaja con un(a) compañero(a) de clase para hablar de sus actividades de la semana pasada.

MODELO Tú: *¿Qué hiciste* (What did you do) *el lunes por la mañana?*
Compañero(a): *Jugué golf. ¿Y tú? ¿Qué hiciste el miércoles por la tarde?*

Gramática útil 2

Talking about what you did: The preterite tense of some common irregular verbs

Cómo usarlo

As you learned in **Gramática útil 1,** the preterite is a Spanish past-tense form that is used to talk about actions that occurred and were completed in the past. It describes actions that began and ended in the past and refers to things that happened and are over with, whether they happened just once or over time.

Fuimos al restaurante.	*We **went** to the restaurant.*
Hicimos deporte todo el día.	*We **played** sports all day.*
¡**Estuvimos** bien cansados!	*We **were** really tired!*

¿**Viste** el partido de fútbol entre Argentina y México ayer?

Cómo formarlo

1. Here are the irregular preterite forms of some frequently used verbs.

	estar	hacer	ir	ser
yo	estuve	hice	fui	fui
tú	estuviste	hiciste	fuiste	fuiste
Ud. / él / ella	estuvo	hizo	fue	fue
nosotros / nosotras	estuvimos	hicimos	fuimos	fuimos
vosotros / vosotras	estuvisteis	hicisteis	fuisteis	fuisteis
Uds. / ellos / ellas	estuvieron	hicieron	fueron	fueron

Notice: True beginners will need help pronouncing these irregular forms. Hearing the rhythm of the irregular preterites will help students mnemonically as well.

	dar	ver	decir	traer
yo	di	vi	dije	traje
tú	diste	viste	dijiste	trajiste
Ud. / él / ella	dio	vio	dijo	trajo
nosotros / nosotras	dimos	vimos	dijimos	trajimos
vosotros / vosotras	disteis	visteis	dijisteis	trajisteis
Uds. / ellos / ellas	dieron	vieron	dijeron	trajeron

Ver is irregular only because it does not carry accents in the **yo** and **Ud. / él / ella** forms. **Dar** is irregular because it uses the regular **-er / -ir** endings rather than the **-ar** endings.

2. Verbs that end in **-cir** follow the same pattern as **traer** and **decir**.

conducir: conduje, condujiste, condujo, condujimos, condujisteis, condujeron

producir: produje, produjiste, produjo, produjimos, produjisteis, produjeron

traducir: traduje, tradujiste, tradujo, tradujimos, tradujisteis, tradujeron

Suggestion: Model a mini-narrative about what you did with whom yesterday. Chat with students about what they did yesterday: **¿Qué hiciste ayer? ¿Dónde estuviste? ¿Adónde fuiste? ¿Con quién estuviste? ¿A quién viste?**

Optional: Have students create a description of all of the things that they did in Spanish class last week using the preterite forms. Cue this with the **nosotros** form.

3. Notice that although these irregular verbs do for the most part use the regular endings, they have internal changes to the stem that must be memorized.

4. Notice that none of these verbs requires accents in the preterite.

5. Notice that **ser** and **ir** have the same forms in the preterite. But because the verbs have such different meanings, it is usually fairly easy to tell which one is being used.

Fuimos estudiantes durante esos años.	*We were students during those years.*
Todos **fuimos** a una fiesta muy alegre.	*We all went to a really fun party.*

ACTIVIDADES

M **5** **¿Qué hicieron?** Haz oraciones completas para decir qué pasó la semana pasada.

MODELO **ir**

ellos / al parque a jugar tenis
Ellos fueron al parque a jugar tenis.

estar

1. tú y yo / en las montañas para hacer alpinismo
2. Mónica y Sara / en el gimnasio todos los días
3. usted / en la costa para hacer surfing

ir

4. ustedes / al gimnasio a entrenarse
5. yo / a la biblioteca a estudiar
6. Jorge / al parque a jugar básquetbol

ver

7. yo / una película muy buena
8. nosotros / a Mónica y a Sara en el gimnasio
9. tú / una serpiente en el parque

traer

10. Luis / su pelota de béisbol a mi casa para jugar
11. ellos / su equipo (*equipment*) para jugar hockey sobre hierba
12. tú / tus pesas para entrenarte

C **6** **¿Quién fue?** Con un(a) compañero(a) de clase, digan quiénes fueron las personas indicadas. (En algunos casos, hay más de una respuesta posible.)

MODELO Abraham Lincoln
¿Quién fue Abraham Lincoln?
Fue presidente de Estados Unidos.

Respuestas posibles: presidente, futbolista, actor / actriz, cantante, científico(a), político(a), revolucionario(a)

1. Monsieur y Madame Curie
2. Albert Einstein
3. Marilyn Monroe y Natasha Richardson
4. Bill Clinton y George W. Bush
5. Henry Kissinger
6. Che Guevara
7. Michael Jackson
8. Diego Maradona

7 Las vacaciones

👫 Averigua qué hizo tu compañero(a) de clase durante
C sus vacaciones del año pasado. Pregúntale si hizo las siguientes cosas y cuánto las hizo.

1. hacer viajes *(trips)* (¿cuántos?)
2. gastar dinero (¿cuánto?)
3. ir a la playa (¿cuántas veces?)
4. ver un partido deportivo (¿cuántas veces?)
5. hacer ejercicio (¿cuántas veces?)

Luego, tu compañero(a) te hace las mismas preguntas. Juntos, determinen la siguiente información.

1. ¿Quién hizo más viajes?
2. ¿Quién gastó más dinero?
3. ¿Quién fue a la playa más?
4. ¿Quién vio más partidos deportivos?
5. ¿Quién hizo más ejercicio?

🔊 ## 8 La reunión

Track 23 Escucha mientras Cecilia describe qué pasó la semana pasada
C en la reunión de ex alumnos de su colegio. Primero, completa la tabla con la información necesaria. Luego, escribe oraciones completas según el modelo.

Persona	¿Qué dijo?
yo (Cecilia)	
tú (Rosa Carmen)	
José María	
Marcos	*Es periodista.*
Laura y Sebastián	
Leticia	
Pilar y Antonio	

MODELO Marcos
Marcos dijo que es periodista.

1. yo   Yo dije que estoy casada y que tengo tres hijos.
2. tú   Tú dijiste que trabajas como enfermera (y que te gusta mucho).
3. José María   José María dijo que es profesor de matemáticas.
4. Laura y Sebastián   Laura y Sebastián dijeron que son profesores de lenguas (en la misma universidad).
5. Leticia   Leticia dijo que ahora vive en Seattle (y que le gusta).
6. Pilar y Antonio   Pilar y Antonio dijeron que se casaron en 1998 y que son médicos (en el mismo hospital).

Optional: For expansion, explain the word **chisme** or *gossip* to students and state: **Dijeron en la tele que [well-known celebrity] se casa.** Ask students to think about any gossip items that they have heard recently and jot them down in Spanish. Call on a few students to read **sus chismes** to the class. If they haven't heard of any good gossip, encourage students to make something up!

Learning objective: Analyzing

Audioscript, Act. 8, La reunión:

Cecilia y su mejor amiga Rosa Carmen hablan por teléfono sobre la reunión de ex alumnos de su colegio.

[Cecilia]: ¿Y qué pensaste de Marcos?
[Rosa Carmen]: Ay, me pareció muy contento. Es periodista, ¿verdad?
[Cecilia]: Sí. Dijo que trabaja para El Nuevo Herald de Miami.
[Rosa Carmen]: ¿Y qué le dijiste de tu vida?
[Cecilia]: Le dije que estoy casada y que tengo tres hijos. ¿Qué le dijiste tú?
[Rosa Carmen]: Que trabajo como enfermera y que me gusta mucho.
[Cecilia]: ¿Hablaste con José María?
[Rosa Carmen]: Sí. Dijo que es profesor de matemáticas.
[Cecilia]: Claro. Siempre fue muy inteligente. ¿Qué tal Laura y Sebastián?
[Rosa Carmen]: Dijeron que son profesores de lenguas en la misma universidad.
[Cecilia]: Ay, ¡tantos profesores!
[Rosa Carmen]: Es raro, ¿verdad? ¿Qué más…? ¿Hablaste con Leticia?
[Cecilia]: Sí, un poco. Dijo que ahora vive en Seattle.
[Rosa Carmen]: Está muy lejos, ¿no?
[Cecilia]: Sí, pero le gusta. También hablé con Pilar y Antonio.
[Rosa Carmen]: ¿Y qué tal ellos? Siempre fueron muy inteligentes también.
[Cecilia]: Bueno, dijeron que se casaron en 1998. Ahora los dos son médicos en el mismo hospital.
[Rosa Carmen]: ¿Te dijeron el nombre del hospital? ¿Es el mismo donde trabajo yo?
[Cecilia]: Ay, no sé. No me dijeron el nombre.

Gramática útil 3

Referring to something already mentioned: Direct object pronouns

Cómo usarlo

LO BÁSICO

A *direct object* is a noun or noun phrase that receives the action of a verb: I buy *a book*. We invite *our friends*. *Direct object pronouns* are pronouns that replace direct object nouns or phrases: I buy *it*. We invite *them*. Often you can identify the direct object of the sentence by asking *what?* or *whom?*: We buy *what? (a book / it)* / We invite *whom*? *(our friends / them).*

You use direct object pronouns in both Spanish and English to avoid repetition and to refer to things or people that have already been mentioned. Look at the following passage in Spanish and notice how much repetition there is.

> **Quiero hablar con María. Llamo a María por teléfono e invito a María a visitar a mis padres. Visito a mis padres casi todos los fines de semana.**

Now read the passage after it's been rewritten using direct object pronouns to replace some of the occasions when the nouns **María** and **padres** were used previously. (The direct object pronouns appear underlined.)

> **Quiero hablar con María. <u>La</u> llamo por teléfono y <u>la</u> invito a visitar a mis padres. <u>Los</u> visito casi todos los fines de semana.**

Cómo formarlo

1. Here are the direct object pronouns in Spanish.

Singular		Plural	
me	me	**nos**	us
te	you (fam.)	**os**	you (fam.)
lo	you (form. masc.), him, it	**los**	you (form. masc.), them, it
la	you (form., fem.), she, it	**las**	you (form. fem.), them, it

2. The third-person direct object pronouns in Spanish must agree in gender and number with the noun they replace.

Compramos **el libro.**	→	**Lo** compramos.
Compramos **la raqueta.**	→	**La** compramos.
Compramos **los libros.**	→	**Los** compramos.
Compramos **las raquetas.**	→	**Las** compramos.

© Cengage Learning 2013

Pues, te perdiste un partido buenísimo. Yo **lo** vi en casa de Arturo.

3. Pay particular attention to the **lo / la** and **los / las** forms, because they can have a variety of meanings. For example, **Lo llamo** can mean *I call you* (formal, male) or *I call him*. **La llamo** can mean *I call you* (formal, female) or *I call her*. Look at the possible meanings for the **los** and **las** forms.

Los llamo. → *I call* **them**. *(at least two men, or a man and a woman)*
              I call **you**. *(formal, at least two people, at least one male)*

Las llamo. → *I call* **them**. *(at least two women)*
              I call **you**. *(polite form, at least two women)*

4. Direct object pronouns always come *before* a *conjugated verb* used by itself.

Me llamas el viernes, ¿no?   *You'll call* **me** *on Friday, right?*
Te invito a la fiesta.   *I'm inviting* **you** *to the party.*

5. When a direct object pronoun is used with an *infinitive* or with the *present progressive*, it may come *before* the conjugated verb or it may be *attached* to the infinitive or to the present participle.

Te voy a llamar.   OR: Voy a llamar**te**.
Te estoy llamando.   OR: Estoy llamándo**te**.

> Notice that when the direct object pronoun attaches to the present participle, you must add an accent to the next-to-last syllable of the present participle to maintain the correct pronunciation: **llamándote**.

6. When a direct object pronoun is used with a *command form*, it *attaches to the end of the affirmative command* but *comes before the negative command* form.

Hágalo ahora, por favor.   BUT: **No lo haga** ahora, por favor.

7. When you use direct object pronouns with *reflexive pronouns*, the *reflexive pronouns come before the direct object pronouns.*

Me estoy lavando **la cara** con jabón.   *I am washing* **my face** *with soap.*
Me **la** estoy lavando con jabón.   *I am washing* **it** *with soap.*

Estoy lavándome **la cara** con jabón.   *I am washing* **my face** *with soap.*
Estoy lavándome**la** con jabón.   *I am washing* **it** *with soap.*

> Again, notice that when the direct object pronoun attaches to the command form, you must add an accent to the next-to-last syllable of command forms of two or more syllables in order to maintain the correct pronunciation: **hágalo**.

ACTIVIDADES

M **9** **El domingo por la tarde** Tú y tu familia tuvieron una reunión en casa el domingo por la tarde. Todos contribuyeron de diferentes maneras. Escribe lo que hicieron todos usando los complementos directos correctos. Sigue el modelo.

MODELO Mi mamá y yo compramos <u>la comida</u>.
         La compramos.

Suggestion: If students have trouble with this activity, have them identify the direct object nouns in each sentence with the whole class before they begin.

1. Mi hermana y yo limpiamos *(cleaned)* <u>la casa</u>.
   <u>La</u> limpiamos.
2. Mi papá invitó a <u>los primos</u>.
   <u>Los</u> invitó.
3. Yo compré <u>los refrescos</u>.
   <u>Los</u> compré.
4. Mi hermano trajo <u>la música</u>.
   <u>La</u> trajo.
5. Mis tíos prepararon <u>la ensalada</u>.
   <u>La</u> prepararon.
6. Mi tía hizo <u>las tortillas</u>.
   <u>Las</u> hizo.

M **10** **El día horrible de Manuel** Lee sobre el día horrible de Manuel. Sustituye las palabras **en negrilla** *(boldface)* con complementos directos, según el modelo.

MODELO Compré **los libros.**
Los compré.

Un día horrible

¡Ayer estuve muy ocupado! Empezaron las clases y tuve que comprar los libros. Compré **los libros** en la librería de la universidad. Pero no encontré el libro para mi clase de cálculo. Tuve que ir a otra librería. Busqué **la librería**, pero, como no me dieron buenas indicaciones para llegar, ¡no encontré **la librería** hasta después de dos horas! Por fin, vi el libro de clase y compré **el libro.**

Después fui al supermercado para comprar algunos comestibles, pero no pude comprar **los comestibles** porque no encontré mi tarjeta de crédito *(credit card).* Volví a la librería para buscar mi tarjeta, pero no encontré **la tarjeta** allí.

Decidí ir a la residencia estudiantil para descansar un poco y hacer un poco de trabajo. Vi a mi compañero de cuarto en la entrada. Saludé a **mi compañero de cuarto.** Él me dijo que me envió un mensaje. Envió **el mensaje** para decirme que la computadora no funciona bien. Examiné **la computadora**, pero no pude *(I couldn't)* reparar **la computadora.** Tenemos que llevar **la computadora** al centro de computación para hacerle reparaciones. ¡Otra cosa que tengo que hacer!

© Cengage Learning 2013

M **11** **Pobre Manuel** Contesta las preguntas sobre el día horrible de Manuel (**Actividad 10**). Usa un complemento directo en tu respuesta.

MODELO ¿Encontró Manuel el libro en la librería de la universidad?
No, no lo encontró.

1. ¿Encontró Manuel la otra librería?
2. ¿Compró los comestibles?
3. ¿Encontró su tarjeta de crédito?
4. ¿Vio a su compañero de cuarto en la residencia estudiantil?
5. Cuando por fin llegó a la residencia estudiantil, ¿pudo hacer su trabajo?
6. ¿Usó la computadora de su cuarto?
7. ¿Llevó la computadora al centro de computaciones?
8. ¿Tuvo un día tranquilo?

M **12** **Natalia** El padre de Natalia y Nico es muy exigente *(demanding)*. Les hace muchas preguntas. Haz el papel de Natalia y contesta las preguntas de su padre.

MODELOS Padre: *¿Limpiaron el baño? (sí)*
Natalia: *Sí, lo limpiamos.*
Padre: *¿Limpiaste tu cuarto? (no)*
Natalia: *No, pero estoy limpiándolo ahora mismo.*

1. ¿Hiciste la tarea? (sí)
2. ¿Prepararon el almuerzo? (no)
3. ¿Hicieron los planes para la fiesta? (no)
4. ¿Leíste la nota de tu mamá? (sí)
5. ¿Viste la lista de comida que debes comprar en el supermercado? (sí)
6. ¿Llamaste a tu abuela? (sí)

ᵗᵗ **13** **¿Lo leíste?** Trabaja con un(a) compañero(a) de clase. Háganse
C preguntas y contéstenlas usando complementos directos. Sigan el modelo.

MODELO leer / el nuevo libro de James Patterson
Compañero(a): *¿Leíste el nuevo libro de James Patterson?*
Tú: *Sí, lo leí. O: No, no lo leí.*

1. ver / la nueva película de Pedro Almodóvar
2. leer / el nuevo libro de Sue Grafton
3. ver / los partidos de básquetbol del WNBA
4. traer / computadora portátil a clase
5. entender / la tarea de la clase de español
6. comprar / las pelotas de tenis
7. descargar / la nueva canción de Calle 13
8. ¿…?

ᵗᵗᵗ **14** **¿Lo tienes?** En grupos de tres, túrnense para hacer y contestar preguntas
C sobre sus actividades recientes. Cuando hacen las preguntas, usen las palabras indicadas con **cuándo** o **dónde**. Cuando contestan, usen un pronombre directo.

MODELOS comprar tu mochila
Tú: *¿Dónde compraste tu mochila?*
Compañero(a): *La compré en la librería de la universidad.*

hacer la tarea para la clase de español
Compañero(a): *¿Cuándo hiciste la tarea para la clase de español?*
Tú: *¡No la hice!*

1. comprar tu computadora
2. hacer la tarea para la clase de ¿…?
3. mirar tus programas favoritos
4. escuchar tu canción favorita
5. llamar a tus padres
6. comer el desayuno *(breakfast)*
7. leer el libro para la clase de ¿…?
8. tomar el café hoy
9. ver a tus amigos
10. lavar la ropa

Sonrisas

 Standards 1.2, 5.2: In **Sonrisas** cartoons, students interpret written language and examine language through humor, irony, and common sense. This technique guides students toward personal enjoyment and life-long uses of the language.

Eduardo le acaba de comprar una computadora nueva a su novia. Quiere empezar una correspondencia romántica con ella por correo electrónico.

El próximo día, a las 7:10 de la mañana

¿Conectaste la computadora?

Sí, la conecté.

... y a las 7:30 ...

¿Conectaste todos los cables?

Sí, los conecté.

... y a las 7:45 ...

¿Conectaste el ratón?

Sí, lo conecté.

... y a las 8:00 ...

¿Conectaste el fax externo y el micrófono?

Sí, los conecté.

... y a las 8:05 ...

¿Instalaste el programa anti-virus?

Sí, lo instalé.

... y a las 8:10 ...

¿Escogiste un proveedor de acceso?

Sí, lo escogí.

... y a las 8:15 ...

¿Tienes tu dirección electrónica?

Sí, la tengo, pero, ¡NO TE LA VOY A DAR A TI!

Expresión En grupos de tres o cuatro estudiantes, hagan una lista de las reglas *(rules)* de cortesía para el teléfono y el correo electrónico. ¿Qué se debe y no se debe hacer?

Learning objectives: Analyzing, Evaluating

MODELO Cuando llamas por teléfono…
No debes llamar muy temprano por la mañana.
Cuando escribes correo electrónico…
Debes escribir mensajes cortos.

Optional: Discuss with the class their own technological preferences and abilities: ¿Prefieres resolver tus propios problemas en tu computadora o prefieres la ayuda de un amigo? ¿Es fácil para ti instalar programas en tu computadora? ¿A quién(es) das tu dirección electrónica? ¿Tienes amigos que pasan demasiado tiempo en Internet?

Gramática útil 4

Telling friends what to do: **Tú** command forms

Photos (left to right): Rihardz/Dreamstime; Sampete/Dreamstime; text: © Cengage Learning 2013

¡No lo intentes en casa!

Haz los saltos y trucos más chéveres – habla con nuestros bicilocos profesionales para elegir la mejor bicicleta BMX para ti.

Calle Eloy Alfaro 27
Casco Antiguo
Ciudad de Panamá
507-516-9997
www.ciclocura.com

CICLOLOCURA

> What are the three **tú** command forms used in this ad for a bike shop in Panamá? Which one is a negative form?
>
> **Answers: intentes** (negative), **Haz, habla**

Suggestion: When presenting command forms, include TPR-like orders to get students moving. **Ve a la pizarra, Levanta la mano,** etc. Or play command-based games like **Simón dice** to get students listening for command forms and responding physically to them. After they have listened to commands, students can author their own commands and "order around" class members in small groups or pairs.

Suggestion: Ask students when they might want to use the informal expressions below. Have them give examples of relevant contexts. Example: You don't want to anger the student in the next dorm room: **¿Te importa bajar el volumen de la música? Tengo examen mañana.**

Cómo usarlo

1. You have already learned the polite and plural (**usted** and **ustedes**) command forms in **Chapter 6**. Now you will learn the informal command form that you use with people you address as **tú**. (You see these forms in activity direction lines.)

   Habla con Claudia. *Talk* to Claudia.
   Pero **no hables** con Leo. *But **don't talk** to Leo.*

2. Remember that when you are addressing more than one person informally you use **ustedes** forms, just as you do when you address more than one person formally. In much of the Spanish-speaking world there is no "plural" **tú** command.

3. Because you mostly use informal command forms to address friends, small children, or animals, you don't need to worry about making your requests sound as polite as in formal settings. However, it never hurts to use a softening expression like the ones that follow.

   ¿Me puedes decir / Me dices…? *Can you tell me . . .?*
   ¿Puedes + *infinitive*…? *Can you + infinitive . . . ?*
   ¿Quieres / Quisieras + *infinitive*…? *Would you like to + infinitive . . . ?*
   ¿Te importa…? *Would / Does it matter to you . . . ?*
   ¿Te molesta…? *Would / Does it bother you . . . ?*

> The **vosotros** command forms, which are the plural informal command forms used in Spain, are not provided in this textbook because **ustedes** forms are used more universally.

Optional: For oral practice, have students imagine that they are preparing for a big Spanish test. Have students come up with advice for each other creating affirmative and negative commands.

Cómo formarlo

1. Unlike the **usted** and **ustedes** forms that you learned in **Chapter 6**, **tú** commands have one form for affirmative commands and one form for negative commands.

2. To form the affirmative **tú** command form, simply use the **usted / él / ella** present-indicative form of the verb.

Affirmative **tú** command forms		
-ar verb	**-er** verb	**-ir** verb
tomar → **toma**	beber → **bebe**	escribir → **escribe**

Notice that the negative **tú** commands are the same as the **usted** command forms, but with an **s** added. **Usted** command: **hable**; negative **tú** command: **no hables**.

3. To form the negative **tú** command form, take the affirmative **tú** command, and replace the final vowel with **es** for **-ar** verbs and with **as** for **-er / -ir** verbs.

Negative **tú** command forms			
	-ar verb **hablar**	**-er** verb **beber**	**-ir** verb **escribir**
affirmative **tú** command	habla	bebe	escribe
negative **tú** command	no **hables**	no **bebas**	no **escribas**

4. These **tú** command forms are irregular and must be memorized.

Notice that the **tú** command for **ser (sé)** is the same as the first person of **saber (sé)**. Context will clarify which is meant: **¡Sé bueno!** vs. **Sé que Manuel es bueno.** The same is true for the command forms of **ir (ve)** and **ver (ve): Ve a clase.** vs. **Ve ese programa.**

	Affirmative **tú** command	Negative **tú**
decir	di	no digas
hacer	haz	no hagas
ir	ve	no vayas
poner	pon	no pongas
salir	sal	no salgas
ser	sé	no seas
tener	ten	no tengas
venir	ven	no vengas

Heritage Learners: Heritage learners will likely know how to use these forms in spontaneous language because they are commonly used at home with children. However, they may not know how to write them correctly. To take advantage of heritage learners' strengths and respond to their needs, pair them with an L2 learner. Ask the L2 learner to produce aural commands and have the heritage learner write them down. This acitivity will help each type of learner develop what they need most. For L2 learners, this is fluidity in spontaneous use of language, and for heritage learners, it is writing skills.

5. As with **usted** command forms, *reflexive pronouns* and *direct object pronouns* attach to affirmative **tú** commands and come before negative **tú** commands. Note that you need to add an accent to the next-to-last syllable of the command form when attaching pronouns.

¡Despiértate, ya es tarde!	*Wake up*, *it's late!*
¡No te acuestes ahora!	*Don't go to bed now!*
Llámame.	*Call me.*
No me llames después de las once.	*Don't call me after 11:00.*

M **15** **El campamento** Tu hermanito va a ir a un campamento de verano. Tú le das algunos consejos. Los primeros cuatro consejos se los das en el afirmativo. Los segundos cuatro consejos se los das en el negativo.

Learning objective: Applying

MODELOS (Acostarse) *Acuéstate* temprano.
No (nadar) *nades* solo.

Afirmativo

1. (Usar) tu casco *(helmet)*.   Usa
2. (Jugar) con los otros niños.   Juega
3. (Ducharse) después de nadar.   Dúchate
4. (Tener) cuidado al nadar.   Ten

Negativo

5. No (correr) en la calle.   corras
6. No (caminar) por la noche.   camines
7. No (hacer) deportes peligrosos.   hagas
8. No (salir) solo por la noche.   salgas

M **16** **¡Primo!** Vas a quedarte en la casa de tu primo. Le haces preguntas sobre la casa y tus quehaceres. Escribe sus respuestas según el modelo.

Answers, Act. 16: **Afirmativo:** 1. Sí, ciérrala, por favor. 2. Sí, ábrelas, por favor. 3. Sí, ponlos en el refrigerador, por favor. 4. Sí, contéstalo, por favor. 5. Sí, apágala, por favor. 6. Sí, sácala, por favor. **Negativo:** 1. No, no la cierres. 2. No, no las abras. 3. No, no los pongas en el refrigerador. 4. No, no lo contestes. 5. No, no la apagues. 6. No, no la saques.

MODELO ¿Apago las luces antes de acostarme?
Sí, apágalas, por favor.

1. ¿Cierro la puerta del garaje por la noche?
2. ¿Abro las ventanas si hace calor?
3. ¿Pongo los comestibles en el refrigerador?
4. ¿Contesto el teléfono cuando no estás en casa?
5. ¿Apago la computadora antes de acostarme?
6. ¿Saco la basura los lunes por la noche?

Ahora, contesta las preguntas de arriba con un mandato informal negativo.

C **17** **Los consejos** Da un consejo (afirmativo o negativo) para cada situación.

Learning objectives: Applying, Analyzing

MODELO Juan quiere desarrollar sus músculos.
Levanta pesas dos veces por semana.

1. María desea perder cinco kilos.
2. Pedro quiere entrenarse para un maratón.
3. Pablo quiere mejorar su capacidad aeróbica.
4. Margarita quiere correr más rápido.
5. Francisco quiere ponerse en forma pero no tiene mucho tiempo para hacer ejercicio.

Check: Quiz students by reading the following commands. Have them identify **usted** or **tú** (formal o familiar): 1. **Levanta la mano (tú).** 2. **No levantes la mano (tú).** 3. **Levante la mano (usted).** 4. **Lave la ropa (usted).** 5. **Explique el problema (usted).** 6. **No expliques el problema (tú).** 7. **Tenlo en mente (tú).** 8. **Págame (tú).** 9. **No me des (tú).** 10. **Habla (tú).**

C **18** **En la residencia** Trabajen en grupos de tres o cuatro personas. Imagínense que un(a) estudiante nuevo(a) acaba de llegar a su residencia estudiantil. Denle consejos para no tener problemas con sus compañeros. Sigan el modelo.

MODELO *No toques música después de las once de la noche.*

¡Explora y exprésate!

Panamá

Standards 2.1, 2.2, 3.1: Throughout *Cuadros*, the **¡Explora y exprésate!** sections explore Spanish-speaking cultures and reinforce and further knowledge of other disciplines—in this case geography, history, ethnicity, and cultural products.

Check: At this point in the chapter, ask students again what they want to know about Panama and Costa Rica. At the end of the chapter, review the student-generated list to see how much has been addressed. You may want to guide students toward other courses on your campus that focus on issues in Latin America in particular.

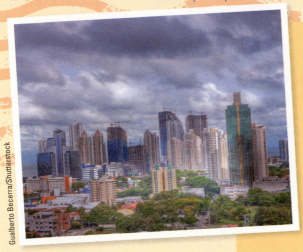

Gualberto Becerra/Shutterstock

Información general

Nombre oficial: República de Panamá

Población: 3.410.676

Capital: Ciudad de Panamá (f. 1519) (900.000 hab.)

Otras ciudades importantes: San Miguelito (300.000 hab.), David (128.000 hab.)

Moneda: balboa

Idiomas: español (oficial), inglés

Mapa de Panamá: Apéndice D

Vale saber…

Jim Lipschutz/Shutterstock

- Vasco Núñez de Balboa y Cristóbal Colón exploraron el país en 1501 y 1502. Buscando el oro y las riquezas de una civilización indígena legendaria, Balboa "descubrió" el océano Pacífico en 1513.

- Las colonias españolas sufrieron ataques de piratas ingleses y holandeses durante el siglo XVII. En 1671 el pirata inglés Henry Morgan destruyó la Ciudad de Panamá y confiscó sus tesoros *(treasures)*.

- Después de ganar la independencia de España en 1821, Panamá pasó por mucha turbulencia política. En 1904, Estados Unidos empezó la construcción del canal de Panamá. En 1999, EEUU cedió el canal al gobierno panameño.

- Tal vez los kunas son la tribu más famosa de Panamá, conocidos por la fabricación *(creation)* de sus molas tradicionales de colores vivos que se venden internacionalmente.

Suggestion: Have students calculate and guess the date of the opening of the Panama Canal in Spanish. The Panama Canal opened in 1914.

Culture: From the 1970s to 1999, the Panama Canal was jointly administered by the U.S. and Panama. Since 1999, Panama has assumed full authority of the Panama Canal.

Costa Rica

Información general

Nombre oficial: República de Costa Rica

Población: 4.516.220

Capital: San José (f. 1521) (1.500.000 hab.)

Otras ciudades importantes: Alajuela (700.000 hab.), Cártago (450.000 hab.)

Moneda: colón

Idiomas: español (oficial), inglés

Mapa de Costa Rica: Apéndice D

Roberto A Sanchez/iStockphoto

Vale saber…

- Cristóbal Colón fue el primer europeo en llegar a esta área en 1502. Esperando encontrar riquezas naturales y otros metales preciosos, observó los adornos de oro de los indígenas y nombró el país Costa Rica.

- Costa Rica ganó la independencia de España en 1821, y después de unos conflictos políticos, llegó a ser una democracia en 1889.

- La gran mayoría de la población es criolla— mestizos de ascendencia española e indígena. Los grupos indígenas componen menos del 1 por ciento de la población y se distinguen en tres etnias indígenas: chorotega, huetar y brunca.

- Costa Rica es famosa por no tener ejército *(army)*, por el café que se vende a nivel mundial *(worldwide)* y por su diversidad biológica.

McPHOTO/age fotostock

 Standards 2.1/Optional: Have students investigate why many Latin Americans refer to Costa Rica as the Switzerland of Central America. (Hint: There are a variety of answers: Costa Rica has no standing army, high mountains, immigrants of northern European descent, etc.)

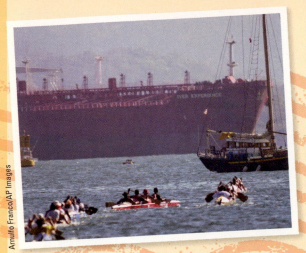

Arnulfo Franco/AP Images

Regata de cayucos *(canoes)* de Océano a Océano

¡En Panamá, puedes remar del océano Atlántico al océano Pacífico a través del canal de Panamá en cayuco! En 1954, un líder de los Boy Scouts que trabajaba para la Compañía del canal de Panamá quiso introducir un grupo de niños exploradores a las tradiciones y cultura de los indígenas panameños que vivían a las orillas *(lived on the shores)* del río Chagres. El principal medio de transporte de los indígenas era el cayuco, una canoa hecha de un tronco de árbol *(tree)* nacional. Pronto, las competencias de cayuco entre los niños exploradores resultan en una regata oficial, la Regata de cayucos de Océano a Océano, tradición que dura 54 años sin interrupción.

Hoy día la regata es organizada por el Club de Remos de Balboa (CREBA). Hay dos categorías: la categoría juvenil (14–21 años) y la categoría abierta (mayores de 22 años) y tres subcategorías: masculina, femenina y mixta. Cada equipo de cuatro deportistas tiene que remar 50 millas en tres días. Maniobrar *(Maneuvering)* un cayuco es un deporte extremo que requiere de los atletas una perseverancia y una exigente *(demanding)* preparación física. ¡Rema de océano a océano! Sólo en Panamá.

El ecoturismo en Costa Rica

DreamPictures/Getty Images

Costa Rica tiene la reputación de practicar una conservación inteligente que atrae *(attracts)* a turistas de todo el mundo. El gobierno ha convertido *(has converted)* los parques nacionales, los bosques y las reservas indígenas en zonas protegidas que cubren 30% del país. El ecoturista puede disfrutar de *(enjoy)* la naturaleza con un impacto mínimo.

En los bosques tropicales puedes observar 850 especies de aves *(birds)*, monos *(monkeys)*, armadillos, jaguares, tapires y diversas especies de mariposas *(butterflies)*. También puedes acampar, hacer alpinismo, montar en bicicleta de montaña o montar a caballo en los parques nacionales como el Poás, el Arenal y el Irazú. Si eres deportista, en las playas y ríos puedes practicar todos los deportes acuáticos: el surfing, la navegación en rápidos, la natación, la pesca, el paseo en bote o en kayak.

Anímate. Transfórmate en ecoturista en Costa Rica, el paraíso del ecoturismo.

Learning objectives: Understanding, Remembering

La información general

1. ¿Quién descubre el océano Pacífico en 1513? Vasco Núñez de Balboa
2. ¿Quién destruye la Ciudad de Panamá? el pirata inglés Henry Morgan
3. ¿En qué año empieza la construcción del canal de Panamá? ¿Cuándo se hace parte del gobierno panameño? 1904; 1999
4. ¿Quién es el primer europeo en llegar a Costa Rica? ¿En qué año? Cristóbal Colón; 1502
5. ¿De qué país gana Costa Rica la independencia? ¿Cuándo llega a ser democracia? España; 1889
6. ¿Por qué se conoce Costa Rica? por no tener ejército, por el café y por su diversidad biológica

El tema de los deportes

1. ¿Qué es el cayuco?
2. ¿Qué tienen que hacer los deportistas en la Regata de cayucos de Océano a Océano?
3. ¿Por qué tiene Costa Rica la reputación de practicar una conservación inteligente que atrae a turistas de todo el mundo?
4. ¿Por qué Costa Rica se puede considerar el paraíso del ecoturismo?

Answers: 1. Es el medio de transporte de los indígenas panameños, una canoa hecha de un tronco de árbol nacional. 2. remar 50 millas en tres días. 3. la conservación de la naturaleza y los valores culturales de los destinos. 4. Porque el gobierno ha convertido los parques nacionales, los bosques y las reservas indígenas en zonas protegidas que cubren 30% del país.

🌐 ¿QUIERES SABER MÁS?

Revisa y rellena la tabla que empezaste al principio del capítulo. Luego, escoge un tema para investigar en línea y prepárate para compartir la información con la clase.

También puedes escoger de las palabras clave a continuación o en **www.cengagebrain.com.**

Palabras clave: (Panamá) Balboa, los kunas, la construcción del canal de Panamá, la dictadura de Manuel Noriega, Rubén Blades; **(Costa Rica)** las plantaciones de café, Juan Mora Fernández, los ticos, por qué Costa Rica decidió abolir las fuerzas armadas, Óscar Arias.

Learning objectives: Analyzing, Evaluating

Standard 5.1: Here students are encouraged to do independent web research on topics that will gradually require more Spanish to carry out the assignments by introducing more participation with Spanish-speaking communities online.

Check: Point out to students that this activity is their opportunity to individualize their inquiries related to Panama and Costa Rica. Review the list of what students stated they wanted to know from the beginning of this section.

🌐 **Tú en el mundo hispano** Para explorar oportunidades de usar el español para estudiar o hacer trabajos voluntarios o aprendizajes en Costa Rica y Panamá, sigue los enlaces en **www.cengagebrain.com**.

🎵 **Ritmos del mundo hispano** Sigue los enlaces en **www.cengagebrain.com** para escuchar música de Costa Rica y Panamá.

A leer

>> ## Antes de leer

ESTRATEGIA

Scanning for detail

In this chapter, you will focus on *scanning*, a complementary skill to *skimming*, which you learned in **Chapter 5**. While skimming is getting the main idea, scanning is looking for specific information. To scan, run your eye over a text while looking for key words about specific pieces of information.

1 Mira el artículo y la foto sobre la navegación en rápidos en Costa Rica y ojea *(scan)* el artículo rápidamente para encontrar la siguiente información.

1. cuántos ríos costarricenses se mencionan   cinco ríos (Reventazón, Pacuare, Sarapiquí, Naranjo, Corobicí)
2. los niveles *(levels)* de dificultad que se usan para describir los rápidos de los ríos   Categorías Clase I a Clase VI

2 Las siguientes palabras aparecen *(appear)* en el artículo. Aunque estas palabras no son cognados, tienen una relación semántica con sus equivalentes en inglés. A ver si puedes identificar el equivalente en inglés de cada palabra a la izquierda.

1. __c__ media docena   a. *co-owner*
2. __d__ principiantes   b. *peaceful*
3. __a__ codueño   c. *half dozen*
4. __f__ haber pasado   d. *beginners*
5. __g__ poblado   e. *stretches*
6. __e__ trechos   f. *to have passed (navigated)*
7. __b__ apacible   g. *town, village*

Suggestion: Warm up for reading with questions like ¿Te gusta navegar en rápidos? Describe tus experiencias.

3 Ahora, lee el artículo rápidamente para buscar la idea principal. Luego mira la **Actividad 4** en la página 262 para ver qué información necesitas para completarla. Vuelve al artículo y busca esa información. No es necesario entender todas las palabras para hacer las **Actividades 4** y **5**.

Excerpt from "Costa Rica: Adventures in White Water Rafting", by David Dudenhoefer, in *Destinos/Miami Aboard*, In-Flight magazine, Taca airlines, January/February 1998, pp. 52-60. © HCP/Aboard Publishing, Miami Herald Media Company, 2011. Used with permission.

LECTURA

Costa Rica

Aventuras en los rápidos

Pocos países pueden contar con tan excelentes condiciones para la navegación en rápidos como Costa Rica, donde los retos de este conocido deporte se complementan con la belleza y diversidad de los bosques tropicales.

Quizás[1] las aguas más bravas del país sean aptas sólo para expertos remeros—media docena de equipos olímpicos de kayaks utilizan a Costa Rica como base de entrenamiento—, pero la mayoría de sus ríos rápidos ofrecen condiciones perfectas también para principiantes.

Los navegantes de balsas y kayaks poseen un sistema para evaluar el grado de dificultad de los rápidos y ríos individuales, en una escala que va de la Clase I a la Clase VI —donde el 0 es similar a una piscina y el VII, a las Cataratas del Niágara. Los rápidos de Clase II y III son, por lo general, suficientes para acelerar el ritmo cardíaco. Los de Clase IV pueden ser un poco más peligrosos, mientras que los de Clase V están ya cerca de lo imposible. Los ríos de Clase II y III son magníficos para principiantes. No obstante, resulta recomendable haber pasado, al menos, por un río antes de intentar lanzarse[2] en los de Clase II–IV. Los de Clase IV–V requieren una buena condición física y más experiencia con las balsas.

Las rutas de navegación

El río **Reventazón** posee numerosos tramos[3] navegables. El más popular es la sección Tucurrique (Clase III), que ofrece una excursión segura y emocionante, lo suficientemente fácil para un viaje de primera vez. La sección Peralta (Clase V) es la ruta más difícil de Costa Rica para este tipo de navegación, con rápidos indetenibles y bastante peligro, razón por la cual sólo está abierta para expertos.

Michael DeYoung/age fotostock

El río **Pacuare** (Clase III–IV) es una de las maravillas naturales más impresionantes de Costa Rica. Es un río emocionante de navegar, con numerosos y provocadores rápidos de Clase IV. El Pacuare se navega mejor en un viaje de dos o tres días, lo cual permite un contacto más cercano con el bosque[4] tropical—un área excelente para la observación de pájaros[5].

El **Sarapiquí** (Clase III) es un río hermoso que fluye por el norte de la Cordillera Montañosa Central. La sección de rápidos entre La Virgen y Chilamae proporciona una aventura de navegación en balsa de Clase III, que pasa a través de muchos bosques tropicales y cataratas. La parte más baja del Sarapiquí es un flotador suave que resulta perfecto para niños pequeños.

El **Naranjo** (Clase III–IV) es un río emocionante y provocador que exige[6] cierta experiencia de navegación en balsa. Puede navegarse sólo en meses lluviosos. Queda[7] a un día desde Manuel Antonio y Quepos.

El **Corobicí** (Clase I–II) es un río completamente apacible. Es excelente para los amantes[8] de la naturaleza y puede ser navegado por personas de cualquier edad. En el bosque que viste sus orillas[9] se pueden ver iguanas, monos[10] y una rica variedad de pájaros.

[1]*Perhaps* [2]**intentar…:** *to try to throw oneself* [3]*sections* [4]*forest* [5]*birds* [6]*demands* [7]*It is located* [8]*lovers* [9]*shores* [10]*monkeys*

Después de leer
Learning objectives: Remembering, Understanding

4 Completa la siguiente tabla con información del artículo. Si te es necesario, vuelve al artículo para buscarla.

Río	Clase	Una cosa interesante
Reventazón	III–V	
	I–II	
		Una parte es perfecta para los niños pequeños.
Naranjo		
		Se navega mejor en un viaje de dos o tres días.

Learning objectives: Applying, Analyzing

5 Trabajen en grupos de tres o cuatro estudiantes para hablar de los cinco ríos que se describen en el artículo. ¿Cuál les interesa más? Escojan *(Choose)* un lugar del artículo para ir de vacaciones con el grupo. Para ayudarles con la decisión, contesten las siguientes preguntas.

1. ¿Cuánta experiencia con la navegación en rápidos tienen las distintas personas del grupo?
2. ¿Van a viajar durante la temporada de lluvia (verano) o durante el invierno?
3. ¿A qué distancia de San José están dispuestos *(willing)* a viajar?
4. ¿Cuánto tiempo quieren pasar en el río?
5. ¿Qué les interesa más, la belleza natural o la aventura de los rápidos?

MODELOS *A mí me gusta…*
Yo prefiero… porque…
Vamos a viajar en…

El río Corobicí

El río Reventazón

>> Antes de escribir

 Standard 1.3: In the writing sections, students present information to readers, who may often consist of their classmates.

ESTRATEGIA

Writing—Freewriting

Once you are ready to write, freewriting is a useful composition strategy. When you freewrite, you don't worry about spelling, punctuation, grammar, or other errors. Instead, you write rapidly, letting the ideas and words flow as quickly as you can. Once you finish, you go back and revise what you've written.

Preparation: You may want to introduce the phrase **escribir sin detenerse** to your students to refer to freewriting in class.

1 Trabaja con un(a) compañero(a) de clase. Van a escribir un artículo de tres párrafos para el periódico universitario en el que describan un pasatiempo interesante que se puede hacer en su pueblo o ciudad. Para empezar, hagan una lista de actividades posibles.

2 Cuando tengan la lista, escojan *(choose)* el pasatiempo que les guste más. Juntos, escojan tres aspectos específicos para desarrollar *(to develop)* en los tres párrafos del artículo. Escriban una oración temática para cada uno. (Usen el artículo de la página 261 como modelo.)

Párrafo 1:
Párrafo 2:
Párrafo 3:

>> Composición

Learning objective: Creating

3 Usando las oraciones temáticas de la **Actividad 2,** escribe los tres párrafos que forman el primer borrador *(draft)* del artículo. Escribe sin detenerte *(freewrite)* y no te preocupes por los errores, la organización, la ortografía ni la gramática.

>> Después de escribir

4 Trabaja con tu compañero(a) otra vez. Intercambien sus borradores y usen las dos versiones para crear un solo artículo.

5 Ahora, miren la nueva versión y revísenla, usando la siguiente lista.

- ¿Tiene el artículo toda la información necesaria?
- ¿Es interesante e informativo también?
- ¿Usaron pronombres de complemento directo para eliminar la repetición?
- ¿Usaron bien el pretérito y otros tiempos gramaticales?
- ¿Hay errores de puntuación o de ortografía?

Vocabulario

Los deportes *Sports*

el básquetbol *basketball*
el béisbol *baseball*
el boxeo *boxing*
el ciclismo *cycling*
el esquí acuático *water skiing*
el esquí alpino *downhill skiing*
el fútbol *soccer*
el fútbol americano *football*
el golf *golf*
el hockey sobre hielo *ice hockey*
el hockey sobre hierba *field hockey*
la navegación en rápidos *whitewater rafting*
la natación *swimming*
el tenis *tennis*
el volibol *volleyball*

Actividades deportivas *Sport activities*

entrenarse *to train*
esquiar *to ski*
hacer ejercicio *to exercise*
jugar (ue) (al) (tenis, béisbol, etc.) *to play (tennis, baseball, etc.)*
levantar pesas *to lift weights*
montar a caballo *to ride horseback*
montar en bicicleta *to ride a bike*
nadar *to swim*
navegar en rápidos *to go whitewater rafting*
patinar en línea *to inline skate (rollerblade)*
patinar sobre hielo *to ice skate*
pescar *to fish*
practicar / hacer alpinismo *to (mountain) climb, hike*
practicar / hacer surfing *to surf*
remar *to row*

Más palabras sobre los deportes *More sports words*

la competencia *competition*
el equipo *team*
ganar *to win*
el lago *lake*
el partido *game, match*
el peligro *danger*
peligroso(a) *dangerous*
la pelota *ball*
la piscina *pool*
el río *river*
seguro(a) *safe*
la tabla de snowboard *snowboard*

Las estaciones *Seasons*

el invierno *winter*
la primavera *spring*
el verano *summer*
el otoño *fall, autumn*

Expresiones con *tener*

tener calor *to be hot*
tener cuidado *to be careful*
tener frío *to be cold*
tener ganas de *to feel like (doing)*
tener hambre *to be hungry*
tener miedo (a, de) *to be afraid (of)*
tener prisa *to be in a hurry*
tener razón *to be right*
tener sed *to be thirsty*
tener sueño *to be sleepy*
tener vergüenza *to be embarrassed, ashamed*

El tiempo *Weather*

¿Qué tiempo hace? *What's the weather like?*
Hace buen / mal tiempo. *It's nice / bad weather.*
Hace calor. *It's hot.*
Hace fresco. *It's cool.*
Hace frío. *It's cold.*
Hace sol. *It's sunny.*
Hace viento. *It's windy.*
Está lloviendo. (Llueve.) *It's raining.*
Está nevando. (Nieva.) *It's snowing.*
Está nublado. *It's cloudy.*

La temperatura *Temperature*

grados Celsio(s) *degrees Celsius*
grados Fahrenheit *degrees Fahrenheit*
La temperatura está a 20 grados Celsio(s). *It's 20 degrees Celsius*
La temperatura está a 68 grados Fahrenheit. *It's 68 degrees Fahrenheit.*

Palabras relativas al tiempo

anoche *last night*
anteayer *the day before yesterday*
el año pasado *last year*
el mes pasado *last month*
la semana pasada *last week*

Preparation: Have students review this material and complete the activities here, in the SAM, and online before they begin **Chapter 8**.

Complete these activities to check your understanding of the new grammar points in **Chapter 7** before you move on to **Chapter 8**.

The answers to the activities in this section can be found in **Appendix B**.

Preterite tense of regular verbs (p. 242)

1 Completa las oraciones con las formas correctas de los verbos en el pretérito para decir qué hizo cada persona durantes sus vacaciones.

1. Tú _montaste_ (montar) a caballo en las montañas.
2. Marilena _leyó_ (leer) cinco novelas de ciencia ficción.
3. Yo _compartí_ (compartir) una cabaña en la playa con unos amigos.
4. Nosotros _navegamos_ (navegar) en rápidos en Costa Rica.
5. Linda y Carmela _corrieron_ (correr) en una maratón.

Preterite tense of some common irregular verbs (p. 245)

2 Escribe oraciones completas con las palabras indicadas para decir qué hicieron estas personas ayer.

1. tú y yo / ir al partido de hockey sobre el hielo   Tú y yo fuimos…
2. Marilena / estar en el hospital todo el día con una amiga enferma   Marilena estuvo…
3. yo / hacer un poco de ejercicio por la mañana   Yo hice…
4. Guille y Paulina / decir que van a casarse   Guille y Paulina dijeron…
5. mis padres / conducir a la universidad para visitarme   Mis padres condujeron…
6. tú / traducir tres poemas españoles al inglés   Tú tradujiste…

Direct object pronouns (p. 248)

Check: The **Repaso** section reviews grammar and vocabulary for the student, and it offers a built-in performance assessment. By doing review activities with students, you can assess concepts that you may need to continue to reinforce in future classes.

Answers, Act. 3: 1. ¿Los perros? Tú los lavaste. 2. ¿El surfing? Victoria lo hizo. 3. ¿La pelota (de golf)? Yo no la encontré. 4. ¿Las mochilas? Nosotros las perdimos. 5. ¿Los refrescos? Ustedes no los bebieron. 6. ¿Las pesas? Esteban y Federico no las levantaron.

3 Mira las ilustraciones y usa las palabras para decir qué hizo cada persona.

MODELOS Raúl / comprar (sí)
¿La computadora? Raúl la compró.
Marina / leer (no)
¿Los libros? Marina no los leyó.

1. tú / lavar (sí)

2. Victoria / hacer (sí)

3. yo / encontrar (no)

4. nosotros / perder (sí)

5. ustedes / beber (no)

6. Esteban y Federico / levantar (no)

Tú command forms (p. 253)

4 Completa los letreros *(signs)* con mandatos de **tú**.

POR FAVOR, NO ___pongas___ (PONER)
BEBIDAS CERCA DE LAS COMPUTA-
DORAS. ___Ten___ (TENER) MUCHO
CUIDADO Y ___lee___ (LEER) TODAS
LAS INSTRUCCIONES ANTES DE
EMPEZAR.

1

___Pon___ (PONER) TU NOMBRE EN
LA LISTA Y ___siéntate___ (SENTARSE)
POR FAVOR. NO ___salgas___ (SALIR)
SIN HABLAR CON UNO DE LOS
ASISTENTES.

2

© Cengage Learning 2013

Preparación para el Capítulo 8

Stem-changing verbs in the present indicative (Chapter 4)

5 Completa las oraciones con las formas correctas de los verbos indicados.

1. Mis amigos ___quieren___ (querer) esquiar.
2. Yo ___me divierto___ (divertirse) en la piscina.
3. Ellos ___se visten___ (vestirse) para entrenarse.
4. Ustedes no ___pueden___ (poder) pescar hoy.
5. Cuando llueve, yo ___duermo___ (dormir) mucho.
6. Tú ___pides___ (pedir) tiempo para descansar.

> Complete these activities to review some previously learned grammatical structures that will be helpful when you learn the new grammar in **Chapter 8**.
>
> Be sure to reread **Chapter 7: Gramática útil 2** and **3** before moving on to the **Chapter 8** grammar sections.
>
> **Learning objective:** Evaluating

Gustar with infinitives (Chapter 2) and with nouns (Chapter 4)

6 Haz oraciones completas para decir qué les gusta a las personas indicadas.

1. a mí / remar
2. a usted / nadar
3. a ti / esos esquíes
4. a ellos / el boxeo
5. a nosotros / pescar
6. a ella / la nieve
7. a ti / entrenarse
8. a mi / las vacaciones
9. a nosotros / la primavera

> **Answers, Act. 6:** 1. A mí me gusta remar. 2. A usted le gusta nadar. 3. A ti te gustan esos esquíes. 4. A ellos les gusta el boxeo. 5. A nosotros nos gusta pescar. 6. A ella le gusta la nieve. 7. A ti te gusta entrenarte. 8. A mí me gustan las vacaciones. 9. A nosotros nos gusta la primavera.

Conocer and saber (Chapter 5), poder and querer (Chapter 4)

7 Completa los comentarios de Lidia con las formas correctas de los verbos indicados.

Yo 1. ___sé___ (saber) hacer muchos deportes diferentes y 2. ___conozco___ (conocer) a muchas personas que 3. ___saben___ (saber) hacerlos también. Cuando nieva, nosotros 4. ___podemos___ (poder) esquiar. Cuando llueve, mis amigos 5. ___pueden___ (poder) venir a mi casa y hacemos ejercicios. Y cuando hace sol, ¡nosotros 6. ___conocemos___ (conocer) las mejores playas para el surfing! Yo 7. ___quiero___ (querer) aprender hacerlo y cuando 8. ___puedo___ (poder), voy con ellos porque necesito la práctica.

¿Cómo defines tu estilo?

ESTILO PERSONAL

Para algunas personas, la ropa es una forma importante de presentarse al mundo e identificarse con los demás. Para otras, solamente sirve para usos prácticos.

¿Tienen mucha importancia para ti la ropa y el estilo personal? ¿Crees que la ropa es una forma de expresión o es solamente para protegerse de los elementos?

Communication

By the end of this chapter you will be able to

- talk about clothing and fashion
- shop for various articles of clothing
- discuss prices
- describe recent purchases and shopping trips
- talk about buying items and doing favors for friends
- make comparisons

AFP/Getty Images

Un viaje por Ecuador y Perú

Ecuador y Perú comparten una frontera y tienen costas en el océano Pacífico. La cordillera *(mountain range)* de los Andes pasa por los dos países.

Learning objectives: See pages AIE-3–AIE-4 for a complete description of the Bloom's Taxonomy learning objectives and an explanation of how they are integrated within *Cuadros*.

País / Área	Tamaño y fronteras	Sitios de interés
Ecuador 276.840 km^2	un poco más pequeño que Nevada; fronteras con Colombia y Perú	las islas Galápagos, la selva *(jungle)* amazónica, el volcán Cotopaxi, los baños termales
Perú 1.280.000 km^2	un poco más pequeño que Alaska; fronteras con Bolivia, Brasil, Colombia, Chile y Ecuador	Machu Picchu, las ruinas de Chan-Chan y el Señor de Sipán en la costa pacífica, el lago Titicaca, la selva amazónica

Check: Interview students to generate what they know about Peru and Ecuador and what they would like to find out. At the end of the chapter, repeat your questions to assess what they have learned.

¿Qué sabes? Di si las siguientes oraciones son ciertas **(C)** o falsas **(F)**.

Learning objective: Understanding

1. Ecuador y Perú son países montañosos. C
2. Perú es más de cinco veces más grande que Ecuador. F
3. No hay volcanes en estos dos países. F
4. La selva amazónica se encuentra en los dos países. C

Lo que sé y lo que quiero aprender Completa la tabla del **Apéndice A**. Escribe algunos datos que **ya sabes** sobre estos países en la columna **Lo que sé**. Después, añade algunos temas que **quieres aprender** a la columna **Lo que quiero aprender**. Guarda la tabla para usarla otra vez en la sección **¡Explora y exprésate!** en la página 297.

Cultures

By the end of this chapter you will have explored
- facts about Peru and Ecuador
- organic cotton from Peru
- a colorful fair that sells traditional clothing in Ecuador
- the ancestral tradition of weaving in the Andes
- attitudes towards jeans around the world

¡Imagínate!

Vocabulario útil 1

Learning objectives: Applying, Analyzing

>>

DEPENDIENTE: ¿En qué puedo servirle, señor?

JAVIER: Pues, estoy buscando un regalo para mi madre pero no sé, no veo nada.

DEPENDIENTE: Pues, si le gusta la **ropa** fina, esta **blusa de seda** es muy bonita y además está rebajada.

JAVIER: No, no le gusta ese color.

DEPENDIENTE: ¿Quizás este **suéter**?

JAVIER: No. Tampoco necesita suéter.

DEPENDIENTE: Y las **joyas**, ¿a quién no le gustan las joyas?… ¿Quizás estos **aretes**? Son de **oro** y le dan ese toque de elegancia a cualquier **vestido.**

Suggestion: Expand discussion of the drawings on this page and the next with ¿Quiénes son las personas en los dibujos? ¿Dónde están? ¿Qué hacen? ¿Qué llevan? ¿Cuántos años tienen (más o menos)? ¿Qué tipo de ropa llevan? ¿Es ropa formal o informal? ¿Llevas este tipo de ropa? ¿Cuándo llevas sudadera / botas / impermeable, etc.?

Optional: Bring in some clothing catalogs or project merchandise from websites. Call attention to the broad selection that we have as U.S. consumers. Have students explore the origin of their own clothing by looking at the tags. Have students continue to think about where these goods come from and how consumers impact the country of origin. Teach the word **etiqueta** for *clothing label.* Do a label check to verify and personalize clothing origin.

>> **Las prendas de ropa**

Labels: el traje, la camiseta, el chaleco, la sudadera, ¡LOCURAS EN LA PLAYA!, los jeans, la falda, el traje de baño, el impermeable, los zapatos, las sandalias, los zapatos de tenis

© Cengage Learning 2013

>> **Las telas**

Suggestion: For some vocabulary words, you can ask about origin: ¿De dónde viene la seda? (Hint: Marco Polo) Answer: **China**; ¿En qué región se cultiva el algodón en EEUU? Answer: **el sureste**; ¿De dónde viene el cuero o la piel? Answer: **los animales**, etc. For other vocabulary words, have students sketch a rayas, de lunares, a cuadros with their books closed.

Está hecho(a) de... *It's made (out) of . . .*
Están hechos(as) de... *They're made (out) of . . .*

el algodón *cotton*
la lana *wool*
el lino *linen*
la mezclilla *denim*
la piel / el cuero *leather*
la seda *silk*

a cuadros *plaid*
a rayas / rayado(a) *striped*
bordado(a) *embroidered*
de lunares *polka-dotted*
de un solo color *solid, one single color*
estampado(a) *print*

>> **Los accesorios**

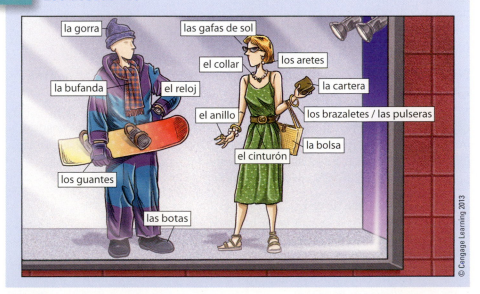

Labels: la gorra, las gafas de sol, el collar, los aretes, la bufanda, el reloj, la cartera, el anillo, los brazaletes / las pulseras, la bolsa, el cinturón, los guantes, las botas

© Cengage Learning 2013

>> **Las joyas**

la cadena... *chain . . .*   **... (de) plata** *. . . (made of) silver*
... (de) oro *. . . (made of) gold*

To say that an item is made of a certain fabric, you need to use **de**: **botas de cuero, abrigo de piel, camiseta de algodón**.

The names for articles of clothing can vary greatly from region to region. For example, *jeans* can also be called **vaqueros, tejanos, bluyines, majones,** or **pantalones de mezclilla**.

Other regional variations: In Spain a handbag is **el bolso** and in Mexico it is **la bolsa**; in some places, **la cartera** can also be a handbag, not just a wallet. Other variations are: **los aretes / los pendientes, el anillo / la sortija, la gorra / el gorro,** and **las gafas / los lentes / los anteojos**.

Heritage Learners: Ask heritage learners if there is a difference in meaning for them between **anillo** *(band)* and **sortija** *(ring with a stone on it)*; and **gorra** *(cap with visor)* and **gorro** *(hat with no visor)*.

Heritage Learners: Words for accessories and articles of clothing show a fair amount of variation throughout the Spanish-speaking world. First, ask students **¿Cómo llamas tú los siguientes objetos en español?** Have students share with the class the terms that they use for items such as earrings, purse, glasses, gym shoes, skirt, swimsuit, and jacket. Involve students in a discussion aimed at showing that, from a linguistic point of view, no word is better than another. Point out that, because of social conventions and historical circumstances, some words are more widely used and accepted than others.

ACTIVIDADES

Preparation: Personalize this type of activity and describe your clothes in detail. Bring an extra funky scarf or tie and/or have some mismatched or outlandish items to illustrate vocabulary visually and to add humor.

Standards: In **Activities 1–7**, answers are going to vary according to the students because in most cases students must provide information and express opinions (C 1.1: Interpersonal Communication). A good follow-up to these activities is to ask which groups or pairs did not agree about fashion or other clothes-related matters. See if students can explain any **desacuerdos**.

Heritage Learners: Ask heritage learners if they perceive a difference in dress codes between the U.S. and Hispanic countries. To get the discussion going, bring in photos from Hispanic magazines and U.S. magazines.

M **1** **¡Llevo…!** Describe qué ropa llevas hoy. ¡No te olvides de incluir los colores!

MODELO *Llevo unos pantalones negros, una camiseta azul y unos zapatos negros.*

M **2** **Me gustan…** Para cada prenda de ropa, indica el tipo de tela y diseño que prefieres. Sigue el modelo.

MODELO el vestido
Me gustan los vestidos de seda.
O: *Me gustan los vestidos estampados.*

1. el suéter
2. los zapatos de tenis
3. la blusa
4. los pantalones
5. el traje
6. la falda
7. la camiseta
8. la chaqueta

C **3** **¿Ropa formal o informal?** Trabaja con un(a) compañero(a) de clase. Digan qué les gusta llevar en las siguientes situaciones. Sean tan específicos como puedan.

1. para estudiar
2. para salir a bailar
3. para trabajar en el jardín
4. para visitar a la familia
5. para ir a clases
6. para ir al gimnasio

C **4** **Las estrellas** Trabajen en grupos de tres o cuatro estudiantes. Primero, hagan una lista de tres personas que son famosas por su manera de vestirse. Luego, usen la imaginación para describir qué llevan en este momento. Incluyan tantos detalles como puedan.

Personas posibles: Lady Gaga, Johnny Depp, Jennifer López, Kanye West, Katy Perry, Beyoncé, etc.

C **5** **Los accesorios** ¿Quién lleva las siguientes cosas? Para cada accesorio indicado, identifica quién(es) en la clase lo lleva(n). Si nadie lleva el accesorio indicado, di a quién le gusta llevarlo generalmente, o da el nombre de una persona famosa que lo lleva frecuentemente.

MODELOS una cadena de oro
Stacy lleva una cadena de oro hoy.
O: *Generalmente Stacy lleva una cadena de oro, pero hoy no la lleva.*
unas gafas de sol
Nadie lleva gafas de sol ahora mismo. A Javier Bardem le gusta llevar gafas de sol.

1. una cadena de oro
2. unos guantes
3. un sombrero
4. un reloj
5. un pañuelo de seda
6. un brazalete
7. un cinturón de cuero
8. aretes de plata

6 ¿Qué me pongo? Descríbele a tu compañero(a) qué ropa y accesorios

C llevas en las siguientes situaciones. Luego, él o ella hace lo mismo.

1. Es tu primera cita *(date)* con alguien que te gusta mucho.
2. Vas a una recepción para recibir un premio *(prize)*.
3. Vas al gimnasio con tu mejor amigo(a).
4. Vas a un concierto de música hip-hop con un grupo de amigos.
5. Vas a una entrevista para un trabajo de verano.
6. Vas a ir a esquiar en las montañas el fin de semana.

7 ¡Qué anticuado! Trabajen en parejas. Juntos hagan una lista de ropa y

C accesorios que están de moda en este momento y otra de los que están pasados de moda. Luego, comparen su lista con la de otra pareja. ¿Incluyeron las mismas prendas?

¡Fíjate! Los tejidos andinos

Sean Sprague/The Image Works

Hoy día puedes ir a los mercados de Perú y Ecuador y comprar prendas de ropa que han sido *(have been)* tejidas a mano usando las técnicas antiguas de los incas, reinterpretadas con nuevas expresiones y tecnologías. Los tejidos pueden verse como un texto histórico, cada sociedad étnica adaptando las técnicas y los diseños para reflejar su estilo, su estética y sus creencias religiosas y sociopolíticas.

Es lógico que vas a encontrar palabras para prendas de ropa en sitios como los Andes que no corresponden a las palabras en tu libro de texto. La gran variedad lingüística de país a país referente a las prendas de ropa se puede notar en la palabra *chompa* de Perú. La chompa es un suéter de lana o algodón de manga larga, pero en Bolivia, Chile, Ecuador y Paraguay es *chomba*, en Argentina y Uruguay es *pulóver*, en Guatemala y Centroamérica es *chumpa* y en España es *jersey*.

¿Tienes alguna prenda de ropa que refleje la cultura de tus antepasados? ¿Qué prendas de ropa varían de nombre a través de Estados Unidos? ¿en otros países de habla inglesa?

Práctica Con un(a) compañero(a), hagan una investigación en Internet sobre uno o dos de los siguientes temas. Compartan su información con la clase.

1. la historia de una prenda de ropa que refleja la cultura de tus antepasados
2. la variedad lingüística de una prenda de ropa en EEUU (escojan una)
3. los símbolos en los diseños de los tejidos andinos

Standards 4.1, 4.2: The **¡Fíjate!** cultural and linguistic notes throughout *Cuadros* encourage students to connect and compare information about cultures, cultural practices, languages, and linguistic history. Topics usually relate to the chapter theme and vocabulary, and help students understand the nature of cultural practices and language usage.

Check: The **¡Fíjate!** readings are intended for cultural comparison; however, you will need to review content and check comprehension before expanding the discussion.

Learning objectives: Applying, Analyzing

Vocabulario útil 2

© Cengage Learning 2013

> **DEPENDIENTE:** Buenas, señorita. **¿En qué puedo servirle?**
>
> **CHELA:** La verdad es que estoy buscando un regalo para el cumpleaños de mi mamá pero no tengo ni la menor idea qué comprarle.
>
> **DEPENDIENTE:** Su mamá seguro es una mujer de muy buen gusto. Tal vez esta blusa de seda…
>
> **CHELA:** Uy, no, ¡a mamá no le gusta ese color!…
>
> **DEPENDIENTE:** ¡Ya sé exactamente lo que busca!… Estos aretes de oro son preciosos y **están a muy buen precio** hoy.
>
> **CHELA:** ¡Qué bonitos! Sí, creo que sí le van a gustar a mamá. **Voy a llevármelos.**

In many countries you will hear an alternate female form for **la dependiente: la dependienta**. Both are used interchangeably.

Notice that when you use the phrases **Voy a probármelo(la / los / las)** and **Voy a llevármelo(la / los / las)**, the pronoun that you use must match the object you are referring to: **Me gusta este <u>vestido</u>. Voy a probárme<u>lo</u>. Me encantan estos <u>zapatos</u>. Voy a llevárme<u>los</u>.**

If you want to know if an item is returnable, you can say **¿Puedo devolverlo si hay un problema?**

>> Ir de compras

El (La) dependiente

¿En qué puedo servirle? *How can I help you?*
¿Cuál es su talla? *What is your size?*
Está rebajado(a). *It's reduced (on sale).*
Está en venta. *It's on sale.*
Es muy barato(a). *It's very inexpensive.*
Está a muy buen precio. *It's a very good price.*
¿Es un regalo? *Is it a gift?*

de buena (alta) calidad *of good (high) quality*
el descuento *discount*
la oferta especial *special offer*

El (La) cliente

¿Cuánto cuesta(n)? *How much does it (do they) cost?*
¿Lo (La / Los / Las) tiene en una talla…? *Do you have this in a size . . .?*
Voy a probármelo(la / las / los). *I'm going to try it / them on.*
Me queda bien / mal. *It fits nicely / badly.*
Me queda grande / apretado. *It's too big / too tight.*
Voy a llevármelo(la / las / los). *I'm going to take it / them.*
Es (demasiado) caro. *It's (too) expensive.*

>> La moda

(no) estar de moda *(not) to be fashionable*

pasado(a) de moda *out of style*

Suggestion: Name some familiar stores from luxury to discount and ask: ¿Dónde te gusta ir de compras? ¿Dónde está la ropa a buen precio? ¿Dónde se encuentra ropa clásica / de moda / cara / barata / deportiva / de alta calidad, etc. ? ¿Dónde (no) se encuentran buenos dependientes listos para servir?

ACTIVIDADES

Learning objective: Applying

M **8** **Por favor…** ¿Qué dices en las siguientes situaciones? Escribe una pregunta o una respuesta para cada situación. En muchos casos, hay más de una respuesta posible.

MODELO Ves una blusa bonita, pero no tiene precio.
¿Cuánto cuesta, por favor?

1. Te pruebas una chaqueta, pero es grande.
2. Decides comprar dos blusas.
3. Ves unos zapatos que te gustan, pero no estás seguro(a) si están rebajados.
4. Te pruebas unos zapatos y decides comprarlos.
5. Quieres probarte un vestido en otra talla y se lo pides a la dependiente.
6. Ves unos pantalones que te gustan, pero quieres otro color.
7. El suéter de vicuña es muy fino, pero no sabes si tienes suficiente dinero para comprarlo.
8. Necesitas una talla más grande.

Answers, Act. 8: *Answers may vary.* 1. Me queda mal. / Me queda grande. 2. Voy a llevármelas. 3. ¿Cuánto cuestan? / ¿Están rebajados? / ¿Están en venta? 4. Voy a llevármelos. 5. ¿Lo tiene en una talla…? 6. ¿Los tiene en otro color? 7. ¿Cuánto cuesta? / ¿Puedo pagar con tarjeta de crédito? 8. Me queda apretado. / ¿Lo tiene en una talla…? / Me queda mal.

Suggestion: Ask students whether they would most likely use informal or formal address with the following people in the contexts indicated: **en una fiesta de amigos, con el presidente de México, con un taxista, con un profesor mayor y honrado, con alguien que ganó el Premio Nóbel de la Paz, con tu mejor amigo(a) por correo electrónico, con un policía en la calle, con tu perro en casa, con un señor mayor, con unos niños de cinco años en una guardería…**

9 **Situaciones** Trabaja con un(a) compañero(a) de clase. Representen las
M siguientes situaciones. Túrnense para hacer los papeles del (de la) dependiente y del (de la) cliente.

Situación 1
Buscas un regalo para tu novio(a). Quieres algo de muy alta calidad pero a muy buen precio.

Situación 2
Tienes que ir a una fiesta formal y no sabes qué llevar. Pídele ayuda al (a la) dependiente y compra lo que necesitas.

Situación 3
Eres un(a) estudiante nuevo(a) en la universidad. Vas a un almacén popular para comprar ropa. ¿Qué debes comprar? Pídele consejos al (a la) dependiente y compra por lo menos dos prendas de ropa.

Situación 4
Tu prima acaba de tener un bebé. Quieres comprarle un regalo, pero no sabes qué comprar. Escucha las sugerencias del (de la) dependiente y luego compra el regalo.

¿Tú o usted? In some Latin American countries, formal address is used even at home, between parents and children, and husbands and wives. In other countries, it is reserved for the elderly and for differences in social class. To be safe, use the formal address until permission to use the informal is granted. Using the informal when the formal is expected can cause negative reactions.

10 **¿Qué me voy a poner?** Tú y tu compañero(a) van a una fiesta muy importante y quieren vestirse apropiadamente. Deciden ir a una tienda de ropa para comprarse algo nuevo. Mientras cada uno(a) se prueba diferentes prendas de ropa y accesorios, comenten sus selecciones. ¡Tengan una conversación auténtica!

Notice: In most cases, **bebé** is masculine. You may encounter some native speakers who say **la bebé** for a baby girl.

 Standards: Here students work on presentational and interpersonal communication. Have students present their favorite situation to the class as a follow-up (**C 1:** Communication).

Optional: Mention (or elicit) other ways of shopping: **por Internet, por catálogos.** ¿Qué método de compras prefieres?

▶ >> Vocabulario útil 3

© Cengage Learning 2013

DEPENDIENTE:	Tiene muy buen gusto, señorita. **¿Cómo desea pagar? En efectivo**, ¿verdad?
CHELA:	Sí, gracias.

Preparation: ¿Cuánto cuesta… aproximadamente? Warm up by asking the class the prices of typical items that cost less than 100 dollars (e.g., **tu bolígrafo, un periódico, un refresco,** etc.) and then present numbers over 100.

Optional: Have students research demographics of Latinos or Hispanics in the U.S. (your state, region, or county) from the most recent U.S. Census and capture these numbers for class discussion. Students can be asked to collect data on the general population as well, so that they work with a variety of large numbers.

>> Métodos de pago

¿Cómo desea pagar? *How do you wish to pay?*
Al contado. / En efectivo. *In cash.*
Con cheque. *By check.*
Con cheque de viajero. *With a traveler's check.*
Con un préstamo. *With a loan.*
Con tarjeta de crédito. *With a credit card.*
Con tarjeta de débito. *With a debit card.*

Cien is used to express the quantity of exactly *one hundred*, as well as before **mil** and **millones**. **Ciento** is used in combination with other numbers to express quantities from 101–199. Note that with numbers using **-cientos,** the number agrees with the noun it modifies: **doscientas tiendas** but **doscientos mercados**.

>> Los números mayores de 100

100 cien	1.000 mil
101 ciento uno	2.000 dos mil
102 ciento dos, etc.	3.000 tres mil
200 doscientos(as)	4.000 cuatro mil
300 trescientos(as)	5.000 cinco mil
400 cuatrocientos(as)	10.000 diez mil
500 quinientos(as)	100.000 cien mil
600 seiscientos(as)	1.000.000 un millón
700 setecientos(as)	2.000.000 dos millones, etc.
800 ochocientos(as)	
900 novecientos(as)	

M **11** **Para pagar** Por lo general, ¿cómo vas a pagar en las siguientes situaciones? Di cuánto crees que te va a costar cada compra.

MODELO   Compras un café grande.
Dos dólares y treinta centavos.

1. Compras un vestido / un traje nuevo.
2. Compras los libros para las clases.
3. Compras un pasaje *(ticket)* de avión.
4. Compras frutas en el mercado.
5. Compras una cadena de oro.
6. Compras unos recuerdos *(souvenirs)* durante tus vacaciones.

7. Cenas en un restaurante muy elegante.
8. Vas al cine para ver una película.
9. Pagas el alquiler *(rent)* de tu apartamento.
10. Compras una casa nueva.
11. Compras un automóvil nuevo.

12 **De compras** Trabaja con un(a) compañero(a) de clase. Juntos escojan
C seis objetos del dibujo y representen una escena como la del modelo. Túrnense para hacer el papel del (de la) dependiente y el (la) cliente. Sigan el modelo.

MODELO   el café
Tú: *Un café grande, por favor.*
Compañero(a): *Muy bien. Son dos dólares y veinticinco centavos.*
    ¿Cómo desea pagar?
Tú: *En efectivo. Aquí lo tiene.*

© Cengage Learning 2013

A ver

Standard 1.2: Through video viewing, students learn interpretive strategies for communication. Activities in this section regularly provide opportunities for students to interpret spoken language.

ESTRATEGIA

Using background knowledge to anticipate content

If you have a rough idea of a video segment's content, you can predict what other information it may contain. Think about the topic and ask yourself what vocabulary you associate with it. By organizing your thoughts in advance, you prepare yourself to understand the content more easily.

Answers, Antes de ver : 1. para su mamá 2. unos aretes (de oro); una blusa, un suéter 3. no; *Answers will vary.*

Learning objective: Evaluating

Antes de ver En el episodio para este capítulo, Chela y Javier independientemente buscan un regalo para sus madres. Mira las páginas 270, 274 y 276.

1. ¿Para quién buscan un regalo Chela y Javier?
2. ¿Cuáles de los accesorios y prendas de ropa del vocabulario pueden ser un regalo bueno para la mamá de Chela y la de Javier? Y, según ellos, ¿cuáles no son un regalo bueno?
3. ¿Los dos se conocen o no? ¿Crees que van a conocerse en este episodio?

▶ **Ver** Mira el video. Usa la información en **Antes de ver** para entenderlo mejor.

Después de ver 1 Contesta las siguientes preguntas sobre el video.

© Cengage Learning 2013

Answers, Después de ver 1: 1. no, no 2. no, no 3. unos aretes 4. No les gusta el color de la blusa. La mamá de Javier no necesita suéter. La mamá de Chela no usa ese estilo. 5. no. 6. en efectivo 7. Piensa que son hermanos.

1. ¿Compró Javier una blusa para su mamá? ¿Y Chela?
2. ¿Compró Javier un suéter para su mamá? ¿Y Chela?
3. ¿Qué compraron Javier y Chela para sus mamás?
4. ¿Por qué no les gustó la blusa a Javier y a Chela? ¿Y el suéter?
5. ¿Sabemos cuánto costaron los aretes?
6. ¿Cómo pagaron Javier y Chela?
7. ¿Qué pensó el dependiente sobre la relación entre Javier y Chela?

Después de ver 2 Escribe un resumen corto de lo que ocurrió en el video para este capítulo. Escribe por lo menos seis oraciones que describan la conversación entre el dependiente y Javier y luego entre el dependiente y Chela. Usa las formas del pretérito que aprendiste en el **Capítulo 7**.

>> Voces del mundo hispano

© Cengage Learning 2013

En el video para este capítulo José, Bruna, Marcela y Alex hablan de la ropa y la moda. Lee las siguientes oraciones. Después mira el video una o más veces para decir si las oraciones son ciertas **(C)** o falsas **(F)**.

1. Cuando José está en Perú, compra su ropa en Marshalls. F
2. A Alex no le gusta mucho la ropa artesanal *(handmade)*. F
3. Las prendas favoritas de José son los suéteres. F
4. A Bruna y a Marcela les gustan las faldas. C
5. A Marcela le gusta combinar accesorios. C
6. A Alex le importa ser original. C

◄)) >> Voces de Estados Unidos

Track 24

Nina García, diseñadora

Valerie Macon/Getty Images

❝El primer paso, y el más importante para desarrollar estilo, es proyectar ese tipo de confianza; el tipo de confianza que les dice a los otros que te respetas a ti misma, te amas *(love)* a ti misma y te vistes para ti misma y no para otros. Tú eres tu propia musa.❞

Los fanáticos de Project Runway la conocen como una de los jurados *(judges)* más perspicaces del programa y como una mujer de un gusto impecable. Pero la fama e influencia de Nina García van mucho mucho más allá de este popular programa de televisión. Nina es una autoridad internacional en la industria de la moda. Ha colaborado *(She has collaborated)* con casas de moda tales como Marc Jacobs y Perry Ellis, fue editora de la revista *Elle* y es autora de cuatro libros de moda que figuran entre los libros con mayor éxito de venta *(bestsellers)* del *New York Times*. Actualmente, Nina reside en Nueva York donde trabaja como directora de modas de la revista *Marie Claire*. Nacida en Colombia, es graduada de Boston University, de La Escuela Superior de Moda de París y del Fashion Institute of Technology de la ciudad de Nueva York.

¿Y tú? ¿Te gusta la idea de vestirte con ropa de diseñadores famosos? ¿Te importan las marcas *(brands)* de tus prendas de ropa? ¿Por qué sí o por qué no?

Standards 2.1, 2.2, 3.2: Students read about successful Spanish speakers in the U.S. and acquire cultural information that features distinctive viewpoints of Spanish-speaking people.

Suggestion, Voces: For a group discussion: ¿Estás de acuerdo con Nina García que la confianza es un elemento esencial del estilo? ¿Te gusta leer revistas de moda? ¿Por qué sí o no? ¿Quiénes llevan ropa de diseño? ¿Quiénes son otros diseñadores? ¿Qué tipo de diseño prefieres (elegante / barroco / simple / clásico / juvenil / lujoso / bohemio / orgánico / práctico / serio / profesional / convencional)? ¿Qué estilo de ropa llevas para ir a una fiesta formal / para una entrevista / para un puesto de gerente en una compañía / para ir de camping?

¡Prepárate!

>> ## Gramática útil 1 **Standards 4.1:** Students compare regular with irregular forms of the Spanish language and the present tense of verbs that have a change in meaning in the preterite.

Talking about what you did: The preterite tense of more irregular verbs

Preparation: Review regular forms and emphasize their *pronunciation* to make it easier to memorize. Emphasize the stressed syllables in the first- and third-person singular in **hablé, leí, visité, habló, leyó, visitó.** Stressing the last syllable helps students internalize the difference between **habló** and **hablo.**

Heritage Learners: When reviewing the preterite of irregular verbs, notice that some heritage language speakers tend to conjugate **venir** in the preterite with an **e** instead of an **i** in the verbal root: **veniste, *venimos, *venieron.* Another verb that is particularly problematic for heritage learners is **caber** in the preterite. Practice the forms of **caber** with groups of high beginners only.

Cómo usarlo

1. In Spanish, as in English, many of the verbs you use most are irregular. In this chapter you will learn the preterite forms of **andar, haber, poder, poner, querer, saber, tener**, and **venir.** Notice that most of these verbs are also irregular in the present indicative.

2. The preterite forms of **conocer, saber, poder**, and **querer** can mean something slightly different from their meaning in the present indicative.

	Present indicative meaning	Different preterite meaning
conocer	*to know someone, to be acquainted with*	*to meet*
saber	*to know a fact*	*to find out some information*
poder	*to be able to do something*	*to accomplish something*
no poder	*to not be able to*	*to try to do something and fail*
querer	*to want; to love*	*to try to do something*
no querer	*to not want, love*	*to refuse to do something*

Elena **quiso** llamarme pero **no pudo** encontrar su celular.

Conocí al padre de Beto y **supe** que Beto está en Colombia.

Pude completar el trabajo pero **no quise** ir a la oficina.

*Elena **tried** to call me but **was unable (failed)** to find her cell phone.*

*I **met** Beto's father and **found out** that Beto is in Colombia.*

*I **succeeded in** finishing the work, but I **refused** to go to the office.*

The preterite can be used here because the focus is on the moment or the duration of the action described.

3. When referring to a specific time period in the past, most of these verbs keep their original meaning in the preterite: **Mi ex novio me quiso mucho, pero mi novio actual me quiere más.**

4. Notice that while the rest of these verbs are irregular in the preterite, **conocer** is regular in this tense. Its only irregularity is its **yo** form in the present tense: **conozco.**

Cómo formarlo

Here are the preterite forms of these irregular verbs. Some verbs are somewhat similar in their irregular stems, so they are grouped together to help you memorize them more easily.

andar:	anduv-	anduve, anduviste, anduvo, anduvimos, anduvisteis, anduvieron
tener:	tuv-	tuve, tuviste, tuvo, tuvimos, tuvisteis, tuvieron
poder:	pud-	pude, pudiste, pudo, pudimos, pudisteis, pudieron
poner:	pus-	puse, pusiste, puso, pusimos, pusisteis, pusieron
saber:	sup-	supe, supiste, supo, supimos, supisteis, supieron
hay:		hubo (invariable)
querer:	quis-	quise, quisiste, quiso, quisimos, quisisteis, quisieron
venir:	vin-	vine, viniste, vino, vinimos, vinisteis, vinieron

Hubo is the preterite equivalent of **hay**. Like **hay**, it is a third-person invariable form that is used whether the subject is singular or plural: **Hubo unas ofertas increíbles en las tiendas la semana pasada. Haber** is the infinitive from which **hay** and **hubo** come.

Notice that although these verbs change their stems, they share the same endings (**-e, -iste, -o, -imos, -isteis, -ieron**).

ACTIVIDADES

M **1** **En el centro comercial** Di qué pasó en el centro comercial hoy según el dibujo. Sigue el modelo.

Optional: Have students expand their statements: **Mario tuvo sed y compró / bebió un refresco enorme.**

MODELO Mario (beber un refresco grande)
Mario bebió un refresco grande.

1. Adela (comer pizza) Adela comió pizza.
2. Ernesto (andar mucho) Ernesto anduvo mucho.
3. Aracely (poder encontrar muchas cosas) Aracely pudo encontrar muchas cosas.
4. Miguel (conocer a Marisa) Miguel conoció a Marisa.
5. Leo (poner la mochila en la mesa) Leo puso la mochila en la mesa.
6. Néstor (querer tomar una siesta pero no poder) Néstor quiso tomar una siesta pero no pudo.
7. Beti (saber las últimas noticias) Beti supo las últimas noticias.

© Cengage Learning 2013

2 **La vida universitaria** Con un(a) compañero(a) de clase, háganse y contesten las siguientes preguntas.

1. ¿Cómo supiste que te habían aceptado *(you had been accepted)* en la universidad? ¿Cuándo lo supiste?
2. ¿Viniste a la universidad como estudiante nuevo(a), estudiante de intercambio o te transferiste de otra universidad? ¿Te gustó la universidad cuando llegaste por primera vez?
3. ¿Pudiste traer todas tus cosas a la universidad? ¿Qué cosas no pudiste traer?
4. ¿Conociste a muchas personas la primera semana de clases? ¿Cuántas, más o menos?
5. ¿Tuviste que estudiar mucho el semestre / trimestre pasado? ¿Recibiste buenas notas?
6. ¿Aprendiste algo interesante el semestre / trimestre pasado? ¿Qué fue?
7. ¿Tuviste tiempo para hacer mucho ejercicio? ¿Anduviste mucho el semestre / trimestre pasado?
8. ¿Pudiste tomar todas tus clases preferidas?

3 **El semestre o trimestre pasado** Mira el siguiente formulario. Luego, pregúntales a tus compañeros de clase si hicieron las actividades indicadas el semestre o trimestre pasado. Si encuentras a alguien que responde que sí, escribe su nombre en el espacio correspondiente. Sigue el modelo.

MODELO   venir a la universidad con mucha ropa nueva
—*¿Viniste a la universidad con mucha ropa nueva?*
—*No, no vine con mucha ropa nueva.*
O: —*Sí, vine con mucha ropa nueva. (Escribe su nombre en el formulario.)*

¿Quién...?	Nombre
tener que estudiar todos los fines de semana	
no conocer a su compañero(a) de cuarto antes de llegar a la universidad	
poner un refrigerador y un televisor en su cuarto	
venir a las clases sin hacer la tarea	
no poder dormir antes de los exámenes importantes	
venir a la universidad con mucha ropa nueva	
tener sueño en las clases	
no querer comer la comida de la cafetería	

Gramática útil 2

Talking about what you did: The preterite tense of -ir stem-changing verbs

Cómo formarlo

1. As you learned in **Chapter 7,** the only stem-changing verbs that also change in the preterite are verbs that end in **-ir.** Present-tense stem-changing verbs that end in **-ar** and **-er** do not change their stem in the preterite.

2. In the preterite, **-ir** stem-changing verbs only experience the stem change in the third-person singular **(usted / él / ella)** and third-person plural **(ustedes / ellos / ellas)** forms.

   ■ Verbs that change **e → ie** in the present change **e → i** in the preterite.

   > **preferir:** preferí, preferiste, **prefirió,** preferimos, preferisteis, **prefirieron**
   > Similar verbs you already know: **divertirse, sentirse**
   > New verb of this kind: **sugerir (ie, i)** *to suggest*

   ■ Verbs that change **e → i** in the present also change **e → i** in the preterite.

   > **pedir:** pedí, pediste, **pidió,** pedimos, pedisteis, **pidieron**
   > Similar verbs you already know: **despedirse, reírse, repetir, seguir, servir, vestir, vestirse**
   > New verbs of this kind: **conseguir (i, i)** *to get, to have;* **sonreír (i, i)** *to smile*

   ■ Verbs that change **o → ue** in the present change **o → u** in the preterite.

   > **dormir:** dormí, dormiste, **durmió,** dormimos, dormisteis, **durmieron**
   > New verb of this kind: **morirse (ue, u)** *to die*

Starting with this chapter, all **-ir** stem-changing verbs will be shown with both of their stem changes in parentheses. The first letter or letters show the present-tense stem change and the second letter shows the preterite stem change.

Heritage Learners: Stem-changing verbs are particularly problematic for heritage language speakers. Emphasize that diphthongs [ie] and [ue] never appear in the root of infinitives. On the other hand, the i / e alternation in forms like sentí and sintió creates uncertainty as to which forms of the verb carry one vowel versus the other. Pay special attention to review and practice these verbs. Practice by moving from infinitive to present to preterite: **pedir: él pide, él pidió; dormir: ella duerme, ella durmió; vestir: yo visto, yo vestí; poder: nosotros podemos, nosotros pudimos; preferir: ustedes prefieren, ustedes prefirieron,** etc.

ACTIVIDADES

M **4** **Olivia y Belkys** Completa la conversación con la forma correcta del pretérito de los verbos indicados. Después, di si, en tu opinión, Belkys tiene razón en sentirse tan avergonzada *(embarrassed)*.

OLIVIA: ¿Qué tal tu día de compras? ¿ ___Te divertiste___ (divertirse)?

BELKYS: No, no ___me divertí___ (divertirse) ni un poquito y además no compré nada.

OLIVIA: ¡No te lo creo! ¿Tú, sin comprar nada? ¡Imposible!

BELKYS: Pero es la verdad. Yo ___fui___ (ir) con Gerardo porque él ___insistió___ (insistir) en acompañarme. Él ___sugirió___ (sugerir) ir al centro porque le gustan los trajes en una tienda allí.

OLIVIA: ¿Pero ustedes no ___consiguieron___ (conseguir) comprar nada?

BELKYS: No. Los dos ___vimos___ (ver) unas cosas bonitas, pero no ___pudimos___ (poder) encontrar nada a buen precio. Por eso, ___preferimos___ (preferir) no comprar nada.

OLIVIA: ¡Qué pena!

BELKYS: Y lo peor es que Gerardo ___se vistió___ (vestirse) con un traje viejo, muy pasado de moda, verde, con rayas amarillas. Yo casi me muero de vergüenza.

OLIVIA: ¡Pobrecita! ¡Imagínate el horror!

BELKYS: Bueno, tú te ríes, ¡pero te digo que yo no ___me reí___ (reírse) en toda la tarde! Nosotros ___seguimos___ (seguir) buscando en todas las tiendas del centro. Por fin ___nos despedimos___ (despedirse) y yo ___vine___ (venir) directamente aquí para contarte toda la historia.

OLIVIA: Ay, chica, tranquila. Por lo menos, ¡tú me ___hiciste___ (hacer) reír un poco!

Learning objective: Understanding

M/C **5** **Me sentí…** Di cómo se sintieron las siguientes personas en las situaciones indicadas. *Answers may vary.*

MODELO tu tía / después de perder el trabajo
Se sintió desilusionada.

Emociones: aburrido(a), animado(a), cansado(a), contento(a), desilusionado(a), feliz, furioso(a), nervioso(a), ocupado(a), preocupado(a), triste

1. tú / antes de tus exámenes finales Me sentí nervioso(a).
2. tú y tu mejor amigo(a) / al final del semestre o trimestre Nos sentimos contentos(as).
3. tu mejor amigo(a) / cuando estuvo enfermo(a) Se sintió cansado(a).
4. tus padres / cuando saliste para la universidad Se sintieron tristes.
5. tu primo(a) / después de perder el partido de fútbol Se sintió furioso(a).
6. tus amigos / en una película de tres horas y media Se sintieron aburridos.
7. tu compañero(a) de cuarto / antes de la visita de sus padres Se sintió nervioso(a).
8. tú / después de conocer a una persona simpática Me sentí animado(a).

Optional: Expand Activity 6 with additional questions: ¿Usaste el Internet para comprar lo básico para la universidad? ¿Los libros? ¿La ropa? ¿Hablaste por celular para contactar a amigos o parientes? ¿Qué hiciste tu primer día en la universidad / de clases?, etc.

6 **En la U** Con un(a) compañero(a) de clase, háganse las siguientes C preguntas sobre su llegada a la universidad y luego contéstenlas.

1. ¿Cómo te sentiste cuando llegaste a la universidad la primera vez?
2. ¿Qué te sugirió tu familia cuando viniste a la universidad?
3. ¿Le pediste ayuda a tu familia para traer todas tus cosas a la universidad?
4. ¿Te divertiste el primer semestre / trimestre? ¿Qué hiciste?
5. ¿Preferiste vivir en una residencia estudiantil o en un apartamento?
6. ¿Conseguiste un trabajo el primer semestre / trimestre?
7. ¿Siguieron tú y tus amigos la misma carrera de estudios?

>> Gramática útil 3

Saying who is affected or involved: Indirect object pronouns

Cómo usarlo

LO BÁSICO

- An *indirect object* is a noun or noun phrase that indicates for whom or to whom an action is done: I bought a gift for *Beatriz*. We asked *the teachers* a question.
- *Indirect object pronouns* are used to replace indirect object nouns: I bought a gift for *her*. We asked *them* a question. Often you can identify the indirect object of the sentence by asking *to* or *for whom*? about the verb: We bought a gift *for whom?* (Beatriz / her) We asked a question *to whom?* (the teachers / them).

1. In **Chapter 7** you learned how to use direct object pronouns to avoid repetition. In this chapter you will learn how you can also use indirect object pronouns to avoid repetition and to clarify to which person you are referring.

2. Look at the following passage and see if you can figure out to whom the boldface indirect object pronouns refer.

> Fui al almacén el miércoles. Tenía una lista larga de compras. **Le** compré unos jeans y una camisa a Miguel. También **le** compré una corbata. A Susana y a Carmen **les** compré unas camisetas. También tuve que comprar**les** calcetines. Además **me** compré una falda bonita y un reloj.

Cómo formarlo

1. Although English uses the same set of pronouns for direct object pronouns and indirect object pronouns, in Spanish there are two slightly different sets.

2. Notice that the only difference between the direct object pronouns and the indirect object pronouns is in the two third-person pronouns. Instead of **lo / la**, the indirect object pronoun is **le**. And instead of **los / las,** the indirect object pronoun is **les**. The indirect object pronouns **le** and **les** do not have to agree in gender with the nouns they replace, as do the direct object pronouns **lo, la, los**, and **las**.

Standard 4.1: Notice that students are asked to compare English and Spanish structures of indirect and direct objects.

Preparation: For visual and kinesthetic learners, bring objects to class to pass around. Illustrate the indirect object pronouns and have students describe actions that they see and do using object pronouns; e.g.: **Le dio el libro nuevo. Me pasaste las llaves. La profesora nos devolvió la tarea.**

¿En qué puedo **servirle,** señor?

Indirect object pronouns			
me	to / for me	**nos**	to / for us
te	to / for you	**os**	to / for you (fam. pl.)
le	to / for you (form. sing) / him / her	**les**	to / for you (form., pl.) / them

Notice that these are the same pronouns you used with **gustar** and similar verbs in **Chapters 2** and **4**.

© Cengage Learning 2013

3. As with direct object pronouns, indirect object pronouns always come before a conjugated verb used alone.

Te traje el periódico.	*I brought **you** the newspaper.*
Nos dieron un regalo bonito.	*They gave **us** a nice gift.*

4. When an indirect object pronoun is used with an infinitive or with the present progressive, it may come before the conjugated verb, or it may be attached to the infinitive or to the present participle.

Te voy a dar el libro.	OR:	Voy a dar**te** el libro.
Te estoy comprando los zapatos.	OR:	Estoy comprándo**te** los zapatos.

5. When an indirect object pronoun is used with a command form, it attaches to the end of the affirmative command but comes before the negative command form.

Cómprame / Cómpreme el libro ahora, por favor.	BUT:	**No me compres / No me compre** el libro ahora, por favor.

6. As you learned in **Chapter 4**, if you want to emphasize or clarify to or for whom something is being done, you can use **a** + the person's name, or **a** + prepositional pronoun: **mí, ti, usted, él, ella, nosotros(as), vosotros(as), ustedes, ellos, ellas**. Note that when a pronoun is used, there is sometimes no direct translation in English.

Les escribo una postal **a ustedes**.	*I'm writing **you** a postcard.*
Le doy el regalo **a Lucas**.	*I'm giving the gift **to Lucas**.*
Les traigo el periódico **a mis padres**.	*I bring the newspaper **to my parents**.*

7. Here are some verbs that are frequently used with indirect object pronouns. Some you already know; others are new: **ayudar** *(to help)*, **comprar, dar, decir, enviar, escribir, gustar** (and verbs like **gustar**), **mandar** *(to send, to order)*, **pedir, prestar** *(to loan or lend)*, **regalar** *(to give a gift)*, **servir**, and **traer**.

ACTIVIDADES

I **7** **Regalos** Varias personas les regalaron varias cosas a diferentes miembros de su familia. Identifica el pronombre del complemento indirecto en cada oración.

1. Yo ___le___ regalé una gorra de lana a mi mamá.
2. Ana ___les___ compró unas pulseras a sus hermanas.
3. Arturo ___te___ dio unos guantes de cuero a ti.
4. Mi tía ___nos___ trajo unas camisetas del Perú a nosotros.
5. Abuela ___les___ mandó una tarjeta postal a mis primos.
6. Papá ___nos___ compró unos pantalones cortos a mí y a mi hermano.
7. Andrés ___te___ trajo una cadena de plata a ti.
8. Nilemy ___le___ regaló un reloj a su tía.

Notice that when the indirect object pronoun attaches to the present participle, you must add an accent to the next-to-last syllable of the present participle to maintain the correct pronunciation.

Again notice that when the indirect object pronoun attaches to the command form, you must add an accent to the next-to-last syllable of command forms of two or more syllables in order to maintain the correct pronunciation.

Prepositional pronouns can follow *any* preposition, not just **a**. Other prepositions you know include **con**: *with* (with **con**, **mí** and **ti** change to **conmigo** and **contigo**); **de**: *from, of;* **sin**: *without*.

M **8** **¡Ay, Hernando!** Completa la siguiente conversación con el complemento indirecto correcto. Después de completarla, léela otra vez para ver si entiendes por qué se usa cada complemento indirecto.

HERNANDO: Oye, tengo que ir al centro. ¿Quieres acompañarme?

SEBASTIÁN: Cómo no. Tengo que (1) comprar___le___ un regalo a mi hermanito para el día de su santo.

HERNANDO: Y yo (2) ___me___ voy a comprar unos jeans y una camiseta nueva.

SEBASTIÁN: ¿Tú con interés en la moda? Hombre, ¿qué (3) ___te___ pasa?

HERNANDO: Es Lidia. Ahora que salimos juntos los fines de semana (4) ___me___ dice que toda mi ropa está pasada de moda.

SEBASTIÁN: ¡No (5) ___me___ digas! A las mujeres… ¡ (6) ___les___ importa demasiado la ropa!

HERNANDO: Y lo peor es que no tengo mucho dinero. ¿Crees que (7) ___me___ den un descuento en la tienda donde trabaja Julio?

SEBASTIÁN: Oye, vale la pena *(it's worthwhile)* ir a ver. ¿(8) ___Le___ dijiste a Julio que necesitas comprar ropa?

HERNANDO: Sí. Pero (9) ___me___ dijo que debemos ir al almacén en el centro. Además dijo que los precios en su tienda son demasiado caros y la calidad no es muy buena.

SEBASTIÁN: Bueno, parece que él no nos puede ayudar. Entonces, ¿vamos directamente al almacén?

HERNANDO: De acuerdo. Oye, ¿no (10) ___me___ puedes prestar un poco de dinero?

SEBASTIÁN: ¡Hombre! Nunca cambias…

9 **De compras** Marisela les compra varias prendas de ropa y accesorios a diferentes miembros de su familia y a varias amistades. Escucha mientras ella describe sus compras. Luego, escribe oraciones que expliquen qué le compró a cada quién. Primero estudia el modelo.

Track 25

M

MODELO Escuchas: A mi tía le encantan las blusas bordadas. Cuando estaba de vacaciones en Ecuador, le compré una blusa bordada muy bonita.

Escribes: *Le compró una blusa bordada a su tía.*

1. ___Le___ compró una cartera a ___su padre___.
2. ___Les___ compró camisetas a ___sus abuelos___.
3. ___Le___ compró una pulsera de oro a ___su madre___.
4. ___Me___ compró unos guantes de piel (___a mí___).
5. ___Les___ compró unos pantalones cortos a ___los niños___.
6. ___Nos___ compró unos zapatos de tenis (___a nosotros___).

Audioscript, Act. 9, De compras:
1. *Busqué un cinturón para mi padre, pero por fin le compré una cartera que vi en la tienda de hombres.*
2. *A mis abuelos les gusta llevar las mismas camisetas. Les compré dos camisetas de la universidad.*
3. *Fui a la joyería a buscarle unos aretes a mi madre, pero al final decidí que le gustaría más una pulsera de oro.*
4. *Sé que te gustan los guantes de piel, por eso te compré unos negros muy bonitos que vi en oferta.*
5. *Fui a la tienda de ropa para comprarles un regalo a los niños. Por fin les compré unos pantalones cortos para el verano.*
6. *Como necesitan unos zapatos de tenis, les compré a ustedes unos que vi en la tienda de deportes.*

10 **De vez en cuando** Con un(a) compañero(a) de clase, digan para quiénes
C hacen las actividades indicadas. Usen cada verbo por lo menos una vez.

> **MODELO** comprar un café
> *De vez en cuando le compro un café a mi compañero(a) de cuarto.*
> O: *Nunca le compro un café a nadie.*

Acción	**Objeto directo**	**Objeto indirecto**
escribir	cartas	mi madre / padre
dar	flores	mis padres
comprar	regalos	mi amigo(a)
contar	chismes *(gossip)*	mis amigos
mandar	notas de agradecimiento	mi profesor(a)
pedir	favores	mis profesores
hacer	chistes *(jokes)*	mi novio(a)
traer	ayuda	mi compañero(a) de cuarto
¿…?	ropa	mis compañeros(as) de cuarto
	¿…?	

Frases útiles: de vez en cuando *(sometimes)*, frecuentemente, muchas veces,
todas las semanas, todos los días, rara vez *(hardly ever)*, nunca, casi

Learning objective: Applying

 11 **¿Quién?** Con un(a) compañero(a), háganse preguntas sobre las acciones
C de sus compañeros de clase. Pueden usar las ideas de la lista o pueden inventar
otras. Asegúrense de usar verbos que requieren el uso del objeto indirecto.

> **MODELO** Tú: *¿Quién le regaló ropa a su novio(a)?*
> Compañero(a): *Dahlia le regaló una chaqueta de cuero a su novio Jesús.*

1. regalar ropa
2. decir siempre la verdad
3. pagar los estudios
4. enviar muchos mensajes de texto
5. ayudar con la tarea
6. ¿…?

 12 **¿Y tú?** Con un(a) compañero(a), túrnense para hacer y contestar
C preguntas sobre las siguientes actividades.

> **MODELOS** tú enviar a tus padres recientemente: *¿qué?*
> Tú: *¿Qué les enviaste recientemente a tus padres?*
> Compañero(a): *Les envié un mensaje de texto la semana pasada.*
> mandar algo a ti por correo recientemente: *¿quién?*
> Compañero(a): *¿Quién te mandó algo por correo recientemente?*
> Tú: *Mi abuela me mandó una tarjeta de cumpleaños ayer.*

1. tú regalar a tu mejor amigo(a) para su cumpleaños: ¿qué?
2. ayudar a ti la última vez que mudaste *(you moved)*: ¿quién?
3. tú prestar algo a un(a) amigo(a) o hermano(a) recientemente: ¿qué?
4. tú traer a tus amigos cuando tuvieron una cena en casa: ¿qué?
5. mandar a ti flores u otro regalo durante el año pasado: ¿quién?
6. decir a ti unos chismes súper interesantes recientemente: ¿quién?

Gramática útil 4

Making comparisons: Comparatives and superlatives

AR MODA

¡Canasta!

LOS BOLSOS DE MIMBRE, RAFIA Y
CUERDA SON EL ACCESORIO BÁSICO
DEL VERANO, TANTO PARA IR A LA
PISCINA COMO SI SALES DE NOCHE

FOTOS: **GEMA LÓPEZ** ESTILISMO: **JUAN ANTONIO FRÍAS**

Revista de Ana Rosa; Photo de Gema Lopez

Can you
find the
comparative
words in this
text? Are
they making
an equal
or unequal
comparison?

**Answers: tanto...
como**; equal
comparison

Cómo usarlo

LO BÁSICO

Comparatives compare two or more objects. *Superlatives* indicate that one
object exceeds or stands above all others. In English we use *more* and *less* with
adjectives, adverbs, nouns, and verbs to make comparisons, and we also add
-er to the end of most one- or two-syllable adjectives: *more expensive, cheaper*.
To form superlatives we use *most / least* with adjectives or add *-est* to the end
of most one- or two-syllable adjectives: *the most expensive, the cheapest*.

1. Comparatives in Spanish use **más** *(more)* and **menos** *(less)* to make
comparisons between people, actions, and things. **Más** and **menos** can be
used with nouns, adjectives, verbs, and adverbs.

Nouns: Hay **más libros** en esta tienda que en aquélla.
*There are **more books** in this store than in that one.*

Adjectives: Este libro es **menos interesante** que ése.
*This book is **less interesting** than that one.*

Verbs: Yo **leo menos** que él.
*I **read less** than he (does).*

Adverbs: Él lee **más lentamente** que yo.
*He reads **more slowly** than I (do).*

2. Superlative forms indicate that something exceeds all others: *extremely, the most, the least.*

Este libro es **interesantísimo**.	*This book is **really interesting**.*
Es **el más interesante** de todos.	*It's the **most interesting** of all of them.*

Cómo formarlo

1. Regular comparatives. Comparisons can be *equal* (as many as) or *unequal* (more than, less than). Comparative forms can be used with nouns, adjectives, adverbs, and verbs.

> Notice that of all the words used in these comparative forms (**tanto, tan, más, menos, como,** and **que**), only **tanto** changes to reflect number and gender.

	Equal comparisons	Unequal comparisons
noun	**tanto** + noun + **como** (**Tanto** agrees with the noun.) Tengo **tanto dinero como** tú. Tengo **tantas tarjetas de crédito como** tú.	**más / menos** + noun + **que** (**Más / menos** do not agree with the noun.) Tengo **más dinero que** tú. Tengo **menos tarjetas de crédito que** tú.
adjective	**tan** + adjective + **como** Este reloj es **tan caro como** ése.	**más / menos** + adjective + **que** Este reloj es **más caro que** ése, pero es **menos caro que** aquél.
verb	verb + **tanto como** **Compro tanto como** tú.	verb + **más / menos** + **que** Ella **compra menos que** yo, pero él **compra más que** yo.
adverb	**tan** + adverb + **como** Pago mis cuentas **tan rápidamente como** tú.	**más / menos** + adverb + **que** Ella paga sus cuentas **más rápidamente que** yo, pero él paga **menos rápidamente que** yo.

2. Irregular comparatives. Some adjectives and adverbs have irregular comparative forms.

> Menor and **mayor** are usually used to refer to people, although they can be used in place of **más grande (mayor)** and **más pequeño (menor)** when referring to objects. If you wish to say that one object is *older* or *newer* than another, use **más viejo** or **más nuevo**.

- Adjectives

bueno → mejor:	Este libro es **bueno**, pero ese libro es **mejor**.
malo → peor:	Esta tienda es **mala**, pero esa tienda es **peor**.
joven → menor:	Los dos somos **jóvenes**, pero Remedios es **menor** que yo.
viejo → mayor:	Martín no es **viejo**, pero es **mayor** que Remedios.

- Adverbs

bien → mejor:	Lorena canta muy **bien**, pero Alfonso canta **mejor**.
mal → peor:	Nosotros bailamos **mal**, pero ellos bailan **peor**.

Notice: Point out to students that **más bueno** and **más malo** are the comparative forms of **bueno** and **malo** when these adjectives refer to the moral quality of people. Therefore, **Pepe es más bueno que su hermano** means that Pepe is a better person (from a moral standpoint) than his brother. On the other hand, **mejor** and **peor** are the comparative forms of **bueno** and **malo** when they refer to the quality of an object (**Esta pluma es mejor que la otra**) or the capacity of an individual within a field of expertise (**Juan es mejor médico que Luis**).

3. Superlatives

- To say that a person or thing is extreme in some way, add **-ísimo** to the end of an adjective. (If the adjective ends in a vowel, remove the vowel first.)

  fácil → **facilísimo** *(very easy)*   contento → **contentísimo** *(extremely happy)*

- To say that a person or thing is the *most . . .* or *the least . . .* use the following formula. (Do not use this formula with the **-ísimo** ending—choose one or the other!)

  article + noun + **más** / **menos** + adjective + **de**

Roberto es **el estudiante más popular de** la universidad.

Ellas son **las dependientes más trabajadoras del** almacén.

These superlative forms must change to reflect the gender and number of the nouns they modify: **unos aretes carísimos, unas camisetas baratísimas**, etc.

Notice that the accent is always on the first **i** of **-ísimo**. If the adjective has an accent, it is dropped when you add **-ísimo**: **difícil → dificilísimo**.

Notice that the article and the adjective must agree with the noun: **el estudiante popular, las dependientes trabajadoras**.

ACTIVIDADES

13 **El almacén Toneti** Escucha el anuncio sobre Toneti, un almacén grande.
Track 26 Pon una X al lado de cada objeto que se menciona. **¡OJO!** Asegúrate de que la descripción de cada objeto es la correcta.

1. _____X_____ las mochilas más baratas
2. _____X_____ las mochilas más grandes
3. _____ la selección más grande de zapatos
4. _____X_____ los zapatos de tenis más populares
5. _____X_____ los pantalones menos caros del centro
6. _____ los pantalones más caros del centro
7. _____X_____ las camisetas de la más alta calidad
8. _____ las camisetas más bonitas del centro

M **14** **La rebaja** Haz comparaciones entre los precios de varias prendas de ropa y accesorios. Sigue el modelo.

Learning objective: Understanding

MODELO caro: las botas ($50) / los zapatos de tenis ($40)
Las botas son más caras que los zapatos de tenis.
Los zapatos de tenis son menos caros que las botas.

1. caro: los suéteres ($25) / las camisetas ($15)
2. caro: las camisetas ($15) / los vestidos ($50)
3. caro: las blusas ($30) / las camisetas ($15)
4. caro: las botas ($50) / los vestidos ($50)
5. barato: los vestidos ($50) / los suéteres ($25)
6. barato: las blusas ($30) / las botas ($50)
7. barato: los vestidos ($50) / los zapatos de tenis ($40)
8. barato: las camisetas ($15) / las blusas ($30)

Audioscript, Act. 13, El almacén Toneti:

Este fin de semana, ¡todo está en oferta en Toneti! ¡Ya tenemos todo lo que necesitas para volver a la escuela! Para los niños, ¡las mochilas más grandes por los precios más bajos! Para toda la familia, ¡los zapatos de tenis en una variedad de colores! ¡Y en los estilos más populares! ¿Los pantalones? ¡Los tenemos para toda la familia! ¡Y son menos caros que en cualquier otra tienda del centro! ¿Necesitas camisetas? ¡Las tenemos todas en oferta! Y son camisetas de la más alta calidad, todas de puro algodón. Todo rebajado, todo en oferta. ¡No te lo pierdas! En Toneti, ¡la tienda de las grandes rebajas!

Answers, Act. 14: 1. Los suéteres son más caros que... / Las camisetas son menos caras que... 2. Las camisetas son menos caras que... / Los vestidos son más caros que... 3. Las blusas son más caras que... / Las camisetas son menos caras que... 4. Las botas son tan caras como... / Los vestidos son tan caros como... 5. Los vestidos son menos baratos que... / Los suéteres son más baratos que... 6. Las blusas son más baratas que... / Las botas son menos baratas que... 7. Los vestidos son menos baratos que... / Los zapatos de tenis son más baratos que... 8. Las camisetas son más baratas que... / Las blusas son menos baratas que...

C ⑮ **Las personas famosas** Haz comparaciones según el modelo.

MODELO cantar: Taylor Swift o Rihanna
Taylor Swift canta peor que Rihanna.
O: *Taylor Swift canta mejor que Rihanna.*
O: *Taylor Swift canta tan bien como Rihanna.*

1. cantar: Lady Gaga o Katy Perry
2. bailar: Usher o Jay-Z
3. cocinar: tu mejor amigo(a) o tu madre
4. jugar tenis: Venus Williams o Serena Williams
5. jugar golf: Lorena Ochoa o tus padres
6. patinar sobre hielo: tú o tu mejor amigo(a)
7. nadar: tú o tu hermano(a)
8. jugar béisbol: Albert Pujols o Edgar Rentería
9. hacer esquí acuático: tú o tus amigos
10. tocar la guitarra: Jack White o Keith Richards

Learning objective: Applying

⑯ **En el centro comercial** Trabaja con un(a) compañero(a) de clase. Juntos
C miren el dibujo y hagan todas las comparaciones que puedan. Usen las palabras
y expresiones útiles por lo menos una vez cada una.

Palabras y expresiones útiles: tanto como, más, menos, tan… como, mejor,
peor, el (la) más… de todos, el (la) menos… de todos

Comparaciones: alto / delgado; hablar; hacer compras; comer

© Cengage Learning 2013

17 Nuestros amigos Trabaja con un(a) compañero(a) de clase. Primero piensen en seis personas que conozcan los dos. Luego hagan comparaciones según el modelo.

C

MODELOS cómico
Sean es más cómico que Jason.
hablar rápido
Sean habla más rápido que Jason.

Palabras y frases útiles: cómico, joven, viejo, alto, extrovertido, introvertido, hablar rápido, comer despacio *(slowly)*, viajar frecuentemente, jugar tenis (u otro deporte) bien, correr rápido, entrenarse frecuentemente

Sonrisas

¿Por qué dice mamá que estoy más loca que un zapato cuando hago algo que no le gusta?

No sé. Es un dicho.

Ya sé, pero la verdad es que los zapatos no tienen nada de loco.

Tienes razón. Es un dicho ridiculísimo.

© Cengage Learning 2013

Expresión En grupos de tres o cuatro estudiantes, trabajen para completar la comparación **"Es más loco(a) que un…"** de una manera diferente. Después de crear una lista de posibilidades, escojan una y hagan una tira cómica semejante a la de arriba.

¡Explora y exprésate!

Perú

Standards 2.1, 2.2, 3.1: Throughout *Cuadros*, the **¡Explora y exprésate!** sections explore Spanish-speaking cultures and reinforce and further knowledge of other disciplines—in this case, products, markets, and marketing. Here students gain knowledge and understanding of Peruvian and Ecuadorean culture and explore cultural products such as clothing and weavings.

Check: Interview students again on what they know and what they would like to know about Perú and Ecuador. Follow up at the end of the chapter to see what has been learned and what may be beyond the scope of this course. Exploring these topics in more detail offers an opportunity to encourage future enrollment in other Spanish classes.

Christian Vinces/Shutterstock

Información general

Nombre oficial: República del Perú

Población: 29.907.003

Capital: Lima (f. 1535) (8.000.000 hab.)

Otras ciudades importantes: Callao (2.000.000 hab.), Arequipa (1.300.000 hab.), Trujillo (1.000.000 hab.)

Moneda: nuevo sol

Idiomas: español y quechua (oficiales), aimara y otras lenguas indígenas

Mapa de Perú: Apéndice D

Although most reference books and written texts usually use just **Perú** to refer to the country, you will often hear native speakers say **el Perú**. This use of **el** sometimes occurs with **Ecuador** also.

Vale saber…

Heritage Learners: Because many heritage learners have had limited practice reading large numbers in Spanish, it is a good idea to practice numbers whenever the opportunity arises. These readings are good practice because they include many dates and population figures.

- La civilización incaica de Perú forma el más grande y poderoso (*powerful*) imperio de Sudamérica en la época prehispánica.

- Otra civilización importante fueron los nazcas, quienes hicieron dibujos en la tierra que sólo se pueden ver desde el aire. El origen y el objetivo de los más de 2000 km. de líneas son un misterio.

Joel Shawn/Shutterstock

- En 1532, Francisco Pizarro captura a Atahualpa, el último emperador inca. Francisco Pizarro funda la ciudad de Lima en 1535. En 1824, Perú gana la independencia de España.

- La mayoría de la población peruana habla español o quechua, las lenguas oficiales, pero también existe una variedad de lenguas nativas, de las cuales el quechua y el aimara son los idiomas más hablados.

Optional: Tell students that during the sixteenth and seventeenth centuries, Peru was the *only* Spanish viceroyalty in South America and a powerful center of government in colonial Latin America.

Ecuador

Información general

Nombre oficial: República del Ecuador

Población: 14.790.608

Capital: Quito (f. 1556) (2.500.000 hab.)

Otras ciudades importantes: Guayaquil (2.200.000 hab.), Cuenca (460.000 hab.)

Moneda: dólar

Idiomas: español (oficial), quechua

Mapa de Ecuador: Apéndice D

Elena Kalistratova/iStockphoto

Vale saber…

- Ecuador toma su nombre de la línea ecuatorial que divide el globo en dos hemisferios: norte y sur.

- Quito forma parte del imperio incaico hasta la conquista de los españoles en 1533. Al ganar la independencia de España, Quito forma la federación la Gran Colombia con Colombia y Venezuela. En 1830, Quito deja la federación y cambia su nombre a la República del Ecuador.

- A 1.000 kilómetros de la costa ecuatoriana están las islas Galápagos, únicas por su belleza y su flora y fauna. Las condiciones naturales de las islas no han cambiado *(have not changed)* desde hace siglos, resultando en ecosistemas permanentes que permitieron a Charles Darwin desarrollar *(to develop)* su teoría de la evolución.

- Hoy día, los idiomas predominantes son el quechua, la lengua de los incas, y el español, la lengua que enseñan en las escuelas. Muchos ecuatorianos son perfectamente bilingües.

Culture: The Galapagos Islands, about 600 miles off the coast of Ecuador, are well known for their unusual plant and animal species. The British biologist Charles Darwin studied on the islands before writing *The Origin of the Species* in 1859.

Michael Zysman/Shutterstock

Check: Test your students' knowledge about the two focus countries in this chapter using comparatives and superlatives with these statements. Cierto o falso. 1. Ecuador es más grande que Perú. (F) 2. Ecuador tiene menos habitantes que Perú. (C) 3. Perú tiene más selva que Ecuador. (C) 4. Las islas Galápagos de Ecuador son famosísimas. (C)

Eye Ubiquitous/Glow Images

Wesley Hitt/Getty Images

Standards: Here students gain knowledge of Peruvian and Ecuadoran culture (C 2.1) and compare and contrast (C 4.2) between these countries and the U. S.

El algodón orgánico

Perú es un país con una industria algodonera importante, un sector principal de la economía del país. Algunos consideran las finas fibras del algodón peruano las mejores del mundo. El cultivo del algodón forma una parte fundamental en la historia de la agricultura peruana. Los agricultores peruanos, localizados en la costa del Pacífico y en los bosques tropicales de la Amazonia, han heredado *(have inherited)* una variedad de técnicas indígenas ancestrales y completamente orgánicas.

El movimiento "verde" ha propulsado el mundo de la moda hacia la producción de materiales orgánicos. El cultivo orgánico del algodón en Perú ha atraído *(has attracted)* la atención de grandes compañías internacionales como Tommy Hilfiger y Nike. Este interés comercial ha abierto *(has opened)* una gran cantidad de posibilidades para aquellos agricultores peruanos que siguen cultivando algodón de una manera natural.

Otavalo, el mercado inolvidable

Ecuador es famoso por sus tejidos de lana de llama y alpaca, dos animales de la región andina. En Otavalo, un pueblo a cincuenta millas al norte de Quito, existe un mercado artesanal que se conoce como la "Plaza de los Ponchos".

La gente viene de toda la provincia vestidos en sus trajes típicos indígenas: los hombres en sus pantalones blancos y sombreros negros y las mujeres en sus blusas bordadas, faldas, chales, collares y pulseras. En cientos de puestos *(stalls)*, ponen a la venta sombreros estilo Panamá, suéteres, blusas bordadas, sacos gruesos de lana tejidos a mano, gorros, guantes, vestidos, bufandas y las famosas fajas *(sashes)* que usan los indígenas como cinturones. Igual se venden productos artesanales en madera y cerámica, tejidos de todo tipo, ponchos, piedras semipreciosas, manteles y mucho más.

La feria *(fair)* dura hasta que baja el sol. Es un espectáculo vibrante, colorido y lleno de vida, ¡tal como las prendas de ropa otavaleñas!

Pictor Pictor/Photolibrary

Remind: Reinforce reading strategies with students before they start this section. Ask them to avoid looking up every word that they don't recognize. Figuring out meaning through context is a skill that can be developed. Students should be encouraged to look up only limited words that are crucial to major comprehension gaps. Select key words are glossed parenthetically.

La información general

1. ¿Qué civilización de Perú es una de las más poderosas de Sudamérica en la época prehispánica? la civilización incaica

2. ¿Qué civilización deja unas líneas misteriosas que solo se pueden ver desde el aire? los nazcas

3. ¿Quién es el último emperador inca en Perú? ¿Quién es el español que conquista el imperio incaico en Perú y funda la ciudad de Lima? Atahualpa, Francisco Pizarro

4. ¿Con qué otros dos países forma Quito la Gran Colombia? Colombia y Venezuela

5. ¿De dónde toma su nombre Ecuador? la línea ecuatorial que divide el globo en dos hemisferios

6. ¿Qué islas famosas permiten a Charles Darwin desarrollar su teoría de la evolución? las islas Galápagos

El tema de las compras

1. ¿Qué producto peruano les interesa a los comerciantes internacionales? el algodón orgánico

2. ¿Qué técnicas han heredado los agricultores peruanos? técnicas indígenas ancestrales

3. ¿Por qué producto es famoso Ecuador? sus tejidos de lana de llama y alpaca

4. ¿Cuáles son tres prendas de ropa que puedes comprar en la Plaza de los Ponchos? ¿Tres accesorios? prendas: suéteres, blusas, sacos, vestidos; accesorios: gorros, guantes, cinturones, bufandas

🌐 ¿QUIERES SABER MÁS?

Revisa y rellena la tabla que empezaste al principio del capítulo. Luego, escoge un tema para investigar en línea y prepárate para compartir la información con la clase. También puedes escoger de las palabras clave a continuación o en **www.cengagebrain.com**.

Palabras clave: (Perú) los incas, los aimaraes, el Inti Raymi, Machu Picchu, Mario Vargas Llosa; **(Ecuador)** José de Sucre, la Gran Colombia, la línea ecuatorial, Rosalía Arteaga, Oswaldo Guayasamín

Learning objectives: Analyzing, Evaluating

Standard 5.1: Here students are encouraged to do independent web research on topics that will gradually require more Spanish to carry out the assignments by introducing more participation with Spanish-speaking communities online.

Check: Reviewing the table of information from earlier in the chapter provides a ready list of student-generated items to research.

🌐 **Tú en el mundo hispano** Para explorar oportunidades de usar el español para estudiar o hacer trabajos voluntarios o aprendizajes en Perú y Ecuador, sigue los enlaces en **www.cengagebrain.com**.

🎧 **Ritmos del mundo hispano** Sigue los enlaces en **www.cengagebrain.com** para escuchar música de Perú y Ecuador.

A leer

 Standards 1.2, 2.1, 2.2, 4.1, 4.2: Throughout the reading sections in *Cuadros*, students learn to interpret the written word and develop insight into the nature of language and culture.

ESTRATEGIA

Using background knowledge to anticipate content

As you learned when watching this chapter's video segment, you can often use prior knowledge to help you understand the content of authentic language, whether it is a video or a reading. When you think about the topic of a piece and compare it with what you already know, you prepare yourself to comprehend more than you might think is possible.

1 Las siguientes palabras están en el artículo de la página 299, que trata de la popularidad de los jeans por todo el mundo. ¿A qué palabras inglesas son similares?

1. overoles   overalls
2. cachemira   cashmere
3. apliques   appliqués

2 El artículo que vas a leer en este capítulo trata de la influencia de los jeans en la moda internacional. Antes de leer el artículo, escribe de cinco a siete palabras que tú asocies con los jeans y con la mezclilla.

Standards 2.1, 2.2: Here students read and reflect about cultural products and practices. In this case, the product is jeans. Ask students to share everything they know about the history of jeans, denim fabric, jeans styles over the years, etc., to warm up for the reading. Whether assigned or read in class, remind students to look for cognates and stress that they needn't understand every word. Encourage multiple readings. Reading out loud offers pronunciation practice.

3 Las siguientes frases del artículo contienen palabras que no conoces. A ver si puedes hacer correspondencia entre las frases de las dos columnas para adivinar el sentido de las palabras **en negrilla**.

1. ___c___ algo moderno, permanente y **novedoso**…
2. ___d___ El jean es muy dúctil… lo puedes **doblar**…
3. ___a___ puedes **guardarlo** sin que ocupe mucho espacio
4. ___b___ Hace ver **varonil** a cualquier hombre.

a. *you can **store** it without it taking up much space*
b. *It makes any man look **manly**.*
c. *something modern, permanent, and **novel**.*
d. *A pair of jeans is very flexible . . . you can **fold** it . . .*

4 Lee el siguiente artículo de un periódico ecuatoriano. ¿Hay palabras que escribiste para la **Actividad 2** en el artículo?

El jean impone su encanto

Los atractivos del jean han sobrepasado[1] los límites del tiempo y de las fronteras. Los clásicos pantalones jeans y los overoles todavía son populares y, además, les dan la posibilidad a sus usuarios de combinarlos de mil maneras. Se pueden usar hasta en ocasiones más elegantes si se usan con una chaqueta o con una blusa de seda o un saco de cachemira. Los beneficios de esta tela son innumerables. Por ejemplo, es común ver carteras de jean, zapatos con tacones de mezclilla y gorras, chalecos, chompas[2], sombreros, mochilas, monederos y otros accesorios de moda que rompen con los diseños tradicionales y se modernizan al usar esta tela tan tradicional y moderna a la vez.

Pero, ¿qué es lo que puede ofrecer el jean a los hombres y a las mujeres de esta época? Escuchemos sus testimonios.

"Usar jean es sentirse más joven, a pesar de la edad real que tengas".

"El jean es muy dúctil, por lo que lo puedes doblar y guardarlo sin que ocupe mucho espacio".

"Es resistente a cualquier trato".

"Se lava y sigue como si nada…"

"Puedes llevar libros o bloques de cemento, sabe cuál es su función".

"El cuero es para gente mayor. El jean siempre será[3] joven".

"Hace ver varonil a cualquier hombre".

"Es de los materiales más durables y que además no pasa de moda. Un jean puedes llevarlo años y mientras más rasgado, más en onda[4]".

Corbis/Glow Images

PhotoNAN/Shutterstock

"Los brazaletes de jean son súper chéveres[5]".

"El jean es discreto cuando debe serlo, pero también sensual cuando le has dado ese papel[6]".

"Sobre el jean puedes poner cualquier tipo de apliques…"

"Es de lo más práctico para vestir. Sólo necesitas un pantalón y falda y la mitad de tus problemas están resueltos[7]".

[1]**han**… *have surpassed* [2]**suéteres** [3]**va a ser** [4]**más rasgado**… *the more ripped, the more in style* [5]*cool*
[6]**le**… *you have given it that role* [7]*solved*

Adapted from "El jean impone su encanto," from El Comercio, Familia Magazine, Numero 643, February 8 1998, Ano XII, pg. 27. Used with approval from El Comercio.

Answers, Act. 6: 1. una chaqueta, una blusa de seda, un saco de cachemira 2. carteras, zapatos con tacones, gorras, chalecos, chompas, sombreros, mochilas, monederos. 3. *Answers will vary. Sample responses:* sentirse más joven, son muy flexibles, son resistentes a cualquier trato, son buenos para todas las situaciones, son varoniles, son durables, no pasan de moda, los puedes llevar años, son discretos pero sensuales, puedes poner apliques sobre los jeans, son muy prácticos.

Learning objectives: Analyzing, Creating

5 Vuelve a la lista de palabras y asociaciones que hiciste para la **Actividad 2.** ¿Te ayudó pensar en este tema antes de leer el artículo? ¿Pudiste predecir algunas de las ideas del texto? ¿Por qué sí o por qué no?

6 Trabaja con un grupo de tres o cuatro estudiantes. Juntos contesten las siguientes preguntas sobre la lectura.

1. ¿Con qué prendas de ropa sugiere el autor combinar los jeans?
2. ¿Qué otras prendas o accesorios son de mezclilla?
3. Hagan una lista de por lo menos cinco aspectos positivos de los jeans que se mencionan en los "testimonios".

7 Haz una encuesta sobre las prendas de ropa y accesorios de mezclilla.

1. Pasa por el salón de clase y pregúntales a tus compañeros las siguientes preguntas.
   - ¿Cuántos pares de jeans tienes? ¿De qué marcas *(brands)*?
   - ¿Tienes otras prendas o accesorios mezclilla? ¿Cuáles?
2. Escribe las respuestas.
3. Después, compara tus resultados con la clase entera. Haz un resumen para decir cuáles son las marcas de jeans más populares y también los accesorios de mezclilla más usados. ¿Son populares los jeans y los accesorios de mezclilla contigo y con tus compañeros de clase?
4. Con un(a) compañero(a) de clase, escriban una cita *(quotation)* como las de la lectura para expresar sus propios sentimientos sobre los jeans.

8 En la opinión de la gente de otros países, los jeans son un símbolo de Estados Unidos (junto con la hamburguesa y los autos grandes). Hablen en grupos sobre las siguientes preguntas. Luego, cada persona debe escribir un resumen corto de la conversación.

1. ¿Hay una diferencia entre una prenda de ropa muy popular y una prenda de ropa "tradicional"? Por ejemplo, en Perú y Ecuador, la ropa tradicional generalmente se refiere a la ropa que usa la gente indígena de la región andina. Los peruanos que viven en las ciudades usan estilos más modernos e internacionales.
2. En la opinión de ustedes, ¿existe una "ropa tradicional" de Estados Unidos"? (Piensen en las regiones geográficas y en los grupos étnicos del país.) Si existe, ¿cómo es?
3. Cuando la gente de otros países piensa en "la ropa típica" de Estados Unidos, ¿a qué tipo de ropa se refieren? En la opinión de ustedes, ¿es correcta o falsa esta imagen del estilo estadounidense?

A escribir

>> Antes de escribir

 Standard 1.3: In the writing sections, students present information to readers, who may often consist of their classmates.

ESTRATEGIA

Revising—Editing your freewriting

In **Chapter 7** you learned how to use freewriting as a way of generating a first draft. Once you have written freely, it's important to edit your work to tighten it up, make it more interesting, and make sure it's all relevant. When you edit your freewriting ask yourself: Is this information necessary? Would it be better placed somewhere else? Is there information missing? Can I tighten this up by omitting words and/or sentences?

1 Vas a escribir una descripción de lo que tienes en tu armario, qué artículos te gustan más y por qué. Antes de empezar, escribe tres categorías (o más) de artículos que contiene. Después añade tres artículos para cada categoría. Luego, pon un adjetivo al lado de cada de los nueve artículos (en total).

>> Composición

Learning objectives: Creating

2 Escribe una descripción de los artículos en tu armario, usando las categorías, artículos y adjetivos que anotaste en la **Actividad 1.** Habla de las categorías y los artículos en cada categoría. ¿Cuál te gusta más y por qué? Escribe sin detenerse y sin pensar demasiado en la gramática, el contenido o la ortografía.

>> Después de escribir

3 Vuelve a tu descripción. Mírala otra vez y contesta las preguntas de la Estrategia. ¿Cómo quieres revisar la información y organización de tu descripción? Analízala con cuidado y escribe la nueva (y probablemente más corta) versión.

4 Mira la nueva versión de tu descripción. Revísala, usando la siguiente lista.

- ¿Está completa la descripción?
- ¿Usaste las formas comparativas y superlativas correctamente?
- ¿Usaste bien los verbos y los tiempos verbales?
- ¿Hay errores de puntuación o de ortografía?

Vocabulario

Las prendas de ropa   *Articles of clothing*

el abrigo *coat*
la blusa *blouse*
las botas *boots*
los calcetines *socks*
la camisa *shirt*
la camiseta *t-shirt*
el chaleco *vest*

la chaqueta *jacket (outdoor non-suit coat)*
la falda *skirt*
el impermeable *raincoat*
los jeans *jeans*
los pantalones *pants*
los pantalones cortos *shorts*

el saco *jacket, sports coat*
la sudadera *sweatsuit, track suit*
el suéter *sweater*
el traje *suit*
el traje de baño *bathing suit*
el vestido *dress*

Los zapatos   *Shoes*

las botas *boots*
las sandalias *sandals*
los zapatos *shoes*

los zapatos de tacón alto *high-heeled shoes*
los zapatos de tenis *tennis shoes*

Las telas   *Fabrics*

Está hecho(a) de... *It's made (out) of . . .*
Están hechos(as) de... *They're made (out) of . . .*
   el algodón *cotton*
   el cuero / la piel *leather*
   la lana *wool*
   el lino *linen*
   la mezclilla *denim*
   la seda *silk*

a cuadros *plaid*
a rayas / rayado(a) *striped*
bordado(a) *embroidered*
de lunares *polka-dotted*
de un solo color *solid (color)*
estampado(a) *print*

Los accesorios   *Accessories*

la bolsa *purse*
la bufanda *scarf*
la cartera *wallet*
el cinturón *belt*

las gafas de sol *sunglasses*
la gorra *cap*
los guantes *gloves*
el sombrero *hat*

Las joyas   *Jewelry*

el anillo *ring*
los aretes / los pendientes *earrings*
el brazalete / la pulsera *bracelet*
la cadena *chain*

el collar *necklace*
el reloj *watch*
el oro *gold*
la plata *silver*

La moda   *Fashion*

(no) estar de moda *(not) to be fashionable*

pasado(a) de moda *out of style*

Ir de compras   *Going shopping*

El (La) dependiente   *The clerk*

¿Cuál es su talla? *What is your size?*
¿En qué puedo servirle? *How can I help you?*
Es muy barato. *It's very inexpensive.*
Está a muy buen precio. *It's a very good price.*
Está en venta. *It's on sale.*
Está rebajado(a). *It's reduced / on sale.*

¿Es un regalo? *Is it a gift?*
de buena (alta) calidad *of good (high) quality*
el descuento *discount*
la oferta especial *special offer*

El (La) cliente *The customer*

¿Cuánto cuesta(n)? *How much does it (do they) cost?*

Es (demasiado) caro. *It's (too) expensive.*

¿Lo (La / Los / Las) tiene en una talla...? *Do you have it / them in a size . . . ?*

Me queda bien / mal. *It fits nicely / badly.*

Me queda grande / apretado(a). *It's too big / too tight.*

Voy a llevármelo(la / los / las). *I'm going to take it / them.*

Voy a probármelo(la / los / las). *I'm going to try it / them on.*

Métodos de pago *Forms of payment*

¿Cómo desea pagar? *How do you wish to pay?*

Al contado. / En efectivo. *In cash.*

Con cheque. *By check.*

Con cheque de viajero. *With a traveler's check.*

Con un préstamo. *With a loan.*

Con tarjeta de crédito. *With a credit card.*

Con tarjeta de débito. *With a debit card.*

Los números mayores de 100 *Numbers above 100*

cien *one hundred*

ciento uno *one hundred and one*

ciento dos, etc. *one hundred and two, etc.*

doscientos(as) *two hundred*

trescientos(as) *three hundred*

cuatrocientos(as) *four hundred*

quinientos(as) *five hundred*

seiscientos(as) *six hundred*

setecientos(as) *seven hundred*

ochocientos(as) *eight hundred*

novecientos(as) *nine hundred*

mil *one thousand*

dos mil *two thousand*

tres mil *three thousand*

cuatro mil *four thousand*

cinco mil *five thousand*

diez mil *ten thousand*

cien mil *one hundred thousand*

un millón *one million*

dos millones, etc. *two million, etc.*

Comparaciones

más [noun / adjective / adverb] **que** *more* [noun / adjective / adverb] *than*

menos [noun / adjective / adverb] **que** *less* [noun / adjective / adverb] *than*

[verb] **más / menos que** [verb] *more / less than*

tan [adjective / adverb] **como** *as* [adjective / adverb] *as*

tanto(a) [noun] **como** *as much* [noun] *as*

tantos(as) [noun] **como** *as many* [noun] *as*

[verb] **tanto como** [verb] *as much as*

mayor *older; more*

mejor *better*

menor *younger; less*

peor *worse*

Pronombres de complemento indirecto

me *to / for me*

te *to / for you (fam. sing.)*

le *to / for you (form. sing.), him, her, it*

nos *to / for us*

os *to / for you (fam. pl.)*

les *to / for you (form., pl.), them*

Pronombres preposicionales

mí *me*

ti *you (fam. sing.)*

usted *you (form. sing.)*

él *him*

ella *her*

nosotros(as) *us*

vosotros(as) *you (fam. pl.)*

ustedes *you (form. pl.)*

ellos *them (male or mixed group)*

ellas *them (female)*

conmigo *with me*

contigo *with you*

Verbos

andar *to walk*

ayudar *to help*

conseguir (i, i) *to get, to obtain*

mandar *to send, to order*

morirse (ue, u) *to die*

prestar *to loan, to lend*

regalar *to give a gift*

sonreír (i, i) *to smile*

sugerir (ie, i) *to suggest*

Repaso y preparación

>> **Repaso del Capítulo 8**

Preparation: Have students review this material and complete the activities here, in the SAM, and online before they begin **Chapter 9.**

Complete these activities to check your understanding of the new grammar points in **Chapter 8** before you move on to **Chapter 9.**

The answers to the activities in this section can be found in **Appendix B.**

Check: The **Repaso** section not only reviews grammar and vocabulary for the student but offers a built-in performance assessment. By doing review activities with students, you can assess concepts that you may need to continue to reinforce in future classes.

Preterite tense of more irregular verbs (p. 280) and preterite tense of -**ir** stem-changing verbs (p. 283)

1 Completa las oraciones para saber qué pasó cuando David se reunió con su viejo amigo Ricardo ayer.

1. ____Supe____ (saber / yo) ayer que mi viejo amigo Ricardo está aquí de visita por una semana. Lo llamé y nosotros 2. ____hicimos____ (hacer) planes para hoy a las nueve de la mañana. Él 3. ____sugirió____ (sugerir) un restaurante para la reunión, pero yo 4. ____preferí____ (preferir) ir a un café. Después de que el camarero nos 5. ____sirvió____ (servir) el café, Ricardo me 6. ____dijo____ (decir) que él 7. ____quiso____ (querer) llamarme pero no 8. ____pudo____ (poder) porque 9. ____tuvo____ (tener) el viejo número. Entonces me 10. ____pidió____ (pedir) el nuevo número y lo 11. ____puso____ (poner) en su lista de contactos.

Salimos del café y 12. ____anduvimos____ (andar) por el centro por unas horas, hablando todo el rato. 13. ____Nos reímos____ (reírse) y 14. ____nos divertimos____ (divertirse) mucho y el tiempo pasó demasiado rápidamente. Al mediodía 15. ____nos despedimos____ (despedirse) y 16. ____dijimos____ (decir) adiós hasta la próxima vez.

Indirect object pronouns (p. 285)

2 Completa las oraciones con los pronombres indirectos correctos para saber qué recibieron las diferentes personas como regalo.

1. Mis padres ____nos____ regalaron unas botas de cuero a mí y a mi hermana.
2. Tu novio ____te____ regaló una bufanda de seda y unos aretes de oro.
3. A mis primos sus padres ____les____ regalaron unas gafas de sol buenísimas.
4. Mi amiga ____me____ regaló una bolsa de piel.
5. A Manuel sus hermanas ____le____ regalaron un abrigo nuevo.

Comparatives and superlatives (p. 289)

3 Completa las oraciones con formas comparativas (1–4) y superlativas (5–6), según el contexto.

1. Yo tengo ____tantos____ zapatos ____como____ tú. (=)
2. Ella compra ____más____ joyas ____que____ nosotras. (>)
3. Esta camisa es ____menos____ barata ____que____ ésa. (<)
4. Estas cadenas son ____tan____ caras ____como____ estas pulseras. (=)
5. Este collar es ____el____ ____más____ bonito de todos. (>)
6. Ella es la dependiente ____más____ popular de la tienda. (>)

>>

Preparación para el Capítulo 9 Learning objective: Evaluating

Preterite tense of regular verbs and some common irregular verbs (Chapter 7)

Complete these activities to review some previously learned grammatical structures that will be helpful when you learn the new grammar in **Chapter 9**.

In addition, be sure to reread **Chapter 8: Gramática útil 1, 2**, and **3** before moving on to the new **Chapter 9** grammar sections.

4 Completa las oraciones con la forma correcta del verbo indicado en el pretérito.

1. Tú ___compraste___ (comprar) la falda.
2. Yo ___vi___ (ver) una blusa bonita.
3. El traje ___estuvo___ (estar) en venta.
4. Ella me ___trajo___ (traer) otra talla.
5. Nosotros ___fuimos___ (ir) a otra tienda de ropa.
6. Tus abuelos te ___dieron___ (dar) los aretes.
7. Tú ___hiciste___ (hacer) esta gorra de lana.
8. Él ___escribió___ (escribir) el nombre de la tienda.

Direct object pronouns (Chapter 7)

5 Di si las personas indicadas compraron (o no) la prenda de ropa o accesorio. Sigue el modelo.

MODELO Marta
Marta no las compró.

Answers, Act. 5: 1. Delfina lo compró. 2. Diego y Eduardo no la compraron. 3. Tú no los compraste. 4. Yo los compré. 5. Nosotros las compramos. 6. Usted no lo compró.

1.

Delfina

2.

Diego y Eduardo

3.

tú

4.

yo

5.

nosotros

6.

usted

Reflexive verbs (Chapter 4)

6 Di qué se pusieron las personas indicadas ayer.

1. yo / un abrigo
2. ellos / unas sandalias
3. tú / un chaleco
4. nosotros / unos jeans
5. ella / una bufanda
6. ustedes / un impermeable

Answers, Act. 6: 1. Yo me puse un abrigo. 2. Ellos se pusieron unas sandalias. 3. Tú te pusiste un chaleco. 4. Nosotros nos pusimos unos jeans. 5. Ella se puso una bufanda. 7. Ustedes se pusieron un impermeable.

¿Qué te apetece?

SABORES

La comida da sabor (*flavor*) a las reuniones entre familia y amigos y juega un papel integral en todas las culturas del mundo.

A ti, ¿te importa mucho, bastante o poco lo que comes todos los días? ¿Comes para vivir o vives para comer?

Communication

By the end of this chapter you will be able to

- talk about food and cooking
- shop for food
- order in a restaurant
- talk about what you used to eat and cook
- say what you do for others

Ron Giling/PhotoLibrary Sabores

Un viaje por Bolivia y Paraguay

Globe Art: Adapted from Shutterstock/irrguest

Learning objectives: See pages AIE-3–AIE-4 for a complete description of the Bloom's Taxonomy learning objectives and an explanation of how they are integrated within *Cuadros*.

Bolivia y Paraguay comparten una frontera. Son los únicos países de Sudamérica que no tienen ni una costa pacífica ni una atlántica. Bolivia es mucho más montañoso que Paraguay, que tiene un clima más tropical y húmedo *(wet)*.

País / Área	Tamaño y fronteras	Sitios de interés
Bolivia 1.084.390 km²	casi tres veces el área de Montana; fronteras con Argentina, Brasil, Chile, Paraguay y Perú	el lago Titicaca, Tiahuanaco, el salar *(salt flat)* de Uyuni, las ciudades de La Paz y Sucre, los Parques Nacionales Amboró y Noel Kempff
Paraguay 397.300 km²	un poco más pequeño que California; fronteras con Argentina, Bolivia y Brasil	los ríos Paraguay y Paraná, la presa *(dam)* Itaipú, la región del Chaco, las misiones jesuitas, la ciudad de Asunción

¿Qué sabes? Di si las siguientes oraciones son ciertas **(C)** o falsas **(F)**.

1. Bolivia es más grande que California. C
2. Paraguay tiene edificios que fueron construidos por los misionarios jesuitas. C
3. Paraguay tiene un lago y unos ríos muy grandes. F
4. Bolivia y Paraguay son sitios buenos para excursiones al mar. F

Lo que sé y lo que quiero aprender Completa la tabla del **Apéndice A**. Escribe algunos datos que **ya sabes** sobre estos países en la columna **Lo que sé**. Después, añade algunos temas que **quieres aprender** a la columna **Lo que quiero aprender**. Guarda la tabla para usarla otra vez en la sección **¡Explora y exprésate!** en la página 335.

Suggestion: Have students describe the photo on the facing page as completely as possible and generate questions and answers about the photo to describe possible interactions. Use interrogatives as cues: ¿Quién(es)?, ¿Qué?, ¿De qué?, ¿Para qué?, ¿Por qué?, ¿Dónde?, ¿Cuánto(a)? ¿Cuántos(as)?

Check: At the beginning of this chapter, interview students to find out what they already know about Bolivia and Paraguay. At the end of the chapter, repeat your questions to assess what they have learned.

Cultures

By the end of this chapter you will have explored

- facts about Bolivia and Paraguay
- **la quinua**, a special food from Bolivia
- **el tereré**, a social tea tradition from Paraguay
- the metric system

¡Imagínate!

>> Vocabulario útil 1

Optional/Standards 2.1, 2.2, 3.1, 4.2: American students typically have little prior knowledge about Bolivia and Paraguay. Have them preview ¡**Explora y exprésate!** and research an aspect of daily life, history, art, or socioeconomic issues in Bolivia and Paraguay to present to the class and help students make connections and comparisons throughout the chapter.

CHELA: Quedamos en vernos a las ocho en punto en el **restaurante**. No llegó hasta las ocho y media. Cuando llegó, no ofreció explicaciones y no se disculpó. El **camarero** nos trajo los **menús** pero en ese momento sonó el celular de Sergio. Habló por teléfono —no sé con quién— por diez minutos enteros mientras yo esperaba. Por fin colgó y **ordenamos**. Yo pedí el **pollo asado** y él pidió el **lomo de res**.

Usage and meaning of **bocadillo** and **sandwich** vary throughout the Spanish-speaking world. In general, a **bocadillo** is made with a crusty bread similar to the French baguette. A **sandwich** is typically made of pre-sliced loaf-style bread.

Food terms vary tremendously from country to country and region to region. For example, *cake* can be **pastel** or **torta**; *pork* can be **puerco** or **cerdo**; *banana* can be **plátano**, **banana**, or **guineo**. When you travel, be prepared to come across a variety of foods that you don't recognize and different names for foods that you do.

Heritage Learners: The term *waiter* or **el camarero** has many variants. Ask students what other words they know for **camarero(a)**. Examples: **mozo(a)**, **garzón**, **mesero(a)**, **mesonero(a)**, etc. Often the variations are tied to dialects and the type of restaurant.

>> En el restaurante

Cómo ordenar y pagar

Camarero(a), ¿me puede traer el menú?	*Waiter (Waitress), could you please bring me the menu?*
Soy vegetariano(a) estricto(a).	*I'm a vegan.*
¿Me puede recomendar algo ligero / algo fuerte / algo vegetariano / algo vegano / la especialidad de la casa?	*Can you recommend something light / something filling / something vegetarian / something vegan / the house specialty?*
Para plato principal, voy a pedir...	*For the main course, I would like to order . . .*
Para tomar, quiero...	*To drink, I want . . .*
De postre, voy a pedir...	*For dessert, I would like to order . . .*
¿Me puede traer la cuenta, por favor?	*Can you bring me the check, please?*
¿Cuánto debo dejar de propina?	*How much should I leave as a tip?*

With a partner, go through all the items on the menu on page 309 and decide whether they are masculine or feminine. Check your answers in the **Vocabulario** section on pages 342–343.

Green beans are referred to as **habichuelas** only in the Caribbean. In Spain, they are referred to as **judías verdes**, and in other countries you might see them referred to as **vainas verdes**.

Notice: In many Spanish-speaking countries the restaurant bill is paid by one person and rarely divided up, as is often the custom in the U.S. You might want to share with your students that friends and relatives use the expression **te (le / os / les) invito** to offer to pay. The rationale is that everyone will pay the bill at some point and the cost will eventually even out. Point out that in some cases, offering to pay one's way might be considered bad manners. Be alert!

Suggestion: As you introduce the words on p. 309 to students, ask them about their preferences in each category: **¿Prefieres caldo de pollo o sopa de fideos?** Ask students which local restaurants specialize in particular items: **¿Qué restaurantes locales se especializan en mariscos / hamburguesas / pasta / pizza?** Have students identify what they would eat on certain occasions: **¿Qué tomas / ordenas / pides para una comida romántica / una comida rápida / una comida vegetariana? ¿Cuándo pagan tus padres o abuelos o cuándo paga otra persona?**

EL MENÚ

Desayuno

cereal	*cereal*
huevos revueltos	*scrambled eggs*
huevos	*eggs,*
estrellados	* sunnyside up*
pan tostado	*toast*

Almuerzo

Ensaladas

ensalada mixta	*mixed salad*
ensalada de	*lettuce and*
lechuga y tomate	* tomato salad*
ensalada de papas	*potato salad*

Sopas

caldo de pollo	*chicken soup*
sopa de fideos	*noodle soup*
gazpacho	*cold, tomato-based*
	* soup (Spain)*

Sándwiches (o bocadillos)

sándwich de	*ham and cheese*
jamón y queso	* sandwich with*
con aguacate	* avocado*
hamburguesa	*hamburger*
hamburguesa	*cheeseburger*
con queso	
perro caliente	*hot dog*
...con papas	*... with French fries*
fritas	

Bebidas y refrescos

café	*coffee*
té o té helado	*hot or iced tea*
agua mineral	*mineral water*
jugo de fruta	*fruit juice*
leche	*milk*
limonada	*lemonade*
vino blanco / tinto	*white / red wine*
cerveza	*beer*

A la carta

Vegetales

frijoles refritos	*refried beans*
zanahorias	*carrots*
bróculi	*broccoli*
espárragos	*asparagus*
guisantes	*peas*
habichuelas	*green beans*

Postres

flan	*custard*
galletas	*cookies*
pastel	*cake*
helado de vainilla /	*vanilla / chocolate*
chocolate	* ice cream*

Frutas

naranja	*orange*
manzana	*apple*
plátano	*banana*
fresas	*strawberries*
uvas	*grapes*
melón	*melon*

Platos principales

Carnes

lomo de res	*prime rib*
bistec	*steak*
chuleta de puerco	*pork chop*
guisado	*beef stew*
pollo asado	*roasted chicken*
pollo frito	*fried chicken*
arroz con pollo	*chicken with rice*

Mariscos

almejas	*clams*
camarones	*shrimp*
langosta	*lobster*

Pescados

atún	*tuna*
salmón	*salmon*
bacalao	*cod*
trucha	*trout*

ACTIVIDADES

Learning objectives: Understanding, Applying

C **1** **¡Tengo hambre!** Tienes mucha hambre. ¿Qué comes y bebes en las siguientes situaciones?

1. Te despertaste tarde y no tienes mucho tiempo para desayunar antes de ir a la oficina.
2. Acabas de correr cinco millas en una carrera para una organización benéfica *(charity)*.
3. Estás en una cita con una persona que es vegetariana y quieres dar una buena impresión.
4. Es tu cumpleaños y estás en un restaurante elegante con varios amigos para celebrarlo.
5. Tu jefe quiere salir a comer contigo para hablar sobre algunos problemas de la oficina.
6. Sales a cenar con tus padres para su aniversario.
7. Estás solo(a) en tu casa o apartamento.

Learning objective: Applying

2 **El menú** Con un(a) compañero(a), preparen un menú para las siguientes
C personas. Incluyan tres comidas y también algunas meriendas *(snacks)* si creen que le hacen falta a esa persona. Incluyan todos los detalles necesarios, incluso lo que debe tomar esa persona con cada comida o merienda.

1. una persona que está a dieta
2. una persona muy activa que necesita muchas calorías
3. una pareja que sale a cenar para celebrar su aniversario
4. un estudiante universitario que no tiene mucho dinero
5. una persona que acaba de despertarse y va a correr un maratón hoy

Standard 1.3:
In **Activities 2** and **3** students are asked to use presentational skills. By presenting through role-play, students will be able to express longer thoughts and ideas with more extended discourse than with the frequent question / answer format in the language class.

Optional: Suggest service learning **(aprendizaje-servicio)** beyond the classroom. Have students explore local opportunities for Spanish practice in community and religious centers in your area.

3 **En el restaurante** En grupos de tres, representen una de las siguientes
C situaciones. Pueden preparar un guión antes de representar la situación a la clase.

Situación 1: Es el cumpleaños de tu novio(a) y están en un restaurante elegante para la celebración. El (La) camarero(a) es un actor (actriz) a quien no le gusta su trabajo y en realidad no debe servirle comida a la gente.

Situación 2: Tu jefe te invita a cenar. Estás un poco nervioso(a) porque no sabes de lo que quiere hablar. El (La) camarero(a) es un(a) viejo(a) amigo(a) tuyo(a) y te hace muchas recomendaciones, pero tú no tienes hambre y no quieres lo que te sugiere.

¡Fíjate! El sistema métrico

Todos los países de habla española usan el sistema métrico para hacer medidas *(measurements)* como volumen, peso y longitud *(length)*. En el **Vocabulario útil 2**, vas a aprender las palabras **kilo**, **medio kilo** y **litro**. Aquí tienes las palabras para otras medidas métricas. (Nota que las medidas métricas se basan en unidades de un mil.)

Volumen Para indicar el volumen de algo, como agua en botella u otro líquido.

	cuartos	pintas	tazas	onzas *(ounces)* líquidas
1 **litro** (1.000 **mililitros**)	1,06	2,11	4,23	33,81
medio litro (500 **mililitros**)	0,53	1,06	2,16	16,91
cuarto litro (250 **mililitros**)	0,27	0,53	1,06	8,45

Peso Para indicar cuánto algo pesa; por ejemplo, doce naranjas o un pedazo de carne.

	libras	onzas
1 **kilo** (**kilogramo**) (1.000 **gramos**)	2,20	35,27
medio kilo (500 **gramos**)	1,10	17,64
cuarto kilo (250 **gramos**)	0,55	8,82

Longitud de cosas ordinarias Para indicar las dimensiones lineares, como un mantel para una mesa.

	yardas	pies *(feet)*	pulgadas *(inches)*
1 **metro** (100 **centímetros**, 1.000 **milímetros**)	1,09	3,28	39,37

Distancia y longitud de cosas grandes Para indicar las distancias y las dimensiones lineares de cosas más grandes.

	millas *(miles)*	yardas	pies
1 **kilómetro** (1.000 **metros**)	0,62	1.083,61	39,37

Práctica Con un(a) compañero(a), hagan conversiones entre las cantidades indicadas. Usen una calculadora o una aplicación si necesitan ayuda y redondeen *(round up)* al número entero más cercano *(round up to the nearest whole number)*. *(Answers round up over 0.5.)*

1. 2 litros = ___68 onzas líquidas___ onzas líquidas
2. 5 litros = ___11 pintas___ pintas
3. 3 kilos = ___7 libras___ libras
4. 125 gramos = ___4 onzas___ onzas
5. 12 metros = ___13 yardas___ yardas
6. 200 centímetros = ___79 pulgadas___ pulgadas
7. 5 kilómetros = ___3 millas___ millas
8. 2 metros = ___7 pies___ pies

Vocabulario útil 2

© Cengage Learning 2013

CHELA: Empezamos a comer. Inmediatamente, Sergio llamó al camarero. ¡Pobre camarero! Sergio fue muy descortés con él. Le dijo que la **sopa** estaba **congelada**, que el **bróculi** no estaba **fresco** ¡y que la **carne** estaba **cruda**! Mandó toda la comida a la cocina. ¡Qué vergüenza! No sabía qué hacer. Mientras esperábamos sus platos, **se enfriaron** los míos.

Suggestion: Practice these verbs by asking students to fill in the blanks orally. Examples: **Tengo que [pelar] las zanahorias para una ensalada (o las papas antes de cocerlas). Tengo que [freír] los huevos para preparar huevos fritos. Tengo que [mezclar] los ingredientes para preparar un pastel. Tengo que [unir] varios ingredientes para preparar una salsa mexicana. Tengo que [hervir] los huevos para hacer huevos duros.**

Suggestion: Have a chat with students about what they like to eat and what they know how to prepare. Lead with questions like: **¿Te gusta preparar la comida? ¿Qué sabes preparar / cocer / freír / hornear? ¿Qué métodos de cocina prefieres: cocinar al horno, a la parrilla, etc.? ¿Sabes preparar la comida al horno / a la parrilla / en el microondas? ¿Te gusta la comida frita? ¿Cuál es un ejemplo de comida frita? ¿Te gusta la comida picante / congelada / fresca / con mucha sal?**

Suggestion: Ask students: **¿Dónde se usan los kilos y dónde se usan las libras? ¿Qué cosas compras por kilo / por litro / …?**

>> Las recetas

Los ingredientes
el aceite de oliva *olive oil*
el ajo *garlic*
el azúcar *sugar*
la cebolla *onion*
la harina *flour*
la mantequilla *butter*
la sal y la pimienta *salt and pepper*
la mayonesa *mayonnaise*
la mostaza *mustard*
el vinagre *vinegar*

Las medidas *Measurements*
un kilo *kilo (approximately 2.2 lbs.)*
medio kilo *half a kilo*
la libra *pound*

el litro *liter*
el galón *gallon*
la cucharada *tablespoonful*
la cucharadita *teaspoonful*
la docena *dozen*
el paquete *package*
el pedazo *piece, slice*
el trozo *chunk, piece*

La preparación
a fuego suave / lento *at low heat*
al gusto *to taste*
al hilo *stringed*
al horno *roasted (in the oven)*
a la parrilla *grilled*
al vapor *steamed*

congelado(a) *frozen*
crudo(a) *raw*
dorado(a) *golden; browned*
fresco(a) *fresh*
frito(a) *fried*
hervido(a) *boiled*
molido(a) *crushed, ground*
picante *spicy*

agregar, añadir *to add*
calentar (ie) (en el microondas) *to heat (in the microwave)*
cocer (ue) *to cook (on the stove)*
enfriarse *to get cold*
freír (i, i) *to fry*
hervir (ie, i) *to boil*
hornear *to bake in the oven*
mezclar *to mix*
pelar *to peel*
picar *to chop, mince*
unir *to mix together, incorporate*

ACTIVIDADES

4 Picadillo boliviano Lee la siguiente receta para un picadillo boliviano. Con un(a) compañero(a), contesten las siguientes preguntas para ver si entendieron las instrucciones.

Learning objective: Understanding

PICADILLO

Ingredientes

15 papas peladas y cortadas al hilo
1/2 kg. de cadera de res
5 vainas de ají colorado molido y frito
2 cebollas
1 tomate
1 cucharadita de pimienta
1/4 cucharadita de comino
aceite
sal

Preparación

Pique la carne muy menuda, el tomate en cuadritos y la cebolla finamente picada. En una sartén con poco aceite, fría la cebolla hasta que esté transparente. Añada la pimienta, el comino, la sal al gusto y la carne. Cuando la carne esté dorada, agregue el tomate, deje cocer 5 minutos e incorpore el ají colorado y 1/2 taza de agua. Deje secar a fuego suave el guiso. Aparte fría las papas en abundante aceite caliente. En el momento de servir, una las papas y el guisado de carne. Mezcle bien.

© Cengage Learning 2013

1. ¿Qué debes hacer con las quince papas?
2. ¿Qué debes hacer con la carne antes de freírla?
3. ¿Cómo debes cortar el tomate?
4. ¿Qué debes hacer con la cebolla?
5. ¿Qué le vas a añadir a la cebolla después de freírla?
6. ¿Cuándo puedes agregar el tomate?
7. Después de agregar el tomate, ¿qué más le tienes que añadir al guiso?
8. Mientras el guiso se seca a fuego suave, ¿qué debes hacer con las papas?
9. ¿Qué debes hacer al final?

5 Telecocina Escoge una receta sencilla, como la del picadillo boliviano, y escríbela en una tarjeta. ¡Vas a explicarle a la clase cómo preparar tu plato favorito! Pero lo vas a tener que hacer sin estufa ni horno. La clase puede hacerte preguntas durante tu demostración. Imagínate que tu presentación se está transmitiendo por televisión.

Picadillo is a mincemeat, often spicy, that is typical of Latin America.

Suggestion: Point out the command forms (third-person singular) in the recipe. Take the opportunity to briefly review them.

Answers, Act. 4: 1. Pelarlas y cortarlas al hilo. 2. Picarla muy menuda. 3. En cuadritos. 4. Picarla finamente y freírla en una sartén con poco aceite hasta que esté transparente. 5. La pimienta, el comino, sal al gusto y la carne. 6. Cuando la carne esté dorada. 7. El ají colorado y media taza de agua. 8. Freírlas aparte en abundante aceite caliente. 9. Unir las papas y el guisado de carne y mezclar bien.

Heritage Learners: Find a recipe for **picadillo** from another country (Cuba, Mexico, etc.) and ask students to compare and contrast the recipes.

Optional, Act. 5: Vary by supplying several other simple recipes for the students to act out. Also, having students role-play a famous chef can add some humor to the presentation. Additionally, students can bring in ingredients and/or a finished product and present.

Preparation: Bringing paper plates, plastic utensils, cups, napkins, tablecloth, etc., is a good way to present and practice these words.

© Cengage Learning 2013

CHELA: Después de la cena, otro desastre. El camarero nos servía el café cuando sonó el celular de Sergio otra vez. Decidió tomar la llamada en privado. Al levantarse, se pegó en la **mesa** y tiró el café por todo el **mantel**.

DULCE: ¡Uy, qué horror! ¡Parece de película!

CHELA: Sí, ¡de película de horror! Y no me lo vas a creer, pero después de todo eso, ¡no le dejó propina al pobre camarero! ¡Yo tuve que regresar a dejársela!

>> **La mesa**

Cómo poner la mesa *Setting the table*

© Cengage Learning 2013

el mantel
el vaso
la taza
el cuchillo
la copa
el tenedor
el plato hondo
la servilleta
la cuchara
el plato

━━ **ACTIVIDADES** ━━

Tomar, not **comer,** is used to refer to eating soup.

Optional: Point out to students that the use of utensils varies in different cultures. For example, in some Spanish-speaking countries, cake is eaten with a spoon, while in others, it is eaten with a fork.

M **6** **¡Necesito un tenedor!** Un(a) amigo(a) da una cena para varios invitados y te pide que lo (la) ayudes. Al oír los comentarios de los invitados, te das cuenta de que necesitan ciertos utensilios. ¿Qué le hace falta a cada persona?

1. "No puedo tomar el caldo de pollo". una cuchara
2. "Me gustaría tomar un té caliente". una taza
3. "Quisiera un poco de agua mineral, por favor". un vaso
4. "Voy a abrir una botella de vino". unas copas
5. "No puedo cortar este bistec". un cuchillo
6. "Este arroz se ve delicioso". un tenedor
7. "¿En qué debo servir el gazpacho?" unos platos hondos
8. "Necesito algo para limpiarme las manos". una servilleta

M/C **7** **En el comedor** Dile a un(a) compañero(a) cómo poner la mesa, según el dibujo en la página 314. Sigue el modelo. (Vas a usar las preposiciones de locación que aprendiste en el **Capítulo 6**.)

MODELO mantel / mesa
Pon el mantel sobre la mesa.

1. cuchara / plato   Pon la cuchara al lado derecho del plato.
2. plato / plato hondo   Pon el plato debajo del plato hondo.
3. cuchillo / tenedor y plato   Pon el cuchillo entre el tenedor y el plato.
4. tenedor y cuchillo / servilleta   Pon el tenedor y el cuchillo sobre la servilleta.
5. taza / plato   Pon la taza enfrente del plato.
6. vaso / taza   Pon el vaso al lado de la taza.

8 **¡Ayúdame!** Necesitas ayuda para poner la mesa antes de que lleguen tus
C cuatro invitados. Pídele ayuda a un(a) compañero(a). Dile qué vas a servir y él o ella te dice qué vas a necesitar para poner la mesa. Sigue el modelo.

MODELO Tú: *Primero voy a servir una ensalada mixta.*
Compañero(a): *Vas a necesitar cuatro platos hondos y cuatro tenedores.*
Tú: *Para beber, voy a servir agua mineral y café.*
Compañero(a): *Vas a necesitar cuatro vasos y cuatro tazas.*

9 **La cena** En grupos de cuatro, representen la siguiente situación: Tú y
C tres amigos van a dar una fiesta para celebrar algo importante. Los cuatro se juntan para planear el menú. No están de acuerdo con varias decisiones:

- dónde va a ser la fiesta
- a quiénes van a invitar
- qué platos van a cocinar
- quién va a preparar qué platos
- cómo los van a preparar
- qué refrescos van a servir

Preparation: To prepare for **Act. 7**, have students use prepositions to tell you where to place items to set the table.

Preparation: To help students with place-setting etiquette, search *place setting placement* in Google images. Both formal and less formal place settings will appear. Some are line drawings that you can adapt and label. These are also useful to show regional differences such as European vs. North American place settings. To guide students in **Activity 7**, project a selected image during this activity.

Learning objective: Applying

Standard 1.3: This activity is in the presentational mode. Also encourage high beginners to research a variety of **menús** that can be found easily online for additional ideas.

A ver

ESTRATEGIA

Using visuals to aid comprehension

You can learn a lot from just looking at the visuals when you watch video. The scenes and images you see help you understand the language that you hear. Be sure to pay attention to the visuals as well as to the spoken conversation.

Antes de ver 1 En el video de este capítulo Chela describe la cena que tuvo con Sergio. Contesta las preguntas sobre lo que ya sabes de Chela y Sergio.

1. ¿Cómo es Chela? Piensa en tres adjetivos que la describan.
2. ¿Cómo es Sergio? Piensa en tres adjetivos diferentes que lo describan.

Antes de ver 2 Antes de ver el video, mira las fotos. Escoge la oración que exprese la idea principal de cada una.

© Cengage Learning 2013

1. ____b____   2. ____a____   3. ____c____

a. Parece que Sergio llegó muy tarde a la cita.
b. A Chela no le gustó nada la conversación telefónica que tuvo Sergio.
c. Sergio fue muy descortés con el camarero.

© Cengage Learning 2013

▶ **Ver** Mira el video. Presta atención a las imágenes mientras lo mires.

Después de ver Pon en el orden correcto estos ejemplos de la descortesía de Sergio.

___1___ "Habló por teléfono… por diez minutos enteros mientras yo esperaba".

___3___ "… Sergio llamó al camarero. ¡Pobre camarero! Sergio fue muy descortés con él".

___2___ "Habló de sí mismo por una eternidad y mientras hablaba no dejaba de arreglarse el pelo".

___4___ "… después de todo eso, ¡no le dejó propina al pobre camarero!"

Optional: Ask a student or two to volunteer a personal experience to the class: **¿Quién tuvo una mala experiencia en un restaurante alguna vez? ¿Qué pasó?**

Optional: Have a group conversation with the class: **¿Prefieres comer / cenar en un restaurante o prefieres comer / cenar en casa?** Introduce the concept of **comida casera** and ask students to give examples.

Learning objectives: Analyzing

Suggestion: Tell students that Chela's body language will be easy to follow in this video segment. Have students make a list of her gestures and facial expressions. There are also examples of expressive intonation that can be pointed out. Students can hear and practice this simple example: **por favor** (polite, pleading, asking for patience) and **por favor** (impolite, don't bother me with this).

▶ >> Voces del mundo hispano

En el video para este capítulo Michelle, Mariana y Cristina hablan de la comida y los restaurantes. Lee las siguientes oraciones. Después mira el video una o más veces para decir si las oraciones son ciertas (**C**) o falsas (**F**).

© Cengage Learning 2013

1. A Michelle le gusta mucho el saisi, que es un plato típico brasileño. F

2. Según Mariana, el silpancho tiene arroz, carne asada, un huevo y una ensalada de cebollas y tomates. C

3. El plato favorito de Cristina es la payagua mascada. F

4. A Michelle le gustan los restaurantes italianos y tailandeses, pero Mariana prefiere comer en restaurantes árabes. F

5. Cristina prefiere las churrasquerías, que son ideales para los vegetarianos. F

6. A Michelle le gusta comer en casa y en restaurantes también. C

◀)) >> Voces de Estados Unidos

Track 27

Aarón Sánchez, especialista en la comida panlatina

❝Hay que pensar en la comida latinoamericana en términos de varias superpotencias culinarias: la influencia afro-caribeña; el maíz, el arroz y los frijoles de Centroamérica; de Suramérica tenemos frutos frescos de mar *(seafood)*; Perú, la cuna *(cradle)* de las papas, y en Chile y Argentina, la influencia europea ❞.

WireImage/Getty Images

Hijo y nieto de dos prominentes chefs mexicanos, Aarón Sánchez es la personificación del proverbio "de tal palo, tal astilla" (*"a chip off the old block"*). Este joven originario de El Paso, Texas, es dueño *(owner)* de dos restaurantes en la ciudad de Nueva York, Paladar, de inspiración panlatina, y Céntrico, de comida mexicana. Además, es co-animador del programa de televisión "Chef vs. City" del Food Network y autor de *La comida del barrio*. En este libro, Sánchez explora la comida y cultura de La Pequeña Habana, Spanish Harlem, The Mission y otros barrios latinos. Sus recetas se enfocan en platillos caseros *(home-cooked dishes)* tales como la ensalada de nopales y camarones, la sopa de frijoles negros y el fricasé de pollo.

Optional: Have students do an informal in-class survey to determine the most popular Latino restaurants in your area. Then choose several restaurants and review directions from **Chapter 6.** Have students work in groups to give directions from campus to the restaurants.

¿Y tú? En tu opinión, ¿es importante mantener las tradiciones culinarias del pasado? ¿Por qué sí o por qué no?

¡Prepárate!

Gramática útil 1

Talking about what you used to do: The imperfect tense

Habló por teléfono, no sé con quién, por diez minutos enteros mientras yo **esperaba**.

Cómo usarlo

1. You have already learned to talk about completed actions and past events using the *preterite tense* in Spanish.

2. Spanish has another past-tense form known as the *imperfect tense*. The imperfect is used to talk about *ongoing actions* or *conditions* in the past.

3. Use the imperfect tense to talk about the following events or situations in the past.

   ■ to talk about what you habitually did or used to do

Todos los días, **desayunaba** a las ocho y luego **caminaba** a la escuela.	*Every day **I used to eat breakfast** at eight and then **I walked** to school.*

   ■ to describe an *action in progress* in the past

Vivíamos en Asunción con mi prima Enedina y sus padres.	*We were living in Asunción with my cousin Enedina and her parents.*

   ■ to *tell the time* in the past

Por lo general, **eran** las diez de la noche cuando **comíamos.**	*It was usually ten at night when we would eat dinner.*

   ■ to describe *emotional or physical conditions* in the past

Todos **estábamos** muy contentos y nadie se enfermó ese año. **Nos sentíamos** muy afortunados.	*We were all very happy and no one got sick that year. We felt very fortunate.*

   ■ to describe *ongoing weather conditions* in the past

Llovía mucho en Paraguay en esa época.	*It rained a lot in Paraguay during that time.*

   ■ to tell someone's *age* in the past

Enedina **tenía** quince años ese año.	*Enedina was fifteen that year.*

4. The imperfect tense is generally translated into English in different ways. For example, **comía** can be translated as *I ate* (routinely), *I was eating, I would eat,* or *I used to eat.*

Cómo formarlo

1. Here are the imperfect forms of regular verbs. Notice that **-er** and **-ir** verbs share the same endings, and that the **yo** and **usted / él / ella** forms are the same.

	cenar	comer	pedir
yo	cen**aba**	com**ía**	ped**ía**
tú	cen**abas**	com**ías**	ped**ías**
usted / él / ella	cen**aba**	com**ía**	ped**ía**
nosotros / nosotras	cen**ábamos**	com**íamos**	ped**íamos**
vosotros / vosotras	cen**abais**	com**íais**	ped**íais**
ustedes / ellos / ellas	cen**aban**	com**ían**	ped**ían**

> Notice the use of accents on the **nosotros / nosotras** form of **-ar** verbs, and on *all* forms of the **-er** and **-ir** verbs.

2. No verbs have stem changes in the imperfect tense, and there are only three verbs that are irregular in the imperfect.

	ir	ser	ver
yo	iba	era	veía
tú	ibas	eras	veías
usted / él / ella	iba	era	veía
nosotros / nosotras	íbamos	éramos	veíamos
vosotros / vosotras	ibais	erais	veíais
ustedes / ellos / ellas	iban	eran	veían

> **Ver** is irregular only in that the **e** is maintained before adding the regular **-er / -ir** imperfect endings.

3. The imperfect form of **hay** is **había**. Like **hay**, it is used with both singular and plural subjects: **Había un restaurante muy bueno allí. / Había algunos restaurantes muy buenos allí.**

> **Heritage Learners:** It is very common for heritage language speakers to spell the imperfect endings -aba, -abas, -ábamos, and -aban with v, rather than b. Call special attention to the correct spelling of these forms. Also, remind students that the imperfect endings -ía, -ías, -íamos, and -ían always take an accent over the i.

> **Heritage Learners:** Do not assume that if heritage learners can conjugate the imperfect, they can use it correctly. Research indicates that heritage learners have better control of the preterite than of the imperfect.

ACTIVIDADES

M **1** **Sergio** Sergio describe su vida cuando tenía catorce años. Cambia los verbos en sus oraciones al imperfecto para saber cómo era su vida.

1. <u>Me levanto</u> a las seis de la mañana todos los días. Me levantaba
2. <u>Tomo</u> el desayuno en casa. Tomaba
3. <u>Salgo</u> a correr dos millas antes de ir al colegio. Salía
4. <u>Voy</u> al colegio en autobús. Iba
5. <u>Almuerzo</u> en la cafetería del colegio. Almorzaba
6. <u>Tengo</u> clases hasta las cuatro de la tarde. Tenía
7. <u>Estudio</u> en la casa de mi novia hasta las ocho y media de la noche. Estudiaba

2 **Nuestros hábitos** Con un(a) compañero(a), túrnense para hacer

M/C oraciones completas con las palabras indicadas para expresar cómo eran sus hábitos con relación a la comida cuando eran niños(as). Sigan el modelo.

MODELO comer (yo) muchos vegetales
Comía muchos vegetales. / No comía muchos vegetales.

1. beber (yo) mucha leche (No) Bebía...
2. preparar (mis hermanos y yo) el desayuno (No) Preparábamos...
3. ir (mi familia) frecuentemente a un restaurante (No) Íbamos...
4. comprar (mis padres) frutas y vegetales orgánicos (No) Compraban...
5. cocinar (mi madre) muchos platos vegetarianos (No) Cocinaba...
6. poner (yo) la mesa para la cena (No) Ponía...
7. buscar (mis padres) recetas para platos nuevos (No) Buscaban...
8. lavar (mis hermanos y yo) los platos después de comer (No) Lavábamos...

Expansion: To practice the learning objective of Analyzing, follow up by having students compare what they did in high school with what they do now. For example, have them write five comparative sentence pairs: **En la secundaria siempre me acostaba antes de las 10 de la noche. Ahora me acuesto a las 2 de la mañana.**

3 **En la secundaria** Entrevista a un(a) compañero(a). Quieres saber más

C de su vida cuando estaba en la secundaria. Puedes usar las siguientes preguntas para tu entrevista, o puedes hacerle las preguntas que quieras. Túrnense para hacer la entrevista.

1. ¿A qué hora empezaban las clases?
2. ¿A qué hora te levantabas / desayunabas?
3. ¿Comías en la cafetería de la escuela o llevabas tu propia comida?
4. Si llevabas tu propio almuerzo, ¿quién lo preparaba?
5. ¿Qué comías de almuerzo?
6. ¿Trabajabas después de la escuela?
7. ¿Cuántas horas de tarea hacías?
8. ¿Participabas en algún deporte?
9. ¿Ibas a fiestas los fines de semana? ¿Solo(a) o con tus amigos?
10. ¿Eras miembro de algún club u organización en tu escuela?
11. ¿Tenías novio(a)?
12. ¿Qué hacías con tus amigos?

4 **Los veranos de mi niñez** ¿Cómo pasabas los veranos cuando eras

C niño(a)? Escribe una descripción de lo que recuerdas de los veranos de tu niñez o de un verano en particular que fue importante u horrible. Léele tu descripción a un(a) compañero(a) y escucha la descripción de él (ella). Usa las siguientes preguntas como guía si quieres.

- ¿Dónde pasabas los veranos? ¿Con quién(es)?
- ¿Qué hacías?
- ¿Qué te gustaba hacer? ¿Por qué?
- ¿Qué no te gustaba hacer? ¿Por qué?
- ¿Cuáles eran tus actividades preferidas del verano?

>> Gramática útil 2

Talking about the past: Choosing between the preterite and the imperfect tenses

Cómo usarlo

1. As you have learned, the preterite tense is generally used in Spanish to express past actions and describe past events that are viewed as completed and over. The imperfect is used to describe past actions or conditions that are viewed as habitual or ongoing.

2. Sometimes the choice between the preterite and the imperfect is not clearcut. It may depend on the speaker's judgment of the event. However, here are some general guidelines for using the two tenses.

No **sabía** qué hacer. Mientras **esperábamos** sus platos, **se enfriaron** los míos.

Preterite	Imperfect
1. Relates a *completed past action* or *a series of completed past actions*. **Comimos** en ese restaurante la semana pasada. Ayer, **fuimos** al restaurante, **pedimos** el menú, **comimos** y luego **salimos** para ir al teatro.	1. Describes *habitual or routine past actions*. **Comíamos** en ese restaurante todas las semanas. Siempre **íbamos** al restaurante, **pedíamos** el menú, **comíamos** y luego **salíamos** para ir al teatro.
2. Focuses on the *beginning* or *end* of a past event. La cena **comenzó** a las nueve, pero no **terminó** hasta medianoche.	2. Focuses on the *duration* of the event in the past, rather than its beginning or end. **Cenábamos** desde las nueve hasta medianoche.
3. Relates a *completed past condition* that is viewed as completely over and done with at this point in time (usually gives a time period associated with the condition). Manuel **estuvo** enfermo por dos semanas después de comer en ese restaurante, pero ahora está bien.	3. Describes *past conditions*, such as time, weather, emotional states, age, and location, that were ongoing at the time of description (no focus on beginning or end of condition). El restaurante **era** famoso por su comida latinoamericana y **estábamos** muy contentos con los platos que pedimos.
4. Relates an *action that interrupted* an ongoing action. Ya comíamos el postre cuando por fin Miguel **llegó** al restaurante.	4. Describes *ongoing background events* in the past that were interrupted by another action. Ya **comíamos** el postre cuando por fin Miguel llegó al restaurante.

Suggestion: Help visual learners by graphically representing the difference between the two tenses, drawing a time line on the board. For the preterite, a pinpointed past action and the beginning and end of a past event can be mapped. For the imperfect, a dotted line can represent time duration, and a habitual past action can be drawn with repeated dots.

Preterite

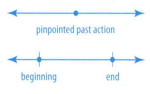

pinpointed past action

beginning   end

Imperfect

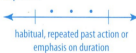

habitual, repeated past action or emphasis on duration

Heritage Learners: Linguistic research suggests that second-generation U.S. Hispanics overextend the use of the imperfect with verbs that refer to states of being: **era, estaba, tenía, había, podía,** and **quería**. On the other hand, these speakers prefer the preterite over the imperfect for the dynamic (action) verbs—**fue, corrió, habló**—and for verbs that occur instantaneously, such as **salir, llegar, sentarse,** and **caerse**. For this reason, it is important to review and practice the preterite–imperfect opposition with heritage language speakers.

Suggestion: Use the following sentences with students and have them justify using the preterite or imperfect: 1. El año pasado yo (visitar) Sucre. 2. (Pasar) dos semanas en la capital de Bolivia. 3. Después yo (ir) a Cochabamba para conocer a una amiga de mis padres. 4. Sabía que ella (ser) muy joven y guapa. 4. Ella (poder) hablar tres lenguas: español, inglés y una lengua indígena. 5. Ella me dijo que (conocer) a mis padres hace tres años. 6. Mis padres la (llamar) a ella para decir que yo iba a visitar Bolivia.

3. Certain words and phrases related to time may suggest when to use the imperfect or the preterite. These are not hard-and-fast rules, but general indicators.

Preterite	Imperfect
de repente (*suddenly*)	**generalmente / por lo general**
por fin (*finally*)	**normalmente**
ayer	**todos los días / meses / años**
la semana pasada	**todas las semanas**
el mes / el año pasado	**frecuentemente**
una vez / dos veces, etc.	**típicamente**

4. In **Chapter 8** you learned that some verbs (**querer, poder, conocer**, and **saber**) sometimes have a different meaning in the preterite tense. This change in meaning does not occur in the imperfect tense.

Cómo formarlo

Review the preterite forms presented in **Chapters 7** and **8**, as well as the imperfect forms presented in **Gramática útil 1** (on page 319 of this chapter).

ACTIVIDADES

I **5** **¿Qué pasó?** Escoge la forma correcta del verbo para completar cada oración.

1. Mis amigos y yo (comimos / comíamos) en ese restaurante todos los días. comíamos
2. Mi amiga me (preparó / preparaba) ese plato ayer. preparó
3. (Estamos / Estábamos) en el café cuando me llamaron. Estábamos
4. Ese restaurante (fue / era) muy popular por mucho tiempo. era
5. Mi hermano (trabajó / trabajaba) como chef por dos años. trabajó
6. Siempre (fuimos / estábamos) muy contentos después de comer allí. estábamos

M **6 Picadillo boliviano** ¡Pobre Amelia! Ella describe lo que le pasó cuando estaba preparando un picadillo boliviano para su familia. Escribe las oraciones según el modelo. Ponle mucha atención al uso del pretérito y el imperfecto.

MODELO   picar la carne / sonar el teléfono
Picaba la carne cuando sonó el teléfono.

1. pelar las papas / empezar a llover
2. freír la cebolla / entrar mi hermano a la cocina empapado (*drenched*)
3. cortar el tomate en cuadritos / llegar papá del trabajo muerto de hambre
4. añadir la sal, la pimienta y el comino / mi hermanito poner la tele
5. agregar el tomate / mi hermanita decidir ayudarme
6. preparar la carne / (ellos) anunciar en la tele que venir un huracán
7. secar el guiso a fuego suave / llegar mamá de la oficina
8. freír las papas en aceite caliente / empezar la tormenta
9. mezclar las papas y el guisado / sentarse todos a la mesa
10. servir el picadillo / cortarse la electricidad

◀)) **7 Los veranos de Chela** Escucha mientras Chela describe cómo pasaba los veranos cuando era niña. En un papel aparte, mira los verbos de la lista (abajo) y escríbelos en dos columnas como las siguientes. Mientras escuchas, escribe las formas de los verbos de la siguiente lista que oyes. Escribe las formas del pretérito en la primera columna y las formas del imperfecto en la segunda columna. **¡OJO!** Vas a escuchar más verbos de los que están en la lista. Sólo presta atención a los verbos de la lista.

Track 28
M

Acciones: visitar a los abuelos, vivir en un pueblo, llevar su computadora, sorprenderse, levantarse muy temprano, ir a dar una vuelta por el centro, estar triste, la computadora no funcionar, salir juntos, jamás usar la computadora

Completed action in the past	Action in progress or habitual action in the past
	visitaba

M **8** **¡Qué decepción!** Anoche, Ricardo y Elena fueron a un restaurante a cenar. Elena le describe la cita a su amiga Fernanda. Completa su descripción con las formas correctas del pretérito y del imperfecto de los verbos entre paréntesis.

Anoche Ricardo y yo (1. ir) a un restaurante elegante. No (2. tener) reservación y por eso no (3. sentarse) hasta las diez de la noche. Los dos (4. estar) muertos de hambre. Yo (5. ordenar) una ensalada mixta, pollo asado con habichuelas, flan y un café. Ricardo (6. pedir) una ensalada de papa, lomo de res y un helado de vainilla. Nosotros (7. hablar) de la película que (8. acabar) de ver cuando (9. regresar) el camarero a la mesa. Él nos (10. explicar) que no (11. haber) ni lomo ni pollo y nos (12. preguntar) si (13. querer) una hamburguesa. Ricardo (14. enojarse) mucho y le preguntó si por favor no nos (15. poder) recomendar algo más apetitoso. El camarero (16. sonreír) y (17. decir) que todo lo que (18. quedar) en la cocina (19. ser) ¡hamburguesas y papas fritas! Con el hambre que (20. tener) los dos, (21. decidir) ordenar las hamburguesas. Yo no (22. querer) dejarle buena propina porque había sido *(had been)* un poco descortés, pero Ricardo (23. insistir) en que no (24. ser) su culpa y le (25. dejar) una propina exagerada.

9 **Mi restaurante favorito** Con un(a) compañero(a), túrnense para hacer y
C contestar las siguientes preguntas sobre la experiencia que tuviste la última vez que comiste en tu restaurante favorito. Pon atención al uso del pretérito y del imperfecto.

1. ¿Con quién fuiste? ¿Qué hora era cuando llegaron al restaurante?
2. ¿Qué platos pidieron? ¿Cómo era la comida?
3. ¿De qué hablaron mientras comían?
4. ¿Comieron un postre? ¿Tomaron café?
5. ¿Cómo era el servicio? ¿Dejaron una propina buena para el (la) camarero(a)?
6. ¿Cómo se sentían al salir del restaurante?

C **10** **¡Qué horror!** A veces salimos con alguien que no conocemos muy bien y la cita es un desastre. Esto le pasó a Chela cuando salió con Sergio en el video. ¿Has tenido alguna vez una cita desastrosa? Escribe una narración que describa esa cita o una cita imaginaria. Incluye muchos detalles y pon atención al uso del pretérito y del imperfecto.

- ¿Adónde fueron?
- ¿Qué hicieron?
- ¿Qué pasó durante la cita?
- ¿Qué hizo él / ella que te avergonzó *(embarrassed you)* o molestó?
- ¿Cómo te sentías?
- ¿Cómo respondiste?
- ¿…?

>> Gramática útil 3

Avoiding repetition: Double object pronouns

Fundación Entreculturas | C/Pablo Aranda 3. 28006 Madrid |902 444 844| noticias@entreculturas.org | **www.entreculturas.org**

Courtesy of ONGD Entreculturas

What are the object pronouns in the name of this organization? Which is the direct object pronoun and which is the indirect object pronoun?

In **Díselo**, **se** is an indirect object pronoun and **lo** is a direct object pronoun. You can tell **se** is indirect because it comes before the direct object pronoun **lo** and because the phrase translates as *Tell it to him/her*. If students ask, the **te** in **Exprésate** is a reflexive pronoun.

Cómo usarlo

1. You studied direct object pronouns (**me, te, lo, la, nos, os, los, las**) in **Chapter 7**. In **Chapter 8** you learned to use indirect object pronouns (**me, te, le, nos, os, les**).

2. Remember that you use direct object pronouns to replace the direct object of a sentence. The direct object receives the action of the verb.

   Preparé **la comida**. → **La** preparé.

3. Remember that you use indirect object pronouns to replace the indirect object of a sentence. The indirect object answers the questions *For whom?* or *To whom?*

   Preparé la comida (para **ti**). → **Te** preparé la comida.

4. When you use direct and indirect object pronouns together, they are called *double object pronouns*.

   Preparé **la comida** (para **ti**). → **Te la** preparé.
   Organicé **un almuerzo** especial (para **ellos**). → **Se lo** organicé.

Cómo formarlo

1. Indirect and direct object pronouns stay the same when used together as double object pronouns, except in the third-person singular and third-person plural (**le** and **les**). In those two cases, the double object pronoun **se** replaces both **le** and **les** when used with the direct objects **lo, la, los,** and **las**.

Indirect object	Direct object
me	me
te	te
le → se	lo / la
nos	nos
os	os
les → se	los / las

2. Follow these rules for using double object pronouns.

- The *indirect object pronoun* always comes *before* the *direct object pronoun*. This is true whether the pronouns are used before a conjugated verb or attached to the end of infinitives, affirmative command forms, and present participles.

  Pedí una sopa. **Me la** sirvieron inmediatamente.
  Le dije al camarero: "Por favor, **tráigamela** con un poco de pan".

- Remember that with *negative command forms*, the double object pronouns must come *before the verb*.

  Quiero un postre, pero **no me lo traiga** inmediatamente.

- When double object pronouns are used with a conjugated verb followed by an infinitive, they may go *before the conjugated verb* or *attach to the infinitive*.

  Me lo van a servir ahora.   O: Van a **servírmelo** ahora.

- When using the direct object pronouns **lo, la, los,** and **las** with the indirect object pronouns **le** or **les,** change **le / les** to **se.** (Notice that you use **se** to replace both **le** and **les.)**

  Susana **le** llevó **los ingredientes** a Elena.

  Susana **se los** llevó (a Elena).

  Ileana y Susana **les** prepararon **la cena** a sus padres.

  Ileana y Susana **se la** prepararon (a sus padres).

ACTIVIDADES

I **11** Escoge los pronombres de doble objeto que mejor completen cada oración.

1. Al señor Martínez le encanta esa sopa. Sírva(sela / selo), por favor.
2. ¡No tienes cuchara! (Te la / Se la) voy a traer ahora mismo.
3. Nuestra abuela hacía un pastel muy rico. Siempre (nos lo / se lo) preparaba cuando veníamos de visita.
4. ¡Este guisado es fabuloso! Quiero la receta. ¿(Me la / Me las) das?
5. Este plato no está listo todavía. No (se lo / te lo) sirvas, por favor.
6. A mí me gusta mucho el flan. ¡Qué bien! Mi mamá esta preparándo(melo / selo) ahora mismo.

M **12** **Dulce en el restaurante** Dulce fue a un restaurante a comer. Completa su descripción de la cena con los pronombres dobles correctos.

1. Pedí el menú. El camarero ___me___ ___lo___ trajo inmediatamente.
2. Para plato principal, pedí una chuleta de puerco. ___Me___ ___la___ sirvieron un poco después.
3. También pedí unos frijoles refritos. ___Me___ ___los___ prepararon precisamente como me gustan.
4. Para postre, pedí unas galletas de chocolate. ___Me___ ___las___ trajeron con helado.
5. Para tomar, pedí un té helado. ___Me___ ___lo___ sirvieron bien frío.
6. Por fin pedí la cuenta. El camarero ___me___ ___la___ trajo rápidamente.

M **13** **Miguel** La mamá de Miguel le pregunta si ha hecho varias cosas para los diferentes miembros de su familia. ¿Cómo contesta Miguel? Sigue el modelo.

MODELO ¿Le serviste la leche a tu prima?
Sí, se la serví.

1. ¿Le preparaste el café a tu abuelo? Sí, se lo preparé.
2. ¿Les compraste las galletas a tus tíos? Sí, se las compré.
3. ¿Le serviste la sopa de fideos a tu hermano? Sí, se la serví.
4. ¿Nos trajiste las servilletas? Sí, se las traje.
5. ¿Te compraste unas galletas en la pastelería? Sí, me las compré.
6. ¿Me imprimiste la receta para el picadillo? Sí, te la imprimí.
7. ¿Les calentaste las tortillas a tus primos? Sí, se las calenté.
8. ¿Les dieron las gracias tus primos a tu hermana y a ti? Sí, nos las dieron.

M **14** **Adán y Adelita** El padre de Adán y Adelita cree que sus hijos sólo deben comer comida nutritiva. Nunca les compra comida rápida y no les permite comer postres llenos de azúcar. Primero, haz el papel del padre y contesta las preguntas de sus hijos. Luego, di si les compró o no les compró las comidas que querían.

MODELO **Adán:** Papá, quiero un perro caliente.
Papá: *Hijo, no te lo voy a comprar. O: Hijo, no voy a comprártelo.*
Tú: *Adán quería un perro caliente. Su papá no se lo compró.*

1. **Adelita:** Papá, quiero un helado.
2. **Adán y Adelita:** Papá, queremos unas hamburguesas.
3. **Adán:** Quiero unos plátanos.
4. **Adelita:** Papá, quiero una ensalada mixta.
5. **Adán y Adelita:** Papá, queremos unas papas fritas.
6. **Adelita:** Papá, quiero unas fresas.
7. **Adán:** Papá, quiero una galleta.

Track 29

M

15 A la hora de comer
Es la hora de comer en casa de Emilia Gutiérrez. La señora Gutiérrez le da instrucciones a Emilia. Escucha lo que le dice y escoge la frase que mejor complete sus instrucciones.

1. ___c___
2. ___h___
3. ___f___
4. ___g___
5. ___d___
6. ___b___
7. ___e___
8. ___a___

a. Ábremelo, por favor.
b. Prepáraselo, por favor.
c. Sírvesela, por favor.
d. Sírveselo, por favor.
e. ¿Nos las calientas, por favor?
f. Llévaselas, por favor.
g. Dáselo, por favor.
h. Tráemelo, por favor.

M/C

16 ¿Me lo haces?
Con un(a) compañero(a), representen la siguiente situación. Un(a) de ustedes está enfermo(a) y le pide unos favores al (a la) otro(a). Sigan el modelo y túrnense para representar los dos papeles.

MODELO preparar una sopa de pollo
Tú: *¿Me preparas una sopa de pollo?*
Compañero: *Claro. Te la estoy preparando / estoy preparándola ahora mismo.*

1. traer un suéter
2. pasar el control-remoto
3. escribir una nota para la farmacia
4. preparar mis platos favoritos
5. lavar los platos
6. mandar un e-mail al profesor

C

17 ¿Qué quieres para tu cumpleaños?
Con un(a) compañero(a), túrnense para representar la siguiente situación. Usen los pronombres dobles por lo menos dos veces en su conversación. Pueden practicar antes de representarle la situación a la clase. (Nota que los verbos **dar, traer, servir, preparar** y **comprar** frecuentemente requieren dos pronombres porque indican una acción hacia otra persona.)

Es tu cumpleaños y tus amigos quieren saber qué regalos quieres. Te van a dar una fiesta y también quieren saber qué comidas quieres. Eres muy exigente *(demanding)*: quieres muchas cosas y te gusta una variedad de cosas. Pide todo lo que te apetezca *(you desire)*.

MODELO Amigo(a): *¿Qué quieres para tu cumpleaños?*
Tú: *Me gustaría tener la nueva versión de Banda de Rock.*
Amigo(a): *Vamos a comprártela. ¿Y qué quieres comer?*
Tú: …

>> Gramática útil 4

Indicating for whom actions are done and what is done routinely: The uses of se

Cómo usarlo

You have used the pronoun **se** in several different ways. Here's a quick review of the uses you already know (items 1 and 2 in the chart), and one new use (item 3).

Al levantarse, **se** pegó en la mesa y tiró el café por todo el mantel.

Suggestion: Ask students if they can identify which use of **se** is demonstrated in the video caption. (reflexive)

Use **se** . . .	
1. to replace **le** or **les** when used with a direct object pronoun.	Marta **le** dio un regalo a Selena. Marta **se** lo dio.
2. with reflexive verbs, when using **usted / ustedes** and **él / ella / ellos / ellas** forms.	Ustedes **se** vistieron y salieron para la oficina. Ella **se** vistió después de duchar**se**.
3. to give general and impersonal information about "what is done."	**Se sirve** comida paraguaya en ese restaurante. ¡**Se come** muy bien allí!

Cómo formarlo

Se can be used to express actions with no specific subject and to say what "one does" in general. **Se** is always used with a third-person form of the verb.

- If a noun immediately follows the **se** + verb construction, the verb agrees with the noun.

  Se sirve el desayuno todo el día.   *Breakfast is served all day.*
  Se venden empanadas aquí.   *Empanadas are sold here.*

- If no noun immediately follows **se** + verb, the third-person singular form of the verb is used.

  Se come muy bien aquí.   *One eats well here.*
  Se duerme mal después de una comida fuerte.   *One sleeps badly after a heavy meal.*

Notice: This is a simplified explanation— a more complete one may confuse students at this level. If you feel your students can understand a higher level of explanation, tell them that the first construction is actually a passive sentence where the agent of the action remains unidentified. Here, the subject of the sentence is the noun that follows the verb, which is why the noun and verb must agree. The second construction has a subject as well, but it is identified only as the non-specific idea of "one" or "you."

Andy Dean Photography/Shutterstock

© Cengage Learning 2013

I **18** **Recomendaciones** Escoge la expresión que mejor complete cada oración.

1. (Se sirve / Se sirven) la cena a las 8:00 hasta las 11:00. Se sirve
2. (Se habla / Se hablan) el español en ese restaurante. Se habla
3. (Se come / Se comen) muy bien en esa cafetería. Se come
4. (Se vende / Se venden) frutas muy frescas en ese mercado. Se venden
5. (Se compra / Se compran) bastante barato en Tienda La Oferta. Se compra
6. (Se duerme / Se duermen) mal en esos hoteles. Se duerme
7. (Se relaja / Se relajan) mucho en el Spa Oasis. Se relaja
8. (Se busca / Se buscan) cocineros con cinco años de experiencia. Se buscan

M **19** **Observaciones** Usando la construcción impersonal con **se**, di cómo es la experiencia de uno en las siguientes situaciones.

MODELO (Ver) muy bien desde aquí.
Se ve muy bien desde aquí.

1. (Trabajar) muy duro en la clase de física. Se trabaja muy duro en la clase de física.
2. (Dormir) muy bien en ese hotel. Se duerme muy bien en ese hotel.
3. (Ver) mucho de la ciudad desde esa ventana. Se ve mucho de la ciudad desde esa ventana.
4. (Aprender) mucho en esa clase. Se aprende mucho en esa clase.
5. (Cenar) muy bien en el restaurante Paraíso. Se cena muy bien en el restaurante Paraíso.
6. (Oír) muy bien con esos audífonos. Se oye muy bien con esos audífonos.

Learning objective: Creating

C **20** **Los anuncios clasificados** Vas a escribir unos anuncios clasificados para el periódico universitario. Algunas personas te describen lo que necesitan o buscan. Escribe la primera línea de cada anuncio según lo que te dicen.

MODELO —Me voy a graduar este año y tengo muchos libros usados que quiero vender.
Se venden libros usados.

1. —Soy director y quiero montar *(put together)* una obra de teatro. Busco tres actores y una actriz. Se buscan tres actores y una actriz para obra de teatro.
2. —Vamos a hacer un Festival Boliviano y necesitamos voluntarios para ayudar con todos los detalles. Se necesitan voluntarios para el Festival Boliviano.
3. —Voy a estudiar al extranjero este semestre y quiero alquilar mi apartamento. Se alquila apartamento.
4. —Para las Navidades queremos darles ropa y juguetes a los niños pobres. Aceptamos donaciones de ropa y juguetes usados. Se aceptan donaciones de ropa y juguetes usados.

Sonrisas

© Cengage Learning 2013

Expresión En grupos de tres o cuatro estudiantes, contesten las siguientes preguntas sobre la tira cómica.

1. ¿Por qué se usa un verbo singular con los dos primeros letreros?
2. ¿Por qué se usa un verbo plural con los dos últimos letreros?
3. ¿Crees que el niño va a recibir dinero de la gente que ve su letrero? ¿Por qué?
4. Piensen en unos letreros cómicos para los siguientes lugares. Luego, compartan sus ideas con otro grupo. ¿Qué grupo tiene los letreros más creativos?
   a. restaurante
   b. tienda
   c. hospital
   d. consultorio *(office)* de un dentista
   e. taller de un mecánico
   f. la pizarra en la clase de español

Standard 5.2: The communities standard is met as learners experience the wit, wisdom, and common sense of a vignette that exemplifies a learning moment for life and humor that promotes personal enjoyment in the target language.

Optional: Have students explain the **Sonrisas** cartoon in their own words in Spanish to check their comprehension.

¡Explora y exprésate!

Bolivia

 Standards 2.1, 2.2: Here students gain knowledge and understanding of Bolivian and Paraguayan culture and explore cultural products such as diverse languages, foods, music, and archaelogical ruins from the pre-Incan period.

Check: Review your list of what students want to know about Bolivia and Paraguay from the beginning of the chapter. Address select items here and during the **¿Quieres saber más?** section. Since cultural information is always evolving, this allows collective classroom knowledge to go beyond the text.

Celso Diniz/Shutterstock

Información general

Nombre oficial: Estado Plurinacional de Bolivia

Población: 9.947.418

Capitales: Sucre (poder judicial) (350.000 hab.) y La Paz (sede del gobierno) (f. 1548) (900.000 hab.)

Otras ciudades importantes: Santa Cruz de la Sierra (1.800.000 hab.), Cochabamba (1.200.000 hab.), El Alto (900.000 hab.)

Moneda: peso (boliviano)

Idiomas: español, quechua, aimara

Mapa de Bolivia: Apéndice D

Image Asset Management/age fotostock

Vale saber…

- Hay varias civilizaciones prehispánicas en Bolivia. Las más importantes son las culturas Chiripa y Wankarani en el altiplano y la de Tiahuanaco cerca del lago Titicaca.

- La colonización española empieza en 1535 y termina en 1826 cuando el libertador Simón Bolívar presenta la primera Constitución al país. Bolivia recibe su nombre del héroe de la independencia de cinco países sudamericanos.

- Es el único país en Latinoamérica con dos capitales. La Paz es la capital administrativa del gobierno y Sucre es la capital constitucional.

- Con la promesa de la justicia social para todos, Evo Morales es el primer miembro de la mayoría indígena elegido presidente en 2005. Fue reelegido en 2009.

Paraguay

Christopher Pillitz/Getty Images

Información general ▶

Nombre oficial: República del Paraguay

Población: 6.375.830

Capital: Asunción (f. 1537) (690.000 hab.)

Otras ciudades importantes: Ciudad del Este (320.000 hab.), San Lorenzo (300.000 hab.)

Moneda: guaraní

Idiomas: español y guaraní (oficiales)

Mapa de Paraguay: Apéndice D

Vale saber...

- Los españoles empiezan a llegar a Paraguay en el siglo XVI. Asunción se funda en 1536 por el explorador español Juan de Salazar de Espinosa.

- Las misiones jesuitas de Latinoamérica fueron construidas *(were constructed)* por la orden religiosa Compañía de Jesús entre 1609 y 1678. Estos misioneros jesuitas españoles y portugueses viajaron a las áreas más remotas de Sudamérica donde establecieron misiones, convirtieron a los indígenas al catolicismo y les enseñaron su idioma.

- Paraguay declara la independencia de España en 1813, siendo el primer país latinoamericano que se proclama república.

Kevin Moloney/Getty Images

- Paraguay siempre ha sido *(has been)* un país bilingüe y bicultural. Se calcula que el 90% de sus habitantes hablan español y guaraní, el idioma de sus pobladores antes de la llegada de los españoles. Las escuelas, las oficinas del gobierno y los medios de comunicación se comunican con el pueblo paraguayo en los dos idiomas.

John Warburton-Lee/Photolibrary

J. Pfeiffer/ ARCO /age fotostock

La quinua boliviana

Bolivia es el primer productor mundial de la quinua, una planta alimenticia que se ha cultivado *(has been grown)* en los Andes desde hace cinco mil años. Para los incas, la quinua era un alimento sagrado *(sacred)*, segundo en importancia solo a la papa. La quinua tiene un gran valor nutricional por varias razones: su contenido de proteína es muy alto; contiene aminoácidos esenciales para el desarrollo humano que no ofrecen ni el arroz ni el trigo *(wheat)*; es pobre en grasas; no contiene gluten; y es fácil de digerir *(digest)*. Por todas sus propiedades nutricionales, NASA está examinando la posibilidad de mandar la quinua al espacio en vuelos *(flights)* de larga duración. De los incas a los astronautas, la quinua sigue alimentando al humano de una manera sabrosa y saludable.

Jorge AdornoReuters /Landov

El tereré paraguayo

El tereré es mucho más que un té, es toda una tradición paraguaya. El tereré se prepara con yerba mate y agua fría. Si hace mucho calor, se añade hielo *(ice)*. Hay muchas maneras de preparar el tereré, hasta se pueden añadir hierbas naturales como la menta para darle distintos sabores. El tereré no es sólo delicioso, refrescante, sano y natural, sino también calma la sed, no contiene azúcar y es una buena alternativa al agua natural para mantenerse hidratado, especialmente en épocas de mucho calor. El tereré se prepara en la guampa, un tipo de vaso de madera *(wood)* o de cuerno de vaca *(cow's horn)*. El rito *(ritual)* de pasar la guampa entre la ronda de amigos es la parte más importante de la costumbre paraguaya, porque el tereré no sólo es un té, es un evento social.

Standards: Here students gain knowledge of Bolivian and Paraguayan culture (C 2.1) and compare and contrast (C 4.2) with the U. S.

La información general

1. ¿En qué capacidad funcionan las dos capitales de Bolivia?
2. ¿Qué heroe de la independencia sudamericana le da su nombre a Bolivia?
3. ¿Cómo se distingue Evo Morales de todos los presidentes bolivianos?
4. ¿Qué orden religiosa tuvo un gran impacto en el idioma de los indígenas paraguayos?
5. ¿Qué hace Paraguay en 1813 que lo distingue de otros países latinoamericanos?
6. El gobierno paraguayo usa dos idiomas para comunicarse con la gente. ¿Cuáles son?

El tema de los alimentos

1. ¿De qué planta alimenticia es Bolivia el primer productor mundial?
2. ¿Por qué la quinua tiene un gran valor nutricional?
3. ¿Por qué el tereré es bueno en épocas de mucho calor?
4. ¿Qué parte del rito de tomar el tereré es la más importante?

⊕ ¿QUIERES SABER MÁS?

Revisa y rellena la tabla que empezaste al principio del capítulo. Luego, escoge un tema para investigar en línea y prepárate para compartir la información con la clase.

También puedes escoger de las palabras clave a continuación o en **www.cengagebrain.com**.

Palabras clave: (Bolivia) los incas, los aimaraes, Carnaval de Oruro, Festival de la Virgen de Urkupiña, Jaime Escalante, Evo Morales; **(Paraguay)** guaraníes, misiones jesuitas, la Guerra del Paraguay, Augusto Roa Bastos, Olga Bliner

---

⊕ **Tú en el mundo hispano** Para explorar oportunidades de usar el español para estudiar o hacer trabajos voluntarios o aprendizajes en Bolivia y Paraguay, sigue los enlaces en **www.cengagebrain.com**.

⊗ **Ritmos del mundo hispano** Sigue los enlaces en **www.cengagebrain.com** para escuchar música de Bolivia y Paraguay.

Learning objectives: Understanding, Remembering

Answers, Act. 1: 1. La Paz es la capital administrativa y Sucre es la capital constitucional. 2. Simón Bolívar 3. Es el primer miembro de la mayoría indígena elegido presidente. 4. La Compañía de Jesús o los jesuitas 5. se reclama república 6. español y guaraní

Answers, Act. 1: 1. la quinua 2. su contenido de proteína es muy alto; contiene aminoácidos esenciales; es pobre en grasas; no contiene gluten; es fácil de digerir 3. porque es refrescante, calma la sed y ayuda mantenerse hidratado 4. pasar la guampa entre la ronda de amigos

Learning objectives: Analyzing, Evaluating

⑤ **Standard 5.1:** Here students are encouraged to do independent web research on topics that will gradually require more Spanish to carry out the assignments by introducing more participation with Spanish-speaking communities online.

Check: Students do research here to be able to investigate other things that they want to know about Bolivia and Paraguay. They can account for what they have learned in the chart from the beginning of the chapter.

Check: Reviewing the table of information from earlier in the chapter provides a ready list of student-generated items for them to research.

A leer

ESTRATEGIA

Setting a time limit

You have learned strategies to help you focus on getting the main idea without becoming too bogged down in the details. Another good way to do this is to set a time limit. Reading under deadline pressure forces you to focus on what's important, rather than on trying to understand every single word.

There are two irregular future tense forms in the reading: **habrá** and **podrán**. Can you guess what they mean? (Hint: they are two irregular verbs used frequently in Spanish.) You will learn more about the future tense in **Chapter 13**.

Recognizing word families helps expand your vocabulary. The word **cría** is used twice in the reading with two different meanings: the raising of a crop and the young trout. Based on this, can you guess what **un criadero** and the phrase **el pescado criado** mean?

1 Vas a leer un artículo sobre la piscicultura, o el cultivo de peces, en una laguna cerca del pueblo boliviano de Botijlaca. La piscicultura da esperanza *(hope)* a los pobladores *(residents)* de Botijlaca, quienes ganan más bolivianos–la moneda nacional de Bolivia–por sus cosechas *(harvests)* de trucha que por el trabajo en las otras industrias de la región.

2 El artículo describe la vida de los residentes de Botijlaca y la región cercana. Para familiarizarte con el vocabulario desconocido, haz correspondencia entre las palabras de la izquierda y la derecha.

1. el centro paceño c
2. el nivel del mar e
3. el pastoreo de llamas y ovejas f
4. las familias madrugan a
5. en cuyas orillas se llevará a cabo la feria i
6. una decena de truchas j
7. son resbalosas y sin escamas d
8. la siembra fue en noviembre pasado b
9. anclar redes y cosechar todos los peces h
10. fueron degustados por un centenar de visitantes g

a. *the families get up early*
b. *the stocking (of fish) was last November*
c. *the center of La Paz*
d. *they are slippery and without scales*
e. *sea level*
f. *the shepherding of llamas and sheep*
g. *they were tasted by about 100 visitors*
h. *to anchor the nets and harvest all the fish*
i. *on whose shores the fair will take place*
j. *(a unit of) ten trout*

Answers, Act. 3: tasty, soft; dry, hard

3 En el artículo se usan varias palabras para describir la carne de trucha, según el método de criarla. Basándote en palabras que ya conoces, ¿puedes adivinar el significado de estas palabras?

- Características positivas: sabrosa, suave
- Características negativas: seca, dura

4 Ahora, vas a leer el artículo por primera vez. Trata de entender sólo las ideas principales y leer el artículo completo en 15 o 20 minutos.

LECTURA

Botijlaca

El pueblo se abre al turismo gracias a la trucha

por Aleja Cuevas Pacohuanca

La producción piscícola devuelve la esperanza a Botijlaca, una pequeña comunidad del Valle de Zongo. En particular, la cría de trucha entusiasma a los pobladores de este lugar, que después de mucho tiempo advierten la posibilidad de mejorar su economía.

Además de consumirlo y venderlo, el pescado de carne rosada promete[1] ser un atractivo para la región. La trucha nada en las aguas frías de la laguna Viscachani.

Botijlaca se encuentra a una hora y media de viaje del centro paceño, es la primera comunidad de las 13 que tiene el Valle de Zongo. Está situada a 3.492 metros sobre el nivel del mar.

La población cuenta con[2] 60 familias. Mientras las mujeres se dedican al pastoreo de llamas y ovejas, los hombres trabajan de manera eventual en una de las plantas hidroeléctricas de la Compañía Boliviana de Energía Eléctrica (Cobee) que se encuentra en el lugar, al norte de la ciudad de La Paz.

La Feria de la Trucha

Muy temprano, las familias madrugan para ser parte de la Primera Feria Productiva y de la Trucha. Domitila Alaña, cargada[3] de su pequeño hijo, camina hacia la laguna Viscachani, en cuyas orillas se llevará a cabo la feria. Dice que allá habrá muchos platos preparados con trucha.

Aurelio Vargas, vicepresidente de la Asociación de Piscicultura de Botijlaca, que cuenta con

Aleja Cuevas

25 socios[4], acaba de pescar una decena de truchas, agarra[5] una y la muestra, son resbalosas y sin escamas. "Hace dos semanas —cuenta— que empezamos a sacar los pescados y ahora estamos promocionando la primera cosecha".

Alaña recuerda que antes no había mucho pescado en la zona, pero gracias a un proyecto piscícola impulsado por el municipio se introdujeron más de 5.000 alevines (crías de truchas) en Viscachani. Ahora, siete meses después, están listos para el consumo. [...]

Así, la producción masiva de truchas abre la posibilidad de desarrollar[6] proyectos turísticos en la comunidad. Por ejemplo, se pretende[7] construir cabañas para dar hospedaje y alimentación[8] a los visitantes. Éstos también podrán pescar. "Mi esposo gana al mes 800 bolivianos en Cobee, ya no conviene, por eso vamos a dedicarnos al turismo", cuenta Domitila. [...]

Según la alcadesa[9] [de Zongo, Erlinda Quispe], un próximo proyecto se orienta a la producción de otros pescados, como las carpas, en la población de Huaylipaya. "En Zongo existe constantemente agua y se tiene que aprovechar[10]".

---

[1]*promises* [2]*includes* [3]*weighed down with* [4]*associates* [5]*grabs* [6]*to develop* [7]*esperan* [8]**hospedaje:** *lodging and food* [9]*mayor* [10]*to take advantage*

Aleja Cuevas

El grande devora al chico

El técnico del Centro de Investigación y Desarrollo Acuícola Boliviano (CIDAB) Santos Saavedra, encargado de hacer la reproducción de la trucha en Botijlaca, indica que en la laguna se colocaron[11] 5.000 alevines de cinco gramos, los que fueron traídos[12] desde las aguas del lago Titicaca.

En ocho meses, la trucha alcanza[13] un peso de 300 gramos, ideal para el consumo y la venta, refiere el técnico. La siembra fue en noviembre pasado. Los peces de los criaderos del lago deben llegar a pesar 700 gramos.

Pero según explica, el pescado criado en una laguna que contiene alimento natural (pequeñas larvas, por ejemplo), como es el caso de Viscachani, alcanza un mejor desarrollo, al menos es más sano. "Con alimento natural, la trucha llega a ser más sabrosa y suave, mientras que en un criadero la carne es seca y dura".

Por su experiencia, lo que corresponde hacer con las truchas de la laguna Viscachani es anclar redes y cosechar todos los peces. "Hay que sacarlas a todas (truchas) —explica Saavedra— para volver a introducir alevines; si colocamos los peces pequeños, los grandes se los devoran, porque las truchas son carnívoras".

En la feria, Aurelio Vargas y otros socios de la Asociación pescaron cerca de dos arrobas[14] de trucha. El pescado fue preparado en diversas formas: frito, ahumado[15], a la parrilla… En tanto, los platos fueron degustados por un centenar de visitantes, quienes, a su vez, disfrutaron de[16] un paisaje de montañas rocosas en medio de las cuales se advierten hilos de agua cristalina.

[11]were placed [12]were brought [13]reaches [14]a unit of measurement that varies between 11 and 16 kilograms; in this region the number is approximately 11.5 kilos [15]smoked [16]enjoyed

5 Di si las siguientes oraciones sobre la lectura son ciertas o falsas.

_____C_____ 1. Botijlaca es una comunidad situada al norte de La Paz.

_____F_____ 2. Antes de la llegada de la industria piscícola, la mayoría de los hombres en Botijlaca trabajaban como pastores *(shepherds)*.

_____C_____ 3. La Primera Feria Productiva y de la Trucha se celebró cerca de la laguna Viscachani.

_____F_____ 4. Siempre había mucho pescado en la laguna, porque es un sitio tradicional para la pesca.

_____F_____ 5. La carne de las truchas de los criaderos es más sabrosa porque las truchas comen alimento natural.

_____C_____ 6. Los pescadores tienen que sacar todas las truchas al mismo tiempo, porque si no lo hacen, las truchas grandes comen los alevines que se introducen en la laguna más tarde.

6 Escoge la respuesta que mejor complete cada oración. Vuelve a la lectura para buscar la respuesta, si es necesario.

1. Los pescadores sacaron la primera cosecha de truchas hace _____b_____.
   a. diez días   b. dos semanas

2. El proyecto piscícolo fue una iniciativa _____b_____.
   a. de Cobee   b. del municipio

3. Los alevines están listos para el consumo _____b_____ después de su introducción a la laguna.
   a. dos semanas   b. siete meses

4. Los hombres ganan 800 bolivianos al mes _____a_____.
   a. en Cobee   b. como parte de este proyecto

5. En el futuro, el próximo proyecto va a ser la producción de _____a_____
   a. otros pescados   b. otros centros para el turismo

6. El peso ideal para el consumo y la venta de la trucha es _____a_____.
   a. 300 gramos   b. 700 gramos

> **Hace** plus a unit of time means *...ago*. Here, **hace diez días** is *ten days ago* and **hace dos semanas** is *two weeks ago*. You will learn more about this structure in **Chapter 10**.

7 En un grupo de tres o cuatro estudiantes, hablen de otros pueblos, ciudades, regiones o países que tengan ferias dedicadas a la comida o la bebida. ¿Conocen algunas de las siguientes? ¿Qué otras conocen? ¿Les gustan las ferias de la comida y la bebida? ¿Por qué sí o no?

- La Feria de la Ostra *(Oyster)*, Galway, Irlandia
- La Feria del Mango, Nuevo Delhi, India
- La Tomatina, Buñol, España
- El Campeonato Mundial del Pastel de Crema, Coxheath, UK
- La Feria de la Hamburguesa, Seymour, Wisconsin
- La Feria del Ajo, Gilroy, California

Expansion, Act. 6: Have students work in pairs to identify and research a famous food festival. Pairs should write a description of the festival and present it to the class.

A escribir

ESTRATEGIA

Writing—Writing a paragraph

You have learned that a paragraph's topic sentence (**oración temática**) tells the reader its main idea. That sentence is followed by examples and details that illustrate it, as you learned in **Chapter 6**. Think of a paragraph as a separate composition that contains a main idea followed by supporting facts and examples. When you move on to a new idea, you create a new paragraph.

1 Trabaja con un(a) compañero(a) de clase. Van a escribir tres párrafos cortos que describan una experiencia con la comida. Escojan uno de los siguientes temas y piensen en una historia que quieren contar:

1. la primera vez que cociné
2. la primera vez que fui a un restaurante elegante
3. mis experiencias culinarias en un país extranjero

2 Después de establecer su tema, miren la tabla y complétenla, usando las oraciones modelo como guía.

	Oración temática (que comunica la idea principal del párrafo)	Detalles y ejemplos que ilustran la oración temática
Párrafo 1: Comienzo / fondo *(background)* de la historia (Recuerden que se usa el imperfecto para describir.)	*Yo tenía trece años y tenía una familia muy grande.*	*Era el menor de seis hijos y a veces me sentía un poco tímido en la presencia de mis hermanos mayores...*
Párrafo 2: La acción de la historia (Por lo general se usa el pretérito para relatar la acción de una historia. Se usa el imperfecto para describir las emociones de los participantes y los estados del pasado.)	*Un día tuve que preparar la cena para mi familia entera.*	*Tenía miedo porque no sabía cocinar muy bien y creía que no podía hacerlo. Miraba los libros de recetas...*
Párrafo 3: El fin de la historia y el resultado	*Aunque la cena estaba muy rica, el postre salió crudo.*	*Mis hermanos se rieron, pero no se burlaron de mí (they didn't make fun of me).*

Composición

3 Ahora, escriban su historia. Usen palabras y expresiones de la siguiente lista mientras escriban.

Pretérito
de repente *(suddenly)*
por fin *(finally)*
ayer
la semana pasada
el mes / el año pasado
una vez / dos veces, etc.

Imperfecto
generalmente / por lo general
normalmente
todos los días / meses / años
todas las semanas
frecuentemente
típicamente

John Burke/Photolibrary

La primera vez que preparé la cena para mi familia, no salió muy bien...

>> Después de escribir

4 Intercambien su borrador con el de otra pareja de estudiantes. Usen la siguiente lista para revisarlo.

- ¿Tiene su historia toda la información necesaria?
- ¿Es interesante?
- ¿Usaron bien las formas del pretérito? ¿Y las del imperfecto?
- ¿Usaron complementos directos e indirectos para eliminar la repetición?
- ¿Hay errores de puntuación o de ortografía?

Vocabulario

En el restaurante *At the restaurant*

el menú *menu*

El desayuno *Breakfast*

el cereal *cereal*
los huevos estrellados *eggs sunnyside up*
los huevos revueltos *scrambled eggs*
el pan tostado *toast*

El almuerzo *Lunch*

Las ensaladas *Salads*

la ensalada de fruta *fruit salad*
la ensalada de lechuga y tomate *lettuce and tomato salad*
la ensalada de papa *potato salad*
la ensalada mixta *tossed salad*

Las sopas *Soups*

el caldo de pollo *chicken soup*
el gazpacho *cold, tomato-based soup (Spain)*
la sopa de fideos *noodle soup*

Los sándwiches (los bocadillos) *Sandwiches*

con papas fritas *with french fries*
la hamburguesa *hamburger*
la hamburguesa con queso *cheeseburger*
el perro caliente *hot dog*
el sándwich de jamón y queso con aguacate *ham and cheese sandwich with avocado*

Los platos principales *Main dishes*

Las carnes *Meats*

el arroz con pollo *chicken with rice*
el bistec *steak*
la chuleta de puerco *pork chop*
el guisado *beef stew*
el lomo de res *prime rib*
el pollo asado *roasted chicken*
el pollo frito *fried chicken*

Los mariscos *Shellfish*

las almejas *clams*
los camarones *shrimp*
la langosta *lobster*

Los pescados *Fish*

el atún *tuna*
el bacalao *cod*
el salmón *salmon*
la trucha *trout*

A la carta *À la carte*

Los vegetales *Vegetables*

el bróculi *broccoli*

los espárragos *asparagus*
los frijoles (refritos) *(refried) beans*
los guisantes *peas*
las habichuelas *green beans*
las zanahorias *carrots*

Los postres *Desserts*

el flan *custard*
la galleta *cookie*
el helado de vainilla / chocolate *vanilla / chocolate ice cream*
el pastel *cake*

Las frutas *Fruit*

las fresas *strawberries*
la manzana *apple*
el melón *melon*
la naranja *orange*
el plátano *banana*
las uvas *grapes*

Las bebidas y los refrescos *Beverages*

el agua mineral *sparkling water*
el café *coffee*
la cerveza *beer*
el jugo de fruta *fruit juice*
la leche *milk*
la limonada *lemonade*
el té / té helado *hot / iced tea*
el vino blanco / tinto *white / red wine*

Cómo ordenar y pagar *How to order and pay*

Camarero(a), ¿me puede traer el menú? *Waiter (Waitress), could you please bring me the menu?*
Soy vegetariano(a) estricto(a). *I'm a vegan.*
¿Me puede recomendar algo ligero / algo fuerte / algo vegetariano / algo vegano / la especialidad de la casa? *Can you recommend something light / something filling / something vegetarian / something vegan / the house specialty?*

Para plato principal, voy a pedir... *For the main course, I would like to order . . .*
Para tomar, quiero... *To drink, I want . . .*
De postre, voy a pedir... *For dessert, I would like to order . . .*

¿Me puede traer la cuenta, por favor? *Can you bring me the check, please?*
¿Cuánto debo dejar de propina? *How much should I leave as a tip?*

Las recetas *Recipes*

Los ingredientes *Ingredients*
el aceite de oliva *olive oil*
el ajo *garlic*
el azúcar *sugar*
la cebolla *onion*
el comino *cumin*
la harina *flour*
la mantequilla *butter*
la mayonesa *mayonnaise*
la mostaza *mustard*
la sal y la pimienta *salt and pepper*
el vinagre *vinegar*

Las medidas *Measurements*
la cucharada *tablespoonful*
la cucharadita *teaspoonful*
la docena *dozen*
el galón *gallon*
el kilo *kilo*
la libra *pound*
el litro *liter*
medio kilo *half a kilo*
el paquete *package*
el pedazo *piece, slice*
el trozo *chunk, piece*

La preparación *Cooking preparation*
a fuego suave / lento *at low heat*
al gusto *to taste*
al hilo *stringed*
al horno *roasted (in the oven)*
a la parrilla *grilled*
al vapor *steamed*
congelado(a) *frozen*
crudo(a) *raw*
dorado(a) *golden; browned*
fresco(a) *fresh*
frito(a) *fried*
hervido(a) *boiled*
molido(a) *crushed, ground*
picante *spicy*
agregar *to add*
añadir *to add*
calentar (ie) *to heat*
cocer (ue) *to cook*
enfriarse *to get cold*
freír (i, i) *to fry*
hervir (ie, i) *to boil*
mezclar *to mix*
pelar *to peel*
picar *to chop, mince*
unir *to mix together, incorporate*

La mesa *The table*

Cómo poner la mesa *Setting the table*
la copa *wine glass*
la cuchara *spoon*
el cuchillo *knife*
el mantel *tablecloth*
el plato *plate*

el plato hondo *bowl*
la servilleta *napkin*
la taza *cup*
el tenedor *fork*
el vaso *glass*

Otras palabras y expresiones

Expresiones para usar con el imperfecto
frecuentemente *frequently*
generalmente / por lo general *generally*
normalmente *normally*
típicamente *typically*
todas las semanas *every week*
todos los días / meses / años *every day / month / year*

Expresiones para usar con el pretérito
ayer *yesterday*
de repente *suddenly*
el mes / el año pasado *last month / year*
por fin *finally*
la semana pasada *last week*
una vez / dos veces, etc. *once, twice, etc.*

>> ## Repaso del Capítulo 9

Preparation: Have students review this material and complete the activities here, in the SAM, and online before they begin **Chapter 10**.

Complete these activities to check your understanding of the new grammar points in **Chapter 9** before you move on to **Chapter 10**.

The answers to the activities in this section can be found in **Appendix B**.

The imperfect tense (p. 318)

1 Di qué hacía cada persona con relación a la comida.

1. la señora Muñoz / preparar unas galletas   La señora Muñoz preparaba unas galletas.
2. yo / freír un huevo   Yo freía un huevo.
3. nosotros / pelar zanahorias para una ensalada   Nosotros pelábamos zanahorias para una ensalada.
4. Manolito / poner la mesa   Manolito ponía la mesa.
5. Sarita y Carmela / picar cebollas para una sopa   Sarita y Carmela picaban cebollas para una sopa.
6. tú / hervir agua para preparar el té   Tú hervías agua para preparar el té.

Choosing between the preterite and the imperfect (p. 321)

2 Escribe la forma correcta (pretérito o imperfecto) de cada verbo para completar la oración.

1. __Eran__ (Ser) las tres de la tarde y yo 2. __quería__ (querer) tomar un café en la cafetería. Cuando 3. __llegué__ (llegar) allí, 4. __vi__ (ver) a mi amiga Lucía. Ella 5. __estaba__ (estar) muy cansada y 6. __tenía__ (tener) ganas de descansar un rato en la cafetería. Yo 7. __me senté__ (sentarse) en su mesa y nosotros 8. __empezamos__ (empezar) a hablar. Mientras 9. __hablábamos__ (hablar), ella me 10. __dijo__ (decir) que tenemos examen mañana en la clase de cálculo. "¡No me digas!" yo 11. __exclamé__ (exclamar). "No lo 12. __sabía__ (saber). ¡Tengo que estudiar!" 13. __Me despedí__ (Despedirme) de ella y 14. __salí__ (salir) corriendo. 15. __Estaba__ (Estar) muy nervioso por el exámen y 16. __quería__ (querer) pasar todo el día estudiando.

Answers, Act. 3: 1. Ábrenosla. 2. Cuéceselos. 3. No me lo compres. 4. No se lo calientes. 5. Pásanosla. 6. No se la prepares.

Double object pronouns (p. 325)

3 Usa cada ilustración y las palabras indicadas para hacer mandatos informales afirmativos y negativos, según la situación. Sigue los modelos.

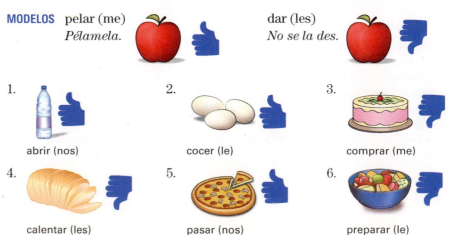

MODELOS   pelar (me)   *Pélamela.*   dar (les)   *No se la des.*

1. abrir (nos)
2. cocer (le)
3. comprar (me)
4. calentar (les)
5. pasar (nos)
6. preparar (le)

All art: © Cengage Learning 2013

The uses of se (p. 329)

4 Complete the sentences with the correct form of the verb indicated.

1. Se __come__ (comer) bien en esa taquería.
2. Se __venden__ (vender) tacos riquísimos.
3. Se __hablan__ (hablar) el español y el inglés.
4. Se __sirve__ (servir) la cena hasta las diez.
5. Se __cierra__ (cerrar) entre las tres y las cinco.
6. Se __duerme__ (dormir) en este hotel.

>> Preparación para el Capítulo 10

Article, noun, and adjective agreement (Chapters 1 and 2)

5 Haz oraciones completas con el artículo definido, el verbo **ser** o **estar** y la forma correcta del adjetivo indicado. Sigue el modelo.

MODELO   copa (ser) / bonito
             La copa es bonita.

1. manteles (ser) / rojo
2. flan (ser) / bueno
3. almejas (estar) / fresco
4. café (estar) / caliente
5. carne (estar) / frito
6. huevos (ser) / blanco
7. pescado (estar) / crudo
8. té (estar) / frío
9. limonada (ser) / dulce
10. platos (estar) / limpio
11. langosta (ser) / caro
12. fresas (ser) / barato

> Complete these activities to review some previously learned grammatical structures that will be helpful when you learn the new grammar in **Chapter 10**.
>
> Be sure to reread **Chapter 9: Gramática útil 1** before moving on to the new **Chapter 10** grammar sections.

> **Answers, Act. 5: 1.** Los manteles son rojos. 2. El flan es bueno. 3. Las almejas están frescas. 4. El café está caliente. 5. La carne está frita. 6. Los huevos son blancos. 7. El pescado está crudo. 8. El té está frío. 9. La limonada es dulce. 10. Los platos están limpios. 11. La langosta es cara. 12. Las fresas son baratas.

Simple possessive adjectives (Chapter 3)

6 Escribe el adjetivo posesivo correcto para cada cosa indicada.

1. __mi__ servilleta (yo)
2. __tus__ galletas (tú)
3. __nuestro__ pan (nosotros)
4. __sus__ uvas (ellos)
5. __sus__ vasos (usted)
6. __su__ mantel (ella)
7. __sus__ platos (ustedes)
8. __su__ menú (él)
9. __nuestras__ tazas (nosotros)
10. __tus__ cuchillos (tú)

Forms of hacer (Chapters 5 and 7)

7 Completa las oraciones con formas de **hacer** en el presente o el pretérito, según el caso.

1. Oye, Maite, ¿qué __hiciste__ para la cena anoche?
2. Yo __hago__ las compras en el supermercado todos los lunes.
3. El año pasado, mi madre __hizo__ un pastel de chocolate para mi cumpleaños.
4. Ustedes ya __hicieron__ las reservaciones en el restaurante, ¿verdad?
5. Nosotros __hacemos__ una excursión al mercado al aire libre esta tarde.

LOS SITIOS

Los sitios y sus ambientes (*atmospheres*) juegan un papel muy importante en nuestras vidas y en nuestras memorias.

¿Tienes recuerdos de la casa o sitio donde te criaste (*you were raised*)? ¿Cómo son?

Communication

By the end of this chapter you will be able to

- talk about your childhood
- describe homes and their furnishings
- talk about household tasks
- indicate numerical order
- express possession
- talk about the duration of past and present events

Maxime Bessieres/Alamy

Un viaje por Guatemala y Nicaragua

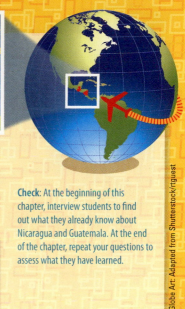

Learning objectives: See pages AIE-3–AIE-4 for a complete description of the Bloom's Taxonomy learning objectives and an explanation of how they are integrated within *Cuadros*.

Guatemala y Nicaragua son países centroamericanos. Nicaragua es el país más grande de Centroamérica. Los dos países tienen costas en el Atlántico y el Pacífico, pero la costa atlántica de Guatemala es muy pequeña. Guatemala es más montañoso que Nicaragua.

Check: At the beginning of this chapter, interview students to find out what they already know about Nicaragua and Guatemala. At the end of the chapter, repeat your questions to assess what they have learned.

País / Área	Tamaño y fronteras	Sitios de interés
Guatemala 108.430 km²	un poco más pequeño que Tennessee; fronteras con Belice, El Salvador, Honduras y México	el lago Atitlán, la ciudad de Antigua, las ruinas mayas de Tikal, la Reserva de la Biosfera de la Sierra de las Minas con su bosque nuboso *(cloud forest)*
Nicaragua 120.254 km²	un poco más pequeño que Nueva York; fronteras con Costa Rica y Honduras	el lago de Nicaragua y sus tiburones *(sharks)*, Bluefields y la Costa de los Mosquitos, la catedral de Santo Domingo en Managua, muchos volcanes (incluso el más alto, San Cristóbal)

¿Qué sabes? Di si las siguientes oraciones son ciertas **(C)** o falsas **(F)**.

Learning objective: Understanding

1. Aunque hay muchos volcanes en Nicaragua, Guatemala es más montañoso. C
2. Guatemala es más pequeño que el estado de Nueva York. C
3. Hay ruinas mayas en Nicaragua. F
4. Los tiburones en Nicaragua están en el lago de Bluefields. F

Lo que sé y lo que quiero aprender Completa la tabla del **Apéndice A**. Escribe algunos datos que **ya sabes** sobre estos países en la columna **Lo que sé**. Después, añade algunos temas que **quieres aprender** a la columna **Lo que quiero aprender**. Guarda la tabla para usarla otra vez en la sección **¡Explora y exprésate!** en la página 369.

Cultures

Standards: In this chapter, students relate their study of culture to the "green movement" and to literature as they learn about Nicaragua and Guatemala.

By the end of this chapter you will have explored

- facts about Guatemala and Nicaragua
- ancient and modern sites in Guatemala and Nicaragua
- a unique recycling program in Guatemala
- Alter Eco: "green" furniture and home decor
- some Hispanic proverbs
- Nicaragua's poetic tradition

Globe Art: Adapted from Shutterstock/rrguest

¡Imagínate!

© Cengage Learning 2013

>> Vocabulario útil 1

Learning objectives: Applying, Analyzing

BETO: Cuando era niño, me gustaba preparar la comida para mi familia.

DULCE: ¿En serio? Yo creía que a los chicos no les gustaba hacer nada en la casa. Mis hermanos siempre decían que el trabajo de casa era para las mujeres.

BETO: ¡Qué anticuado! Yo no pienso así. Me crié en **el centro de la ciudad**. Somos muy modernos los hombres de la ciudad.

DULCE: ¿De veras? Qué bueno. En mi casa, mis hermanas y yo teníamos que hacer los quehaceres domésticos, mis hermanos sólo hacían lo que tenía que ver con **el garaje** o **el jardín**.

Suggestion: This vocabulary lends itself to a discussion of ¿Dónde vives? ¿Vives en el centro o en las afueras (o en el campo)? Have students interview a classmate about where they live now.

Optional: To review tenses, expand this discussion to where students lived in the past and where they plan to live in the future.

Ordinal numbers must agree in gender with the nouns they modify: **el segundo piso, la tercera oficina**. They are usually used in front of the noun. **Primero** and **tercero** shorten to **primer** and **tercer** when used before a masculine singular noun: **primer piso, tercer dormitorio** (but **primera casa, tercera ciudad**).

Ordinal numbers can be used without nouns when it is clear what they are referring to: **Mi casa es *la cuarta* de la calle. Primero** and **tercero** are not shortened when used without a noun: **Este piso *es el tercero*, pero vamos *al primero*.**

>> Áreas de la ciudad

las afueras *the outskirts*
el apartamento *apartment*
el barrio *neighborhood*
...comercial *business district*
...residencial *residential neighborhood*
el centro de la ciudad *downtown*
los suburbios *suburbs*
los vecinos *neighbors*

>> Números ordinales

primer(o) *first*
segundo *second*
tercer(o) *third*
cuarto *fourth*
quinto *fifth*
sexto *sixth*
séptimo *seventh*
octavo *eighth*
noveno *ninth*
décimo *tenth*

>> La casa

el garaje *garage*
el jardín *garden, yard*
la lavandería *laundry room*
el pasillo *hallway*
el patio *patio*
el sótano *basement, cellar*

Notice: Los suburbios can have a negative connotation in some parts of the Spanish-speaking world, where it may refer to ghettos or shantytowns on the outskirts of a town or city.

Heritage Learners: As is the case with English, the vocabulary for parts of the house varies from one Spanish-speaking country to the other. Have heritage learners work as a group to pool the words they use and also interview native speakers they know to gather as many variants as possible. As a follow-up, students can place these variants on a map of the Spanish-speaking world.

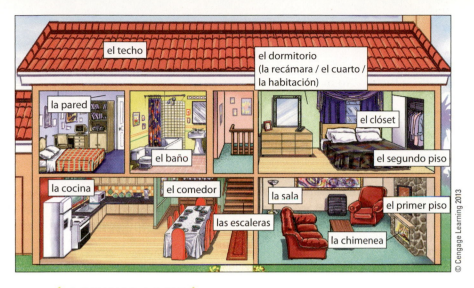

el techo

el dormitorio
(la recámara / el cuarto /
la habitación)

la pared

el clóset

el baño

el segundo piso

la cocina

el comedor

la sala

el primer piso

las escaleras

la chimenea

© Cengage Learning 2013

ACTIVIDADES

1 **¿En qué cuarto estás?** Di en qué cuarto o lugar de la casa está tu
M compañero(a) de clase basándote en lo que él (ella) te dice que está haciendo.

MODELO Compañero(a): *Estoy preparando la comida.*
Tú: *Estás en la cocina.*

1. Estoy lavando la ropa.
2. Estoy mirando la tele.
3. Estoy cenando con mi familia.
4. Me estoy lavando los dientes.
5. Estoy subiendo al segundo piso.
6. Estoy cambiándole el aceite al carro.
7. Estoy regando *(watering)* las plantas.
8. Estoy en la computadora.

2 **¿Dónde vives?** En grupos de cuatro, describan el barrio donde viven,
C qué tipo de casa o apartamento tienen y cómo llegan a la universidad de su
casa. Añadan todos los detalles personales que quieran. Tus compañeros
pueden hacerte preguntas si no les das suficiente información.

MODELO *Yo vivo en un barrio residencial en las afueras de la ciudad. Hay
apartamentos y también casas individuales. Vivo en un apartamento en el segundo piso. Manejo para llegar a la universidad.*

Al final, informen a otro grupo o a la clase quién vive más lejos de la
universidad y cuál es el modo de transporte más común.

3 **Mi casa** En grupos de tres, háganse preguntas y describan su casa o
C apartamento. Averigüen cómo es, cuántos cuartos tiene, si hay jardín y garaje,
etc. Pueden describir la casa de su niñez o donde vive su familia ahora.

MODELOS Compañero(a): *¿Cuántos dormitorios hay en tu casa?*
Tú: *Hay tres dormitorios, dos en el segundo piso y uno en el primero.*

>> Vocabulario útil 2

BETO: No me parece justo. Yo **tendía las camas, pasaba la aspiradora, lavaba los platos** igual que mis hermanas.

DULCE: Pues eres único.

BETO: Sí, mi mamá decía que yo era su ayudante preferido. **Barría el piso, sacaba la basura, ponía la mesa, limpiaba los baños, planchaba, sacudía las alfombras…**

DULCE: Oye, me estás tomando el pelo, ¿verdad? Yo no conozco a ningún niño tan trabajador.

Optional: Throughout this chapter there are vocabulary words that lend themselves to graphics. Bring visuals of homes and floor plans with or without furniture and/or have students sketch and label their living spaces to present, reinforce, and make the vocabulary words three-dimensional.

Mention to students that in some countries, native speakers say **tender la cama** instead of **hacer la cama**.

>> Los quehaceres domésticos

Dentro de la casa

arreglar el dormitorio

limpiar el baño

hacer la cama

lavar los platos

sacudir los muebles

barrer el suelo / el piso

Dentro de la casa

lavar la ropa

planchar

guardar la ropa

trapear el piso

pasar la aspiradora

poner y quitar la mesa

poner sus juguetes en su lugar

preparar la comida

© Cengage Learning 2013

Fuera de la casa

darle de comer al perro y al gato

regar (ie) las plantas

sacar la basura

sacar a pasear al perro

cortar el césped

hacer el reciclaje

© Cengage Learning 2013

Notice: Although the word **persiana** can be translated as *Venetian blind,* **persiana** conjures different visual images depending on the country. Writer Julia Álvarez, from the Dominican Republic, calls attention to the nuance of the term **persiana** in the first poem in "Bilingual Sestina" *(The Other Side / El Otro Lado).* "Bilingual Sestina" is written principally in English.

Optional: ¿Participas en juegos virtuales como "SimCity" donde puedes planear una ciudad virtual? ¿Qué tipo de casa / ciudad te gustaría crear? Suggest that interested students do a **búsqueda** of "SimCity Spanish" and download old versions for free.

Heritage Learners: Many of the communication objectives of this chapter focus on areas of linguistic knowledge familiar to heritage learners, e.g., childhood experiences and vocabulary about the home. While many heritage learners can converse on these topics, they have difficulty writing about them if they have had limited schooling in Spanish. One way to take advantage of their expertise and to address their literacy needs is to do paired activities with L2 learners. Ask L2 learners to provide answers to questions in aural form while heritage learners write the answers. This will give L2 learners practice making spontaneous use of vocabulary and structures while giving heritage learners writing practice.

Answers, Act. 4: *Answers may vary.* Sample answers: 1. ¿Dónde pongo el sofá? Pon el sofá en la sala, por favor. 2. ¿Dónde pongo la mesita de noche? Pon la mesita de noche en el dormitorio, por favor. 3. ¿Dónde pongo el tocador / la cómoda? Pon el tocador / la cómoda en el dormitorio, por favor. 4. ¿Dónde pongo la lámpara? Pon la lámpara en la mesita de noche, por favor. 5. ¿Dónde pongo el espejo? Pon el espejo en el baño, por favor. 6. ¿Dónde pongo la alfombra? Pon la alfombra en el pasillo, por favor.

>> Los muebles y decoraciones

el cuadro · la alfombra · el tocador / la cómoda · el sillón · la persiana · la cama · la mesita de noche · la silla · la lámpara · el espejo · la mesa · las cortinas · el sofá

© Cengage Learning 2013

ACTIVIDADES

4 ¿Dónde pongo esto? Un(a) amigo(a) acaba de mudarse *(has just moved)* a un nuevo apartamento. Tú le vas a ayudar a poner todos sus muebles y decoraciones en su lugar. Pregúntale dónde van ciertas cosas. Él (Ella) va a decirte dónde quiere cada cosa.

MODELO Tú: *¿Dónde pongo el sillón?*
Compañero(a): *Pon el sillón en la sala, por favor.*

1.

2.

3.

4.

5.

6.

© Cengage Learning 2013

M **5** **Los quehaceres** Ves que hay un problema en casa. ¿Qué quehacer le pides a tu hermano(a) que haga? Sigue el modelo.

Answers, Act. 5: 1. ¿Puedes preparar la comida? 2. ¿Puedes poner la mesa? 3. ¿Puedes lavar la ropa? 4. ¿Puedes hacer la cama? 5. ¿Puedes hacer el reciclaje? 6.¿Puedes arreglar el dormitorio? 7. ¿Puedes planchar la blusa? 8. ¿Puedes cortar el césped?

MODELO Hay muchos juguetes en el piso.
¿Puedes poner los juguetes en su lugar?

1. Es hora de comer.
2. Estamos listos para cenar.
3. Acabamos de llegar del gimnasio y hay mucha ropa sucia *(dirty)*.
4. La cama necesita sábanas limpias *(clean sheets)*.
5. Hay varias botellas plásticas en la cocina que están vacías *(empty)*.
6. Hay ropa, zapatos y libros por todo el dormitorio.
7. La blusa está arrugada *(wrinkled)*.
8. El césped está demasiado alto.

6 **¿A quién le toca?** En grupos de tres, representen la siguiente situación.

C Ustedes tres son compañeros(as) de cuarto ¡y su apartamento es un desastre! Decidan entre sí *(among yourselves)* quién va a hacer cada quehacer. Pueden negociar si quieren.

Learning objective: Applying

MODELO No hay platos limpios para la cena.
Compañero(a) #1: *¿Quién va a lavar los platos?*
Compañero(a) #2: *Yo los puedo lavar si* [Compañero(a) #3] *hace las compras.*
Compañero(a) #3: *Estás loco(a). Prefiero sacar la basura.*
Compañero(a) #1: *Bueno, los lavo yo.*

Problema	Nombre / Tarea
No hay platos limpios para la cena.	[Nombre] va a lavar los platos.
El perro tiene mucha hambre.	
Las plantas están secas.	
El suelo de la cocina está sucio *(dirty)*.	
Hay mucho polvo *(dust)* en los muebles.	
Mañana es día de reciclaje.	
Hay varias bolsas de basura.	
El perro tiene que salir.	
La alfombra está sucia.	
El baño es un desastre.	

BETO: Pues, exagero un poco, pero sí me gustaban algunos de los quehaceres.

DULCE: ¿Como cuáles?

BETO: Pues, a ver, me gustaba limpiar **el refrigerador**…

© Cengage Learning 2013

Suggestion: When introducing appliances, ask questions like: **¿En qué cuarto / habitación de la casa se encuentra…? ¿Para qué se usa…?**

>> **Los electrodomésticos**

el abrelatas eléctrico *electric can opener*	**el microondas** *microwave*
la aspiradora *vacuum cleaner*	**la plancha** *iron*
el congelador *freezer*	**el procesador de comida** *food processor*
la estufa *stove*	**el refrigerador** *refrigerator*
la lavadora *washer*	**la secadora** *dryer*
el lavaplatos *dishwasher*	**el televisor** *television set*
la licuadora *blender*	**la tostadora** *toaster*

━━━━━| ACTIVIDADES |━━━━━

Answers, Act. 7: 1. la lavadora 2. el abrelatas eléctrico 3. la plancha 4. la tostadora 5. la licuadora 6. el microondas 7. el refrigerador 8. la aspiradora

M **7** **¿Qué necesitas?** Identifica el electrodoméstico que necesitas en cada situación.

1. Tienes que lavar ropa esta noche porque no tienes nada que ponerte mañana.
2. Tienes que abrir una lata *(can)* de atún.
3. Tu ropa está muy arrugada *(wrinkled)* porque la acabas de sacar de la maleta.
4. Quieres pan tostado con los huevos revueltos.
5. Tienes ganas de tomar un batido de frutas *(smoothie)*.
6. No tienes mucho tiempo para preparar la cena, así que decides comer un paquete de comida preparada.
7. Quieres enfriar la botella de vino.
8. Quieres limpiar la alfombra.

Optional: This activity can be done as **La casa de mis sueños** using an example from **Las casas de los ricos y famosos.**

 8 **La casa nueva** En grupos de tres, representen la siguiente situación

C a la clase. Pueden preparar un guión si quieren: Tres amigos(as) van a ser compañeros(as) de casa. Tienen que comparar qué tienen y qué necesitan para la casa nueva. La casa tiene tres dormitorios, una sala grande, una cocina y dos baños.

- ¿Qué muebles y electrodomésticos tienen entre los tres?
- ¿Qué necesitan comprar?
- ¿En qué cuartos quieren poner los distintos muebles y electrodomésticos?

¡Fíjate! Los refranes en español

Los refranes (*proverbs*) reflejan las actitudes psicológicas, religiosas, espirituales, prácticas, tradicionales y humorísticas de la cultura originaria. Sin embargo, hay unos refranes universales que se conocen por todo el mundo y no pertenecen (*don't belong*) a una cultura en particular. Un refrán que se oye por dondequiera en Estados Unidos y que probablemente conoces es **Mi casa es tu casa**. Aquí están otros refranes que usan como metáfora el hogar, los muebles y los quehaceres:

Si quieres que te vengan a ver, ten la casa sin barrer.
(Expect a surprise visit if the house is a mess.)

Con promesas no se cubre la mesa.
(You can't eat promises!)

El amigo viejo es el mejor espejo.
(An old friend is the best reflection.)

Las paredes oyen.
(The walls have ears.)

© Cengage Learning 2013

Práctica En grupos de tres o cuatro personas, hablen de los siguientes temas.

1. ¿Qué actitud refleja cada refrán?
2. Escriban un refrán de su cultura que usa el hogar cómo metáfora; o un refrán que usan entre familia o amigos con frecuencia. Escriban el refrán en su lengua original; tradúzcanlo al español si está en otro idioma.
3. Compartan los refranes más interesantes con la clase.

A ver

Standard 1.2: Through video viewing, students learn interpretive strategies for communication. Activities in this section regularly provide opportunities for students to interpret spoken language.

ESTRATEGIA

Listening to tone of voice

Listening carefully to a speaker's tone of voice **(el tono de voz)** helps you understand what lies beneath their surface commentary. In this chapter's video segment, pay particular attention to Dulce and Beto's tone of voice. In many cases, what they say may contradict what they are actually thinking and feeling!

Notice: You may want to point out that non-native speakers rely heavily on this type of *extra-linguistic* information to figure out situations in which they do not understand every word. Besides **el tono de voz**, what other nonverbal clues do you see in the clip that communicate attitude or information?

Antes de ver Piensa en lo que ya sabes de Beto y Dulce. ¿Cómo es la personalidad de Beto? ¿Cómo es la personalidad de Dulce?

Ver Mientras ves el video, presta atención al tono de voz de Beto y Dulce.

Después de ver 1 Lee los siguientes comentarios del video y mira el video otra vez. Si crees que el tono contradice *(contradicts)* el comentario, escribe **C**; si crees que añade más información, marca **A**. Si crees que el tono no afecta el comentario, no escribas nada. **Learning objective:** Analyzing

1. ___—___ Dulce: Hace mucho tiempo que no voy de picnic.
2. ___A___ Beto: Sí, mi mamá decía que yo era su ayudante preferido.
3. ___C___ Dulce: ¡Vas a ser un padre excelente!
4. ___A___ Beto: Mira, prueba éstos, los compré en el supermercado.
5. ___C___ Dulce: ¡Planchabas! ¡Limpiabas los baños! ¡Cocinabas! ¡Súper-Chico!

Optional: To personalize, survey who does which domestic chores in your class. Are there any trends regarding age of students or gender? **Pensando en la limpieza, ¿quiénes son los trabajadores y quiénes son los perezosos en casa?**

Después de ver 2 Di si los siguientes comentarios sobre el video son ciertos **(C)** o falsos **(F)**.

1. ___C___ Beto dice que preparaba la comida para su familia.
2. ___F___ En la familia de Dulce, los hijos también preparaban la comida.
3. ___C___ Beto se crió *(was raised)* en el centro de la ciudad y se considera un hombre moderno.
4. ___F___ En realidad, Beto sí hacía las camas, pasaba la aspiradora y lavaba los platos.
5. ___C___ Dulce cree que Beto está exagerando.
6. ___C___ Beto está nervioso y confiesa que no preparó la comida.

© Cengage Learning 2013

Voces de la comunidad

>> Voces del mundo hispano

En el video para este capítulo Winnie y Carlos hablan de dónde viven ahora y qué quehaceres hacían de niño(a). Lee las siguientes oraciones. Después mira el video una o más veces para decir si las oraciones son ciertas **(C)** o falsas **(F)**.

1. Winnie tiene una casa en la Ciudad de Guatemala y vive con su hermana. F
2. Carlos vive en un apartamento de dos cuartos. C
3. En el cuarto de Winnie hay muchos recortes *(clippings)* de artistas y deportistas. F
4. Carlos tiene cuadros de cultura de Nicaragua en las paredes de su habitación. C
5. A Carlos le gustaba hacer todos los mandados (quehaceres) de la casa cuando era niño. F
6. De niña Winnie compartía los quehaceres con su prima. F

> Carlos uses the words **mandados** and **quehaceres** interchangeably. **Mandados** can also be used more specifically to mean errands.

>> Voces de Estados Unidos

Track 30

César y Rafael Pelli, arquitectos

❝Lo que importa es la ciudad. Los edificios son secundarios. Los arquitectos no entienden esto. Creen que su edificio es el más importante en el mundo. Pero un edificio es parte de una ciudad. ❞

El World Financial Center en Nueva York, la Torre de Carnegie Hall y las Torres Gemelas Petronas de Kuala Lumpur (Malasia). Estos edificios, que figuran entre los más altos del mundo, son algunas de las obras maestras del famoso arquitecto argentino César Pelli. Después de licenciarse *(earned a degree)* en arquitectura en su país natal, Pelli vino a Estados Unidos a seguir sus estudios y luego decidió quedarse. Considerado uno de los arquitectos vivos *(living)* más importantes, ha recibido más de 200 premios por la excelencia en diseño y se han publicado numerosos libros y artículos sobre su obra. Fue decano de la escuela de arquitectura de Yale, ha sido premiado con la medalla de oro del American Institute of Architects (Instituto Estadounidense de Arquitectos) y tiene una de las firmas de arquitectura más solicitadas del mundo (Pelli Clarke Pelli), donde colabora con su hijo, Rafael, que también es un arquitecto de renombre *(renowned)*, y que ha enseñado arquitectura en la Universidad de Harvard, Parsons The New School of Design en Nueva York, y el Instituto de Arquitectura del Sur de California.

> The forms **ha recibido, se han publicado,** and **ha sido premiado** are all forms of the present perfect tense, which you will learn in **Chapter 14**. Their English equivalents are *has received, has published,* and *has been awarded.*

¿Y tú? ¿Te interesa la arquitectura? ¿Hay unos ejemplos de casas o edificios históricos o únicos en tu comunidad?

 Standards 2.1, 2.2, 3.2: Students read about successful Spanish speakers in the U.S. and acquire cultural information that features distinctive viewpoints of Spanish-speaking people.

¡Prepárate!

>> Gramática útil 1

Emphasizing ownership: Stressed possessives

Cómo usarlo

Heritage Learners: The stressed possessives present two spelling challenges for heritage language speakers. Many heritage language speakers tend to spell **tuyo** and **suyo** with an **i** rather than a **y**. Second, students tend to forget that the forms of **mío** always carry an accent. Be sure to remind students of correct spelling.

1. You have already learned how to express possession in Spanish using possessive adjectives and phrases with **de.**

   Es **tu** habitación.   It's *your* bedroom.
   Es la habitación **de Nati**.   It's *Nati's* bedroom.

2. When you wish to emphasize, contrast, or clarify who owns something, you can also use stressed possessives.

Stressed possessives		Unstressed possessive	
Es la casa **mía**.	*It's **my** house.*	Es **mi** casa.	*It's **my** house.*
¡La casa es **mía**!	*The house is **mine**!*		
La casa es **mía**, no **suya**.	*The house is **mine**, not **yours / his / hers**.*		

3. Stressed possessives must agree in number and gender with the noun they modify: **un libro mío, la calculadora mía, los platos míos, las mochilas mías**.

4. Stressed possessives may be used as adjectives with a noun, in which case they follow the noun: **Es el coche <u>mío</u>**. If it's clear what is being referred to, the noun may be dropped: **—¿De quién es el coche? —Es <u>mío</u>**.

5. Stressed possessives can also be used as pronouns that replace the noun. Notice that the article is maintained: **Le gusta <u>el coche mío</u>. Le gusta <u>el mío</u>.**

English uses inflection and vocal stress to emphasize something: *These are **my** books*. In Spanish, inflection and vocal stress are not used the way they are in English. Instead, stressed possessive forms play this role. For example, if you want to emphasize ownership in Spanish, you would say **Estos libros son <u>míos</u>**, but never **Estos son mis libros**.

Cómo formarlo

Here are the stressed possessive forms in Spanish.

	Singular	Plural	
yo	**mío, mía**	**míos, mías**	*my, mine*
tú	**tuyo, tuya**	**tuyos, tuyas**	*your, yours*
usted / él / ella	**suyo, suya**	**suyos, suyas**	*your, yours, his, her, hers, its*
nosotros / nosotras	**nuestro, nuestra**	**nuestros, nuestras**	*our, ours*
vosotros / vosotras	**vuestro, vuestra**	**vuestros, vuestras**	*your, yours*
ustedes / ellos / ellas	**suyo, suya**	**suyos, suyas**	*your, yours, their, theirs*

ACTIVIDADES

M **(1)** **Organizando la casa** Sigue el modelo para decir qué pertenece *(belongs)* a cada persona indicada.

1.

MODELO él
Es suya.

yo Es mía.

2.

nosotros Son nuestras.

3.

usted Es suyo.

4.

tú Es tuya.

5.

ellos Son suyas.

© Cengage Learning 2013

🔊 **(2)** **María, Elena y yo** Un amigo quiere saber de quién son ciertos muebles y

Track 31 decoraciones. Contesta sus preguntas según el modelo.

M

MODELO Ves: *yo*
Escuchas: ¿De quién es esta lámpara?
Escribes: *Es mía.*

1. María Es suyo.
2. Elena Son suyas.
3. tú Es tuya.
4. Elena Son suyos.
5. María Es suya.
6. yo Es mío.

Audioscript, Act. 2, María, Elena y yo:
1. ¿De quién es este espejo? 2. ¿De quién son las cortinas? 3. ¿De quién es esta silla? 4. ¿De quién son estos cuadros? 5. ¿De quién es esta alfombra? 6. ¿De quién es este sillón?

M **(3)** **La fiesta** Después de la fiesta, el anfitrión *(host)* encuentra algunas cosas de los invitados. Contesta sus preguntas con **no**, según el modelo.

MODELO Anfitrión: ¿Es éste el impermeable de Martín? (gris)
Tú: *No, no es suyo. El suyo es gris.*

1. ¿Es éste tu abrigo? (negro) No, no es mío. El mío es negro.
2. ¿Es ésta la bufanda de María? (azul) No, no es suya. La suya es azul.
3. ¿Son éstos los guantes de Miguel? (de piel) No, no son suyos. Los suyos son de piel.
4. ¿Son éstas las botas de ustedes? (de otra marca) No, no son nuestras. Las nuestras son de otra marca.
5. ¿Son éstas las bolsas de Ana y Adela? (verdes) No, no son suyas. Las suyas son verdes.

👤👤👤 **(4)** **¿De quién es?** En grupos de cuatro, hagan lo siguiente.

C

Learning objective: Understanding

1. Cada persona escribe una descripción corta de su posesión favorita en un trocito de papel *(slip of paper)*.
2. Júntense con otro grupo para intercambiar los trocitos de papel. Túrnense para elegir un trocito del otro grupo y tratar de adivinar de quién es.

MODELO mi chaqueta de cuero negro, estilo motocicleta
Tú: *Sean, ¿es tuya?*
Compañero: *Sí, es mía. O: No, no es mía.*

Standard 4.1: Compare Spanish and English constructions of expressions with time. Point out that Spanish uses **hace** + *present* whereas English uses *has / have been* + *verb ending in -ing* to express the same idea. Likewise, Spanish uses **hacía** + *imperfect* whereas English uses *had been* + *verb ending in -ing.*

>> Gramática útil 2

Expressing ongoing events and duration of time: Hace / Hacía with time expressions

Hace mucho tiempo que **no voy** de picnic.

Cómo usarlo

1. **Hace** and **hacía** are used to talk about ongoing actions and their duration. They can also be used to say how long it has been since someone has done something or since something has occurred. Look carefully at the following formulas and model sentences.

- To express *an action that has been occurring over a period of time and is still going on*

> **hace** + period of time + **que** + present indicative

Hace tres años que vivimos en este barrio.   *We've been living in this neighborhood for three years.*

- To say *how long it has been since you have done something*

> **hace** + period of time + **que** + **no** + present indicative

Hace seis meses que no salimos de la ciudad.   *We haven't left the city in six months.*

- To express *how long ago an event took place*

> preterite + **hace** + period of time

Vine aquí **hace tres años**.   *I came here three years ago.*

- To say *how long an action had been going on in the past* before another more recent past event

> **hacía** + period of time + **que** + imperfect

Cuando nos mudamos a esta nueva casa, **hacía cinco años que vivíamos** en ese apartamento.   *When we moved to this new house, we had been living in that apartment for five years.*

2. Use the following formulas to ask *questions* with **hace** and **hacía**.

- To ask *how long an action or event has been going on* (**hace** + present indicative)

¿Cuánto tiempo hace que vives aquí?   *How long have you been living here?*

- To ask *how long it has been since an action or event last occurred* (**hace** + **no** + present)

¿Cuánto tiempo hace que no hablas con tus abuelos?   *How long has it been since you spoke to your grandparents?*

Point out that when **hace** + time period comes at the end of a sentence expressing *ago*, **que** is not used: **Vine aquí hace tres años.**

You can also say **Hace tres años que vine aquí.** Notice that **que** precedes the verb in this case.

Heritage Learners: Do not assume that heritage language speakers know how to use **hace / hacía**. In fact, some may need as much practice as the second language learners. Use this construction to remind students that all forms of the verb **hacer** are written with an **h**.

Suggestion: Have students answer questions to practice **hace: ¿Cuánto tiempo hace que vives aquí / vives en el mismo sitio / estudias español / asistes a nuestra universidad** / etc. ?

- To ask *how long ago an action took place* (**hace** + preterite)

  ¿Cuánto tiempo hace que hablaste con tus abuelos?

  How long ago did you speak to your grandparents?

- To ask *how long an action or event had been going on in the past* (**hacía** + imperfect)

  ¿Cuánto tiempo hacía que no podías ir a las clases cuando decidiste ir al médico?

  How long had you not been able to go to classes when you decided to go to the doctor?

Notice that in all these examples only the forms **hace** and **hacía** are used.

ACTIVIDADES

M **5** **¡Odio los quehaceres!** Odias los quehaceres. Di cuánto tiempo hace que no haces ciertos quehaceres en tu casa.

MODELO ...no pasar la aspiradora (dos meses)
Hace dos meses que no paso la aspiradora.

1. ...no limpiar el baño (tres semanas)
2. ...no preparar la comida en casa (una semana)
3. ...no cortar el césped (seis semanas)
4. ...no trabajar en el jardín (un mes)
5. ...no lavar el auto (tres meses)
6. ...no arreglar el sótano (dos años)
7. ...no trapear el piso (un mes)

Preparation: Emphasize that in **Activity 5**, the actions are still going on.

Answers, Act. 5: 1. Hace tres semanas que no limpio... 2. Hace una semana que no preparo... 3. Hace seis semanas que no corto... 4. Hace un mes que no trabajo... 5. Hace tres meses que no lavo... 6. Hace dos años que no arreglo... 7. Hace un mes que no trapeo...

M **6** **Hacía cinco años que…** Manuel y su familia se mudaron de Guatemala a Estados Unidos hace muchos años. Manuel recuerda cuando él se graduó del colegio. ¿Qué dice?

MODELO nosotros / vivir en Estados Unidos (5)
Cuando me gradué del colegio, hacía cinco años que vivíamos en Estados Unidos.

1. yo / estudiar inglés (10)
2. mamá / estudiar computación (3)
3. mi novia y yo / conocerse (1)
4. nosotros / alquilar nuestra casa (2)

Preparation: In **Act. 6**, stress that the actions had been going on for a period of time when Manuel graduated.

Answers, Act. 6: Cuando me gradué del colegio…: 1. …hacía diez años que (yo) estudiaba inglés. 2. …hacía tres años que mamá tomaba clases de computación. 3. …hacía un año que mi novia y yo nos conocíamos. 4. …hacía dos años que alquilábamos nuestra casa.

👥 **7** **¿Y tú?** Túrnense para preguntarle a un(a) compañero(a) cuánto tiempo
C hace que él o ella no hace los quehaceres de la **Actividad 5**.

MODELO Tú: *¿Cuánto tiempo hace que no pasas la aspiradora?*
Compañero(a): *Hace dos semanas que no paso la aspiradora.*

👥 **8** **¿Cuánto tiempo hace?** Túrnense para preguntarle a un(a) compañero(a)
C cuánto tiempo hace que participó en ciertas actividades. Puedes usar ideas de la lista o puedes inventar tus propias preguntas.

Ideas: estudiar español en…, comprar tu carro, hablar con tus abuelos, mudarte a tu apartamento, conocer a tu novio(a), ¿…?

MODELO Tú: *¿Cuánto tiempo hace que estudiaste español en Nicaragua?*
Compañero(a): *Estudié español en Nicaragua hace cinco años.*

Preparation: Emphasize that the word *ago* will appear in the English translations of these statements.

Sonrisas

Pasé los últimos diez años en un monasterio budista en Nepal.

Hace diez años que no viajo en avión.

© Cengage Learning 2013

Hace diez años que no leo una novela moderna.

Como dicen los budistas: Lo único que no cambia es que ¡TODO cambia!

††† **Expresión** En grupos de tres o cuatro estudiantes, imaginen que pasaron los últimos diez años en un sitio donde el mundo tecnológico no existe como existe hoy en sus vidas diarias. Vuelvan a escribir *(Rewrite)* la tira cómica con las cosas que les sorprende cuando vuelven al mundo de hoy.

Learning objective: Creating

¿Conoces a alguien como el hombre en la tira, que no sabe mucho del mundo de hoy? ¿Qué cosas le sorprenden?

Standards 1.2, 5.2: In Sonrisas cartoons, students interpret written language and examine language through humor, irony, and common sense. This technique guides students toward personal enjoyment and life-long uses of the language. Learners experience the wit, wisdom, and common sense in this vignette. This brief scene stimulates life-long learning using the language and cultural knowledge beyond the classroom.

Suggestion: The vignette can launch a discussion of how quickly the world is changing due to technology and other factors. Ask students, **¿Cuántos años hace que . . .?**

Optional: To review technology and further develop the theme, pose the following: **¿Crees que hay lugares en el mundo que no tienen acceso al mundo moderno? ¿Qué clase de cosas das por hecho *(take for granted)* que muchas personas del mundo no tienen? (calefacción, aire acondicionado, agua limpia, etc.) ¿Qué pensarían de tu vida?**

>> Gramática útil 3

Expressing yourself correctly: Choosing between **por** and **para**

Cómo usarlo

1. You have already learned some expressions that use the prepositions **por** (por favor, por lo general) and **para** (Para plato principal, voy a pedir…).

2. **Por** and **para** are often translated with the same words in English, but they are not used interchangeably in Spanish. Here are some guidelines to help you use them correctly.

por dentro la belleza y elegancia de las maderas nobles naturales de roble o sapelly barnizadas.

por fuera el acabado y la dureza del aluminio lacado al fuego.

Use **por**...	
to describe the *method by which an action is carried out.*	Viajamos **por** avión. Hablamos **por** teléfono. Nos comunicamos **por** Internet.
to give a *cause or reason.*	Miguel está preocupado **por** su salud. Elena está nerviosa **por** el examen.
to give a *time of day.*	Vamos al café **por** la tarde. **Por** las noches, comemos en casa.
to describe *motion through or around* a place.	Pasamos **por** la playa todas las mañanas. Vas **por** el centro de la ciudad y luego doblas a la izquierda.
to express the idea of an *exchange.*	Pagué doce dólares **por** el espejo. ¡Gracias **por** todo!
to say that something was done on *behalf of someone else.*	Lo hice **por** mi hermano porque estaba enfermo. Puedo hablar **por** ellos.
to express *units of measurement.*	Venden las naranjas **por** kilo. Venden la harina **por** gramos.
to express *duration of time.*	Estuvimos en el restaurante **por** dos horas. Fuimos a Bolivia **por** tres semanas.
in certain *fixed expressions.*	**por ejemplo** (for example) **por eso** (so, that's why) **por favor** (please) **por fin** (finally) **por lo menos** (at least) **por supuesto** (of course)

Can you figure out why **por** is used in this ad and not **para**?

Answer: Por is used because it is expressing motion through or around a place.

Optional: For high beginners, you may want to add more idioms with **por: por aquí, por algo, por casualidad, por suerte, por todas partes, por otra parte, por si acaso.**

Optional: With heritage learners and high beginners, you may want to introduce **estar para** = *to be about to /* **estar por** = *to be in favor of.*

Use **para**...

to indicate *destination*.	Salimos **para** un parque en las afueras y nos perdimos.
to indicate a *recipient* of an object or action.	El cuadro es **para** Angélica. Limpié la casa **para** mis padres.
to indicate a *deadline or specific time in the future*.	Hicimos reservaciones en el restaurante **para** la próxima semana.
to express *intent or purpose*.	Estas lámparas son **para** la sala. Vinieron temprano **para** limpiar la casa.
to indicate an *employer*.	Trabajo **para** la universidad.
to make a *comparison* or state an *opinion*	**Para** estudiante, tiene mucho dinero. **Para** mí, la sopa de ajo es la mejor de todas.

3. To aid your understanding of these two prepositions, here are some ways they are translated into English.

Por	Para
(in exchange) for	*for* (deadline)
during, in	*toward, in the direction of*
through, along	*for* (recipient or purpose)
on behalf of	*in order to* + verb
for (duration of an event)	*for . . .* (in comparison with others)
by (transportation)	*for* (employer)

ACTIVIDADES

Audioscript, Act. 9, ¿Por qué?:
1. Uy, ¡tenemos que arreglar la casa entera para mañana! 2. Héctor trabaja para el jardinero que cuida nuestro jardín. 3. ¡No lo creo! ¡Lavé la ropa por dos horas y todavía hay más! 4. Para ellos, el quehacer más aburrido es sacudir los muebles. 5. ¡Por fin hiciste todos tus quehaceres! ¿Puedes salir con nosotros ahora? 6. ¿Cuánto pagaron ustedes por esos sillones? ¡Son súper cómodos!

🔊 **9** **¿Por qué?** Escucha las oraciones. Indica si usan **por** o **para** y escoge la
Track 32   razón correcta.

1. ___para___ Razón: ☐ cause or reason   ☒ deadline
2. ___para___ Razón: ☒ employer   ☐ time of day
3. ___por___ Razón: ☒ duration of time   ☐ destination
4. ___para___ Razón: ☐ method   ☒ state opinion
5. ___por___ Razón: ☐ recipient   ☒ fixed expression
6. ___por___ Razón: ☐ intent or purpose   ☒ exchange

M **10** **¡Vamos a Nicaragua!** Ernesto va a viajar a Nicaragua. Completa su descripción con **por** o **para** para saber más de su viaje con su familia.

1. Vamos a ir a Nicaragua ___para___ las vacaciones.
2. Vamos principalmente ___para___ visitar a mis tíos.
3. Hicimos las reservaciones ___por___ Internet.
4. Pagamos muy poco ___por___ los boletos.
5. Mi tío trabaja ___para___ una compañía de telecomunicaciones en Nicaragua.
6. Nos vamos a quedar en Managua ___por___ un mes.

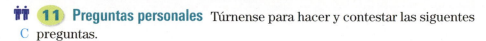

11 **Preguntas personales** Túrnense para hacer y contestar las siguientes

C   preguntas.

1. ¿Qué cosas necesitas para tu cuarto, apartamento o casa? ¿Por qué? ¿Para qué los vas a usar?

2. ¿A qué hora normalmente regresas a tu cuarto, apartamento o casa? ¿Por la tarde? ¿Por la noche?

3. Piensa en cuatro de tus posesiones favoritas. ¿Recuerdas cuánto pagaste por cada una?

4. Para ti, ¿cuál es la cosa más importante que necesitas cuando buscas un apartamento o casa? ¿Por qué?

5. ¿Qué quehaceres domésticos necesitas hacer? ¿Para cuándo debes hacerlos?

6. Si tienes compañero(a) de cuarto, ¿qué haces para ayudarle a él o ella? ¿Qué hace él o ella para ayudarte a ti?

7. Durante un día normal, ¿por cuántas horas estás en tu cuarto, apartamento o casa?

12 **¿Por o para?** Vas a hacerle cinco preguntas a tu compañero(a). Usa

C   elementos de las cuatro columnas para formar las preguntas. Luego, él o ella te va a hacer cinco preguntas a ti. Sé creativo(a) con tus preguntas y sincero(a) con tus respuestas.

MODELOS   *¿Te gusta hacer compras por Internet?*

Cuando haces reservaciones, ¿prefieres hacerlas por Internet o por teléfono?

Cuando termines la universidad, ¿quieres trabajar para una compañía internacional o nacional?

Columna A	Columna B	Columna C	Columna D
¿Te gusta...?	hacer compras	por	Internet o en persona
¿Vas a...?	hacer reservaciones	para	un restaurante, el cine, etc.
¿Quieres...?	esperar a un amigo		media hora, una hora, dos horas, etc.
¿...?	viajar		avión (autobús, tren, etc.)
	comprar un regalo		[nombre de persona]
	trabajar		una compañía (de..., multinacional, etc.)
	comunicarte		teléfono (correo electrónico, mensaje de texto, etc.)
	¿...?		¿...?

Guatemala

De Agostini/Getty Images

Información general

Nombre oficial: República de Guatemala

Población: 13.550.440

Capital: Guatemala (f. 1775) (1.104.890 hab.)

Otras ciudades importantes: Mixco (410.000 hab.), Villa Nueva (400.000 hab.)

Moneda: quetzal

Idiomas: español (oficial), lenguas mayas y otras lenguas amerindias

Mapa de Guatemala: Apéndice D

Vale saber…

- La gran civilización maya florece en grandes ciudades como Tikal, Uaxactún y Dos Pilas. Cuando llega el explorador español Pedro de Alvarado a Guatemala en 1524, la civilización maya ya está en declive *(decline)*.

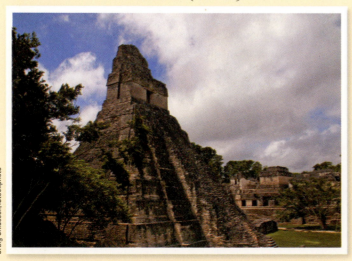

Craig Chiasson/iStockphoto

- Guatemala gana la independencia de España en 1821. Guatemala pasa por una guerra civil en los años 1960–1996. La guerra termina con un acuerdo de paz facilitado por las Naciones Unidas.

- La gran mayoría de la población o es de ascendencia maya (más del 40%), o es mestiza (59%). Hoy día en el país se hablan más de veinte lenguas de la familia maya-quiché.

- "La biblia" de los maya-quiché es el *Popol Vuh*. Este libro sagrado describe la creación de los hombres, las mujeres y el mundo entero.

Nicaragua

Información general ▶

Nombre oficial: República de Nicaragua

Población: 5.995.928

Capital: Managua (f. 1522) (2.000.000 hab.)

Otras ciudades importantes: León (200.000 hab.), Chinandega (180.000 hab.)

Moneda: córdoba

Idiomas: español (oficial), mosquito, inglés y lenguas indígenas en la costa atlántica

Mapa de Nicaragua: Apéndice D

Andoni Canela/Photolibrary

Vale saber…

- Antes de la llegada de Cristóbal Colón, varios grupos indígenas vivían en Nicaragua: los nicaraos, los chorotegas, los chontales y los mosquitos (llamados también 'misquitos' en otras partes de Centroamérica). Hoy día, el 69% de la población de Nicaragua es mestiza.

- Cristóbal Colón llega a la región en 1502, aunque las primeras colonizaciones españolas no se fundan hasta 1524. En 1838, Nicaragua se hace república independiente.

- Nicaragua ha tenido *(has had)* varios dictadores, pero la de la dinastía de Anastasio Somoza entre 1926–1979 fue la más larga. La Revolución Sandinista ocurre en 1978 y resulta en ponerle fin a la dictadura de la familia Somoza.

- En 1990, Violeta Barrios Chamorro fue la primera mujer presidenta elegida democráticamente en las Américas.

- En Acahualinca, a orillas *(on the shores)* del lago de Managua, hay unas famosas huellas *(footprints)* antiguas que tienen más de seis mil años. Una hipótesis de su origen sugiere que se formaron cuando unas personas pisaron *(they stepped on)* la lava caliente mientras escapaban de una erupción volcánica.

Nik Wheeler/Photolibrary

Bruno Domingos/Reuters/Landov

Standards: Here students gain knowledge of the Guatemalan and Nicaraguan culture (C 2.1: Practices of Culture) and compare and contrast (C 4.2: Cultural Comparisons) between multicultural Guatemala and the U. S.

Construcciones creativas

Cuando Mateo Paneitz, un voluntario del Cuerpo de Paz, llegó a San Juan Comalapa, en Guatemala, se encontró con una situación desagradable: todos echaban la basura al río, incluso él. Para resolver dos problemas a la vez, la contaminación y el desempleo, tuvo la idea de usar la basura como materia prima *(raw material)* para la construcción de edificios. Su proyecto de reciclaje ha recibido *(has received)* atención internacional por su innovación y su doble objetivo de preservar el medio ambiente *(environment)* y crear puestos de trabajo para la gente de la comunidad. La idea central de la organización *Long Way Home*, empezada por Paneitz en 2004, es construir edificios con desechos *(waste)* reciclados. En seis años, han construido una escuela, una casa, una cocina y tienen planes para construir más hogares y edificios con llantas *(tires)*, botellas, bolsas y tubos de plástico. Su primera obra, La Escuela Técnica Maya, existe como testimonio de lo que se puede hacer con una buena idea, mucha cooperación y bastante pasión.

LA PRENSA/DIANA NIVIA. Used with permission.

Hogar, verde hogar *(home)*

Las ocho mujeres superpoderosas *(powerful)* que formaron el conglomerado Alter Eco decidieron que querían crear una sinergía entre sus pequeños negocios *(businesses)* para ofrecer una nueva alternativa verde y nacional. Las seis tiendas forman un mini-centro comercial y tienen un compromiso *(obligation)* con la mujer, la naturaleza y los artesanos nicaragüenses. El lema de Alter Eco, "alianza hecha a mano *(handmade)*", lo dice todo. Carla Fjeld, una de las propietarias, explica: "…en los malls te venden cosas de todas partes del mundo y jamás conoces a las personas que las elaboran, mientras que aquí las cosas están hechas a mano, por artesanos que los clientes pueden conocer…". Puedes hacer de tu casa un hogar verde al comprar una lámpara o un bello mueble hecho de madera *(wood)* de fuentes sostenibles, o puedes decorar tu cocina con cerámicas sin plomo *(lead-free)* diseñadas por pintores nicaragüenses. El que hace sus compras en Alter Eco invita la armonía con la naturaleza a su propio hogar.

La información general

1. ¿Qué gran civilización está en declive cuando llegan los españoles a Guatemala en 1524?
2. ¿En qué año gana Guatemala la independencia de España?
3. ¿Cómo termina la guerra civil de Guatemala?
4. ¿Cuándo se hace república independiente Nicaragua?
5. ¿Qué revolución le pone fin a la dictadura de la familia Somoza?
6. ¿Quién fue la primera mujer presidenta elegida democráticamente en las Américas?

El tema de la vivienda

1. ¿Cuál es la idea central del proyecto de reciclaje de *Long Way Home?*
2. ¿Qué dos problemas intenta resolver el programa de reciclaje de *Long Way Home?*
3. ¿Qué es Alter Eco?
4. Al crear Alter Eco, ¿qué tres cosas son importantes para las propietarias?

🌐 **¿QUIERES SABER MÁS?**

Revisa y rellena la tabla que empezaste al principio del capítulo. Luego, escoge un tema para investigar en línea y prepárate para compartir la información con la clase. También puedes escoger de las palabras clave a continuación o en **www.cengagebrain.com**.

Palabras clave: (Guatemala) los dialectos maya-quiché, *Popol Vuh,* Efraín Ríos Montt, la familia de Rigoberta Menchú Tum, Augusto Monterroso, Miguel Ángel Asturias, Carlos Mérida; **(Nicaragua)**; Mosquitos, Anastasio Somoza, Sandino, Revolución Sandinista; el modernismo**,** Rubén Darío, Ernesto Cardenal, Violeta Chamorro

---

🌐 **Tú en el mundo hispano** Para explorar oportunidades de usar el español para estudiar o hacer trabajos voluntarios o aprendizajes en Guatemala y Nicaragua, sigue los enlaces en **www.cengagebrain.com**.

🎵 **Ritmos del mundo hispano** Sigue los enlaces en **www.cengagebrain.com** para escuchar música de Guatemala y Nicaragua.

Learning objectives: Understanding, Remembering

Answers, La información general.
1. la civilización maya 2. 1821 3. con un acuerdo de paz facilitado por las Naciones Unidas 4. 1838
5. la Revolución Sandinista 6. Violeta Barrios Chamorro

Answers, El tema de la vivienda:
1. construir edificios con desechos reciclados 2. la contaminación y el desempleo 3. es un conglomerado de seis tiendas 4. la mujer, la naturaleza y los artesanos nicaragüenses

Learning objectives: Analyzing, Evaluating

Standard 5.1: here students are encouraged to do independent web research on topics that will gradually require more Spanish to carry out the assignments by introducing more participation with Spanish-speaking communities online.

Check: This activity offers a built-in assessment of what the students know as they record it in **Lo que aprendí** and then allows them to expand into additional topics and subtopics through independent research.

A leer

 Standards 1.2, 2.1, 2.2, 4.1, 4.2: Throughout the reading sections in *Cuadros*, students learn to interpret the written word and develop insight into the nature of language and culture.

ESTRATEGIA

Understanding poetry

Many poems feature rhyme **(la rima)**. Words rhyme when they share similar sounds, for example, **pino** and **fino**. Blank verse **(El verso libre)** is a kind of poetry that does not follow the usual rules of rhyme. Instead, it relies on the sounds of words and the division of lines to create its own sense of rhythm and motion.

AFP/Getty Images

Valga in this context loosely means *let this (page) serve*. **Intentar** means *to try*.

Answers, Act. 2: 1. both, no 2. espero / quiero, eres / mujeres, María / mía; todo / lodo, cielo / anhelo, vida / encendida, abismos / mismos 3. nada, que, para; amo / amas / amar, con 4. el amor

1 Vas a leer un poema de Rubén Darío (1867–1916), considerado el poeta más importante de Nicaragua, y un poema en dos partes de un poeta nicaragüense vanguardista, José Coronel Urtecho (1906–1994). Estos poemas, entre otros, aparecen en un sitio web que se llama "Dariana". Lee el siguiente comentario del sitio web sobre Darío y contesta las preguntas a continuación.

"Se ha dicho que el mejor producto de exportación de Nicaragua es su poesía. Y toda nuestra mejor poesía y, por qué no, nuestra misma nicaraguanidad nacen *(are born)* y se fundamentan en Rubén Darío… Darío pronosticó que un día su poesía, indefectiblemente, iría a las muchedumbres *(would reach the masses)*. Valga esta humilde página y esta todo-abarcante *(all-encompassing)* tecnología para intentarlo".

1. Según este comentario, ¿cuál es el mejor producto de exportación de Nicaragua? la poesía

2. ¿Creía Darío que muchas o pocas personas leerían *(would read)* su poesía? muchas

2 Lee las siguientes preguntas. Después, lee los poemas de la página 371 rápidamente para buscar las respuestas. (Luego vas a leer los poemas otra vez.)

1. ¿Cuál(es) de los poemas se escribe(n) en rima? ¿Se escribe uno en verso libre?

2. Busca un ejemplo de dos palabras que riman.

3. Busca el uso de la repetición de palabras en los dos poemas. Escribe dos ejemplos de la repetición de una palabra o de palabras semejantes.

4. ¿Cuál es el tema principal de los dos poemas?

3 Ahora lee los poemas con más detalle. Escucha los sonidos *(sounds)* de las palabras y trata de entender la idea principal de cada poema.

"Dos Canciones de Amor Para El Otoño, I and II" by José Coronel Urtecho. Used with permission of the author's estate. "Amo, amas" from *Abrojos*, Imprenta Cervantes, Santiago de Chile, 1887.

LECTURA

Suggestion: Encourage reading the poems aloud to hear rhythm and make connections between content and form.

 Standard 2.2: Here students demonstrate an understanding of a literary "product and perspective" of the target culture.

Dos canciones de amor para el otoño

José Coronel Urtecho

I Cuando ya nada pido
y casi nada espero
y apenas puedo nada[1]
es cuando más te quiero.

II Basta[2] que estés, que seas
Que te pueda llamar, que te llame María
Para saber quién soy y conocer quién eres
Para saberme tuyo y conocerte mía
Mi mujer entre todas las mujeres.

Amo, amas

Rubén Darío

Amar[3], amar, amar siempre, con todo
el ser y con la tierra y con el cielo[4],
con lo claro del sol y lo oscuro del lodo[5]:
amar por toda ciencia y amar por todo anhelo[6].

Y cuando la montaña de la vida
nos sea dura y larga y alta y llena de abismos,
amar la inmensidad que es de amor encendida[7]
¡y arder[8] en la fusión de nuestros pechos[9] mismos!

[1]**apenas…:** *There's nothing to be done, I can do no more.* [2]**Basta…:** Es bastante [3]*to love* [4]**con la tierra…:** *with the earth and with the sky* [5]*mud* [6]*wish, desire* [7]*burning, on fire* [8]*to burn* [9]*hearts (literally, chests)*

 Después de leer

Learning objectives: Remembering, Understanding, Analyzing, Evaluating

4 Trabaja con un(a) compañero(a) para contestar las preguntas de comprensión.

"Dos canciones de amor para el otoño, I, II" de Coronel Urtecho

1. ¿Cuál de las siguientes oraciones mejor expresa la idea central del primer poema?
   a. Cuando el autor no tiene esperanza es cuando está más enamorado.
   b. El autor no pide ni espera el amor, porque no lo quiere.
   c. El autor no puede querer a nadie porque no tiene esperanza.

2. ¿Es optimista o pesimista la actitud del poeta? ¿Por qué? *optimista; Answers will vary.*

3. ¿Cuál de los poemas les gustó más? ¿Por qué? *Answers will vary.*

"Amo, amas" de Darío

4. ¿Cuál de las siguientes oraciones mejor expresa la idea central del poema?
   a. El amor es duro *(hard)* y difícil.
   b. El amor es como una montaña alta que es difícil escalar.
   c. El amor verdadero es eterno, como la naturaleza.

5. ¿Es optimista o pesimista la actitud del poeta? ¿Por qué? *optimista; Answers will vary.*

6. ¿Están de acuerdo con el mensaje del poema? *Answers will vary.*

A escribir

Antes de escribir

 Standard 1.3: In writing sections, students present information to readers, who may often consist of their classmates.

ESTRATEGIA

Writing—Adding transitions between paragraphs

You have learned how to write paragraphs that contain a topic sentence and supporting detail. Often the shift from one paragraph to another may sound choppy without transition words and phrases that make a thematic link **(enlace)** between the content of the two paragraphs. In that case you may need to write an opening transition sentence for a new paragraph that is then followed by the topic sentence, or add a transitional phrase to the beginning of your topic sentence.

1 Vas a escribir una descripción de tres párrafos. Escoge tu sitio preferido en tu cuarto, residencia estudiantil, apartamento o casa y descríbelo. Después, habla de lo que haces allí y explica por qué es tu sitio preferido. Organiza la información según la siguiente tabla.

Párrafo 1: ¿Cómo es el sitio?	Párrafo 2: ¿Qué haces allí?	Párrafo 3: ¿Por qué es tu sitio preferido?
Oración temática:	Oración temática:	Oración temática:
Detalles interesantes:	Detalles interesantes:	Detalles interesantes:

Marcos Welsh /age fotostock

Composición   Learning objective: Creating

2   Escribe el borrador de tu composición, escribiendo sin detener *(freewriting)* y sin preocuparte por el momento por las transiciones entre párrafos.

Después de escribir

3   Ahora vas a crear las transiciones entre los párrafos. Mira tu composición y copia las oraciones indicadas en otra hoja de papel.

1. Última oración del Párrafo 1:
2. Primera oración del Párrafo 2:

3. Última oración del Párrafo 2:
4. Primera oración del Párrafo 3:

4   Mira las oraciones que escribiste para la **Actividad 3** y añade las transiciones entre los párrafos. Aquí tienes algunas palabras y expresiones que pueden servir como enlaces.

a pesar de que	*in spite of*
afortunadamente	*fortunately*
al contrario	*on the contrary*
como resultado	*as a result*
de esta manera / de este modo	*(in) this way*
de igual importancia	*of equal importance*
de la misma manera / del mismo modo	*in the same way*
desgraciadamente	*unfortunately*
por un lado	*on one hand*
por el otro lado	*on the other hand*
por esta razón	*for this reason*
sin decir más / demasiado	*without saying more / too much*
sin embargo	*nevertheless*

1. Enlace entre Párrafo 1 y Párrafo 2:
2. Enlace entre Párrafo 2 y Párrafo 3:

5   Revisa la composición y añade tus nuevos enlaces. Usa la siguiente lista para ayudarte a revisar la composición entera otra vez.

- ¿Ayudan los enlaces a clarificar la transición entre los párrafos?
- ¿Usaste algunas de las palabras y expresiones de la lista para los enlaces?
- ¿Hay algo que no es necesario? ¿Hay algo que falta *(is missing)*?
- ¿Usaste bien las formas posesivas?
- ¿Usaste **por** y **para** correctamente?
- ¿Hay errores de puntuación o de ortografía?

Vocabulario

Áreas de la ciudad   *Parts of the city*

las afueras *the outskirts*
el apartamento *apartment*
el barrio *neighborhood*
...comercial *business district*
...residencial *residential neighborhood*

el centro de la ciudad *downtown*
los suburbios *suburbs*
los vecinos *neighbors*

La casa   *The house*

el baño *bathroom*
la chimenea *fireplace*
el clóset *closet*
la cocina *kitchen*
el comedor *dining room*
el dormitorio (el cuarto, la habitación, la recámara) *bedroom*
las escaleras *stairs*
el garaje *garage*
el jardín *garden, yard*

la lavandería *laundry room*
la oficina *office*
la pared *wall*
el pasillo *hallway*
el patio *patio*
el primer piso (segundo, etc.) *first floor (second, etc.)*
la sala *living room*
el sótano *basement, cellar*
el techo *roof*

Números ordinales   *Ordinal numbers*

primer(o) *first*
segundo *second*
tercer(o) *third*
cuarto *fourth*
quinto *fifth*

sexto *sixth*
séptimo *seventh*
octavo *eighth*
noveno *ninth*
décimo *tenth*

Los quehaceres domésticos   *Household chores*

Dentro de la casa   *Inside the house*
arreglar el dormitorio *to straighten up the bedroom*
barrer el suelo (el piso) *to sweep the floor*
guardar la ropa *to put away the clothes*
hacer la cama *to make the bed*
lavar los platos (la ropa) *to wash the dishes (the clothes)*
limpiar el baño *to clean the bathroom*
pasar la aspiradora *to vacuum*
planchar *to iron*
poner los juguetes en su lugar *to put the toys away*
poner y quitar la mesa *to set and to clear the table*
preparar la comida *to prepare the food*
sacudir los muebles *to dust the furniture*
trapear el piso *to mop the floor*

Fuera de la casa   *Outside the house*
cortar el césped *to mow the lawn*
darle de comer al perro (gato) *to feed the dog (cat)*

hacer el reciclaje *to do the recycling*
regar (ie) las plantas *to water the plants*
sacar a pasear al perro *to take the dog for a walk*
sacar la basura *to take out the garbage*

Los muebles y decoraciones   *Furniture and decorations*
la alfombra *rug, carpet*
la cama *bed*
las cortinas *curtains*
el cuadro *painting, print*
el espejo *mirror*
la lámpara *lamp*
la mesa *table*
la mesita de noche *night table*
la persiana *Venetian blind*
la silla *chair*
el sillón *armchair*
el sofá *sofa*
el tocador (la cómoda) *dresser*

Los electrodomésticos *Appliances*

el abrelatas eléctrico *electric can opener*
la aspiradora *vacuum cleaner*
el congelador *freezer*
la estufa *stove*
la lavadora *washer*
el lavaplatos *dishwasher*
la licuadora *blender*

el microondas *microwave*
la plancha *iron*
el procesador de comida *food processor*
el refrigerador *refrigerator*
la secadora *dryer*
el televisor *television set*
la tostadora *toaster*

Adjetivos posesivos

mío, mía, míos, mías *my, mine*
tuyo, tuya, tuyos, tuyas *your, yours*
suyo, suya, suyos, suyas *your, yours, his, her, hers, its, their, theirs*
nuestro, nuestra, nuestros, nuestras *our, ours*
vuestro, vuestra, vuestros, vuestras *your, yours*

Otras palabras y expresiones

para *for, by* (a deadline); *toward, in the direction of; for* (a specific recipient, employer, or purpose); *in order to* (+ verb); *for. . .* (in comparison with others)
por (in exchange) *for; during; through, along; on behalf of; for* (duration of an event); *by* (a means of transportation)
por ejemplo *for example*
por eso *so, that's why*
por favor *please*
por fin *finally*
por lo menos *at least*
por supuesto *of course*

Repaso y preparación

>> **Repaso del Capítulo 10** Preparation: Have students review this material and complete the activities here, in the SAM, and online before they begin **Chapter 11**.

Complete these activities to check your understanding of the new grammar points in **Chapter 10** before you move on to **Chapter 11**.

The answers to the activities in this section can be found in **Appendix B**.

Check: The **Repaso** section not only reviews grammar and vocabulary for the student but it offers a built-in performance assessment. By doing review activities with students, you can assess concepts that you may need to continue to reinforce in future classes.

Answers, Act. 1: 1. ¿La aspiradora? No es tuya. Es suya. 2. ¿Las licuadoras? No son suyas. Son mías. 3. ¿Las planchas? No son nuestras. Son suyas. 4. ¿La tostadora? No es mía. Es suya. 5. ¿Los microondas? No son suyos. Son nuestros. 6. ¿El lavaplatos? No es suyo. Es tuyo.

Answers, Act. 2: 1. Hace un año que Sarita no va de vacaciones. 2. Hace seis meses que ellos viven en esa casa. 3. Ellos limpiaron el baño hace dos semanas. 4. Hacía tres meses que Luis no podía trabajar en la casa. 5. Los abuelos vinieron de visita hace dos años.

Stressed possessives (p. 358)

1 Escribe oraciones con posesivos enfáticos según el modelo.

MODELO yo (no) / tú (sí)
¿La licuadora? No es mía. Es tuya.

1.

tú (no) / ellos (sí)

2.

usted (no) / yo (sí)

3.

nosotros (no) /
ustedes (sí)

4.

yo (no) / ella (sí)

5.

él (no) / nosotros (sí)

6.

ellos (no) / tú (sí)

Hace / Hacía with time expressions (p. 360)

2 Contesta las preguntas con oraciones que contengan **hace** o **hacía** para expresar la duración de un evento o situación. Presta atención al contexto para ver si se refiere al momento presente o al pasado.

1. ¿Cuánto tiempo hace que Sarita no va de vacaciones? (un año)
2. ¿Cuánto tiempo hace que ellos viven en esa casa? (seis meses)
3. ¿Cuánto tiempo hace que ellos limpiaron el baño? (dos semanas)
4. ¿Cuánto tiempo hacía que Luis no podía trabajar en la casa? (tres meses)
5. ¿Cuánto tiempo hace que los abuelos vinieron de visita? (dos años)

Por and para (p. 363)

3 Completa las oraciones con **por** o **para**, según el caso.

1. ¡Pagué sólo cuarenta dólares ___por___ ese sillón!
2. ___Para___ mí, es importante tener una casa limpia.
3. ¡___Por___ fin arreglaste tu dormitorio!
4. Limpiamos la casa ___por___ tres horas ayer.
5. Compré esta lámpara ___para___ Angelita.
6. ___Por___ la mañana, normalmente lavo la ropa.
7. ¡Tenemos que organizar y limpiar la sala ___para___ mañana!
8. Mi madre trabaja ___para___ una tienda que vende muebles.

All art: © Cengage Learning 2013

Preparación para el Capítulo 11 Learning objective: Evaluating

Complete these activities to review some previously learned grammatical structures that will be helpful when you learn the new grammar in **Chapter 11**.

In addition, be sure to reread **Chapter 10: Gramática útil 1** before moving on to the new **Chapter 11** grammar sections.

Regular and stem-changing present-indicative **yo** forms (Chapters 2, 3, and 4)

4 Completa las oraciones con las formas correctas de **yo** de los verbos indicados.

Todas las semanas, tengo mucho que hacer en casa.

1. _____Lavo_____ (lavar) los platos.
2. _____Plancho_____ (planchar) la ropa.
3. _____Barro_____ (barrer) el suelo.
4. _____Sacudo_____ (sacudir) los muebles.
5. _____Hiervo_____ (hervir) el agua para el café.
6. _____Riego_____ (regar) las plantas.

7. _____Sirvo_____ (servir) la comida a la familia.
8. _____Vuelvo_____ (volver) a lavar los platos.
9. Les _____pido_____ (pedir) ayuda a los hijos.
10. Al final del día, ¡_____duermo_____ (dormir) muy bien!

Irregular-**yo** forms and **yo** forms of irregular verbs (Chapters 1, 3, 4, and 5)

5 Completa las oraciones con la forma **yo** del verbo indicado.

1. _____Estoy_____ (estar) en el jardín.
2. _____Conduzco_____ (conducir) al centro.
3. A las seis, le _____doy_____ (dar) de comer al perro.
4. Le _____digo_____ (decir) "Hola" a mi vecino.
5. _____Oigo_____ (oír) el tono de la secadora.
6. _____Vengo_____ (venir) para cortar el césped.

7. _____Veo_____ (ver) al jardinero los lunes.
8. _____Sé_____ (saber) reparar la tostadora.
9. _____Pongo_____ (poner) la mesa para la cena.
10. _____Tengo_____ (tener) una sofá y dos sillones.

Negative tú commands (Chapter 7)

6 Completa las oraciones con los mandatos negativos informales correctos.

1. Por favor, no _____laves_____ (lavar) los platos ahora mismo.
2. ¡Ay, no _____planches_____ (planchar) esa blusa de seda!
3. No _____saques_____ (sacar) a pasear al perro cuando hace mucho frío.
4. No _____pases_____ (pasar) la aspiradora mientras los niños están durmiendo.
5. ¡No _____pongas_____ (poner) la mesa con esas copas sucias!
6. No _____uses_____ (usar) ese microondas; está roto.
7. No _____trapees_____ (trapear) el piso cuando estoy preparando la comida.
8. No _____sacudas_____ (sacudir) los muebles con ese trapo sucio.
9. ¡No _____comas_____ (comer) dulces antes de la cena!
10. No _____insistas_____ (insistir) en ver ese programa; ya es tarde.

Reference Materials

Appendix A: KWL Chart

Lo que sé	Lo que quiero saber	Lo que aprendí

Capítulo 1 (pp. 40–41)

Act. 1: 1. la 2. X 3. la 4. X 5. X 6. X 7. unos 8. una 9. los

Act. 2: 1. Tú 2. Nosotros 3. Yo 4. es 5. son 6. somos

Act. 3: 1. Hay dos chicas. 2. Hay un hombre. 3. Hay una mujer. 4. No hay niño. 5. No hay computadora. 6. No hay mochila. 7. Hay una serpiente. 8. No hay elefante.

Act. 4: 1. tienes 2. tiene 3. tengo 4. tenemos 5. tienen 6. tienes

Act. 5: 1. tengo que 2. tienen que 3. tenemos que 4. tiene que 5. tienes que 6. tienen que

Act. 6: *Answers will vary depending on current year.* 1. Tú tienes… años. 2. Ellos tienen… años. 3. Usted tiene… años. 4. Ella tiene… años. 5. Yo tengo… años. 6. Nosotros tenemos… años. 7. Ustedes tienen… años. 8. Tú y yo tenemos… años.

Capítulo 2 (pp. 80–81)

Act. 1: 1. Esteban y Carolina caminan. 2. Usted pinta. 3. Loreta levanta pesas. 4. Yo saco fotos. 5. Nosotros tomamos el sol. 6. Tú cocinas. 7. Ustedes hablan por teléfono. 8. Tú y yo patinamos.

Act. 2: 1. A mí me gusta estudiar. 2. A ti te gusta mirar televisión. 3. A usted le gusta visitar a amigos. 4. A nosotras nos gusta pintar. 5. A ustedes les gusta practicar deportes.

Act. 3: 1. Gretchen y Rolf son alemanes. Son muy sinceros. 2. Brigitte es francesa. Es muy divertida. 3. Nosotras somos españolas. Somos simpáticas. 4. Yo soy estadounidense. Soy muy generosa. 5. Usted es japonesa. Es muy interesante. 6. Tú eres italiano. Eres muy activo.

Act. 4: 1. las 2. El 3. la 4. unos 5. la 6. una 7. un 8. la 9. la 10. las

Act. 5: 1. f, es 2. d, es 3. a, es 4. g, son 5. b, somos 6. e, eres 7. c, soy

Capítulo 3 (pp. 118–119)

Act. 1: 1. qué 2. Por qué 3. Cuál 4. cuándo 4. Cuántas 5. Quién

Act. 2: 1. escribe 2. debemos 3. como 4. viven 5. lee

Act. 3: 1. mis 2. tus 3. nuestra 4. sus 5. sus 6. mi

Act. 4: 1. voy, van 2. va, vamos 3. vas

Act. 5: 1. A mí me gusta leer. 2. A nosotros nos gusta comer. 3. A ustedes les gusta bailar. 4. A ti te gusta cocinar. 5. A él le gusta patinar. 6. A mí me gusta cantar.

Act. 6: 1. estudia 2. cocina 3. toca 4. canta 5. levantan 6. practican 7. miramos 8. alquilamos 9. trabajo 10. visito 11. paso

Act. 7: 1. Rogelio y Mauricio son muy egoístas. 2. Tú eres muy impaciente. 3. Nosotros somos muy perezosos. 4. Yo soy muy activo(a). 5. Sandra es muy generosa. 6. Néstor y Nicolás son muy tímidos.

Capítulo 4 (pp. 158–159)

Act. 1: 1. les gustan 2. me encanta 3. le molesta 4. nos interesan 5. te importa 6. le gusta

Act. 2: 1. estás 2. estamos 3. soy 4. son 5. Estoy 6. Está 7. es 8. es 9. está 10. son 11. es 12. están

Act. 3: 1. Tú duermes mucho. 2. Yo cierro la computadora portátil. 3. Ella entiende las instrucciones. 4. Nosotras jugamos el juego interactivo. 5. Usted repite la contraseña. 6. Ellos quieren un MP3 portátil. 7. Yo puedo instalar el programa. 8. Nosotros preferimos ir a un café con wifi.

Act. 4: 1. lentamente 2. rápidamente 3. Generalmente 4. fácilmente

Act. 5: debe, envias, recibes, grabas, instalas, llevas, trabajas, hablan, funciona, bajo, subo, pesa, saco, accedo, leo, usamos, comentan, ofrecemos, vendemos, debes

Capítulo 5 (pp. 194–195)

Act. 1: *Answers will vary for **Sí/No** column.* 1. Sé 2. Conozco 3. Conduzco 4. Hago 5. Salgo 6. Veo

Act. 2: 1. Tú conoces Buenos Aires. 2. Ellos saben jugar golf. 3. Yo sé todas las respuestas. 4. Usted conoce a mis primos. 5. Nosotras conocemos al chef. 6. Ella sabe cocinar bien.

Act. 3: 1. se maquilla 2. me acuesto 3. se reunen 4. te levantas 5. nos enfermamos 6. se pelean

Act. 4: 1. Ella está hablando con un paciente. 2. Yo estoy escribiendo un artículo. 3. Ellos están preparando la comida. 4. Nosotros estamos pintando. 5. Usted está sirviendo la comida. 6. Él está trabajando en la computadora.

Act. 5: 1. grande 2. extrovertidas 3. simpáticas 4. tonto 5. contentos 6. nerviosos 7. viejos 8. divertidos 9. triste

Act. 6: 1. Mi tío lava su auto todas las semanas. 2. Mis abuelos no duermen mucho. 3. Mis primas prefieren estudiar en la residencia estudiantil. 4. Mi hermano y yo corremos en el parque los sábados. 5. Tú manejas todos los días. 6. Mi madre viste a mi hermanita por las mañanas. 7. Yo miro una película. 8. Mi madre y yo vivimos en un apartamento grande.

Act. 7: 1. La mujer de negocios está en la oficina. 2. Tú y yo estamos en el salón de clase. 3. El Doctor Méndez está en el hospital. 4. Los programadores están en el centro de computación. 5. La policía está en el parque. 6. Yo estoy en la biblioteca. 7. Los cocineros están en el restaurante. 8. Tú estás en el gimnasio.

Capítulo 6 (pp. 228–229)

Act. 1: El perro está lejos del auto. 2. El perro está delante del auto. 3. El perro está detrás del auto. 4. El perro está debajo del auto. 5. El perro está dentro del auto. 6. El perro está entre los autos.

Act. 2: 1. Vengan, pierdan 2. Ponga, Hable 3. Haga, Llame

Act. 3: 1. Siempre, 2. También, 3. algunos 4. nada 5. algo 6. nadie

Act. 4: 1. estos, ésos 2. aquella, ésta 3. esos, aquéllos 4. esta, ésa 5. aquellas, éstas 6. este, ése

Act. 5: 1. salgo 2. traigo 3. Pongo 4. conduzco 5. veo 6. conozco 7. Oigo 8. hago 9. digo 10. sé

Act. 6: 1. te preparas 2. me acuesto 3. nos preocupamos 4. se están divirtiendo / están divirtiéndose 5. se quejen 6. Siéntese, relájese

Capítulo 7 (pp. 266–267)

Act. 1: 1. montaste 2. leyó 3. compartí 4. navegamos 5. corrieron

Act. 2: 1. Tú y yo fuimos... 2. Marilena estuvo... 3. Yo hice... 4. Guille y Paulina dijeron... 5. Mis padres condujeron... 6. Tú tradujiste...

Act. 3: 1. ¿Los perros? Tú los lavaste. 2. ¿El surfing? Victoria lo hizo. 3. ¿La pelota (de golf)? Yo no la encontré. 4. ¿Las mochilas? Nosotros las perdimos. 5. ¿Los refrescos? Ustedes no los bebieron. 6. ¿Las pesas? Esteban y Federico no las levantaron.

Act. 4: 1. pongas, Ten, lee 2. Pon, siéntate, salgas

Act. 5: 1. quieren 2. me divierto 3. se visten 4. pueden 5. duermo 6. pides

Act. 6: 1. A mí me gusta remar. 2. A usted le gusta nadar. 3. A ti te gustan esos esquíes. 4. A ellos les gusta el boxeo. 5. A nosotros nos gusta pescar. 6. A ella le gusta la nieve. 7. A ti te gusta entrenarte. 8. A mí me gustan las vacaciones. 9. A nosotros nos gusta la primavera.

Act. 7: 1. sé 2. conozco 3. saben 4. podemos 5. pueden 6. conocemos 7. quiero 8. puedo

Capítulo 8 (pp. 304–305)

Act. 1: 1. Supe 2. hicimos 3. sugirió 4. preferí 5. sirvió 6. dijo 7. quiso 8. pudo 9. tuvo 10. pidió 11. puso 12. anduvimos 13. Nos reímos 14. nos divertimos 15. nos despedimos 16. dijimos

Act. 2: 1. nos 2. te 3. les 4. me 5. le

Act. 3: 1. tantos, como 2. más, que 3. menos, que 4. tan, como 5. el más 6. más

Act. 4: 1. compraste 2. vi 3. estuvo 4. trajo 5. fuimos 6. dieron 7. hiciste 8. escribió

Act. 5: 1. Delfina lo compró. 2. Diego y Eduardo no la compraron. 3. Tú no los compraste. 4. Yo los compré. 5. Nosotros las compramos. 6. Usted no lo compró.

Act. 6: 1. Yo me puse un abrigo. 2. Ellos se pusieron unas sandalias. 3. Tú te pusiste un chaleco. 4. Nosotros nos pusimos unos jeans. 5. Ella se puso una bufanda. 7. Ustedes se pusieron un impermeable.

Capítulo 9 (pp. 344–345)

Act. 1: 1. La señora Muñoz preparaba unas galletas. 2. Yo freía un huevo. 3. Nosotros pelábamos zanahorias para una ensalada. 4. Manolito ponía la mesa. 5. Sarita y Carmela picaban cebollas para una sopa. 6. Tú hervías agua para preparar el té.

Act. 2: 1. Eran 2. quería 3. llegué 4. vi 5. estaba 6. tenía 7. me senté 8. empezamos 9. hablábamos 10. dijo 11. exclamé 12. sabía 13. Me despedí 14. salí 15. Estaba 16. quería

Act. 3: 1. Ábrenosla. 2. Cuéceselos. 3. No me lo compres. 4. No se lo calientes. 5. Pásanosla. 6. No se la prepares.

Act. 4: 1. come 2. venden 3. hablan 4. sirve 5. cierra 6. duerme

Act. 5: 1. Los manteles son rojos. 2. El flan es bueno. 3. Las almejas están frescas. 4. El café está caliente. 5. La carne está frita. 6. Los huevos son blancos. 7. El pescado está crudo. 8. El té está frío. 9. La limonada es dulce. 10. Los platos están limpios. 11. La langosta es cara. 12. Las fresas son baratas.

Act. 6: 1. mi 2. tus 3. nuestro 4. sus 5. sus 6. su 7. sus 8. su 9. nuestras 10. tus

Act. 7: 1. hiciste 2. hago 3. hizo 4. hicieron 5. hacemos

Capítulo 10 (pp. 376–377)

Act. 1: 1. ¿La aspiradora? No es tuya. Es suya. 2. ¿Las licuadoras? No son suyas. Son mías. 3. ¿Las planchas? No son nuestras. Son suyas. 4. ¿La tostadora? No es mía. Es suya. 5. ¿Los microondas? No son suyos. Son nuestros. 6. ¿El lavaplatos? No es suyo. Es tuyo.

Act. 2: 1. Hace un año que Sarita no va de vacaciones. 2. Hace seis meses que ellos viven en esa casa. 3. Ellos limpiaron el baño hace dos semanas. 4. Hacía tres meses que Luis no podía trabajar en la casa. 5. Los abuelos vinieron de visita hace dos años.

Act. 3: 1. por 2. Para 3. Por 4. por 5. para 6. Por 7. para 8. para

Act. 4: 1. Lavo 2. Plancho 3. Barro 4. Sacudo 5. Hiervo 6. Riego 7. Sirvo 8. Vuelvo 9. pido 10. duermo

Act. 5: 1. Estoy 2. Conduzco 3. doy 4. digo 5. Oigo 6. Vengo 7. Veo 8. Sé 9. Pongo 10. Tengo

Act. 6: 1. laves 2. planches 3. saques 4. pases 5. pongas 6. uses 7. trapees 8. sacudas 9. comas 10. insistas

Regular Verbs

Simple Tenses

Infinitive	Past participle / Present participle	Indicative					Subjunctive	
		Present	Imperfect	Preterite	Future	Conditional	Present	Imperfect*
cantar *to sing*	cantado cantando	canto cantas canta cantamos cantáis cantan	cantaba cantabas cantaba cantábamos cantabais cantaban	canté cantaste cantó cantamos cantasteis cantaron	cantaré cantarás cantará cantaremos cantaréis cantarán	cantaría cantarías cantaría cantaríamos cantaríais cantarían	cante cantes cante cantemos cantéis canten	cantara cantaras cantara cantáramos cantarais cantaran
correr *to run*	corrido corriendo	corro corres corre corremos corréis corren	corría corrías corría corríamos corríais corrían	corrí corriste corrió corrimos corristeis corrieron	correré correrás correrá correremos correréis correrán	correría correrías correría correríamos correríais correrían	corra corras corra corramos corráis corran	corriera corrieras corriera corriéramos corrierais corrieran
subir *to go up, to climb up*	subido subiendo	subo subes sube subimos subís suben	subía subías subía subíamos subíais subían	subí subiste subió subimos subisteis subieron	subiré subirás subirá subiremos subiréis subirán	subiría subirías subiría subiríamos subiríais subirían	suba subas suba subamos subáis suban	subiera subieras subiera subiéramos subierais subieran

*In addition to this form, another one is less frequently used for all regular and irregular verbs: cantase, cantases, cantase, cantásemos, cantaseis, cantasen; corriese, corrieses, corriese, corriésemos, corrieseis, corriesen; subiese, subieses, subiese, subiésemos, subieseis, subiesen.

Commands

Person	Affirmative	Negative	Affirmative	Negative	Affirmative	Negative
tú	canta	no cantes	corre	no corras	sube	no subas
usted	cante	no cante	corra	no corra	suba	no suba
nosotros	cantemos	no cantemos	corramos	no corramos	subamos	no subamos
vosotros	cantad	no cantéis	corred	no corráis	subid	no subáis
ustedes	canten	no canten	corran	no corran	suban	no suban

Stem-Changing Verbs: -ar and -er Groups

Type of change in the verb stem	Subject	Indicative Present	Subjunctive Present	Commands Affirmative	Commands Negative	Other -ar and -er stem-changing verbs
-ar verbs **e > ie** pensar *to think*	yo	pienso	piense	—	—	atravesar *to go through, to cross;* cerrar *to close;* despertarse *to wake up;* empezar *to start;* negar *to deny;* sentarse *to sit down* Nevar *to snow* is only conjugated in the third-person singular.
	tú	piensas	pienses	piensa	no pienses	
	él/ella, Ud.	piensa	piense	piense	no piense	
	nosotros/as	pensamos	pensemos	pensemos	no pensemos	
	vosotros/as	pensáis	penséis	pensad	no penséis	
	ellos/as, Uds.	piensan	piensen	piensen	no piensen	
-ar verbs **o > ue** contar *to count, to tell*	yo	cuento	cuente	—	—	acordarse *to remember;* acostarse *to go to bed;* almorzar *to have lunch;* colgar *to hang;* costar *to cost;* demostrar *to demonstrate;* mostrar *to show;* encontrar *to find;* mostrar *to show;* probar *to prove, to taste;* recordar *to remember*
	tú	cuentas	cuentes	cuenta	no cuentes	
	él/ella, Ud.	cuenta	cuente	cuente	no cuente	
	nosotros/as	contamos	contemos	contemos	no contemos	
	vosotros/as	contáis	contéis	contad	no contéis	
	ellos/as, Uds.	cuentan	cuenten	cuenten	no cuenten	
-er verbs **e > ie** entender *to understand*	yo	entiendo	entienda	—	—	encender *to light, to turn on;* extender *to stretch;* perder *to lose*
	tú	entiendes	entiendas	entiende	no entiendas	
	él/ella, Ud.	entiende	entienda	entienda	no entienda	
	nosotros/as	entendemos	entendamos	entendamos	no entendamos	
	vosotros/as	entendéis	entendáis	entended	no entendáis	
	ellos/as, Uds.	entienden	entiendan	entiendan	no entiendan	
-er verbs **o > ue** volver *to return*	yo	vuelvo	vuelva	—	—	mover *to move;* torcer *to twist* Llover *to rain* is only conjugated in the third-person singular.
	tú	vuelves	vuelvas	vuelve	no vuelvas	
	él/ella, Ud.	vuelve	vuelva	vuelva	no vuelva	
	nosotros/as	volvemos	volvamos	volvamos	no volvamos	
	vosotros/as	volvéis	volváis	volved	no volváis	
	ellos/as, Uds.	vuelven	vuelvan	vuelvan	no vuelvan	

Stem-Changing Verbs: -ir Verbs

Type of change in the verb stem	Subject	Indicative			Subjunctive		Commands	
		Present	Preterite		Present	Imperfect	Affirmative	Negative
-ir verbs e > ie or i **Infinitive:** sentir *to feel* **Present participle:** sintiendo	yo tú él/ella, Ud. nosotros/as vosotros/as ellos/as, Uds.	siento sientes siente sentimos sentís sienten	sentí sentiste sintió sentimos sentisteis sintieron		sienta sientas sienta sintamos sintáis sientan	sintiera sintieras sintiera sintiéramos sintierais sintieran	— siente sienta sintamos sentid sientan	— no sientas no sienta no sintamos no sintáis no sientan
-ir verbs o > ue or u **Infinitive:** dormir *to sleep* **Present participle:** durmiendo	yo tú él/ella, Ud. nosotros/as vosotros/as ellos/as, Uds.	duermo duermes duerme dormimos dormís duermen	dormí dormiste durmió dormimos dormisteis durmieron		duerma duermas duerma durmamos durmáis duerman	durmiera durmieras durmiera durmiéramos durmierais durmieran	— duerme duerma durmamos dormid duerman	— no duermas no duerma no durmamos no durmáis no duerman

Other similar verbs: advertir *to warn;* arrepentirse *to repent;* consentir *to consent, pamper;* convertir(se) *to turn into;* divertir(se) *to amuse (oneself);* herir *to hurt, wound;* mentir *to lie;* morir *to die;* preferir *to prefer;* referir *to refer;* sugerir *to suggest*

Type of change in the verb stem	Subject	Indicative		Subjunctive		Commands	
		Present	Preterite	Present	Imperfect	Affirmative	Negative
-ir verbs e > i **Infinitive:** pedir *to ask for, to request* **Present participle:** pidiendo	yo tú él/ella, Ud. nosotros/as vosotros/as ellos/as, Uds.	pido pides pide pedimos pedís piden	pedí pediste pidió pedimos pedisteis pidieron	pida pidas pida pidamos pidáis pidan	pidiera pidieras pidiera pidiéramos pidierais pidieran	— pide pida pidamos pedid pidan	— no pidas no pida no pidamos no pidáis no pidan

Other similar verbs: competir *to compete;* despedir(se) *to say good-bye;* elegir *to choose;* impedir *to prevent;* perseguir *to chase;* repetir *to repeat;* seguir *to follow;* servir *to serve;* vestir(se) *to dress, to get dressed*

Verbs with Spelling Changes

	Verb type	Ending	Change	Verbs with similar spelling changes
1	buscar *to look for*	-car	• Preterite: yo busqué • Present subjunctive: busque, busques, busque, busquemos, busquéis, busquen	comunicar, explicar *to explain* indicar *to indicate*, sacar, pescar
2	conocer *to know*	*vowel +* -cer or -cir	• Present indicative: conozco, conoces, conoce, and so on • Present subjunctive: conozca, conozcas, conozca, conozcamos, conozcáis, conozcan	nacer *to be born*, obedecer, ofrecer, parecer, pertenecer *to belong*, reconocer, conducir, traducir
3	vencer *to win*	*consonant +* -cer or -cir	• Present indicative: venzo, vences, vence, and so on • Present subjunctive: venza, venzas, venza, venzamos, venzáis, venzan	convencer, torcer *to twist*
4	leer *to read*	-eer	• Preterite: leyó, leyeron • Imperfect subjunctive: leyera, leyeras, leyera, leyéramos, leyerais, leyeran • Present participle: leyendo	creer, poseer *to own*
5	llegar *to arrive*	-gar	• Preterite: yo llegué • Present subjunctive: llegue, llegues, llegue, lleguemos, lleguéis, lleguen	colgar *to hang*, navegar, negar *to negate, to deny*, pagar, rogar *to beg*, jugar
6	escoger *to choose*	-ger or -gir	• Present indicative: escojo, escoges, escoge, and so on • Present subjunctive: escoja, escojas, escoja, escojamos, escojáis, escojan	proteger, *to protect*, recoger *to collect, gather*, corregir *to correct*, dirigir *to direct*, elegir *to elect, choose*, exigir *to demand*
7	seguir *to follow*	-guir	• Present indicative: sigo, sigues, sigue, and so on • Present subjunctive: siga, sigas, siga, sigamos, sigáis, sigan	conseguir, distinguir, perseguir
8	huir *to flee*	-uir	• Present indicative: huyo, huyes, huye, huimos, huis, huyen • Preterite: huí, huiste, huyó, huimos, huisteis, huyeron • Present subjunctive: huya, huyas, huya, huyamos, huyáis, huyan • Imperfect subjunctive: huyera, huyeras, huyera, huyéramos, huyerais, huyeran • Present participle: huyendo • Commands: huye (tú), huya usted, huyamos (nosotros), huid (vosotros), huyan (ustedes), (negative) no huyas (tú), no huya (usted), no huyamos (nosotros), no huyáis (vosotros), no huyan (ustedes)	concluir, contribuir, construir, destruir, disminuir, distribuir, excluir, influir, instruir, restituir, substituir
9	abrazar *to embrace*	-zar	• Preterite: yo abracé • Present subjunctive: abrace, abraces, abrace, abracemos, abracéis, abracen	alcanzar *to achieve*, almorzar, comenzar, empezar, gozar *to enjoy*, rezar *to pray*

Compound Tenses

	Indicative					Subjunctive	
	Present perfect	Past perfect	Preterite perfect	Future perfect	Conditional perfect	Present perfect	Past perfect
	he	había	hube	habré	habría	haya	hubiera
	has	habías	hubiste	habrás	habrías	hayas	hubieras
cantado	ha	había	hubo	habrá	habría	haya	hubiera
corrido	hemos	habíamos	hubimos	habremos	habríamos	hayamos	hubiéramos
subido	habéis	habíais	hubisteis	habréis	habríais	hayáis	hubierais
	han	habían	hubieron	habrán	habrían	hayan	hubieran

(cantado / corrido / subido combine with each form)

All verbs, both regular and irregular, follow the same formation pattern with **haber** in all compound tenses. The only thing that changes is the form of the past participle of each verb. (See the chart below for common verbs with irregular past participles.) Remember that in Spanish, no word can come between **haber** and the past participle.

Common Irregular Past Participles

Infinitive	Past participle	
abrir	**abierto**	opened
caer	caído	fallen
creer	creído	believed
cubrir	**cubierto**	covered
decir	**dicho**	said, told
descubrir	**descubierto**	discovered
escribir	**escrito**	written
hacer	**hecho**	made, done
leer	leído	read

Infinitive	Past participle	
morir	**muerto**	died
oír	oído	heard
poner	**puesto**	put, placed
resolver	**resuelto**	resolved
romper	**roto**	broken, torn
(son)reír	(son)reído	(smiled) laughed
traer	traído	brought
ver	**visto**	seen
volver	**vuelto**	returned

Reflexive Verbs

Regular and Irregular Reflexive Verbs: Position of the Reflexive Pronouns in the Simple Tenses

Infinitive	Present participle	Reflexive pronouns	Indicative					Subjunctive	
			Present	Imperfect	Preterite	Future	Conditional	Present	Imperfect
lavarse	lavándome	me	lavo	lavaba	lavé	lavaré	lavaría	lave	lavara
to wash	lavándote	te	lavas	lavabas	lavaste	lavarás	lavarías	laves	lavaras
oneself	lavándose	se	lava	lavaba	lavó	lavará	lavaría	lave	lavara
	lavándonos	nos	lavamos	lavábamos	lavamos	lavaremos	lavaríamos	lavemos	laváramos
	lavándoos	os	laváis	lavabais	lavasteis	lavaréis	lavaríais	lavéis	lavarais
	lavándose	se	lavan	lavaban	lavaron	lavarán	lavarían	laven	lavaran

Regular and irregular reflexive verbs: Position of the reflexive pronouns with commands

Person	Affirmative	Negative	Affirmative	Negative	Affirmative	Negative
tú	lávate	no te laves	ponte	no te pongas	vístete	no te vistas
usted	lávese	no se lave	póngase	no se ponga	vístase	no se vista
nosotros	lavémonos	no nos lavemos	pongámonos	no nos pongamos	vistámonos	no nos vistamos
vosotros	lavaos	no os lavéis	poneos	no os pongáis	vestíos	no os vistáis
ustedes	lávense	no se laven	pónganse	no se pongan	vístanse	no se vistan

Regular and irregular reflexive verbs: Position of the reflexive pronouns in compound tenses*

	Indicative						Subjunctive	
Reflexive Pronoun	Present Perfect	Past Perfect	Preterite Perfect	Future Perfect	Conditional Perfect		Present Perfect	Past Perfect
me	he	había	hube	habré	habría		haya	hubiera
te	has	habías	hubiste	habrás	habrías	lavado	hayas	hubieras
se	ha	había	hubo	habrá	habría	puesto	haya	hubiera
nos	hemos	habíamos	hubimos	habremos	habríamos	vestido	hayamos	hubiéramos
os	habéis	habíais	hubisteis	habréis	habríais		hayáis	hubierais
se	han	habían	hubieron	habrán	habrían		hayan	hubieran

(participles: lavado, puesto, vestido)

*The sequence of these three elements—the reflexive pronoun, the auxiliary verb **haber**, and the present perfect form—is invariable and no other words can come in between.

Regular and irregular reflexive verbs: Position of the reflexive pronouns with conjugated verb + infinitive**

	Indicative						Subjunctive	
Reflexive Pronoun	Present	Imperfect	Preterite	Future	Conditional		Present	Imperfect
me	voy a	iba a	fui a	iré a	iría a		vaya a	fuera a
te	vas a	ibas a	fuiste a	irás a	irías a	lavar	vayas a	fueras a
se	va a	iba a	fue a	irá a	iría a	poner	vaya a	fuera a
nos	vamos a	íbamos a	fuimos a	iremos a	iríamos a	vestir	vayamos a	fuéramos a
os	vais a	ibais a	fuisteis a	iréis a	iríais a		vayáis a	fuerais a
se	van a	iban a	fueron a	irán a	irían a		vayan a	fueran a

(infinitives: lavar, poner, vestir)

The reflexive pronoun can also be placed after the infinitive: voy a lavarme**, voy a poner**me**, voy a vestir**me**, and so on. Use the same structure for the present and the past progressive: **me** estoy lavando / estoy lavándo**me**; **me** estaba lavando / estaba lavándo**me**.

Irregular Verbs

andar, caber, caer

Infinitive	Past participle / Present participle	Indicative — Present	Indicative — Imperfect	Indicative — Preterite	Indicative — Future	Indicative — Conditional	Subjunctive — Present	Subjunctive — Imperfect
andar *to walk; to go*	andado andando	ando andas anda andamos andáis andan	andaba andabas andaba andábamos andabais andaban	anduve anduviste anduvo anduvimos anduvisteis anduvieron	andaré andarás andará andaremos andaréis andarán	andaría andarías andaría andaríamos andaríais andarían	ande andes ande andemos andéis anden	anduviera anduvieras anduviera anduviéramos anduvierais anduvieran
caber *to fit; to have enough space*	cabido cabiendo	quepo cabes cabe cabemos cabéis caben	cabía cabías cabía cabíamos cabíais cabían	cupe cupiste cupo cupimos cupisteis cupieron	cabré cabrás cabrá cabremos cabréis cabrán	cabría cabrías cabría cabríamos cabríais cabrían	quepa quepas quepa quepamos quepáis quepan	cupiera cupieras cupiera cupiéramos cupierais cupieran
caer *to fall*	caído cayendo	caigo caes cae caemos caéis caen	caía caías caía caíamos caíais caían	caí caíste cayó caímos caísteis cayeron	caeré caerás caerá caeremos caeréis caerán	caería caerías caería caeríamos caeríais caerían	caiga caigas caiga caigamos caigáis caigan	cayera cayeras cayera cayéramos cayerais cayeran

Commands

Person	andar — Affirmative	andar — Negative	caber — Affirmative	caber — Negative	caer — Affirmative	caer — Negative
tú	anda	no andes	cabe	no quepas	cae	no caigas
usted	ande	no ande	quepa	no quepa	caiga	no caiga
nosotros	andemos	no andemos	quepamos	no quepamos	caigamos	no caigamos
vosotros	andad	no andéis	cabed	no quepáis	caed	no caigáis
ustedes	anden	no anden	quepan	no quepan	caigan	no caigan

dar, decir, estar

Infinitive	Past participle / Present participle	Indicative					Subjunctive	
		Present	Imperfect	Preterite	Future	Conditional	Present	Imperfect
dar *to give*	dado / dando	doy	daba	di	daré	daría	dé	diera
		das	dabas	diste	darás	darías	des	dieras
		da	daba	dio	dará	daría	dé	diera
		damos	dábamos	dimos	daremos	daríamos	demos	diéramos
		dais	dabais	disteis	daréis	daríais	deis	dierais
		dan	daban	dieron	darán	darían	den	dieran
decir *to say, to tell*	dicho / diciendo	digo	decía	dije	diré	diría	diga	dijera
		dices	decías	dijiste	dirás	dirías	digas	dijeras
		dice	decía	dijo	dirá	diría	diga	dijera
		decimos	decíamos	dijimos	diremos	diríamos	digamos	dijéramos
		decís	decíais	dijisteis	diréis	diríais	digáis	dijerais
		dicen	decían	dijeron	dirán	dirían	digan	dijeran
estar *to be*	estado / estando	estoy	estaba	estuve	estaré	estaría	esté	estuviera
		estás	estabas	estuviste	estarás	estarías	estés	estuvieras
		está	estaba	estuvo	estará	estaría	esté	estuviera
		estamos	estábamos	estuvimos	estaremos	estaríamos	estemos	estuviéramos
		estáis	estabais	estuvisteis	estaréis	estaríais	estéis	estuvierais
		están	estaban	estuvieron	estarán	estarían	estén	estuvieran

Commands

Person	dar Affirmative	dar Negative	decir Affirmative	decir Negative	estar Affirmative	estar Negative
tú	da	no des	di	no digas	está	no estés
usted	dé	no dé	diga	no diga	esté	no esté
nosotros	demos	no demos	digamos	no digamos	estemos	no estemos
vosotros	dad	no deis	decid	no digáis	estad	no estéis
ustedes	den	no den	digan	no digan	estén	no estén

haber*, hacer, ir

Infinitive	Past participle / Present participle	Indicative						Subjunctive	
		Present	Imperfect	Preterite	Future	Conditional		Present	Imperfect
haber* / *to have*	habido / habiendo	he has ha hemos habéis han	había habías había habíamos habíais habían	hube hubiste hubo hubimos hubisteis hubieron	habré habrás habrá habremos habréis habrán	habría habrías habría habríamos habríais habrían		haya hayas haya hayamos hayáis hayan	hubiera hubieras hubiera hubiéramos hubierais hubieran
hacer / *do*	hecho / haciendo	hago haces hace hacemos hacéis hacen	hacía hacías hacía hacíamos hacíais hacían	hice hiciste hizo hicimos hicisteis hicieron	haré harás hará haremos haréis harán	haría harías haría haríamos haríais harían		haga hagas haga hagamos hagáis hagan	hiciera hicieras hiciera hiciéramos hicierais hicieran
ir / *to go*	ido / yendo	voy vas va vamos vais van	iba ibas iba íbamos ibais iban	fui fuiste fue fuimos fuisteis fueron	iré irás irá iremos iréis irán	iría irías iría iríamos iríais irían		vaya vayas vaya vayamos vayáis vayan	fuera fueras fuera fuéramos fuerais fueran

*Haber also has an impersonal form, hay. This form is used to express "There is, There are." The imperative of haber is not used.

Commands

Person	hacer		ir	
	Affirmative	Negative	Affirmative	Negative
tú	haz	no hagas	ve	no vayas
usted	haga	no haga	vaya	no vaya
nosotros	hagamos	no hagamos	vamos	no vayamos
vosotros	haced	no hagáis	id	no vayáis
ustedes	hagan	no hagan	vayan	no vayan

jugar, oír, oler

Infinitive	Past participle / Present participle	Indicative					Subjunctive	
		Present	Imperfect	Preterite	Future	Conditional	Present	Imperfect
jugar *to play*	jugado jugando	**juego** **juegas** **juega** jugamos jugáis **juegan**	jugaba jugabas jugaba jugábamos jugabais jugaban	**jugué** jugaste jugó jugamos jugasteis jugaron	jugaré jugarás jugará jugaremos jugaréis jugarán	jugaría jugarías jugaría jugaríamos jugaríais jugarían	**juegue** **juegues** **juegue** **juguemos** **juguéis** **jueguen**	jugara jugaras jugara jugáramos jugarais jugaran
oír *to hear, to listen*	oído oyendo	**oigo** **oyes** **oye** oímos oís **oyen**	oía oías oía oíamos oíais oían	oí oíste **oyó** oímos oísteis **oyeron**	oiré oirás oirá oiremos oiréis oirán	oiría oirías oiría oiríamos oiríais oirían	**oiga** **oigas** **oiga** **oigamos** **oigáis** **oigan**	oyera oyeras oyera oyéramos oyerais oyeran
oler *to smell*	olido oliendo	**huelo** **hueles** **huele** olemos oléis **huelen**	olía olías olía olíamos olíais olían	olí oliste olió olimos olisteis olieron	oleré olerás olerá oleremos oleréis olerán	olería olerías olería oleríamos oleríais olerían	**huela** **huelas** **huela** olamos oláis **huelan**	oliera olieras oliera oliéramos olierais olieran

Commands

Person	jugar		oír		oler	
	Affirmative	Negative	Affirmative	Negative	Affirmative	Negative
tú	juega	no juegues	**oye**	no oigas	huele	no huelas
usted	juegue	no juegue	**oiga**	no oiga	huela	no huela
nosotros	juguemos	no juguemos	**oigamos**	no oigamos	olamos	no olamos
vosotros	jugad	no juguéis	**oíd**	no oigáis	oled	no oláis
ustedes	jueguen	no jueguen	**oigan**	no oigan	**huelan**	no huelan

poder, poner, querer

Infinitive	Past participle / Present participle	Indicative					Subjunctive	
		Present	Imperfect	Preterite	Future	Conditional	Present	Imperfect
poder *to be able to, can*	podido pudiendo	puedo puedes puede podemos podéis pueden	podía podías podía podíamos podíais podían	pude pudiste pudo pudimos pudisteis pudieron	podré podrás podrá podremos podréis podrán	podría podrías podría podríamos podríais podrían	pueda puedas pueda podamos podáis puedan	pudiera pudieras pudiera pudiéramos pudierais pudieran
poner* *to put*	puesto poniendo	pongo pones pone ponemos ponéis ponen	ponía ponías ponía poníamos poníais ponían	puse pusiste puso pusimos pusisteis pusieron	pondré pondrás pondrá pondremos pondréis pondrán	pondría pondrías pondría pondríamos pondríais pondrían	ponga pongas ponga pongamos pongáis pongan	pusiera pusieras pusiera pusiéramos pusierais pusieran
querer *to want, to wish, to love*	querido queriendo	quiero quieres quiere queremos queréis quieren	quería querías quería queríamos queríais querían	quise quisiste quiso quisimos quisisteis quisieron	querré querrás querrá querremos querréis querrán	querría querrías querría querríamos querríais querrían	quiera quieras quiera queramos queráis quieran	quisiera quisieras quisiera quisiéramos quisierais quisieran

*Similar verbs to poner: imponer, suponer.

Commands**

Person	poner		querer	
	Affirmative	Negative	Affirmative	Negative
tú	pon	no pongas	quiere	no quieras
usted	ponga	no ponga	quiera	no quiera
nosotros	pongamos	no pongamos	queramos	no queramos
vosotros	poned	no pongáis	quered	no queráis
ustedes	pongan	no pongan	quieran	no quieran

Note: The imperative of **poder is used very infrequently and is not included here.

saber, salir, ser

Infinitive	Past participle / Present participle	Indicative					Subjunctive	
		Present	Imperfect	Preterite	Future	Conditional	Present	Imperfect
saber *to know*	sabido / sabiendo	sé sabes sabe sabemos sabéis saben	sabía sabías sabía sabíamos sabíais sabían	supe supiste supo supimos supisteis supieron	sabré sabrás sabrá sabremos sabréis sabrán	sabría sabrías sabría sabríamos sabríais sabrían	sepa sepas sepa sepamos sepáis sepan	supiera supieras supiera supiéramos supierais supieran
salir *to go out, to leave*	salido / saliendo	salgo sales sale salimos salís salen	salía salías salía salíamos salíais salían	salí saliste salió salimos salisteis salieron	saldré saldrás saldrá saldremos saldréis saldrán	saldría saldrías saldría saldríamos saldríais saldrían	salga salgas salga salgamos salgáis salgan	saliera salieras saliera saliéramos salierais salieran
ser *to be*	sido / siendo	soy eres es somos sois son	era eras era éramos erais eran	fui fuiste fue fuimos fuisteis fueron	seré serás será seremos seréis serán	sería serías sería seríamos seríais serían	sea seas sea seamos seáis sean	fuera fueras fuera fuéramos fuerais fueran

Commands

Person	saber		salir		ser	
	Affirmative	Negative	Affirmative	Negative	Affirmative	Negative
tú	sabe	no sepas	sal	no salgas	sé	no seas
usted	sepa	no sepa	salga	no salga	sea	no sea
nosotros	sepamos	no sepamos	salgamos	no salgamos	seamos	no seamos
vosotros	sabed	no sepáis	salid	no salgáis	sed	no seáis
ustedes	sepan	no sepan	salgan	no salgan	sean	no sean

sonreír, tener*, traer

Infinitive	Past participle / Present participle	Indicative					Subjunctive	
		Present	Imperfect	Preterite	Future	Conditional	Present	Imperfect
sonreír *to smile*	sonreído sonriendo	sonrío sonríes sonríe sonreímos sonreís sonríen	sonreía sonreías sonreía sonreíamos sonreíais sonreían	sonreí sonreíste sonrió sonreímos sonreísteis sonrieron	sonreiré sonreirás sonreirá sonreiremos sonreiréis sonreirán	sonreiría sonreirías sonreiría sonreiríamos sonreiríais sonreirían	sonría sonrías sonría sonriamos sonriáis sonrían	sonriera sonrieras sonriera sonriéramos sonrierais sonrieran
tener* *to have*	tenido teniendo	tengo tienes tiene tenemos tenéis tienen	tenía tenías tenía teníamos teníais tenían	tuve tuviste tuvo tuvimos tuvisteis tuvieron	tendré tendrás tendrá tendremos tendréis tendrán	tendría tendrías tendría tendríamos tendríais tendrían	tenga tengas tenga tengamos tengáis tengan	tuviera tuvieras tuviera tuviéramos tuvierais tuvieran
traer *to bring*	traído trayendo	traigo traes trae traemos traéis traen	traía traías traía traíamos traíais traían	traje trajiste trajo trajimos trajisteis trajeron	traeré traerás traerá traeremos traeréis traerán	traería traerías traería traeríamos traeríais traerían	traiga traigas traiga traigamos traigáis traigan	trajera trajeras trajera trajéramos trajerais trajeran

*Many verbs ending in -tener are conjugated like tener: contener, detener, entretener(se), mantener, obtener, retener.

Commands

Person	sonreír		tener		traer	
	Affirmative	Negative	Affirmative	Negative	Affirmative	Negative
tú	sonríe	no sonrías	ten	no tengas	trae	no traigas
usted	sonría	no sonría	tenga	no tenga	traiga	no traiga
nosotros	sonriamos	no sonriamos	tengamos	no tengamos	traigamos	no traigamos
vosotros	sonreíd	no sonriáis	tened	no tengáis	traed	no traigáis
ustedes	sonrían	no sonrían	tengan	no tengan	traigan	no traigan

valer, venir*, ver

Infinitive	Past participle / Present participle	Indicative					Subjunctive	
		Present	Imperfect	Preterite	Future	Conditional	Present	Imperfect
valer *to be worth*	valido valiendo	valgo vales vale valemos valéis valen	valía valías valía valíamos valíais valían	valí valiste valió valimos valisteis valieron	valdré valdrás valdrá valdremos valdréis valdrán	valdría valdrías valdría valdríamos valdríais valdrían	valga valgas valga valgamos valgáis valgan	valiera valieras valiera valiéramos valierais valieran
venir* *to come*	venido viniendo	vengo vienes viene venimos venís vienen	venía venías venía veníamos veníais venían	vine viniste vino vinimos vinisteis vinieron	vendré vendrás vendrá vendremos vendréis vendrán	vendría vendrías vendría vendríamos vendríais vendrían	venga vengas venga vengamos vengáis vengan	viniera vinieras viniera viniéramos vinierais vinieran
ver *to see*	visto viendo	veo ves ve vemos veis ven	veía veías veía veíamos veíais veían	vi viste vio vimos visteis vieron	veré verás verá veremos veréis verán	vería verías vería veríamos veríais verían	vea veas vea veamos veáis vean	viera vieras viera viéramos vierais vieran

*Similar verb to venir: prevenir

Commands

Person	valer		venir		ver	
	Affirmative	Negative	Affirmative	Negative	Affirmative	Negative
tú	vale	no valgas	ven	no vengas	ve	no veas
usted	valga	no valga	venga	no venga	vea	no vea
nosotros	valgamos	no valgamos	vengamos	no vengamos	veamos	no veamos
vosotros	valed	no valgáis	venid	no vengáis	ved	no veáis
ustedes	valgan	no valgan	vengan	no vengan	vean	no vean

AMÉRICA DEL SUR

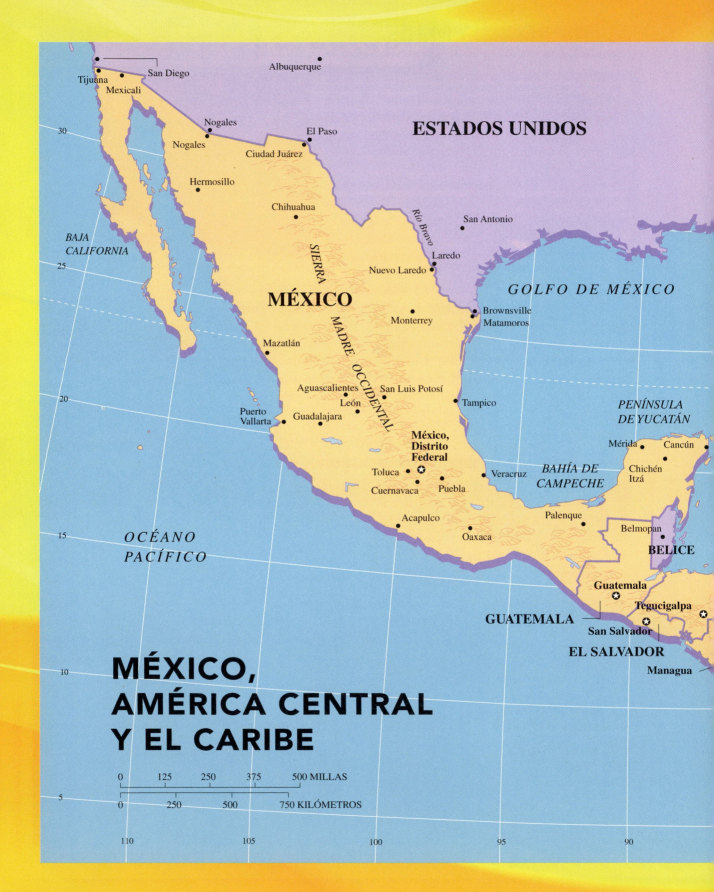

ESTADOS UNIDOS

Albuquerque

San Diego
Tijuana
Mexicali

30

Nogales
Nogales
El Paso
Ciudad Juárez

Hermosillo

Chihuahua

San Antonio

Río Bravo

BAJA
CALIFORNIA

Laredo
Nuevo Laredo

25

GOLFO DE MÉXICO

SIERRA

MÉXICO

Monterrey

Brownsville
Matamoros

Mazatlán

MADRE

Aguascalientes
León

San Luis Potosí

OCCIDENTAL

20

Puerto
Vallarta

Guadalajara

Tampico

*PENÍNSULA
DE YUCATÁN*

Mérida
Cancún

**México,
Distrito
Federal**

Veracruz

*BAHÍA DE
CAMPECHE*

Chichén
Itzá

Toluca
Cuernavaca
Puebla

Palenque

Belmopan

Acapulco

Oaxaca

BELICE

15

*OCÉANO
PACÍFICO*

Guatemala

Tegucigalpa

MÉXICO,
AMÉRICA CENTRAL
Y EL CARIBE

GUATEMALA

San Salvador

EL SALVADOR

Managua

10

| 0 | 125 | 250 | 375 | 500 MILLAS |

| 0 | 250 | 500 | 750 KILÓMETROS |

5

110   105   100   95   90

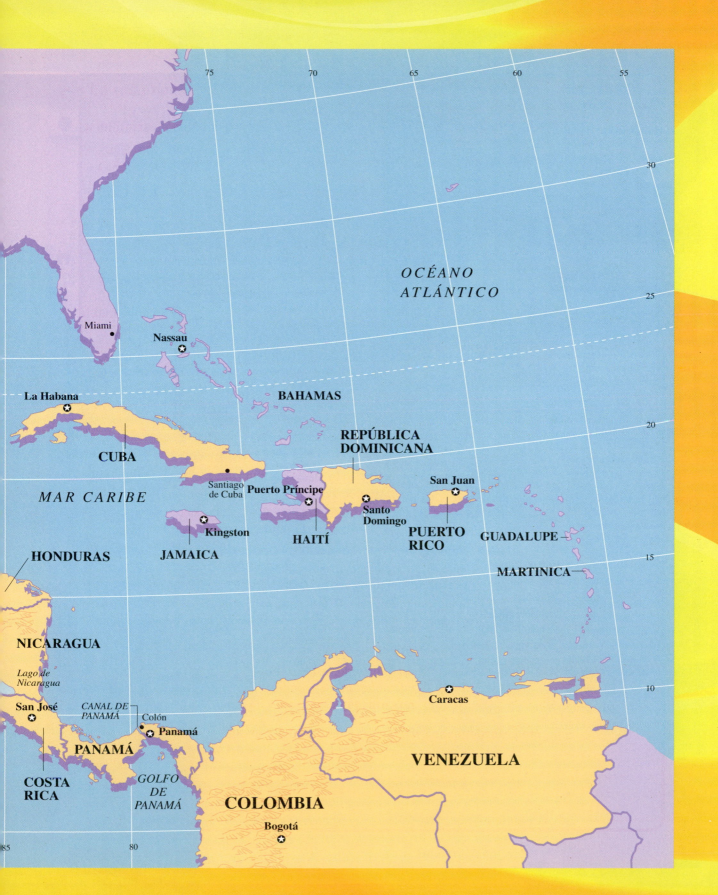

OCÉANO
ATLÁNTICO

Miami

Nassau

BAHAMAS

La Habana

CUBA

MAR CARIBE

Santiago
de Cuba

Puerto Príncipe

REPÚBLICA
DOMINICANA

San Juan

Santo
Domingo

GUADALUPE

Kingston

JAMAICA

HAITÍ

PUERTO
RICO

MARTINICA

HONDURAS

NICARAGUA

Lago de
Nicaragua

Caracas

San José

CANAL DE
PANAMÁ

Colón

Panamá

PANAMÁ

VENEZUELA

COSTA
RICA

GOLFO
DE
PANAMÁ

COLOMBIA

Bogotá

75

70

65

60

55

30

25

20

15

10

85

80

ESPAÑA

FRANCIA

ANDORRA

200 MILLAS
150
100
50
0

300 KILÓMETROS
200
100
0

OCÉANO
ATLÁNTICO

MAR CANTÁBRICO

Santander

PRINCIPADO
DE ASTURIAS
Santiago de Compostela

GALICIA

CORDILLERA CANTÁBRICA

CANTABRIA   PAÍS VASCO
Bilbao

CASTILLA
Y LEÓN

Valladolid

Salamanca

Segovia

SIERRA DE
GUADARRAMA

PIRINEOS

NAVARRA
Pamplona

LA RIOJA

Río Ebro

Zaragoza

ARAGÓN

CATALUÑA
Lérida

Gerona

Barcelona

Costa
Brava

MENORCA

MALLORCA

Palma

ISLAS
BALEARES

IBIZA

MAR MEDITERRÁNEO

★ Madrid

MADRID

Toledo

Río Tajo

CASTILLA-LA MANCHA

Ciudad Real

COMUNIDAD
VALENCIANA

Valencia

Alicante

MURCIA
Murcia

Cartagena

Costa del Sol

GIBRALTAR (Br.)

CEUTA (Sp.)

MELILLA (Sp.)

EXTREMADURA

PORTUGAL

★ Lisboa

Río Guadalquivir

Córdoba

Sevilla

ANDALUCÍA
Granada

SIERRA NEVADA

Málaga

Cádiz

Estrecho
de Gibraltar

Tanger

MARRUECOS

ÁFRICA

ISLAS CANARIAS

MILLAS
100   150

KILÓMETROS
150

LANZAROTE

FUERTEVENTURA

LA
PALMA

TENERIFE

GOMERA

HIERRO

GRAN
CANARIA

Las
Palmas

Appendix E: Grammar Review

Chapter 1

>> ## Gramática útil 1

Identifying people and objects: Nouns and articles

Cómo usarlo

Nouns identify people, places, and things: **señora Velasco, calle,** and **teléfono** are all nouns. *Articles* supply additional information about the noun.

1. *Definite* articles refer to a specific person, place, or thing.

   La Avenida Central es **la** calle   *Central Avenue is **the** most*
   más importante de **la** universidad.   *important street in **the** university.*
   (You already know which avenue
   and university you are talking about.)

2. *Indefinite* articles refer to a noun without identifying a specific person, place, or thing.

   Un amigo es **una** persona que te gusta.   ***A** friend is **a** person you like.*
   (You are making a generalization,
   true of any friend.)

Cómo formarlo

LO BÁSICO

- *Number* indicates whether a word is singular or plural: **la calle** *(sing.)*, **las calles** *(pl.)*, **un escritorio** *(sing.)*, **unos escritorios** *(pl.)*
- *Gender* indicates whether a word is masculine or feminine: **una avenida** *(fem.)*, **el teléfono** *(masc.)*

3. Noun gender and number

   - **Gender:** Often you can tell the gender of a Spanish noun by looking at its ending. Here are some general guidelines.

Masculine	Feminine
1. Nouns ending in **-o: el amigo, el muchacho**	Exception to rule #1: **la mano** *(hand)*
Exceptions to rule #2: words ending in **-ma: el sistema, el problema, el tema, el programa;** also **el día, el mapa**	2. Nouns ending in **-a: la compañera de cuarto, una chica**
Exceptions to rule #3: **el avión, el camión**	3. Nouns ending in **-ión, -dad, -tad,** and **-umbre** are usually feminine: **la información, una universidad, una costumbre** *(custom)*

> The idea of gender for non-person nouns and for articles does not exist in English, although it is a feature of Spanish and other languages. When learning new Spanish words, memorize the article with the noun to help remember gender.

> When nouns ending in **-ión** become plural, they lose the accent on the o: **la corporación,** but **las corporaciones.**

Nouns referring to people often reflect gender by changing a final **o** to an **a** (**chico / chica, amigo / amiga**) or adding an **a** to a final consonant (**profesor / profesora**). For nouns ending in -**e,** -**ista,** or -**a** that refer to people, the article or context indicates gender (**el estudiante / la estudiante, el guitarrista / la guitarrista, Juan / Juanita es atleta**).

- **Number:** Spanish nouns form their plurals in several ways.

Singular	Plural
Ends in vowel: **calle**	Add **s: calles**
Ends in consonant: **universidad**	Add **es: universidades**
Ends in -**z: lápiz**	Change **z** to **c** and add **es: lápices**

4. Definite and indefinite articles

- Here are the Spanish definite articles, which correspond to the English article *the*.

In the past, **los** and **unos,** rather than **las** and **unas,** were used to refer to groups containing one or more males. The **Real Academia de la Lengua Española** recently ruled that the feminine forms should be used for groups with more females than males, but usage is changing slowly.

	Singular	Plural
Masculine	**el amigo** *the friend (male)*	**los amigos** *the friends (male or mixed group)*
Feminine	**la amiga** *the friend (female)*	**las amigas** *the friends (female)*

- Here are the Spanish indefinite articles, which correspond to the English articles *a, an,* and *some*.

	Singular	Plural
Masculine	**un amigo** a friend *(male)*	**unos amigos** some friends *(male or mixed group)*
Feminine	**una amiga** a friend *(female)*	**unas amigas** some friends *(female)*

- Remember that you use masculine articles with masculine nouns and feminine articles with feminine nouns. When a noun is in the plural, the corresponding plural article (masculine or feminine) is used: **el hombre, los hombres.**
- When referring to a person's *profession*, the article is omitted: **Liana es profesora y Ricardo es dentista.**

When the noun is modified, the article is used: **Liana es una profesora excelente.**

- However, when you use a *title* to refer to someone, the article is used: **Es el profesor Gómez.** When you address that person directly, using their title, the article is not used: **Buenos días, profesor Gómez.**

The following titles are typically used with the article when referring to a person, and without the article when addressing that person directly.

señor (Sr.)	*Mr.*	**señorita (Srta.)**	*Miss / Ms.*
señora (Sra.)	*Mrs. / Ms.*	**profesor / profesora**	*professor*

Gramática útil 2

Identifying and describing: Subject pronouns and the present indicative of the verb ser

Cómo usarlo

The Spanish verb **ser** can be used to identify people and objects, to describe them, to make introductions, and to say when something will take place. It is one of two Spanish verbs that are the equivalents of the English verb *to be*.

Mi teléfono **es** el 2-39-71-49.	*My telephone number **is** 2-39-71-49.*
Yo **soy** Mariela y ella **es** Elena.	*I **am** Mariela and this **is** Elena.*
La fiesta **es** el miércoles.	*The party **is** on Wednesday.*

> **Estar,** which you have already used in the expression **¿Cómo estás?**, also means *to be*. You will learn other ways to use **estar** in **Chapter 4.**

Cómo formarlo

LO BÁSICO

- *Pronouns* are words used to replace nouns. (Some English pronouns are *it, she, you, him*, etc.)
- Verbs change form to reflect *number* and *person*. *Number* refers to singular versus plural. *Person* refers to different subjects.
- A verb's *tense* indicates the time frame in which an event takes place (for example, *talk, talked, will talk*). The *present indicative tense* refers to present-time events or conditions (*I talk, I am talking*).

1. Subject pronouns

- Subject pronouns are pronouns that are used as the subject of a sentence. Here are the subject pronouns in Spanish.

Singular		Plural	
yo	*I*	**nosotros / nosotras**	*we*
tú	*you (fam.)*	**vosotros / vosotras**	*you (fam.)*
usted (Ud.)	*you (form.)*	**ustedes (Uds.)**	*you (fam., form.)*
él, ella	*he, she*	**ellos, ellas**	*they*

> In Spanish, it is not always necessary to use the subject pronoun with the verb, as long as the subject is understood. For example, it's less common to say **Yo soy Rafael**, because **Soy Rafael** is clear enough on its own.

- The **vosotros / vosotras** forms are primarily used in Spain. They allow speakers to address more than one person informally. In most other places, Spanish speakers use **ustedes** to address several people, regardless of the formality of the relationship. The **vosotros** forms of verbs are provided in *Cuadros* so that you can recognize them, but they are not included for practice in activities.

2. Formal vs. familiar

English has a single word—*you*—to address people directly, regardless of how well you know them. As you have already seen, Spanish has two basic forms of address: the **tú** form and the **usted** form.

- **Tú** is used to address a family member, a close friend, a child, or a pet.
- **Usted** (often abbreviated **Ud.**) is a more formal means of address used with older people, strangers, acquaintances, and sometimes with colleagues.
- Remember that the **ustedes** form is normally used to address more than one person in both *informal* and *formal* contexts (except in Spain, where **vosotros**(as) is used in informal contexts).

Levels of formality vary throughout the Spanish-speaking world, so it's important when traveling to listen to how **tú** and **usted** are used and to follow the local practice.

In some countries, you will hear **vos** forms (Argentina and parts of Uruguay, Chile, and Central America). This is a variation of **tú** that is used only in these regions.

To show respect, you sometimes hear the titles **don** and **doña** used with people you address as **usted**. **Don** and **doña** are used with the person's first name: **don Roberto, doña Carmen**.

3. The present tense of the verb **ser**

The present indicative forms of the verb **ser** are as follows. Note the subject pronouns associated with each form.

ser *(to be)*	
Singular	
yo soy	*I am*
tú eres	*you (s. fam.) are*
usted es	*you (s. form.) are*
él es	*he is*
ella es	*she is*
Plural	
nosotros / nosotras somos	*we are*
vosotros / vosotras sois	*you (pl. fam.) are*
ustedes son	*you (pl. form. or pl. fam.) are*
ellos son	*they (masc. or mixed) are*
ellas son	*they (fem.) are*

Gramática útil 3

Expressing quantity: **Hay** + nouns

Cómo usarlo

1. **Hay** is the Spanish equivalent of *there is* or *there are* in English.

Hay una reunión en la cafetería.	***There is*** *a meeting in the cafeteria.*
Hay tres estudiantes en la clase.	***There are*** *three students in the class.*
Hay unos libros en la mesa.	***There are*** *some books on the table.*
Hay una fiesta el viernes.	***There is*** *a party on Friday.*

2. **Hay** is used with both singular and plural nouns, and in both affirmative and negative contexts.

   Hay un bolígrafo, pero no **hay** lápices en la mesa.

3. **Hay** can be used with numbers or with indefinite articles (**un, una, unos, unas**), but it is never used with definite articles (**el, la, los, las**).

¡**Hay** tres profesores en la clase, pero sólo **hay** una estudiante!	*There are three professors in the class, but **there is** only one student!*

4. With a plural noun or negative, typically no article is used with **hay** unless you are providing extra information.

Hay papeles en la mesa.	***There are papers*** *on the table.*
No hay libros en el escritorio.	***There aren't (any) books*** *on the desk.*
Hay quince personas en la clase.	***There are fifteen people*** *in the class.*

   BUT:

Hay unas personas interesantes en la clase.	***There are some interesting people*** *in the class.*

Cómo formarlo

Hay is an *invariable verb form* because it never changes to reflect number or person. That is why **hay** can be used with both singular and plural nouns.

Gramática útil 4

Expressing possession, obligation, and age: **Tener, tener que, tener + años**

Cómo usarlo

1. The verb **tener** means *to have*. It is used in Spanish to express possession and to give someone's age. You can also use it with **que** and another verb to say what you have to do: **Tengo que irme.** *(I have to go.)*

Tengo dos teléfonos en casa.	*I **have** two telephones in my house.*
Elena **tiene** veinte años. ¿Cuántos años **tienen** Sergio y Dulce?	*Elena **is** twenty years old. How old **are** Sergio and Dulce?*
Tengo que irme porque **tengo** clase.	*I **have to** go because I **have** class.*

2. When **tener** is used to express possession, the article is usually omitted, unless number is emphasized or you are referring to a specific object.

3. Note that where Spanish uses **tener... años** to express age, the English equivalent is *to be . . . years old.*

Cómo formarlo

1. Here are the forms of the verb **tener** in the present indicative tense.

tener *(to have)*			
yo	**tengo**	nosotros / nosotras	**tenemos**
tú	**tienes**	vosotros / vosotras	**tenéis**
Ud., él, ella	**tiene**	Uds., ellos, ellas	**tienen**

> Remember, it's better to use the verb without a subject pronoun unless the subject is unclear or you want to emphasize it.

2. When talking about age, it's helpful to know the months of the year so that you can say when people's birthdays are celebrated.

¿Cuándo es tu cumpleaños? *When is your birthday?*

enero	julio
febrero	agosto
marzo	septiembre
abril	octubre
mayo	noviembre
junio	diciembre

> In Spanish the word for birthday is **cumpleaños**, which literally means "completes (**cumple**) years (**años**)." Many Spanish speakers celebrate their saint's day (**el día de su santo**), which is the birthday of the saint whose name is the same as or similar to their own. For example: **El 19 de marzo es el día de San José**.

3. When giving dates in Spanish, the day of the month comes first: **el quince de abril** = *April 15th.* When writing the date with numbers, the day always comes before the month: 15/4/10 = **el quince de abril de 2010**.

Chapter 2

>> Gramática útil 1

Describing what you do or are doing: The present indicative of regular -ar verbs

Cómo usarlo

In English we use a variety of structures to express different present-tense concepts. In Spanish many of these are communicated with the same grammatical form. The present indicative tense in Spanish can be used. . .

- to describe routine actions:

    ¡Estudias mucho!   *You study a lot!*

- to say what you are doing now:

    Estudias matemáticas hoy.   *You are studying mathematics today.*

- to ask questions about present events:

    ¿**Estudias** con Enrique todas las semanas?   *Do you study with Enrique every week?*

- to indicate plans in the immediate future:

    Estudias con Enrique el viernes, ¿no?   *You're going to study with Enrique on Friday, right?*

> The use of the present tense to talk about future plans is used more in some regions of the Spanish-speaking world than others.

Notice how the same form in Spanish, **estudias**, can be translated four different ways in English.

Cómo formarlo

LO BÁSICO

- An *infinitive* is a verb before it has been conjugated to reflect person and tense. **Bailar** *(To dance)* is an infinitive.
- A *verb stem* is what is left after you remove the **-ar, -er,** or **-ir** ending from the infinitive. **Bail-** is the verb stem of **bailar.**
- A conjugated verb is a verb whose endings reflect person *(I, you, he/she, we, you, they)* and tense *(present, past, future, etc.)*. **Bailas** *(You dance)* is a conjugated verb (person: *you familiar singular;* tense: *present*).

1. Spanish infinitives end in **-ar**, **-er**, or **-ir**. For now, you will learn to form the present indicative tense of verbs ending in **-ar**. To form the present indicative tense of a regular **-ar** verb, simply remove the **-ar** and add the following endings.

bailar *(to dance)*			
yo	bail**o**	nosotros / nosotras	bail**amos**
tú	bail**as**	vosotros / vosotras	bail**áis**
Ud., él, ella	bail**a**	Uds., ellos, ellas	bail**an**

2. Remember, as you learned in **Chapter 1**, you do not need to use the subject pronouns (**yo, tú, él, ella**, etc.) unless the meaning is not clear from the context of the sentence, or you wish to clarify, add emphasis, or make a contrast.

   Camino en el parque todos los días.   *I walk in the park every day.*
   But:
   Yo camino en el parque, pero Lidia camina en el gimnasio.   *I walk in the park, but Lidia walks in the gymnasium.*

3. You may use certain conjugated present-tense verbs with infinitives. However, do not use two conjugated verbs together unless they are separated by a comma or the words **y** *(and)*, **pero** *(but)*, or **o** *(or)*.

   Necesitamos trabajar el viernes.   *We have to work on Friday.*
   Los sábados, **trabajo, practico** deportes y **visito** a amigos.   *On Saturdays I work, play sports, and visit friends.*
   Los domingos, **dejo de trabajar**.   *On Sundays I stop working.*
   ¡**Bailo, canto** o **escucho** música!   *I dance, sing, or listen to music!*

Notice that in this usage, Spanish infinitives are often translated into English as *-ing* forms: *I stop working.*

4. To say what you don't do or aren't planning to do, use **no** before the conjugated verb.

   ¡**No estudio** los fines de semana!   *I don't study on the weekends!*

5. Add question marks to turn a present-tense sentence into a *yes/no* question.

   ¿**No estudias** los fines de semana?   *Don't you study on the weekends?*
   ¿**Tienes que estudiar** este fin de semana?   *Do you have to study this weekend?*

6. Other regular **-ar** verbs:

The expression **acabar de** can be used with any infinitive to say what activity you and others have just completed: **Acabo de llegar.** *(I just arrived.)* **Acabamos de cenar.** *(We just ate dinner.)*

apagar	*to turn off*	**llegar**	*to arrive*
acabar de (+ infinitive)	*to have just done something*	**necesitar** (+ infinitive)	*to need (to do something)*
buscar	*to look for*	**pasar**	*to pass (by); to happen*
cenar	*to eat dinner*	**preparar**	*to prepare*
comprar	*to buy*	**regresar**	*to return*
dejar de (+ infinitive)	*to leave; to stop (doing something)*	**usar**	*to use*
descansar	*to rest*	**viajar**	*to travel*
llamar	*to call*		

Gramática útil 2

Saying what you and others like to do: **Gustar** + infinitive

Cómo usarlo

The Spanish verb **gustar** can be used with an infinitive to say what you and your friends like to do. Note that **gustar**, although often translated as *to like*, is really more similar to the English *to please*. **Gustar** is always used with pronouns that indicate *who is pleased* by the activity mentioned.

—**Me gusta bailar** salsa.	**I like to dance** salsa. (**Dancing** salsa **pleases me.**)
—¿**Te gusta bailar** también?	**Do you like to dance**, too? (**Does dancing please you**, too?)
—No, pero a **Luis le gusta** mucho.	No, but **Luis likes it** a lot. (No, but it pleases Luis a lot.)

Cómo formarlo

LO BÁSICO

The pronouns used with **gustar** are indirect object pronouns. They show the person who is being pleased or who likes something. You will learn more about them in **Chapter 8.**

1. When **gustar** is used with one or more infinitives, it is always used in its third-person singular form **gusta**. Sentences with **gusta** + *infinitive* can take the form of statements or questions without a change in word order.

—**Nos gusta cocinar** y **cenar** en restaurantes.	**We like to cook** and **to eat** dinner in restaurants.
—¿**Te gusta cocinar** también?	**Do you like to cook** also?

2. **Gusta** + *infinitive* is used with the following pronouns.

gusta + *infinitive*	
Me gusta cantar. *I like to sing.*	**Nos** gusta cantar. *We like to sing.*
Te gusta cantar. *You like to sing.*	**Os** gusta cantar. *You (fam. pl.) like to sing.*
Le gusta cantar. *You (form.) / He / She like (s) to sing.*	**Les** gusta cantar. *You (pl.) / They like to sing.*

¡OJO! Do not confuse **me, te, le, nos, os,** and **les** with the subject pronouns **yo, tú, él, ella, Ud., nosotros, vosotros, ellos, ellas,** and **Uds.** that you have already learned.

3. When you use **gusta**, you can also use **a** + *person* to emphasize or clarify *who* it is who likes the activity mentioned. Clarification is particularly important with **le** and **les,** because they can refer to several people.

Le gusta navegar por Internet.	*He/She likes to browse the Internet. (Who does?)*
A Beto / A él le gusta navegar por Internet.	*Beto / He likes to browse the Internet.*
A ellos les gusta cantar.	*They like to sing.*
A nosotros nos gusta conversar.	*We like to talk.*
A Sergio y a Anilú les gusta bailar.	*Sergio and Anilú like to dance.*

> Notice that **mí** has an accent, but **ti** does not.

4. If you want to emphasize or clarify what you or a close friend like, use **a mí** (with **me gusta**) and **a ti** (with **te gusta**).

A mí me gusta alquilar películas, pero **a ti te gusta** mirar televisión.	*I like to rent movies, but you like to watch television.*

5. To create negative sentences with **gusta** + *infinitive*, place **no** before the *pronoun* + **gusta**.

No nos gusta trabajar.	*We don't like to work.*
A Roberto **no le gusta cocinar**.	*Roberto doesn't like to cook.*

6. To express agreement with someone's opinion, use **también**. If you want to disagree, use **no** or **tampoco**. If you want to ask a friend if they like an activity you've already mentioned, ask **¿Y a ti?**

—¿Te gusta cocinar?	*Do you like to cook?*
—**A mí, no.** No me gusta. Me gusta comer en restaurantes. **¿Y a ti?**	*No, not me. I don't like it. I like to eat in restaurants. And you?*
—**A mí también.** Pero no me gusta comer en restaurantes elegantes.	*Me too. But I don't like to eat in fancy restaurants.*
—¡**A mí tampoco!**	*Me neither!*

>> Gramática útil 3

Describing yourself and others: Adjective agreement

Cómo usarlo

As you learned in **Chapter 1,** Spanish nouns must agree with definite and indefinite articles in both gender and number. This agreement is also necessary when using Spanish adjectives. Their endings change to reflect the number and gender of the nouns they modify.

Anilú es **delgada**.	*Anilú is **thin**.*
Sergio y Beto son **inteligentes**.	*Sergio and Beto are **intelligent**.*
Sergio es un hombre **alto**.	*Sergio is a **tall** man.*
Dulce y Anilú son mujeres **jóvenes**.	*Dulce and Anilú are **young** women.*

Notice that in these cases the adjectives go *after* the noun, rather than before, as in English.

Cómo formarlo

LO BÁSICO

A *descriptive adjective* is a word that describes a noun. It answers the question *What is . . . like?*

To modify is to limit or qualify the meaning of another word. A descriptive adjective *modifies* a noun by specifying characteristics that apply to that noun: **un estudiante** vs. **un estudiante inteligente**.

1. **Gender**: If an adjective is used to modify a masculine noun, the adjective must have a masculine ending. If it is used to modify a feminine noun, it must have a feminine ending.

   - The masculine ending for adjectives ending in **-o** is the **o** form.
   - The feminine ending for adjectives ending in **-o** is the **a** form.
   - Adjectives ending in **-e** or most consonants don't change to reflect gender.
   - Adjectives ending in **-or** add **a** to the ending for the feminine form.

Un professor	Una profesora
simpátic**o**	simpátic**a**
interesant**e**	interesant**e**
trabajad**or**	trabajad**ora**

2. **Number**: If an adjective is used to modify a plural noun or more than one noun, it must be used in its plural form.

   - To create the plural of an adjective ending in a vowel, add **s**.
   - To create the plural of an adjective ending in a consonant, add **es**.
   - To create the plural of an adjective ending in **-or**, add **es** to the masculine form and **as** to the feminine form.
   - To create the plural of an adjective ending in **-z**, change the **z** to **c** and add **es**.

Numbers do not change to match the number or gender of the nouns they describe. They go *before* the noun, rather than after.

El profesor	Los profesores	Las profesoras
simpátic**o**	simpátic**os**	simpátic**as**
interesant**e**	interesant**es**	interesant**es**
trabajad**or**	trabajad**ores**	trabajad**oras**
feli**z**	feli**ces**	feli**ces**

3. As with articles and subject pronouns, adjectives that apply to mixed groups of males and females typically use the masculine form.

4. Most descriptive adjectives are used *after* the noun, rather than before.

5. If you want to use more than one adjective, you can use **y** *(and)* or **o** *(or).*

El estudiante es simpático **y** trabajador.
¿Es el profesor alto **o** bajo?
Mis amigos son activos, generosos **y** cómicos.
¿Son ellas extrovertidas **o** introvertidas?

- If **y** appears before a word that begins with an **i**, it changes to **e**.
  La instructora es divertida **e** interesante.

- If **o** appears before a word that begins with an **o**, it changes to **u**.
  Hay siete **u** ocho estudiantes buenos en la clase.

6. Adjectives of nationality follow slightly different rules. These adjectives add **a / as** feminine endings for nationalities whose names end in **-l, -s,** and **-n**. See the nationalities in the following group for examples. Adjectives of nationality are always used after the noun.

Nacionalidades		
África		
ecuatoguineano(a) Guinea Ecuatorial		
Asia		
chino(a) China	**indio(a)** India	
coreano(a) Corea	**japonés, japonesa** Japón	
Australia		
australiano(a) Australia		
Centroamérica y el Caribe		
costarricense Costa Rica	**guatemalteco(a)** Guatemala	**panameño(a)** Panamá
cubano(a) Cuba	**hondureño(a)** Honduras	**puertorriqueño(a)** Puerto Rico
dominicano(a) República Dominicana	**nicaragüense** Nicaragua	**salvadoreño(a)** El Salvador
Europa		
alemán, alemana Alemania	**francés, francesa** Francia	**italiano(a)** Italia
español, española España	**inglés, inglesa** Inglaterra	**portugués, portuguesa** Portugal
Norteamérica		
canadiense Canadá	**estadounidense** Estados Unidos	**mexicano(a)** México
Sudamérica		
argentino(a) Argentina	**colombiano(a)** Colombia	**peruano(a)** Perú
boliviano(a) Bolivia	**ecuatoriano(a)** Ecuador	**uruguayo(a)** Uruguay
chileno(a) Chile	**paraguayo(a)** Paraguay	**venezolano(a)** Venezuela

7. Several adjectives in Spanish may be used *before* or *after* the noun they modify. Three common adjectives of this type are **bueno** *(good)*, **malo** *(bad)*, and **grande** *(big, large)*. When **bueno** and **malo** are used before a singular masculine noun, they have a special shortened form. Whenever **grande** is used before any singular masculine or feminine noun, its shortened form **gran** is used. Note that **grande** has different meanings when used *before* the noun *(great, famous)* and *after* the noun *(big, large)*.

un estudiante bueno una estudiante buena	BUT:	un **buen** estudiante una buena estudiante
un día malo una semana mala	BUT:	un **mal** día una mala semana
un hotel grande	BUT:	un **gran** hotel
una universidad grande	BUT:	una **gran** universidad

Chapter 3

>> # Gramática útil 1

Asking questions: Interrogative words

Cómo usarlo

You have already seen, learned, and used a number of interrogative words to ask questions. **¿Cómo te llamas?**, **¿Cuál es tu dirección electrónica?**, **¿Dónde vives?**, and **¿Qué tal?** are all questions that begin with interrogatives: **cómo, cuál, dónde, qué.**

As in English, we use interrogatives in Spanish to ask for specific information. Here are the Spanish interrogatives.

¿Cuál(es)?	What? Which one(s)?	**¿Dónde?**	Where?
¿Qué?	What? Which?	**¿Adónde?**	To where?
¿A qué hora?	(At) What time?	**¿De dónde?**	From where?
¿De qué?	About what? Of what?	**¿Quién(es)?**	Who?
¿Cuándo?	When?	**¿De quién(es)?**	Whose?
¿Cuánto(a)?	How much?	**¿Cómo?**	How?
¿Cuántos(as)?	How many?	**¿Por qué?**	Why?

1. **¿Qué?** and **¿cuál?** may appear interchangeable at first sight, but they are used in very specific ways.

   ¿Qué? is . . .

   ■ used to ask for a definition: **¿Qué es el reloj de veinticuatro horas?**

   ■ used to ask for an explanation or further information: **¿Qué vas a estudiar este semestre?**

- generally used when the next word is a noun: **¿Qué libros te gustan más? ¿Qué clase tienes a las ocho?**

¿Cuál? is . . .

- used to express a choice between specified items: **¿Cuál de los libros prefieres?**
- used when the next word is a form of **ser** but the question is *not* asking for a definition: **¿Cuál es tu número de teléfono? ¿Cuáles son tus clases favoritas?**

2. **¿Dónde?** is used to ask where something is.

¿Dónde está la biblioteca?	*Where is the library?*

Notice that **dónde** and **adónde** are both translated the same way into English.

3. **¿Adónde?** is used to ask where someone is going.

¿Adónde vas ahora?	*Where are you going now?*

4. **¿De quién es?** and **¿De quiénes son?** are used to ask about possession. You answer using **de**.

—**¿De quién** es la computadora?	*Whose computer is this?*
—**Es de** Miguel.	*It's Miguel's.*
—**¿De quiénes** son los libros?	*Whose books are these?*
—**Son de** Anita y Manuel.	*They're Anita's and Manuel's.*

Note that the interrogative is two separate words with an accent on **qué**. **Porque** is one single word with no accent.

5. Questions using **¿por qué?** can be answered using **porque** (*because*).

—**¡Por qué** tienes que trabajar?	*Why do you have to work?*
—**¡Porque** necesito el dinero!	*Because I need the money!*

Cómo formarlo

1. Interrogatives are always preceded by an inverted question mark (**¿**). The question requires a regular question mark (**?**) at the end.

2. Notice that in a typical question the subject *follows* the verb.

¿Dónde **estudia Marcos**?	*Where does **Marcos study**?*
¿Qué instrumento **tocan** ustedes?	*What instrument do **you play**?*

3. **¿Quién?** and **¿cuál?** change to reflect number.

¿**Quién** es el hombre alto? / ¿**Quiénes** son los hombres altos?
¿**Cuál** de los libros tienes? / ¿**Cuáles** son tus idiomas favoritos?

4. **¿Cuánto?** changes to reflect both number and gender.

¿**Cuánto** dinero tienes?	*How much money do you have?*
¿**Cuánta** comida compramos?	*How much food should we buy?*
¿**Cuántos** años tienes?	*How many years old are you? / How old are you?*
¿**Cuántas** personas hay?	*How many people are there?*

5. When you want to ask *how much* in a general way, use **¿cuánto?**

¿**Cuánto** es?	¿**Cuánto** necesitamos?

6. Note that interrogatives always require an accent.

7. You have already learned how to form simple *yes/no* questions by adding **no** to a sentence.

¿**No escribes** e-mails hoy?	***Aren't you writing*** *any e-mails today?*

8. You can also form simple *yes/no* questions by adding a tag question, such as ¿**verdad?** *(Isn't that right?)* and ¿**no?** to the end of a statement.

Cantas en el coro con Ana, ¿**no?**	*You sing in the chorus with Ana,* ***right?***
Enrique baila salsa muy bien, ¿**verdad?**	*Enrique dances salsa very well,* ***right?***

When a Spanish speaker adds ¿**verdad?** or ¿**no?** to a question, he or she is expecting an affirmative answer.

>> Gramática útil 2

Talking about daily activities: The present indicative of regular -er and -ir verbs

Cómo usarlo

In **Chapter 2,** you learned how to use the present indicative of regular **-ar** verbs to talk about daily activities. The present indicative of **-er** and **-ir** verbs are used in the same contexts.

Remember:

1. The present indicative, depending on how it is used, can correspond to the following English usages: *I read* (in general), *I am reading, I am going to read, I do read,* and, if used as a question, *Do you read?*

2. You can often omit the subject pronoun when the subject is clear from the verb ending used or from the context of the sentence.

Leo en la biblioteca todos los días.	***I read*** *in the library every day.*
Lees en la residencia estudiantil, ¿no?	***You read*** *in the dorm, right?*

3. You may use an infinitive after certain conjugated verbs.

¿**Tienes que imprimir** esto?	***Do you have to print*** *this?*
¿**Necesitas leer** este libro?	***Do you need to read*** *this book?*
¡**Dejo de leer** después de medianoche!	***I stop reading*** *after midnight!*

4. However, do not use two verbs conjugated in the present tense together unless they are separated by a comma or the words **y** *(and)* or **o** *(or)*.

Leo, estudio y **escribo** composiciones en la biblioteca.	***I read, study***, *and* ***write*** *compositions in the library.*

5. Remember that you can negate sentences in the present indicative tense to say what you don't do or aren't planning to do.

No comemos en la cafetería hoy.	***We're not eating*** *in the cafeteria today.*
No leo todos los días.	***I don't read*** *every day.*

Cómo formarlo

To form the present indicative tense of **-er** and **-ir** verbs, simply remove the **-er** or **-ir** and add the following endings.

comer *(to eat)*			
yo	**como**	nosotros / nosotras	**comemos**
tú	**comes**	vosotros / vosotras	**coméis**
Ud. / él / ella	**come**	Uds. / ellos / ellas	**comen**

vivir *(to live)*			
yo	**vivo**	nosotros / nosotras	**vivimos**
tú	**vives**	vosotros / vosotras	**vivís**
Ud. / él / ella	**vive**	Uds. / ellos / ellas	**viven**

> Notice that the present indicative endings for **-er** and **-ir** verbs are identical except for the **nosotros** and **vosotros** forms.

Here are some commonly used **-er** and **-ir** verbs.

-er verbs			
aprender a (+ infinitive)	*to learn to (do something)*	**creer (en)**	*to believe (in)*
beber	*to drink*	**deber** (+ infinitive)	*should, ought (to do something)*
comer	*to eat*	**leer**	*to read*
comprender	*to understand*	**vender**	*to sell*
correr	*to run*		

-ir verbs			
abrir	*to open*	**escribir**	*to write*
asistir a	*to attend*	**imprimir**	*to print*
compartir	*to share*	**recibir**	*to receive*
describir	*to describe*	**transmitir**	*to broadcast*
descubrir	*to discover*	**vivir**	*to live*

>> Gramática útil 3

Talking about possessions: Simple possessive adjectives

Cómo usarlo

1. You already have learned to express possession using **de** + a noun or name.

Es la computadora portátil **de la profesora**.

*It's **the professor's** laptop computer.*

2. You can also use possessive adjectives to describe your possessions, other people's possessions, or items that are associated with you. You are already familiar with some possessive adjectives from the phrases **¿Cuál es tu** **dirección?** and **Aquí tienes mi número de teléfono**.

—¿Cuándo es **tu** clase de historia?	*When is **your** history class?*
—A las dos. Y **mi** clase de español es a las tres.	*At two. And **my** Spanish class is at three.*

3. When you use **su** (which can mean *your, his, her, its,* or *theirs*), the context will usually clarify who is meant. If not, you can follow up with **de** + name.

Es **su** libro. Es **de la profesora**.	*It's **her** book. It's **the professor's**.*

Cómo formarlo

LO BÁSICO

Possessive adjectives modify nouns in order to express possession. In other words, they tell who owns the item.

1. Here are the simple possessive adjectives in Spanish.

mi mis	*my*	nuestro / nuestra nuestros / nuestras	*our*
tu tus	*your (fam.)*	vuestro / vuestra vuestros / vuestras	*your (fam. pl.)*
su sus	*your (form.), his, her, its*	su sus	*your (pl.), their*

The subject pronoun **tú** *(you)* has an accent on it to differentiate it from the possessive adjective **tu** *(your)*.

Tú trabajas los lunes, ¿verdad?

Tu libro está en mi casa.

2. Notice that . . .

- all possessive adjectives change to reflect number: **mi clase, mis clases; nuestro compañero de cuarto, nuestros compañeros de cuarto.**

- **mi, tu**, and **su** do not change to reflect gender, but **nuestro** and **vuestro** do: **nuestro libro, nuestros amigos, vuestras clases**, but **mi libro, mi clase.**

- unlike other adjectives, which often go after the noun they modify, simple possessive adjectives always go before the noun: **su profesora, nuestras amigas.**

Gramática útil 4

Indicating destination and future plans: The verb ir

Cómo usarlo

You can use the Spanish verb **ir** to say where you and others are going. You can also use it to say what you and others are going to do in the near future.

Vamos a la biblioteca mañana.   *We're going to the library tomorrow.*
Vamos a estudiar.   *We're going to study.*

Cómo formarlo

LO BÁSICO

> An *irregular verb* is one that does not follow the normal rules, such as **tener**, which you learned in **Chapter 1**.
>
> A *preposition* links nouns, pronouns, or noun phrases to the rest of the sentence. Prepositions can express location, time sequence, purpose, or direction. *In, to, after, under,* and *for* are all English prepositions.

> You have already used similar expressions: **necesitar** + infinitive *(to need to do something),* **tener que** + infinitive *(to have to do something),* and **dejar de** + infinitive *(to stop doing something).*

1. Here is the verb **ir** in the present indicative tense. **Ir**, like the verbs **ser** and **tener** that you have already learned, is an irregular verb.

ir *(to go)*			
yo	**voy**	nosotros / nosotras	**vamos**
tú	**vas**	vosotros / vosotras	**vais**
Ud. / él / ella	**va**	Uds. / ellos / ellas	**van**

2. Use the preposition **a** with the verb **ir** to say where you are going.

   Voy a la cafetería.   *I'm going to the cafeteria.*

3. When you want to use the verb **ir** to say what you are going to do, use this formula: **ir** + **a** + *infinitive*.

   Vamos a comer a las cinco hoy.   *We're going to eat at 5:00 today.*
   Después, **vamos a ir** al concierto.   *Afterward, we're going to go to the concert.*

4. When you use **a** together with **el**, it contracts to **al**. The same holds true for **de** + **el**: **del**.

   a + el = **al**   de + el = **del**

   Voy **a la** biblioteca y luego **al** gimnasio. Después, **al** mediodía, voy a estudiar en la biblioteca **del** centro de comunicaciones.

Chapter 4

>> ## Gramática útil 1

Expressing likes and dislikes: **Gustar** with nouns and other verbs like **gustar**

Cómo usarlo

As you learned in **Chapter 2,** you can use **gustar** with an infinitive to say what activities you and other people like to do.

Me gusta estudiar en la biblioteca,
pero **a Vicente le gusta estudiar**
en la cafetería.

I like to study in the library,
but *Vicente likes to study*
in the cafeteria.

You can also use **gustar** with nouns, to say what thing or things you (and others) like or dislike. In this case, you use **gusta** with a single noun and **gustan** with plural nouns or a series of nouns.

—¿**Te gusta** esta **computadora?**
—Sí, ¡pero **me gustan** más estas
portátiles!

Do you like this *computer?*
Yes, but I like these *laptops*
more!

When you make negative sentences with **gusta** and **gustan,** you use **no** before the pronoun + **gusta / gustan.**

Nos gustan los programas de
diseño gráfico, pero **no nos**
gustan los programas de arte.

We like the graphic design
programs, but *we don't like* the
art programs.

> Remember that when you use **gustar** + infinitive you only use **gusta: Les gusta comer en la cafetería.**

Cómo formarlo

LO BÁSICO

- In Spanish, an *indirect object pronoun* is used with **gustar** to say who likes something. Because **gustar** literally means to *please*, the indirect object answers the question: *Pleases whom?*

- A *prepositional pronoun* is a pronoun that is used after a preposition, such as **a** or **de**.

1. As you have already learned, you must use forms of **gustar** with the correct indirect object pronoun.

> You will learn more about Spanish indirect object pronouns in **Chapter 8.**

Me gusta	el foro.	**Nos gusta**	el foro.
Me gustan	los foros.	**Nos gustan**	los foros.
Te gusta	el foro.	**Os gusta**	el foro.
Te gustan	los foros.	**Os gustan**	los foros.
Le gusta	el foro.	**Les gusta**	el foro.
Le gustan	los foros.	**Les gustan**	los foros.

2. As you have learned, if you want to *emphasize* or *clarify* who likes what, you can use **a** + name or noun, or **a** + prepositional pronoun. Note that when **a** + prepositional pronoun is used, there is often no direct translation in English. Notice that except for **mí** and **ti**, the prepositional pronouns are the same as the subject pronouns you already know.

Notice that while **mí** takes an accent, **ti** does not.

Prepositional pronoun	Indirect object pronoun	Form of gustar + noun
A mí	**me**	gustan los videojuegos.
A ti	**te**	gustan los videojuegos.
A Ud. / a él / a ella	**le**	gustan los videojuegos.
A nosotros / a nosotras	**nos**	gustan los videojuegos.
A vosotros / a vosotras	**os**	gustan los videojuegos.
A Uds. / a ellos / a ellas	**les**	gustan los videojuegos.

A mí me gustan los MP3 portátiles pero **a Elena** no le gustan.

A ella le gustan los teléfonos inteligentes que también tocan MP3s.

*I like MP3 players, but **Elena** doesn't like them.*

***She** likes smartphones that also play MP3s.*

3. A number of other Spanish verbs are used like **gustar.** These verbs are usually just used in two forms, as is **gustar.**

—**Me interesan** mucho estos celulares.

—¿No **te molesta** la recepción mala aquí?

***I'm interested** in these cell phones.*

*Doesn't the bad reception here **bother you**?*

Other verbs like gustar	
encantar *to like a lot*	¡**Me encanta** la tecnología!
fascinar *to fascinate*	A Ana **le fascinan** esos sitios web.
importar *to be important to someone; to mind*	**Nos importa** tener acceso a Internet. ¿**Te importa** si usamos la computadora?
interesar *to interest, to be interesting*	A ellos **les interesan** las redes sociales.
molestar *to bother*	**Nos molestan** las computadoras viejas.

In Spanish-speaking cultures, courtesy is of utmost importance. It is very common to use phrases like **¿Le importa?** or **¿Le molesta?** to ask someone a question. **¿Le importa si uso la computadora?** would be more likely heard than **Voy a usar la computadora** or **¿Puedo usar la computadora?** It's also common to use **por favor** when asking a question and **gracias** upon receiving the answer. Other common expressions of courtesy are:

¡Perdón! / ¡Disculpe! / ¡Lo siento! *Pardon me! / Excuse me! / I'm sorry!*

No hay de qué. / No se preocupe.

No problem. / Not to worry.

Con permiso. *Excuse me. . . / With your permission. . .*

Cómo no. *Of course. / Certainly.*

Gramática útil 2

Describing yourself and others and expressing conditions and locations: The verb estar and the uses of ser and estar

Cómo usarlo

You already know that the verb **ser** is translated as *to be* in English. You have already used the verb **estar**, which is also translated as *to be*, in expressions such as **¿Cómo estás?** While both these Spanish verbs mean *to be*, they are used in different ways.

1. Use **estar** . . .

   ■ to express location of people, places, or objects.

La profesora Suárez **está** en la biblioteca.	*Professor Suárez **is** in the library.*
Los libros **están** en la mesa.	*The books **are** on the table.*

   ■ to talk about a physical condition.

—¿Cómo **está** usted?	*How **are** you?*
—**Estoy** muy bien, gracias.	*I'm well, thank you.*
—Yo **estoy** un poco cansada.	*I'm a little tired.*

   ■ to talk about emotional conditions.

El señor Albrega **está** un poco nervioso hoy.	*Mr. Albrega **is** a little nervous today.*
Estoy muy ocupada esta semana.	*I'm very busy this week.*

2. Use **ser** . . .

   ■ to identify yourself and others.

Soy Ana y ésta **es** mi hermana Luisa.	*I'm Ana and this **is** my sister Luisa.*

   ■ to indicate profession.

Pablo Picasso **es** un artista famoso.	*Pablo Picasso **is** a famous artist.*

   ■ to describe personality traits and physical features.

Somos altos y delgados.	*We **are** tall and thin.*
Somos estudiantes buenos.	*We **are** good students.*

   ■ to give time and date.

Es la una. Hoy **es** miércoles.	*It **is** one o'clock. Today **is** Wednesday.*

   ■ to indicate nationality and origin.

—**Eres** española, ¿no?	*You **are** Spanish, right?*
—Sí, **soy** de España.	*Yes, I **am** from Spain.*

   ■ to express possession with **de.**

Este celular **es de Anita.**	*This **is** Anita's cell phone.*

   ■ to give the location of an event.

La fiesta **es** en la residencia estudiantil.	*The party **is** in the dorm.*

> Notice that expressing the location of people, places, and things (other than events) requires the use of **estar. Ser** is used only to indicate *where an event will take place.*

Cómo formarlo

1. Here are the forms of the verb **estar** in the present indicative tense.

estar *(to be)*			
yo	**estoy**	nosotros / nosotras	**estamos**
tú	**estás**	vosotros / vosotras	**estáis**
Ud. / él / ella	**está**	Uds. / ellos / ellas	**están**

2. In the **¡Imagínate!** section you learned some adjectives that are commonly used with **estar** to describe physical and emotional conditions.

aburrido(a)	nervioso(a)
cansado(a)	ocupado(a)
contento(a)	preocupado(a)
enfermo(a)	seguro(a)
enojado(a)	triste
furioso(a)	

Don't forget that when you use adjectives with **estar,** as with any other verb, they need to agree with the person or thing they are describing in both gender and number.

Los estudiantes están preocupados por Miguel.	*The students are worried about Miguel.*
Elena está nerviosa a causa del examen.	*Elena is nervous because of the exam.*

>> Gramática útil 3

Talking about everyday events: Stem-changing verbs in the present indicative

Cómo usarlo

In **Chapters 1** and **2** you learned the present indicative forms of regular **-ar, -er,** and **-ir** verbs in Spanish. There are other Spanish verbs that use the same endings as regular **-ar, -er,** and **-ir** verbs in this tense, but they also have a small change in their stem. (Remember that the stem is the part of the infinitive that is left after you remove the **-ar / -er / -ir** ending.)

—¿Qué **piensas** de este MP3 portátil?	*What **do you think** of this MP3 player?*
—Me gusta, pero **prefiero** éste.	*I like it, but I **prefer** this one.*
—¿Verdad? Bueno, ¿por qué no le **pides** el precio al dependiente?	*Really? Well, why don't **you ask** the sales clerk the price?*

Cómo formarlo

1. There are three categories of stem-changing verbs in the present indicative.

	o → ue: encontrar *(to find)*	e → ie: preferir *(to prefer)*	e → i: pedir *(to ask for)*
yo	encuentro	prefiero	pido
tú	encuentras	prefieres	pides
Ud. / él / ella	encuentra	prefiere	pide
nosotros / nosotras	encontramos	preferimos	pedimos
vosotros / vosotras	encontráis	preferís	pedís
Uds. / ellos / ellas	encuentran	prefieren	piden

2. Note that the stem changes in all forms except the **nosotros / nosotras** and **vosotros / vosotras** forms.

3. Remember, all the endings for the present indicative are the same for these verbs as for the other regular verbs you've learned: **-o, -as, -a, -amos, -áis, -an** for **-ar** verbs; **-o, -es, -e, -emos / -imos, -éis / -ís, -en** for **-er** and **-ir** verbs. The only thing that is different here is the change in the stem.

4. Here are some commonly used Spanish verbs that experience a stem change in the present indicative tense.

e → ie

cerrar	*to close*
comenzar (a)	*to begin (to)*
empezar (a)	*to begin (to)*
entender	*to understand*
pensar de	*to think (of), have an opinion about*
pensar en	*to think about, to consider*
perder	*to lose*
preferir	*to prefer*
querer	*to want, to love*
sentir	*to feel*

o → ue

contar	*to tell, to relate; to count*
dormir	*to sleep*
encontrar	*to find*
jugar*	*to play*
poder	*to be able to*
sonar	*to ring, to go off (phone, alarm clock, etc.)*
soñar (con)	*to dream (about)*
volver	*to return*

e → i

pedir	*to ask for something*
repetir	*to repeat*
servir	*to serve*

*Jugar is the only **u → ue** stem-changing verb in Spanish. It's grouped with the **o → ue** verbs, because its change is most similar to those.

>> Gramática útil 4

Describing how something is done: Adverbs

Cómo usarlo

When you want to say how an activity is carried out (slowly, thoroughly, generally, etc.), you use an adverb.

Generalmente, prefiero usar una contraseña secreta.

__Generally__, I prefer to use a secret password.

Escribo más **rápido / rápidamente** en computadora que con bolígrafo.

I write more __rapidly__ on the computer than I do with a pen.

Este programa es **muy** lento.

This program is __very__ slow.

Cómo formarlo

LO BÁSICO

An adverb is a word that modifies a verb, an adjective, or another adverb. (Sometimes adjectives can also be used as adverbs—for example, *fast*). *Generally, rapidly,* and *very* are all adverbs. You can identify an adverb by asking the question, *"How?"*

1. To form an adverb from a Spanish adjective, it is often possible to add the ending **-mente** to the adjective: **fácil → fácilmente**. If the adjective ends in an **-o**, change it to **-a** before adding **-mente: rápido → rápidamente**.

2. Here are some frequently used Spanish adjectives that can be turned into **-mente** adverbs.

fácil *(easy)*	→ **fácilmente**
difícil *(difficult)*	→ **difícilmente**
lento *(slow)*	→ **lentamente**
rápido *(fast)*	→ **rápidamente**

> **Lento** and **rápido** can also be used with **muy** for the same effect: **Esta computadora se conecta a Internet muy rápido / muy lento / rápidamente / lentamente.**

3. The following **-mente** adverbs are also useful to talk about your routine and what you normally do.

frecuentemente	*frequently*	**normalmente**	*normally*
generalmente	*generally*		

4. Here are some other common Spanish adverbs.

bastante	*somewhat, rather*	Este sistema es **bastante** lento.
bien	*well*	Tu computadora funciona **bien**.
demasiado	*too much*	Navego **demasiado** por Internet.
mal	*badly*	¡Mi cámara web funciona muy **mal**!
mucho	*a lot*	Me gustan **mucho** los juegos interactivos.
muy	*very*	Guardo archivos **muy** frecuentemente.
poco	*little*	Chateo **poco** por Internet.

> Remember, adverbs can be used to modify other adverbs, so it's perfectly acceptable to use **muy** with **frecuentemente** or **mal**, for example!

Chapter 5

Gramática útil 1

Describing daily activities: Irregular-yo verbs in the present indicative, saber vs. conocer, and the personal a

Cómo usarlo

1. You have already learned the present indicative tense of many verbs. These include regular **-ar, -er,** and **-ir** verbs (**hablar, comer, vivir,** etc.), some irregular verbs (**ser, tener, ir**), and some stem-changing verbs (**pensar, poder, dormir,** etc.).

2. Now you will learn some verbs that are regular in all forms of the present indicative except the **yo** form. Like other verbs in the present indicative tense, these verbs can be used to say what you routinely do, what you are doing at the moment, or what you plan to do in the future.

Todos los días **salgo** para la universidad a las ocho.

Every day I leave for the university at 8:00.

Ahora mismo, **pongo** mis libros en la mochila y **digo** "hasta luego" a mi compañera de cuarto.

Right now, I put / I'm putting my books in my backpack and I say / I'm saying, "See you later" to my roommate.

Esta noche, **traigo** mis libros a casa otra vez y **hago** la tarea.

Tonight, I bring / I'll bring my books home again and I do / I'll do my homework.

Cómo formarlo

Irregular-**yo** verbs

Many irregular-**yo** verbs in the present indicative fall into several recognizable categories. Others have to be learned individually.

1. **-go** endings:

hacer	to make; to do	**hago**, haces, hace, hacemos, hacéis, hacen
poner	to put	**pongo**, pones, pone, ponemos, ponéis, ponen
salir	to leave, to go out (with)	**salgo**, sales, sale, salimos, salís, salen
traer	to bring	**traigo**, traes, trae, traemos, traéis, traen

2. **-zco** endings:

conducir	to drive; to conduct	**conduzco**, conduces, conduce, conducimos, conducís, conducen
conocer	to know a person; to be familiar with	**conozco**, conoces, conoce, conocemos, conocéis, conocen
traducir	to translate	**traduzco**, traduces, traduce, traducimos, traducís, traducen

Conducir is used more frequently in Spain to talk about driving. In most of Latin America, the verbs **manejar** and **guiar** (both regular -ar verbs) are used. (**Guiar** uses an accent on the **i** in these forms: **guío, guías, guía, guían.**)

3. Other irregular-**yo** verbs:

dar	to give	**doy**, das, da, damos, dais, dan
oír	to hear	**oigo**, oyes, oye, oímos, oís, oyen
saber	to know a fact; to know how to	**sé**, sabes, sabe, sabemos, sabéis, saben
ver	to see	**veo**, ves, ve, vemos, veis, ven

Note that **oír** requires a **y** in the **tú, él / ella / Ud.,** and **ellos / ellas / Uds.** forms.

4. Two irregular-**yo** verbs (**-go** verbs) with a stem change:

decir	to say, to tell	**digo**, dices, dice, decimos, decís, dicen
venir	to come, to attend	**vengo**, vienes, viene, venimos, venís, vienen

5. Remember that most of these verbs are irregular only in the **yo** form. Otherwise, they follow the rules for regular **-ar, -er**, and **-ir** verbs that you have already learned. **Oír** uses the regular endings but includes a spelling change: the addition of **y** to all forms except the **yo** form. **Decir** and **venir** also have a stem change in addition to the irregular-**yo** form, but they still use **-ir** present-tense endings.

Saber vs. conocer

Saber and **conocer** both mean *to know*. It's important to know when to use each one.

■ Use **saber** to say that you know a fact or information, or that you know how to do something.

Eduardo **sabe** hablar alemán, jugar tenis y bailar flamenco. Además **sabe** dónde están todos los restaurantes buenos de la ciudad.

*Eduardo **knows how** to speak German, play tennis, and dance flamenco. He also **knows** where all the good restaurants in the city are.*

One way to remember the difference between **saber** and **conocer** is that **saber** is usually followed by either a verb or a phrase, while **conocer** is often followed by a noun and is never followed by an infinitive.

■ Use **conocer** to say that you know a person or are familiar with a thing.

—¿**Conocen** a Sandra?
—No, pero **conocemos** a su hermana.

*Do you **know** Sandra?*
*No, but we **know** her sister.*

—¿**Conoces** bien Tegucigalpa?
—Sí, pero no **conozco** las otras ciudades de Honduras.

*Do you **know** Tegucigalpa well?*
*Yes, but I don't **know** the other cities in Honduras.*

The personal **a** can also be used with pets: **Adoro a mi perro.**

The personal a

When you use **conocer** to say that you know a person, notice that you use the preposition **a** before the noun referring to the person. This preposition is known as the personal **a** in Spanish and it must be used whenever a person receives the action of any verb (not just **conocer**). It has no equivalent in English.

In **Chapter 3** you learned that **a** + **el** = **al**. The personal **a** is no exception: **Veo al profesor.**

Conocemos **a** Nina y **a** Roberto.
¿Ves **a** tus amigos frecuentemente?

We know Nina and Roberto.
Do you see your friends frequently?

Gramática útil 2

Describing daily activities: Reflexive verbs

Cómo usarlo

1. So far, you have learned to use Spanish verbs to say what actions people are doing or to describe people and things.

Elena **habla** por teléfono.	*Elena **talks** on the phone.*
Tu hermano **está** cansado.	*Your brother **is** tired.*

2. Spanish has another category of verbs, called *reflexive* verbs, where the action of the verb *reflects back* on the person who is doing the action. When you use reflexive verbs in Spanish, they are often translated in English as *with* or *to myself, yourself, himself, herself, ourselves, yourselves, themselves.*

Lidia **se maquilla**.	*Lidia **puts makeup on (herself)**.*
Antes de ir a clase, yo **me ducho,** **me visto** y **me peino**.	*Before going to class, **I shower, get dressed**, and **comb my hair**.*

3. Notice how a reflexive verb is always used with a reflexive pronoun. These pronouns always match the subject of the sentence. The action of the verb *reflects back* on the person when the pronoun is used.

Yo me acuesto a las once.	***I go to bed (put myself to bed)*** *at eleven.*
Tú te despiertas a las diez los fines de semana.	***You get up (wake yourself up)*** *at ten on the weekends.*
Nosotros nos bañamos antes de salir de casa.	***We bathe (ourselves) before*** *we leave the house.*
Ellos se afeitan todos los días.	***They shave (themselves)*** *every day.*

> The reflexive pronoun and verb must always match the subject of the sentence: **Nosotros nos bañamos, Ellos se afeitan, Mateo se lava**, etc.

4. Most reflexive verbs can also be used without the reflexive pronoun to express non-reflexive actions, that is, actions that are performed on someone other than oneself.

Mateo **se baña** todos los días.	*Mateo **bathes** every day.*
Mateo **baña** a su perro.	*Mateo **bathes (washes)** his dog.*

5. Reflexive pronouns can also be used to indicate *reciprocal actions*.

Leo y Ali **se cortan** el pelo.	*Leo and Ali **cut each other's** hair.*

Cómo formarlo

LO BÁSICO

- A *reflexive verb* is one in which the action described reflects back on the subject.
- A *reflexive pronoun* is a pronoun that refers back to the subject of the sentence. English reflexive pronouns are *myself, herself, ourselves,* etc.

1. You conjugate reflexive verbs the same way you would any other verb. The only difference is that you must always include the reflexive pronoun.

2. Here is the reflexive verb **lavarse** conjugated in the present indicative tense.

lavarse *(to wash oneself)*	
yo	**me lavo**
tú	**te lavas**
Ud. / él / ella	**se lava**
nosotros(as)	**nos lavamos**
vosotros(as)	**os laváis**
Uds. / ellos / ellas	**se lavan**

3. The only difference in the way that reflexive and non-reflexive verbs are conjugated is the addition of the reflexive pronoun to the verb form. Verbs that are irregular or stem-changing when used non-reflexively have the same irregularities or stem changes when used with a reflexive pronoun.

Me despierto a las seis y media.   *I wake (myself) up at 6: 30.*
Despierto a mi esposo a las siete.   *I wake my husband up at 7: 00.*

> Remember that when you use a reflexive verb as an infinitive, you still need to change the pronoun to match the subject of the sentence: **Voy a acostarme a las once, pero tú vas a acostarte a medianoche**.

4. When you use a reflexive verb in its infinitive form, the reflexive pronoun may attach at the end of the infinitive (most commonly) or go at the beginning of the entire verb phrase.

Voy a acostarme a las once.   OR: **Me voy a acostar** a las once.
Necesito acostarme a las once.   **Me necesito acostar** a las once.
Tengo que acostarme a las once.   **Me tengo que acostar** a las once.

Notice that with **gustar** (and similar verbs), the reflexive pronoun *must* be attached at the end of the infinitive.

Me gusta acostarme a las once.

5. Here are some common reflexive verbs, many of which refer to daily routine. Many reflexive verbs have a stem change, which is indicated in parenthesis.

acostarse (ue) *to go to bed*	**levantarse** *to get up*
afeitarse *to shave oneself*	**maquillarse** *to put on makeup*
bañarse *to take a bath*	**peinarse** *to brush / comb one's hair*
cepillarse el pelo *to brush one's hair*	**ponerse (la ropa)** *to put on (clothing)*
cepillarse los dientes *to brush one's teeth*	**prepararse** *to get ready*
despertarse (ie) *to wake up*	**quitarse (la ropa)** *to take off (clothing)*
ducharse *to take a shower*	**secarse el pelo** *to dry one's hair*
lavarse *to wash oneself*	**sentarse (ie)** *to sit down*
lavarse el pelo *to wash one's hair*	**vestirse (i)** *to get dressed*
lavarse los dientes *to brush one's teeth*	

6. Some Spanish verbs are used with reflexive pronouns to emphasize a change in state or emotion. Spanish has many more verbs that are used this way than English does. Note that some of these verbs (**casarse, comprometerse,** etc.) are usually used to express reciprocal actions, due to the nature of their meaning.

casarse *to get married*	**irse** *to leave, to go away*
comprometerse *to get engaged*	**pelearse** *to have a fight*
despedirse (i) *to say goodbye*	**preocuparse** *to worry*
divertirse (ie) *to have fun*	**quejarse** *to complain*
divorciarse *to get divorced*	**reírse (i)** *to laugh*
dormirse (ue) *to fall asleep*	**relajarse** *to relax*
enamorarse *to fall in love*	**reunirse** *to meet, to get together*
enfermarse *to get sick*	**separarse** *to separate*

7. Here are some common words and phrases to use with these verbs.

a veces *sometimes*	**siempre** *always*
antes *before*	**todas las semanas** *every week*
después *after*	**todos los días** *every day*
luego *later*	**...veces al día / ... times a day /**
nunca *never*	**por semana** *per week*

>>

Gramática útil 3

Describing actions in progress: The present progressive tense

Cómo usarlo

1. The present progressive tense is used in Spanish to describe actions that are in progress at the moment of speaking. It is equivalent to the *is / are + -ing* structure in English.

En este momento **estamos llamando** a los abuelos.	*Right now,* ***we are calling*** *the (our) grandparents.*
Están comiendo ahora.	***They are eating*** *right now.*

2. Note that the present progressive tense is used *much* more frequently in English than it is in Spanish. Whereas in English it is used to describe future plans, in Spanish the present indicative or the **ir** + **a** + infinitive structure is used instead.

Salimos con la familia este viernes.	***We are going out*** *with the family this Friday.*
Vamos a salir con la familia este viernes.	***We are going to go out*** *with the family this Friday.*

3. Use the present progressive in Spanish only to describe actions in which people are engaged at the moment. Do not use it to describe routine ongoing activities (use the present indicative), to describe generalized action (use the infinitive), or to describe future actions.

Right now:	No puedo hablar. **Estamos estudiando.**	*I can't talk.* ***We're studying*** *(right now).*
BUT:		
Routine:	**Estudio** español, biología, historia e informática.	***I am studying / I study*** *Spanish, biology, history, and computer science.*
Generalized action:	**Estudiar** es importante.	***Studying*** *is important.*
Future:	**Estudio** con Mario el lunes.	***I will study*** *with Mario on Monday.*

Cómo formarlo

LO BÁSICO

A *present participle* is the verb form that expresses a continuing or ongoing action. In English, present participles end in *-ing*: *laughing, reading.*

1. Form the present progressive tense by using the present indicative forms of the verb **estar** (which you learned in **Chapter 4**) and the present participle.

estoy / estás / está / estamos / estáis / están + present participle

2. Here's how to form the present participle of regular **-ar, -er**, and **-ir** verbs.

-ar verbs	-er / -ir verbs
Remove the **-ar** from the infinitive and add **-ando**.	Remove the **-er** / **-ir** from the infinitive and add **-iendo**.
caminar → **caminando**	ver → **viendo**
	escribir → **escribiendo**

Estamos caminando al centro.   ***We're walking*** *downtown.*
Estoy viendo la televisión.   ***I'm watching*** *television.*
Chali **está escribiendo** su trabajo.   *Chali **is writing** her paper.*

3. A few present participles are irregular.

leer: **leyendo**   oír: **oyendo**

4. All **-ir** stem-changing verbs show a stem change in their present participle as well.

e → i			
despedirse	**despidiéndose**	reírse	**riéndose**
divertirse	**divirtiéndose**	repetir	**repitiendo**
pedir	**pidiendo**	servir	**sirviendo**
o → u			
dormir	**durmiendo**	morir	**muriendo**

5. As you may have noticed in the list above, to form the present participle of reflexive verbs, you may attach the reflexive pronoun to the end of the present participle, or place it before the entire verb phrase, the same as when you use reflexive verbs in the infinitive. Note that when the pronoun is attached, the new present participle form requires an accent to maintain the correct pronunciation.

Lina **está levantándose** ahora mismo. /   *Lina **is getting up** right now.*
Lina **se está levantando** ahora mismo.

Estoy divirtiéndome mucho. /   *I'm having a lot of fun.*
Me estoy divirtiendo mucho.

Spanish–English Glossary

The vocabulary includes the active vocabulary presented in the chapters and many receptive words. Exceptions are verb conjugations, regular past participles, adverbs ending in **-mente**, superlatives, diminutives, and proper names of individuals and most countries. Active words are followed by a number that indicates the chapter in which the word appears as an active item. **P** refers to the opening pages that precede Chapter 1.

The gender of nouns is indicated except for masculine nouns ending in **-o** and feminine nouns ending in **-a.** Stem changes and spelling changes are shown for verbs, e.g., **dormir (ue, u); buscar (qu).**

The following abbreviations are used. Note that the *adj.*, *adv.*, and *pron.* designations are used only to distinguish similar or identical words that are different parts of speech.

adj.	adjective	*fam.*	familiar	*irreg.*	irregular verb	*p.p.*	past participle
adv.	adverb	*form.*	formal	*m.*	masculine	*pron.*	pronoun
f.	feminine	*inf.*	infinitive	*pl.*	plural	*s.*	singular

A

a to; ~ **cambio de** in exchange for; ~ **nivel mundial** worldwide; ~ **pesar de** in spite of; ~ **pie** on foot, walking, 6; ~ **través de** across, throughout
abogado(a) lawyer, 5
abrelatas eléctrico (*m. s.*) electric can opener, 10
abrigo coat, 8
abril April, 1
abrir to open, 3; **Abran los libros.** Open your books. P
abuelo(a) grandfather (grandmother), 5
abundancia abundance
aburrido(a) boring, 2; bored, 4
aburrimiento boredom
acabar de (+inf.) to have just (*done something*), 2
académico(a) academic
acceder to access, 4
accesorio accessory, 8
acción (*f.*) action, 5
aceite (*m.*) **de oliva** olive oil, 9
acero steel
aconsejar to advise, 10
acostarse (ue) to go to bed, 5
acrecentar (ie) to strengthen; to increase
actividad (*f.*) activity, P; ~ **deportiva** sports activity, 7
activo(a) active, 2
actor (*m.*) actor, 5
actriz (*f.*) actress, 5

actualidad (*f.*): **en la** ~ at the present time
acudir to go; to attend
adelantar to get ahead, to promote
adelante ahead
además besides
adinerado(a) rich, wealthy
adiós goodbye, 1
adivinar to guess; **Adivina.** Guess. P
administración (*f.*) **de empresas** business administration, 3
¿adónde? (to) where?
adquisición (*f.*) acquisition
aeropuerto airport, 6
afán (*m.*) desire
afeitarse to shave oneself, 5
afueras (*f. pl.*) outskirts, 10
agosto August, 1
agregar (gu) to add, 9
agrícola agricultural
agua (*f.*) (*but:* **el agua**) water; ~ **dulce** fresh water; ~ **mineral** sparkling water, 9
aguacate avocado, 9
ajedrez (*m.*) chess
ajo garlic, 9
al (a + el) to the, 3
albergar (gu) to shelter
albóndiga meatball
alcalde (alcaldesa) mayor
alcanzar (c) to achieve
alemán (alemana) German, 2
alemán (*m.*) German language, 3
alfabeto alphabet

alfombra rug, carpet, 10
algo something, 6
algodón (*m.*) cotton, 8
alguien someone, 6
algún, alguno(a)(s) some, any, 6
alistar to recruit; to enroll
allá over there, 6
allí there, 6
alma (*f.*) (*but:* **el alma**) soul
almacén (*m.*) store, 6
almeja clam, 9
almohada pillow
almuerzo lunch, 9
¿Aló? hello (*on the phone*), 1
alpinismo: practicar / hacer ~ to hike, to (mountain) climb, 7
alquilar videos / películas to rent videos / movies, 2
alquiler (*m.*) rent
alrededor de around
altitud (*f.*) altitude, height
altivo(a) arrogant
alto(a) tall, 2
altoparlante (*m., f.*) speaker, 4
altura height
amanecer (zc) to dawn
amante (*m., f.*) lover
amar to love
amarillo(a) yellow, 4
ambiente (*m.*) atmosphere; **medio** ~ (*m.*) environment
ambigüedad (*f.*) ambiguity
ambos(as) both
amenaza threat
amigo(a) friend, P
amor (*m.*) love
anaranjado(a) orange (*in color*), 4
andar (*irreg.*) to walk, 8

anexo attachment
anfitrión (*m.*) host
anhelo wish, desire
anillo ring, 8
anoche last night, 7
anónimo(a) anonymous
Antártida Antarctica
anteayer the day before yesterday, 7
antecesor(a) ancestor
anteojos (*m. pl.*) eyeglasses
antepasado(a) ancestor
anteponer to give preference
antes before, 5
anticuado(a) antiquated, old-fashioned
antipático(a) unpleasant, 2
antros bar or club; the "in" place
anuncio personal personal ad
añadir to add, 9
año year, 3; **~ pasado** last year, 7; **tener** (*irreg.*) ... **~** to be . . . years old, 1
apacible mild, gentle
apagar (gu) to turn off, 2
aparatos electrónicos electronics, 4
aparecer (zc) to appear
apariencia física physical appearance
apartamento apartment, 6
apenas scarcely
apetecer (zc) to long for
aplicación (*f.*) application, 4
apodo nickname
apoyar to support
apreciar to appreciate
aprender to learn, 3
aprendizaje (*m.*) learning
apropiado(a) appropriate
apto(a) apt, fit
apuntes (*m.*) notes, P
aquel / aquella(s) (*adj.*) those (over there), 6
aquél / aquélla(s) (*pron.*) those (over there), 6
aquí here, 6
árbol (*m.*) tree; **~ genealógico** family tree
archivar to file, 4
archivo file, 4; **~ PDF** PDF file, 4
arder to burn
arete (*m.*) earring, 8
argentino(a) Argentinian, 2
arquitecto(a) architect, 5

arquitectura architecture, 3
arreglar el dormitorio to straighten up the bedroom, 10
arroz (*m.*) **con pollo** chicken with rice, 9
arrugado(a) wrinkled
arte (*m.*) art, 3
artesanía handicrafts
artículo article, 1
artista (*m., f.*) artist, 5
asado(a) grilled
asco disgusting
asegurarse to make sure
asistente (*m., f.*) assistant, 5; **~** (*m.*) **electrónico** electronic notebook, 4
asistir a to attend, 3
aspiradora vacuum cleaner, 10
ataque (*m.*) attack
atardecer (*m.*) late afternoon
atún (*m.*) tuna, 9
audiencia audience
audífonos (*m. pl.*) earphones, 4
audio audio, P
auditorio auditorium, 6
aumentar to increase
aun even
aún yet (*in negative contexts*); still
australiano(a) Australian, 2
autobús: en ~ by bus, 6
automóvil: en ~ by car, 6
avenida avenue, 1
avergonzado(a) embarrassed
avergonzar (ue) (c) to embarrass
avión (*m.*) airplane; **en ~** by airplane, 6
aviso warning
ayer yesterday, 3
ayuda help
ayudar to help, 8
azúcar (*m., f.*) sugar, 9; **caña de ~** sugar cane
azul blue, 4

B

bacalao codfish, 9
bailar to dance, 2
baile (*m.*) dance, 3
bajar to get down from, to get off of (*a bus, etc.*), 6; to download, 4
bajo(a) short (*in height*), 2
balay large basket
baldosa paving stone

banco (commercial) bank, 6
bañador(a) bather
bañar to swim; to give someone a bath, 5; **bañarse** to take a bath, 5
baño bathroom, 10
barato: Es muy ~. It's very inexpensive. 8
barco boat
barrer el suelo / el piso to sweep the floor, 10
barrio neighborhood, 1; **~ residencial** residential neighborhood, suburbs, 10; **~ comercial** business district, 10
básquetbol (*m.*) basketball, 7
basta it is enough
bastante somewhat, rather, 4
Bastante bien. Quite well. 1
basura garbage, 10; **sacar la ~** to take out the garbage, 10
basurero wastebasket
batir to beat; to break
beber to drink, 3
bebida beverage, 9
béisbol (*m.*) baseball, 7
belleza beauty
bello(a) beautiful
berro watercress
besar to kiss
bicicleta: en ~ on bicycle, 6; **montar en ~** to ride a bike, 7
bien well, 4; **~, gracias.** Fine, thank you. 1; **(no) muy ~** (not) very well, 1
bienestar (*m.*) well-being
bienvenido(a) welcome
bilingüe bilingual
biología biology, 3
bistec (*m.*) steak, 6
blanco(a) white, 4
blog blog, 4
blusa blouse, 8
bocadillo sandwich, 9
boda wedding
bodegón (*m.*) tavern
bolígrafo ballpoint pen, P
boliviano(a) Bolivian, 2
bolsa purse, 8
bombero(a) fire fighter, 5
bondadoso(a) kind; good
bonito(a) pretty
bordado(a) embroidered, 8
borrador (*m.*) rough draft

bosquejo outline

bota boot, 8

botar to throw out

bote (*m.*) boat

boxeo boxing, 7

brazalete (*m.*) bracelet, 8

breve brief

bróculi (*m.*) broccoli, 9

broma joke

bueno(a) good, 2; **Buenas noches.** Good night. Good evening. 1; **Buenas tardes.** Good afternoon. 1; **Buenos días.** Good morning. 1

bufanda scarf, 8

buscador (*m.*) search engine, 4

buscar (qu) to look for, 2

buzón (*m.*) **electrónico** electronic mailbox, 4

C

caballo: montar a ~ to ride horseback, 7

cable (*m.*) cable, 4

cabo end

cacao chocolate

cachemira cashmere

cadena chain, 8

caer (*irreg.*) to fall

café (*m.*) coffee, 9; (*adj.*) brown, 4

cafetería cafeteria, 3

caimán (*m.*) alligator (*cayman*)

cajero automático automated bank teller, ATM, 6

cajón (*m.*) large box; drawer

calcetín (*m.*) sock, 8

calculadora calculator, P

cálculo calculus, 3

caldo de pollo chicken soup, 9

calentar (ie) to heat, 9

calidad (*f.*) quality; **de buena (alta) ~** of good (high) quality, 8

calificación (*f.*) evaluation

calle (*f.*) street, 1

calor: Hace ~. It's hot., 7; **tener** (*irreg.*) **~** to be hot, 7

caluroso(a) warm

cama bed, 10; **hacer la ~** to make the bed, 10

cámara: ~ digital digital camera, 4; **~ web** webcam, 4

camarero(a) waiter (waitress), 5

camarón (*m.*) shrimp, 9

cambio change; exchange rate; **a ~ de** in exchange for

caminar to walk, 2

camisa shirt, 8

camiseta t-shirt, 8

campestre rural

campo: ~ de estudio field of study, 3; **~ de fútbol** soccer field, 6

caña de azúcar sugar cane

canadiense (*m., f.*) Canadian, 2

canasta basket

cancha soccer field, 6; **~ de tenis** tennis court, 6

canela cinnamon

cansado(a) tired, 4

cantante (*m., f.*) singer

cantar to sing, 2

capítulo chapter, P

característica trait; **~ de la personalidad** personality trait, 2; **~ física** physical trait, 2

Caribe (*m., f.*) Caribbean (sea)

cariño love, fondness, affection

carne (*f.*) meat, 9

cargar to upload, 4

carnicería butcher shop, 6

caro: Es (demasiado) caro(a). It's (too) expensive. 8

carpintero(a) carpenter, 5

carrera career, 5

carreta wooden cart

carro: en ~ by car, 6

carta: a la ~ à la carte, 9

cartera wallet, 8

cartón (*m.*) cardboard

casa house, 6

casarse to get married, 5

casco helmet

casero(a) homemade

castaño brown, 2

catarata waterfall

catorce fourteen, P

cebolla onion, 9

celebración (*f.*) celebration

celos: tener (*irreg.*) **~** to be jealous

celosamente jealously

celoso(a) jealous

cena dinner

cenar to eat dinner, 2

censo census

centavo cent

centro center; **~ comercial** mall, 6; **~ de computación** computer center, 3; **~ de comunicaciones** media center, 3; **~ de la ciudad** downtown, 10; **~ estudiantil** student center, 6

Centroamérica Central America

cepillarse el pelo to brush one's hair, 5

cepillo brush, 5; **~ de dientes** toothbrush, 5

cerca de close to, 6

cereal (*m.*) cereal, 9

cero zero, P

cerrar (ie) to close, 4; **Cierren los libros.** Close your books. P

cerveza beer, 9

chaleco vest, 8

champú (*m.*) shampoo, 5

chaparrón (*m.*) cloudburst, downpour

chaqueta jacket (*outdoor; non-suit coat*), 8

chatear to chat online, 4

Chau. Bye, Goodbye, 1

cheque (*m.*) check; **pagar con ~ / con ~ de viajero** to pay by check / with a traveler's check, 8

chévere terrific, great, cool (*Cuba, Puerto Rico*)

chico(a) boy (girl), P

chileno(a) Chilean, 2

chimenea fireplace, 10

chino Chinese language, 3

chino(a) Chinese, 2

chisme (*m.*) gossip

chismoso(a) gossiping

chompa sweater

chuleta de puerco pork chop, 6

ciberespacio cyberspace, 4

ciclismo cycling, 7

ciego(a) blind; **cita a ciegas** blind date

cien one hundred, P; **~ mil** one hundred thousand, 8

ciencias (*f. pl.*) science, 3; **~ políticas** political science, 3

científico(a) scientific

ciento uno one hundred and one, 8

cierto(a) certain

cinco five, P; **~ mil** five thousand, 8

cincuenta fifty, P

cine (*m.*) cinema, 6
cinturón (*m.*) belt, 8
cita quotation; **~ a ciegas** blind date
ciudad (*f.*) city, 6
claridad (*f.*) clarity
clase (*f.*) class, P; **~ baja** lower class
clic: hacer ~ / doble ~ to click / double click, 4
cliente (*m., f.*) customer, 8
clóset (*m.*) closet, 10
cobre (*m.*) copper
cocer (-z) (ue) to cook, 9
coche: en ~ by car, 6
cocina kitchen, 10
cocinar to cook, 2
cocinero(a) cook, chef, 5
código code
colectivo bus
cólera anger
collar (*m.*) necklace, 8
colombiano(a) Colombian, 2
colonia neighborhood, 1
color (*m.*) color, 4; **de un solo ~** solid (colored), 8
coma comma
comedor (*m.*) dining room, 10
comenzar (ie) (c) to begin, 4
comer to eat, 3; **darle de ~ al perro / gato** to feed the dog / cat, 10
cómico(a) funny, 2
comida food, 6
comino cumin, 9
¿cómo? how? 3; **¿~ desea pagar?** How do you wish to pay? 8; **¿~ es?** What's he / she / it like? 2; **¿~ está (usted)?** (*s. form.*) How are you? 1; **¿~ están (ustedes)?** (*pl.*) How are you? 1; **¿~ estás (tú)?** (*s. fam.*) How are you? 1; **¿~ te / le / les va?** How's it going with you? 1; **~ no.** Of course. 6; **¿~ se dice…?** How do you say . . . ? P; **¿~ se llama?** (*s. form.*) What's your name? 1; **¿~ te llamas?** (*s. fam.*) What's your name? 1
cómoda dresser, 10
compañero(a) de cuarto roommate, P
comparación (*f.*) comparison, 8
compartir to share, 3
competencia competition, 7

competir (i, i) to compete
complicidad (*f.*) complicity
comportamiento behavior
comprar to buy, 2
compras: hacer las ~ to go shopping, 6
comprender to understand, 3
comprensión (*f.*) understanding
comprometerse to get engaged, 5
computación (*f.*) computer science, 3
computadora computer, P; **~ portátil** laptop computer, P
común common
comunicación (*f.*) **pública** public communications, 3
con with
concordancia agreement
concurso contest
conducir (zc) to drive, to conduct, 5
conectar to connect, 4
conexión (*f.*) connection, 4; **hacer una ~** to go online, 4
confección (*f.*) confection
conferencista (*m., f.*) speaker
congelado(a) frozen, 9
congelador freezer, 10
conjunto group; **en ~** as a group
conmigo with me, 8
conocer (zc) to meet; to know a person, to be familiar with, 5
conseguir (i, i) to get, to obtain, 8
contabilidad (*f.*) accounting, 3
contado: al ~ in cash, 8
contador(a) accountant, 5
contar (ue) to tell, to relate, 4; to count; **~ con** to be certain of
contento(a) happy, 4
contestar to answer; **Contesten.** Answer. P
contigo with you (*fam.*), 8
contracción (*f.*) contraction, 3
contrario: al ~ on the contrary
contraseña password, 4
conversación (*f.*) conversation
convertir (ie, i) to change
copa wine glass, goblet, 9
coraje (*m.*) courage
cordillera mountain range
coreano(a) Korean, 2
corregir (i, i) (j) to correct
correo electrónico e-mail, 4
correr to run, 3 to mow the lawn, 10; **~ la conexión** to go offline, 4

cortesía courtesy, 4
cortina curtain, 10
corto(a) short (*in length*)
costarricense (*m., f.*) Costa Rican, 2
cotidiano(a) daily
crear to create
creativo(a) creative
crecimiento growth
creer (en) to believe (in); to think, 3
cronología chronology
crucero cruise ship
crudo(a) raw, 9
cruzar (c) to cross, 6
cuaderno notebook, P
cuadra (city) block, 6
cuadro painting; print, 10
cuadros: a ~ plaid, 8
¿cuál? what? which one? 3; **¿~ es tu / su dirección (electrónica)?** (*s. fam. / form.*) What's your (e-mail) address? 1; **¿~ es tu / su número de teléfono?** (*s. fam. / form.*) What is your phone number? 1
¿cuáles? what? which ones? 3
cualquier whatever
¿cuándo? when? 3; **¿~ es tu cumpleaños?** When is your birthday? 1
¿cuánto(a)? how much? 3; **¿Cuánto cuesta(n)?** How much does it (do they) cost? 8
¿cuántos(as)? how many? 3
cuarenta forty, P
cuarto room, P; bedroom, 10
cuarto(a) fourth, 10
cuate(a) friend, buddy
cuatro four, P
cuatrocientos(as) four hundred, 8
cubano(a) Cuban, 2
cuchara spoon, 9
cucharada tablespoonful, 9
cucharadita teaspoonful, 9
cuchillo knife, 9
cuenta check, bill, 9
cuento de hadas fairy tale
cuero leather, 8
cuestionario questionnaire
cuidado: tener (*irreg.*) **~** to be careful, 7; **¡~!** careful!
cuidadoso(a) cautious, 2
culinario(a) culinary

cultura culture
cuna cradle
cuñado(a) brother-in-law (sister-in-law), 5
curso básico basic course, 3
cuy (*m.*) guinea pig
cuyo(a) whose

D

dar (*irreg.*) to give, 5; **~ información personal** to give personal information, 1; **~ la hora** to give the time, 3; **~ un papel** to give (play) a role; **~le de comer al perro / gato** to feed the dog / cat, 10; **~le mucha dicha** to give one a lot of happiness
dato fact; piece of information
De nada. You're welcome. 1
debajo de below, underneath, 6
deber (+ *inf.*) should, ought to (*do something*), 2
décimo(a) tenth, 10
decir (*irreg.*) to say, to tell, 5; **~ cómo llegar** to give directions, 6; **~ la hora** to tell the time, 3; **Se dice...** It's said . . . , P
decoración (*f.*) decoration, 10
definido(a) definite, 1
dejar to leave, to stop, 2; **~ de** (+ *inf.*) to stop (*doing something*), 2
del (**de + el**) from the, of the, 3
delante de in front of, 6
delgado(a) thin, 2
demasiado(a) too much, 4
demostrar (ue) to demonstrate, to show
demostrativo(a) demonstrative, 6
dentista (*m., f.*) dentist, 5
dentro de inside of, 6; **~ la casa** inside the house, 10
dependiente (*m., f.*) salesclerk, 5
deporte (*m.*) sport, 7
derecha: a la ~ to the right, 6
derecho: (todo) ~ (straight) ahead, 6
desarrollar to develop
desayuno breakfast, 9
descalificar (qu) to disqualify
descalzo(a) barefoot
descansar to rest, 2
descargar to download, 4

descortés rude
describir to describe, 2
descubrir to discover, 3
descuento discount, 8
desear to want; to wish, 10
desempeñarse to manage; to work (as)
desengaño disillusionment
desilusión (*f.*) disappointment
desodorante (*m.*) deodorant, 5
despachar to dispatch; to wait on; to work (from a home office)
despacio (*adv.*) slowly; (*adj.*) slow
despedido(a) fired (*from a job*)
despedirse (i, i) to say good-bye, 1
despertar (ie) to wake someone up, 5; **despertarse (ie)** to wake up, 5
después after, 5
destacar (qu) to emphasize
detalle (*m.*) detail
detrás de behind, 6
día (*m.*) day, 3; **~ de la semana** day of the week, 3; **~ de las Madres** Mother's Day, 3; **todos los días** every day, 3
dialecto dialect
dibujo drawing, P
diccionario dictionary, P
dicha happiness
dicho saying
diciembre December, 1
diecinueve nineteen, P
dieciocho eighteen, P
dieciséis sixteen, P
diecisiete seventeen, P
diez ten, P; **~ mil** ten thousand, 8
diferencia difference
difícil difficult, 4
dinero money
director(a) de social media social media director, 5
dirección (*f.*) address
disco duro hard drive, 4
Disculpe. Excuse me. 4
diseñador(a) gráfico(a) graphic designer, 5
diseño design; **~ gráfico** graphic design, 3
disfrutar (la vida) to enjoy (life)
disponibilidad (*f.*) availability
dispuesto(a) willing

diversidad (*f.*) diversity
diversión (*f.*) amusement
divertido(a) fun, entertaining, 2
divertirse (ie, i) to have fun, 5
dividir to divide
divorciarse to get divorced, 5
doblar to turn, 6; to fold
doce twelve, P
docena dozen, 9
doctor(a) doctor
dólar (*m.*) dollar
domesticado(a) tame, tamed
domingo Sunday, 2
dominicano(a) Dominican, 2
don (doña) title of respect used with male (female) first name, 1
¿dónde? where? 3; **¿~ tienes la clase de... ?** Where does your . . . class meet? 3; **¿~ vives / vive?** (*s. fam. / form.*) Where do you live? 1
dondequiera: por ~ everywhere
dorado(a) golden, browned, 9
dormir (ue, u) to sleep, 4; **dormirse (ue, u)** to fall asleep, 5
dormitorio bedroom, 10; **~ estudiantil** dormitory, 6
dos two, P; **~ mil** two thousand, 8
doscientos(as) two hundred, 8
ducharse to take a shower, 5
duelo pain
dueño(a) owner, 5
dulce (*adj.*) sweet
duro(a) hard

E

economía economics, 3
ecuador (*m.*) equator
ecuatoriano(a) Ecuadoran, 2
edad (*f.*) age
edificio building, 6
educación (*f.*) education, 3
efectivo: en ~ in cash, 8
egoísta selfish, egotistic, 2
ejemplo example, 10; **por ~** for example, 10
ejercicio: hacer ~ to exercise, 7
el (*m.*) the, 1
él he, 1; him, 8
electricidad (*f.*) electricity
electrodoméstico appliance, 10
elefante (*m.*) elephant

ella   she, 1; her, 8

ellos(as)   they, 1; them, 8

e-mail (*m.*)   e-mail, P

embajador(a)   ambassador

emoción (*f.*)   emotion, 4

empapado(a)   drenched

emparejar   to match

empezar (ie) (c)   to begin, 4

empresas (*pl.*)   business

en   in, on, at; ~ **autobús /
   tren**   by bus / train, 6;
   ~ **bicicleta**   on bicycle,
   6; ~ **carro / coche /
   automóvil**   by car,
   6; ~ **línea**   online, 4;
   ~ **metro**   on the subway, 6;
   ~ **realidad**   actually

enamorarse   to fall in love, 5

Encantado(a).   Delighted to meet
   you. 1

encargado de   in charge of

encendida   burning, on fire

encima de   on top of, on, 6

encontrar (ue)   to find, 4

encuentro   encounter; meeting

encuesta   survey

enero   January, 1

enfatizar (c)   to emphasize

enfermarse   to get sick, 5

enfermero(a)   nurse, 5

enfermo(a)   sick, 4

enfrente de   in front of,
   opposite, 6

enfriarse   to get cold, 9

engañar   to fool

engaño   hoax

enlace (*m.*)   link, 4

enojado(a)   angry, 4

ensalada   salad, 9; ~ **de fruta**
   fruit salad, 9; ~ **de lechuga y
   tomate**   lettuce and tomato
   salad, 9; ~ **de papa**   potato
   salad, 9; ~ **mixta**   tossed
   salad, 9

ensayo   essay

enseñar   to teach

entender (ie)   to understand, 4

entonces   then

entre   between, 6

entregar (gu)   to turn in;
   Entreguen la tarea.   Turn in
   your homework. P

entrenador(a)   trainer

entrenarse   to train, 7

entresemana   during the week,
   on weekdays, 3

entretener (*like* **tener**)   to
   entertain

enviar   to send, 4

equilibro: poner en ~   to balance

equipo   team, 7

erupción (*f.*) **volcánica**   volcanic
   eruption

escaleras (*f. pl.*)   stairs, 10

esclavo(a)   slave

escoger (j)   to choose

esconder   to hide

escribir   to write, 3; **Escriban en
   sus cuadernos.**   Write in your
   notebooks. P

escritorio   desk, P

escuchar   to listen; ~ **música**   to
   listen to music, 2; **Escuchen el
   audio / el CD.**   Listen to the
   tape / CD. P

escuela   school, 3

ese (esa) (*s. adj.*)   that, 6

ése (ésa) (*s. pron.*)   that one, 6

eso   that, 6; **por ~**   so, that's
   why, 10

esos (esas) (*pl. adj.*)   those, 6

ésos (ésas) (*pl. pron.*)   those
   (ones), 6

España   Spain

español (a)   Spanish, 2

español (*m.*)   Spanish
   language, 3

espárragos (*m.pl.*)   asparagus, 9

especialidad de la casa   house
   special, 9

especie (*f.*)   species

espejo   mirror, 10

esperanza   wish, hope

esperar   to hope, 10

esposo(a)   husband (wife), 5

esquí (*m.*)   ski, skiing;
   ~ **acuático**   water skiing, 7;
   ~ **alpino**   downhill skiing, 7

esquiar   to ski, 7

esquina   corner, 6

estación (*f.*)   season, 7
   de trenes / autobuses   train /
   bus station, 6

estacionamiento   parking lot, 6

estadio   stadium, 6

estadística   statistics, 3

estado   state, 5; ~ **civil**   marital
   status

Estados Unidos   United States

estadounidense (*m., f.*)   U. S.
   citizen, 2

estampado(a)   print, 8

estancia   ranch

estar (*irreg.*)   to be, 1;

estatura   height (*of a person*)

este (esta) (*s. adj.*)   this, 6

éste (ésta) (*s. pron.*)   this one, 6

estilo   style

estos(as) (*pl. adj.*)   these, 6

éstos(as) (*pl. pron.*)   these
   (ones), 6

estrategia   strategy

estudiante (*m., f.*)   student, P

estudiar   to study; ~ **en la
   biblioteca (en casa)**   to study
   at the library (at home), 2;
   **Estudien las páginas…
   a…**   Study pages . . . to . . . P

estudio   studio, 3

estufa   stove, 10

etapa   era

Europa   Europe

evitar   to avoid

exhibir   to exhibit

exigir (j)   to demand

éxito   success

exótico(a)   exotic, strange

expresar preferencias   to
   express preferences, 2

expresión (*f.*)   expression, 1

extrovertido(a)   extroverted, 2

F

fácil   easy, 4

falda   skirt, 8

falso(a)   false

familia   family;
   ~ **nuclear**   nuclear family, 5;
   ~ **política**   in-laws, 5

fantasía   fantasy

farmacia   pharmacy, 6

fascinar   to fascinate, 4

fatal   terrible, awful, 1

favor: por ~   please, 1

febrero   February, 1

fecha   date, 3; **¿A qué
   ~ estamos?**   What is today's
   date? 3

felicidad (*f.*)   happiness

femenino(a)   feminine

feo(a)   ugly, 2

ferrocarril (*m.*)   railroad

filantrópico(a)   philanthropic

filosofía   philosophy, 3

fin (*m.*)   end; intention; ~ **de
   semana**   weekend, 2; **por ~**
   finally, 9

final final
financiero(a) financial
física physics, 3
físico(a) physical, 5
flan (*m.*) custard, 9
flor (*f.*) flower
florecer (zc) to flower, to flourish
flotador(a) floating
fondo background
fortaleza fortress
foro forum, 4
foto (*f.*) photo, P; **sacar fotos** to take photos, 2
francés (francesa) French, 2
francés (*m.*) French language, 3
frecuentemente frequently, 4
freír (i, i) to fry, 9
frente a in front of, facing, opposite, 6
fresa strawberry, 9
fresco(a) fresh, 9; **Hace fresco.** It's cool. 7
frijoles (*m.*) **(refritos)** (refried) beans, 9
frío(a) cold; **Hace frío.** It's cold. 7; **tener** (*irreg.*) **frío** to be cold, 7
frito(a) fried, 9
frontera border
fruta fruit, 6
fuego fire; **a ~ suave / lento** at low heat, 9
fuente (*f.*) source
fuera de outside of, 6; **~ de la casa** outside the house, 10
fuerte strong, filling (*e.g., a meal*), 9
funcionar to function, 4
funciones (*f. pl.*) **de la computadora** computer functions, 4
fundador(a) founder
fungir to work
furioso(a) furious, 4
fútbol (*m.*) soccer, 7; **~ americano** football, 7

G

gafas (*f. pl.*) **de sol** sunglasses, 8
galleta cookie, 9
galón (*m.*) gallon, 9
ganadería cattle, livestock
ganado cattle
ganar to win, 7

ganas: tener (*irreg.*) **~ de** to have the urge to, to feel like, 7
garaje (*m.*) garage, 10
gato(a) cat, 2
gazpacho cold tomato soup (*Spain*), 9
general: por lo ~ generally, 9
género genre
generoso(a) generous, 2
gente (*f.*) people
geografía geography, 3
gerente (*m., f.*) manager, 5
gimnasio gymnasium, 3
gobernador(a) (*m.*) governor
golf (*m.*) golf, 7
gordo(a) fat, 2
gorra cap, 8
gozar (c) to enjoy
grabador (*m.*) **de discos compactos / DVD** CD / DVD recorder, 4
grabar to record, 4
gracias: Muchas ~. Thank you very much. 1
grado degree; **~ Celsio(s)** Celsius degree, 7; **~ Fahrenheit** Fahrenheit degree, 7
gráfica graph
grande big, great, 2
grano: al ~ to the point
gris gray, 4
gritar to shout, to scream
grito scream
grupo group; **~ de conversación** chat room, 4; **~ de noticias** news group, 4
guagua bus (*Cuba, Puerto Rico*)
guante (*m.*) glove, 8
guapo(a) handsome, attractive, 2
guardar to store; **~ la ropa** put away the clothes, 10; to save, 4
guatemalteco(a) Guatemalan, 2
guión (*m.*) script
guionista (*m., f.*) script writer
guisado beef stew, 9
guisante (*m.*) pea, 9
guitarra guitar, 2
gustar: A mí / ti me / te gusta . . . I / You like . . . , 2; **A . . . le gusta . . .** He / She likes . . . , 2; **A . . . les gusta . . .** They / You (*pl.*) like . . . , 2; **Me gustaría (+ *inf.*) . . .** I'd like (+ *inf.*) . . . , 6

gusto taste; **al ~** to individual taste, 9; **El ~ es mío.** The pleasure is mine. 1; **Mucho ~.** My pleasure. 1; **Mucho ~ en conocerte.** A pleasure to meet you. 1

H

haba (*f.*) (*but:* **el haba**) bean
habichuela green bean, 9
habitación (*f.*) bedroom, 10
habitante (*m., f.*) inhabitant
hablar por teléfono to talk on the telephone, 2
hacer (*irreg.*) to make, to do, 5; **Hace buen / mal tiempo.** It's nice / bad weather. 7; **Hace calor / fresco / frío.** It's hot / cool / cold. 7; **Hace sol / viento.** It's sunny / windy. 7; **~ alpinismo** to hike, 7; **~ caso** to pay attention, to obey; **~ clic / doble clic** to click / double click, 4; **~ ejercicio** to exercise, 7; **~ el reciclaje** to do the recycling, 10; **~ la cama** to make the bed, 10; **~ las compras** to go shopping, 6; **~ preguntas** to ask questions, 3; **~ surfing** to surf, 7; **~ una conexión** to go online, 4; **Hagan la tarea para mañana.** Do the homework for tomorrow. P
hambre (*f.*) (*but:* **el hambre**) hunger; **tener** (*irreg.*) **~** to be hungry, 7
hamburguesa hamburger, 9; **~ con queso** cheeseburger, 9
hardware (*m.*) hardware, 4
harina flour, 9
hasta until; **~ luego.** See you later, 1; **~ mañana.** See you tomorrow. 1; **~ pronto.** See you soon. 1
hay there is, there are, 1
hecho fact
hecho(a) (*p. p.*): **Está ~ de...** It's made out of . . . , 8
helado de vainilla / chocolate vanilla / chocolate ice cream, 9
herencia heritage
hermanastro(a) stepbrother (stepsister), 5

hermano(a) (menor, mayor) (younger, older) brother (sister), 5

hermoso(a) handsome, beautiful

hervido(a) boiled, 9

hervir (ie, i) to boil, 9

hierro iron

hijo(a) son (daughter), 5

hilo: al ~ stringed, 9

himno hymn

hispano(a) Hispanic

hispanohablante Spanish-speaking

historia history, 3

hockey (*m.*) **sobre hielo / hierba** ice / field hockey, 7

hogar (*m.*) home; **sin ~** homeless

hoja de papel sheet of paper, P

hola hello, 1

hombre (*m.*) man, P; **~ de negocios** businessman, 5

hondureño(a) Honduran, 2

honesto(a) honest

hora hour; time; **dar** (*irreg.*) **la ~** to give the time, 3; **decir la ~** to tell the time, 3

horario schedule

horno oven; **al ~** roasted (in the oven), 9

hospital (*m.*) hospital, 6

hoy today, 3; **~ es martes treinta.** Today is Tuesday the 30th. 3; **¿Qué día es ~?** What day is today? 3

huella footprint

huevo egg, 6; **~ estrellado** egg sunny-side up, 9; **~ revuelto** scrambled egg, 9

humanidades (*f. pl.*) humanities, 3

húmedo(a) humid

humilde humble

I

ícono del programa program icon, 4

identidad (*f.*) identity

idioma (*m.*) language, 3

iglesia church, 6

Igualmente. Likewise. 1

impaciente impatient, 2

impermeable (*m.*) raincoat, 8

importar to be important to someone; to mind, 4

impresionante impressive

impresora printer, 4

imprimir to print, 3

impulsivo(a) impulsive, 2

incendio forestal forest fire

increíble incredible

indefinido(a) indefinite, 1

índice (*m.*) index

indio(a) Indian, 2

indígena indigenous

influencia influence

influir (y) to influence

informática computer science, 3

informe (*m.*) report

ingeniería engineering, 3

ingeniero(a) engineer, 5

inglés (inglesa) English, 2

inglés (*m.*) English language, 3

ingrediente (*m.*) ingredient, 9

ingreso revenue

inmigración (*f.*) immigration

insistir to insist, 10

instalar to install, 4

instructor(a) instructor, P

inteligente intelligent, 2

intentar to attempt

intercambiar to exchange

interesante interesting, 2

interesar to interest, to be interesting, 4

Internet (*m. or f.*) Internet

intérprete (*m., f.*) interpreter

íntimo(a) intimate

introvertido(a) introverted, 2

invertir to invest

invierno winter, 7

ir (*irreg.*) to go, 3; **~ a** (+ *inf.*) to be going to (*do something*), 3; **~ de compras** to go shopping, 8; **irse** to leave, to go away, 5

irresponsable irresponsible, 2

italiano(a) Italian, 2

italiano (*m.*) Italian language

izquierda: a la ~ to the left, 6

J

jabón (*m.*) soap, 5

jamás never, 6

jamón (*m.*) ham, 6

japonés (japonesa) Japanese, 2

japonés (*m.*) Japanese language, 3

jardín (*m.*) garden, 10

jeans (*m. pl.*) jeans, 8

jornada laboral workday

joven young, 2

joyas (*f. pl.*) jewelry, 8

joyería jewelry store, 6

juego interactivo interactive game, 4

jueves (*m.*) Thursday, 3

jugar (ue) (gu) to play, 4; **~ tenis (béisbol, etc.)** to play tennis (baseball, etc.), 7

jugo de fruta fruit juice, 9

juguete (*m.*) toy, 10

juguetón (juguetona) playful

julio July, 1

junio June, 1

juntar to group

juntarse to join

juventud (*f.*) youth

K

kilo kilo, 9; **medio ~** half a kilo, 9

L

la (*f.*) the, 1

labio lip

lado side; **al ~ de** next to, on the side of, 6

ladrillo brick

lago lake, 7

lámpara lamp, 10

lana wool, 8

langosta lobster, 9

lanzarse (c) to throw oneself

lápiz (*m.*) pencil, P

lavadora washer, 10

lavandería laundry room, 10

lavaplatos (*m. s.*) dishwasher, 10

lavar to wash, 5; **~ los platos (la ropa)** to wash the dishes (the clothes), 10

lavarse to wash oneself, 5; **~ el pelo** to wash one's hair, 5; **~ los dientes** to brush one's teeth, 5

le to / for you (*form. s.*), to / for him, to / for her, 8

lección (*f.*) lesson, P

leche (*f.*) milk, 6

lector (*m.*) **de CD-ROM / DVD** DVD / CD-ROM drive, 4

leer (y) to read, 3; **Lean el Capítulo 1.** Read Chapter 1. P

lejos de far from, 6

lema (*m.*) slogan

lentes (*m. pl.*) eyeglasses

lento(a) slow, 4

les to / for you (*form. pl.*), to / for them, 8
letrero sign
levantar to raise, to lift, 5; **~ pesas** to lift weights, 2
levantarse to get up, 5
libra pound, 9
libre free
librería bookstore, 3
libro book, P; **~ electrónico** e-book, P
licencia de manejar driver's license
licuado de fruta fruit shake, smoothie
licuadora blender, 10
ligero(a) light, lightweight, 9
limonada lemonade, 9
limpiar el baño to clean the bathroom, 10
lindo(a) pretty, 2
línea: en ~ online, 4
lingüístico(a) linguistic
lino linen, 8
literatura literature, 3
litro liter, 9
llamar to call, 2; **llamarse** to name, 2; **Me llamo . . .** My name is . . . , 1
llano(a) flat
llanura plain
llegar (gu) to arrive, 2
llenar to fill
llevar to take, to carry **llover** to rain; **Está lloviendo. (Llueve.)** It's raining. 7
lobo wolf
lodo mud
lograr to achieve
lomo de res prime rib, 9
los (las) (*pl.*) the, 1
luego later, 5
lugar (*m.*) place; **~ de nacimiento** birthplace
lujoso(a) luxurious
lunares: de ~ polka-dotted, 8
lunes (*m.*) Monday, 3
luz (*f.*) light; **~ solar** sunlight

M

madera wood
madrastra stepmother, 5
madre (*f.*) mother, 5
maestro(a) teacher, 5

maíz (*m.*) corn
mal badly, 4
malo(a) bad, 2
mamá mother, 5
mañana morning, 3; tomorrow, 3; **de la ~** in the morning (*with precise time*), 3; **por la ~** during the morning, 3
mandar to send; to order, 8
mandato command
manejar to drive, 5
mantel (*m.*) tablecloth, 9
mantener (*irreg.*) to keep, maintain
mantequilla butter, 9
manzana apple, 9
maquillaje (*m.*) makeup, 5
maquillarse to put on makeup, 5
máquina de afeitar electric razor, 5
maravilla wonder
marcar (qu) to mark; to point out
marisco shellfish, 9
marrón brown, 4
martes (*m.*) Tuesday, 3
marzo March, 1
más more; **~ que** more than, 8
masculino(a) masculine
matemáticas (*f. pl.*) mathematics, 3
mayo May, 1
mayonesa mayonnaise, 9
mayor older, greater, 8
mayoría majority
mayúsculo(a) capital (letter)
me to / for me, 8
mecánico(a) mechanic, 5
medio(a) hermano(a) half-brother (half-sister), 5
medianoche (*f.*) midnight, 3
medicina medicine, 3
médico(a) doctor, 5
medida measurement, 9
medio ambiente (*m.*) environment
mediodía (*m.*) noon, 3
medios de transporte means of transportation, 6
medir (i, i) to measure
meditación (*f.*) meditation
mejilla cheek
mejor better, 8
melón (*m.*) melon, 9
memoria flash flash drive, 4
menor younger; less, 8

menos: ~ que less than, 8; **por lo ~** at least, 10
mensajero(a) messenger
mentiroso(a) dishonest, lying, 2
menú (*m.*) menu, 9
mercadeo marketing, 3
mercado market, 6; **~ al aire libre** open-air market, farmer's market, 6
merecer (zc) to deserve
merienda snack
mes (*m.*) month, 3; **~ pasado** last month, 7
mesa table, P; **poner la ~** to set the table, 9; **quitar la ~** to clear the table, 10
mesita de noche night table, 10
meta goal
metro: en ~ on the subway, 6
mexicano(a) Mexican, 2
mezcla mix
mezclar to mix, 9
mezclilla denim, 8
mi (*adj.*) my, 3
mí (*pron.*) me, 8
micro bus (*Chile*)
micrófono microphone, 4
microondas (*m. s.*) microwave, 10
miedo: tener (*irreg.*) **~ (a, de)** to be afraid (of), 7
mientras while, during
miércoles (*m.*) Wednesday, 3
mil (*m.*) one thousand, 8
miles (*pl.*) thousands
millón (*m.*): **un ~** one million, 8; **dos millones** two million, 8
mío(a) (*adj.*) my, 10; (*pron.*) mine, 10
mirar televisión to watch television, 2
misionero(a) missionary
mismo(a) same; **lo mismo** the same (thing)
mitad (*f.*) half
mixto(a) mixed
mochila backpack, P; knapsack
moda fashion, 8; **(no) estar de ~** (not) to be fashionable, 8; **pasado(a) de ~** out of style, 8
modales (*m. pl.*) manners
modas: de ~ (*adj.*) fashion
módem (*m.*) **externo / interno** external / internal modem, 4
molestar to bother, 4

molido(a) crushed, ground, 9
monitor (*m.*) monitor, 4
mono monkey
montañoso(a) mountainous
montar to ride; **~ a caballo** to ride horseback, 7; **~ en bicicleta** to ride a bike, 7
monte (*m.*) mountain
morado(a) purple, 4
morirse (ue, u) to die, 8
mortalidad (*f.*) mortality
mostaza mustard, 9
mostrar (ue) to show
MP3 portátil portable MP3 player, P
muchacho(a) boy (girl), P
muchedumbre (*f.*) crowd
mucho a lot, 4; **~ que hacer** a lot to do; **No ~.** Not much. 1
mudarse to move (*change residence*)
muebles (*m. pl.*) furniture, 10
mujer (*f.*) woman, P; **~ de negocios** businesswoman, 5
mundo world
muñeca doll
museo museum, 6
música music, 3
muy very, 2

N

nacer (zc) to be born
nacionalidad (*f.*) nationality, 2
nada nothing, 1; **De ~.** You're welcome. 1
nadar to swim, 7
nadie no one, nobody, 6
naranja orange (*fruit*), 9
narrador(a) narrator
natación (*f.*) swimming, 7
naturaleza nature; **~ muerta** still life
navegación (*f.*) navigation; **~ en rápidos** whitewater rafting, 7
navegar (gu): ~ en rápidos to go whitewater rafting, 7; **~ por Internet** to browse the Internet, 2
necesitar to need, 2
negocio business, 3; (*pl.*) business
negro(a) black, 4
nervioso(a) nervous, 4
nevar to snow, 7; **Está nevando. (Nieva.)** It's snowing. 7

ni... ni neither . . . nor, 6
nicaragüense (*m., f.*) Nicaraguan, 2
nieto(a) grandson (granddaughter), 5
niñero(a) baby-sitter
ningún, ninguno(a) none, no, not any, 6
niño(a) boy (girl), P
nivel (*m.*) level
noche (*f.*) night, 3; **de la ~** in the evening (*with precise time*), 3; **por la ~** during the evening, 3
nombre (*m.*) name; **Mi ~ es…** My name is . . . , 1; **~ completo** full name
normal normal, 4
Norteamérica North America
norteamericano(a) North American
nos to / for us, 8; **¿~ vemos donde siempre?** See you at the usual place? 1
nosotros(as) we, 1; us, 8
nota grade, P
novato(a) newbie, novice
novecientos(as) nine hundred, 8
novedoso(a) novel, new
novelista (*m., f.*) novelist
noveno(a) ninth, 10
noventa ninety, P
noviembre November, 1
novio(a) boyfriend (girlfriend)
nublado: Está ~. It's cloudy. 7
nuera daughter-in-law, 5
nuestro(a) (*adj.*) our, 3; (*pron.*) ours, 10
nueve nine, P
número number, 8; **~ ordinal** ordinal number, 10
nunca never, 5

O

o... o either . . . or, 6
ochenta eighty, P
ocho eight, P
ochocientos(as) eight hundred, 8
octavo(a) eighth, 10
octubre October, 1
ocupado(a) busy, 4
ocupar to live in
odio hatred
oferta especial special offer, 8

oficina office, 6; **~ de correos** post office, 6
oír (*irreg.*) to hear, 5
ojear to scan
ola wave
ómnibus (*m.*) bus
once eleven, P
onda: en ~ in style
oprimir to push
opuesto(a) opposite
oración (*f.*) sentence
ordenar to order, 9
organización (*f.*) **benéfica** charity
orgulloso(a) proud
originar to originate
orilla shore
oro gold, 8
ortografía spelling
os to / for you (*fam. pl.*), 8
otoño fall, autumn, 7

P

paciente (*m., f.*) patient, 2
padrastro stepfather, 5
padre (*m.*) father, 5; **padres** (*m. pl.*) parents, 5
pagar (gu) to pay, 9
página page, P; **~ web** web page, 4
pago: método de ~ form of payment, 8**país** (*m.*) country
paisaje (*m.*) scenery
pájaro bird
pan (*m.*) bread, 6; **~ tostado** toast, 9
panameño(a) Panamanian, 2
pandilla gang
pantalla screen, 4
pantalones (*m. pl.*) pants, 8; **~ cortos** shorts, 8
pañuelo handkerchief
papá (*m.*) father, 5
papas fritas (*f. pl.*) French fries, 9
papel role; paper; **hoja de ~** sheet of paper, P
papelería stationery store, 6
papitas fritas (*f. pl.*) potato chips, 6
paquete (*m.*) package, 9
para for, toward, in the direction of, in order to (+ *inf.*), 10
paracaídas (*m.*) parachute
parada stop

paraguayo(a) Paraguayan, 2
parar to stop
parecer (zc) to seem
pared (*f.*) wall, P
pariente (*m., f.*) family member, relative, 5
parque (*m.*) park, 6
párrafo paragraph
parrilla: a la ~ grilled, 9
partido game, match, 7
pasar to pass (by), 2; **~ la aspiradora** to vacuum, 10
pasear: sacar a ~ al perro to take the dog for a walk, 10
pasillo hallway, 10
pasta de dientes toothpaste, 5
pastel (*m.*) cake, 9
patinar to skate, 2; **~ en línea** to inline skate (rollerblade), 7; **~ sobre hielo** to ice skate, 7
patio patio, 10
patrocinador(a) sponsor
pavo turkey, 6
paz (*f.*) peace
pedazo piece, slice, 9
pedir (i, i) to ask for (*something*), 1; to request, 10; **~ la hora** to ask for the time, 3
peinarse to brush / comb one's hair, 5
peine (*m.*) comb, 5
pelar to peel, 9
pelearse to have a fight, 5
peligro danger, 7
peligroso(a) dangerous, 7
pelirrojo(a) redheaded , 2
pelo hair; **~ castaño / rubio** brown / blond hair, 2
pelota ball, 7
peluquero(a) barber / hairdresser, 5
pendiente (*m.*) earring, 8
pendrive (*m.*) flash drive, 4
pensar (ie) to think, 4; **~ de** to have an opinion about, 4; **~ en (de)** to think about, to consider, 4
penúltimo(a) next-to-last
peor worse, 8
pequeño(a) small, 2
perder (ie) to lose, 4; **perderse (ie)** to lose oneself, to get lost
Perdón. Excuse me. 4
perejil (*m.*) parsley
perezoso(a) lazy, 2

periódico newspaper
periodismo journalism, 3
periodista (*m., f.*) journalist, 5
permiso: Con ~. Pardon me. 4
permitir to permit, to allow, 10
pero but, 2
perro(a) dog, 2; **perro caliente** hot dog, 9
persiana Venetian blind, 10
personalidad (*f.*) personality
peruano(a) Peruvian, 2
pesar: a ~ de in spite of
pesas: levantar ~ to lift weights, 2
pescado fish (*caught*), 9
pescar (qu) to fish, 7
pez (*m.*) fish (*alive*)
piano piano, 2
picante spicy, 9
picar (qu) to chop, to mince, 9
pie (*m.*): **a ~** on foot, walking, 6
piel (*f.*) leather, 8
pimienta pepper, 9
pingüino penguin
pintar to paint, 2
pintoresco(a) picturesque
pintura painting, 3
pirata (*m.*) pirate
pisar to step on
piscina swimming pool, 6
piso floor; **primer (segundo, etc.) ~** first (second, etc.) floor, 10
pista de atletismo athletics track, 6
pizarra interactiva interactive whiteboard, P
pizzería pizzeria, 6
placer: Un ~. My pleasure. 1
plancha iron, 10
planchar to iron, 10
plata silver, 8
plátano banana, 9
plato plate, 9; **~ hondo** bowl, 9; **~ principal** main dish, 9
plaza plaza, 6
plomero(a) plumber, 5
poblar (ue) to populate
pobre poor
poco little, small amount, 4; **muy ~** very little
poder (*m.*) power; (*irreg.*) to be able to, 4
poderoso(a) powerful
poesía poetry
poeta (poetisa) poet

policía (*m., f.*) policeman (policewoman), 5
político(a) political
pollo chicken, 6; **~ asado** roasted chicken, 9; **~ frito** fried chicken, 9
polvo dust
poner (*irreg.*) to put, 5; **~ en equilibro** to balance; **~ la mesa** to set the table, 9; **~ mis juguetes en su lugar** to put my toys where they belong, 10 to put on (clothing), 5
por for, during, in, through, along, on behalf of, by, 10; **~ avión** by plane, 6; **~ ejemplo** for example, 10; **~ eso** so, that's why, 10; **~ favor** please, 1; **~ fin** finally, 9; **~ lo menos** at least, 10; **~ supuesto** of course, 10
¿por qué? why? 3
porcentaje (*m.*) percentage
porque because, 3
portarse to behave
portátil: MP3 ~ portable MP3 player, P; **computadora ~** laptop computer, P
portugués (portuguesa) Portuguese, 2
postre (*m.*) dessert, 9
pozo well; hole
practicar (qu) to practice; **~ alpi-nismo** to hike, to (mountain) climb, 7; **~ deportes** to play sports, 2; **~ surfing** to surf, 7
precio: Está a muy buen ~. It's a very good price. 8
preferencia preference
preferir (ie, i) to prefer, 4
pregunta: hacer preguntas to ask questions, 3
premio prize
prenda de ropa article of clothing, 8
preocupado(a) worried, 4
preocuparse to worry, 5
preparación (*f.*) preparation, 9
preparar to prepare, 2; **~ la comida** to prepare the food, 10; **prepararse** to get ready, 5
preposición (*f.*) preposition, 6
presa dam
presentar a alguien to introduce someone, 1
préstamo loan, 8

prestar to loan, 8

primavera spring, 7

primer(o)(a) first, 10; **primer piso** first floor, 10

primo(a) cousin, 5

principiante(a) beginner

prisa haste, hurry; **tener** (*irreg.*) ~ to be in a hurry, 7

probarse (ue): Voy a probármelo / la(los / las). I'm going to try it (them) on. 8

procesador de comida food processor, 10

producto electrónico electronic product, 4

profesión (*f.*) profession, 5

profesor(a) professor, P

programa (*m.*) program; ~ **antivirus** anti-virus program, 4; ~ **de procesamiento de textos** word-processing program, 4

programador(a) programmer, 5

prohibir to forbid, 10

promover (ue) to promote

pronombre (*m.*) pronoun, 1

propina tip, 9

propósito purpose

proveedor (*m.*) **de acceso** Internet service provider, 4

provocador(a) provocative

próximo(a) next

proyector projector, P

psicología psychology, 3

publicidad (*f.*) public relations, 3

publicitario(a) (*adj.*) pertaining to advertising

pueblo town, 6

puerta door, P

puerto de USB USB port, 4

puertorriqueño(a) Puerto Rican, 2

pulgada inch

pulsera bracelet, 8

punto de vista viewpoint

punto period

Q

¿qué? what? which? 3; **¿~ hay denuevo?** What's new? 1; **¿~ hora es?** What time is it? 3; **¿~ significa…?** What does . . . mean? P; **¿~ tal?** How are things going? 1; **¿~ te gusta hacer?** What do you like to do? 2

quedar to fit; **Me queda bien / mal.** It fits nicely / badly. 8; **Me queda grande / apretado.** It's too big / too tight. 8; **quedar(se)** to remain; to be

quehacer (*m.*) **doméstico** housechore, 10

quejarse to complain, 5

querer (*irreg.*) to want, to love, 4; to wish, 10

queso cheese, 6

¿quién(es)? who? 3; **¿De ~ es?** Whose is this? 3; **¿De ~ son?** Whose are these? 3

química chemistry, 3

quince fifteen, P

quinientos(as) five hundred, 8

quinto(a) fifth, 10

quisiera (+ *inf.*) I'd like (+ *inf.*), 6

quitar to take off, to remove 5; ~ **la mesa** to clear the table, 10; **quitarse (la ropa)** to take off (one's clothing), 5

quizás perhaps

R

raíz (*f.*) root

rango rank

rápido(a) fast, 4

rasgado torn up

rasgar (gu) to tear up

rasuradora razor, 5

ratón (*m.*) mouse, 4

rayado(a) striped, 8

rayas: a ~ striped, 8

razón (*f.*) reason; **tener** (*irreg.*) ~ to be right, 7

realidad: en ~ actually

realizarse (c) to take place

rebajado(a): estar ~ to be reduced (in price) / on sale, 8

recámara bedroom, 10

recibir to receive, 3

reciclaje (*m.*) recycling, 10

recomendar (ie) to recommend, 10

reconocer (zc) to recognize

recordar (ue) to remember

recorte (*m.*) cutting

recuerdo souvenir

recurrir to fall back on, to resort to

red (*f.*) web, Internet; ~ **mundial** World Wide Web, 4; ~ **social** social networking site, 4

redactar to edit

reflejar to reflect

reflexión (*f.*) reflection

refresco soft drink, 6; beverage, 9; **tomar un ~** to have a soft drink, 2

refrigerador (*m.*) refrigerator, 10

regalar to give (as a gift), 8

regalo present, gift, 8

regar (ie) (gu) las plantas to water the plants, 10

regla rule

regresar to return, 2

regular so-so, 1

reina queen

reírse (*irreg.*) to laugh, 5

relajarse to relax, 5

reloj (*m.*) watch, 8

remar to row, 7

remero(a) rower

renombre (*m.*) renown

renovar (ue) to renovate

repente: de ~ suddenly, 9

repetir (i, i) to repeat, 4; **Repitan.** Repeat. P

reproductor (*m.*) **de discos compactos / DVD** CD / DVD recorder, 4

requerir (ie, i) to require, 10

residencia estudiantil dorm, 3

respirar to breathe

responder to respond, 1

responsable responsible, 2

restaurante (*m.*) restaurant, 6

resumen: en ~ in short, to sum up

reto challenge

reunión (*f.*) meeting

reunirse to meet, to get together, 5

revista magazine; ~ **de moda** fashion magazine

rey (*m.*) king

riesgo risk

rima rhyme

río river, 7

riqueza wealth

rodeado(a) surrounded

rojo(a) red, 4

ropa clothing, 5

rosa rose, 4

rosado(a) pink, 4

rubio(a) blond(e), 2
rueda wheel
ruta route

S

sábado Saturday, 2
saber (*irreg.*) to know (*a fact, information*), 5; **~** (+ *inf.*) to know how (*to do something*), 5
sabor (*m.*) flavor
sacar (qu) to take out; **~ a pasear al perro** to take the dog for a walk, 10; **~ fotos** to take photos, 2; **~ la basura** to take out the garbage, 10
sacerdote (*m.*) priest
saco jacket, sports coat, 8
sacudir los muebles to dust the furniture, 10
sal (*f.*) salt, 9
sala living room, 10
salchicha sausage, 6
salir (*irreg.*) to leave, to go out, 5
salmón (*m.*) salmon, 9
salón (*m.*) **de clase** classroom, P
salud (*f.*) health, 3
saludable healthy
saludar to greet, 1
saludo greeting
salvadoreño(a) Salvadoran, 2
salvaje wild, untamed
salvavidas (*m. s.*) lifejacket
sandalia sandal, 8
sandwich (*m.*) sandwich, 9; **~ de jamón y queso con aguacate** ham and cheese sandwich with avocado, 9
secadora dryer, 10
secar (qu) to dry (*something*), 5; **secarse (qu) el pelo** to dry one's hair, 5
secretario(a) secretary, 5
secreto secret
sed (*f.*) thirst; **tener** (*irreg.*) **~** to be thirsty, 7
seda silk, 8
seguido(a) continued
seguir (i, i) to continue, 6; **~ derecho** to go straight ahead
según according to
segundo(a) second, 10
seguro(a) sure, 4; safe, 7
seis six, P
seiscientos(as) six hundred, 8

semana week, 3; **~ pasada** last week, 7; **fin** (*m.*) **de ~** weekend, 2; **todas las semanas** every week, 5
semejanza similarity
sencillo(a) simple; single (*room*)
sentarse (ie) to sit down, 5
sentir (ie, i) to feel, 4; **Lo siento.** I'm sorry. 4
señalar to point out
señor (*abbrev.* **Sr.**) Mr., Sir, 1
señora (*abbrev.* **Sra.**) Mrs., Ms., Madam, 1
señorita (*abbrev.* **Srta.**) Miss, Ms., 1
separarse to get separated, 5
septiembre September, 1
séptimo(a) seventh, 10
ser (*irreg.*) to be, 1
serio(a) serious, 2
servicio service **servilleta** napkin, 9
servir (i, i) to serve, 4; **¿En qué puedo servirle?** How can I help you? 8
sesenta sixty, P
setecientos(as) seven hundred, 8
setenta seventy, P
sexto(a) sixth, 10
sí yes, 1
siempre always, 5
siete seven, P
siglo century
significar (qu): Significa... It means . . . , P
significado meaning
siguiente following, next
silla chair, P
sillón (*m.*) armchair, 10
símbolo symbol
simpático(a) nice, 2
sin without; **~ control** uncontrolled
sincero(a) sincere, 2
sino but instead
sistemático(a) systematic
sitio place; **~ web** website, 4
smartphone smartphone, 4
snowboarding snowboarding, 7
soberanía sovereignty
sobre on, above, 6
sobrepasar to surpass
sobresaliente outstanding
sobrino(a) nephew (niece), 5
sofá (*m.*) sofa, 10

software (*m.*) software, 4
sol (*m.*) sun; **Hace ~.** It's sunny. 7
soltero(a) single (unmarried)
sombrero hat, 8
sonar (ue) to ring, to go off (*phone, alarm clock, etc.*), 4
sonido sound
sonreír (*irreg.*) to smile, 8
sonrisa smile
soñar (ue) con to dream about, 4
sopa soup, 9; **~ de fideos** noodle soup, 9
sorpresa surprise
sorteo raffle; evasion
sortija ring
sótano basement, cellar, 10
su (*adj.*) your (*s. form., pl.*), his, her, their, 3
suave soft
subir to go up, to get on, 6; to upload, 4
suburbio suburb, 10
sucio(a) dirty
sudadera sweatsuit, track suit, 8
Sudamérica South America
suegro(a) father-in-law (mother-in-law), 5
sueño dream; **tener** (*irreg.*) **~** to be sleepy, 7
suéter (*m.*) sweater, 8
sugerencia suggestion
sugerir (ie, i) to suggest, 8
superación (*f.*) overcoming
supermercado supermarket, 6
supuesto: por ~ of course, 10
surfing: hacer / practicar (qu) ~ to surf, 7
sustantivo noun
sustituir (y) to substitute
suyo(a) (*adj.*) your (*form. s., pl.*), his, her, its, their, 10; (*pron.*) yours (*form. s., pl.*), his, hers, its, theirs, 10

T

tabla de snowboard snowboard, 7
tableta tablet computer, 4
tal vez perhaps
talla size, 8
taller (*m.*) workshop
también also, 2
tampoco neither, not either, 2
tan... como as . . . as, 8
tanto(a)(s)... como as much (many) . . . as, 8

tarde (*f.*) afternoon, 3; **de la ~** in the afternoon (*with precise time*), 3; **por la ~** during the afternoon, 3; (*adv.*) late, 3

tarea homework, P

tarjeta **~ de crédito** credit card, 8; **~ de débito** (bank) debit card, 8

te to / for you (*fam. s.*), 8

té hot tea, 9; **~ helado** iced tea, 9

teatro theater, 6

tecnología technology, 4

techo roof, 10

tecla key (*on a keyboard*), 4

teclado keyboard, 4

tejer to weave

tejido weaving

tela fabric, 8

teléfono inteligente smartphone, 4

televisor (*m.*) television set, 10

temperatura temperature, 7; **La ~ está a 20 grados Celsio(s) (Fahrenheit).** It's 20 degrees Celsius (Fahrenheit). 7

temporada: ~ de lluvias rainy season; **~ de secas** dry season

temprano early, 3

tender to tend (to)

tenedor (*m.*) fork, 9

tener (*irreg.*) to have, 1; **~ ... años** to be . . . years old, 1; **~ calor** to be hot, 7; **~ cuidado** to be careful, 7; **~ frío** to be cold, 7; **~ ganas de** to have the urge to, to feel like (doing), 7; **~ hambre** to be hungry, 7; **~ miedo (a, de)** to be afraid (of), 7; **~ prisa** to be in a hurry, 7; **~ que** (*+ inf.*) to have to (*+ verb*), 1; **~ razón** to be right, 7; **~ sed** to be thirsty, 7; **~ sueño** to be sleepy, 7; **~ vergüenza** to be embarrassed, ashamed, 7

tenis (*m.*) tennis, 7

teoría theory

tercer(o, a) third, 10

término term

terrible terrible, awful, 1

tesoro treasure

texto text

tez (*f.*) skin, complexion

ti you (*fam. s.*), 8

tiburón (*m.*) shark

tiempo weather, 7; **¿Qué ~ hace?** What's the weather like? 7

tienda store, 6; **~ de equipo deportivo** sporting goods store, 6; **~ de juegos electrónicos** electronic games store, 6; **~ de ropa** clothing store, 6

tierra earth, ground

tímido(a) shy, 2

tinto: vino ~ red wine, 9

tío(a) uncle (aunt), 5

típico(a) typical, 9

tira cómica comic strip

tiroteo shooting

titular to title

título title, 1

tiza chalk, P

toalla towel, 5; **~ de mano** handtowel, 5

tocador (*m.*) dresser, 10

tocar (qu) un instrumento musical to play a musical instrument, 2

todavía still

todo everything

todo(a) all, every; **todas las semanas** every week, 5; **todos los días (años)** every day (year), 9

tomar to take; **~ un refresco** to have a soft drink, 2; **~ el sol** to sunbathe, 2

tonto(a) silly, stupid, 2

tormenta thunderstorm

torpe awkward

tostadora toaster, 10

trabajador(a) (*adj.*) hard-working, 2; (*noun*) worker, 5

trabajar to work, 2

traducir (zc) to translate, 5

traer (*irreg.*) to bring, 5

traje (*m.*) suit, 8; **~ de baño** bathing suit, 8

trama plot

tramos sections

transmitir to broadcast, 3

trapear el piso to mop the floor, 10

tratar de to try

tratarse de to be a matter of; to be

través: a ~ de across, throughout

trece thirteen, P

trecho distance, period

treinta thirty, P

tren: en ~ by train, 6

tres three, P

trescientos(as) three hundred, 8

trigo wheat

tripulación (*f.*) crew

triste sad, 4

triunfar to triumph

trompeta trumpet, 2

trozo chunk, 9

trucha trout, 9

truco trick

tu your (*fam.*), 3

tú you (*fam.*), 1

tuyo(a) (*adj.*) your (*fam.*), 10; (*pron.*) yours (*fam.*), 10

U

ubicado(a) located

Ud. (*abbrev. of* **usted**) you (*form. s.*), 8

Uds. (*abbrev. of* **ustedes**) you (*fam. or form. pl.*), 8

último: lo ~ the latest (thing)

un(a) a, 1

único(a) only, unique

unido(a) united

unir to mix together, to incorporate, 9

universidad (*f.*) university, 6

uno one, P

unos(as) some, 1

uruguayo(a) Uruguayan, 2

usar to use, 2

usted you (*s. form.*), 1

ustedes you (*fam. or form. pl.*), 1

usuario(a) user, 4

útil useful

uva grape, 9

V

vacío(a) empty

valer (*irreg.*) **la pena** to be worthwhile

valioso(a) valuable

valle (*m.*) valley

valor (*m.*) value

vanidoso(a) vain

vapor: al ~ steamed, 9

vaquero cowboy

variedad (*f.*) variety

varios(as) various, several

varonil   manly

vaso   glass, 9

veces (*f. pl.*)   times; **a ~** sometimes, 5; **(dos) ~ al día / por semana**   (two) times a day / per week, 5

vecino(a)   neighbor, 6

vegano: algo ~ something vegan, 9

vegetal (*m.*)   vegetable, 6

vegetariano(a)   vegetarian; **~ estricto**   vegan, 9

vehículo   vehicle

veinte   twenty, P

veintiuno   twenty-one, P

vender   to sell, 3

venezolano(a)   Venezuelan, 2

venir (*irreg.*)   to come, 5

venta: estar en ~   to be on sale, 8

ventana   window, P

ver (*irreg.*)   to see, 5; **Nos vemos.**   See you later. 1

verano   summer, 7

veras: de ~   truly, really

verbo   verb, 3

verdad   true; **~** (*f.*)   truth

verde   green, 4

vergüenza shame;   **tener** (*irreg.*) **~** to be embarrassed, ashamed, 7

verso libre   blank verse

vestido   dress, 8

vestir (i, i)   to dress (*someone*), 5; **vestirse (i, i)**   to get dressed, 5

veterinario(a)   veterinarian, 5

vez (*f.*)   time; **de ~ en cuando**   sometimes; **en ~ de**   instead of; **rara ~**   hardly ever; **tal ~** perhaps; **una ~**   once, 9

viajar   to travel, 2

vida   life

videocámara   videocamera, 4

viejo(a)   old, 2

viento   wind; **Hace ~.**   It's windy. 7

viernes (*m.*)   Friday, 2

vinagre (*m.*)   vinegar, 9

vino: ~ blanco   white wine, 9; **~ tinto**   red wine, 9

violín (*m.*)   violin, 2

viraje (*m.*)   turn

visitante (*m., f.*)   visitor

visitar a amigos   to visit friends, 2

vivienda   housing

vivir   to live, 3

volibol (*m.*)   volleyball, 7

volver (ue)   to return, 4

vosotros(as)   you (*fam. pl.*), 1

voz (*f.*)   voice

vuestro(a) (*adj.*)   your (*fam. pl.*), 3; (*pron.*)   yours (*fam. pl.*), 3

W

wifi (*m.*)   wifi, wireless connection, 4

Y

yerno   son-in-law, 5

yo   I, 1

yogur (*m.*)   yogurt, 6

Z

zanahoria   carrot, 9

zapato   shoe, 8; **~ de tacón alto**   high-heeled shoe, 8; **~ de tenis**   tennis shoe, 8

English–Spanish Glossary

A

a un(a), 1
à la carte a la carta, 9
above sobre, 6
abundance abundancia
academic académico(a)
access acceder, 4
accessory accesorio, 8
according to según
accountant contador(a), 5
accounting contabilidad (*f.*), 3
achieve alcanzar (c), lograr
acquisition adquisición (*f.*)
across a través de
action acción (*f.*), 5
active activo(a), 2
activity actividad (*f.*), P
actor actor (*m.*), 5
actress actriz (*f.*), 5
actually en realidad
ad: personal ~ anuncio personal
add agregar, añadir, 9
address dirección (*f.*)
advertising (*adj.*) publicitario(a)
advise aconsejar, 10
affection cariño
afternoon tarde (*f.*), 3;
   during the ~ por la tarde, 3;
   Good ~. Buenas tardes. 1;
   in the ~ (*with precise time*)
   de la tarde, 3;
   late ~ atardecer (*m.*)
age edad (*f.*)
agreement concordancia
agricultural agrícola (*m.*, *f.*)
ahead adelante
airport aeropuerto, 6
all todo(a)
alligator aligátor (*m.*), caimán
   (*m.*)
along por, 10
alphabet alfabeto
also también, 2
altitude altitud (*f.*)
always siempre, 5
ambassador embajador(a)
ambiguity ambigüedad (*f.*)
amusement diversión (*f.*)
ancestor antecesor(a),
   antepasado(a)
anger cólera

angry enojado(a), 4
anonymous anónimo(a)
answer contestar;
   Answer. Contesten. P
Antarctica Antártida
antiquated anticuado(a)
any algún, alguno(a) 6
apartment apartamento, 6
appear aparecer (zc)
apple manzana, 9
appliance electrodoméstico, 10
application aplicación (*f.*), 4
appreciate apreciar
appropriate apropiado(a)
April abril, 1
apt apto(a)
architect arquitecto(a), 5
architecture arquitectura, 3
Argentinian argentino(a), 2
armchair sillón (*m.*), 10
around alrededor de
arrive llegar, 2
arrogant altivo(a)
art arte (*m.*), 3
article artículo, 1
artist artista (*m.*, *f.*), 5
as como; **~ . . . ~** tan... como, 8;
   ~ many . . . ~ tantos(as)...
   como, 8; **~ much . . . ~**
   tanto(a)(s)... como, 8
ask: ~ questions hacer
   (*irreg.*) preguntas, 3; **~ for**
   something pedir (i, i), 1; **~ for**
   the time pedir (i, i) la hora, 3
asparagus espárragos (*m. pl.*), 9
at en; **~ least** por lo menos, 10;
   ~ low heat a fuego suave /
   lento, 9
athletics track pista de
   atletismo, 6
atmosphere ambiente (*m.*)
attachment anexo
attack ataque (*m.*)
attempt intentar
attend acudir; asistir a, 3
attractive guapo(a), 2
audio audio, P
audiotape cinta, P
auditorium auditorio, 6
August agosto, 1
aunt tía, 5
Australian australiano(a), 2

automated bank teller
   (ATM) cajero automático, 6
autumn otoño, 7
availability disponibilidad (*f.*)
avenue avenida, 1
avoid evitar
awful fatal, terrible, 1
awkward torpe

B

baby-sitter niñero(a)
background fondo
backpack mochila, P
bad malo(a), 2
badly mal, 4
balance poner (*irreg.*) en
   equilibro
ball pelota, 7
ballpoint pen bolígrafo, P
banana plátano, 9
bank (commercial) banco, 6
barber peluquero(a), 5
barefooted descalzo(a)
baseball béisbol (*m.*), 7
basement sótano, 10
basket canasta
basketball básquetbol (*m.*), 7
bather bañador(a)
bathing suit traje (*m.*) de baño, 8
bathroom baño, 10
be estar (*irreg.*), ser (*irreg.*), 1;
   ~ . . . years old tener (*irreg.*)...
   años, 1; **~ a matter of** tratarse
   de; **~ able to** poder (*irreg.*),
   4; **~ afraid (of)** tener
   (*irreg.*) miedo (a, de), 7;
   ~ ashamed tener (*irreg.*)
   vergüenza, 7; **~ born** nacer
   (zc); **~ careful** tener (*irreg.*)
   cuidado, 7; **~ certain of** contar
   (ue) con; **~ cold** tener (*irreg.*)
   frío, 7; **~ embarrassed** tener
   (*irreg.*) vergüenza, 7; **~ familiar**
   with conocer (zc), 5; **~ going**
   to ir a, 3; **~ hot** tener (*irreg.*)
   calor, 7; **~ hungry** tener
   (*irreg.*) hambre, 7;
   ~ important importar, 4; **~ in**
   a hurry tener (*irreg.*) prisa,
   7; **~ interesting** interesar, 4;
   ~ jealous tener (*irreg.*) celos;

~ **right**   tener (*irreg.*) razón, 7;
~ **sleepy**   tener (*irreg.*) sueño,
7; ~ **thirsty**   tener (*irreg.*) sed,
7; ~ **worthwhile**   valer (*irreg.*)
la pena

bean   haba (*f. but* el haba);
(**green**) ~   habichuela, 9;
refried beans
frijoles refritos, 9

beat   batir

beautiful   bello(a), hermoso(a)

beauty   belleza

because   porque, 3

bed   cama, 10

bedroom   cuarto, dormitorio,
habitación (*f.*), recámara, 10

beef stew   guisado, 9

beer   cerveza, 9

before   antes, 5

begin   comenzar (ie) (c), empezar
(ie) (c), 4

beginner   principiante

behave   portarse

behavior   comportamiento

behind   detrás de, 6

believe (in)   creer (en), 3

below   debajo de, 6

belt   cinturón (*m.*), 8

besides   además

better   mejor, 8

between   entre, 6

beverage   bebida, refresco, 9

bicycle: on ~   en bicicleta, 6

big   grande, 2

bilingual   bilingüe

bill   cuenta, 9

biology   biología, 3

bird   pájaro

birthplace   lugar (*m.*) de
nacimiento

black   negro(a), 4

blank verse   verso libre

blender   licuadora, 10

blind   ciego(a); ~ **date**   cita a
ciegas

block   cuadra, 6

blog   blog, 4

blond(e)   rubio(a), 2

blouse   blusa, 8

blue   azul, 4

boat   barco, bote (*m.*)

boil   hervir (ie, i), 9

boiled   hervido(a), 9

Bolivian   boliviano(a), 2

book   libro, P

bookstore   librería, 3

boot   bota, 8

border   frontera

boredom   aburrimiento

bored   aburrido(a), 4

boring   aburrido(a), 2

both   ambos(as)

bother   molestar, 4

bowl   plato hondo, 9

box: large ~   cajón (*m.*)

boxing   boxeo, 7

boy   chico, P; muchacho, P;
niño, P

boyfriend   novio

bracelet   brazalete (*m.*),
pulsera, 8

bread   pan (*m.*), 6

break (a record)   batir

breakfast   desayuno, 9

breathe   respirar

brick   ladrillo

brief   breve

bring   traer (*irreg.*), 5

broadcast   transmitir, 3

broccoli   bróculi (*m.*), 9

brother (younger, older)
hermano (menor, mayor), 5

brother-in-law   cuñado, 5

brown   castaño, 2; café,
marrón, 4

browse: the Internet   navegar
por Internet, 2

brush   cepillo, 5; ~ **one's**
hair   cepillarse el pelo,
peinarse, 5; ~ **one's**
teeth   lavarse los dientes, 5

buddy   cuate(a)

building   edificio, 6

burn   arder

burning   encendida

bus   ómnibus (*m.*), colectivo,
guagua (*Cuba, Puerto Rico*),
micro (*Chile*)

business   negocio,
3; ~ **administration**
administración (*f.*) de empresas,
3; ~ **district**   centro comercial,
10

businessman   hombre (*m.*) de
negocios, 5

businesswoman   mujer (*f.*) de
negocios, 5

busy   ocupado(a), 4

but   pero, 2; ~ **instead**   sino

butcher shop   carnicería, 6

butter   mantequilla, 9

buy   comprar, 2

by   por, 10; ~ **bus**   en autobús, 6;
~ **car**   en carro / coche /
automóvil, 6; ~ **check**   con
cheque, 8; ~ **plane**   por avión,
6; ~ **train**   en tren, 6

Bye.   Chau. 1

C

cable   cable (*m.*), 4

cafeteria   cafetería, 3

cake   pastel (*m.*), 9

calculator   calculadora, P

calculus   cálculo, 3

call   llamar, 2

can opener (electric)   abrelatas
(*m.*) (eléctrico), 10

Canadian   canadiense (*m., f.*), 2

cap   gorra, 8

capital (letter)   mayúsculo(a)

card   tarjeta; **credit** ~   tarjeta de
crédito, 8; **debit** ~   tarjeta de
débito, 8

cardboard   cartón (*m.*)

career   carrera, 5

Careful!   ¡Cuidado!

Caribbean (Sea)   Caribe (*m., f.*)

carpenter   carpintero(a), 5

carpet   alfombra, 10

carrot   zanahoria, 9

carry   llevar

cash: in ~   en efectivo,
al contado, 8

cashmere   cachemira

cat   gato(a), 2

cattle   ganado, ganadería

cattle-raising industry   industria
ganadera

cautious   cuidadoso(a), 2

CD: CD / DVD recorder
grabador (*m.*) de discos
compactos / DVD, reproductor
(*m.*) de discos compactos /
DVD, 4

celebration   celebración (*f.*)

cellar   sótano, 10

Celsius degree   grado Celsio(s), 7

census   censo

cent   centavo

center   centro

Central America   Centroamérica

century   siglo

cereal   cereal (*m.*), 9

certain   cierto(a)

chain   cadena, 8

chair   silla, P

chalk tiza, P
challenge reto
change cambio; convertir (ie, i);
chapter capítulo, P
charity organización (*f.*) benéfica
chat chatear (*online*),
    4; **~ room** grupo de
    conversación, 4
check cheque (*m.*); (*restaurant
    check*) cuenta, 9
cheek mejilla
cheese queso, 6
cheeseburger hamburguesa con
    queso, 9
chef cocinero(a), 5
chemistry química, 3
chess ajedrez (*m.*)
chicken pollo, 6; **~ soup** caldo
    de pollo, 9; **~ with rice** arroz
    (*m.*) con pollo, 9; **fried ~** pollo
    frito, 9; **roasted ~** pollo
    asado, 9;
Chilean chileno(a), 2
Chinese chino(a), 2;
    ~ language chino, 3
chocolate cacao
choose escoger (j)
chronology cronología
chunk trozo, 9
church iglesia, 6
cinema cine (*m.*), 6
cinnamon canela
city ciudad (*f.*), 6
clam almeja, 9
clarity claridad (*f.*)
class clase (*f.*), P; **lower ~** clase
    baja
classroom salón (*m.*) de clase, P
clean the bathroom limpiar el
    baño, 10
clear the table quitar la mesa, 10
click hacer (*irreg.*) clic, 4; **double ~**
    hacer (*irreg.*) doble clic, 4
close cerrar (ie), 4; **~ your
    books.** Cierren los libros. P
close to cerca de, 6
closet clóset (*m.*), 10
clothing ropa, 5; **article
    of ~** prenda de ropa, 8;
    ~ store tienda de ropa, 6
cloudburst chaparrón (*m.*)
cloudy: It's ~. Está nublado. 7
coat abrigo, 8
code código
codfish bacalao, 9
coffee café (*m.*), 9

cold (*adj.*) frío(a); **It's ~.** Hace
    frío. 7
Colombian colombiano(a), 2
color color (*m.*), 4; **solid ~** de
    un solo color, 8
comb peine (*m.*), 5; **~ one's
    hair** peinarse, 5
come venir (*irreg.*), 5
comic strip tira cómica
comma coma
command mandato
compact disc CD, disco
    compacto (*m.*)
comparison comparación (*f.*), 8
compete competir (i, i)
competition competencia, 7
complain quejarse, 5
complexion tez (*f.*)
complicity complicidad (*f.*)
computer computadora, P;
    ~ center centro
    de computación, 3;
    ~ functions funciones (*f. pl.*)
    de la computadora, 4;
    ~ science computación (*f.*),
    informática, 3
conduct conducir (zc), 5
confection confección (*f.*)
connect conectar, 4
connection conexión (*f.*), 4
consider pensar (ie) en (de), 4
contest concurso
continue seguir (i, i), 6
continued seguido(a)
contraction contracción (*f.*), 3
contrary: on the ~ al contrario
conversation conversación (*f.*)
cook cocinar, 2; cocer (-z) (ue), 9;
    cocinero(a), 5
cookie galleta, 9
cool, chévere; It's cool. Hace
    fresco. 7
copper cobre (*m.*)
corn maíz (*m.*)
corner esquina, 6
correct corregir (i, i) (j)
Costa Rican costarricense
    (*m., f.*), 2
cotton algodón (*m.*), 8
country país (*m.*)
courage coraje (*m.*)
course: basic ~ curso básico, 3
courtesy cortesía, 4
cousin primo(a), 5
cowboy vaquero
cradle cuna

create crear
creative creativo(a)
crew tripulación (*f.*)
crowd muchedumbre (*f.*)
cruise ship crucero
crushed molido(a), 9
Cuban cubano(a), 2
culinary culinario(a)
culture cultura
cumin comino, 9
cup taza, 9
curtain cortina, 10
custard flan (*m.*), 9
customer cliente (*m., f.*), 8
cutting recorte (*m.*)
cyberspace ciberespacio, 4
cycling ciclismo, 7

D

daily cotidiano(a)
dam presa
dance bailar, 2; baile (*m.*), 3
danger peligro, 7
dangerous peligroso(a), 7
date fecha, 3; **blind ~** cita a
    ciegas
daughter hija, 5
daughter-in-law nuera, 5
dawn amanecer (zc)
day día (*m.*), 3; **~ before
    yesterday** anteayer, 7;
    ~ of the week día de la
    semana, 3; **every ~** todos
    los días, 3
December diciembre, 1
decoration decoración (*f.*), 10
definite definido(a), 1
degree grado
Delighted to meet you.
    Encantado(a). 1
demand exigir (j)
demonstrate demostrar (ue)
demonstrative demostrativo(a),
    6
denim mezclilla, 8
dentist dentista (*m., f.*), 5
deodorant desodorante (*m.*), 5
describe describir, 2
deserve merecer (zc)
design diseño; **graphic ~** diseño
    gráfico, 3
designer: graphic ~ diseñador(a)
    gráfico(a), 5
desire afán (*m.*); anhelo
desk escritorio, P

dessert postre (*m.*), 9
detail detalle (*m.*)
determined resuelto (*p.p. of* resolver)
develop desarrollar
dialect dialecto
dictionary diccionario, P
die morirse (ue, u), 8
difference diferencia
difficult difícil, 4
digital camera cámara digital, 4
dining room comedor (*m.*), 10
dinner cena
dirty sucio(a)
disappointment desilusión (*f.*)
disaster desastre (*m.*)
discount descuento, 8
discover descubrir, 3
disgusting asco
dish: main ~ plato principal, 9
dishonest mentiroso(a), 2
dishwasher lavaplatos (*m. s.*), 10
disillusionment desengaño
dispatch despachar
disqualify descalificar (qu)
distance trecho
diversity diversidad (*f.*)
divide dividir
do hacer (*irreg.*), 5; **a lot to ~** mucho que hacer; **~ the homework for tomorrow.** Hagan la tarea para mañana. P; **~ the recycling** hacer el reciclaje, 10
doctor doctor(a); médico(a), 5
dog perro(a), 2
doll muñeca
dollar dólar (*m.*)
Dominican dominicano(a), 2
door puerta, P
dorm residencia estudiantil, 3; dormitorio estudiantil, 6
download descargar, bajar, 4
downpour chaparrón (*m.*)
downtown centro de la ciudad, 10
dozen docena, 9
drawing dibujo, P
dream sueño; **~ (about)** soñar (ue) con, 4
drenched empapado(a)
dress vestido, 8; **~ (someone)** vestir (i, i), 5; **get dressed** vestirse (i, i), 5
dresser cómoda, tocador (*m.*), 10
drink beber, 3
drive manejar, conducir (zc), 5

driver's license licencia de manejar
dry (something) secar (qu), 5; **~ one's hair** secarse (qu) el pelo, 5
dryer secadora, 10
during mientras, por, 10
dust polvo; **~ the furniture** sacudir los muebles, 10
DVD / CD-ROM drive lector (*m.*) de CD-ROM / DVD, 4

E

early temprano, 3
earphones audífonos (*m. pl.*), 4
earring arete (*m.*), pendiente (*m.*), 8
earth tierra
easy fácil, 4
eat comer, 3; **~ dinner** cenar, 2
e-book libro electrónico, P
economics **economía, 3**
Ecuadoran ecuatoriano(a), 2
edit redactar
education educación (*f.*), 3
egg huevo, 6; **~ sunny-side up** huevo estrellado, 9; **scrambled ~** huevo revuelto, 9
egotistic egoísta, 2
eight ocho, P; **~ hundred** ochocientos(as), 8
eighteen dieciocho, P
eighth octavo(a), 10
eighty ochenta, P
either . . . or o... o, 6
electricity electricidad (*f.*)
electronic electrónico(a); **~ games store** tienda de juegos electrónicos, 6; **~ mailbox** buzón (*m.*) electrónico, 4; **~ notebook** asistente (*m.*) electrónico, 4; **electronics** aparatos electrónicos, 4
elephant elefante (*m.*)
eleven once, P
e-mail correo electrónico, e-mail (*m.*), P
embarrass avergonzar (ue) (c)
embarrassed avergonzado(a)
embroidered bordado(a), 8
emotion emoción (*f.*), 4

emphasize destacar (qu), enfatizar (c)
empty vacío(a)
encounter encuentro
end cabo; fin (*m.*)
engineer ingeniero(a), 5
engineering ingeniería, 3
English inglés (inglesa), 2; **~ language** inglés (*m.*), 3
enjoy gozar (c); **~ (life)** disfrutar (la vida)
enough: it is ~ basta
enroll alistar
entertain entretener (*like* tener)
entertaining divertido(a), 2
environment medio ambiente (*m.*)
equator ecuador (*m.*)
era etapa
essay ensayo
Europe Europa
evaluation calificación (*f.*)
evasion sorteo
even aun
evening noche (*f.*); **during the ~** por la noche, 3; **Good ~.** Buenas noches. 1; **in the ~** (*with precise time*) de la noche, 3
everything todo
everywhere por dondequiera
example ejemplo, 10
exchange intercambiar; **in ~ for** a cambio de; **~ rate** cambio
Excuse me. Disculpe. Perdón. 4
exercise hacer (*irreg.*) ejercicio, 7
exhibit exhibir
exotic exótico(a)
expensive: It's (too) ~. Es (demasiado) caro(a). 8
express preferences expresar preferencias, 2
expression expresión (*f.*), 1
extroverted extrovertido(a), 2
eyeglasses lentes (*m. pl.*), anteojos (*m. pl.*)

F

fabric tela, 8
fact dato, hecho
Fahrenheit degree grado Fahrenheit, 7
fairy tale cuento de hadas

fall caer (*irreg.*);
(*autumn*) otoño, 7;
~ asleep dormirse (ue, u), 5;
~ back on recurrir; **~ in
love** enamorarse, 5
false falso(a)
family familia;
~ member pariente (*m., f.*), 5;
nuclear ~ familia nuclear, 5;
~ tree árbol (*m.*) genealógico
fantasy fantasía
far from lejos de, 6
fascinate fascinar, 4
fashion (*adj.*) de modas
fashion moda, 8;
~ magazine revista de moda
fashionable: (not) to be ~ (no)
estar de moda, 8
fast rápido(a), 4
fat gordo(a), 2
father padre (*m.*), papá (*m.*), 5
father-in-law suegro, 5
fax: external / internal ~ fax
(*m.*) externo / interno, 4
February febrero, 1
feed the dog darle de comer al
perro, 10
feel sentir (ie, i), 4; **~ like
(doing)** tener (*irreg.*) ganas
de, 7
feminine femenino(a)
field of study campo de estudio, 3
fifteen quince, P
fifth quinto(a), 10
fifty cincuenta, P
file archivar, 4; archivo, 4
fill llenar
final final
finally por fin, 9
financial financiero(a)
find encontrar (ue), 4
find out averiguar (gü)
Fine, thank you. Bien, gracias. 1
fire fuego; **~ fighter**
bombero(a), 5
fired despedido(a)
fireplace chimenea, 10
first primer(o)(a), 10;
~ floor primer piso, 10
fish pescar (qu), 7; pez (*m.*)
(*alive*); pescado (*caught*), 9
fit apto(a); **It fits nicely /
badly.** Me queda bien / mal. 8
five cinco, P;
~ hundred quinientos(as), 8;
~ thousand cinco mil, 8

flash drive la memoria flash, el
pendrive, 4
flat llano(a)
flavor sabor (*m.*)
floating flotador(a)
floor piso; **first ~**
primer piso, 10
flour harina, 9
flourish florecer (zc)
flower florecer (zc); flor (*f.*)
fold doblar, 6

following siguiente
fondness cariño
food comida, 6
food processor procesador
(*m.*) de comida, 10
fool engañar
foot: **on ~** a pie, 6
football fútbol americano, 7
footprint huella
for para, por, 10; **~ example** por
ejemplo, 10
forbid prohibir, 10

fork tenedor (*m.*), 9
fortress fortaleza
forty cuarenta, P
forum foro, 4
founder fundador(a)
four cuatro, P; **~ hundred**
cuatrocientos(as), 8
fourteen catorce, P
fourth cuarto(a), 10
free libre
freezer congelador (*m.*), 10
French francés (francesa), 2;
~ fries papas fritas, 9;
~ language francés (*m.*), 3
frequently frecuentemente, 4
fresh fresco(a), 9
Friday viernes (*m.*), 2
fried frito(a), 9
friend amigo(a), P; cuate(a)
from the del (de + el), 3
front: in ~ of delante de, frente a,
enfrente de, 6
frozen congelado(a), 9
fruit fruta, 6; **~ juice** jugo de
fruta, 9; **~ salad** ensalada
de fruta, 9; **~ shake** licuado
de fruta
fry freír (i, i), 9
fun divertido(a), 2
function funcionar, 4
funny cómico(a), 2

furious furioso(a), 4
furniture muebles (*m. pl.*), 10

G

gallon galón (*m.*), 9
game partido, 7; **interactive ~**
juego interactivo, 4
gang pandilla
garage garaje (*m.*), 10
garbage basura, 10
garden jardín (*m.*), 10
garlic ajo, 9
generally por lo general, 9
generous generoso(a), 2
genre género
gentle apacible
geography geografía, 3
German alemán (alemana), 2;
~ language alemán (*m.*), 3
get conseguir (i, i), 8;
~ ahead adelantar;
~ cold enfriarse, 9;
~ divorced divorciarse, 5;
~ down from bajar, 6;
~ dressed vestirse (i, i), 5;
~ engaged comprometerse, 5;
~ married casarse, 5;
~ off of (*a bus, etc.*) bajar, 6;
~ on subir, 6;
~ ready prepararse, 5;
~ separated separarse, 5;
~ sick enfermarse, 5;
~ together reunirse, 5;
~ up levantarse, 5
gift regalo
girl chica, P; muchacha, P; niña, P
girlfriend novia
give dar (*irreg.*), 5;
~ as a gift regalar, 8;
~ directions decir (*irreg.*)
cómo llegar, 6; **~ personal
information** dar (*irreg.*)
información personal, 1;
~ preference anteponer;
~ someone a bath bañar, 5;
~ the time dar (*irreg.*) la
hora, 3
glass vaso, 9
glove guante (*m.*), 8
go acudir; ir (*irreg.*), 3;
~ away irse (*irreg.*), 5;
~ off (*alarm clock, etc.*) sonar
(ue), 4; **~ offline** cortar la
conexión, 4; **~ online** hacer
(*irreg.*) una conexión, 4;

~ out salir (*irreg.*), 5;
~ shopping hacer (*irreg.*)
las compras, 6; ir de compras,
8; **~ straight** seguir (i, i) (g)
derecho; **~ to bed** acostarse
(ue), 5; **~ up** subir, 6
goal meta
gold oro, 8
golden dorado(a), 9
golf golf (*m.*), 7
good bueno(a), 2; bondadoso(a)
goodbye adiós, 1
gossip chisme (*m.*)
gossiping chismoso(a)
governor gobernador(a)
grade nota, P
granddaughter nieta, 5
grandfather abuelo, 5
grandmother abuela, 5
grandson nieto, 5
grape uva, 9
graph gráfica
gray gris, 4
great chévere (*Cuba, Puerto Rico*); grande, 2
greater mayor, 8
green verde, 4
greet saludar, 1
greeting saludo
grilled asado(a); a la parrilla, 9
ground molido(a), 9; tierra
group (*m.*) conjunto; **group** (*v.*) juntar
growth crecimiento
Guatemalan guatemalteco(a), 2
guess adivinar;
Guess. Adivina. P
guinea pig cuy (*m.*)
guitar guitarra, 2
gymnasium gimnasio, 3

H

hair: blond ~ pelo rubio, 2;
brown ~ pelo castaño, 2
hairdresser peluquero(a), 5
half mitad (*f.*)
half-brother medio hermano, 5
half-sister media hermana, 5
hallway pasillo, 10
ham jamón (*m.*), 6
hamburger hamburguesa, 9
handicrafts artesanía
handkerchief pañuelo
handsome hermoso(a); guapo(a), 2

handtowel toalla de mano, 5
happiness dicha; felicidad (*f.*)
happy contento(a), 4
hard duro(a); **~ drive** disco duro, 4
hardly ever rara vez
hardware hardware (*m.*), 4
hard-working trabajador(a), 2
haste prisa
hat sombrero, 8
hatred odio
have tener (*irreg.*), 1; **~ a fight** pelearse, 5; **~ a soft drink** tomar un refresco, 2; **~ fun** divertirse (ie, i), 5; **~ the urge to** tener (*irreg.*) ganas de, 7; **~ to** (+ *inf.*) tener (*irreg.*) que (+ *inf.*), 1
he él, 1
health salud (*f.*), 3
healthy saludable
hear oír (*irreg.*), 5
heat calentar (ie), 9
heavy fuerte, 9
height altitud (*f.*), altura; (*of a person*) estatura
hello hola, ¿Aló? (*on the phone*), 1
helmet casco
help ayudar; ayuda
her (*pron.*) ella, 8; (*adj.*) su, 3; suyo(a), 10; **to / for ~** le, 8
here aquí, 6
heritage herencia
hers (*pron.*) suyo(a), 10
hide esconder
hike hacer (*irreg.*) alpinismo, practicar (qu) alpinismo, 7
him (*pron.*) él, 8; **to / for ~** le, 8
his (*adj.*) su, 3; (*adj., pron.*) suyo(a), 10
Hispanic hispano(a)
history historia, 3
hoax engaño
hockey: field ~ hockey (*m.*) sobre hierba, 7; **ice ~** hockey (*m.*) sobre hielo, 7
hole pozo
home hogar (*m.*)
homeless sin hogar
homemade casero(a)
homework tarea, P
Honduran hondureño(a), 2
honest honesto(a)
hope esperanza; esperar, 10
hospital hospital (*m.*), 6

hot: be ~ tener (*irreg.*) calor, 7;
~ dog perro caliente, 9;
It's ~. Hace calor. 7
hour hora
house casa, 6; **the ~ special** la especialidad de la casa, 9
housechore quehacer (*m.*) doméstico, 10
housing vivienda
how? ¿cómo? 3; **~ are things going?** ¿Qué tal? 1; **~ are you?** (*form. s.*) ¿Cómo está (usted)? / (*form. pl.*) ¿Cómo están (ustedes)? / (*s. fam.*) ¿Cómo estás (tú)? 1; **~ can I help you?** ¿En qué puedo servirle? 8; **~ do you say . . . ?** ¿Cómo se dice…? P; **~ do you wish to pay?** ¿Cómo desea pagar?, 8; **~ many?** ¿cuántos(as)? 3; **~ much?** ¿cuánto(a)? 3; **~ much does it cost?** ¿Cuánto cuesta? 8; **How's it going with you?** ¿Cómo te / le(s) va? 1
humanities humanidades (*f. pl.*), 3
humble humilde
humid húmedo(a)
hunger hambre (*f. but* el hambre)
hurry prisa; **be in a ~** tener (*irreg.*) prisa, 7
husband esposo, 5
hymn himno

I

I yo, 1
ice: (vanilla / chocolate) ~ cream helado (de vainilla / de chocolate), 9;
~ hockey hockey (*m.*) sobre hielo, 7; **~ skate** patinar sobre hielo, 7
identity identidad (*f.*)
immigration inmigración (*f.*)
impatient impaciente, 2
impressive impresionante
impulsive impulsivo(a), 2
in en; por, 10; **~ charge of** encargardo de; **~ order to** (+ *inf.*) para, 10; **~ relation to** en cuanto a; **~ short** en resumen; **~ spite of** a pesar de; **~ the direction of** para, 10; **the "in" place** "antro"

inch pulgada
increase acrecentar (ie), aumentar
incredible increíble
indefinite indefinido(a), 1
index índice (*m.*)
Indian indio(a), 2
indigenous indígena
influence influir (y); influencia
ingredient ingrediente (*m.*), 9
inhabitant habitante (*m., f.*)
in-laws familia política, 5
inline skate (rollerblade) patinar en línea, 7
inside of dentro de, 6; **~ the house** dentro de la casa, 10
insist insistir, 10
install instalar, 4
instead of en vez de
instructor instructor(a), P
intelligent inteligente, 2
intention fin (*m.*)
interactive whiteboard pizarra interactiva, P
interest interesar, 4
interesting interesante, 2
Internet Internet (*m.* or *f.*), red (*f.*); **~ provider** proveedor (*m.*) de acceso, 4
interpreter intérprete (*m., f.*)
intimate íntimo(a)
introduce someone presentar a alguien, 1
introverted introvertido(a), 2
invest invertir
iron planchar, 10; (*metal*) hierro; (*appliance*) plancha, 10
irresponsible irresponsable, 2
Italian italiano(a), 2; **~ language** italiano, 3
its (*adj.*) su, 3; (*pron.*) suyo(a), 10

J

jacket (*suit jacket, blazer*) saco; (*outdoor, non-suit coat*) chaqueta 8
January enero, 1
Japanese japonés (japonesa), 2; **~ language** japonés (*m.*), 3
jealous celoso(a); **be ~** tener (*irreg.*) celos
jealously celosamente
jeans jeans (*m. pl.*), 8
jewelry store joyería, 6
jewelry joyas (*f. pl.*), 8

join juntarse
joke broma
journalism periodismo, 3
journalist periodista (*m., f.*), 5
July julio, 1
June junio, 1

K

keep: (oneself) separate mantenerse apartado
key (*on a keyboard*) tecla, 4
keyboard teclado, 4
kilo kilo, 9; **half a ~** medio kilo, 9
kind bondadoso(a)
king rey (*m.*)
kiss besar
kitchen cocina, 10
knapsack mochila, P
knife cuchillo, 9
know: ~ a person conocer (zc), 5; **~ a fact, ~ how to** saber (*irreg.*), 5
Korean coreano(a), 2

L

lake lago, 7
lamp lámpara, 10
language idioma (*m.*), lengua, 3
laptop computer computadora portátil, P
late tarde, 3
later luego, 5
latest: the ~ lo último
laugh reírse (*irreg.*), 5
laundry room lavandería, 10
lawn césped (*m.*), 10; **mow the ~** cortar el césped, 10
lawyer abogado(a), 5
lazy perezoso(a), 2
learn aprender, 3
learning aprendizaje (*m.*)
leather piel (*f.*), cuero, 8
leave dejar, 2; salir (*irreg.*), irse (*irreg.*), 5
left: to the ~ a la izquierda, 6
lemonade limonada, 9
less menor, 8; **~ than** menos que, 8
lesson lección (*f.*), P
level nivel (*m.*)
life vida
lifejacket salvavidas (*m. s.*)

lift levantar, 5; **~ weights** levantar pesas, 2
light luz (*f.*); (*adj.*) ligero(a), 9
like gustar; **~ a lot** encantar, 4; (**They / You** [*pl.*]) **~ . . .** A... les gusta... 2; **He / She likes . . .** A... le gusta... 2; **I / You ~ . . .** A mí / ti me / te gusta... 2; **I'd ~** (+ *inf.*) quisiera (+ *inf.*), 6; Me gustaría (+ *inf.*)... 6
Likewise. Igualmente. 1
linen lino, 8
linguistic lingüístico(a)
link enlace (*m.*), 4
lip labio
listen escuchar; **~ to music** escuchar música, 2; **~ to the audio** Escuchen el audio. P
liter litro, 9
literature literatura, 3
little poco, 4
live vivir, 3, ocupar
livestock ganadería
living room sala, 10
loan préstamo, 8; (*v.*) prestar, 8
lobster langosta, 9
located ubicado(a); **is ~** queda
long for apetecer (zc)
look: ~ for buscar (qu), 2
lose perder (ie), 4; **~ oneself** perderse (ie)
love querer (*irreg.*), 4; amar; amor (*m.*), cariño
lover amante (*m., f.*)
lunch almuerzo, 9
luxurious lujoso(a)
lying mentiroso(a), 2

M

made: It's ~ out of . . . Está hecho(a) de... 8; **They're ~ out of . . .** Están hechos(as) de... 8
magazine revista
mailbox buzón (*m.*)
majority mayoría
make hacer (*irreg.*), 5; **~ sure** asegurarse; **~ the bed** hacer la cama, 10
makeup maquillaje (*m.*), 5
mall centro comercial, 6
man hombre (*m.*), P
manager gerente (*m., f.*), 5
manly varonil

manners modales (*m. pl.*)

March marzo, 1

marital status estado civil

mark marcar (qu)

market mercado, 6; **open-air ~, farmer's ~** mercado al aire libre, 6

marketing mercadeo, 3

masculine masculino(a)

match emparejar; (*sports*) partido, 7

mathematics matemáticas (*f. pl.*), 3

matter (to someone) importar, 4

May mayo, 1

mayonnaise mayonesa, 9

mayor alcalde (alcaldesa)

me mí, 8; **to / for ~** me, 8; **with ~** conmigo, 8

mean: It means . . . Significa… P

meaning significado

means of transportation medios de transporte, 6

measure medir (i, i)

measurement medida, 9

meat carne (*f.*), 9

meatball albóndiga

mechanic mecánico(a), 5

media center centro de comunicaciones, 3

medicine medicina, 3

meditation meditación (*f.*)

meet conocer (zc), reunirse, 5

meeting encuentro, reunión (*f.*)

melon melón (*m.*), 9

menu menú (*m.*), 9

messenger mensajero(a)

Mexican mexicano(a), 2

microphone micrófono, 4

microwave microondas (*m. s.*), 10

midnight medianoche (*f.*), 3

mild apacible

milk leche (*f.*), 6

mine (*pron.*) mío, 10

mirror espejo, 10

Miss señorita (*abbrev.* Srta.), 1

missionary misionero(a)

mix mezclar, 9; mezcla

mixed mixto(a)

modem: external / internal ~ módem (*m.*) externo / interno, 4

Monday lunes (*m.*), 3

money dinero

monitor monitor (*m.*), 4

monkey mono

month mes (*m.*), 3; **last ~** mes pasado, 7

mop the floor trapear el piso, 10

more más; **~ than** más que, 8

morning mañana, 3; **during the ~** por la mañana, 3; **Good ~.** Buenos días. 1; **in the ~** (*with precise time*) de la mañana, 3

mortality mortalidad (*f.*)

mother madre (*f.*), mamá, 5; **Mother's Day** día (*m.*) de las Madres, 3

mother-in-law suegra, 5

mountain monte (*m.*); **~ range** cordillera

mountainous montañoso(a)

mouse ratón (*m.*), 4

move (*change residence*) mudarse

mow the lawn cortar el césped, 10

Mr. señor (*abbrev.* Sr.), 1

Mrs. señora (*abbrev.* Sra.), 1

Ms. señorita (*abbrev.* Srta.), 1

much mucho, 4

mud lodo

museum museo, 6

music música, 3

mustard mostaza, 9

my (*adj.*) mi, 3; (*pron.*) mío(a), 10; **~ pleasure.** Mucho gusto. Un placer. 1

N

name llamar, 2; nombre (*m.*); **full ~** nombre (*m.*) completo; **My ~ is . . .** Me llamo…, Mi nombre es…, 1

napkin servilleta, 9

narrator narrador(a)

nationality nacionalidad (*f.*), 2

nature naturaleza

navigation navegación (*f.*)

necklace collar (*m.*), 8

need necesitar, 2

neighbor vecino(a), 6

neighborhood barrio, colonia, 1

neither tampoco, 2; **~ . . . nor** ni… ni, 6

nephew sobrino, 5

nervous nervioso(a), 4

never nunca, 5; jamás, 6

nevertheless sin embargo

new novedoso(a)

news: **~ group** grupo de noticias, 4

newspaper periódico

next próximo(a); **~ to** al lado de, 6; **~ to last** penúltimo(a)

Nicaraguan nicaragüense (*m., f.*), 2

nice simpático(a), 2

nickname apodo

niece sobrina, 5

night noche (*f.*), 3; **Good ~.** Buenas noches. 1; **last ~** anoche, 7

nine hundred novecientos(as), 8

nine nueve, P

nineteen diecinueve, P

ninety noventa, P

ninth noveno(a), 10

no one nadie, 6

nobody nadie, 6

none ningún, ninguno(a), 6

noodle soup sopa de fideos, 9

noon mediodía (*m.*), 3

normal normal, 4

North America Norteamérica

not: **~ any** ningún, ninguno(a), 6; **~ either** tampoco, 2; **~ much** no mucho, 1

notebook cuaderno, P

notes apuntes (*m. pl.*), P

nothing nada, 1

noun sustantivo

novel novedoso(a)

novelist novelista (*m., f.*)

November noviembre, 1

novice novato(a)

number número, 8

nurse enfermero(a), 5

O

obey hacer (*irreg.*) caso

obtain conseguir (i, i), 8

October octubre, 1

of: **~ course** cómo no, 6; por supuesto, 10; **~ the** del (de + el), 3

offer: special ~ oferta especial, 8

office oficina, 6

old viejo(a), 2

old-fashioned anticuado(a)

olive oil aceite (*m.*) de oliva, 9

on en, sobre, encima de, 6; **~ behalf of** por, 10

once una vez, 9

one uno, P; **~ hundred** cien, P; **~ hundred and ~** ciento uno, 8; **~ hundred thousand** cien mil, 8; **~ million** millón (*m.*), un millón, 8; **~ thousand** mil (*m.*), 8

onion cebolla, 9

online en línea, 4

only único(a)

open abrir, 3; **~ your books.** Abran los libros. P

opposite enfrente de, frente a, 6; opuesto(a)

orange (*color*) anaranjado(a), 4; (*fruit*) naranja, 9

order ordenar, 9; mandar, 10

ordinal number número ordinal, 10

originate originar

ought deber (+ *inf.*), 3

our (*adj.*) nuestro(a)(s), 3

ours (*pron.*) nuestro(a)(s), 10

outline bosquejo

outside of fuera de, 6; **~ the house** fuera de la casa, 10

outskirts afueras (*f. pl.*), 10

outstanding sobresaliente

oven horno

overcoming superación (*f.*)

owner dueño(a), 5

P

package paquete (*m.*), 9

page página, P

paint pintar, 2

painting pintura, 3; cuadro, 10

Panamanian panameño(a), 2

pants pantalones (*m. pl.*), 8

paper papel (*m.*), P

parachute paracaídas (*m. s.*)

paragraph párrafo

Paraguayan paraguayo(a), 2

Pardon me. Con permiso. 4

parents padres (*m. pl.*), 5

park parque (*m.*), 6

parking lot estacionamiento, 6

parsley perejil (*m.*)

pass (by) pasar, 2

password contraseña, 4

patient paciente (*m., f.*), 2

patio patio, 10

paving stone baldosa

pay pagar (gu), 9; **~ attention** hacer (*irreg.*) caso

payment: form of ~ método de pago, 8

PDF file archivo PDF, 4

pea guisante (*m.*), 9

peace paz (*f.*)

peel pelar, 9

pencil lápiz (*m.*), P

penguin pingüino

people gente (*f.*)

pepper pimienta, 9

percentage porcentaje (*m.*)

perhaps quizás, tal vez

period (*punctuation*) punto; trecho

permit permitir, 10

personality personalidad (*f.*); **~ trait** característica de la personalidad, 2

Peruvian peruano(a), 2

pharmacy farmacia, 6

philanthropic filantrópico(a)

philosophy filosofía, 3

photo foto (*f.*), P

physical físico(a), 5; **~ appearance** apariencia física; **~ trait** característica física, 2

physics física, 3

piano piano, 2

picturesque pintoresco(a)

piece pedazo, 9

pillow almohada

pink rosado(a), 4

pirate pirata (*m.*)

pizzeria pizzería, 6

place lugar (*m.*), sitio

plaid a cuadros, 8

plain llanura

plate plato, 9

play jugar (ue) (gu), 4; **~ a musical instrument** tocar (qu) un instrumento musical, 2; **~ sports** practicar (qu) deportes, 2; **~ tennis (baseball, etc.)** jugar tenis (béisbol, etc), 7

playful juguetón (juguetona)

plaza plaza, 6

please por favor, 1

pleasure: A ~ to meet you. Mucho gusto en conocerte. 1

plot trama

plumber plomero(a), 5

poet poeta (poetisa)

poetry poesía

point: ~ out marcar (qu), señalar; **to the ~** al grano

policeman (policewoman) policía (*m., f.*), 5

political político(a); **~ science** ciencias políticas (*f. pl.*), 3

polka-dotted de lunares, 8

poor pobre

populate poblar (ue)

pork chop chuleta de puerco, 6

portable CD / MP3 player CD portátil / MP3, P

Portuguese portugués (portuguesa), 2

post office oficina de correos, 6

potato: ~ chips papitas fritas, 6; **~ salad** ensalada de papa

pound libra, 9

power poder (*m.*)

powerful poderoso(a)

practice practicar (qu)

prefer preferir (ie, i), 4

preference preferencia

prenuptual agreement contrato prenupcial

preparation preparación (*f.*), 9

prepare preparar, 2; **~ the food** preparar la comida, 10

preposition preposición (*f.*), 6

present (*gift*) regalo; **at the ~ time** en la actualidad

pretty bonito(a); lindo(a), 2

price: It's a very good ~. Está a muy buen precio. 8

priest sacerdote (*m.*)

prime rib lomo de res, 9

print imprimir, 3; (*patterned fabric*) estampado(a), 8; (*art*) cuadro, 10

printer impresora, 4

prize premio

profession profesión (*f.*), 5

professor profesor(a), P

program programa (*m.*); **antivirus ~** programa antivirus, 4; **~ icon** ícono del programa, 4

programmer programador(a), 5

projector proyector, P

promote adelantar, promover (ue)

pronoun pronombre (*m.*), 1

proud orgulloso(a)

provocative provocador(a)

psychology psicología, 3

public: ~ communications comunicación (*f.*) pública, 3; **~ relations** publicidad (*f.*), 3

Puerto Rican puertorriqueño(a), 2

purple morado(a), 4

purpose propósito
purse bolsa, 8
push oprimir
put poner (*irreg.*), 5; **~ away the clothes** guardar la ropa, 10; **~ my toys where they belong** poner mis juguetes en su lugar, 10; **~ on (clothing)** ponerse (la ropa), 5; **~ on makeup** maquillarse, 5

Q

quality calidad (*f.*); **of good (high) ~** de buena (alta) calidad, 8
queen reina
questionnaire cuestionario
quotation cita

R

raffle sorteo
railroad ferrocarril (*m.*)
rain llover (ue);
    ~ forest bosque (*m.*) tropical, bosque (*m.*) pluvial; **It's raining.** Está lloviendo. (Llueve.), 7
raincoat impermeable (*m.*), 8
raise levantar, 5
ranch estancia
rank rango
rather bastante, 4
raw crudo(a), 9
razor rasuradora, 5; **electric ~** máquina de afeitar, 5
read leer (y), 3; **~ Chapter 1.** Lean el Capítulo 1. P
really de veras
reason razón (*f.*)
receive recibir, 3
recipe receta, 9
recognize reconocer (zc)
recommend recomendar (ie), 10
record grabar, 4
recruit alistar
recycling reciclaje (*m.*), 10
red rojo(a), 4
redheaded pelirrojo(a), 2
reduced: It's ~. Está rebajado(a). 8
reflect reflejar
reflection reflexión (*f.*)
refrigerator refrigerador (*m.*), 10
relate contar (ue), 4
relative pariente (*m.*, *f.*), 5

relax relajarse, 5
remain quedar(se)
remember recordar (ue)
renovate renovar (ue)
renown renombre (*m.*)
rent alquiler (*m.*);
    ~ videos alquilar videos, 2;
    ~ movies alquilar películas, 2
repeat repetir (i, i), 4;
    ~. Repitan. P
report informe (*m.*)
request pedir (i, i), 10
require requerir (ie, i), 10
residential neighborhood barrio residencial, 10
resort to recurrir
respond responder, 1
responsible responsable, 2
rest descansar, 2
restaurant restaurante (*m.*), 6
return regresar, 2; volver (ue), 4
revenue ingreso
rhyme rima
rich adinerado(a)
ride montar; **~ a bike** montar en bicicleta, 7;
    ~ horseback montar a caballo, 7
right: to the ~ a la derecha, 6
ring sonar (ue), 4; anillo, 8; sortija
ripped rasgado
risk riesgo
river río, 7
roasted (in the oven) al horno, 9
role papel (*m.*)
roof techo, 10
room cuarto,
    P**roommate** compañero(a) de cuarto, P
root raíz (*f.*)
rose rosa, 4
rough draft borrador (*m.*)
route ruta
row remar, 7
rower remero(a)
rude descortés
rug alfombra, 10
rule regla
run correr, 3
rural campestre

S

sad triste, 4
safe seguro(a), 7

said: It's said . . . Se dice…, P
salad ensalada, 9; **lettuce and tomato ~** ensalada de lechuga y tomate, 9; **tossed ~** ensalada mixta, 9
sale: It's on ~. Está en venta. 8
salesclerk dependiente (*m.*, *f.*), 5
salmon salmón (*m.*), 9
salt sal (*f.*), 9
Salvadoran salvadoreño(a), 2
same mismo(a); **~ (thing)** lo mismo
sandal sandalia, 8
sandwich bocadillo, sandwich (*m.*), 9; **ham and cheese ~ with avocado** sandwich de jamón y queso con aguacate, 9
Saturday sábado, 2
sausage salchicha, 6
save guardar, 4
say decir (*irreg.*), 5; **~ good-bye** despedirse (i, i), 1
saying dicho
scan ojear
scarcely apenas
scarf bufanda, 8
scenery paisaje (*m.*)
schedule horario
school escuela, 3
science ciencia, 3
scientific científico(a)
scream gritar; grito
screen pantalla, 4
script guión (*m.*);
    ~ writer guionista (*m.*, *f.*)
search engine buscador (*m.*), 4
season estación (*f.*), 7; **dry ~** temporada de secas; **rainy ~** temporada de lluvias
second segundo(a), 10
secret secreto
secretary secretario(a), 5
sections tramos
see ver (*irreg.*), 5; **~ you at the usual place?** ¿Nos vemos donde siempre? 1; **~ you later.** Hasta luego. Nos vemos. 1; **~ you soon.** Hasta pronto. 1; **~ you tomorrow.** Hasta mañana. 1
seem parecer (zc)
selfish egoísta, 2
sell vender, 3
send enviar, 4; mandar, 8
sentence oración (*f.*)
separate apartado

September septiembre, 1
serious serio(a), 2
serve servir (i, i), 4
set the table poner (*irreg.*) la mesa, 9
seven siete, P; **~ hundred** setecientos(as), 8
seventeen diecisiete, P
seventh séptimo(a), 10
seventy setenta, P
several varios(as)
shame vergüenza
shampoo champú (*m.*), 5
share compartir, 3
shark tiburón (*m.*)
shave oneself afeitarse, 5
she ella, 1
sheet of paper hoja de papel, P
shellfish marisco, 9
shelter albergar (gu)
shirt camisa, 8
shoe zapato, 8; **high-heeled ~** zapato de tacón alto, 8; **tennis ~** zapato de tenis, 8
shooting tiroteo
shore orilla
short (*in length*) corto(a); (*in height*) bajo(a), 2
shorts pantalones (*m. pl.*) cortos, 8
should deber (+ *inf.*), 3
shout gritar
show demostrar (ue), mostrar (ue)
shred picar (qu), 9
shrimp camarón (*m.*), 9
shy tímido(a), 2
sick enfermo(a), 4
side lado; **on the ~ of** al lado de, 6
sign letrero
silk seda, 8
silly tonto(a), 2
silver plata, 8
similarity semejanza
simple sencillo(a)
sincere sincero(a), 2
sing cantar, 2
singer cantante (*m., f.*)
single soltero(a)
sister (younger, older) hermana (menor, mayor), 5
sister-in-law cuñada, 5
sit down sentarse (ie), 5
six seis, P; **~ hundred** seiscientos(as), 8

sixteen dieciséis, P
sixth sexto(a), 10
sixty sesenta, P
size talla, 8
skate patinar, 2
ski esquiar, 7; esquí (*m.*)
skiing esquí (*m.*); **downhill ~** esquí alpino, 7; **water ~** esquí acuático, 7
skin tez (*f.*)
skirt falda, 8
slave esclavo(a)
sleep dormir (ue, u), 4
slice pedazo, 9
slogan lema (*m.*)
slow lento(a), 4
slowly despacio
small pequeño(a), 2; **a ~ amount** un poco, 4
smartphone teléfono inteligente, smartphone, 4
smile sonreír (*irreg.*), 8; sonrisa
snack merienda
snow nevar (ie); **It's snowing.** Está nevando. (Nieva.), 7
snowboard tabla de snowboard, 7
snowboarding snowboarding, 7
so por eso, 10
soap jabón (*m.*), 5
soccer fútbol (*m.*), 7; **~ field** cancha, campo de fútbol, 6
social: media director director(a) de social media, 5; **~ networking site** red social, 4
sock calcetín (*m.*), 8
sofa sofá (*m.*), 10
soft suave; **~ drink** refresco, 6
software software (*m.*), 4
solved resuelto
some unos(as), 1; algún, alguno(a), 6
someone alguien, 6
something algo, 6; **~ vegan** algo vegano, 9
sometimes de vez en cuando; a veces, 5
somewhat bastante, 4
son hijo, 5
son-in-law yerno, 5
sorry: I'm sorry. Lo siento. 4
So-so. Regular. 1
soul alma (*f.*) (*but* el alma)
sound sonido
soup sopa, 9; **cold ~** gazpacho (*Spain*), 9

source fuente (*f.*)
South America Sudamérica
souvenir recuerdo
sovereignty soberanía
spa balneario
Spain España
Spanish español (a), 2; **~ language** español (*m.*), 3
Spanish-speaking hispanohablante
speaker conferencista (*m., f.*); altoparlante (*m., f.*), 4
species especie (*f.*)
spelling ortografía
spicy picante, 9
sponsor patrocinador(a)
spoon cuchara, 9
sport deporte (*m.*), 7; **~ activity** actividad (*f.*) deportiva, 7
sporting goods store tienda de equipo deportivo, 6
sports coat saco, 8
spring primavera, 7
stadium estadio, 6
stairs escaleras (*f. pl.*), 10
state estado, 5
station estación (*f.*); **train / bus ~** estación de trenes / autobuses, 6
stationery store papelería, 6
statistics estadística, 3
steak bistec (*m.*), 6
steamed al vapor, 9
steel acero
step on pisar
stepbrother hermanastro, 5
stepfather padrastro, 5
stepmother madrastra, 5
stepsister hermanastra, 5
still todavía; **~ life** naturaleza muerta
stop (*e.g., bus stop*) parada; **~ (doing something)** dejar de (+ *inf.*), 2; parar (de), 3
store guardar; almacén (*m.*), tienda, 6; **music (clothing, video) ~** tienda de música (ropa, videos), 6
stove estufa, 10
straight ahead todo derecho, 6
straighten out the bedroom arreglar el dormitorio, 10
strategy estrategia
strawberry fresa, 9

street calle (*f.*), 1
strengthen acrecentar (ie)
stringed al hilo, 9
striped rayado(a), a rayas, 8
strong fuerte
student estudiante (*m.*, *f.*), P;
~ **center** centro estudiantil, 6
studio estudio, 3
study estudiar; ~ **at the library
(at home)** estudiar en la
biblioteca (en casa), 2;
~ **pages . . . to . . .**
Estudien las páginas . . .
a . . ., P
stupid tonto(a), 2
style estilo; **in ~** en onda; **out
of ~** pasado(a) de moda, 8
substitute sustituir (y)
suburb barrio residencial,
suburbio, 10
subway: on the ~ en metro, 6
success éxito
suddenly de repente, 9
sugar azúcar (*m.*, *f.*), 9;
~ **cane** caña de azúcar
suggest sugerir (ie, i), 8
suggestion sugerencia
suit traje (*m.*), 8; **bathing ~**
traje (*m.*) de baño, 8
summer verano, 7
sun sol (*m.*)
sunbathe tomar el sol, 2
Sunday domingo, 2
sunglasses gafas (*f. pl.*)
de sol, 8
sunlight luz (*f.*) solar
sunny: It's ~. Hace sol. 7
supermarket supermercado, 6
support apoyar
sure seguro(a), 4
surf hacer (*irreg.*) surfing,
practicar (qu) surfing, 7
surpass sobrepasar
surprise sorpresa
surrounded rodeado(a)
survey encuesta
sweater suéter (*m.*), 8;
chompa
sweatsuit sudadera, 8
sweep the floor barrer el suelo /
el piso, 10
sweet dulce (*m.*); (*adj.*)
dulce
swim bañar, 5; nadar, 7
swimming natación (*f.*), 7;
~ **pool** piscina, 6

symbol símbolo
systematic sistemático(a)

T

table mesa, P; **night ~** mesita
de noche, 10; **set the ~** poner
(*irreg.*) la mesa, 9
tablecloth mantel (*m.*), 9
tablespoon cucharada, 9
tablet: ~ **computer** tableta, 4
take tomar, llevar; ~ **a
bath** bañarse, 5; ~ **a
shower** ducharse, 5; ~ **off
clothing** quitarse la ropa, 5;
~ **out the garbage** sacar (qu)
la basura, 10; ~ **photos** sacar
(qu) fotos, 2; ~ **place** realizarse
(c); ~ **the dog for a walk**
sacar (qu) a pasear al
perro, 10
talk hablar; ~ **on the telephone**
hablar por teléfono, 2
tall alto(a), 2
tamed domesticado(a)
taste gusto; **to individual ~** al
gusto, 9
tavern bodegón (*m.*)
tea: hot ~ té (*m.*), 9; **iced ~** té
(*m.*) helado, 9
teach enseñar
teacher maestro(a), 5
team equipo, 7
tear up rasgar (gu)
teaspoon cucharadita, 9
technology tecnología, 4
television: ~ **set** televisor
(*m.*), 10;
tell contar (ue), 4; decir (*irreg.*),
5; ~ **the time** decir la hora, 3
temperature temperatura, 7
ten diez, P; ~ **thousand** diez
mil, 8
tend tender
tennis tenis (*m.*), 7;
~ **court** cancha de tenis, 6;
~ **shoes** zapatos (*m. pl.*) de
tenis, 8
tenth décimo(a), 10
term término
terrible fatal, terrible, 1
terrific chévere (*Cuba, Puerto
Rico*)
text texto
Thank you very much. Muchas
gracias. 1

that (*adj.*) ese(a), 6; (*pron.*)
ése(a), 6; ~ **over there** (*adj.*)
aquel (aquella), 6; (*pron.*) aquél
(aquélla), 6
that's why por eso, 10
the el, la, los, las, 1
theater teatro, 6
their su, 3; suyo(a), 10
theirs (*pron.*) suyo(a), 10
them ellos(as), 8; **to / for ~** les, 8
then entonces
theory teoría
there allí, 6; **over ~** allá, 6; ~ **is /
~ are** hay, 1
these (*adj.*) estos(as), 6; (*pron.*)
éstos(as), 6
they ellos(as), 1
thin delgado(a), 2
think (about) pensar (ie)
(en, de), 4
third tercer(o, a), 10
thirst sed (*f.*)
thirsty: be ~ tener (*irreg.*) sed, 7
thirteen trece, P
thirty treinta, P
this (*adj.*) este(a), 6; (*pron.*)
éste(a), 6
those (*adj.*) esos, 6; (*pron.*)
ésos(as), 6; ~ **(over there)**
(adj.) aquellos(as), 6; (*pron.*)
aquéllos(as), 6
thousands miles
threat amenaza
three tres, P; ~ **hundred**
trescientos(as), 8
through por, 10
throughout a través de
throw: ~ **oneself** lanzarse (c);
~ **out** botar
thunderstorm tormenta
Thursday jueves (*m.*), 3
time hora; vez (*f.*)
times veces (*f. pl.*); **(two, three,
etc.) ~ a day / per week** (dos,
tres, etc.) veces al día / por
semana, 5
tip propina, 9
tired cansado(a), 4
title titular; título, 1
to a; **to the** al (a + el), 3
toast pan (*m.*) tostado, 9
toaster tostadora, 10
today hoy, 3; ~ **is Tuesday the
30th.** Hoy es martes treinta. 3
tomorrow mañana, 3
too much demasiado, 4

toothbrush cepillo de dientes, 5
toothpaste pasta de dientes, 5
top: on ~ of encima de, 6
toward para, 10
towel toalla, 5
town pueblo, 6
toy juguete (*m.*), 10
track suit sudadera, 8
train (*for sports*) entrenarse, 7; tren, 6
trainer entrenador(a) (*m.*)
trait característica
translate traducir (zc), 5
traveler's check cheque (*m.*) de viajero, 8
treasure tesoro
tree árbol (*m.*)
trick truco
triumph triunfar
trout trucha, 9
true verdad
truly de veras
trumpet trompeta, 2
try intentar, tratar de; **I'm going to ~ it on.** Voy a probármelo(la). 8
t-shirt camiseta, 8
Tuesday martes (*m.*), 3
tuna atún (*m.*), 9
turkey pavo, 6
turn cruzar (c), doblar, 6; viraje (*m.*); **~ in** entregar; **~ in your homework.** Entreguen la tarea. P; **~ off** apagar (gu), 2
twelve doce, P
twenty veinte, P
twenty-one veintiuno, P
twice dos veces, 9
two dos, P; **~ hundred** doscientos(as), 8; **~ million** dos millones, 8; **~ thousand** dos mil, 8
typical típico(a), 9

U

U.S. citizen estadounidense (*m., f.*), 2
ugly feo(a), 2
uncle tío, 5
underneath debajo de, 6
understand comprender, 3; entender (ie), 4
understanding comprensión (*f.*)
unique único(a)

unite unir, 9
united unido(a); **~ States** Estados Unidos
university universidad (*f.*), 6
unpleasant antipático(a), 2
untamed salvaje
upload subir, cargar, 4
Uruguayan uruguayo(a), 2
us nosotros(as), 8; **to / for ~** nos, 8
use usar, 2
useful útil
user usuario(a), 4

V

vacuum (*verb*) pasar la aspiradora, 10; **~ cleaner** aspiradora, 10
vain vanidoso(a)
valley valle (*m.*)
valuable valioso(a)
value valor (*m.*)
variety variedad (*f.*)
various varios(as)
vegan vegetariano(a) estricto(a), 9
vegetable vegetal (*m.*), 6
vegetarian vegetariano(a)
vehicle vehículo
Venetian blind persiana, 10
Venezuelan venezolano(a), 2
verb verbo, 3
very muy, 2; **~ little** muy poco
vest chaleco, 8
veterinarian veterinario(a), 5
videocamera videocámara, 4
videotape (*noun*) video
viewpoint punto de vista
vinegar vinagre (*m.*), 9
violin violín (*m.*), 2
visit friends visitar a amigos, 2
visitor visitante (*m., f.*)
voice voz (*f.*)
volcanic eruption erupción (*f.*) volcánica
volleyball volibol (*m.*), 7

W

waiter camarero, 5
waitress camarera, 5
wake up despertarse (ie), 5; **wake someone up** despertar (ie), 5
walk caminar, 2; andar (*irreg.*), 8

walking a pie, 6
wall pared (*f.*), P
wallet cartera, 8
want desear, querer (*irreg.*), 10
warm caluroso(a)
warning aviso
wash lavar, 5; **~ one's hair** lavarse el pelo, 5; **~ oneself** lavarse, 5; **~ the dishes (the clothes)** lavar los platos (la ropa), 10
washer lavadora, 10
wastebasket basurero
watch reloj (*m.*), 8; **~ television** mirar televisión, 2
water agua (*f.*) (*but:* el agua); **fresh ~** agua dulce; **sparkling ~** agua mineral, 9; **~ skiing** esquí acuático, 7; **~ the plants** regar (ie) las plantas, 10
watercress berro
waterfall catarata
wave ola
we nosotros(as), 1
wealth riqueza
wealthy adinerado(a)
weather tiempo, 7; **It's nice / bad ~.** Hace buen / mal tiempo. 7
weave tejer
weaving tejido
web red (*f.*); **~ page** página web, 4
webcam cámara web, 4
website sitio web, 4
wedding boda
Wednesday miércoles (*m.*), 3
week semana, 3; **during the ~** entresemana, 3; **every ~** todas las semanas, 5; **last ~** semana pasada, 7
weekend fin (*m.*) de semana, 2
welcome bienvenido(a); **You're ~.** De nada. 1
well bien, 4; **(Not) Very ~.** (No) Muy bien. 1; **Quite ~.** Bastante bien. 1; (*for drawing water*) pozo
well-being bienestar (*m.*)
what? ¿cuál(es)? ¿qué? 3; **~ day is today?** ¿Qué día es hoy? 3; **~ do you like to do?** ¿Qué te gusta hacer? 2; **~ does . . . mean?** ¿Qué significa…? P; **~ is today's date?** ¿A qué

fecha estamos? 3; **~ is your phone number?** ¿Cuál es tu / su número de teléfono? (*s. fam. / form.*), 1; **~ time is it?** ¿Qué hora es? 3; **~'s he / she / it like?** ¿Cómo es? 2; **~'s the weather like?** ¿Qué tiempo hace? 7; **~'s your (e-mail) address?** ¿Cuál es tu / su dirección (electrónica)? (*s. fam. / form.*), 1; **~'s your name?** ¿Cómo se llama (*s. form.*) / te llamas (*s. fam.*)? 1; **~ 's new?** ¿Qué hay de nuevo? 1

whatever cualquier

which? ¿qué? 3; **~ one(s)?** ¿cuál(es)? 3

wheat trigo

wheel rueda

when? ¿cuándo? 3; **~ is your birthday?** ¿Cuándo es tu cumpleaños? 1

where? ¿dónde? 3; **~ (to)?** ¿adónde?; **~ do you live?** ¿Dónde vives / vive? (*s. fam. / form.*), 1; **~ does your . . . class meet?** ¿Dónde tienes la clase de… ? 3

while mientras

white blanco(a), 4

whitewater rafting: go ~ navegar en rápidos, 7

who? ¿quién(es)? 3

whose cuyo(a)(s); **~ are these?** ¿De quiénes son? 3; **~ is this?** ¿De quién es? 3

why? ¿por qué? 3

wife esposa, 5

wifi wifi, 4

wild salvaje

willing dispuesto(a)

win ganar, 7

wind viento

window ventana, P

windy: It's ~. Hace viento. 7

wine: red ~ vino tinto, 9; **white ~** vino blanco, 9

wineglass copa, 9

winter invierno, 7

wireless connection wifi, 4

wish desear, querer (*irreg.*), 10; esperanza

with con

wolf lobo

woman mujer (*f.*), P

wonder maravilla

wood madera

wooden cart carreta

wool lana, 8

word-processing program programa (*m.*) de procesamiento de textos, 4

work trabajar, 2

workday jornada laboral

worker trabajador(a), 5

workshop taller (*m.*)

world mundo; **~ Wide Web** red (*f.*) mundial, 4; **~wide** a nivel mundial

worried preocupado(a), 4

worry preocuparse, 5

worse peor, 8

wrinkled arrugado(a)

write escribir, 3; **~ in your notebooks.** Escriban en sus cuadernos. P

Y

year año, 3; **every ~** todos los años, 9; **last ~** año pasado, 7

yellow amarillo(a), 4

yes sí, 1

yesterday ayer, 3

yogurt yogur (*m.*), 6

you vosotros(as) (*fam. pl.*), tú (*fam. s.*), usted (Ud.) (*form. s.*), ustedes (Uds.) (*fam. or form. pl.*), 1; ti (*fam. s.*), Ud(s). (*form.*), 8; **to / for ~** os (*fam. pl.*), te (*fam. s.*), le (*form. s.*), les (*form, pl.*), 8; **with ~** contigo (*fam.*), 8

young joven, 2

younger menor, 8

your (*adj.*) tu (*fam.*), su (*s. form. pl.*), vuestro(a) (*fam.*), 3; suyo(a) (*form. s., pl.*), tuyo(a) (*fam.*), 10

yours (*pron.*) vuestro(a) (*fam. pl.*), suyo(a) (*form. s., pl.*), tuyo(a) (*fam. s.*), 10

youth juventud (*f.*)

Z

zero cero, P

Index